Dance Words

compiled by

Valerie Preston-Dunlop

harwood academic publishers
Australia • Austria • Belgium • China • France • Germany • India • Japan • Luxembourg •
Malaysia • Netherlands • Russia • Singapore • Switzerland • Thailand • United Kingdom •
United States

Harwood Academic Publishers
Poststrasse 22
7000 Chur
Switzerland

British Library Cataloguing in Publication Data

Dance Words. — (Choreography & Dance
Studies, ISSN 1053-380X; Vol. 8)
  I. Preston-Dunlop, Valerie   II. Series
792.8

   ISBN 3-7186-5601-9 (hardcover)
   ISBN 3-7186-5605-1 (softcover)

CONTENTS

Chapter 9   Space-in-the-body and The Dancer in Space

Chapter 10   Notation

PART FOUR: CHOREOGRAPHY

Chapter 11   Choreographic Form

Chapter 12   Some Ensemble, Group, Duo and Solo Dance Concerns

Chapter 13   Choreographic Processes

INTRODUCTION TO THE SERIES

Choreography and Dance Studies is a book series of special interest to dancers, dance teachers and choreographers. Focusing on dance composition, its techniques and training, the series will also cover the relationship of choreography to other components of dance performance such as music, lighting and the training of dancers.

In addition, *Choreography and Dance Studies* will seek to publish new works and provide translations of works not previously published in English, as well as publish reprints of currently unavailable books of outstanding value to the dance community.

ROBERT P. COHAN

ACKNOWLEDGEMENTS

The research, of which this book is the end product, has been generously supported. The Laban Centre for Movement and Dance, London, through its Research Committee, has financially assisted me by allowing me some research time over a period of three years, and by supporting the initial research assistants Jane Carr, Elizabeth Charman and Nichola Stapleton. The Laban Centre faculty have co-operated copiously as have post-graduate students.

The Radcliffe Trust has grant aided the project. It was their support which enabled the decision to go ahead to be made. Research facilities provided by the Gulbenkian Foundation to the Laban Centre research work have been shared by this project.

Interviewees have been exceptionally co-operative, but The Birmingham Royal Ballet especially so. Through the generosity of Sir Peter Wright, the company allowed me to use them as the model of a large classical company and enabled me to listen and talk to all departments. Through Robert Cohan, London Contemporary Dance Theatre have been the major contemporary company studied. Scholars and artists in all domains of dance have been listened to and watched in action and have spoken of their work. My appreciation of their contribution, their painstaking verification of their entries, is warmly stated. Wherever possible they have been consulted and many have assisted me on the wording used.

The contributors whose written word has been researched have generously agreed to be included. Robert Robertson and his colleagues at Gordon and Breach have supported in all the professional ways one would expect and more. So too has Peter Bassett, Senior Librarian of the Laban Centre Library. Muriel Topaz and Robert Cohan have provided welcome comments on the completed text, and at earlier stages Dorothy Madden, Roderyk Lange and Rona Sands have given wise counsel.

A project such as this is electronically daunting. Liz Cooke and Diana Ball set up the data base originally, but John Dunlop is the keyboarding wizard who has dealt with the daily chore, over five years, of entering, exiting, rearranging, correcting, and checking every entry, as the project took shape, a job for a husband disguised as a saint.

INTRODUCTION

THE NATURE OF THE BOOK

The entries in this book have been collected from classes, rehearsals, workshops, and dance events; from written materials in published books, journals, newspapers, programme notes; from unpublished materials and research theses on dance; from discussions on television and radio, and texts of dance films; and from many interviews with individuals in dance. In effect, from anywhere and everywhere that dance people communicate verbally.

The words and phrases found to be used by dance people in their work can best be described as a mixture of agreed technical terms, subcultural vernacular expressions, and idiosyncratic utterances. The rich melange represents the breadth of attitude to language and practice which the dance community appears to have. Some contributors were concerned to 'get it right'. Others used words simply as a means to achieve what really mattered to them — the dance. How they spoke was more important than what was said. Some were poetic, some prosaic. All were dealing with the exceptional problem of sharing, through verbal means, events and ideas which, by their nature, are non-verbal.

The project set out originally with a focused objective to compile a dictionary with definitions of terms used in dance practice. Limiting the collection to definitions was soon found to be an error. Artists talking about dance in their own words offered insights which complemented those found through defining. Carefully studied meanings of words were found to be regarded as essential wherever the safeguarding of a tradition, or the establishment of a new concept, or attempts to unify diversity were the goals. Hence dance people attached to one artist, one school, one system were conscious of how language could aid or inhibit their purpose; indeed some contributors in these domains were particular 'to the comma'.

On the other hand, choreographers created idiosyncratic expressions for their own work. They and dance directors communicated with performers in all manner of both personal and traditional terms. Both are included. They encapsulate working methods and concerns directly, without mediation from a dance writer's definition of what was meant.

There are more entries from dance as a theatre art than as a recreational or social form, more from serious theatre than entertainment, more from innovative dancers than traditional ones. While this must somewhat reflect the choice of sources researched, it also shows where talking about dance was found, where discussion was included in work, and in what diversity of language.

For some readers the mix of more and less objective entries may seem uneven, but it is intentional, as a reflection of how artists, teachers, researchers, and technicians speak. The dance domain is broad, the people in it individual, and the diversity of their language reflects their concerns and their style.

Traditionally, dance people and dance books divide their art into genres and styles of work, of which tap dancing, clog dancing, ballet, and tanztheater might be examples. Inevitably, practitioners within each group use distinct terminology and expressions. It would seem that some dance people know little about the language of others and may believe that their own terminology is common practice. This book aims to diminish rather than strengthen the divisions, by the manner in which the entries are arranged, placing side by side ways of expressing similar concerns, and so showing commonality, diversity, and controversy.

Since dance is increasingly multicultural, has cross-art forms, and no longer has hard-edged parameters, the main problem for the compiler was deciding where to stop. The criteria applied were:

a)   that terms of present-day dance should be the starting point, working back in time but stopping at 1900. In the early part of the century, only individuals and concepts that dance people speak of as seminal should be included;

b)   that since the book is being compiled in Great Britain, the mix of dance activity there should be reflected in the entries;

c)   that copious influences from overseas are evident in dance activity, and where that influence is talked about, it should be included;

d)   that the language of established dance practitioners, of dance academics, of younger dancers, and of the amateur would all be included, to reflect the range of people who dance and who talk about it;

e)   that where already-published detailed dictionaries of technical terms in specialist areas such as classical Indian dance, classical ballet, or notation exist, this book would avoid duplication, by including entries in which the usage of terms be given rather than the description of the terms themselves.

The aim of the book is to present language in use in the dance domain in such a way that dance people might have available a verbal resource with which to discuss their subject and with which to work and practice. The present volume can only be regarded as a beginning. Inevitably a somewhat unpredictable balance of British and American terms and examples are given. It is hoped that other compilers may follow suit, so that the international nature of dance activity and dance scholarship can be made more widely available.

THE CHOREOLOGICAL PERSPECTIVE

Not everything that dance people talk about and write about is in this volume. The perspective is a choreological one. What, may be asked, is that? It is the perspective of the developing subject known as choreological studies. Since the 1920s spasmodically and haltingly, choreology has grown, appearing first in 1923 in Moscow in the work of the Choreological Laboratory, in Germany in 1926 at Laban's Choreographic Institute, in the United States in 1956 through Kurath's anthropological work, in London in the same year through Benesh Notation, in Europe more widely from 1962 as ethnochoreology through ethnologists. Louis Horst called for 'a science of dance' in 1925, for choreographers, and he did not mean kinesiology but the equivalent of musicology, and especially of musical composition theory. In 1986 Choreological Studies commenced at the Laban Centre for Movement and Dance, in London, transforming a loosely associated group of courses which were proving inadequate for the study of dance for the 1980s and 1990s, including Movement Study, Dance Analysis, Dance Workshops, Labanotation, Documentation and Reconstruction, into a subject which has become a coherent area for dance practitioners, and both academic and practical scholars. In symbiotic relationship to it, cluster Technique, Repertory, Reconstruction, Choreography, History, Politics and Sociology of Dance, Dance Education, Aesthetics of Dance, Production and Design, and Music for Dance.

A choreological perspective embraces first and foremost a view of dance from the point of view of those who do it. The popular view of a work as movement material, interpreted by dancers supported by production, while seen as adequate for some traditional dances and ballets, is regarded as inadequate for the present practice of all those choreographers for whom the interactions of all the ingredients of a dance work are in a more dynamic and fluid relationship. Dance is approached as a nexus of performer/ movement/sound/and space, manifest in highly individual forms and statements. In a choreological perspective, these views from within the art meet others looking in from without, views of people who are not practitioners but spectators, critics or researchers. The concept that research and practice overlap and inform each other, may be undertaken by the same people and may even be sometimes indistinguishable from each other, is valued.

In choreological study, how the dancer creates the dance is the concern, how s/he turns what there is to be said by the dance into a performance is central, be it an avant garde performance art piece, a Morris dance, or a Latin American programme. What means are at the disposal of the choreographer and reconstructor is central. The conventions of dance, the media of dance, its structuring processes, and the collaborations with fellow art makers are all of crucial interest. The structural elements of movement, the things that can be notated, are included, and so too are the interpretative elements of the performers and the spectators, which leads to an interest in issues of style, meaning and communication.

The central concepts of choreological study have been the guiding principle for the organisation of this book, while sectioning and subsectioning were not predetermined before collecting began. These developed during the research and were dictated by the content and focus of the contributions.

The book opens with THE DANCE DOMAIN. The first chapter 'The Dance Domain' outlines the field of operation. The historical focus is on present-day practice and moves back over the 20th century to scan the language of practice that is evident in the dance literature, and that is retained in dance discussion, and present practice. To go further back historically is beyond the resources of the present project. Exceptions are made for outstanding figures whose terminology is still current. The geographical focus is the wealth of dance activity in Great Britain, through indigenous dance forms and received vocabularies, and Britain's growing multicultural nature, together with extensive influences from the United States and Europe. The chapter 'Dance People' follows. Included are terms for those who participate in the dance domain, and titles which individuals use to describe themselves and each other, in terms of their work within the domain.

THE PERFORMER is the overarching topic of the second part of the book, with 'The Performer', 'The Performer and Movement', 'Technique', and 'Costume' as chapters. In this part the choreological perspective becomes evident. Neither the traditional categorisation according to dance type and activity as in the opening chapters, nor an alphabetical listing did justice to the contributions. The entries appeared to cluster under areas of interest. These topics dictate the order in which entries are placed. Only where no common topic can be detected are entries arranged alphabetically. The language of casting, of bodies, of feeling and sensation, of audition requirements and talents, of the complex nexus of the dancer and the dance is included. The entries reflect the technical and artistic concerns of being, becoming, looking at, and co-operating with, the people who do the dancing. This part enlarges upon the entries under 'Dancers' in 'Dance People'. Contributors are from all walks of the dance domain, with technique specialists and costume designers given a clear place.

MOVEMENT overarches the third part with the language of 'The Moving Body', 'Dynamics and Timing', 'Space-in-the-Body and the Dancer in Space', and 'Notation' as the chapters. Here, language which focuses on what the dancer might be doing, vocabularies, components of movement, and how these are communicated verbally and in symbol systems is the subject. There was some difficulty in deciding where to place some entries, because movement is dynamic, is made by a moving body and is in space, always. The organisation of the entries accommodates this overlap by looking for overall focus of the statements. Entries from choreographers, dancers, dance teachers, and notators predominate.

Concerns of CHOREOGRAPHY are fourth. 'Choreographic Form', including the devices that are embedded in works, is the opening chapter; some language specific to 'Ensemble, Group, Duo and Solo' work follows, with examples of 'Choreographic Processes' in the making of works concluding. New works and the form of traditional dances are included, with historians and choreographers being the main contributors. This part expands on the entries under 'Dance Makers' in the chapter 'Dance People' and on the formal subdivisions of dance works in the chapter 'Dance Domain'.

Part Five, THE DANCE SOUND AND THE DANCE SPACE, introduces the language of people engaged in the 'Sound' of dance, the interrelationship of 'Sound and Movement', and the dance 'Space'. The language of musicians, designers for dance, and video collaborators is included.

Part Six deals with THE DANCE EVENT itself, starting with the beginning rehearsal processes, to the moment of presentation of whatever is being danced. Here, the language of choreologists, rehearsal directors, stage managers and performers intermingle as the collaboration proceeds towards its product. Language on the style of the performed work is presented as 'The Nexus and the Emergence of Style', that is as the nexus of the elements already contained in the previous chapters, together with issues in style discussed by scholars, notators, film makers, repertory companies, and traditional groups, and by individuals for whom style is a concern. The concluding chapter includes the language of how, and if, dances communicate, audiences' perceptions, and issues of meaning for the choreographer, the performer, and the spectator, under 'Communication'.

Finally, in Part Seven, an overview of some language in current approaches to DANCE RESEARCH is offered.

Bibliographical details of each publication cited are given at the end of the book. For oral contributions, a brief biographical note is given in the list of contributors.

THE ENTRIES

The book contains terms each of which is followed by a sentence or two, under which is the name of the contributor. They fall roughly into the following categories. They explain a procedure, illustrate a practice, raise a problem, reflect a theoretic stand, define a use, and offer a point of view.

The entries have one of four formats:

1) Entries which are credited as a name followed by the word Interview (or Seminar or Rehearsal) were collected through discussion, in many cases after a rehearsal or a workshop or a performance. The entries are not direct quotations of what was said, unless inverted commas are used, but a distillation of the content of the interview, giving the format of term and explanatory statement. These were verified and/or edited by each interviewee and constitute their personal view. Interviews have all taken place recently, between 1992 and 1994, so no dates are added.

2) Entries which are a term followed by sentences in inverted commas are direct quotations, usually from written sources. In almost all cases, except where an author could not be traced or is deceased, the authors have agreed to the selection of quotations. The date of the publication in which the source can be found follows the author's name and, if the subject is known to have arisen earlier, that date is given in brackets.

3) Entries that are a term followed by sentences in which inverted commas appear spasmodically are incomplete quotations. They arise from writings in which the term was used but not directly explained. For the format of term and explanatory statement required for this book, it has been necessary to turn sentences round and to make implicit content explicit. Wherever possible the original writers have authorised the change.

4) Entries with no inverted commas, a name and a date are interpretations of content, mostly from single sentences or paragraphs in which terminology and dance concepts were presented and discussed. The term and the explanation pull out the main issue and condense/paraphrase/enlarge/translate the content. Every effort has been made to ensure agreement to all of these; the wishes of contributors have been respected in all cases.

Some terms in common use are attributed to 'Editors', as it seemed impossible to attribute them to any one individual. In rare instances, owners of copyright ask for a particular formula of acknowledgement; the consequence is a departure from the uniform treatment of sources. Original spelling is used, so that both 'theatre' and 'theater' appear, and so on. Occasionally an entry appears in two places, if its content merits that treatment.

Some contributors expressed concern that, by taking verbal material out of context the reader could be confused and possibly the author misrepresented. It is felt that the new context provided by the topic-based organisation of entries safeguards authors. Even short entries are contextualised by similarities or differences, so focusing the reader's attention to the content of each.

HOW TO USE THIS BOOK

This is not a book to read from the beginning to the end; rather it is one in which to search specifically, in the first instance. To aid the reader, a contents list and two indices are provided. The 'Contents' shows how the book is divided into subject sections, which can be read as a whole, or searched through for specific information. The 'Index of Terms' lists all the terms in the book, by which it is possible to see where a dance word, and words similar to it, might be found, sometimes in several sections. The 'Index of Names' lists the entries contributed by, or mentioning, dance artists and scholars, so that it is possible to locate all entries associated with one person.

Having studied a term, the reader is advised to consult those adjacent to it, for contrasting or similar views may be nearby. It is recommended that the brief biographies of contributors be referred to so that a statement is seen in the context from which it emerges, for the same term may be used by a choreographer and an anthropologist, a feminist writer or a notator, and that context may throw light on the perspective offered. The reader is advised also to note the date of the publication from which the entry is taken, to gain a historical perspective on it. Further reading from the publications cited is facilitated through the bibliography.

PART ONE: THE DANCE DOMAIN

Chapter 1, THE DANCE DOMAIN, gives examples of what people consider dance to be. It sets out titles, words and phrases for the diverse genres and styles into which dance is divided. The divisions, as the entries show, have boundaries which some dance people largely ignore, creating cross-art forms and cross-genre styles. Other dance people hold to the boundaries with tenacity. At one time in the compilation of this book, entries on the various forms of dance as a theatre art were to be the only entries, social dance being seen as beyond the scope of the present research. However, that rapidly became a foolish limitation, for dance artists made it clear that they make much use of social dance forms in their work. Where one starts and the other finishes is not clear cut.

Education and training, and administration, were not in the first brief either, but the practice and talk of dance artists spills over into these fields, and vice versa. So they are in, but not exhaustively, there being a national flavour to the language of funding and branches of dance training, while a more widely used international language prevails elsewhere.

Titles for DANCE PEOPLE, and their explanations, form Chapter 2. Here the wealth of professions within the dance domain shows itself and the nomenclature within it. What dance artists entitle themselves is indicative of the content of their work, and their attitude to it, for by no means all dance performers call themselves dancers, and dance makers do not all regard themselves as choreographers, but something else. Boundaries are broken here, as in Chapter 1. Who, for instance, is regarded as a dance scholar? Only academics? It would seem not.

Chapter 1 THE DANCE DOMAIN

1. DANCE IN GENERAL

Dance

"...it is impossible to define..."
Curt Sachs, 1937.

Idiom of dance

"...the idiom of dance is non-verbal and any verbal description of it fails: it is inadequate."
Roderyk Lange, 1980.

Physical creative process

"Dance is a form of art which deals with that which cannot be verbalized...the physical creative process."
Jerome Robbins in Simone Dupuis, 1987.

Dancing

"...is no more than knowing how to bend and straighten the knees at the proper time."
Pierre Rameau, trans. 1931 (1725).

Dance

"The art of expressing emotion by means of rhythmic bodily movements."
Émile Jaques Dalcroze (1921) in Suzanne Shelton, 1981.

Dance

That which is stimulated by music.
Émile Jaques Dalcroze (1921) in Vera Maletic, 1987.

Dance

"Far from being a futile amusement, far from being a speciality confined to putting on a show now and then for the amusement of the eyes that contemplate it or the bodies that take part in it, it is quite simply a poetry that encompasses the action of living creatures in its entirety."
Paul Valéry, (1936), 1964.

Dance

"The mother of the arts."
Curt Sachs, 1937.

2

Dance, A

"...it is not a symptom of a dancer's feeling but an expression of its composer's knowledge of many feelings."
Susanne K. Langer, 1957.

Dance, A

"A dance is movements guided by certain principles. It doesn't have to mean anything."
Louis Horst, 1958.

Dancing

"A language whose words are movements of the body."
Peggy van Praagh and *Peter Brinson*, 1963.

Dance

"A constellation of motor behaviors."
Joann W. Kealiinohomoku, 1965.

Dance

The art of motion where the motion is an end in itself and has no need to justify itself. Time/space/shape interacting in a dynamic relationship.
Alwin Nikolais, 1969.

Dance

"...is everything that a human being is able to do musically, with every part of the body...eyelids and eyeballs (Balinese), little finger (mudras), feet (classical European), animalistic gesticulation of the whole body (modern Western expressionism)."
Karlheinz Stockhausen in Mya Tannenbaum, 1987 (1979–81).

Dance

"Dance might...be defined as any movement designed to be looked at."; said with reference to the Judson Church experiments.
Roger Copeland and *Marshall Cohen*, 1983.

Dancing

"Dancing, for me, is movement in time and space."
Merce Cunningham in Richard Fraser, 1989.

Dance

"Formalised human behaviour."
Jane Dudley, 1992.

Dance

"...the noble art of Terpsichore...."
Vivi Flindt and *Knud Arne Jürgensen*, 1992.

Dance

Activity which "displays bodies in a condition of special use, bodies that are doing something out of the ordinary" containing "the merging of contradictory extremes of complete control over the body and complete loss of control"; said of the Black Swan and the Mevlevi Dervishes.

Roger Copeland, 1992.

Dance

"Whatever the people say it is; an attempt to avoid a biased definition of what dance might mean to a particular community, an attitude adopted by anthropologists."

Andrée Grau, Interview.

Dance

"A visual art whose raw material is the body."

Judith Mackrell, Interview.

Dance

"A sensorial art, as are all arts."

Doris Rudko, Interview.

Dance

An art form in which the body is both presenting and representing, and in some ways challenging, the culture from which it emerges.

Helen Thomas, Interview.

Dance and theatre

"They have to be magic."

Carla Maxwell, Interview.

Dance as art

Dance which has to be approached, understood, and appreciated, within the constraints of the craft and techniques, conventions, and traditions of the day, for its own sake and for its individual meaning.

Pauline Hodgens, 1988(a).

Art

"Art results from the impassioned human under the most rigorous discipline. That's the art I know about and love."

José Limón quoted by Carla Maxwell, Interview.

Dance as an autonomous art

"An art form in its own right, not dependent on music or design or even on individual dancers."

Peter Brinson, 1991.

Dance as a fine art
"Enjoying dance intuitively through the senses and with the mind through understanding form. That's what makes it a fine art."
Louis Horst, 1958.

Dance as an art discipline
A subject in the education system, frequently wrongly placed as a subordinate part of Physical Education.
"An aesthetic discipline belonging generically with the other great arts disciplines."
Peter Abbs in Peter Brinson, 1991.

Dance as appearance
[Dance] "...springs from what the dancers do, yet it is something else, an appearance...a display of interacting forces, by which the dance seems to be lifted, driven, drawn, closed, or attenuated."
Susanne K. Langer, 1957.

Dance as transformation of life
"You don't stop living, so you don't stop dancing. I think of dance as a constant transformation of life itself."
Merce Cunningham in Merce Cunningham and Jacqueline Lesschaeve, 1985.

Dance as a means of communication
"Dance cannot and does not exist by itself as technique; for it requires human activity to produce it. In short, dance is people communicating something to people."
Alan Merriam, 1974.

Dance as entertainment
"I think that dance should primarily be entertainment...It's a visual theater and an aural theater...beautiful people, beautifully dressed, doing beautiful and meaningful things."
Alvin Ailey in Joseph Mazo, 1977.

Mainstream dance
Dance work which is established, which takes place in expected places such as theatres for art dances, dance halls for social dances, and which has recognisable forms.
Andrée Grau, Interview.

Fringe dance
Dance work which is in contrast to mainstream dance, usually taking place in unusual or experimental venues, and having experimental or unusual form; it may also become part of the establishment as a recognised and expected fringe activity.
Andrée Grau, Interview.

Marginalisation of dance
> The location of dance at the fringe of contemporary culture and hence perceived as trivial by those at the centre of that culture.
> *Paul Filmer*, Interview.

Fragility
> The quality of dance works in that they can be damaged at every point.
> "...ballets are fragile."
> *David Bintley*, Interview.

Impermanence of dance
> "Isn't it just great, the way dances are so easy to erase."
> *Robert Rauschenberg* in Paul Taylor, "Private Domain" 1987.

Ephemeral nature of dance
> "A ballet dies every night as every performance ends."
> *Clement Crisp*, Interview.

2.   OTHER WORDS FOR DANCE

Ceremony
> The title given to the performance of a Butoh work.
> *Ushio Amagatsu*, Interview.

Choreography, A
> A dance work: said of a work in the making or newly made.
> *Dorothy Madden*, Interview.

Dynamic Image, The
> The virtual image which the actual dance creates.
> "What dancers create is a dance; and a dance is an apparition of active powers, a dynamic image."
> *Susanne K. Langer*, 1957.

Fertility rite
> A ritual with which the Morris dance is associated, although not all teams agree, preferring to see it as having entertainment as the goal.
> *Anthony G. Barrand*, 1991.

Kinetic sculpture
> What dance is from the designer's point of view.
> *Beatrice Hart*, Interview.

Movement system
> A rule-governed way of moving with boundaries, which is regarded as dancing or miming, or sport, or courting systems or whatever, by a community.
> *Andrée Grau*, Interview.

Music
> The same word as "dance" in many cultures, a label covering a complex comprising dance, drama, singing, mime, etc.
> *Andrée Grau*, Interview.

Pleasurable pastime
> What dance is seen as by some members of the public, especially intellectuals, in contrast to a serious communicating art form.
> *Chris de Marigny*, Interview.

Ritual
> A dance in which an aspect of human life is imitated for the purpose of mediating to some divine power.
> *Jane Harrison*, 1913.

Saltation
> Dance: literally from the Latin "saltare", to jump.
> *Havelock Ellis*, 1923.

Terpsichore
> "The Greek muse of dancing and choral song"; used also for dance in general.
> '*Webster*', 1993.

Time-based arts
> Polytechnic jargon for theatre, music, and dance.
> *John Ashford*, Interview.

Visual feeling
> "He [Paul Taylor] accepts the definition of dancing as 'visual feeling'."
> *Clive Barnes*, in Clive Barnes, Noel Goodwin, and Peter Williams, 1965.

3. DANCE EVENTS

Dance concert
> A dance performance, maybe a solo concert, a one-artist show, a company performance, or a school show.
> *John Ashford*, Interview.

Recital
   A solo presentation of poetry, dance or piano music, at the end of the 19th/beginning of the 20th century, common in European salons and drawing rooms as entertainment for guests.
   Walter Sorell, 1981.

Group exhibition
   Several live installation works, choreographed and made collaboratively with visual artists, presented in the same gallery; viewed as separate visual arts works in an exhibition; said of "Body as Site, Image as Event" (1993).
   Rosemary Butcher, Interview.

Solo dance recital
   A dance form, developed from the salon recital, appearing in Europe in the first years of the 20th century, used by Loie Fuller, Jane Arne, Isadora Duncan and Anna Pavlova at that time.
   Walter Sorell, 1981.

Gala
   A special dance performance, usually in aid of a good cause and in the presence of somebody well known.
   Clement Crisp, Interview.

Showcases
   Opportunities to perform work through a season or festival or even simply an evening of choreographic works; said of the London South Bank's " Hothouse" showcase, 1992.
   Allen Robertson, 1993.

Repertoire
   A series of works or roles which a company or a solo dancer is ready and prepared to put on.
   Eds.

Heavy repertory
   The series of dance works which a company has prepared and can perform, which require considerable contribution and concentration from the audience, in contrast to light works which entertain and amuse.
   Dorothy Madden, Interview.

Programme, A
   A selection of dances chosen for a particular place, time and audience, usually referring to works for performance in a theatre space, but can also be used for any pre-sentation, e.g. video, folk dance, festival.
   Dorothy Madden, Interview.

Programme

In Latin-American dance, a term used for a group of routines, each based on one Latin-American dance form, prepared and presented by a couple in competitions.
Ruud Vermey, Interview.

Ham and eggs programme

Used in America as a term to identify a programme of tried and true audience favourites that touring ballet companies presented in "the sticks".
"American Ballet Theater and Ballets Russes de Monte Carlo used to identify 'Sylphides' (or 'Lac' II), then a serious work, and closing with a Massine romp, or 'Fancy Free', or some equally happy piece."
Clement Crisp, Interview.

Programme order

The order in which dances will be presented in a programme; a concern of choreographers and directors in which the audience's appreciation of each work is considered, together with pragmatic concerns: of dancer energy, costume and set changes, music, and so on.
Dorothy Madden, Interview.

Programming

The order in which the works in the programme will be shown.
"Kurt Jooss decreed that 'Green Table' should be the last work because he wanted audiences...to leave the theatre with its tragic message."
Mary Clarke, 1993.

Performance platform

An organised opportunity for dance people to show their work, possibly through a festival, or a teaching institution, an alternative theatre venue, a collective of individuals, et al.
Eds.

Platform

A one-off performance opportunity given at the invitation of the producer.
John Ashford, Interview.

Series

Several works given in one theatre, events that take place not by invitation but because individuals buy the building and risk the box office receipts, while benefitting from joint publicity; an example is " Resolutions" at The Place Theatre, London.
John Ashford, Interview.

Season

A period of time during which a company is in residence at a theatre and presents repertory; ranges from two weeks to six months.
Sadlers Wells Theatre, 1993.

Season, A
A period of time in a theatre where a variety of independent dance companies are invited to present their work; examples are "Spring Loaded" at The Place Theatre, London, "New Moves" at the Centre for Contemporary Art, Glasgow, "Bare Essentials" at the Institute for Contemporary Art, London.
John Ashford, Interview.

Curate a season, To
To invite and present a variety of dance companies in one season; artistic choice by the curator is implicit.
John Ashford, Interview.

Programming a season
Matching the works chosen to the size of the venue and its audience profile.
John Ashford, Interview.

Workshop jam sessions
Contact improvisation sessions in which any number of 'democratic duets' sharing the same space take place simultaneously.
Stephanie Jordan, 1992.

Company workshops
Opportunities for dance company members to give participants an experience of high level technical work and to try performing excerpts from the company's repertory; said of Transitions Dance Company.
Marion North, Interview.

Company workshops
Company members making work which is shown informally to give opportunity to developing choreographers, to allow their work to be seen and possibly be taken into the regular repertory.
Robert Cohan, Interview.

Workshops
Classes which go beyond technique into dance; used with any style of dance and may be a jazz workshop, an improvisation workshop, a choreology workshop, a workshop for children, etc.
Eds.

Mixed media project
Workshops and courses provided by community arts workers in video, photography, dance, drama, music, and design.
"Animated", 1992.

Lecture-demonstration

An event undertaken with an audience, usually by the education department of a company or by a dance conservatoire.

Jonathan Higgins, Interview.

Lecture-demonstration

A mode of promoting understanding of the training procedures and creative processes of a dance company.

Marion North, Interview.

Congress

A gathering, usually annual, of dance people with a common interest, such as members of the Imperial Society of Teachers of Dancing, where demonstrations, performances, reports, discussions and informal exchange are the activities undertaken.

Eds.

Dance festivals

Gatherings of dance people to share their dance; the work may be in any genre, or mixed genres, may be competitive or fiercely non-competitive; opportunities for choreographers and dancers to show their work.

Eds.

Folk dance festivals

Gatherings for the public display of folk dance from many countries, held both in public halls, and outside (Sidmouth).

Hugh Rippon, 1993.

Folk festivals

Events where groups from different countries perform to each other, ranging from "primitive but authentic which some participants find boring, to highly skilled but often removed from the original spirit which may have more impact."

Robert Harrold, Interview.

Ceilidhs

An evening of traditional music, song, and dance, held locally for all to take part.

Hugh Rippon, 1993.

Carnival

"An instance of merrymaking, feasting, masquerading."

'Webster', 1993.

Pageant

"An elaborate colorful exhibition or spectacle, often with music, that consists of a series of tableaux, of a loosely unified drama, or of a procession usually with floats."

'Webster', 1993.

Procession
> A group of people moving in an orderly way, usually in the open, of which a dance may be a component, possibly mounted on a mobile stage.
> *Michael Heaney* and *John Forrest*, 1991.

Cabaret and street acts
> Created and rehearsed acts based on a persona specific to each artist, presented usually as a solo or duo performance in which movement expression plays a part and which involves direct contact with an audience.
> *Helen Crocker* and *Bim Mason*, Interview.

Trade show
> Extravaganzas organised by firms to launch a new product or model car — often choreographed; the use of song and dance to sell the product.
> *Stuart Hopps*, Interview.

4. GENRES AND STYLES, BALLET-DERIVED

Dance genres
> "Groups of dances, the individual members of which have enough in common to make them collectively distinctive."
> *Pauline Hodgens* in Janet Adshead, 1988.

Genres of dance
> ..."crystallisations" of specific knowledge, beliefs, ideas, techniques, preferences, or values around which particular traditions and conventions for producing and receiving dance have grown.
> *Pauline Hodgens*, 1988(a).

Genres and styles
> The characteristic selections and patterning of basic components of the dance as directed by conventions and traditions derived from socio-cultural life.
> *Janet Adshead*, 1988.

Ballet
> "Ballet is about dancing to music not painting to pantomime."
> *George Balanchine* in Bernard Taper, 1974.

Ballet
> "Ballet is an art of example."
> *George Balanchine* in Bernard Taper, 1974.

Ballet
Theatrical blending of four component arts: drama, music, design and dance. "The perfect blending."
Peggy van Praagh and *Peter Brinson*, 1963.

Ballet
"A synthesis of human anatomy, solid geometry, and musical composition."
Lincoln Kirstein and *Muriel Stuart*, 1977 (1952).

Ballet
"Organised dynamism creating beauty."
André Levinson (1992) in Joan Acocella and Lynn Garafola, 1991.

Operatic dancing
The term used for ballet by Espinosa.
Édouard Espinosa, 1935.

Ballet d'action
"I have dared to fathom the art of devising ballets with action; to re-unite action with dancing; to accord it some expression and purpose."
Jean Georges Noverre, tr. 1966 (revised original 1803).

Ballet d'action
Type of 18th century ballet in which expression was emphasised in the quest for dramatic cohesiveness. If these ballets were viewed today they would seem to rely on conventional gesture to convey story and expression.
Jane Carr, Interview.

Romantic ballet
"...the so-called Romantic ballet is not a department of the dance, but merely a localized theatrical echo of a transient influential literary and artistic movement."
Lincoln Kirstein, 1939.

Romantic ballet
Ballet influenced by the Romantic movement in the arts generally; Romanticism in ballet attained its peak between 1830 and 1850.
Ivor Guest, Contributed.

Traditional ballet
A technique of refined difficulty which gives expression primarily to concepts of grace, control, fluidity, speed and balance.
A. V. Coton, 1946.

Classic ballet

"The classic dance is not merely a department of theatrical dancing opposed to the 'romantic', but rather a central line, or governing attitude which links the purest developments in traditional stage practice, whatever the epoch."
Lincoln Kirstein, 1939.

Classical ballet

An expression most commonly used as a name for ballet in the tradition of which Marius Petipa (ballet master at St. Petersburg 1869–1903) was a leading figure; this tradition evolved from the Romantic movement.
Ivor Guest, Contributèd.

Classicism

A living tradition, developing and changing from one era to the next, the acrobatics of a previous time often coming to belong to the classicism of the next.
Alistair Macaulay, 1988.

Dance classicism

"All of Ashton's ballets reflect a single passionate concern — the concern of any dance classicist — to assert that the classical ballet offers the core of its expression in its dances."
Alistair Macaulay, 1988.

Classical ballet

"...classical dancing is part constant, and part progressive. Today's classical dancers reaffirm the same principles that gave rise to the art in the first place ... simultaneously they work at extending the powers of their given means."
Robert Greskovic, 1984.

Classics

A term used, confusingly, for ballets associated with the music of Tchaikovsky and danced with classical ballet vocabulary, but also for ballets by Cunningham and Graham with their own technique.
Norman Morrice, Interview.

Neo-classicism (Balanchine)

"Into the classical ballet vocabulary Balanchivadze (Balanchine) introduced elements from the popular dance, from acrobatic arts, from the cabaret, from Goleizovsky, and even...from Isadora Duncan."
Bernard Taper, 1974.

Neo-classicism (Balanchine)

"At the height of the jazz age...[Balanchine] evolved a new classicism, which serenely embodied the classical virtues of clarity and grandeur and yet in spirit and in style of movement was more up-to-date and adventurous that the run of ultra-modern ballets."
Bernard Taper, 1974.

Ballets Russes style (c. 1930's)

"Compared to ours (American Ballet 1940's) its atmosphere was more hot and bothered, its rhythm in dance scenes made more sweeping climaxes, its techniques looked more casual and undefined and its temperament was more exotically fiery."

Edwin Denby, 1944.

American ballet

"America has its own spirit — cold, luminous, hard as light. Good American dancers can express clean smooth emotion in a manner that might almost be termed angelic."

George Balanchine in George Balanchine (ed. Thomas Schoff), 1984.

New Age ballet

The Balanchine-inspired period when the choreography diminished the stage designer's importance by using throwaway costumes and a designless plain stage, in which lighting dominated, with quasi-nudity.

Richard Buckle, 1981.

New ballet

Fokine's term for his developments in ballet, c. 1905–1914, in which he pursued the ideal that ballet should be presented as an expressive and cohesive whole.

Eds from *Michel Fokine*, 1961 (1914).

New Ballet, The

A term used to describe the amalgam of technical dance-forms, especially classic ballet, with dramatic material in the work of Kurt Jooss.

A. V. Coton, 1946.

Modern ballet

"Robbins...thinks that the best way to make a modern work is to integrate the perspectives of the present with the proved techniques of the past."

S. Kauffmann, 1961.

Modern Ballet

The works made between 1909 and the present day, Diaghilev and after; works which are music, designs, dancing as well as choreography.

Richard Buckle, 1981.

Contemporary ballet, A

A ballet by a choreographer working now, with present-day themes, not to be confused with a dance work made in both contemporary and ballet vocabularies.

Norman Morrice, Interview.

Character dance

Folk dance derived material adapted and elaborated for theatre performances, especially in the classical ballet genre.

Robert Harrold, Interview.

Character dance

Originally based on folklore but refined and adapted for stage use, found generally in traditional classical ballets as peasant and court dances and as vocabulary for characters.

"...the eccentric old man...", "...the robust, seductive but good-humoured woman...."

Jurgen Pagels, 1984.

Character ballets

Ballets whose main material is derived from character dancing, not main dance d'école classical ballet; said of Diaghilev's early works.

Richard Buckle, 1981.

Dance ballet

A term used by Edwin Denby.

"...focuses the attention...on a suite of dances.... The parts that show you the heart of the subject, that are the most expressive, are in the form of dance numbers, of dance suites. They are like arias in an opera."

Edwin Denby, 1944.

Ballet drama

A theatre piece which combines the presentation of complex human relationships with the traditional ballet vocabulary, a term used of Kenneth Macmillan's work.

John Percival, Contributed.

Pop-youth ballets

A group of contemporary ballets, with which the Joffrey Ballet (New York) were identified through choreographers such as Jerome Robbins and Twyla Tharp, "which show us people dancing about their time and in the idiom of their time."

Marcia Siegel, 1979.

Third stream style

"It intentionally combines elements of both classical ballet and modern dance genres."

Clive Barnes, 1987.

5.   MODERN DANCE AND CONTEMPORARY DANCE

Modern dance

Dance since the 1920's which is expressionistic in a non-balletic, often idiosyncratic style.

Sally Banes in Janet Adshead, 1986.

Modern dance

"...the discarding of all traditional requirements of form and the establishment of a new principle upon which each dance makes its own form...its resistance to the past, its response to the present, its constant redefining of the idea of dance..."

Marcia Siegel, 1969.

Modern dance

"...there is absolutely nothing modern about modern dance. It is...virtually basic dance, the oldest of all dance forms. The modern dancer, instead of employing the cumulative resources of academic tradition, cuts through directly to the source of all dancing."

John Martin, 1946.

Modern dance

A title given to the British dance after World War II which attempted to establish an alternative to the established ballet tradition.

"An alternative to ballet stemming from both Central European and American dance from the 1930's."

Stephanie Jordan, 1992.

Plastique

'Artistic movement', dance not derived from steps and established vocabularies but from the rhythm of the moving body; a term used in Russian experimental dance in the 1920's.

Nancy van Norman Baer, 1991.

Plastique

"Sculptural posing."

Ruth St. Denis (ca 1915) in Suzanne Shelton, 1981.

Living Art, The

A "new social art", the vision of a new form of theatre which commented on world issues through a pageant form in which the community was the players and simultaneously the appreciators.

Adolphe Appia (1921) in Denis Bablet and Marie-Louise Bablet, 1982.

Natural Movement

The title of a form of theatre dance created by Madge Atkinson, for which Art Nouveau's linear forms were the style, and Isadora Duncan the inspiration.

Francine M. Watson Coleman, Interview.

Barefoot dance

A term used of modern 20th century dance, starting with Isadora Duncan, in which no shoes were worn, which reflects "the escape of an imprisoned and tormented soul into the most natural and simple language of the body."

Walter Sorell, 1981.

Ausdruckstanz (Ger.)

The expressionist dance which began with Laban's innovations in freeing dance from music, set vocabularies and mime, in Germany from 1912.
Kurt Jooss, 1956.

Expressionistic dance

A translation of 'Ausdruckstanz', also translated as 'expressive dance', the New German Dance of the 1920's, which was associated with Expressionism in the visual arts but long after visual artists had moved away from concern with raw emotion.
Valerie Preston-Dunlop and *Susanne Lahusen*, 1990.

American modern dance

"The art of dancing has become almost entirely objective. I am trying to make it subjective", a statement which became the credo of American modern dance.
Ruth St. Denis (1939) in Suzanne Shelton, 1981.

Modern dance

"The scheme of modern dancing is all in the direction of individualism and away from standardization.... The modern dance is not a system; it is a point of view."
John Martin, 1972 (1933).

Modern dance

"[The modern dance] is movement devised not for spectacular display, as was the ballet, nor for self expression...but it is movement made to externalise personal authentic experience."
John Martin in Selma Jeanne Cohen, 1977.

Modern dance

"It is an individual quest for an individual expression of life."
Anna Sokolow in Selma Jeanne Cohen, 1977.

Modern dance choreographers

"We are not representational, we are imaginative."
Anna Sokolow in Selma Jeanne Cohen, 1977.

Modern dance

"To me modern dance is a licence to do what I feel is worth doing, without someone saying that I can't do it because it does not fit into a category."
Paul Taylor in Selma Jeanne Cohen, 1977.

Contemporary dance

Used in Britain to describe a dance genre which includes the techniques of the American and German modern dancers (e.g. Graham, Cunningham, Leeder) and developments of the modern dance, Post-modernism, avant-garde dance, and the New Dance of British choreographers who use release-based techniques. The term "Contemporary dance" was coined following the setting up, by Robin Howard, of the Contemporary Ballet Trust in 1966, and later London Contemporary Dance Theatre.
Peter Bassett, Interview.

Contemporary ballet

A term used by Robin Howard in the early 1960's to distinguish what he wanted to promote in Britain from the existing "modern dance", that is the Central European modern dance and ballroom dancing; a term which rapidly became "Contemporary dance."

Jack Anderson, 1990.

Jazz dance

Dance classes, choreographed works, and arranged routines, performed with music; interpreted by individual dancers and dance teachers as their own particular mix of jazz experience.

Thea Barnes, Interview.

Jazz dance

A controversial title for a range of dance activity which stems from African-American social dance of the 1920's and 1930's, might include street dancing and/or today's popular dance forms; what is essential is that it is performed to jazz music.

Fred Tragath, 1983.

6. ABSTRACT AND NON-LITERAL DANCES

Pure dance

"Pure dance is a dance without a support — no music, no narrative, just the dance."

Louis Horst, 1958.

Absolute Dance

A Wigman term for a dance genre free from subservience to music and theatricality, a dance that would take its impulse from the primordial sources of the body and space.

Walter Sorell, 1975.

Pure or absolute dance

Choreographic ideas which work only with movement, shape and form.

A. V. Coton, 1946.

Pure dance

"Pure dance integrates force, time and space patterns into a meaningful whole. This whole is the abstract form of the dance."

Barbara Mettler, 1980.

Abstract

"A term used as a level of understanding different from that of "literal'."

Alwin Nikolais, 1963.

Abstract theater

A term used by Nikolais for the nature of his creative output — total theatre in which shape, colour, sound, and motion are equal forces.
Alwin Nikolais, 1963.

Modernist dances

Dances about dancing.
Stephanie Jordan, 1992.

Abstract dance

"We present the event and leave it up to the audience to decide what is and what is not expressed. I have a feeling it produces some kind of atmosphere."
Merce Cunningham, 1968.

Abstract piece

"...[Cunningham] was inventing this kind of abstract, non-coherent, non-logically coherent, non-narrative piece...."
Edwin Denby, 1968.

Abstract mime

A term used by Alexander Sakharoff and his wife Clothilde van Derp for their style (about 1910) reflecting the introduction of the abstract into the visual arts.
Walter Sorell, 1981.

Movement-based work

Kinetic work, not necessarily regarded as dance, which arises out of movement exploration rather than as a response to sound or to the embodiment of a narrative.
Rosemary Butcher, Interview.

Presentational dance

"For me, the subject of dance is dancing itself. It is not meant to represent something else, whether psychological, literary, or aesthetic." "The dance isn't directed to them, or done for them. It's presented for them."
Merce Cunningham in Merce Cunningham and Jacqueline Lesschaeve, 1985.

Dehumanisation of the arts

"It shows as atonality in music, non-representation in art, the cerebral in dance, abstract."
Louis Horst, 1958.

Cerebral dance

"Dehumanization in movement, all from the head and nothing from the heart; it avoids all living forms and denies all personal emotions."
Louis Horst, 1957.

Objective dance, An
> Said of Bharatha Natyam Nritta, which is abstract in content, being geometric in form to give an aesthetic pleasure in technical achievement of the form.
> *"Dance Theatre Journal"*, 1991.

Non-literal dance
> "... an emphasis on movement and motion as communication, a concern with attitudes, images, relationships, shapes and form that can be communicated directly through the senses."
> *Eleanore W. Gwynne*, 1978.

Dances of action
> "...those dances that have their source in feeling states of motor origin."
> *Margaret H'Doubler*, 1957 (1940).

7. DANCE THEATRE AND DANCE DRAMA

Theater
> "Theater was a verb before it was a noun. It was an act before it was a building."
> *Martha Graham* in Elinor Rogosin, 1980.

Theatre
> Usually narrowly defined in Western culture as 'a play', giving rise to terms which express the broader view of theatre in other cultures; hence fringe theatre, cross arts activity, work with text, music, and movement.
> *John Ashford*, Interview.

Dance theatre
> "[A genre which fuses]...vivid metaphor with drastic realism."
> *Nadine Meisner*, 1989.

Dance theatre
> A body of work from the Eighties that represents a rediscovery of theatrical traditions after the dominance of the anti-expression, anti-narrative Sixties and post-Sixties dance.
> *Lesley-Anne Sayers*, 1988.

Dance theatre
> A way of working, exemplified by Ian Spink for Second Stride company, in which the traditions and devices of both theatre and dance are used together; linked to its German counterpart Tanztheater through its media and devices.
> *Eds.*

Dance theatre
How Christopher Bruce describes his work.
"I make dances, my works are theatrical events."
Christopher Bruce, Interview.

Dance theater
"Theater of movement drawn from mixed genres, the combination of elements from dance, opera, spoken theater and mime, becomes established as an uncompromising dance theater art form"; in the work of Pina Bausch.
Norbert Servos and *G. Weigelt*, 1984.

Tanztheater (Ger.)
The style of contemporary dance used to identify the work of Pina Bausch and the Wuppertal Tanztheater, and more broadly the works of those, primarily European, choreographers influenced by her.
Develops from the concern about what "of being human" can be expressed via the medium of dance. The experience is given a multiple context which explains the use of elements outside of the dance medium belonging to opera, vaudeville, musical, theatre, and film, all of which are seen "as representations" of that "experience."
Ana R. Sanchez-Colberg, 1992.

Spectacle
An art work in which the elements of dance, decor, and music combine to give an aurally, visually, and kinetically powerful experience to the audience, said of Bausch's "Orpheus and Eurydice."
Nadine Meisner, Contributed.

Theater piece
A mixed-media work using both dancers and actors, accomplished dance movement as well as pedestrian vocabulary, designed to provoke a response from the audience.
Dorothy Madden, Interview.

Voiceless Theatre, The
How Coton describes dance in the context of Kurt Jooss whose concern was to combine drama with elements of the established ballet vocabulary.
A. V. Coton, 1946.

Earth theater
A Pearl Primus term, for her approach to her art through her reliance on her roots.
Walter Sorell, 1986.

Total theater

The creation, and emphasis, of a complete audio-visual environment in which all theatrical elements operate integrally. The dancers are dehumanised and lose dominance over other elements.

Alwin Nikolais, 1971.

Total theater

"... the balance of music, drama and dance to create a harmonious whole in which no art form is subordinated to another and in which the intention of the original idea is paramount ..."

Walter Sorell, 1976.

Gesamtkunstwerk (Ger.)

A form of theatre in which many art forms combine to provide a 'total work of art'; associated with Richard Wagner, Adolphe Appia, Gordon Craig around the end of the nineteenth century and beginning of the twentieth.

Walter Sorell, 1981.

Butoh

A Japanese form of Gesamtkunstwerk (total theatre) in which the director is responsible for the movement, the costume, the lighting, and co-operates with a musical composer.

Raimund Hoghe, Interview.

Theatrical apparatus

The traditional constraints of theatre; the compulsion to communicate, to present the illusion of perfection, to divide audience from performer, to have a continuous dramaturgical concept, to present product and hide process, the passive expectation of the audience, etc.

Norbert Servos and *G. Weigelt*, 1984.

Theatre of the absurd

Theatre that seeks to represent the absurdity of man's existence in a meaningless universe by bizarre or fantastic means. [Eds. a term applied to some choreographic work].

Peter Brook, 1988.

Theatre of the Invisible-made-Visible

Based on the idea that the stage is a place where the invisible can appear.

"We are all aware that most of life escapes our senses: a most powerful explanation of the various arts is that they talk of patterns which we can only begin to recognise when they manifest themselves as rhythms and shapes."

Peter Brook, 1990 (1968).

Lyric theater, The
   A new kind of theater, in a total integration of dance, drama and music.
   Alwin Ailey in Walter Sorell, 1986.

Ballet drama
   A theatre piece which combines the presentation of complex human relationships
with the traditional ballet vocabulary, a term used of Kenneth MacMillan's work.
   John Percival, Contributed.

Dance drama
   A genre used primarily to interpret and transmit epic content, originally of a
religious sort.
   Roderyk Lange, 1975.

Dance drama
   "...has a story to tell and does so by means of several dramatic dance episodes
or scenes sequentially arranged."
   Jacqueline M. Smith, 1980.

Character pieces
   Dance works with a narrative centred around people, not archetypes but people
with costumes and names which are specific.
   Eds.

Dances of characterisation
   "...are those whose movements take on the qualities of another character.... He
designs his movements to portray another's actions and feelings."
   Margaret H'Doubler, 1957 (1940).

Play
   The title given to a theatrical dance work in which the participants regard
themselves as actors, although they may move both with and without words; the product
they present is regarded by them as theatre, while other cultures might see it as dance.
   Andrée Grau, Interview.

Mimesis
   "That form of theater in which a dramatist-actor delineates characters of his own
creation with or without speech; also known as pantomime."
   Angna Enters in Walter Sorell, 1951.

Nritya
   "The Bharatha Natyam technique together with stylised facial mime, in the
service of drama."
   "Dance Theatre Journal", 1991.

Mime
        An art form with a vocabulary that is made not from the dancers' movement, nor the acrobats', nor the old gamut of Pantomime gestures and grimaces, but the natural movement of all things that move, human beings or waterfalls, said of Étienne Decroux's work.
        Alvin Epstein, 1958.

8.   DANCE   THEATRE,   CROSS-CULTURAL

Heritage art
        Productions which focus on or evolve in the style of a defined cultural heritage, such as Indian dance, and are presented in another cultural environment, where the traditional meaning of the work may be difficult to read.
        "Dance Theatre Journal", 1992.

Pan-African classical dance
        Traditional dance forms from throughout Africa, a resource for some Black dance companies, such as "Adzido" in Great Britain.
        Maggie Semple, 1992.

Black dance
        Dance work choreographed and danced by Black people but not necessarily accessible only to Black audiences, said of "Adzido" company's work.
        Maggie Semple, 1992.

Fusion
        A blend of African-based, Afro-Cuban, Haitian jazz, with much hip swing and many isolations.
        Thea Barnes, Interview.

Butoh
        A term for a group of Japanese artists who direct dance work in a similar way, who share a common awareness, and create a common trend; it is not regarded as a style.
        "A milieu for the presentation of humanity, of the commonalities within different cultures."
        Ushio Amagatsu, Interview.

Dance of Darkness, The
        The translation of 'Ankoko Butoh', the title given to his new art form by Butoh's founder Tatsumi Hijkata.
        Ushio Amagatsu, Interview.

Nritta and Nritya
        The pure dance form of South India, "the heartbeat of the dance style"; and the interpretative dance form, "its very soul."
        U.S. Krishna Rao, 1990.

Cross-cultural work
        A dance piece which includes styles from more than one cultural heritage; said of Shobana Jeyasingh's work on the amalgam of Bharatha Natyam and Western theatrical dance.
        Shobana Jeyasingh, 1993.

Multiculture movement forms
        Forms of dance which cross the culture-specific barriers, "Kabuki to ballet, modern to Indian"; said of Joseph Houseal's work.
        "Time Out", 1993.

9.   POST-MODERN, NEW DANCE, AND CROSS-ART FORMS

Post-modern dance
        Works which post-date, and comment upon, modernist work, such as Cunningham and Balanchine, and play radically with their own conventions, arriving at a range of styles and aesthetics.
        David Michael Levin, 1991.

Post-modern dance (phase one) and (phase two)
        Sally Banes's suggested terms to distinguish dance in the U.S.A. which essentially rethought the defining parameters of dance, asking: "What is dance, who does it, where?" in the 1960's and early 70's, from that taking place in the 1980's.
        Judith Mackrell, 1991.

Post-modernistic dance
        Dance since 1979, as Post-modern but with differences in regard to technical virtuosity, permanence of repertory, elements of theatricality, the use of the media, the relationship of dance and music, the influence of mass culture, choice.
        Sally Banes in Janet Adshead, 1986.

Post-modern dance (in Britain)
        A movement beginning concurrently with modern trends in ballet in the 1970's, whose sources were the American minimalists and improvisors, performance art, and release technique.
        Judith Mackrell, 1991.

Independent dance scene

Dance activity which is not attached to a company or to a school; usually alternative in nature with a radical streak, such as X6 Collective in the 1960's in London.
Stephanie Jordan, 1992.

Independent contemporary dance

"A minority form of a minority form."
John Ashford, Interview.

New Dance

A term originally applied to the dance work of Emilyn Claid, Maedée Duprès, Fergus Early, Jacky Lansley and Mary Prestidge, founder members of the X6 Collective, who started the magazine "New Dance" in 1977 in Britain, and applied also to others who featured in the pages of "New Dance."
Stephanie Jordan, 1992.

Physical Theatre

A mode of theatrical presentation in dance in which verbal ideas are expressed in a vocabulary of physical movement, this being a deeper and more powerful method than words themselves.
"DV8's physical theatre is uncompromising in its immediacy."
Christopher Winter and *Leslie-Ann Sayers*, 1989.

Contact improvisation

"...an improvisational form in which the movement and structures of a work are generated by the responses of two or more performers to moments of physical contact between them."
Sarah Rubidge, 1986.

Contact improvisation

The democratic duet form with clearly stated criteria of aesthetic and function introduced by Steve Paxton.
"...the ideal of active, reflexive, harmonic, spontaneous, mutual forms."
Steve Paxton in Sally Banes, 1980(a).

Boundaries

The barriers between art forms, the delineation of what is considered to be dance, what to be kinetic sculpture, what to be clowning, what to be puppetry or mime, and so on "but we work across them."
Dorothy Madden, Interview.

Performance

"...by its very nature, performance defies precise or easy definition beyond the simple declaration that it is live art by artists. Any stricter definition would immediately negate the possibility of performance itself. For performance draws freely on any number of references — literature, theatre, drama, music, architecture, peotry, film and fantasy — deploying them in any combination.", "...its base has always been anarchic."

RoseLee Goldberg, 1979.

Performance art

A theatrical form derived from the visual arts which emphasises visual images and very often dispenses with text — usually lacking any kind of story line.

Chris De Marigny, 1991.

Live installations

Works which are essentially non-theatrical, are collaborations with visual artists, take place in art galleries, are movement-based around concepts associated with the visual contribution, made for an audience who function like gallery visitors.

Rosemary Butcher, Interview.

Live art

Similar to performance art, more theatre than dance, but the performers may be dance-trained.

John Ashford, Interview.

Cross arts activity

Works which mix performance genres, especially in experimental ways.

John Ashford, Interview.

Dance-gymnastics

The adaptation of dance skills to meet the needs of the gymnastic environment; the inclusion of dance in the competitive gymnast's training to retain an element of "elegance" to go with the "risk and diffculty".

Denise A. Gula, 1990.

Cross-art form

A way of working which uses traditional circus skills and an extended area of the performance skills used in physical theatre.

Helen Crocker and *Bim Mason,* Interview.

Cross-art form

"...dancers who speak, actors who dance, roller skating, eating a meal...", the content of a work which opens the traditional boundaries between art forms.

Elizabeth Keen, Interview.

Dreamtime choreography

"...dance that is not dance, scenes that are not scenes, snippets of narrative, comic ability, multi-media skills, objects, real time not 'acted' time, montage structure."; said of Wim Vandekeybus's "Always The Same Lies" (1992).
Andrea Phillips, 1992.

Alternative choreographer

One who experiments with new forms in contrast to those of the established dance styles of both ballet and mainstream contemporary dance.
Stephanie Jordan, 1992.

Clowning/fooling

"The art of making people laugh by being, as a performer, naïve, socially grace-less, accident-prone, pretentious, illogical, and disruptive."
'Fool Time', 1992/93.

Equilibristics

That part of circus skills which consists in the variety of stilt walking, unicycling, rola bola, slack wire, tight wire, walking globe, etc.
'Fool Time', 1992/93.

Aerial Work

That part of circus skills which consists in movement suspended above the ground on static and swinging trapeze, flying, and web rope cradle, etc.
'Fool Time', 1992/93.

Acrobatics

Physical work which comes from circus skills, consisting in tumbling, hand balances, flight, and balances in pairs and groups, etc.
'Fool Time', 1992/93.

Manipulation

Movement material from circus which consists in the skill of manipulating two or more objects, such as juggling, devil stick, club swinging, diabolo, balancing objects, etc.
Helen Crocker and *Bim Mason*, Interview.

Robotics

A movement art form in which highly controlled body isolations and smooth travelling over the floor represent a merging of man and the machine in robot-like action; includes robot costuming and make-up.
Helen Thomas, Interview.

10. DANCE IN MUSICALS, OPERAS, ETC.

Musical

"A film or theatrical production typically of a sentimental or humorous nature that consists of musical numbers and dialogue based on a unifying plot"; called also "musical comedy."
'Webster', 1993.

Musical comedy

A branch of dance with limited skills, taught in the 1930's in the U.K., preparing dancers for shows and pantomime; used in contrast to highly skilled tap dancing.
Jane Nicholas, Interview.

Dansical

"...involving an original score, a constant stream of dancing and mime, and a spoken text to parallel them both"; used of Tharp's "When We Were Very Young."
Robert Coe, 1985.

Dansical

Used of "West Side Story" (Robbins, 1957), being the first time that a musical is said to have dance as the primary art form.
Eds.

Musical theatre

A named branch of the theatrical profession in which singing, dancing, and acting are combined skills; Gershwin's "Crazy for You", Lloyd Webber's "Cats" are examples.
Eds. from the Programme for "Crazy for You" 1993.

Shows

Musical theatre productions, in which the elements include music, comedy, dancing, and girls.
Eugenia Volz Schoettler, 1979.

Microphone dances

The show business type of dance with a soloist and a backing group.
Richard Alston in Stephanie Jordan, 1992.

Jazz dance

An open style of dance based on the personal response to Jazz of leading teachers, such as Matt Maddox, Walter Nicks, Donald McKayle, Gus Giordiano, or Luigi, and in which individuality plays an important part.
Fred Tragath, 1978.

Jazz

"Of unknown origin, a term first used in the early 1900's to describe social dances and popular music that evolved from African-American traditional movement patterns and rhythms modified by the impact of Euro-American culture."
Walter Nicks, Contributed.

Vernacular jazz dance

"Movement patterns of African-Americans that date back to the importation of African slaves, plantation mores, minstrel shows and vaudeville. These dance phrases continue to contribute to current social and theatrical jazz dance forms."
Walter Nicks, Contributed.

Tap dancing

"A style of dance in which the percussive sound of the footwork is the distinguishing characteristic; the steps are performed in intricate rhythmical combinations derived from the distinctive sounds of the basic vocabulary."
James Siegelman in Mary Clarke and David Vaughan, 1977.

Music hall

An evening's entertainment made up of some 15 acts, including comedians, singers, dancers, circus acts, etc., with a compere.
Eds.

Dance in plays

The movement material in plays, which has to bring together the ingredients of "the story line, the steps, the character, and the period."
Geraldine Stephenson, Interview.

Movement for actors

The material that actors can cope with and make their own, approached through dynamic qualities, touch and relationships, spatial qualities rather than steps and set moves.
"Press into the ground.", "Use the space between you.", "Grasp her arm lightly.", "Thrust out.".
Geraldine Stephenson, Interview.

Movement directing

In opera, film and theatre, devising steps, the groupings and the movement of "traffic" of large groups of performers, as well as their gestural content, all at a level of complexity capable of being performed by actors, singers and extras, who are not dancers.
"Getting people expressively moving through space."
Stuart Hopps, Interview.

Tumbling
    Acrobatic skills in some musical theatre as part of the choreography, for which specialist performers are engaged; said of work in "Barnum" and "Crazy for You."
    Programme of "Crazy for You", 1993.

11.   VIDEO DANCE AND FILM

Video dance, A
    A work commissioned for video, designed jointly by the choreographer and the video director, which has no stage existence.
    "It exists on screen."
    Bob Lockyer, Interview.

Dance on video
    "Dance on video is a video performance of a stage ballet."
    Bob Lockyer, 1983.

Relay, A
    A live or recorded as live television transmission of a dance performance as it is given in the theatre, with audience.
    "A football match covering."
    Bob Lockyer, Interview.

TV version of a commissioned stage work
    A dance suitable for TV, created for stage space, which then is re-worked for the camera with care that the restructuring may be true to the original stage performance.
    "You may lose the work."
    Bob Lockyer, Interview.

Dance on screen
    The art form which emerges through collaborative relationship of choreographer and director, in which dance, visual qualities, camera, and editing techniques play a part.
    The Video Place, 1993.

Screening
    A showing of dance on screen, a performance of dances on screen.
    The Video Place, 1993.

Screen work, A
    A dance piece conceived of and scripted as a work for TV.
    The Video Place, 1993.

Dance cinema
>An experimental new way of working with non-dance cinematic materials, interspersed with dance materials, structured with both filmic and choreographic devices.
>*Mark Murphy*, Interview.

Pop music video
>Video made of pop groups in which dance usually plays a part, as either loose improvised rhythmic accompaniment to the music or as choreographed dance material; intended to promote the song and the group.
>*Jayne Dowdeswell*, 1993.

Videography
>The video records of performances and rehearsals of a dance company (Cunningham).
>*David Vaughan*, Conversation with Valerie Preston-Dunlop.

12. DANCE AS A SPIRITUAL ACTIVITY

Dance
>The vehicle for spiritual activity.
>*Roderyk Lange*, 1975.

Dance
>"Dance is the impulse of the spirit to move rhythmically, proportionally, and perpetually."
>*Ruth St. Denis* (1939) in Walter Terry, 1969.

Dancing
>"A magical operation for the attainment of real and important ends of every kind."
>*Havelock Ellis*, 1923.

Dancing
>"The primitive expression alike of religion and love."
>*Havelock Ellis*, 1923.

Sacred dance
>A genre of dance originating in prehistoric times which can be seen as a rite performed at all the crises of life.
>*W. E. O. Oesterley*, 1923.

Secular dances
>Dances not associated with the religious life of a community.
>*Havelock Ellis*, 1923.

Religious dances

"A savage does not preach his religion, he dances it."
Havelock Ellis, 1923.

Religious dance

"An expression of spiritual joy...expressing feelings of adoration or of supplication."
J. G. Davies, 1984.

Circle Dance

Sacred dance expressed through dancing group material derived from folk dances using a circular form, performed "to improve and enrich our lives physically, mentally, emotionally, and spiritually."
Anna Barton, 1992.

Vehicle of worship

What a dance can be when used in liturgy where it is not only a sign of spirituality but an instrument to spiritual experience.
J. G. Davies, 1984.

Trance dances

Dances in which the dancer achieves a state of disassociation from his surroundings and association with his spirit world through, usually, hyperventilation, exhaustion, dizziness from whirling, and head movements leading to autohypnosis, ecstasy, and trance.
Erika Bourguignon in Roderyk Lange, 1975.

Numinous in dance, The

The spiritual in dance; dancing and dance making in which the attraction and awe in religion and of God are paramount features giving rise to forms of dance which embody the spiritual.
Janet Adshead-Lansdale, Interview.

Dance as meditation

A form of dance which emphasises "the spiritual quest for inner stillness", is "a celebration", is about "reconciliation and hope", and is open to anyone who wishes to participate.
Stanley Hamilton, 1992.

Ecstasy of the dance

The way man bridges the chasm between this and the other world of demons, spirits and God.
Curt Sachs, 1937.

Mystic dance

"A dance symbolic of cosmic powers in its expression and form when the personal life experience of the choreographer yields to the dance visualisation of the incomprehensible and eternal."

Mary Wigman in Walter Sorell, 1968.

Ecstatic dance

A genre of dance in which the performer dances to such an extent that he becomes unconscious; by this he honours the deity, offering something in the nature of sacrifice, and makes his body a fit temporary abode for his god.

W. E. O. Oesterley, 1923.

Whirling Dervishes

A ritual dance performed by the followers of Mevlana Jalal al-din Rumi, a Sufi, in which they turn with arms outstretched, right palm up to receive the spirit and left palm down transmitting it to the earth, serving as a vessel through which divine grace can pass.

Roger Copeland, 1992.

T'ai Chi Ch'uan

A movement form which aims at a state of harmony on a physical, emotional, mental, and spiritual level.

Katherine Allen, Interview.

Cosmic dance

The universe seen as a series of dances of the heavenly bodies, in their various orbits.

E. M. W. Tillyard, 1944.

Divine dance

The dance of the stars around the sun, the circular form, round dance or 'Reigen', associated with the dances of deities.

Havelock Ellis, 1923.

Eurhythmy

A Rudolph Steiner term for Marie Steiner's system of movement (c. 1914.).

"Eurhythmy wishes to visualize the spiritual law and quality of word and tone through gesture and movement and raise them to the level of an artistic experience."

Anthroposophist Society in Walter Sorell, 1981.

13. DANCE AS A CULTURAL AND SOCIAL ACTIVITY

Dance

"Dance is a transient mode of expression, performed in a given form and style by the human body moving in space. Dance occurs through purposefully selected and controlled rhythmic movements; the resulting phenomenon is recognised as dance both by the performer and the observing members of a given group."

Joann Kealiinohomoku in Roger Copeland and Marshall Cohen, 1983.

Dance

One of the cultural manifestations of man, created by man in his own environment.

Roderyk Lange, Interview.

Sub-cultural dance

The significant dance practice of specific social groups, for instance in leisure, in liturgical dance, in acid house dance, in competitive dance.

Paul Filmer, Interview.

Dance as a mediating practice

A medium through which the tension between two parts of culture can be expressed, such as between a sub-cultural group and fashion in popular dance forms, or between women and concepts of the body in aerobics.

Paul Filmer, Interview.

Ethnic dance

The dance of a group "which holds in common genetic, linguistic, and cultural ties with special emphasis on cultural tradition"; said of every dance form and argued to include ballet.

Joann Kealiinohomoku, 1969.

Vernacular dance

Dance in the United States which arose out of the Negro community, starting with touring medicine shows, gilly shows in a tent, carnivals with side shows and animal acts, as a means of earning.

Marshall and *Jean Stearns*, 1968.

Dance in a traditional rural community

An integral part of group life, an organising factor of the community, a medium of control of the group, a medium of social ritual, magical, recreational significance.

Roderyk Lange, Interview.

Dance event in an ethnochoreological context

A meaningful culture-text, characterised by several simultaneous and interrelated modes of expression. A dance event has an aim (such as entertainment, ceremonial, ritual, etc.) and a code according to which the entire communicative process is structured and understood.

Anca Giurchescu, 1987.

Ceremonial dances
Dances executed at particular times of the year in a performer/audience context.
Theresa Buckland, 1983.

Ceremonial dances
Display dances which fulfil some of the criteria of purpose, place, performer, time of year associated with ceremonial forms, but not all; some men's dances may be performed by women, or be freer in time and place of performance.
Theresa Buckland, Interview.

Ritual-ceremonial
The linked sword dance, the hobby horse dance, the Cotswold Morris, and the processional Morris dance, from the North West, East Anglia, or the Border Counties (Hereford, Worcestershire).
"Ceremonial dancing performed by special teams of men and women for a ritual purpose."
Hugh Rippon, 1993.

Fertility dance
A traditional dance aimed at invoking the fertility of the district, such as the Abbots Bromley horn dance in which a wooden phallic-shaped object is carried by 'Maid Marion' with the other characters and six dancers dressed in Tudor costume, and each carrying antlers or horns, dancing movements symbolising the battle of Good and Evil.
Hugh Rippon, 1993.

Hobby Horse (Obby Oss)
A May 1st ceremony in which a man with a Hobby Horse over his head and shoulders, with Mayers who summon the citizens and decorate the streets with May boughs, dance all day; preceded by a 'Teaser' character and musicians; he lies down, 'dies', and revives from time to time.
Hugh Rippon, 1993.

Primitive dance
"Dance in a society which is autonomous and self-contained with its own set of customs and institutions."
Robert Redfield in Roger Copeland and Marshall Cohen, 1983.

Folk dance
Dance in a society which is, in contrast to a so-called primitive society, not autonomous but one which is in symbiotic relationship with the larger soceity with which it constantly interacts.
Robert Redfield in Roger Copeland and Marshall Cohen, 1983.

Folk dances
What is identified within urbanised cultures as the dances of rural communities, which in fact were taken out of their rural context and are executed by urban dance groups.
Roderyk Lange, 1980.

Folk dance

     Dances performed for recreational and social purposes; "should be fun to do."
Robert Harrold, Interview.

Folk dance content

     Community dances that are forms of communication and co-operation, done for
a purpose (at marriages, births) and in public places (the street, the taverna).
Robert Harrold, Interview.

Folk dance demonstrations

     National groups who keep alive a folk dance tradition by training a demon-
stration team and so emphasise technique and remove the dance from its original milieu.
Robert Harrold, Interview.

Traditional dance

     Said to have three types in England, the Morris, the sword dance, and the country
dance.
Cecil Sharp, quoted by Theresa Buckland, Interview.

True traditional form

     An aim of Cecil Sharp in founding the English Folk Dance Society, to preserve
and promote the practise of English folk dances in their "true traditional form."
Hugh Rippon, 1993.

Living folk form

     The natural evolution of folk dances and community dances even when written
down, where people are encouraged to interpret the instructions liberally and so keep the
spontaneity of the form alive.
Peter Kennedy, 1964.

Fit the occasion, To

     Choosing the community dances appropriate to the kind of venue and people
taking part, so that a programme of sufficient interest, difficulty, energy is offered by the
caller.
Michael Bell, 1977 (1957).

Evolving folk art form

     Some of the modern teams of traditional dancers, such as the girls' "fluffy
Morris" in the North West of England, and Molly Dancers in East Anglia, exemplify a
process in folk dance in which the traditions shift in light of changing circumstances.
Hugh Rippon, 1993.

Revival, The
The renewed interest in English Folk dance, started by Cecil Sharp at the turn of the century, which has resulted in new forms evolving from the originals which had all but died out.
Roy Judge, Interview.

Cotswold Morris, The
Originally an all-male performance dance, recently also danced by all-women sides, at certain times of the year, in public places, in uniform, usually white clothing with bells, using intricate step patterns, sticks and handkerchiefs, and dancing to live music.
Anthony G. Barrand, 1991.

Morris Dance
"...a ceremonial, spectacular and professional dance...performed by men only ... a formal, official dance performed only on certain days in each year, such as Whitsun Week, wake or fair day."
Cecil J. Sharp, 1934 (1909).

Morris Dance
An English country dance for six men, with energetic leaps and leg gestures; using sticks and bells on the legs with peripatetic musicians, often violin, accordion, drum and pipe of some kind.
Curt Sachs, 1937.

Morris, The
"When one says 'Morris' one usually means the Cotswold or South Midlands variant, but not always. There is a N.W. Morris, a Derbyshire Morris, a Border Morris, a Molly (Morris)."
Roy Judge, Interview.

Street theatre
What a few Morris dancers say their dance is, not a ritual, but a performance for an audience in a public place, usually a space outside a public house.
Anthony G. Barrand, 1991.

Country dancing
Dances evolved from revivals of rural community dances, sometimes producing new dance forms, such as some of the Scottish country dances.
Roderyk Lange, 1980.

Country dance
A form of dance originating in rural communities, easily learnt, performed for the pleasure of doing it and the opportunity of social intercourse.
Cecil J. Sharp, 1934 (1909).

Country Dance

"...is pre-eminently a figure dance depending in the main for its expressiveness upon the weaving of patterned concerted evolutions rather than upon intricate steps or elaborate body movements."
Cecil J. Sharp, 1934 (1909).

English Country Dance

Dance performed by two or more couples, usually facing each other in squares or, later, in lines, originally danced to popular tunes of the day, with coordinated pathways and a limited vocabulary of steps forming the main material of the dance.
Peter Buckman, 1978.

Contras

American community dances from New England, arranged in long sets of any number of couples, made up of figures danced with a light walking step to a brisk tempo; a form originally developed from English Country Dancing and now re-appearing in England as American Contra Dance.
Ralph Page, 1969.

Maypole dances

A form of country dance introduced in late 19th century, consisting in dancing with plaited ribbons around a maypole, a form introduced deliberately to teachers for children in school; not an indigenous, dance form, although the pole itself, hoisted on the village green in May, is traditional.
Hugh Rippon, 1993.

Step Dancing

In the British tradition this is a percussive form of dancing in which rhythms are beaten out with the feet. There are two broad categories: regulated, in which the dancer usually performs a sequence of steps to a specified number of musical bars, concluding with a distinctive regular motif; and improvised, in which the dancer has a freer relation with the music and performs less obviously codified material. It may appear as a solo or group display or form part of social dancing. Clog Dancing is a form of step dancing in which the dancer wears clogs and tends to follow the regulated variety.
Theresa Buckland, Contributed.

Clog Dancing

In the British and North American traditions, this consists of rhythmic patterns, usually to music and beaten out by the feet by a dancer wearing clogs. It appears to have been particularly popular in the nineteenth and early twentieth centuries in vernacular and stage contexts and is currently enjoying a revival amongst amateur dancers.
Theresa Buckland, Contributed.

Scottish dancing

A recreational social dance form using all manner of reels, largely organised in clubs and danced in the kilt for a foursome, a sixsome, or an eightsome, traditionally to the bagpipes or the fiddle.
Peter Buckman, 1978.

Highland dances

Traditional Scottish dances with an established vocabulary and style, danced as recreation and also in Highland Games and competitions; the Highland Fling, Sword Dance, Seann Triubhas, Strathspey, and Reels.

Scottish Official Board of Highland Dancing, 1955.

Competitions

A way to discover "the best all-round dancers" in Highland dancing, for which rules and conditions of entry are laid down, titles of championships are established, amateur and professional status clarified, judges appointed who allot marks for Timing, Technique, and General Deportment.

Scottish Official Board of Highland Dancing, 1955.

Competitions

One kind of folk dance event, in which teams compete with their version of a dance, such as the rapper from Tyneside, in which short, flexible, two-handled swords are used.

Hugh Rippon, 1993.

Irish step-dance

A solo dance genre, with emphasis on the feet stepping intricately to musical accompaniment. The Reel, Jig, and Hornpipe are the main categories. These are danced by both men and women, boys and girls. Posture is always held erect. Hands are held loosely by the sides. For convenience purposes the above dances may be divided into two broader categories — Light Shoe dances and Hard Shoe dances.

Catherine Foley, 1988.

Light shoe dances (Irish)

Soft black pumps are worn for the Reel, Slip Jig, Light Jig and Single Jig. Hence, these dances are termed "the Light Shoe dances."

Catherine Foley, 1988.

Hard shoe dances (Irish)

The Hornpipe, Jig, and solo set dances are regarded as "the Hard Shoe dances" as hard-soled, black shoes (laced or buckled) with either nailed leather tips, or fibreglass tips, allow the beats of the dance to be heard.

Catherine Foley, 1988.

14.   EARLY DANCE

Early Dance

Social and theatrical dancing before the establishment of a separate ballet technique, and social dance prior to the development of modern ballroom dancing.

Chris Rogers, Conversation with Larraine Nicholas.

Pre-classic dance forms

Pre-classic refers to the classic court dances, classic in form and highly stylized in the highly decorous court manner of the early sixteenth century. "Classic" refers to the classic ballet of the pointe, skirts, and five positions of Beauchamps of the court of Louis XIV.
Louis Horst, 1960 (1937).

Renaissance dances

A term applied to court dances current from the late fifteenth through the sixteenth and early seventeenth centuries, commencing in Italy and Burgundy.
"...pavanes, galliards, branles, canaries, figure dances, and the volta..."
Ingrid Brainard in CORD, 1972.

Sarabande

An example of the pre-classic dance forms taught by Louis Horst whose qualities are "arrogant, dominating, dictatorial, majestic, and authoritative."
Jane Dudley, Interview.

Baroque dances

A term applied to court dances current in the seventeenth and eighteenth centuries.
"...minuet, courante, bourrée, sarabande, passepeid, L'Allemande, gigue, gavotte..."
Shirley Wynne and *Wendy Hilton* in CORD, 1972.

Contredanse (baroque)

Ballroom dance performed by more than one couple.
Wendy Hilton, 1981.

Baroque dance (revived)

Contemporary dance individuals and ensembles who specialise in the research and practice of dances from the seventeenth and eighteenth centuries.
Imperial Society of Teachers of Dancing, 1972.

15.   20TH CENTURY SOCIAL DANCE

Social dancing

Recreative dancing by the populace, secular in nature.
Joann Kealiinohomoku (1969) in Roger Copeland and Marshall Cohen, 1983.

Community dancing

Essentially dancing in which the individual loses his 'self' in the common bond of unanimous expression; the social element of give and take is paramount.
Douglas Kennedy, 1949.

Barn dance

An all-age social gathering, usually in an informal setting, at which a variety of folk and square dances are used, not for performance, but for sheer enjoyment.

Ron Saunders, Interview.

Dances at a barn dance

Specified dances enjoyed at social occasions for the whole community.

"A modern barn dance programme would be: Waves of Tory, Drops of Brandy, Nottingham Swing, The Gay Gordons, Circassian Circle."

Hugh Rippon, 1993.

Square dancing

A recreational dance for four male/female couples, lively music and a "caller", originating in the U.S.A.

Betty Casey, 1976.

Old Time Dancing

A set form of social dance, both amateur and competitive, based on foot positions, steps, and holds, and an etiquette to be observed; it includes, amongst others, the Valeta, Regis Waltz, the Saunter, Schottische, various Two Steps.

Derek Young, 1991.

Old time dancing

A general term for a recreational dance genre using the dances of the 19th century, such as the Lancers, the Dashing White Sergeant, the Polka, the Valeta.

Peter Buckman, 1978.

Old-fashioned ballroom dancing

The waltzes, quadrilles, cotillions, and the polka, introduced into the ballroom in the early 19th century in place of the indigenous country dance forms.

Hugh Rippon, 1993.

Ballroom dancing

Forms of social dance which arise from musical rhythms.

"A new dance is born of a new rhythm. It is a rhythm to which the steps of no existing dance can be satisfactorily fitted without some subtle change which alters the whole nature of the steps."

Victor Silvester, 1942.

Contact dancing

A retrospective term for the swing-era jive dancing of couples where touch, dependency, leaps, and lifts were part of the vocabulary; said in contrast to the disco dance way of dancing without physical contact. May also be used for traditional ballroom-hold dances.

Laura Thompson, 1993.

Dance craze

A feature of the popular culture in which a new dance or new dance movement is introduced which "everyone" does and wants to become proficient in.

Paul Filmer, Interview.

Thé dansant

An elegant mid-afternoon social occasion popular in the 1920's and 1930's, which a dance adviser may re-create in a period play.

"...in 'The House of Elliot'...."

Geraldine Stephenson, Interview.

Novelty dances

Short-lived ragtime dances which imitated the gait of animals, such as the Monkey Dance, the Bunnyhug, the Grizzly Bear, the Turkey Trot, the Fishtail, the Eagle Rock, the Buzzard Lope.

Peter Buckman, 1978.

Novelty dances

Dances which arose in the 1930's, mostly processional dances, such as the Lambeth Walk, the Hokey Cokey, the Palais Glide and Boomps-a-daisy, the Conga.

Peter Buckman, 1978.

Standard dancing

The Waltz, Foxtrot, Tango, Quickstep, and Viennese Waltz, the five techniqes in ballroom dancing, all of which are danced by a couple while staying in the ballroom hold.

Geoffrey Hearn, Interview.

Latin American dancing

The Rumba, Cha Cha Cha, Samba, Paso Doble, and Jive, which constitute the five rhythms and techniques of competitive and social Latin American dance, none of which stay in the ballroom hold and so allow more freedom of composition than standard ballroom dancing.

"Cuban style dancing."

Geoffrey Hearn, Interview.

Sport dance

Latin American and ballroom dancing which is competitive, having medals and championships, and set techniques to be presented by couples to judges.

Geoffrey Hearn, Interview.

Medal dancing

Ballroom and Latin American classes in which young people learn their techniques for the established examinations.

Geoffrey Hearn, Interview.

Sequence dancing

In a sequence the various movements have to be made in a set order. As a result the same step is being executed by all the couples in the room simultaneously.

Victor Silvester, 1942.

Modern Sequence Dancing

A recent introduction to social dance, using the ballroom and Latin forms as a popular pastime.

Derek Young, 1991.

"Come Dancing"

The title of an exceptionally long-running television series on competitive ballroom dancing in a style which the participants themselves mould into its own look and aesthetic, one which gives pleasure to them and to the fully involved spectators.

Helen Thomas, Interview.

Authentic jazz dance

Those dances performed in the 1920's and 1930's in African-American social dance.

K. Hazzard-Gordon, 1990.

Ragtime dances

Social dances from the U.S.A. which came to Europe at the turn of the 19th/20th centuries.

"...the Brazilian Maxixe, the Onestep, the Turkey Trot, the Cakewalk...."
Walter Sorell, 1981.

Lindy, The

A swing dance for couples, with breakaways, pushaways, flips, slide-unders and partner lifts, using a slow/slow/quick/quick rhythm, with room for "your own breaks and routines."

Lani Van Ryzin, 1979.

Conga

A social dance in which the dancers form a long line with hands on each other's hips and, with simple repetitive step, weave in and around in curving floor patterns, sometimes from dance floor to dance floor.

Jack Villari and *Kathleen Sims Villari*, 1979.

Boogie, To

To dance in a social context, especially in the 1960's; including all manner of short-lived dances.

"The Watusi, the Pony, the Boogaloo, the Frug, the Funky Broadway, the Slop, the Mashed Potato, the Monkey, the Hitchhiker, the Swim, the Shake."
Jack Villari and *Kathleen Sims Villari*, 1979.

Disco dancing
A 1970's version of the "age-old desire for men and women in engage in dance as celebration, as recreation, and as expression".
Jack Villari and *Kathleen Sims Villari*, 1979.

Disco dancing
Jitterbug, Rock 'n' Roll and the Twist, dances which made the transition from couple dances to solo dances in which improvisation around the beat of the music is the main ingredient.
Peter Buckman, 1978.

Break dancing
A style of competitive, acrobatic and pantomimic dancing game which arose in New York in the late 1970's, was performed by black and hispanic teeenage crews in parks or subways to rap music.
Sally Banes, 1985.

Break dancing
The urban vernacular dance game which became a media-made theatrical art form with a technique and vocabulary capable of expansion.
Sally Banes, 1985.

Breaking jam
An unscheduled happening, occurrence or performance by a crew of break dancers; onlookers form an impromptu circle as dancers enter the ring singly for a brief 10–30 second turn.
Sally Banes, 1985.

Body popping
"...the muscles and joints of the body 'pop' or explode on the beat of the music; the music is funk music, danceable Black soul music."
Julie Tolley and *Ramsay Burt*, 1983.

Bopping
The style of dance performed by the motorbikers of the 1970's which was rooted in the Rock 'n' Roll tradition of the 1950's.
"The male swings the female around with a flick of his hand or spins her by holding her hand over her head. The beat is followed in an exaggerated way by movements of the head, hands and the whole body."
Paul Willis, 1978.

Clubbing
Going to night clubs to dance, listening to particular popular music, wearing subculture clothing, using the in-language of that kind of music.
"Solid soul and funky dance classics", "garage and house party", "up-front jazz and funky rap", "leather-clad trendies", "tuff house and advance dance."
"Time Out", 1993.

Frontin'

A clubbing term for the manoeuvre of winning a female dancing partner through dance. The male dancer moves to within close proximity of the female dancer, who will shift her orientation so as to be dancing with the male, if his attention and intention is welcome.

Donna Taylor, Observation and interview with Portsmouth clubbers.

Having a slice

Being successful in attracting and dancing with a girl when frontin'.

Donna Taylor, Interview with Portsmouth clubbers.

Pullin'

To attract successfully a member of the opposite sex. The act of pullin' is often the intention behind going out clubbing.

"...going out on the pull."

Donna Taylor, Interview with Portsmouth clubber (Stewart).

Blown out

To have failed to win a girl's interest when frontin'.

Donna Taylor, Interview with Portsmouth clubbers.

Crash and burn

Another term for being 'blown out', i.e. having failed to attract a girl's interest through frontin'.

Donna Taylor, Interview with Portsmouth clubbers.

Chillin'

A derivative of 'to chill out', meaning relaxing, taking it easy.

Donna Taylor, Interview with Portsmouth clubbers.

Rave culture

Youth culture with its own aesthetic, with dancing to pop music in a one-off venue specially chosen for the occasion, associated with loud noise, strobe lighting, Ecstacy, and continuous trance-inducing dancing.

Helen Thomas, Interview.

Moves and grooves

The title given to popular dance forms which clubbers relish, each venue offering a particular sound and look and kind of dance; for example lambada, merengue, cumbia and salsa at the "Salsa-Fusion".

"Time Out", 1993.

Slam Dancing

A dance style that has progressed from the Punk era to the New Age Punks. It is for males only, who dance close to each other, thrashing their arms and legs, intentionally knocking into each other, with the aim of knocking each other over.

"[Slam Dancing] is like a mating ritual, the men having to prove their machoness by staying on their feet and seeing how many they can push over."
Donna Taylor, Interview with New Age Punk (Brian).

"Dances"

Illegal occasions, unlicensed all-night raves; music is connoisseur soul, the crowd followers of their 'sound', that is the music 'selector' and 'm.c.'; the present urban version of the 1980's ravers.
"Touch", 1993.

Global Dance

The international move in music and dance, cutting across cultural barriers: "World Music",

"...everything from African and salsa to reggae and zouk...".
"Time Out", 1993.

Ball

Prestigious function such as charity ball, hunt ball, Queen Charlotte's ball, May ball, Caledonian ball, for which formal dress is worn, a professional band is engaged, and at which social dancing is the central feature; customarily, a ball goes on into the early hours or dawn.
Valerie Preston-Dunlop, Interview.

16.   DANCE IN THE COMMUNITY

Community dance

Dance activity designed for the population as a whole, run in Great Britain in conjunction with local authority and Arts Council funding, which caters for a wide range of dance activity including professional choreographers working with amateur dancers.
Peter Brinson, 1991.

Community dance

An opportunity provided for anyone to take part in dance; dance made accessible, "for everyone to dance, or watch and appreciate, or create", primarily in dance as art, rather than conventional social dance.
Alysoun Tomkins, Interview.

Community dance project

A locally organised, funded, dance initiative, may be one-off or on-going, with a stated purpose "to reflect the diverse environments...from industrialised and urban areas to rural communities."; said of community dance in Wales.

Sally Varrall, 1992.

Community initiative

An experiment in the 1950's in community arts in which workers from a factory and their families participated in art activities, including dance, of a recreational and celebratory kind following the model pioneered by Rudolf Laban for the regeneration of community arts.

Marion North, Interview.

Community Dance styles

A complete mix of dance styles from theatre and musical theatre, to ethnic specific styles; Kurdish, Afro-Caribbean, Chinese ribbon dance, Scottish reels; from body therapies, to tap dance, any form which requires a space and a teacher.

Alysoun Tomkins, Interview.

Dance in a multi-cultural society

Dance forms from diverse cultural origins, such as T'ai Chi, Capoeira, Yemenite folk dance, contact improvisation, introduced into a society such as Great Britain, which itself contains people from many cultural origins; both promoted by private initiative and sponsored by local government organs.

Valerie Preston-Dunlop, Interview.

Capoeira

A Brazilian game in which partners exchange movements of attack and defence in a constant flow, exploring the strength and weakness of the opponent; it is accompanied by the berimbau, a one-string bow-shaped musical instrument.

"...a dance-like fight, a fight-like dance...traditional ritualised combat.".

Bira Almeida, 1986.

Dance culture

The diverse ways in which dance occurs and is catered for in a community, reflecting the gamut of its social, creative and artistic commitment.

"Street dance", "Bhangra dance", "ballet."

Jeanette Siddall, 1992.

Health and fitness

A category of adult education classes in which dance is offered alongside body therapies, martial arts, and a variety of exercise to music.

"Callanetic type exercise. Aerobics stretch and tone. Lunchtime ballet. Fun in Fitness. Move with Medau. Yoga for all. T'ai Chi. Ballroom Dancing. Circle dancing. Alexander Technique."

Kent County Council, 1992.

Aerobics
A form of movement exercise to pop music offered for the general public.
"Low impact, fat-burning stamina work. Strengthen, tone and stretch the muscles — abdominal work — floor work."
Kent County Council, 1992.

Education and Community Unit
A company-based unit which works with people of all ages throughout the year, tours nationally alongside the Company, and delivers an outreach programme promoting knowledge and understanding of classical ballet, most often focusing on their rich and varied repertoire.
English National Ballet, Education Office, Contributed.

Outreach
A programme of work from a dance company to the community at large, designed to make connections between the professional dance world and the general population.
English National Ballet, 1992.

17. DANCE EDUCATION AND TRAINING

Dance education
"Dance Education is a process of interaction which empowers individuals to develop dance skills and activity by means of the integrating elements of composing, performing, and appreciating."
Marion Gough, Correspondence.

Dance education
A process of developing the individual's talents as a human being in a society while initiating him or her into the form of life which the dance domain offers.
June Layson, Interview.

Professional dance education
A process requiring co-ordination of the knowledge of what makes a physically healthy dancer, with what choreographers require from performers, with the liberating knowledge that the individual needs to facilitate their own creativity.
Richard Ralph, Interview.

Dance training
The preparation in a vocational school of the young dancer to take a place in the dance profession, a process which often removes him or her from the contemporary cultural context during this formative period.
June Layson, Interview.

Dance training

Preparation of the body for dancing, but also a political act, "leading dancers to think and work in a particular way which may enhance or diminish their autonomy, which may encourage technical eloquence or creative fervour."

Peter Dunleavy, Interview.

Dance education and training

A process promoted by some dance institutions of higher education in which there is a reconciliation between the rigorous training needs of the professional performer and the wider educational and cultural needs of the student.

June Layson, Interview.

Director of a Dance Education and Training Academy

The person who enables and encourages dance education and training to take place by anticipating trends, developing and responding to ideas, initiating experimentation and new areas of work, liaising with other academies at home and overseas, by developing creative work through choreography; said of the Laban Centre for Movement and Dance.

Marion North, Interview.

Professor of dance

The person appointed to a Chair of Dance at a British University, responsible for a programme in dance in higher education with an opportunity to employ whatever mix of theory and practice he wishes to promote.

Richard Ralph, 1993.

Dance in education

Dance in the public education system, at primary, secondary and tertiary level, in both curriculum and extra-curriculum provision.

Valerie Preston-Dunlop, 1980.

Art of dance in education

A programme of dance in the school curriculum which favours dance as an art form, providing methods and materials which contribute to the artistic, aesthetic and cultural education of the child.

Jacqueline Smith-Autard, Interview.

Physical education

The curriculum subject in schools with which, traditionally, dance is associated, and within which it is catered for in the National Curriculum of the U.K.

Jeanette Siddall, 1992.

Dance as education

Dance as a means to the education of the person, through both formal and informal learning modes, a concept promoted early this century especially by Rudolf Laban, and presently in the United Kingdom by Peter Brinson.

Peter Brinson, 1991.

Professional training

Training for an actual job (in the dance domain) by which the focus of the course is on the acquisition of work-specific skills and attitudes; may be a performer, dance archivist, company education unit, teacher, lighting designer for dance, dance administrator, etc.

Janet Adshead-Lansdale, Interview.

Vocational dance training

Education in a specialist dance academy, conservatoire or college which is intended to provide the skills and understanding necessary to pursue a career in dance; usually seen as training for performance but may also be for any of the professional work in the domain of dance, such as choreography, or lighting design, or choreology.

Eds.

Vocationalisation of dance education

The current move towards teaching, including dance teaching, with learning skills as paramount aims through which students are seen as more employable generally; seen as contrasted with study of dance in its own right, for its own sake, or professional training.

Janet Adshead-Lansdale, Interview.

Dance academy

A training centre specialising in dance with an emphasis on performance, usually associated with particular dance styles; examples are the Royal Academy of Dancing, the Urdang Academy.

Royal Academy of Dancing and *Urdang Academy*, 1993.

Dance centre

A place where dance lessons, tea dances, social dances, group classes, and professional coaching take place, which may also act as a social centre for a locality.

Spencer Dance Centre, 1992(a) and 1992(b).

Ballet school

A centre for the training of ballet as a technique, and ultimately as a performance art form. These centres range from local schools which children attend once or twice a week, to the ballet conservatoires.

Ying-Pi Chiang, 1991.

Ballet company schools

The most efficient schooling for young dancers, one attached to a company from which they learn the essentials of the life of the professional dancer.

"...from familiarity with make-up, the wearing of wigs and costumes, theatrical emergency and an opera-house climate."

Lincoln Kirstein, 1977 (1952).

Theatre Arts

Dance, drama and singing; usually refers to vocational courses of training towards work in commercial musical theatre, and television.

Eds., from school prospectuses and advertisements.

Performing Arts

Dance, music and drama; usually refers to courses in which the broad education of the three arts is offered in performing, making and appreciating modes; offered in secondary and tertiary education institutions.

Eds., GCSE, A levels, and degree course syllabi.

Performing Arts College

A training establishment in which courses designed to prepare people to work in the performing arts are offered, including subject categories of Modern, Drama, Ballet, Tap, Musical theatre, Stage dancing, Singing, etc.

Doreen Bird College, 1993.

University dance department

An institution with a responsibility to "spearhead the advance of the frontiers of dance knowledge" through a commitment to research in Dance.

June Layson, Interview.

Dance teacher training

Full-time three-year courses offered to prepare dancers to teach 'junior and senior students' and to become professional teachers of dance within the styles offered.

Royal Academy of Dancing, 1993.

International summer school

The two- to six-week courses offered in the academic vacation which many colleges and organisations offer as a mixture of serious study, holiday, and a chance to work with well-known dance people.

Royal Academy of Dancing, 1993.

Dance degree

A BA or BA(Honours) degree course offered in both private and public higher education institutions, each course offering its own emphasis in theory and practice, its own range of dance styles, its own innovations and research base; equally applies to MA degrees.

Peter Brinson, 1991.

Practice-based degree

Undergraduate dance courses focused on studio work contextualised in cultural and critical discussion.

Richard Ralph, Interview.

Research degree in dance

Practice-based work in which the experience of the investigative artist is the process, expressed physically and intellectually, with the relation between the two being rigorously monitored and placed in wider critical contexts — individual and cultural.
Richard Ralph, Interview.

Accreditation

The validation for a course offered at an educational institution, by a body appointed to visit, review and safeguard standards of the course; used in the U.K. for the former Council for National Academic Awards validation of Further and Higher degrees in dance, for the Council for Dance Education and Training validation, and for Universities' validation of degree courses.
"Dancing Times", passim.

Grades

Standards of dance work divided according to syllabi, offered from the youngest age, Grade I to the Major syllabus levels, Elementary to Advanced for the older student; offered in stated genres of dance.
"RAD Elementary", "ISTD Grade 5 in Modern Stage Dancing."
"Dancing Times", passim.

Graded examinations

Carefully prepared syllabi, teaching methods, and examination procedures, organised for the progressive education of dancers at pre-vocational, recreational, and vocational levels; used in the Cecchetti Method of Classical Ballet training.
Imperial Society of Teachers of Dancing, 1993(f).

Competitions

Competitive events held by dance societies, especially the Imperial Society of Teachers of Dancing, for children and vocational students for the awards offered in the various branches; the Mabel Ryan Award for Cecchetti ballet, the Marjorie Davies Star Tap Award, the Ruby Ginner Award in Greek Dancing, the Kathleen Browning Award in choreography are examples.
Imperial Society of Teachers of Dancing, 1993(a).

Test

The first Imperial Society of Teachers of Dancing assessment for children, in which a broadly based activity at an elementary level is taught and presented for award.
Robert Harrold, Interview.

Choreographic portfolio

Dances made by a student and presented as part of the requirements for an undergraduate, postgraduate, or research degree in Dance.
June Layson, Interview.

Vocational dance curricula

Planned courses in dance education and training institutions in which named subjects are taught and accredited examinations are taken, selected according to the aims of the institution and the expertise of the faculty.

"Ballet, contemporary, character, tap", "body conditioning, classical ballet, Spanish, Tap, Modern Jazz, Drama", or "acrobatics, aerobics", or "ballet, tap, Greek, and modern stage", etc.

"Dancing Times", passim.

Dance curriculum

A programme of study for dance 'for ages five to sixteen' to be taught in schools through Physical Education or Performing Arts departments.

Jeanette Siddall, 1992.

Service, To

What an educational institution for professional dance does, to provide trained dance people for mainstream companies, animateurs, teaching, administration, dance video and film, work in commercial theatre as well as "the spiky end of the independent scene".

Richard Ralph, Interview.

Artistic core

An area of dance which some teachers maintain cannot be explained, verbalised or understood by any means other than practice, which some other teachers may question.

"...passing down arcane knoledge as holy inviolable truth..."

Richard Ralph, Interview.

Theoretical practice/practical theory

The idea that it is unhelpful to distinguish between the practical and the theoretical study of dance; they may happen at the same time or separately, students may excel in both or one.

"...the practice of dance as academic study...".

Christopher Bannerman in Richard Ralph, 1993.

Marrying theory and practice

A dance study method which links theoretical class content with studio work, encouraging dancers to think vigorously while working practically; an aim especially necessary in a modular curriculum system.

Stephanie Jordan, Interview.

Theoretical practice

Work in the studio seen as theoretical practice through using creative, appreciative, kinetic, and rational faculties while dancing.

Valerie Preston-Dunlop, Interview.

Cross feeding
     Making links across dance 'subjects', so that a dance student's writing is informed by what she has danced, and vice versa.
     Stephanie Jordan, Interview.

Dance processes and products
     Composing, performing and viewing of dance material seen as non-assessable processes in dance education, with compositions, performances and appreciation of dance material seen as assessable products.
     Jacqueline Smith-Autard, Interview.

Mid-way model
     A suggested model for dance educators, especially those in secondary education, which combines elements from the process-focused 'educational model' inherited from modern educational dance and the product-oriented professional model of the dance conservatoire.
     Jacqueline Smith-Autard, Interview.

Multicultural dance styles
     The forms of dance being offered in classes and performances which span the range of the cultural heritage of the 1990's.
     "Afro-contemporary", "Jazz", "Afro-Brazilian contemporary", "Samba", "Afro-Cuban dance", "Capoeira", "Chinese ribbon dances", "Kurdish dance."
     "Time Out", passim.

National Dancing
     The practice of folk dancing from many countries, especially European, associated with dance teaching rather than a spontaneous social event; a branch of the Imperial Society of Teachers of Dancing.
     Sheila Dickie and *Lesley Anne Sayers*, 1992/93.

National dance
     One dance which everyone in a country knows and regards as their national symbol.
     "Kalamatianos in Greece, Mazurka in Poland."
     Robert Harrold, Interview.

Tap Branch
     A branch of the Imperial Society of Teachers of Dancing which caters for the amateur and professional dancer, promoting 'good rhythm, style and technique' in the tap vocabulary, including American Tap.
     Imperial Society of Teachers of Dancing, 1993(b).

Modern Theatre Dance

A branch of the Imperial Society of Teachers of Dancing centred on modern and jazz dance which, through keeping close ties with the profession, adapts the syllabi when necessary to reflect trends in theatre practice while maintaining standards.

Imperial Society of Teachers of Dancing, 1993(c).

Sequence dancing

The title of a branch of the Imperial Society of Teachers of Dancing which aims to encourage the practice of dancing in sequences, including those in the authentic Old Time style, and sequences of Ballroom and Latin American style, 'as pastime', as well as providing examination and medals for those who wish to improve their standard.

Imperial Society of Teachers of Dancing, 1993(d).

Repertory

A curriculum subject in a dance conservatoire, the student learning to dance and interpret the work to performance standard (Juilliard School), (Royal Ballet School), (London School of Contemporary Dance).

Eds.

Repertory

Works made for particular dance student groups to give them performance education and experience, works designed for their level of expertise, and group logistics.

Eds.

Repertory in education

A term for a body of work capable of being performed, in which students study how a choreographer dealt with aspects of dance making, such as exits and entrances, group designs, relationships of dancers, rhythmic phrasing, by dancing extracts and whole dances.

Janet Adshead-Lansdale, Interview.

Repertory

This can be a course in which dancers not only learn to work accurately in a style, but it is also a rigorous activity both conceptually and for the body.

Stephanie Jordan, Interview.

Composition

Drawing out students' ideas, giving them the opportunity to put their ideas into movement, providing a secure atmosphere in which to do it, giving them courage to 'live dangerously', to dig into their own resources, monitoring and guiding them toward artistic clarity.

"The inventiveness of the human being is a constant surprise."

Dorothy Madden, Interview.

Dynamic interplay

The interactive process of young choreographer and teacher/mentor by which the choreographer takes the next steps in the art of making dances.

Bonnie Bird, Interview.

Tools

What the composition teacher can give; what the dance maker with talent, intuition and taste can use successfully.

Jane Dudley, Interview.

Dance appreciation method

A curriculum subject in which students learn to overlay the history of a work with their own life history and so come to understand the complex layering of dance interpretation.

Janet Adshead-Lansdale, Interview.

Dance score as source

Using notated dance as a starting point for asking all manner of questions on the nature of the original work and how, if at all, it might be re-found.

"Establish a relationship to the score."

Stephanie Jordan, Interview.

Language of Dance Teaching Approach

A method developed by Ann Hutchinson Guest of exploring movement to discover basic possibilities, using as visual aids the symbols of Labanotation.

Ann Hutchinson Guest, Interview.

Dancing lessons

Classes for beginners to advanced held in most localities in privately-owned Dance Schools, Ballet Schools, or simply offered in the church hall or through evening classes by a dance teacher, usually qualified through one of the main dance teachers organisations.

Spencer Dance Centre, 1992(a) and 1992(b).

Dance class

The main way in which a traditon of dance is passed on, be it tap dance, ballet, Kathak, jazz, the teacher being the vehicle through which the heritage is carried.

Eds.

Dance class

A process through which the would-be dancer becomes an instrument of the dance, acquiring the necessary skills, stamina, and physique, and also learning the basic vocabularies of dance material for the profession.

Eds.

Dance class
> The mode through which most amateurs engage in dance activity as recreation, in which a teacher provides the movement material and the sound is provided by a musician or audio equipment.
> *Eds.*

Movement and sound classes
> The variety of ways that sound and dance are offered in classes, both for participation and for the preparation of dance composition.
> "Drums for self-expression" (Jason Wood), "mixing the elements of movement and dance" (Sue MacLellan), "personal development through movement and sound" (Keith Brazil).
> *"Time Out"*, 1993.

Natural Movement
> The dance form initiated by Madge Atkinson and developed in the 1930's by Anita Hayworth as a systematic training of the body through dance, which took nature as an infinite stimulus to artistic activity; used primarily in teacher training and schools.
> *Francine M. Watson Coleman*, Interview.

Natural Movement
> A movement training system in which the unnatural exercises of virtuosic dance were replaced by fundamental movement forms healthy to the body, lyrical in style, practised in expressive studies and dances as an art form.
> *Francine M. Watson Coleman*, Interview.

Eurhythmics (also **Eurythmics**)
> The music and movement education of Emile Jaques-Dalcroze, introduced at the beginning of the century, and developed and developing today.
> *Marie-Laure Bachmann*, 1992.

Principles of Eurhythmic practice
> "Learning through personal experience, harmonizing body and mind, the moving body as the origin of the rhythmic sense; the time — space — energy relationship of music and movement."
> *Selma Landen Odom*, 1992.

Dalcroze method
> To experience music through the rhythmic expression of the body and, at the same time, to "loosen and heighten all mental and creative forces in man."
> *Walter Sorell*, 1986.

Modern Educational Dance

A form of dance widely used in the U.K. from the early 1940's, initiated by Rudolf Laban's "danse libre" concepts; a form in which the experience of the participants in creative dance was valued as a means to the education of the "whole" person — prowess or the presentation of theatrical dance works as art being less valued.

"In schools where art education is fostered, it is not the artistic perfection or the creation and performance of sensational dances that is aimed at, but the beneficial effect of the creative activity of dancing upon the personality of the pupil."

Rudolf Laban, 1948.

Central European Dance

A genre of dance introduced into general education in Britain, and some dance studios, in the later 1930's and early 1940's, stemming from 'the New German Dance' of Rudolf Laban and Mary Wigman.

Elsie Palmer, 1958.

Art of movement

The English translation of 'Bewegungskunst', the term coined by Laban in the 1910's for a range of movement spheres, especially theatre dance, dance drama, and choric movement. The English term, coined in the 1940's, embraced not only Laban's style of theatre, but also movement in schools and in industry.

Laban Art of Movement Guild, passim.

Art of movement

The expressive arts of mime, drama, dance, and ritual which "communicate man's inner life and energy".

Joan Russell, 1958.

Dance Drama

A form of group dance in which motives, incidents, climaxes, mood, interactions, characterisation all play a part; a dance form widely used in schools and particularly appropriate for boys and young men.

Joan Russell, 1958.

Greek dancing

Form of dancing developed by Ruby Ginner using the Hellenic ideal of the dance as its inspiration; no authenticity was claimed for these dances, but descriptions from Greek literature and the paintings and sculptures of Hellenic dancing figures were used as its basis.

Ruby Ginner, 1944.

Classical Greek Dance

A branch of the Imperial Society of Teachers of Dancing in which the pioneering work of Ruby Ginner is furthered, including 'lyrical, athletic, pyrrhic, bacchic, choric, ritual and tragic' aspects, and improvisation.

Imperial Society of Teachers of Dancing, 1993(e).

Basic Dance

A revival of the consciousness in the body as it reflects the root of the movement impulse which is a response to every experience both sensory and emotional; awareness of this prevents the individual from becoming "conventionalised into a mass product"; said of Isadora Duncan's work.

John Martin, 1977 (1947).

Dance studios

Dance spaces which can be hired for classes, rehearsals, practice, auditions, which may also act as a centre for professional dancers to keep in touch with events.

Pineapple Dance Studios, 1990.

18. ADMINISTRATION AND FUNDING

Artistic policy (of a company)

The strategy adopted by a ballet or dance company in relation to its repertory and its audiences.

"...to take classical ballet to a wide audience...", "...to perform the 19th century classics...", "...to stage heritage works within the ballet style of the 20th century...", "...to mount new works..."; said of The Birmingham Royal Ballet.

Derek Purnell, Interview.

Dance research organisations

National and international bodies who promote research into dance, holding conferences, reconstruction platforms, publishing papers and videos of dance, supporting innovative and scholarly research methods; examples are the Committee on Research in Dance (CORD), the Society for Dance Research, U.K.

Eds.

Folk dance society

A central body whose function is to promote folk dance activity, providing information, publications, training, a library, a shop, a meeting place, and a space to dance in.

English Folk Song and Dance Society, 1993.

International co-operation

Organisations which promote international interaction in dance with stated objectives and area of work; said of Fédération Internationale de Danse, Dance and the Child International, International Dance Teacher's Association, International Dance Council, World Dance Alliance, International Council for Kinetography Laban, etc.

Eds.

Management

The multi-layered controlling systems which a company or ensemble has to engage with, such as the management of the theatre, of the company itself, the cultural administration of the city visited, the fund raisers and grant givers, the political lobbyists.
Norman Morrice, Interview.

Foundation

Organisation that administers, manages, and supports the activities of its Dance Company and its School.
Merce Cunningham Foundation, 1993.

Umbrellas

Management organisations who promote particular aspects of the dance domain, such as "Dance Umbrella"'s annual international dance festival, "Dance U.K." which provides a national forum for discussion of dance problems, "ADiTi", the national organisation for South Asian Dance, Community Dance and Mime Foundation.
Jane Nicholas, Interview.

Dance agency

A community dance initiative where policy making, funding, and administrative assistance is offered to practitioners in the field by a central agency associated with a city or a region.
Birmingham National Dance Agency, 1992.

Dance agency

Often but not invariably building-based, dance agencies are focal points for dance development, offering residencies, classes and projects, as well as a developing performance programme. In some cases they also offer advice and information.
Arts Council of Great Britain, Dance Department, 1993.

National Dance Agencies

"National Dance Agencies (NDAs) are a main plank of the Dance Panel's strategy for building a healthy infrastructure for dance. NDAs commission and promote regional, national and international artists, provide space, professional training, community classes, information and advice, and focal points for the development of a community of dance artists."
Arts Council of Great Britain, Dance Department, 1993.

Access

The availability of dance to the community through public provision of classes, performances, events, without privilege.
Peter Brinson, Interview.

Access

A portmanteau word which includes the "accessibility" of a building, e.g. wheelchair access, induction loop or big print; and, an attempt to reach sections of the community not often served by theatres etc. Paul Hamlyn Week at Covent Garden is an example of an access attempt by targeting audiences, limiting ticket prices, lifting rules about who can come; encouraging first-time attenders.

Lynn Maree, Contributed.

Safe house

A rehearsal and performance space for dancers where there is a supportive staff and the core of an interested audience.

Lynn Maree, Contributed.

Marketing dance

Selling dance performances and companies by packaging them and publicising them in a way which will bring new audiences as well as retaining the present ones.

Jane Nicholas, Interview.

Build a public, To

To present works which attract an audience to come to performances on a regular basis.

"...to excite, amuse, and move an audience...".

Christopher Bruce in John Percival, Contributed.

Ambassadors

What a prestigious company, or well-known artists, become when sent on foreign tours organised to coincide with or precede a political event; said of the Royal Ballet invited to Mexico City for "U.K. week".

Norman Morrice, Interview.

Cultural export

A ballet company used as a glamorous export to enhance international relations, who include social occasions in their schedule of appearances.

Norman Morrice, Interview.

Packaging dance events

A marketing device whereby certain free activities, possibly dance workshops, open rehearsals, pre-performance talks, are available with the purchase of tickets for performances, but not without a purchase.

Jane Nicholas, Interview.

Invisible to the public

Unnoticed, what performances often are, for which festivals are a possible solution, to make dance visible.

John Ashford, Interview.

Festivalisation of culture

A marketing device through festivals whereby critics and the public will come to performances which otherwise they would miss or overlook.

John Ashford, Interview.

Multicultural policy

Statements made by an advisory and funding body, such as the Arts Council of Great Britain, to encourage dance people to pay more attention to the percentage of the population who have multicultural dance interests, both as performers and spectators.

Jane Nicholas, Interview.

Demands

The requirements imposed on a company by entrepreneurs and impresarios who dictate which works shall be played and which artists, especially stars, shall perform for the tour they have organised.

Norman Morrice, Interview.

Three-acter

A full evening three-act ballet, a problematic work for management because of huge financial outlay and forward planning it requires, but which, being attractive to the established dance audience, brings in revenue and so must be mounted. If successful, can remain in the reportoire for many years.

Jane Nicholas, Interview.

Ballet triple bill

An evening of ballet with three one-act works, programming which is difficult to market, the public generally preferring 3-act ballets.

Jane Nicholas, Interview.

Council

An appointed body whose major responsibility is to allot state financial support to the internal culture and to the export of the culture; said of the Arts Council of Great Britain and the British Council.

Norman Morrice, Interview.

Panel

An advisory body of people regarded as experts in the field (of dance) who advise councils on how to spend their money.

Normal Morrice, Interview.

Advisory structure

The way the funding bodies seek advice about policy-making, strategy, assessment, and funding decisions: usually a group of 'peers' — artists, promoters, administrators, critics — representing a range of opinion and interest.

Lynn Maree, Contributed.

Regional Arts Board: function

Originally established to fund at local level because the Arts Council was too far away and too 'national', R.A.B.s have developed advisory and development roles — working to establish partnerships often with local authorities, for instance in the setting up of a dance animateur post.

Lynn Maree, Contributed.

Regional Arts Board: structure

"There were 12 Regional Arts Associations, semi-autonomous, able to choose their own governing structures and decide their own policies. There are now ten R.A.B.s whose chairs are appointed by the Minister of National Heritage and who have to submit detailed spending plans to the Arts Council, which adhere to Arts Council guidelines and priorities, in order to receive their Arts Council grant: which is usually around 90% of their funds."

Lynn Maree, Contributed.

Dance status, Change of

The relative importance of Dance within the subsidy system. E.g. Recognition by the Arts Council of Great Britain of Dance as an independent Art-Form with its own Panel, Department, and Budget in 1978–79 whereas it had hitherto come under the aegis of Music's Panel, Department and Budget.

Jane Nicholas, Interview.

Status of dance

Although now perceived as a distinct art form with specialist staff (i.e. Dance Officers), the low status of Dance within the funding system is still a concern.

Julia Carruthers, Contributed.

Priorities

Policies developed by all arts funding bodies, in consultation with advisers and artists' forums; within those policies they have priorities which are areas of work which are seen as especially important and necessary for development, areas in which funders want to encourage applications, or see the need to initiate work themselves.

Lynn Maree, Contributed.

Clients

Arts organisations/artists, in receipt of regular funding from an arts funding body.

Lynn Maree, Contributed.

Arts budgets

Means by which funds within a funding body are broken up into categories which can be by art form or by the nature of the work: e.g. New Work/Touring within an art form budget. There can be further classification according to policy: e.g. dance commissioning.

Lynn Maree, Contributed.

Ballet budget

Planned financial resources for a ballet company working within an Opera House may be subsumed under a general opera house budget, but may be organised separately and so under the control of the ballet administration and advisers.

Jane Nicholas, Interview.

Heritage

A term used in arts funding.

"This ought to be understood to mean the preservation of past glories, including those of the recent past, and the addition to that heritage of current glories, which can come at all scales of work, in all combination of art forms, and from all cultural origins and mixes."

Lynn Maree, Contributed.

Innovation

"This ought to mean work created now by choreographers and directors, which is not a re-working of existing work, but which does not require creators to always be totally different from how they worked before."

Lynn Maree, Contributed.

Dance projects

Many, if not most, of these are by their nature multi-art form, often collaborations where artists from a number of art forms work together as equals, a fact which may prove problematic for funding bodies of 'dance'.

Lynn Maree, Contributed.

Cultural diversity

As used at present by the Arts Council the term implies a recognition that there are many cultures in Great Britain and that all need recognition and respect from the funding agencies. In dance this includes African, Carribbean, South Asian work, and disability culture.

Lynn Maree, Contributed.

Multi-disciplinary/Combined arts/Performance Art/Live art

Changing names given by funders for work which does not fit easily into art-form categories, and has venues and organisation which programme and do projects with artists from a number of art forms.

Lynn Maree, Contributed.

Negotiated terms

The arrangement made between a theatre and a dance company/group/artist where the costs and income are shared; one example might be the company take 60% of the returns, the theatre 40%, and each pays their own staff and they share marketing costs at an agreed ratio.

Jane Nicholas, Interview.

Wall-to-wall

One way of hiring a theatre for dance performances, for which the hirer pays all expenses, including the marketing of the date and the payment of the stage crew.
Jane Nicholas, Interview.

Papering the house

To fill the theatre by giving out free passes.
Eds.

Criteria

The statement of what value system is being applied for the successful application funding for dance; necessary for the administration of public funds for the arts.

"...to enable creative work to take place to professional standards.", "...in professional circumstances...".
Jane Nicholas, Interview.

Annual funding

Financial support for a company or an artist renewed every twelve months, so that forward planning is inevitably limited in scope.
Jane Nicholas, Interview.

Franchise client, A

A company, group, or individual to be given an amount of funding for a fixed period of time, say 2 years, followed by a review, after which the franchise may or may not be renewed.
Jane Nicholas, Interview.

Project funding

Financial support for one specified endeavour, may be over a 3 week period or 3 months, or more or less.
Jane Nicholas, Interview.

Revenue funded company

A company receiving major on-going financial support, so allowing planning a year (or more) ahead. Security fluctuates with the quality of artistic work, management and financial position of the company, and the policies of the funding body; said of Arts Council funding.
Jane Nicholas, Interview.

Commission

A paid opportunity to create a work to be performed, may be a choreography commission or a musical score commission.
"Animated", 1992.

Awards and Commissions

Alternative terms for fees given to companies, choreographers and to musicians, based on criteria set up by the funding body, to encourage creativity.
Jane Nicholas, Interview.

Dance award

Prize, usually of money, but also of publicity and the opportunity to perform or choreograph or write, offered to the winner of a competition set up for the purpose of encouraging and stimulating excellence in some field of dance.
"Dance Theatre Journal", 1992(a).

Study Award

A monetary award to an emerging choreographer who applies to undertake a period of study or research or to work on a piece, a time which is intended to develop artistic progress, to stretch him or her in some way; said of the Bonnie Bird Choreographic Award.
Bonnie Bird, Interview.

Commissioning Award

An award, to create a work for a company; for Transitions Dance Company the criteria are "...given to a young choreographer with an established track record who evidences freshness of vocabulary, an ability to structure and to communicate, with musicality or style or wit, able to work with emerging contemporary dancers."
Bonnie Bird, Interview.

Grants

Money distributed by funders. These can be 'one off', often referred to as 'project grants', with no guarantee of further funds, or annual, or revenue. These later involve greater and greater commitment to future funding and can embrace "funding agreements".
Lynn Maree, Contributed.

Retraining grants

Financial support for dancers who wish to gain alternative skills to work in the dance domain in another capacity, such as arts administration, or teaching, sometimes known as bursaries.
Jane Nicholas, Interview.

Accountability

Because funding bodies' funds are taxpayer and ratepayer money: funders are responsible, through local authorities and central government, to the public (in which artists are included) for how they spend the money. An important concept in the consciousness of a funder.
Lynn Maree, Contributed.

Enquiry, An

An influential document on the findings of an investigation initiated by Government sources, possibly a Minister for the Arts, with an appointed Chairman supported by a body of independent advers, to look into costs, resources, efficiency, et al. of the funded sector of the dance domain; said of The Wilding Review, 1989, and Opera and Ballet Enquiry, 1969.

Jane Nicholas, Interview.

Appraisal system

A five-year rolling programme of assessment by a funding body of all companies receiving revenue and annual support, covering finance, management, marketing, and artistic concerns, resulting in recommendations for the company's policies for the next 5-year period and beyond.

Jane Nicholas, Interview.

Monitoring process

Regular review by a subsidising body of all client/project activities, including dance; more intensively conducted when new schemes are being piloted.

Jane Nicholas, Interview.

Quality

At present this is seen as "the improvement of creative standards", and requires a vigilance on "fit for purpose"; there is therefore not only one definition of quality: for instance quality in classical ballet maintenance of heritage has one notion of creative standards, while youth dance has another — not lower, but different.

Lynn Maree, Contributed.

19.   DANCE AS THERAPY

Dance as a therapeutic tool

Dance activity in which a patient is encouraged to become interested in and to participate in a dance experience which acts as an integrating factor and a means of expression.

Marion North, Interview.

Dance Movement Therapy

"The use of expressive movement in dance as a medium through which the individual can engage creatively in a process of personal integration and growth."

Association for Dance Movement Therapy, quoted in Penelope A. Best, 1993.

Dance Movement Therapy

"A psycho-therapeutic technique which uses movement as a process to further the emotional, cognitive, and physical integration of the individual."

American Dance Therapy Association, quoted in Penelope A. Best, 1993.

Function of dance therapy

Not a cure, but: "One of the ways in which people who are mentally ill can be with one another without too much fear of defeat", as practised at St. Elizabeth's Hospital for Mental Diseases, Washington DC.

Marion Chase, 1952.

Professional practice as a therapist

A range of skills, qualifications, and clinical methods which may use 'pure' movement activity for some clients or largely verbal activity informed by movement for others.

Penelope A. Best, 1993.

Reciprocal interaction

One essential concept to dance movement therapy, that the body and mind are in constant "reciprocal interaction", so that making a connection between verbally expressed insight and movement experience is a key therapeutic practice.

Trudi Schoop, 1974.

Personality in movement

An essential concept in dance movement therapy, that the individual personality, and stages of personal development, are reflected in movement behaviour.

Kristina Stanton-Jones , 1992.

Movement profiling

Writing a profile of a person from their movement behaviour, observed and analysed according to various established methods, such as Laban/Kestenberg method and Lamb's Action Profiling.

Penny Lewis Bernstein, 1984.

Client and therapist

The person undergoing dance movement therapy, and the professional person leading the session.

Kristina Stanton-Jones, 1992.

Therapist/patient relationship

The way a dance movement therapist interacts with a client, a crucial ingredient to the effectiveness of the treatment.

Clare Schmais in K. Mason, 1974.

Communication in therapy

The way a therapist and client interact, the way the client communicates through movement unconsciously and with symbolic content.

Helen Payne, 1992.

Creativity as therapy
       A concept in dance movement therapy leading to the practice of movement improvisation, through which novel ways of moving generate a "new experience of being-in-the-world".
       Kristina Stanton-Jones, 1992.

Movement and the unconscious
       A concept that movement reflects "those contents of the mind that are not present in the field of conscious awareness, including repressed ideas, feelings, and images"; a Dance Movement Therapy concept.
       H. Ellenberger, 1970.

Relationship play
       A practice in Sherborne's Developmental Movement system in which a mature person partners a less able youngster, possibly parent/child, in which physically supported interactions with 'with' relationship, an 'against' relationship, or a mutual shared relationship form the central concept.
       Veronica Sherborne, 1990.

Movement experiences
       A central concept to Veronica Sherborne's Developmental Movement system, rather than movement exercises, experiences which combine both physical and psychological learning in children.
       Veronica Sherborne, 1990.

Body awareness
       A term originated by Rudolf Laban's work, and used centrally in Sherborne's work to provide children, especially those with special needs, a means of relating to their own bodies, put into practice through movement play activities.
       Veronica Sherborne, 1990.

Awareness of others
       A central concept in Sherborne Developmental Movement work with children with special needs for which relationship play experiences are used to assist the youngster to form relationships and to trust physically, emotionally, and socially.
       Veronica Sherborne, 1990.

20. DANCERS' HEALTH

Dancers' health
       The ability to work to top capacity, achieved through attention to physical condition, nutrition, injury prevention and treatment, emotional health, sensible clothing.
       Dance UK, 1992.

Medical practitioners

Those who give dancers advice and treatment from a variety of orthodox and alternative medical spheres, such as exercise physiology, osteopathy, sports medicine, acupuncture, dietetics, etc.
Dance UK, 1992.

Schools of body education

Followers of the exponents of various approaches to body alignment and re-education which have stated criteria, theory, and practices.
"Alexander Technique, Todd Method, Selver's organismic functioning, Moshe Feldenkreis, Dorothy Vislocky, Valerie Hunt, Joseph Pilates."
Valentina Litvinoff, 1973.

Alexander Technique

A body education developed by F. Matthias Alexander focusing on the maintainance of the poise of the head and the total lengthening of the spine, undertaken in one-to-one lessons combining verbal instruction and gentle touch.
"An educational process for learning about how to change the habits you want to change."
Judith Leibowitz and *Bill Connington*, 1991.

Use and function

Two key terms in the Alexander technique, for the deep level of co-ordination in neuro-muscular interplay that can be altered through learning to evaluate the experienes of the senses, and for the bodily activities which result in articular interplay.
Hans Atle Svenheim, Seminar.

Debauched kinaesthesia

A state of kinaesthetic awareness which is undependable through sustained poor uses of the neuro-muscular system, so providing an unreliable source for changing unsatisfactory movement habits.
F. Matthias Alexander quoted by Hans Atle Svenheim, Seminar.

Bartenieff Fundaments (TM)

"...an approach to basic body training that deals with principles of anatomical body function within a context that encourages personal expression and full psychophysical functioning as an integral part of total body mobilization."
Peggy Hackney, 1984.

Inner connectivity and outer expressivity

The "lively interplay" between these two states of awareness in the moving person and dancer constitutes the goal of Bartenieff Fundamentals (TM).
Peggy Hackney, 1984.

Feldenkreis method, The

A method of education and awareness developed by Moshe Feldenkreis through the medium of movement education.

"...uses a teacher to remind one and extrapolate on modes of learning already used during infancy."

Scott Clark quoting Moshe Feldenkreis, 1984 (1972).

Pilates technique

A body therapy system designed to heighten kinaesthetic awareness and encourage efficient movement patterns.

"Lengthen the spine", "Relax the ribs", "Widen the back", "No tension in the shoulders", "Inhale, exhale."

Susanne Lahusen, Class.

Chapter 2   DANCE PEOPLE

1.   DANCERS

Dancer

"A person who performs a dance", "a person whose profession is dancing."
'Concise Oxford Dictionary', 1990.

Dancer

Someone who dances, who moves in a way which the maker of the dance thinks of as dancing or a way that the place he or she is in suggests that the dance should be: hence, tap dancer, ballet dancer, disco dancer, barn dancer.
Eds.

Dancer

A dancing body, gendered and cultured.
Helen Thomas, Interview.

Company dancer

The personification of the vision of the artistic director, through his selection of company members, his company class, his choice or creation of dance works in which the dancer will function.
Robert Cohan, Interview.

Dance theatre artist

A term used by Yolande Snaith about herself and fellow performers to distinguish them from 'dancer'.
Yolande Snaith, Interview.

Artist

A term used of Loie Fuller (1890) instead of 'dancer' to reflect her way of moving which was "spontaneous and natural as a gifted child", "unburdened by technically trained knowledge."
Walter Sorell, 1981.

Dance artist

A trained dancer who can function creatively as a performer within the domain of a professional ensemble.
Marion North, Interview.

Pool of dancers

A resource of trained performers whom an independent choreographer can call upon to make his/her work, for the kind of participation both parties are familiar with.
Rosemary Butcher, Interview.

Bunch of dancers

A group of dancers collected by a workshop director, or a choreographer, to work with on a new piece for a workshop; usually from a professional studio or a university dance department.

Bessie Schoenberg, Interview.

Solo performer

A dancer who presents work as the only performer; said in contrast to "soloist" which may mean a performer with a solo role amongst other performers; said of Laurie Booth.

Dance Umbrella, 1992.

Categories of classical dancer

Traditionally dancers were put into one of three categories depending on their height, appearance and personality: I. The serious, noble of heroic dancer; 2. The demicaractère dancer; 3. The character or grotesque dancer.

"The genius of the three dancers who take up these particular styles should be as different as their heights, their features and their type of mind. The first should be tall, the second gallant and the last comic..."

Jean Georges Noverre, 1966 (1803).

High, medium, and low dancer

A classification of dancers by Laban in the 1930's, developing from Blasis's division of 'noble', 'demicaractère', and 'caractère' dancers, and of singers into Soprano (Tenor), Mezzo (Baritone), and Contralto (Bass), according to innate movement characteristics.

Vera Maletic, 1987.

Ballerina

"...the female figure who is traditionally the pinnacle of the ballet...", "...the apex of a pyramid formed by the traditional ballet company and the traditional repertory...".

Mary Clarke and *Clement Crisp*, 1987.

Ballerina

A term for an étoile of the ballet, the criteria for achieving the status of ballerina being somewhat arbitrary; at one time "if you had danced Aurora you were automatically 'a ballerina'", but the criterion no longer holds, there being outstanding artists of ballerina class who never would dance Aurora or the equivalent for valid reasons.

Norman Morrice, Interview.

Superstars

Artists who become more than a 'star', acquiring international reputations of excellence which bring demands for performances on an unprecedented scale, so reducing the artist to a commodity; said of Margot Fonteyn and Rudolf Nureyev.

Norman Morrice, Interview.

Star system
A hierarchy valued for those with outstanding talent who deserve international fame, but a system which can be distorted by publicity and the media, possibly making it unnaturally hard for up-and-coming artists who are expected to compete with media-maintained stars.
Ninette de Valois, 1977.

Dollarinas
British ballerinas who were successful stars in the United States and so earned the country copious dollars in revenue, thereby becoming commodities; said of Fonteyn in her first New York season, 1949.
Norman Morrice, Interview.

Danseur Noble
A male ballet dancer in the noble classical style who interprets the major roles in the traditional repertoire.
Glossary in *Mary Clarke* and *David Vaughan*, 1977.

Principals and soloists
Titles given to dancers who have identified roles in a work; the same titles used to identify dancers' status within a company.
Monica Parker, Interview.

Principal dancer
A ballet soloist who dances not only the major roles in the classics, which a ballerina does, but also a wider repertory.
"...an all-rounder...".
Marion Tait, Interview.

Character dancer
A performer, usually in a supporting role, who specialises in the portrayal of characters in ballets, with ability to act as well as dance and to make a personal contribution to the 'business' of his or her role.
Ashley Page, Interview.

Soubrette
A small female dancer with a strong technique and dramatic ability; said by van Praagh of her own qualities.
Peggy van Praagh, 1984.

Porteur
A male dancer in a pas de deux, whose function is to display the ballerina, by supporting, lifting and balancing her.
Peggy van Praagh and *Peter Brinson*, 1963.

My girls
   The pas de deux partners of a male soloist; after learning a particular coaching point with one female soloist, he may "pass it on to my girls".
   Joseph Cipolla in Desmond Kelly, Coaching.

Coryphée
   "A (ballet) dancer (of either sex) who has moved out of the corps de ballet to dance minor solo roles."
   Glossary in *Mary Clarke* and *David Vaughan*, 1977.

Corps de ballet
   "The ensemble of dancers in a ballet company who appear in support of the soloists."
   Glossary in *Mary Clarke* and *David Vaughan*, 1977.

Cast
   Up to five complete groups of soloists for a ballet, each of which perform during a season, first cast dancing on opening night, all casts being backed up by covers.
   The Birmingham Royal Ballet, 1992.

Covers
   Members of the company who learn parts and roles by working at the back of the studio; and who may have to step in to dance them.
   The Birmingham Royal Ballet, 1992.

Cover dancer
   The extra dancer in opera, always in the house ready to go on if necessary, who has to know everyone's part.
   Lynn Robertson Bruce, Interview.

Understudy
   The dancer who rehearses a work, is not first cast, and may or may not perform the role.
   Bonnie Bird, Interview.

Walking wounded
   Dancers who are returning to company class or to conservatoire class after injuries, and for whom special care has to be taken for the safe recuperation of their bodies back to full working order as efficient artistic instruments.
   Norman Morrice, Interview.

Ladies and gentlemen
   What the chorus, and dancers, are called in an opera house; the principals would be named individually.
   Lynn Robertson Bruce, Interview.

Girls and boys
>   The dancers in a classical ballet company.
>   *Judith Maelor Thomas*, Rehearsing.

Associates
>   Boys and girls who have successfully auditioned for classes run by a school attached to or associated with a contemporary or ballet company, and who may have small parts in performances by the company, such as "Nutcracker"; a Royal Ballet School term.
>   *"Dancing Times"*, Passim.

Chorus girl, chorus boy
>   The chorus (boys and girls) who perform the interest behind the lead roles, giving their musical numbers substance. Often chosen for their average height in order that precision work in lines "looks good". The job of chorus boy/girl may be seen as the only way into the theatre.
>   *Eugenia Volz Schoettler*, 1979.

Hoofer
>   Originally an American term for chorus dancers, dancers in musicals and cabaret.
>   *Norman Morrice*, Interview.

Tappers
>   Proficient tap dancers.
>   *Roy Castle*, 1986.

Supporting artists
>   Dancers, or extras employed to dance and move, used in plays to surround the leading characters.
>   *Geraldine Stephenson*, Interview.

Non-dancers in theatre and opera
>   The singers and actors and extras who have to be directed to move expressively, even to appear to be dancing, usually in two rehearsals only.
>   *Stuart Hopps*, Interview.

Extra
>   A stand-in or walk-on in films, television, or photography.
>   *Lynn Robertson Bruce*, Interview.

Amateur and professional dancer
>   The status of an unpaid or paid couple in the world of competitive dance such as ballroom and Latin American dancing regardless of their ability.
>   *British Broadcasting Corporation*, 1992.

Star
The actor/actress performing the role of the principal character in a musical theatre production, usually required to sing and maybe to dance.
Eugenia Volz Schoettler, 1979.

Partner
In Latin American dance, the term used by a dancer for another of the opposite sex with whom he or she dances as a couple.
Ruud Vermey, Interview.

Couples
In Latin American dance, the term used for dancers, which are always male/female, never two females or two males.
Ruud Vermey, Interview.

Couple, The
The dancers in English country dancing where a pair of opposite sex is the essential unit whatever the formation.
Cecil J. Sharp, 1934.

Gent and lady
Rock 'n' Roll terms for the two dancers.
Derek Young, 1991.

Partnership
A male/female soloist pair who dance regularly together, developing a smoothness of technicality, and removing the anxiety of "going wrong" in major roles.
Marion Tait, Interview.

Dance captain
A chorus dancer responsible for the other members of the group; a term used in musicals.
Lynn Robertson Bruce, Interview.

Leader
The dancer in charge of a social dance event, who signals the dance figures, the tempo, and the beginning and ending of the dance event.
Robert Harrold, Interview.

Beautiful Girl Dancers
Heading to advertisements for dubious cabaret, night club, summer season, and nude revue shows, in which the dancing skills required are limited, probably erotic, and the "beauty" is equated with "sexy".
Eds. from *"The Stage"*, passim.

Champions and Runners-up

In competitive dancing, such as ballroom or Latin American, the couples who score the highest marks for such elements as technical proficiency, musicality, originality within the constraints of the obligatory style, and 'artistic merit'.

British Broadcasting Corporation, 1992.

Champion

A dancer who has won a competition at least at the level of county up to international championships.

"UK amateur IO dance Champions, Come Dancing Formation Winners, World Professional Ballroom Champions."

The Spencer Dance Centre, 1992.

Flappers

Young women of the 1920's, often associated with the dances named the Charleston, the Suzy Q, the Shimmy, and the Black Bottom.

Jack Villari and *Kathleen Sims Villari*, 1979.

Wanaby

A white man who emulates black men in every way: dress, attitude, dancing; a clubbing term.

Portsmouth clubbers interviewed by *Donna Taylor*.

Home boy

Mate, good friend, one of the crowd who dance in a club.

Portsmouth clubbers interviewed by *Donna Taylor*.

Participant

A person dancing for the enjoyment of taking part; may perform or may not; a term used largely in recreational and amateur dance work.

Eds.

Participant

A person, not necessarily a trained dancer, who takes part in a session or workshop of contact improvisation, moving in contact with another person in the physical way that is necessitated by the democratic duet form; usually a non-performance situation, 'participant' being used in contrast to 'performer'.

Eds. from Cynthia J. Novack, 1990.

Aerialist

Someone who either develops an act specialising on one of the aerial skills or who uses aerial skills amongst other performance skills as and when the choreographer/ director decides.

"Web, Spanish lunge, a cloud swinging act, the perch, the cradle, the Russian swing."

Helen Crocker and *Bim Mason*, Interview.

Buskers

British street entertainers who may include dance in their act.
Eds.

Actors

A title given to performers who might otherwise be regarded as dancers, by people for whom dance has an unacceptable image, possibly too narrow, specialised, or stylised.
Andrée Grau, Interview.

Dancer/actor

The performer of a role in a ballet in which both 'steps' and characterisation have to appear spontaneous.
Judith Mackrell, Interview.

Singer/dancer

The combination of two art forms within one artist or as two separate but connected artists; said of Lisa Minelli in "Cabaret" and of Malou Airaudo and Veronika Waldner in Bausch's "Orpheus and Eurydice".
Nadine Meisner, Contributed.

Mime

"The mime is not an imitator. He enlarges, emphasizes, particularizes, accents, comments upon the characters he portrays."
Angna Enters in Walter Sorell, 1951.

Improvisor

A dancer engaged in the spontaneous production of movement around thematic material; may be working alone or as a group in a workshop or a performance.
Dorothy Madden, Interview.

Capoeiristas

People who engage as both opponents and partners in the Brazilian duo art form of Capoeira, for which techniques, physical conditioning, ritual skills and manners, musical knowledge and experience of 'playing the jôgo' (engaging in the fight/dance) are the means of expressing creativity and personality in the 'jôgo de capoeira'. A traditionally male pastime, Capoeira now has many women players.
Bira Almeida, 1986.

Traditional dancer

A person working with dance material that is handed down from one generation to another; said of folk and country dancers, of ethnic specific dance traditions, and of any received dance vocabularies, including ballet.
Eds.

Traditional dancer
Performing within the received tradition of Kathak dance in every respect — technique, improvised form, music and costume.
Alpana Sengupta, Interview.

Player
A T'ai Chi Ch'uan practitioner.
Katherine Allen, Interview.

2. GROUPS

Company
A group of dancers with an identity, a name, who perform together; a relatively permanent association of people concerned with presenting dance together.
Eds.

Dance company
"...a hive of creative industry..."; said by Christopher Bruce of his priorities for Rambert Dance Company, 1993.
Christopher Bruce, Interview.

Dance in Education Company
A dance company making work solely for young people, whose company members create, perform, and teach dance in school and community settings; said of Ludus Dance Company.
"The Stage", 1993.

Democratic company
One in which the members have mutual responsibility for the work that it produces, for how it is shown, for how they work together.
Peter Dunleavy, Interview.

Integrated dance company
A group of dancers some of whom have disabilities, some may be wheelchair users, who make dance works and present them.
"Dance Theatre Journal", 1992.(b).

Integrated companies
Dance companies, such as Candoco, in which some performing artists are disabled and others are able-bodied, where the emphasis is on the art works made and not on the difficulties to be overcome, and criterion of membership is ability as a performer.
Candoco Company, 1993.

Novice company

A repertory company for talented but inexperienced dancers preparing to take their place as professionals in the field.

Bonnie Bird, Interview.

Opera House based company

A ballet company which, being part of an opera house, is subject to the whims of the director of the house who may regard ballet as of far less significance than opera; a company who perform sandwiched between opera performances, a situation that is difficult for the rhythm of the dancers.

Norman Morrice, Interview.

Repertory company

An ensemble for which dance works are made and who perform their repertoire, remounting the works with meticulous care on the performers of the next season.

Marion North, Interview.

Resident company

A ballet or dance company attached to a particular theatre or opera house who regularly perform there as well as touring; said of The Royal Ballet in London.

Norman Morrice, Interview.

Single choreographer company

An ensemble designed to perform the works of one artist, who is probably the artistic director and may or may not be a principal soloist.

Bonnie Bird, Interview.

Touring company

A dance or ballet company who have no theatre of their own but who perform by touring their repertoire in residences and seasons; said of Rambert Dance Company.

Norman Morrice, Interview.

Group

A small performing dance company, usually in the contemporary or fringe genre; may be professional or amateur.

Dance Umbrella, 1992.

One-off concert group

A group of performers who work together for one production only, disband to earn a living through other means, and regroup for another single concert.

Bonnie Bird, Interview.

State Folk Dance Ensembles

Troupes concerned with adapting rural community dance forms for theatrical shows, sponsored by governments, and often used in the former Eastern Bloc as a means of propaganda.

Roderyk Lange, 1980.

Folk dance companies

Highly skilled national companies who present folk dance as a spectacle with enhanced technique and choreographic elements to make the dance attractice on a stage.

"Cossack men showing off; soldiers vying with each other."
Robert Harrold, Interview.

Team

The name given to the group of people in a Morris dance club who are the dancers, out of which six dance together as 'the side'.
Roy Judge, Interview.

Morris-men

(Dancers in) "...something of an exclusive art, confined (until very recently) not only to men but often to the men of certain families and their connection."
Peter Buckman, 1978.

Crew

The name for a group of break dancing youngsters, identified by shared vocabulary, sharing a dance mat and an insignia on their T-shirt, usually black or hispanic boys.
Sally Banes, 1985.

Posse

Group of friends dancing together in a club.
Portsmouth clubbers interviewed by *Donna Taylor.*

Sub-culture

The specific social group who participate in an identified way of dancing: ravers, house, Morris men, clog dancers.
Paul Filmer, Interview.

Primitive dance cultures

So-called 'primitive' are cultures with a highly integrated social structure, usually inferior in material, economic, and technological development, where dance holds a deep relevance to the life of the community.
Roderyk Lange, 1975.

Collective

A term established within the Judson Church body defining a group of people (dancers, choreographers, musicians, artists) who worked within a democratic or 'collective' process to produce creative methods that "metaphorically seemed to stand for freedom (like improvisation, spontaneous determination, chance)".
Sally Banes, 1980.

Dance circle

An amateur group of dancers who meet regularly for recreational dancing, which may be creative or centre around a traditional dance form.

"Laban Art of Movement Guild Magazine", 1955.

Folk dance clubs

Groups which hold public events in local halls, with a caller who introduces and runs through each dance.

Hugh Rippon, 1981.

Lay people

Amateur dancers who are not trained but who enjoy dancing together within their own capacity; a term used for both performers and audience members.

Geraldine Stephenson, Interview.

3. DANCE MAKERS

Choreographers

People who make dances.

Janet Adshead and *June Layson*, 1983.

Dance maker

What some contemporary dancers prefer to call themselves rather than 'choreographer'.

Jane Dudley, Interview.

Choreographer

"The person setting the ballet."

Marion Tait, Interview.

Choreographer

The person who puts routines together in ballroom dancing.

Geoffrey Hearn, Interview.

Choreographer

Someone with something to say, someone not into it for reasons of inflating their ego.

Jane Dudley, Interview.

Choreographer

A person who makes movement-based work that is not necessarily regarded as a dance, i.e. not work that carries all the expectations and limitations associated with the word 'dance'.

Rosemary Butcher, Interview.

Community choreographers

Dance makers who work with dancers from all corners of the community such as youth dance, mentally and physically disabled dancers, children, amateur dancers; creators of dances as art works which suit the capabilities of the community performers.

Peter Brinson, 1991.

Company choreographer

"It would seem that a good choreographer for major company works has to come out of a big company; it takes years before one can work successfully for those circumstances."

Robert Cohan, Interview.

House choreographer

A dance maker attached to a company or a theatre, whose responsibility is to provide new works of quality and with the staff contribute to a repertory which attracts an audience.

Christopher Bruce in John Percival, Contributed.

Jobbing choreographer

A dance and movement maker who can be effective in the various genres which offer work: opera, theatre, film, cabaret, pantomime, trade shows.

Stuart Hopps, Interview.

Master choreographer

A dance maker who sustains a career of creating major works of acclaimed value; said of Bournonville.

Clement Crisp, Interview.

Proscenium choreographer

A choreographer operating in the established traditional theatre.

Stephanie Jordan, 1992.

Screen-literate choreographer

A dance maker who has the necessary vision and skills to make works for television.

The Video Place, 1993.

Street choreographers

Dance makers who have learnt their craft from dancing socially rather than from professional training.

"... involved with Hip Hop and Vogueing."

Chris de Marigny, 1992.

'Arty' and 'Commercial'

The labels given to choreographers who specilise in different areas of the choreographic domain; for example directing the movement of the classic "The Orestia" or devising the numbers for the pantomime "Mother Goose".

Stuart Hopps, Interview.

Dance arranger

What a choreographer is sometimes called in the credits of a play or film; also credited as 'dance adviser' or 'movement by'.
Geraldine Stephenson, Interview.

Dance author

"A maker of dances, a choreographer; someone who is the founder, the originator, the main cause of something, someone who makes a work of art."
Lorrina Niclas in Rencontres Chorégraphiques Internationales de Bagnolet, 1992.

Author

"...the person who conceives the idea of the ballet. He may be the choreographer. He may be some else."
Peggy van Praagh and *Peter Brinson*, 1963.

Choréauteur (Fr.)

An author of dances, much used by Serge Lifar (1935); a choreographer.
Clement Crisp, Interview.

Artist in Residence

A dance person, usually a performer/choreographer, who is attached to a venue and funded to work creatively there for a fixed period; example: Emilyn Claid at the Yorkshire Dance Centre.
Chris de Marigny, 1993.

Movement director

The person in opera responsible for both the choreography of the dance numbers and the directing of the movement of the performers, especially the chorus; usually subject to the director of the whole piece with more, or less autonomy.
Stuart Hopps, Interview.

Player-manager

A term Mark Murphy uses of himself, as performer in his own works and as director of the works, which are a mixture of given choreographed material and collaborations with his performers and artistic team.
Mark Murphy, Interview.

Dancer-choreographer

A dancer who makes works in which he or she performs a major role; said of Martha Graham and of Doris Humphrey.
Walter Sorell, 1971.

Professional stiffener

What a professional choreographer can be for an amateur group, a function for which public funds might be provided.
Jane Nicholas, Interview.

4.   COLLABORATING ARTISTS

Collaborator
What the choreographer (movement director) is in an opera, musical or theatre work, working with a director who may rely heavily on the choreographer for all movement, may block movement sequences and so share out responsibility clearly, may use the choreographer's ideas either with due recognition given or pass them off as his own.
Stuart Hopps, Interview.

Collaborators
"Performers, lighting designer, designer, composer, administrator, and choreographer."
"I like a set of independent minds."
Mark Murphy, Interview.

Composer/performer
Two roles which one person can undertake in the same work; "creating the music and playing the central character in Janet Smith's 'Another Man Drowning'; dancing and playing the violin."
Chris Benstead, Interview.

Collaborations
Pieces in which more than one artist work together from the inception; choreographer with designer, choreographer with lighting designer, choreographer with musicians, and so on.
Eds.

Collaborations
Several artists in contributing media working in partnership to create a visual kinetic whole; used of Laurie Booth's co-operative works.
Judith Mackrell, Interview.

Collaboration of designer/choreographer
The co-operative work of two artists in ballet; of Yolanda Sonnabend and Kenneth MacMillan it is said that she "provides him with settings and costumes which are both a portrait and reflection of what he is formulating in movement", implicitly showing the mutual influence of one artist on the other.
Clement Crisp, 1985.

Collaborators
A composer working with a choreographer in a two-way co-coperative creative process; said of the making of Christopher Bruce's/Philip Chambon's "Swan Song."
Philip Chambon, Interview.

Composer for dance

A person who creates a musical score for a dance, usually in collaboration with the choreographer and following a suggested outline or, possibly, given a free hand within the limits of a duration.

Dorothy Madden, Contributed.

Visual artist

A person who contributes to the environment in which or with which the dance will happen; may be a fine artist, a theatre set designer.

Eds.

Designers

"We designers interpret, accommodate and reinforce and illuminate."

S. Loquasto in Nancy Vreeland Dalva, 1989.

Easel painters

A term used for theatre designers who were, or may combine being, painters per se as well as painters of sets.

Barry Kay, 1981.

Designer's eye, The

The visual artistry of the designer in dance.

Beatrice Hart, Interview.

Director/designer

An artist who sees a work as a whole and so both directs its action and designs it visually; said of Lindsay Kemp.

Yolanda Sonnabend, Interview.

Design assistants

The apprentice collaborators who assist the designer in making the model of the set, and parts of the actual scenery.

Yolanda Sonnabend, Interview.

Lighting designer

The creative artist who envisages and decides upon the lighting effects for production, translating them into a lighting plot through co-operation with the chief electrician; a collaborator in ballet and dance productions.

Eds.

Lighting designer

A visual artist, a computer buff, and an engineer.

Ross Cameron, Interview.

Video master
 The person responsible for all the artistic aspects of the video operations connected with a major company.
 The Dutch National Ballet, 1993.

Television director
 The person who, with the choreographer, directs the shot-by-shot creation of the record or the "video" dance or whatever collaborative effort is being undertaken.
 Bob Lockyer, Interview.

Dance/tele director
 A choreographer who is also a director of work on television, someone who works in both media, able to adapt a stage work for video and possibly adapt a video dance for the stage; said of Gillian Lynne.
 Gillian Lynne, Interview.

Television producer
 The person who "begets" the work, enables it to be made, raises the money, engages the dance artists.
 Bob Lockyer, Interview.

Master carpenter
 In a ballet or dance company, the person who translates the set design into usable scenery which can be set and transported and stored with the minimum of difficulty.
 John Hart, Interview.

Stage carpenter and scene painter
 Traditional craftsmen in the theatre for the construction of the set, now supplemented by metal workers, sculptors or engineers because of modern designs.
 Kenneth Rowell in Mary Clarke and David Vaughan, 1977.

5.   COMPANY STAFF

Founder
 A choreographer, or teacher, who initiates a company or school that goes on to become an established institution; said of Ninette de Valois and Frederick Ashton.
 Norman Morrice, Interview.

Artistic director
 "... leader of the whole ballet team ... creative organiser whose job it is to pursue the new, to be always thinking of prospects for the development of ballet as a whole."
 Peggy van Praagh and *Peter Brinson*, 1963.

Artistic director
> The person responsible for artistic decisions in a course for dance artists and/or a company of dance artists; said of Bonnie Bird and Transitions Dance Company.
> *Valerie Preston-Dunlop* and *Bonnie Bird*, Discussion.

Artistic director
> A person leading and nurturing a company of dancers who have to be able to trust that he will not "violate their own passions", but rather "funnel all the visions into one image"; said in contrast to imposing a personal vision.
> *Robert Cohan*, Interview.

Artistic director
> A dance person directing a company, who is responsible for the long-term health, style and look of the company's dancers, as well as nurturing choreographic talent from within the company and overseeing the company repertory.
> *Robert Cohan*, Interview.

Company director
> The head of a dance or ballet company, from whom the artistic policy of the company emanates; the chief administrator being responsible for the promotion of that policy and its day-to-day functioning.
> *Derek Purnell*, Interview.

Company choreographer
> A person able to make first-class work for a repertory company, able to cope with casting, rehearsal schedules, collaborations with musicians, scenic artists, has a developed style, knows how to work with first-class dancers and has some burning desire to do so.
> *Robert Cohan*, Interview.

Rehearsal director
> The person responsible for rehearsing works in a company's repertoire, who has to understand the meaning of a work as well as its form, meaning which may have layers beyond that perceived or intended by the choreographer but apparent in context.
> *Marion North*, Interview.

Rehearsal director
> The person in a company who takes care of and maintains the intention of a dance work after the choreographer has completed it, solving any dancers' problems with the work, helping them to articulate their role.
> *Marion North*, Interview.

Call director
> At an opera rehearsal, the person responsible for that rehearsal, that call, together with the call prompters there especially for the singers.
> *Teresa Kelsey*, Interview.

Ballet staff, The

Company members who are responsible for the dancing part of a ballet company's activities; they include the ballet master and mistress, regisseur, teachers, repetiteur, and notators.

The Birmingham Royal Ballet, 1992.

Repetiteur

The person who starts the rehearsals of a work, "teaching the steps in the book", and also rehearsing the crowd scenes and linking material.

Desmond Kelly, Interview.

Regisseur

The administrator of the ballet department of a company, responsible for rehearsal scheduling, cast lists, guest teachers for class.

Desmond Kelly, Interview.

Ballet master and mistress

The man and woman who teach class in a company and who also rehearse and coach dancers, and may play small character roles in narrative ballets.

Desmond Kelly, Interview.

Company teacher

Someone equipped to take responsibility for the training of company members in a strong, visibly distinct and safe way; a person able to travel with the company and remain in place long enought to allow company confidence to be established.

Robert Cohan, Interview.

Choreologist

A dance notator and reconstructor from the dance score, especially said of a person on the staff of a ballet or contemporary company; a person literate in a dance notation system, used more frequently of a Benesh notator than a Labanotator.

Eds.

Dance director

The new profession of dancers working from the score to create a repertoire of dance classics.

"The task of the director essentially is to direct, advise, coach, exhort, and inspire — it seems terribly simple but it is terribly difficult."

Ray Cook, 1980's.

Company physiotherapist

The person responsible for treating the injuries of the members of the dance company.

Monica Mason, Interview.

6. MUSICIANS AND SPEAKERS

Musical director
> Member of a company staff, responsible to conduct performances, fix the musicians, organise sound for rehearsals, collaborate with choreographers, discuss the musical balance of the repertory, play for class.
> *Nicholas Mojsiejenko*, Interview.

Music staff
> The conductor, chorus master, assistant conductor, prompter, and several others, who contribute to the music side of an opera house's activity, and may include auditions of dancers.
> *Lynn Robertson Bruce*, Interview.

Conductor
> The orchestral conductor who is in charge of the music, who may conduct piano rehearsals, and who negotiates the tempo with whoever is directing the production of the work.
> *Jonathan Higgins*, Interview.

Company pianist
> The pianist who organises and coordinates the rehearsal pianists of a ballet company and the pianists to play with the orchestra and who may also play the solo part of concertos at rehearsals and performances.
> *Jonathan Higgins*, Interview.

Rehearsal pianist
> The musician who plays for the company class and for rehearsals both in the studio and for stage calls.
> *Jonathan Higgins*, Interview.

Band, The
> How the musicians for a dance work are referred to, especially by the backstage department.
> *Robert Coleridge*, Interview.

Musos, The
> A slang term for the musicians in a dance work.
> *Robert Coleridge*, Interview.

Sound technician
> A term used by dancers of a musician working physically with the electro-acoustic sound making, who may see himself as a composer.
> *Philip Chambon*, Interview.

Peripatetic instrumentalist

A musician who is part of the action of the choreography, taking part aurally, visually and kinetically by moving from place to place in the performing space.

Robert Coleridge, Interview.

On-stage musicians

The players placed on stage, visible from the audience, possibly interacting with the dancers; a way of working which has to be an integral part of the work to succeed.

Chris Benstead, Interview.

Musician (of the Morris)

A player of the accordion, concertina, melodeon or fiddle, or pipe and tabor; an essential member of the Morris team who plays the tunes belonging to the repertoire of the side.

Roy Judge, Interview.

Disc jockey

The person in charge of the overall sound and pace of the music at a discotheque, who chooses and controls the discs, raising and calming the energy levels, and organising the dance contests and the requests.

Jack Villari and *Kathleen Sims Villari*, 1979.

Compere

In Latin American dance, the person (almost always male) who introduces the couples, the various dances, and successive rounds in competitions.

Ruud Vermey, Interview.

Master of ceremonies

The "M.C.", the person on whom the responsibility lies for the memorising of the figures of a dance; usually named the "Caller", who chants or calls rhythmically the steps and patterns of each dance as the dancers do them.

Douglas Kennedy, 1949.

M.C.

Microphone Controller — replacing the term 'D.J.' = Disc Jockey; a clubbing term.

Portsmouth clubbers interviewed by *Donna Taylor*.

Caller

The person who directs American square dance and has the prerogative of extemporaneously choosing patterns from known basic movements and terminology, or making up new ones.

"...not an entertainer, but is the leader who teaches and calls the directions for dancers' movements while they are dancing...".

Betty Casey, 1976.

7. WARDROBE PEOPLE

Theatre costumier

The person who interprets the design of the costume, turning it into an actual costume to be worn by a speccific dancer; a creative process enhanced by "the feeling you put into the costume".

The Birmingham Royal Ballet, 1992.

Theatrical costumier

A person who makes or deals in theatre costume; for dance, a person who understands the cut necessary to accommodate movement, especially of the arms and legs and at the waist.

Eds.

Outworkers

Costumiers hired regularly by the costume department of large companies with complex repertoire, such as Covent Garden, when a new production is being made.

Barry Kay, 1981.

Wardrobe, The

The people in theatre responsible for costume provision and running repairs.

Lynn Robertson Bruce, Interview.

Running wardrobe

The department of a company which stores and maintains and sets the costumes in the current repertory.

Lili Sobieralska, Interview.

Shoe master

The person in a ballet company responsible for ordering, dyeing, and maintaining the pointe shoes, canvas shoes, character shoes or boots, which are made individually for the performers.

Michael Clifford, Interview.

Wigmaster

The person responsible for creating and maintaining the wigs, moustaches and beards for a ballet company.

Henry Menary, Interview.

Wigs

The people responsible for hats and wigs, in opera, ballet or theatre.

Lynn Robertson Bruce, Interview.

Dressers

The people in a theatre who assist costume changes and costume care.

Lynn Robertson Bruce, Interview.

8. PRODUCTION

Stage management team

Four or five people on stage responsible for the smooth running of the performance/rehearsal, to whom dancers turn with any problem.

Lynn Robertson Bruce, Interview.

Stage manager

The person in a large company who is the liaison between all departments during rehearsals and performances, the person through whom the choreographer or the person in charge of the production communicates with the prop master, the stage carpenter, the contume and wig departments, between the dancers and the stage crew, and so on.

Diana Childs, Interview.

Production Crew

The people responsible for the practical staging of the show, the lighting, the sound, and any set and props.

Mickie Mannion, Interview.

Stage Crew

The people who position, change, and strike the sets, a term associated wtih large houses.

Lynn Robertson Bruce, Interview.

Chief electrician

The person who is responsible for setting up the lighting rig for a production, making the lighting plot with the designer, focusing the lights and running the lighting at a performance in collaboration with the stage manager.

John Hart, Interview.

Sound Designer, Engineer, and Crew

The people responsible for the production and reproduction of the sound score, both live and recorded, installation of microphones, the setting of sound levels, co-ordination of the sources of sound for that production.

Mickie Mannion, Interview.

9. TEACHERS

Coach

In Latin American dance, the term used for the person who devises the routines and rehearses the couples in preparation for competitions.

Ruud Vermey, Interview.

Master
>A level in the heirarchy of T'ai Chi Ch'uan practitioners, from grand master, an exceptionally long-term practitioner, a master, probably 20 years as teacher/student, teacher (or sifu), and student; the levels are tacitly agreed, no belts or general assessment are offered.
>*Katherine Allen*, Interview.

Mentor
>A person who "through experience and age, is able to ignite without interfering, impersonal while being sensitive to the character of the dance artist (choreographer) at hand, persuading, never indoctrinating."
>*Bessie Schoenberg*, Interview.

Teacher (of ballet)
>"The teacher embodies the link with tradition."
>*George Balanchine* in Bernard Taper, 1974.

Expert/apprentice
>Terms for the teacher/learner relationship of the dance conservatoire which emphasises the passing on of a tradition by the teacher rather than the learner's own creativity.
>*Jacqueline Smith-Autard*, Interview.

Guide/agent-of-own-learning
>Terms for the teacher/learner relationship in one model of dance education which emphasises the creativity of the learner over the passing down of a dance tradition by the teacher.
>*Jacqueline Smith-Autard*, Interview.

Teaching staff
>The term used by conservatoires and centres of dance excellence for teachers with a specialism, such as ballet, contemporary, jazz, character, and tap; for example at the Arts Educational London schools.
>*"Dancing Times"*, 1993.

Faculty
>Teachers in a dance school, university department, college, conservatoire, et al, who put their institution's curriculum into practice; used primarily in tertiary education.
>*Eds.*

Associate, Licentiate and Fellow
>Terms for the status of dance teachers based on the executant examinations of, for example, the Cecchetti Society.
>*Imperial Society of Teachers of Dancing*, 1993(f).

Guest teachers

Specialist teachers invited to a dance institution, a common practice amongst the international community of dance in order to share the expertise in different styles of work.

Eds.

Feldenkreis practitioner

A person trained in the method of Moshe Feldenkreis who aimed to promote awareness through movement; a person using these methods as a body therapist or applying them in the teaching of dance.

Scott Clark, Interview.

Maître/maîtresse de ballet

Ballet master/mistress. According to C.W. Beaumont (in his edition of Noverre's *Letters*) the old usage of this term referred to the person who composed the dances in divertissements and ballets. Now indicates the person responsible for training the dancers and maintaining their technique through giving class.

Jean Georges Noverre, 1966 (1803).

Head of movement

The person responsible for the dancers at an opera house, especially concerning auditions, warm up for performance, and notes; may also be known as Opera Ballet Mistress.

Lynn Robertson Bruce, Interview.

Dance Artist in Education

A scheme to place professional dance artists in schools through residencies and joint projects.

Jane Nicholas, Interview.

10.   SCHOLARS

Choreologists

Writers who, over the years, have recorded dances in whatever systems were available to them, be it notation, film, or the written word, for both social dances and theatre dance, usually combining these skills with those of reconstruction or ethnology or anthropology or archiving.

Valerie Preston-Dunlop, Interview.

Collector

A person who, out of special interest, assembles over a period of years materials relating to one artist, one dance subject, one historical period, or whatever their focus in dance is; said of Rolf de Maré, Derra de Moroda, David Leonard.

Peter Bassett, Interview.

Counselling eye
A person giving some guidance to a choreographer, an outsider who can discern the elusive qualities of form in relation to what 'works' for an audience and/or for the idea.
Mary Brennan, 1992.

Dance aesthetician
A person principally concerned with appreciating the form of dance works rather than their function; seen as contrasted with the anthropologist for whom the cultural function is paramount.
Roger Copeland, 1992.

Dance anthropologist
A researcher who focuses on the concepts behind the dance, the belief, systems operative within it; a researcher who aims to understand a society and culture through its dance.
Andrée Grau, Interview.

Dance archivist
Any person appointed responsible for collecting, holding, and preserving materials of historical interest; said of company archives, theatre archives, or of any dance institution's materials; may, cover business, artistic, personal and stage management items or whatever will identify the activities of the group concerned.
Peter Bassett, Interview.

Foundation archivist
The person responsible for the collecting, cataloguing and dissemintion of documents, visual material, both graphic and electronic, sound and production materials, scenery, costumes; said of the Cunningham Foundation.
David Vaughan, Conversation with Valerie Preston-Dunlop.

Dance consultant
A person considerably experienced in one or more fields of dance activity, who is called upon to give professional advice or an opinion.
Dorothy Madden, Interview.

Dance ethnologist
A researcher who attempts to understand the dance of a community, contextualising it within the general culture of that community and the wider culture.
Andrée Grau, Interview.

Dance historian
A scholar who looks at dance through the perspective of progressing time.
Walter Sorell, 1981.

Dance historian

A historian who places dance in the foreground.
"The mediator between the present and the past."
June Layson, Interview.

Dance librarian

The person responsible for collecting, classifying, indexing, and retrieving materials which provide information about dance, including books, periodicals, videos, scores, press cuttings, photographs, manuscripts, sound recordings, and for communicating with the user.
Peter Bassett, Interview.

Dance sociologist

A dance practitioner who combines his professional knowledge of both dance and sociology.
Paul Filmer, Interview.

Sociologist of dance

A sociologist who applies the methods of his discipline to dance.
Paul Filmer, Interview.

Practical choreologist

A dance person engaged in using the structural principles of choreology in their daily work in dance practice; said of Rosemary Brandt's teaching of ballet and contemporary dance, and Ruud Vermey's coaching of Latin American international competitors.
Valerie Preston-Dunlop, Interview.

Practical scholar

Dance people who work with scholarly rigour in the studio and theatre, combining practical dexterity with understanding of their subject; they may work as choreographers, reconstructors, choreologists, performers, or teachers.
Valerie Preston-Dunlop, Interview.

Practical researchers

Intelligent dancers who not only perform material given to them, but also work at translating choreographic instructions into original movement material.
Rosemary Butcher, Interview.

Semasiologist

A term used by Drid Williams to describe a researcher who studies dance as a system of meaningful signs.
Andrée Grau, Interview.

11. DANCE WRITERS

Dance writer
A person engaged in writing about dance, who may use the whole spectrum of styles from journalistic to scholarly, there being no clear dividing line between styles.
Stephanie Jordan, Interview.

Dance writer
A person who comments on what is happening in dance, who aims to communicate issues in dance in several formats and from more than one point of view, for both specialist and non-specialist readers.
Chris de Marigny, Interview.

Notator
A person engaged in transcribing human movement on paper using movement notation.
Roderyk Lange, 1985.

Notator
"It should be appreciated that to become a good notator means that there must be present a certain talent as specific and highly specialised as that which is found in a good teacher, repetiteur, or choreographer."
Ninette de Valois, 1977.

Notators
Notators may work with various companies on a per-project basis, as is usual for Labanotation writers, or work full-time for one company, as is often the case for Benesh writers.
Ilene Fox, Interview.

Dance magazine publishing
The field is a specialist one but it is also very wide spread. "The Dancing Times" reached its 1000th issue in January 1994 and attributes its long life to its endeavours to cater for a very wide readership, from the young pupil to the professional, from the 'general reader' to the most serious and academic historian. In addition, the publishing company has to be economically viable to sustain an efficient and qualified staff in all departments.
Mary Clarke, Interview.

Dance editor
The person responsible for a dance magazine or journal; who conceives the rationale and image of it, commissions articles, gives detailed briefs to contributors and the designer, reviews the content overall.
Chris de Marigny, Interview.

Dance editor

The member of an editorial staff of a journal or magazine responsible for the listings and reviews of dance events; said of Allen Robertson of "Time Out".
"Time Out", 1993.

Dance journalist

Writer whose job is to "add to the buzz" around a dance event, both as publicity and by adding an extra dimension to the work through a review written off the cuff immediately after the event.
Judith Mackrell, Interview.

Dance journal

A magazine for people who work in the dance profession, able to include specialised language and articles which a magazine for dance audiences could not; said of "Dance Theatre Journal".
Chris de Marigny, Interview.

Academic dance journal

A vehicle for sharing research in dance through publishing scholarly papers and reports of scholarly practice; aims to generate a dialogue between researchers.
Chris de Marigny, Interview.

Dance critic

One who "...attempts to define precisely what struck me as important or interesting about that work..."; "...to evoke the experience again..."; "...to provide those who enjoy thinking and talking about dance with new fodder for argument."
Deborah Jowitt, 1977.

Dance critic

A writer who discusses dance events through longer articles than reviews, written after reflection, in which an argument and an analysis are developed.
Judith Mackrell, Interview.

Ballet critic

A writer who concentrates on ballet performances rather than dance performances in general.
"I go to the performance of the ballet, and write about it, and tell people what I've seen."
Clement Crisp, Interview.

Dance photographer

Exponent of the difficult art of capturing motion in stills and turning them into 'potent images' which, if they are of the popular avant-garde dance, could become 'icons'.
Allen Robertson, 1993.

12.   SPECTATORS

Public, The
>The people who watch dances, both in a theatrical setting and in street dancing.
>*Eds.*

Dance audience
>The audience who attend a specific location, such as Riverside Studios or The Royal Opera House, who are there primarily because of the place, rather than the actual works being shown there.
>*Norman Morrice*, Interview.

Them
>The audience.
>*Judith Maelor Thomas*, Rehearsing.

Regulars
>The loyal audience who come to every performance and see every cast, spectators on whom the company can rely.
>*Norman Morrice*, Interview.

Crowd, The
>In Latin American dance, a term used for the public in competitions who participate in the event by shouting and encouraging their favourite couples.
>*Ruud Vermey*, Interview.

Balletomanes
>People devoted to ballet, usually said of supporters but also used of entrepreneurs.
>*Eds.*

Fans
>The audience members who are devotees, who travel to see "their" company and "their" dancers, on countless occasions.
>*Norman Morrice*, Interview.

Claque
>People hired, or self-appointed, to applaud one artist rather than another.
>"...a group of devoted admirers who make an inordinate response to their favourites...".
>*Norman Morrice*, Interview.

Bums on seats
>The name given to audiences from the point of view of the number of people who might come to a performance; said in connection with financial issues and company's artistic policies.
>*Eds.*

Non-attenders

People who, by choice, do not come to dance performances, seen as potential new audiences whom a company marketing body might wish to find ways to encourage to attend.

Jane Nicholas, Interview, 1993.

First-time comers

Spectators on their first visit to a dance performance; people whom marketing managers in dance wish to pursuade to become regular audience members.

Jane Nicholas, Interview.

13.　ADMINISTRATORS AND FUNDERS

Dance administrators

People concerned with supporting the dance through management and supervision skills.

Eds.

Company administrator

A facilitator, working to enable the three elements of ballet — the choreography, the design, and the music — to culminate in the ballet performance, especially by securing and budgeting finances from the government, sponsors, and the box office.

Derek Purnell, Interview.

Intendant

The director of a theatre in continental European countries, who has the final say on what shall and shall not be done in his venue by a visiting company.

Norman Morrice, Interview.

Production manager (of a theatre)

The person responsible "to satisfy the potentially conflicting needs" of the show coming in and the economics of a theatre.

Ross Cameron, Interview.

Presenter

The person who provides a space and an audience for a touring event, an administrative role, not an artistic role.

John Ashford, Interview.

Producer in dance

"The person who forms the bridge between the artist and the audience."

The person who raises the finance; often commissions the work; may offer artistic ideas which the artist might not otherwise consider.

John Ashford, Interview.

Producer's role

In dance, a role annexed by the funding authorities who decide which artists receive support, leaving only the role of presenter.

John Ashford, Interview.

Curator

A person who chooses who to put on, with a purpose to make an argument about those artefacts presented and those omitted; a practice common in exhibitions of contemporary art and now beginning in dance.

John Ashford, Interview.

Community dance animators

People in Britain responsible for promoting, providing, enabling, and supporting dance activity in their region for the local community.

Peter Brinson, 1991.

Dance animateur

Dance activists working in the community in Britain, in receipt of subsidy, whose main function is to stimulate the dance culture of their locality.

Community Dance and Mime Foundation, 1992.

Dance Officer

A term used in some districts of Britain for an animateur in community dance, also called "Dance Development Officer", occasionally "Dance Worker".

Alysoun Tomkins, Interview.

Dance Worker

A community dance leader, usually with a particular special commitment such as "dance, disability, and equal opportunities", which is the focus of Stanley Hamilton's work.

Stanley Hamilton, 1992.

Dance Fellows/Co-ordinators

A title given in the U.K. by Local Authorities and Regional Arts Associations to dance people, who were usually co-funded, to initiate activities in a specific area. Used before the term "Dance Animateur" came into fairly common use.

Jane Nicholas, Interview.

Angel

"A financial backer of an entreprise, esp. in the theater."

'Webster', 1993.

Sponsor

"A person or organisation that promotes or supports an artistic or sporting activity."

'Concise Oxford Dictionary', 1990.

Impresario

"An organiser of public entertainments esp. the manager of an operatic, theatical or concert company".

'Webster', 1993.

Entrepreneur

The person who buys the product, that is the repertoire of a company, and its dancers, and tours it; a person who takes the financial risk, who persuades others to back the product; said of Sol Hurok.

Norman Morrice, Interview.

Agent

The person whose essential role is to negotiate the contract of a choreographer or a performer; may also mould their career and may get them work.

Stuart Hopps, Interview.

Dance Director

A title given to the person who carries the responsibility for dance on high-level advisory and funding bodies.

Jane Nicholas, Interview.

Dance voice

The dance person on a funding council for the arts generally, whose job is to put the case for dance, to ensure that the needs of dance are taken into account in policy and financial decision making.

Jane Nicholas, Interview.

PART TWO: THE PERFORMER

Providing a chapter on the performer could be seen as dualist, for the dancer is the dance. They are one. But while the movement cannot come into being without the mover, the mover can be looked at independently of the movement. The performer adds to the dance over and above the act of dancing through kinetic, visual, aural, and creative capacities. These are the subject of acute interest to dance people, and all manner of attitudes to the issues of casting, training, interpretation, sensing, oneness of the dancer and the dance, reification, gender, costuming, auditions, and so on are contributed.

In THE PERFORMER, these capacities are collected together, and, because one cannot divide the dancer from the dance, some entries that flow over into the performer/ movement relationship of the next chapter are there, with emphasis on the performer's lived experience or consciousness-body. How dancers perceive what they are doing has given rise to sections of entries.

In THE PERFORMER AND THE MOVEMENT the dualist or unitary issues in dance become evident in the entries. Capacities of interpretation and creation by the dancer are of interest to the contributors. So too are ways in which the choreographer and the dancer might collaborate. See also the section on the "Choreographer/dancer dependency" in the chapter CHOREOGRAPHIC PROCESSES, which looks at their collaboration from the choreographer's viewpoint. Further entries in Part Three in the movement chapters include references to how the dancer dances the movement.

TECHNIQUE is placed in this Part, rather than in the movement chapters, because the entries are taken fundamentally from the performer's point of view. Techniques are customarily described as movement systems, but also as the means of making dancers. Most techniques have textbooks, in which the verbal vocabulary of their movement content is explained and defined. The bibliography lists several to which the reader's attention is drawn. Here, talk about teaching class and working in class, purposes of class, the structure of class, are given. Different views are evident, and diverse value systems at work. Ballet takes pride of place because it is so widely used, modern and contemporary techniques being represented primarily by Graham and Humphrey-Limón, and lesser-used techniques giving rise to a smaller number of entries.

COSTUME is crucial to how the spectator perceives the dancer dancing. The designers' point of view on what is worn was collected, and their language and making practice is introduced here. Entries on the designer's role in decor are included later, in THE DANCE SPACE.

Chapter 3   THE PERFORMER

1.   THE PERFORMER

Performers

Dancers and anyone who participates visibly in the work, including musicians and the audience, if they become part of the work itself.
Valerie Preston-Dunlop, Interview.

Performer

A singer and dancer in the pop scene.
Michael Jackson, 1993.

Performers as material

An attitude to performers in which their energies, personas, they themselves, are regarded as the material of the work, and not only as instruments or interpreters of movement.
Yolande Snaith, Interview.

Dancers as visual dance material

"He [Paul Taylor] saw them as texture, colour, weight, design, contour..."
Caroline Adams, Lecture.

Dancer

A person for whom the whole network of needs relating to movement, from the physicality to the emotional demands, are paramount, for whom plummeting through space as well as the moment of stillness are an ecstacy.

"People mad enough to starve themselves to a shadow and break their body in the service of their art."
Dorothy Madden, Interview.

Dancer

"A performer with good proportions to the body, technical capacity, musicality, who can pick up steps quickly and retain them, with a creative streak."
Marion Tait, Interview.

Dancer

"A specific individual, a specific woman, not a girl."
Twyla Tharp, Informal talk.

Dancer
    A person, a human being, a man or a woman who expresses ideas through movement and gesture; said of the Limón dancer.
    Carla Maxwell, Interview.

Dancers
    Movers who give quality to the movement, can use a variety of qualities both dynamic and dramatic, who have control both technically and emotionally.
    Christopher Bruce, Interview.

Dancers
    Re-creators; through their own sensitivity to the material of the movement, they are able to realise the intentions of the choreography, as it is expressed in its physical form.
    Doris Rudko, Interview.

Non-dancers as dancers
    Performers who are not technically trained but who nevertheless dance in the work, with material made to suit their limited capacity as dancers.
    Stuart Hopps, Interview.

Non-dancers as performers
    Performers who are not trained technically as dancers but who contribute to the work through their own skills; a conjurer in Bausch's "1980", stuntmen in Bausch's "Carnations", a violinist in de Keersmaeker's "Rosas", movers in Rainer's "Trio A".
    Eds.

Celestial messengers
    "In his [Balanchine's] cosmogony, dancers were like angels: celestial messengers who may communicate emotions but do not themselves experience the joys or griefs of which they bring tidings."
    Bernard Taper, 1974 (1960).

Divine normal
    Martha Graham's term for a dancer, one who does "what the human body is capable of doing" for which "it takes 10 years of study".
    Martha Graham, 1957.

Protagonist
    What performers become when they take on the roles that they are to dance in the work.
    Eds.

Stage persona

The person who a performing artist is on stage, not the person he is pretending to be, but actially is, usually a character who is a larger than life "version of yourself"; said of clowning, fooling and performance arts.

Helen Crocker and *Bim Mason*, Interview.

Be people, To

What dancers have to be in plays and films where they need a sense of drama and character; said in contrast to dancers as dancers.

Geraldine Stephenson, Interview.

Roles

Particular functions which artists incorporate into performance arts in which movement plays a large part, such as fooling.

"...the straight man and the comic, the white clown, the juggler and the feed, flyer and catcher on trapeze."

Helen Crocker and *Bim Mason*, Interview.

2. INDIVIDUALITY AND PERSONALITY

Dancer as individual

"[Tharp] is peripherally intrigued with dancers as individuals and their special individual qualities which she works into her choreography."

Don McDonagh, 1969.

Personal style

"The outstanding artist is invariably endowed with a highly personal style."

John Martin, 1972 (1933).

Dancer as human being

"He [Paul Taylor] used dancers as total human beings, often looking for their idiosyncracies."

Caroline Adams, Lecture.

Idiosyncratic style

The highly personal movement style of a dancer who is or who becomes a choreographer, and whose choreographic style contains the possibilities of his own body; said of Paul Taylor.

Deborah Jowitt, 1977.

Soloist

A dancer capable of giving a solo recital; a dancer with charisma, able to invest the movement with meaning, and to have developed a personal signature.

Jane Dudley, Interview.

Dancer as soloist

A Cunningham term, implying an attitude to the dancer as an individual person, acting with his or her own social sense.

"...each in the company is a soloist, and in a given dance we may act sometimes separately and sometimes together.... Each person, observant of the others, is allowed to act freely."

Carolyn Brown, 1968.

Cunningham dancers

They "are not pretending to be other than themselves. They are, in a way, realising identities through the act of dancing. Rather then being someone they are doing something."

Merce Cunningham, 1974.

Quality of stardom

The "...inner fire..." of Rudolf Nureyev.

Ninette de Valois, 1977.

Fire

The quality which some dancers have to "blaze" on stage, to convey "a hidden volcano" which might and does erupt in passionate feeling; said of Hugh Laing and Rudolf Nureyev.

Maude Lloyd, 1984.

Aura

The quality of stardom which a performer adopts, "transcending her physical being"; said of Miss Ruth (St. Denis).

"...eleven feet tall, iridescent, surrounded by a five-foot magnetic force... radiant, magic...".

Murray Louis, 1980.

Dancer (as god figure)

"What dance audiences want to watch an ordinary person? Audiences expect, maybe deserve, a blow-up of reality — a god or goddess, a veritable miracle in the shape of a human being, which is what a good dancer is."

Paul Taylor, "Private Domain" 1987.

Charisma

The quality in a performer which draws the audience towards him or her; an innate capacity.

Jane Dudley, Interview.

Magnetism

A physical and emotional quality which a dancer may possess through which he makes tangible the dance by drawing the spectator into a spiritual, emotional intention; said of Laurie Booth.

Judith Mackrell, Interview.

Authority
     A quality which a dancer can give to a role, so making the audience completely believe in the character she is playing.
     Judith Mackrell, Interview.

Effort habits
     Habitual ways of moving dynamically typical of each individual; the range of an individual, his dynamic 'palette'.
     Rudolf Laban, 1950.

Range
     The intensity and available number of movement elements used by an individual are compared with the number of possible elements to give a profile of an individual's preferred range and lack.
     Janis Pforsich, Ellen Goldman, John Chanik and *Lynn Wenning*, Contributed.

Proportion
     The frequency with which some elements of effort and shape appear in an individual's repertoire, compared with the frequency of other elements gives some sense of the proportional importance of one or another in a personal profile.
     Cecily Dell, 1970.

Posture-gesture-merger mode of expression
     The unique pattern of an individual's way of moving in terms of his posture-gesture merging behaviour; the behaviour which a person will exhibit as a way of expressing his personality.
     Warren Lamb and *Elizabeth Watson*, 1979.

Personal style
     The way an individual moves, embodying attitudes in the choices made, from the host of possible nuances so that authentic movement expression results.
     Marion North, Interview.

Personal language of dance
     "It is an organic statement of the person...which must be stretched so that it does not remain static."
     Anna Sokolow in Selma Jeanne Cohen, 1977.

Performance style of a dancer
     The unique style of a performer which results from personal movement characteristics and physical, technical and interpretative abilities.
     Janet Adshead, 1990.

Awkwardness

A quality in a dancer valued by Merce Cunningham; a quality of awkwardness, some individual quality; maybe in how they walk or turn their head, over and above their technical capacity.

David Vaughan, Conversation.

Personality, A

The individuality of each dancer, not androgenous, not an automoton, not stereotypically "macho or glamorous", but a unique individual; said of José Limón's choice of dancer.

Carla Maxwell, Interview.

Style

"We do not mean polish, that is perfected physical movement, but rather the air, the manner with which physical movements are executed;...[through] the dancer's personality and the character of the dance itself."

Cecil J. Sharp, 1934.

Artistic merit

An indescribable quality in competitive dance separate from the merit of performance of the figures themselves, which centres on the way each couple present their routine by making it distinctively their own.

"...characterisation through personality...".

Geoffrey Hearn, Interview.

Talent

A quality beyond technique, one which "not all agree on", which has to be nurtured by the choregrapher.

Twyla Tharp, Informal talk.

Dancer of substance

A performer with talent but no conceit, who engages with the job at hand.

Elizabeth Keen, Interview.

3. BODIES

Body, The

The dancer's instrument, his raw material.

"The body...has more personal and limiting associations in the inner mind of his audience than color, tone, texture, shape or ever words can have."

Louis Horst in Louis Horst and Carroll Russell, 1961.

Body, The
> The raw material of the dance, to which an audience will respond strongly.
> "...powerful, attractive, magical...".
> *Judith Mackrell*, Interview.

Body
> "The body has always been to me a thrilling wonder, a dynamo of energy, exciting, courageous, powerful; a delicately balanced logic and proportion."
> *Martha Graham* in Frederick Rand Rogers, 1941.

Beautiful body
> "I would like to show...that these bodies of ours, which most of the time are used for dull, ordinary things, can be beautiful...".
> *George Balanchine* in Bernard Taper, 1974.

Negro body
> It is the physical bone structure which is unique.
> *Alvin Ailey* in Walter Sorell, 1986.

Normal body, The
> The body of a person who has not undergone such rigorous dance training that s/he has taken on the tailored look of the professionally trained dancer in body shape, musculature, and carriage; not, as Graham puts it, an acrobat of God.
> *Valerie Preston-Dunlop*, Interview.

Perfect body, A
> The aim of the ballet dancer's training, which is essential for the genre, and without which "however strongly the spirit moves, very little can be achieved."
> *Ninette de Valois*, 1977.

Imperfect body
> A valued physical attribute by people working in clowning and performance arts in which the bodily imperfections are used as an integral part of the development of a 'persona' for an act.
> *Helen Crocker* and *Bim Mason*, Interview.

Grotesque, The
> One presentation of the dancer's body, exemplified by Bausch's work; said in contrast to "the classical body".
> "...a body which has orifices, genitals and protuberances...".
> *Janet Woolf*, 1990.

Body shape
The physical carriage and musculature of the body which is moulded/developed through cultural activities from childhood onwards, such as crouching on the ground as opposed to sitting on a sofa, attending ballet classes or dancing barefoot on the open ground.
Andrée Grau, Interview.

Instrument
The dancer's body, trained to function as an efficient machine by some dance technique methods; said in contrast to 'the person'.
Andrée Grau, Interview.

Homogeneous physique
The body of dancers which reflects a reduction of individual differences to a norm of similarity; a body type either looked for by a company or definitely not looked for by choreographers who value individual differences in performances.
Laurie Booth, Interview.

Stereotype
The standardised physique, stance, and vocabulary of mainstream contemporary dancers in the 1990's which a teacher may wish her students to achieve; alternatively she may not wish to mould them in that direction.
Erica Stanton, Interview.

Heterogeneous group
A dance ensemble, in which differences of age, physique, personal styles and gender are valued.
Laurie Booth, Interview.

Body shape
"...I try not to have an idea about how they [the dancers] should be. Tall and thin, or short and thin.... Mostly, if they can dance, then I get interested...".
Merce Cunningham in Merce Cunningham and Jacqueline Lesschaeve, 1985.

Bodies
The cast for a piece with non-dancers of every kind of physique.
"...the incredible assortment of bodies, the any old bodies, in our any old lives ...in their any old clothes."
Jill Johnson of a Steve Paxton work, in Sally Banes, 1980.

Broad bracket
Widely varied physiques which a choreographer might prefer for his work, which nevertheless have to converge on a goal in order to become a collaborative working team of performers.
Mark Murphy, Interview.

Body type

The classification of the physique for ballet into one with long or short ligaments and muscles, so allowing too little or too much movement in the joints for the flexibility and control required by the technique.

Anna Paskevska, 1990.

Lyrical dancer

A long-limbed romantic female dancer typically used in lead roles in ballets; said of Maude Lloyd.

Peggy van Praagh, 1984.

Smaller dancers' vocabulary

The petit allegro work which smaller, more compact dancers excel in.

Monica Mason, Interview.

Muscular build

The kind of physique which both male and female dancers need, to participate successfully in the physicality of some contemporary theatrical work, while nevertheless retaining gender differences through their performance.

Mark Murphy, Interview.

Womanly qualities

"...the woman's quality is tender, protective, conservative, conciliatory, delicate and tentative."

Ted Shawn, 1946.

Manly qualities

"...the man's quality is positive, aggressive, forceful, definite, explicit...".

Ted Shawn, 1946.

Bournonville men and women

"Bournonville stands for natural movements. He wants male dancers to look like males and females to look feminine."

Kirsten Ralov, 1979.

Individual instrument

"Doris Humphrey knew that every dancer, being an individual, has an instrument unique and distinct from any other, and that in consequence each dancer must ultimately find his own dance, as she has."

José Limón in Selma Jeanne Cohen, 1977.

Make it work

To adapt and synthesize the Graham exercise to your instrument (body) so that "the gamut of physiques" can accommodate and participate.

Thea Barnes, Susan Sentler, and *Brenda Baden-Semper*, Interview.

State of the body

A major concern of dancers in terms of the sensation and health of their instrument, its muscle soreness, its fatigue, its tension, its general well-being.

Laurie Booth, Interview.

Socially constructed body, A

A view of the body influenced by the society in which the person lives; there being no such thing as one concept of the human body.

Andrée Grau, Interview.

Celebration of the body

Part of what the dancer does in terms of the possibilities of the body as a mode of human expression, contrasted to and simultaneous with what the dancer has to go through to become an instrument of dance production, the oppression of her/his body.

Paul Filmer, Interview.

4. APPROACHES TO KINAESTHETIC AWARENESS

4a. SENSING AND PERCEIVING ONE'S OWN MOVEMENT

Sense of motion, A

"We may speak of a sense of motion but in reality this requires the cooperation of several [senses]."; "...in addition to kinetics, motion is also seeing, feeling, hearing, balance, gravity, sound, light, color, shape, smell and other senses as well."

Alwin Nikolais, 1964.

Bodily perspective

The physical experience of moving, not the view of that movement by an observer.

Rudolf Laban, 1966 (1939).

Experiencing

"Until the reader has actually experienced the feeling of a dance movement, description and discussion cut little ice."

Douglas Kennedy, 1949.

Experience

"The puritanical concept of life has always ignored the fact that the nervous system and the body as well as the mind are involved in experience, and art cannot be experienced except by one's entire being."

Martha Graham, 1956.

Feeling and sensation

"Feeling is subjective, 'I think I am feeling stretched', while sensation is objective, it is the real sensing of what it is like to stretch muscularly and motionally."
Robert Cohan, Interview.

Think-feeling

"A state of mutual balance and interdependence between intellectual understanding of a movement and the simultaneous direct, sensual experience of it. A powerful component of a heightened kinaesthetic awareness in which one strives to remain fully conscious of the sensation of the degree of muscle tone moment by moment; relates to the Zen concept of 'suchness' or 'thus-ness'"; said of Erick Hawkins technique.
Mark Lintern Harris, Contributed.

Sensation equation, The

Feeling individual muscle action (m) which alone does not give the sensation of movement, but grouped together can.
"$m + m + m = x$ sensation".
Robert Cohan, Interview.

Sensation body

What a dancer is, a person whose primary attitude to his body is what it perceives of its actions.
"That which allows space and time to come into formation."
Laurie Booth, Interview.

Compression and decompression

The basic sensation of the legs during walking as the weight is transferred from one leg to the other.
Laurie Booth, Interview.

Comfortable participation

How the parts of the body should feel during a movement; awareness of this kind of co-ordination is the aim of a Feldenkreis practitioner.
Scott Clark, Interview.

Manipulation of the skeleton

How a Feldenkreis practitioner works with a dancer/client to aid consciousness of changes within the body as the position changes.
Scott Clark, Interview.

Sensing

The ability of the dancer to know his/her own and others' movements using perceptual channels other than the visual.
Gregory Nash, Interview.

Feeling

Sensing exactly what is happening in the body.

"Feel the separation of chest and hip. Let it move on its own." (said of the paso doble); "Get the feeling of the poise." (said of the waltz).

Geoffrey Hearn, Instructing.

Narrow and wide

The sensation of the crossing over and the opening out of leg or arm gestures in a continuous sequence of dance.

Scott Clark, Class.

Physicality

The depth of involvement of the physique in the movement, through the experience and control of the muscularity of the body.

Stuart Beckett, Class.

Physical knowledge

"Knowledge that lives inside the dancer which can be used, while it is growing imaginatively, in the making of a work."

Siobhan Davies, Contributed.

Volume of knowledge, A

An attitude to the body based on knowledge of the way the body works automatically.

"It's whether or not they know where their pelvis is, or where their tail-bone is — it's a volume of knowledge...the dancers that I work with professionally have the same volume of knowledge to me, and in rehearsal I can call on that."

Gregory Nash, Interview.

Discover sensation, To

To make the transition from doing movements to sensing their motional content, a process aided by images of movement.

"The energy goes out through the hollowed bones, water streaming through a hose pipe."

Robert Cohan, Company class.

Inner focus

An awareness in the performer of what each and every part of the body is doing.

Hanya Holm in Walter Sorell, 1976.

Spatial distinctions

What a Feldenkreis practitioner wants a mover to be able to discern, in detail.

Scott Clark, Interview.

Three-dimensional focus

The inner sensation of the spatial co-ordination of dance material which a performer needs to work with to support and enrich the actual doing of the steps.

Robert Cohan, Interview.

Motional blindness

"Motional blindness precludes knowledge by the performer of the context of the event. He is virtually left with a blank page or a movement doodle of symbols without meaning," because he ignores that "Motion demands by its definition, the detail values of its itinerary."

Alwin Nikolais, 1964.

Tactile incapacity

The increasing inability of modern man to experience movement fully through his propensity for reflection and distancing himself from his own body and isolating himself from his surroundings.

Rudolf Laban, 1966 (1939).

Kinaesthetic perception

A complex mix of proprio- and exteroception providing information and sensation about the perceiver's own movement.

James J. Gibson, 1966.

Proprioception

The perception of self.

James J. Gibson, 1966.

Exteroception

The perception of the environment.

James J. Gibson, 1966.

Exteroception

Attending to the environment, which for a dancer is everything and everybody in the space plus all sound plus all tactile feeling, a formidable array of potential experience.

Valerie Preston-Dunlop, 1992.

Active perception

An active process of searching for sensory experience.

James J. Gibson, 1966.

Passive perception

Energies, such as heat, light, colour, motion, which impinge on the senses without the person actively seeking them out.

James J. Gibson, 1966.

Focal attention

Attending to the component parts of an experience, e.g. parts of a movement phrase, by which the sense of the phrase as a whole will be lost (contrasted with subsidiary attention).

Eds. from *Michael Polanyi*, 1983.

Subsidiary knowledge

Knowing a movement phrase as a whole, in contrast to focusing on its component parts (contrasted with focal attention).

Eds. from *Michael Polanyi*, 1983.

Notice, To

A term used in classes with a Feldenkreis base, in which the awareness of the proprioceptive and exteroceptive content is paramount.

"Notice what you do with the chest when you chassé."

Scott Clark, Class.

Sensory awareness

The efficient use of the sensory apparatus in the body; a key concept in the Alexander technique teacher's practice where unreliable sensory awareness is identified and re-educated so that troublesome movement habits are experienced, intuited, and new ways of moving instituted, which promote efficiency of body and mind.

Judith Leibowitz and *Bill Connington*,1991.

Give instructions and ask questions, To

The method used by Feldenkreis practitioners to promote awareness through movement; the instructions are spatial and the questions are concerned with sensing change in the body.

Scott Clark, Interview.

Pilates technique

A body therapy system designed to heighten kinaesthetic awareness and encourage efficient movement patterns.

"Lengthen the spine", "Relax the ribs", "Widen the back", "No tension in the shoulders", "Inhale, exhale".

Susanne Lahusen, Class.

4b. PHENOMENAL EXPERIENCE

Phenomenology

This "...strives to capture pre-reflective experience, the immediacy of being-in-the-world. I think of this initial impulse of phenomenology (the basis of phenomenological reduction) as poetic and subliminal, containing moments of insight into an experience when the details of 'being there' are vivid in feeling, but have not had time to focus in thought."

Sondra Fraleigh, 1991.

Pre-reflective experience
> The experience of being fully and exclusively responsive to what is taking place, being made, now.
> *Valerie Preston-Dunlop*, Interview.

Lived experience of dance
> "An experience of a sheer dynamic flow of force."
> *Maxine Sheets-Johnstone*, 1979.

Movement
> "The basic experience of existence."
> *Rudolf Laban*, 1966 (1939).

Movement quality
> "Movement imbued with the inner quality you find in the wonderous immediate knowledge of existence, that you find in the pure fact of movement."
> *Erick Hawkins* in Selma Jeanne Cohen, 1977.

Horizon of time
> The ways in which time is lived — compressed, elongated, endless, a long time, a short time, barely enough time, etc. Lived time does not refer to clock time, but to how time feels. A concept applied to "existence and the arts".
> *Sondra Fraleigh*, 1991.

Phenomenological experience and time
> "Central to phenomenology is the understanding that we never perceive a phenomenon in static unchanging perspectives, but rather as existing through time. Time and motion are ever present conditions influencing attention and perspective. Nevertheless, consciousness can unify experience."
> *Sondra Fraleigh*, 1991.

Present
> The totally aware state of being in the action as it evolves, rather than moving towards a planned goal or moving away from the previous state.
> *Katherine Allen*, Interview.

Moment
> The attitude to the phenomenon of time in improvisation, living in the present moment as it occurs.
> *Laurie Booth*, Interview.

Sensitivity
> "In life, heightened nerve sensitivity produces that concentration on the instant which is true living. In dance this sensitivity produces action timed to the present moment."
> *Martha Graham* in Frederick Rand Rogers, 1941.

Dancer's clock

"Inside, at a million miles per hour or more, corpuscles are zipping around and filling me with a sensation of great speed. Otherwise, I'm experiencing a feeling of superslow ooziness. This, of course, has little to do with actual rates of speed but is because of something that, for want of a better term, I'll call the dancer's clock. Focus and concentration makes time different for when you dance and for when you don't."

Paul Taylor, "Private Domain" 1987.

4c. IMAGING AND MEMORY

Body image

An image formed by an individual of himself as a physical person, a long-term concept of his body built up while growing up, but vulnerable to change throughout life.

Lynette Young Overby, 1990.

Body image

The image a person has of their own body, which is usually socially determined, that is by the interest people around us give to the body, but which, in pathological states, is distorted by the 'peculiar ideas' a patient may develop of his own body; an area of interest to the dance movement therapist.

Marion Chase, 1952.

Body schema

"The diagram of the body that is built up in the brain by which coordinated purposeful movements are carried out and by which the body parts and the body itself are oriented in space."

Lynette Young Overby, 1990.

Imaging

A means of finding a way of moving by imagining lines of energy in the body.

Susanne Lahusen, Class.

Choreological imaging

Using choreological principles as images for expression.
"Plié — slide down your own verticality." (not "bending your knees")
"Extending — give vitality to the leg." (not "pointing your feet").

Rosemary Brandt, Interview.

Thinking high

An image used to achieve verticality of the body.

Margaret Lloyd, 1974 (1949).

Opposition
Using the five points of opposition to create a feeling of length and stretch in the entire body. The points, in the standing body, are: the head, the right and left hand and the right and left foot. The stretch is felt pulling out from the top of the head, away from the palms of out-turned hands and down through the feet.
Daniel Lewis, 1984.

Image of kinetic sensation
Imagined feeling, particularly of a tactile sensation of moving around within a spherical surface, used to generate spontaneous movement material.
Laurie Booth, Interview.

Ideokinesis
"The imagined movement" of one's neuro-muscular-skeletal process, used as a teaching device, dependent upon a "...thorough knowledge of the universal laws of mechanics, the skeletal structure, and the principles of the muscular and neurological function."
"In the cerebral cortex it is the movements that are pictured, not individual muscle actions."
Jones Quain in Lulu E. Sweigard, 1974.

Imagined movement
The ideokinetic perspective by which you "visualise yourself growing tall and, in so doing, stand upright with greater ease. If you forcefully stretch up to make yourself taller, however, you will find your body taut and unyielding."
Lulu E. Sweigard, 1974.

Mapping the body
Getting a sense of the body in motion through using anatomical and kinaesthetic imagery.
"The sun filling the room of your body", "let the feet be soft, see through the ground as if it were water".
Miranda Tufnell and *Chris Crickmay, 1990.*

Golden cord
The image in T'ai Chi of being suspended from above by "a golden cord" so that the vertebrae are like "a string of pearls".
Katherine Allen, Interview.

Dance memory, The
"Each new movement experience, engendered by the previous one, or an initial impress of the action of the body upon time, must be discovered, felt and made meaningful to its fullest in order to enrich the dance memory."
Merce Cunningham in Walter Sorell, 1951.

Muscle memory
    What a dancer relies on in performance, where it is no longer profitable to think about the movement but s/he has to simply "go for it".
    Joseph Cipolla, Interview.

Muscle memory
    The retention of the knowledge of a movement within the muscles of the body themselves, allowing a movement to be reperformed without being relearned.
    Daniel Lewis, 1984.

4d. COMPLEX EXPERIENCE OF THE CONSCIOUSNESS OF DANCING

Moving in space
    An attention which the dancer needs to use to develop awareness and care when entering the space, gauging it to get a sense of himself and other dancers in it.
    Robert Cohan, 1986.

Visual cue
    Knowing when to move on with the next material, not by counting or by the sound, but by some visually apparent information.
    Anna Markard, Rehearsal.

Time pattern
    "...is established by the relative duration of movement impulses. It can be accurately sensed without being mathematically measured (counted)...".
    Merce Cunningham in Merce Cunningham and Jacqueline Lesschaeve, 1985.

Time awareness
    "...if you paid attention to the timing, then, even if you weren't facing them [other dancers], you knew they were there. And that made a relationship...".
    Merce Cunningham in Merce Cunningham and Jacqueline Lesschaeve, 1985.

Speed
    The tempo of each movement, something which dancers can remember with great accuracy and use with uncountable music, so knowing just when to complete a movement.
    "I put the foot back down in fifth, NOW."
    Monica Mason, Interview.

Space-time imagery
    "The space-time imagery of the body in motion represents the rhythmic design of a remembered action-feeling."
    F. Mary Fee, 1971.

Sensation of qualities

Something dealt with in dance "before you are able to verbalise about it", the intense kinaesthetic awareness of actual sensation and then of imagined sensation.

"Feel what texture you might be lying on or standing on."

Siobhan Davies in National Resource Centre for Dance, 1988.

Rhythmic awareness

The discrimination and relating of the sound the body makes, especially of the feet on the floor, with the sensation of the movement that created the sound.

F. Mary Fee, 1971.

Effort awareness

The perception by the individual of his own dynamic potential for qualitative change.

Rudolf Laban, 1950.

Dance consciousness

An awareness, induced by dancing, of an alternative consciousness to that of the practicalities of every day.

"...the ever-changing forms and shapes about things and realities important to us all...", "...the land of silence...", "...a forgotten landscape...", "...the riches of the soul...".

Rudolf Laban, 1975 (1935).

Creating the dance

"What you do is move, what you create is the dance...they are crucially different experiences."

Valerie Preston-Dunlop, Interview.

Verve

The feeling of aliveness in a moment of stillness, of ongoing-ness, of continued vibration.

Thea Barnes, Susan Sentler, and *Brenda Baden-Semper*, Interview.

Dance state

Deep concentration on the body in motion induced by prolonged improvisation focusing on the sensations of the moving body during simple movement activities; said of Ann Halprin's method.

"A state of enchantment."

Simone Forti in Sally Banes, 1980(a).

Interior world

The sensate private world of the dancer to which only he is privy and which is rich in sensation and imagery.

Laurie Booth, Interview.

Experiential understanding

Knowledge in dance which can only be deepened to understanding through the active process of perceiving what you are creating.

Ernestine Stodelle, 1978.

Significance of the movement, The

A term used for the import the movement has for the mover, a concept used in teaching dance in the process of awakening a dance student to the meaning content of her own movement.

Marion North, Interview.

Play back

The way in which the content of movement is sensed by the mover and carries some significance for him/her.

"The sensation plays back."

Marion North, Interview.

Intensity

What a dancer needs to feel as she leaves the wings and enters the stage; said of the experience of dancing an early Graham work.

Bonnie Bird in a Reconstruction by Brenda Baden-Semper.

Spontaneity in performance

"...is not wholly dependent on emotion at that instant. It is the condition of emotion objectified...it illumines. It excites.... It is the result of perfect timing to the Now."

Martha Graham, 1956.

Texture, harmony

"Texture and harmony are the feeling in the dance, the way in which one gesture affects the rest of the body, the top of the head or the left heel."

Louis Horst, 1958.

Dancewise

Cunningham term meaning dance intelligence, or solving a dance problem "by dancing".

"You see how to get from one point to another from dancing it, you figure it out dancewise."

Merce Cunningham in Merce Cunningham and Jacqueline Lesschaeve, 1985.

Dancer's craft

"The understanding of the organisation of movement is the high point of the dancer's craft."

Merce Cunningham in Walter Sorell 1951.

Center (awareness of)

In Graham technique, "integration of mind and body is required along with awareness of the relationships between all body parts and center.... Awareness of center has a dramatic as well as a physical advantage. It assures a sense of identity...".

Alice J. Helpern, 1981.

Before the habit forms

Before a mistaken way of moving, that is, one not in the style of the work being rehearsed, becomes ingrained and so difficult to eradicate; a term used early on in rehearsal.

Judith Maelor Thomas, Rehearsal.

5. ENDEAVOUR

Confidence

A helpful quality for major performances which can be jeopardised by fatigue, anxiety of a first night, sudden change of partner, injury, et al.

Monica Mason, Interview.

In peak condition

A dancer's readiness to perform, especially difficult in an opera-house-based ballet company where the performances are not in seasons but are interspersed with opera performances; said of The Royal Ballet.

Monica Mason, Interview.

Keep pushing, To

What a young professional dancer has to do through self-motivation, to make the most of the learning opportunities even where, as a junior member of a company, there may not be many opportunities to perform.

Thomas Paton, Interview.

Commitment

The quality of personal involvement which a performer brings to his work, so building the confidence needed to interpret a role, "To go for broke", "To really pitch in".

Bonnie Bird, Interview.

Competition

The drive for success which each dancer has to have, and to maintain, in order to overcome the physical and emotional strains of becoming, and remaining, a professional dancer.

Martha Graham, 1957.

Perishable things

"At the peak of his power he (a dancer) has two lovely, fragile, perishable things — one is spontaneity; the other is simplicity."
Martha Graham, 1958.

Performer's responsibility

The onus on the performer, which starts in the classroom, not simply to 'do' what is given, but to "make" the dance: "making by doing".
Rosemary Brandt, Interview.

Creative responsibility

The quality which dancers in training have to bring to their work in readiness for surviving in the profession.
Bonnie Bird, Interview.

Take responsibility

To know how company dancers should behave, rehearse each other, arrive on time, retain material, work together.
Lea Anderson, Interview.

Personal discipline

The quality of self-discipline required by a professional dancer, to stand up to strains of performing, the hazards of touring, the vagaries of choreographers, injury, fatigue,....
Bonnie Bird, Interview.

Self-imposed discipline

A way of working which dancers have to learn in order to successfully graduate from relying on the discipline imposition by a teacher, and to tolerate the physical and mental hardships of dance training; said of professional dancers and also aerobics participants.
Helen Thomas, Interview.

6.   REIFICATION

Reify (the dancer), To

"To convert a person into a thing."
'Concise Oxford Dictionary', 1990.

Things

What dancers, especially ballet students, may be treated like, so eroding their confidence and their development as interpreters.
Bonnie Bird, Interview.

Reification/humanness

A continuum on which choreographers seem to place their dancers, through complex layers of choices, so that they appear both dehumanised and fully human in ways which are typical of that choreographer.

Valerie Preston-Dunlop, Interview.

Artist as commodity

Artists listed as sets of vital statistics, e.g. "Nigel Charnock, 36:28:36, Brown hair, blue eyes, 5′ 6″, 9.5 stone. British, Single".

Programme Note quoted by *Lesley-Anne Sayers*, 1988.

Be 'darling', To

What a dancer is called in commercial work for some weeks, unlike opera, where you are named individually as M/s so-and-so.

Lynn Robertson Bruce, Interview.

Objectified body

The body developed as an object through some dance technique training methods.

Andrée Grau, Interview.

Regimented

The quality of rigorous control and conformity which some Eastern European trained dancers are expected to comply with, and which some Eastern choreographers expect from Western dancers but do not find.

Teresa Kelsey, Interview.

Dancer, A

"I have never liked to see dancers on stage, but people. I have always told my dancers 'don't look like a dancer, be a vessel for the human emotions, try to look like a human being'."

Alvin Ailey in Walter Sorell, 1986.

Asexual works

Dance pieces in which role reversal, androgyny and traditional partnering are taken for granted, not presented as an issue.

Stephanie Jordan, 1992.

Classical body, The

A dancer's body which "excludes bodily functions and privatises specific bodily areas" (particularly those associated with sexuality).

Janet Woolf, 1990.

Gender-specific
Clear male and female content of a work, through casting, costume, and movement quality, for instance; typical examples are ballerina roles for women and macho male folk dance troupes.
Helen Thomas, Interview.

Dehumanization
A process in the arts which dispenses with human content and lived reality.
José Ortega y Gasset in Roger Copeland and Marshall Cohen, 1983.

Dehumanisation
"...Alwin Nikolais — by costuming and lighting — dehumanised his dancers into abstractions...".
Clive Barnes, 1968.

Oppression of the body
The reduction of the dancer to an instrument of dance production; counter-balanced by the dance making possible a celebration of human expression through the body.
Paul Filmer, Interview.

Kunstfigur (Ger.)
What Oskar Schlemmer called his dancer figures.
They were "sexless figures or eternal types of humans moving like mechanical puppets in a variety of moods through space...within geometric patterns."
Walter Sorell, 1981.

Life forces, or energies, brush strokes
How dancers might be seen in a non-narrative work especially by a designer.
Beatrice Hart, Interview.

Abstract perfection
The striving to become a perfect human being, often manifested by dancers through losing individuality.
"Abstract perfection is something which I think hounds a lot of people in a lot of ways...which is the case with many dancers."
Twyla Tharp in British Broadcasting Corporation, 1983.

Using the mirror
Surveying yourself in the mirror of a studio, a negative force operating in aerobics classes where the individual sees herself as a body with a shape, a weight, a look, rather than a person.
Helen Thomas, Interview.

Mirror
       An authoritative structure which gives negative reinforcement to the dancer, telling him he is not as good as he should be, a diminishing rather than supportive element in studio life.
       Laurie Booth, Interview.

7. THE AUDITION

Audition
       A theatrical convention in which the dancers present their wares to a casting director/choreographer.
       Norbert Servos and *G. Weigelt*, 1984.

Aesthetics of the body
       An issue in casting dance on video and video dance where close up shots reveal age and body physique, creating problems for casting not encountered in theatre work; you try and cast for "best in a video version", not necessarily a big name or the same person who is "best in the theatre version".
       Bob Lockyer, 1992.

Audition criteria
       The priorities which a company or dance academy may have to guide them in selecting dancers at an audition; these might include range and versatility of movement style, and ability to pick up speedily, an ability to translate movement into meaningful performance, to be able to work with others, to possess a mainstream physique.
       Marion North, Interview.

Conduct the audition, To
       To give movement material which will tell you which dancers have a feel for what you are needing.
       Stuart Hopps, Interview.

Performer potential
       An audition criterion set for recruiting new dancers into a single-choreographer company; put into practice not through a formal audition but by seeing dancers in performance; Lea Anderson's method.
       Lea Anderson, Interview.

Performer qualities
       "Dance ability taken for granted, a creative mind, quick witted, with physical strength, able to work in physical contact with other people."
       Mark Murphy, Interview.

Bring in, To
> To invite a potential new company member to a workshop as part of the auditioning process, to see how s/he responds to the movement material, the company atmosphere, and way of working.
> *Lea Anderson*, Interview.

Sell yourself
> An attitude in the jazz dance class which a student learns quickly to adopt; namely to say with his movement "I'm good, hire me."
> *Thea Barnes*, Interview.

Take direction, To
> To respond to a choreographer or rehearsal director in the way that they need you to respond for the style of the work.
> *Lea Anderson*, Interview.

Invited audition (in opera)
> An audition which one is invited to attend for work as a dancer in an opera season.
> *Lynn Robertson Bruce*, Interview.

Open audition
> An audition open to all comers for work as a dancer in opera; an audition which several hundreds attend.
> *Lynn Robertson Bruce*, Interview.

Commercial auditions
> A cattle market: where dancers are given numbers, never referred to by name, not told what the job is until hired.
> *Lynn Robertson Bruce*, Interview.

Placed in the room, To be
> To be given a place in an audition, which you stay in and return to, in order to facilitate the task of the casting panel identifying you.
> *Lynn Robertson Bruce*, Interview.

Put yourself forward, To
> What you have to do in an audition in order to be seen amongst the crowd.
> *Lynn Robertson Bruce*, Interview.

Putting movers together in groupings
> What may happen in auditions as the panel try out several dancers together to see how they look as a group.
> *Lynn Robertson Bruce*, Interview.

'Book ends'

Dancers of similar physique and general look, qualities needed for some unison ensemble work, and hence those who are selected in audition primarily on looks rather than ability.

Stuart Hopps, Interview.

Use your voice, To

What dancers have to be able to do in commercial work and some opera work.

Lynn Robertson Bruce, Interview.

Audition outfit

What you wear at an audition: i) which conveys that you know the scene; ii) which draws attention to you in a suitable way.

Lynn Robertson Bruce, Interview.

Look, A (for contemporary audition)

The kind of clothing, hair, make up, shoes to wear in an audition for contemporary dance work, which is different from the look for an opera audition.

Lynn Robertson Bruce, Interview.

Eliminate, To

What happens in an audition, as gradually less and less dancers remain to be chosen.

Lynn Robertson Bruce, Interview.

Self-eliminating

T'ai Chi Ch'uan students who decide for themselves that the form is not for them, compared with the eliminating processes of dance auditions.

Katherine Allen, Interview.

Pick up, To

The ability of a dancer to learn steps/material quickly; a skill which is looked for in dancers at audition by choreographers.

Elizabeth Keen, Rehearsal.

'Dancability'

A quality which a choreographer may be looking for in a dancer, not necessarily highly skilled technically, but capable of working as a dance artist, of making the movement material his own.

Stuart Hopps, Interview.

Line up

In an open commercial audition, standing in a line after the class, waiting to be asked to step forward, or not.

Lynn Robertson Bruce, Interview.

Right, To be
The right dancer for that particular role, according to the criteria in the mind of the choreographer; may be tall and leggy, squat and strong, able to jump well, to interpret a role, be an all-rounder; especially to be responsive to the choreographer's ways of working.
Stuart Hopps, Interview.

Sylphs and heavies
The casting types which a movement director of a play or film might need, essentially a person who can play a character and also dance, their physique being germane to their character role.
Geraldine Stephenson, Interview.

Recalls
In the audition procedure, being asked to audition several times more before the choice is made by the panel.
Lynn Robertson Bruce, Interview.

Panel
At an audition, the group of people selecting the dancers for the work.
Lynn Robertson Bruce, Interview.

Take a reserve
What a panel does when a dancer successful in an audition cannot, or will not, undertake the job offered.
Lynn Robertson Bruce, Interview.

Contract
The agreement presented to you after successful audition, in which remuneration and conditions are stated.
Lynn Robertson Bruce, Interview.

Schedule
The times and commitment outlined to you before an audition for opera, and after the audition for commercial work.
Lynn Robertson Bruce, Interview.

Pool of dancers
The group of dancers known to the Head of Movement at an opera house, on whom s/he can draw to audition for work.
Lynn Robertson Bruce, Interview.

Chapter 4 THE PERFORMER AND THE MOVEMENT

1. THE PERFORMER/MOVEMENT RELATIONSHIP

Execution

> The actual performance of the movement.
> *Lucas Hoving*, 1969.

Instrument and medium

> "The instrument of the dance is the human body; the medium is the movement."
> *Martha Graham*, 1956.

Subject and object

> What the performer is in dance, namely, simultaneously, the one who does the dancing and the one who is seen to dance.
> *Laurie Booth*, Interview.

Inseparability of dancer and dance

> "The body is the dance, as the dancer is the dance; the body is concretely there in the dance. The body is not the instrument of dance; it is the subject of dance. The body cannot be an instrument, because it is not an object as other instruments are. Even when it is objectified in dance, it retains its subjectivity."
> *Sondra Fraleigh*, 1987.

Moving or dancing

> The crucial difference between moving about and dancing: "...if you separate what is done from who is doing it you lose the dance."
> "You are the dance."
> *Rosemary Brandt*, Interview.

Dancer's role

> A double role, as creator and as externaliser of concepts created in his own mind; as instrument revealing his spiritual experience; he both creates and externalises the creation.
> *Roderyk Lange*, 1975.

Dance performance

The practical skills and the interpretation of a dance work.
Janet Adshead and *June Layson*, 1983.

Informing the movement

The personality, musicality, and expressiveness of the dancer strongly influencing the way the dance looks.
Judith Mackrell, Interview.

Utterance

The act of dancing which adds the dancer's own layer of meaning to the dance material.
Valerie Preston-Dunlop, 1987.

Speaking through the movement

"Communicating gesturally, body-wise, floor pattern-wise, and through steps"; what a performer should do.
Jane Dudley, Interview.

Communicability of dance

The inherent ability of dance to communicate through the mix of performer and movement.

"By failing to find a completely objective approach, and by failing to disguise the dancer's individual body language, my awareness of the communicability of dance has increased."
Paul Taylor, "Private Domain", 1987.

Interpretation

The process when a dancer takes the steps and makes them his own, concerned with how they will look best on him.

"...the way my facility will allow...".
Joseph Cipolla, Interview.

Work it through, To

The job of the performers to find out how they can do the dance material with their facility.
Mark Murphy, Interview.

Interpret, To

"To make a dance come to life."
Bonnie Bird, Interview.

Meaningful performance

A way of learning to dance a role in which the given form is translated into dance material which carries its innate meaning.
Marion North, Interview.

Interpretation

Finding the meaning that is in the movement rather than adding to it.
"It is all in the choreography."
Monica Mason, Interview.

Finding the meaning

Refining the details of movement by referring to the choreographer's intention and the narrative on which he has based his work.
"Do I touch my body here or not?"; said in The Royal Ballet's rehearsal of Glen Tetley's "La Ronde".
Monica Mason, Interview.

Find the gesture, To

"I want to dig beneath the empty formalisms and technical displays of technical virtuosity and the slick surface, to probe the human entity for the powerful and often crude beauty of the gesture that speaks of man's humanity."
Carla Maxwell, quoting José Limón, Interview.

Intention

The reason for a movement, whether formal or dramatic; information from the choreographer which a dancer needs in order to make an informed move.
"Why am I bending over?", said rehearsing Darshan Singh Bhuller's "Fall Like Rain" for London Contemporary Dance Theatre (1993).
Kate Coyne, Rehearsing.

What the choreography should say

What the rehearsal director, the coach, and the dancers work towards while studying roles; that bit of the meaning which it is the performer's responsibility to convey.
Desmond Kelly, Coaching.

Structure and Content

Structure is given to the dancer by the choreographer, while content is found by the dancer from the structure.
Jack Moore, 1969.

Inner demand of the movement

The requirements of the movement, over and above technique; the inner impetus of the movement understood by the inner focus of the body.
Hanya Holm in Walter Sorell, 1976.

Know material inside out

To work as a performer on material so long that the content becomes visible as the form.
Yolande Snaith, Interview.

How of a movement, The

The spirituality of the movement which is not made manifest by the movement itself but by the manner in which it is performed by the dancer.

Hanya Holm in Walter Sorell, 1976.

Interpretive dancer

"[One] dedicated to the belief that behind each physical gesture was an emotional or spiritual innovation."

Ruth St. Denis (1939) in Suzanne Shelton, 1981.

2.   COMMITMENT

Acknowledge, To

To dance in such a way that the premise of the movement is communicated; used particularly of acknowledging gravity in Limón style.

Carla Maxwell, Interview.

All the concern (of the dancer)

The dancer's focus of attention, what he has to commit himself to, in image and motion; said as a way of overcoming fragmented or ornamented moving habits.

Anna Markard, Rehearsal.

Artistry

Bringing dynamics and responsiveness to the craftsmanship.

Walter Sorell, 1976.

Assemble yourself

To collect yourself together in readiness to move; said within a class to a dancer who appeared not totally prepared.

"Assemble yourself."

Hanya Holm in Dorothy Madden, Interview.

Attack

A way of working with dance material with a positive attitude and dynamic; said of Davies's "Rushes".

Siobhan Davies, 1988.

Attitude, Your

The dancer's intention reflected in the way s/he supports the gesture with the torso.

Anna Markard, Rehearsal.

Attitude and attack

A dancer's use of her material, how she dances it, with whatever attitude and level of energy is needed.

Twyla Tharp, Informal talk.

Consciousness/body relationship

The essential inner/outer relatedness which the performer of Butoh must find to provide the style of movement commitment in the genre.

Ushio Amagatsu, Interview.

Conviction

What a dancer must have in her own performance to rise above routine rendering.

Judith Mackrell, Interview.

Dance full out, To

To dance with the vigour and expression demanded of the ballet; a term used in rehearsal in contrast to "marking".

Michael Somes, Rehearsal.

Dancing in the present

"When they [good dancers] are onstage there is no waste, no moment of halfheartedness. Each millisecond is danced with commitment and largesse."

Paul Taylor, "Private Domain", 1987.

Delicate line of consciousness

The quality in Butoh which the dancers need to find, through specific images which aid concentration on the interior of the work.

Ushio Amagatsu, Interview.

Doing a movement

Performing a movement with a oneness of purpose; performing a gesture, however small, and making it 'right'; 'doing' rather than 'acting' a movement, no superfluous movements.

Hanya Holm in Walter Sorell, 1976.

Dynamic commitment

"The strength is produced, effectively, by his [the dancer's] personal commitment to the forces in his body. He has to feel them, control them, project them, simultaneously, three distinct processes. The four motion factors [weight, time, flow, space] all require this treatment...".

Valerie Preston-Dunlop, 1980.

Felt or guided movement
Movement achieved with the full concentration of mind and body; movement performed with purpose.
Margaret Lloyd, 1974 (1949).

Find the movement
To "push yourself through the choreography" and come to what makes the essence of the movement, and so find the expressive possibility of the work.
Judith Mackrell, Interview.

Heightened awareness
A recognition by the dancer of the fast moment-by-moment decisions that s/he must make to ensure that the next move is inevitable.
"Reach that point in the body where something else must happen."
Robert Cohan, Company class.

Holding
Coming into a position and retaining it, sustaining and expanding, totally focusing into it.
"...an inner stirring...", "...the resonance...".
Thea Barnes, Susan Sentler, and *Brenda Baden-Semper*, Interview.

Inflect the movement, To
A form of interpolation by the performer in which the motoric elements are strengthened, such as "suspended", "darkened", "sharpened".
Jane Dudley, Interview 1992.

Intention
The moment by moment changing focus, image, objective which dancers have to find in the movement given to them.
Bonnie Bird, Interview.

Internal dynamics/inner rhythm
The element of interpretation available to the baroque performer, within the required dynamics of the step pattern. Subtlety of internal dynamics makes for a more accomplished performance.
Philippa Waite, Interview.

Live into the movement, To
To perform the movement with the whole body and spirit; to focus the whole body on a particular movement at a particular moment.
Margaret Lloyd, 1974 (1949).

Marking

What dancers do as one process of learning material, walking it through without high energy or personal commitment, concentrating on various aspects of what has to be danced, in preparation for the full-out performance.

Eds.

Motivation (for the movement)

The emotional/spiritual and intellectual reason for moving, which the dancer must find and through which the expressiveness emerges.

Laverne Meyer, Interview.

Physical conviction

What a dancer has to find in preparation for performing a work, after s/he has the form of the material in his/her body and is searching for its content.

Elizabeth Keen, Rehearsal.

Positive

A quality of attack, definite and with conviction, required of a dancer by the choreographer in rehearsal.

Christopher Bruce, Rehearsal.

Proper execution

For some choreographers, Tudor in particular, the way the steps should be performed, the details of performance being the embodiment of the character being danced; contrasted to the concept of overlaying 'acting' on top of the steps.

Muriel Topaz, 1986.

Resonance of a movement

To allow the dancer to complete the movement and to not stop it short of its intended timing or space.

Dorothy Madden, Interview.

Speaking through the movement

"Communicating gesturally, body-wise, floor patern-wise, and through steps"; what a performer should do.

Jane Dudley, Interview.

Strands of interest of the dancer

"Dynamics, space and time — the dancer may call one or the other to your attention, but actually she keeps these three strands of interest going all the time, for they are all simultaneously present in even the simplest dancing."

Edwin Denby, 1968.

3. TECHNICAL EXPERTISE

Technical expertise
Such a level of technical mastery that the inner personality can move in any way it chooses.
Walter Sorell, 1976.

Technical dancer
"One who likes to conquer a difficulty, to take on a technical challenge, has joy in getting on top of the material."
Peter Dunleavy, Interview.

Technique
The stunning control and capacity to move which a dancer may possess and to which an audience will initially strongly respond, but which is surpassed in interest by what the dancer does with her technique.
Judith Mackrell, Interview.

Technical expertise of the performer
The control, alignment, clarity of movement, physical articulation, precise beginnings and endings which provide a base for performing.
Helen Crocker and *Bim Mason*, Interview.

Eloquent
The quality of some dancers who have an outstanding technical facility, who are able to articulate virtuosic movement with apparent ease.
Peter Dunleavy, Interview.

Poise
A moment of stillness involving both the technical skill of balance, and the self-presentation of the dancer.
Stephen Preston, Interview.

Performance skills
An ability which empowers performers, strengthens them, in order to use their technical expertise with confidence on stage.
Helen Crocker and *Bim Mason*, Interview.

Partnering
An innate feeling which some male dancers have, an instinctive ability to dance with and support a female soloist.
Marion Tait, Interview.

In control, To be

In partnering, what some female soloists want their male partners to be, while others prefer to be followed.

"to start me off", "a firm grip", "to give clear signals".

Marion Tait, Interview.

Good dancer

Said of a social 'folk' dancer that has such an economy of effort that he is able to give the impression that he is never tired and could dance all night long.

Douglas Kennedy, 1949.

Slammin'

Adjective applied to someone appreciated as a good dancer in a club.

"He's slammin'."

Stewart (Portsmouth clubber), Interviewed by Donna Taylor.

Amenable to moving

The essential capacity of both non-dancers and dancers who are working in theatre.

Stuart Hopps, Interview.

4. HOLDING THE STAGE

Take the stage, To

"I want each dancer to take the stage. What the audience watches is the dancer and not the choreographer."

Paul Taylor in Arthur Todd, 1964.

Take control of the space, To

A quality in a performer which aids the audience to connect with the work.

Mary Brennan, 1992.

Here

The presence on stage of the dancer, occupying and filling the space beyond her mere size with her energy.

"Every pore of your body is saying 'I'm here'."

Elizabeth Keen, Rehearsal.

To be

To have presence, especially to find the essence of stillness; said in contrast to 'to do'.

Rosemary Butcher, Interview.

Presence
> The quality of a dancer who can hold the stage.
> "You've got a good presence but you don't use it."
> *Michael Somes*, Rehearsal.

Project, To
> To make visible, through movement, the feelings and intentions in the material.
> *Bonnie Bird*, Interview.

Dramatic power
> The ability of the dancer to convey dramatic meaning, to interpret the role through the 'steps', which is achieved by "two intricate technicalities: the skill and the intelligence behind the *timing* of the movement, and, the sensitivity towards the amount of emphasis required in the gesture." (said of Margot Fonteyn).
> *Ninette de Valois*, 1977.

Showmanship
> The knack of presenting showy steps in a routine, so as to astonish and impress the audience.
> *Roy Castle*, 1986.

Work your face
> Use facial expression as part of the attitude of a jazz dancer, to go out there and communicate.
> *Thea Barnes*, Interview.

Cosmic centre
> For the Butoh dancer, this is where he is, at the centre of the world for the duration of the ceremony.
> *Ushio Amagatsu*, Interview.

Foreground and background
> The role a performer has to know that he is fulfilling in a work, either as the centre of interest for the audience, or retreating to a peripheral place; the quick changes from foreground and background which a character dancer has to make while to stage.
> "...dead places...".
> *Ashley Page*, Interview.

Amplifying a stage presence
> The physical language which a performer uses to enlarge the presentation of the persona which he or she adopts for the act.
> *Helen Crocker* and *Bim Mason*, Interview.

Calculate the energy, To

To assess how much dynamic to put into a movement, to one step, one arm, a shoulder, a head turn, so that that move is what will register; the responsibility of the dancers.

"Don't miscalculate."

Lea Anderson, Interview.

Important movement

"...to be able to phrase a look with your eye and your finger and to know which is the important movement, and not to give each one equal emphasis."

Lea Anderson, in Arts Council of Great Britain, 1990.

Emphasis of the movement, The

From a range of possible motional alternatives, the intention which a mover gives to the performance of an action, giving minor variations in detail which affect the movement's expressive content.

Ann Hutchinson Guest, Interview.

Energetic connection (or direction), within the body

The ability to direct energy around the body, based on knowledge of three things — 'weight falling', release of tension, and direction.

Gregory Nash, Interview.

Uniformity of group movement

Clean execution by every dancer.

Lucas Hoving, 1992.

Semaphore signals

The exaggerated expressiveness which ordinary theatricality can look like on video, so that some performers have to "tone down" their interpretation.

"To suit the performance to the shots."

Bob Lockyer, 1992.

Bring it up, To

In dance on video, what some performers have to do with the interpretation of their role, in order to take into account the essential narrative-telling nature of the television medium.

Bob Lockyer, 1992.

7.   SPONTANEITY

Spontaneity

The illusion of the dancers discovering things as they move, a step, a relationship, a place, which dancers give to a performance, a seemingly improvised quality.

Judith Mackrell, Interview.

Spontaneity
Moving so that the audience feels that it has 'just occurred to you' to move like that.
Lea Anderson, Interview.

Spontaneity in performance
"...is not wholly dependent on emotion at that instant. It is the condition of emotion objectified...it illumines. It excites.... It is the result of perfect timing to the Now."
Martha Graham, 1956.

Spontaneity in performance
"[the dancer's] motions look spontaneous, as if they suited her particular body, her personal impulses, as if they had been invented that very moment.... The original dancer vivifies the dance...that the choreographer has set."
Edwin Denby, 1968.

Spontaneous performance
The so-called unrehearsed look of a work, actually achieved through meticulous rehearsal, in which the layers of meanings are carefully judged.
Maude Lloyd, 1984.

Holy white instant of performance
"For a dancer to be able to perform well, most of his waking hours must be devoted to preparing for the holy white instant of performance. Preparing your body comes first, your soul second, and your brain a relatively unimportant third."
Paul Taylor, "Private Domain" 1987.

In the now, To be
The attitude that a dancer needs to cultivate: being present, completely, when working.
Jane Dudley, Interview.

Fresh
The quality of movement which is achieved by "surprising yourself every time you move on from where you are".
"That is the only way you will sense it and so inform it."
Robert Cohan, Company class.

Re-living the movement
"You have to make a movement awkward for yourself, as though you didn't know how to do it, so that when you come back to it, you can be lively again."
Merce Cunningham in Merce Cunningham and Jacqueline Lesschaeve, 1985.

8.   FEELING

Alive

A quality in a performer in which the radiance of feeling alive is adding to the movement.

Judith Mackrell, Interview.

Blatant

A quality of the jazz dancer.

"...sensual, no holds barred, raw and gutsy...".

Thea Barnes, Interview.

Charm and animation

"Among the more difficult of Korean words to translate, they (*mot* and *heung*) refer to an inner spiritual quality of charm or grace and a feeling of lively animation or interest, both of which lead to an almost irrepressible joy or giddiness. This is the ultimate quality the Korean dancer strives to achieve, and specific movement characteristics either contribute to the achievement of this desired state or are the physical manifestation of its having been achieved."

Judy Van Zile, 1993.

Dispassionate

An interpretative attitude by which material which contains passion of some sort is danced with cool aloofness, so giving the material emotional distance; said of Paul Taylor.

"...funny dances funnier, lewd ones more depraved...".

Deborah Jowitt, 1977.

Evoke a reaction, To

A rehearsal term used to aid a dancer to respond to the given material, by letting it touch something in the memory, something which might evoke a feeling or an image, which will be transmitted to the audience through the way in which they perform the movement.

Elizabeth Keen, Rehearsal.

Express themselves, To

What singers have to do in opera, what the movement rehearsal director has to find a way to help them to do.

Teresa Kelsey, Interview.

Expressive dancer

"One who wants to communicate the feelings of dance, wants to touch many people, wants to use his own facility to say not only what the choreographer wants, but also what he believes in, himself."

Peter Dunleavy, Interview.

Feel, To

Said in rehearsal in order to get dancers to shift out of a pedestrian 'doing' mode into a theatrical mode of being, by being acutely aware of their relative place in space.

"...feel your relationship to the group; feel the distance between you and the sixth row; feel the space between you and the tabs."

Elizabeth Keen, Rehearsal.

Giving

A quality in the ballet dancer, who aims at generosity of movement and never self-indulgence.

Mirella Bartrip and *Teresa Kelsey*, Interview.

Intensify, To

In a rehearsal, to work on the quality of a held position; whatever its qualities are, to give more of it from yourself as a performer.

"Strike, intensify it."

Elizabeth Keen, Rehearsal.

Leave your imprint on the air, To

To leave the audience with an after-image of your performance.

Elizabeth Keen, Rehearsal.

Musicality

A valued quality in a dancer in which "the music sings through her body".

Judith Mackrell, Interview.

Passion

To speak through the body with passion, allowing yourself to come through the movement, to "become visible from inside".

Bonnie Bird, Interview.

Passionate

"How performers may be, should be, in interpreting a role, in identifying with a role."

Gillian Lynne, Interview.

Sensitivity of mind and body

Sensitivity is more than mere physical feeling leading to control. It includes awareness of and sympathy towards [other dancers], spontaneity and insight [of action], all leading to freedom of expression.

Diana Jordan, 1938.

Sensual

The quality a dancer can give to the movement irrespective of a gender-specific appearance, overriding androgeny.

Mark Murphy, Interview.

Subterranean emotions
    The feelings behind a character which a performer has to find, or which the director may identify for him with which he creates the role.
    Gillian Lynne, Interview.

Turn it on, To
    A rehearsal term, said to dancers to get feeling into the performance of their material.
    Elizabeth Keen, Rehearsal.

Uninhibited
    A quality of work which is valued through the passionate involvement of the performers in what they are doing.
    Gillian Lynne, Interview.

9.   CREATING A ROLE

Role
    What a dancer dances in a work, whether it is a dramatic piece with named roles or an abstract ensemble work; involves finding out what part 'your role' plays in the fabric of the work, in contrast to working in isolation.
    Bonnie Bird, Interview.

Playing a role
    Becoming a character, giving quality to the choreographic material, by providing yourself with a scenario of who you are, a process each dancer has to do for themselves; said of the Lemon Seller in the Town Square scene of "Romeo and Juliet".
    Monica Mason, Interview.

Become, To
    The process of changing from doing the steps to taking on the role; a feeling which, in performance, "starts with putting on make-up".
    Marion Tait, Interview 1992.

Creating a role
    Choreographing with a dancer who, although having material which is strong in shapes and rhythms, is to be read as a person, albeit "shadowy", for which choreographer and dancer share sources and imaginative ideas.
    "A Beckett character, can't cope with light, shut off, sometimes panicked."
    Richard Alston, Rehearsing Darshan Singh Bhuller.

What the choreography should say

What the rehearsal director, the coach, and the dancers work towards while studying roles; that bit of the meaning which it is the performer's responsibility to convey.
Desmond Kelly, Coaching.

Illusion of mime

The mime-actor's ability to suggest through his physical "play" all manner of characters and places, changing rapidly from one situation to another.
Alvin Epstein, 1958.

Movement quality

The ways of using the choreography of a ballet which dancers have to find to suit the role, coping with character shoes, not pointes, finding more weight, feeling the period, walking naturally; qualities which the rehearsal director must ensure are there.
Monica Mason, Interview.

Dancer as interpreter

"Dancers give the dance shades of character, quality and meanings which are not necessarily prescribed by the choreography."
Pauline Hodgens in Janet Adshead, 1988(a).

Interpret, To

What a dancer has to do with a role, paying close attention to the way that that choreographer likes dancers to work.
"Look at the role, understand it, and be an individual; respect for the steps but not bound by them."
David Bintley, Interview.

Definitive interpretation

The way of dancing a role by an artist which is regarded as more than just ONE interpretation among many, but rather is seen as one giving the role those qualities and meanings which define the work.
"'Le Spectre de la Rose' is forever associated with Nijinsky and 'The Dying Swan' with Pavlova."
Pauline Hodgens in Janet Adshead, 1988(a).

Characterisation

The process of building an interpretation of a role to be created for, or maintained in, a dance scene in a play; dancing as a character.
"Avoid her gaze", "How would Lord Briggs do it?", "You are very bold.", "Wouldn't you pull away from him?".
Geraldine Stephenson, Interview.

Finding your way into the dance drama

What dancers have to do in works which have dramatic content and character roles, finding the integration of personal interpretation with the constraints of style which constitutes successful identification with a work.

Anna Markard, Rehearsal.

Subtext

The images surrounding a character which a dancer or actor is asked to perform; an understanding of the role provided by the choreographer.

"In 'A Simple Man', it was the relationship of Lowry with his mother that was explored."

Gillian Lynne, Interview.

Scenarios

The description of characters to be played, which the choreographer or director will provide, so that the dancers know what they are trying to achieve.

Gillian Lynne, Interview.

Images

Narrative given to a dancer to aid his interpretation of the role.

"You've got nothing better to do, you're just waiting", said to Kenneth Tharp; "...weary with the years...", to Elizabeth Fancourt.

Christopher Bruce, Rehearsal.

Give colour, To

To add a layer to the movement material given, in audition, class or rehearsal, and so turn a piece of movement into something worth looking at.

Bonnie Bird, Interview.

Acting qualities

Abilities needed for dramatic roles, to prepare the dynamics, timing and focus, for the finesse of the narrative; needed in MacMillan's "Judas Tree".

Monica Mason, Interview.

Conjure the dance, To

A process whereby a choreographer weans actors from self-consciousness and apathy to movement, to become creative artists using steps, characterisation and sometimes dialogue in the movement scenes of plays.

Geraldine Stephenson, Interview.

Plot and character

"His steps are his plot, his dancers are his characters, regardless of whether the ballet is plotless or a narrative work."; said of Ashton's choreography.

Alistair Macaulay, 1988.

Performing an 'act'
The skills of a performing artist who presents an act, including mime, dance, mask work, movement qualities, themes, and moods, providing a means to present the specific technical skills, usually circus-derived, on which the act is based.
Helen Crocker and *Bim Mason*, Interview.

10.   CASTING

Instruments
"The choreographer has to work with the instruments he finds.... He finds some dancers who are more responsive than others to his ideas."
Peggy van Praagh and *Peter Brinson*, 1963.

Develop, To
The invitation to dancers to extend their talents, which a choreographer may offer to his collaborating cast.
Ashley Page, Interview.

Casting
"De Valois selects dancers of the correct physical type to be instruments of the choreographer and not interpreters of roles."
Peggy van Praagh and *Peter Brinson*, 1963.

Casting
"Balanchine thinks of his dancers impersonally, as clay for the moulding or like notes of music waiting to be assembled."
Peggy van Praagh and *Peter Brinson*, 1963.

Casting
Robbins chooses dancers that are different from each other, physically and temperamentally."
Peggy van Praagh and *Peter Brinson*, 1963.

Type casting
Casting someone for a specific role because they have talent in that area, are receptive to the idea of the role, show an attitude which is conductive to a particular role; used by Hanya Holm.
Don Redlich, Informal discussion.

Aesthetics of the body
An issue in casting dance on video and video dance where close-up shots reveal age and body physique, creating problems for casting not encountered in theatre work; you try and cast for "best in a video version", not necessarily a big name or the same person who is "best in the theatre version".
Bob Lockyer, Interview.

Favourite dancers

"...that dancer, those talents, that facility...".
Ashley Page, Interview.

Dancer's qualities

"Beauty, vigour, plasticity, vivacity and an ear for music; Intellectual qualities: taste, energy, perserverance, imagination and a rhythmical sense; Artistic qualities: grace, lightness, aplomb, sensitivity and precision; Dramatic qualities: stature, physiognomy, emotion, firmness and gesture; Technical qualities: placement, turn-out, high instep, ballon and brilliance."
August Bournonville (ca. 1878) in Viva Flindt and Knud Arne Jürgensen, 1992.

Performer qualities

"...intelligence with understanding of the ideas being presented to them...";
"...precision, control, presence, an understanding of performance ...".
Rosemary Butcher, Interview.

Cunningham dancers

"two legs and two arms and so on", "with a way of thinking" which copes with "my ideas which are not all familiar", coping "with no music", "independent", "with an instinctual awareness of the area he is in" in the space.
Merce Cunningham, 1979.

Company continuity

The coherence of a company (such as Sankai Juko) in which the members remain the same for 10 years or more.
Ushio Amagatsu, Interview.

Use the dancers, To

"It is my job to create a ballet and simply use the dancers in the ways they move best. Different bodies have different shapes, different qualities."
George Balanchine in George Balanchine, 1984.

Put a dance on another dancer

Changing cast so that an already-created work is danced by a different dancer, with the danger that something might be felt to be missing through interpretation, physique, or personal style.
Christoper Bruce, Rehearsal.

Performer dependency

The problem of re-staging a work, such as Bausch's "Orpheus and Eurydice", where the original performers contributed personally in the process of creating their roles.
"...Inviting the original performers back to their roles...".
Nadine Meisner, Contributed.

11.   WORKING WITH A CHOREOGRAPHER

Able to contribute
A desirable characteristic of an ensemble dancer or an actor in a crowd scene, essentially an ability not to be "a star" but to know their place as one of a large group.
Geraldine Stephenson, Interview.

At risk
The vulnerability of performers which is part of the event; said of artists who allow their personal lives to be part of the dance material, and of artists who break new ground.
Judith Mackrell, Interview.

Autonomy of the dancers
"...each person and the work he does is independent, and he acts with the others, not competitively, but complementarily...each person, observant of the others, is allowed to act freely."
Merce Cunningham in Selma Jeanne Cohen, 1968.

Contemporary dancer
A performer, with a contemporary technical facility, who is a creative artist in his own right through the way he collaborates in the creation of new works.
Peter Dunleavy, Interview.

Creative dancer
A company member who can interpret and expand what is given, without "overstepping the mark and setting the role off at a tangent".
Marion Tait, Interview.

Dancer's role
The dancer should not only meet the choreographer's demands but also be totally receptive to his ideas.
"A choreographer's doormat."
Lynn Seymour quoted in Monica Parker, Interview.

Dancer as individual
"I definitely encourage the individual because people left to their own devices, within certain parameters, will function much better than people forced to do something in ways they don't understand."
Twyla Tharp in British Broadcasting Corporation, 1983.

De-train, To
The process undertaken by a choreographer of opening up some of the strict stylistic habits which a dancer acquires in conservatoire or studio training.
Rosemary Butcher, Interview.

Dynamic range

The varied approach to dynamics and phrasing which choreographers have and which dancers have to learn to adapt to and respond to.

Bonnie Bird, Interview.

Get it, To

The performer's goal, to be able to do what it is that he is being asked to do; what the choreographer or director has to achieve and has to make each performer believe that he can achieve.

"If they know I will be there until they do it, they will find a way to do it."

Gillian Lynne, Interview.

Input

What you may or may not be expected to provide for a choreographer in opera; you have to learn immediately whether or not s/he welcomes contributions.

Lynn Robertson Bruce, Interview.

Leave it with them, To

To give dancers movement which they find difficult to cope with, which is not working, and to give them time to solve it, come to terms with it.

"Don't give up."

Ashley Page, Interview.

Performing disciplines

"The dancers of the company perform as actors and as singers; the boundaries between the performing disciplines are eliminated through their incorporation into dance theater (of Bausch)."

Norbert Servos and *G. Weigelt*, 1984.

Play, To

The capacity a dance artist is required to possess in order to respond to a choreographer who works by getting the movement material from the dancer.

Marion North, Interview.

Pick it up, To

To empathise with the teacher, in rehearsal or class, and, not only to take in what is said and shown, but to look for what is essentially intended.

Jane Dudley, Interview.

Professionalism

"Working as a performer in the way a choreographer wants you to work, whether you like it or not; finding a way to apply what you believe in, even in a situation you can't believe in."

Peter Dunleavy, Interview.

Read, To

To see and understand movement which has to be picked up, in audition, in rehearsal, in class.

Bonnie Bird, Interview.

Rehearsal techniques

In addition to picking up the material given, functioning effectively in rehearsing a new work with a choreographer by reading his non-verbal signals and listening for the images he might use.

Bonnie Bird, Interview.

Room to manoeuvre

Letting the performer assemble or assimilate the material given to him in rehearsal, making use of his inventive artistry as well as his ability to perform.

Dorothy Madden, Interview.

Show me my ideas, To

What a choreographer wants a dancer to do, to make visual the imagined ideas, movement and 'look' that is in his head.

Elizabeth Keen, Rehearsal.

Without disturbing

A quality in a dancer's contribution to the journey he and the choreographer make together, adding something to the material which the choreographer would not have found by himself while not disrupting the style or progression of the piece.

Ashley Page, Interview.

12.   WHAT NOT TO DO

Abstract perfection

The striving to become a perfect human being, often manifested by dancers through losing individuality.

"Abstract perfection is something which I think hounds a lot of people in a lot of ways...which is the case with many dancers."

Twyla Tharp in British Broadcasting Corporation, 1983.

Bit of spaghetti

A dancer's muddled transition, especially in the feet, which s/he has to sort out.

Anna Markard, Rehearsal.

Blank

A correct performance of the shape of the movements with no risk, no passion, no commitment, no focus.

Bonnie Bird, Interview.

Dance academically, To

To perform movement within a set of rules, without breath or life. To be afraid to break the rules.

Hanya Holm in Walter Sorell, 1976.

Hide behind technique, To

What some dancers do and so provide a competent, even acceptable, performance without ever putting themselves at risk by exposing themselves emotionally.

Judith Mackrell, Interview.

Hold back, To

What dancers may do when asked to become involved in a role; what a choreographer finds unresponsive in a dancer with whom she wants to work on an emotionally strong piece.

Gillian Lynne, Interview.

Locked into a speed

The way in which a performer may only have one tempo in which s/he works. The lock must be released for new material to be generated.

Yolande Snaith, Interview.

Marking

Not dancing full out, something a performer should only do, in rehearsal, when expressly asked to.

Bonnie Bird, Interview.

Obey orders, To

What a dancer should NOT feel she is doing in class, but rather doing something much more self-motivated, making the given combinations her own.

"You're not just obeying orders."

Elizabeth Keen, Rehearsal.

Overdance, To

To use working movements or behavioural vocabulary and to somehow turn them into supposedly dance-like movement, rather than leaving the movement in its raw state.

"Don't overdance it."

Royston Muldoon, Interview.

Prima donna-ish

An ensemble dancer behaving inappropriately as if she or he were a star.

Bonnie Bird, Interview.

Projection

"Projection in serious dancing is a mild and stready force; the dancer who goes out to the audience with a bang cuts herself off from the rest of the stage action."

Edwin Denby, 1968.

Qualify movement for the audience, To

A way of performing movement material with some showmanship, rather than identifying with the role honestly.

Anna Markard, Rehearsal.

Rushing the movement

"When I talk about not rushing, it has to do with the weight, giving time to giving in to your weight."

Della Davidson, Rehearsal.

Stripped, To be (of a style)

A process, when learning a new style, for a ballet dancer who is used to being "a prince"; he has to be helped to have the archetypal noble image taken away so that he can start afresh to fill out the framework given to him in the new steps.

Joseph Cipolla, Interview.

Suspend your intelligence, To

What dancers sometimes do in technique class and so allow themselves to move in ways which they neither consider nor understand.

Laurie Booth, Interview.

Chapter 5 TECHNIQUE

1. TECHNIQUE AS STYLE

Technique
"Through technique, one acquires the discipline that, in turn, allows total freedom and a sense of well being." "...technique prepares your body to speak in dance".
Martha Graham in Elinor Rogosin, 1980.

Craft, The
A term used synonymously with technique.
"To learn the craft", or "to acquire proficiency in the technique".
Anna Paskevska, 1990.

Gymnastic exercises
The early 20th century modern dancer's way of referring to technical training; "a way of preparing the body for dancing through limbering exercises", after which expressive studies were undertaken.
Irma Duncan, 1970.

Metakinesis
"Because of this [metakinetic] close relationship between movement and personal experience, temperament, mental and emotional equipment, it is manifestly impossible for everyone to be taught to do the same type of movement".
John Martin, 1972 (1933).

Pulled up technical dancer
The establishment dancer's basic body attitude, contrasted to the more pedestrian, relaxed carriage common in much Post Modern and New Dance work.
Stephanie Jordan, 1992.

Strong physical technique
Something that can inhibit both a choreographer and a dancer.
"...may be a barrier to hide behind...".
Siobhan Davies in National Resource Centre for Dance, 1988.

Maintaining tradition
What a ballet master has to do through class, to keep the style of work of the company, or school, safe and alive.
"Think classical, don't embellish."
Alan Dubreuil, Class.

Motivation

An essential ingredient of any style of dance, the principles from which the form of the style grew in the first place and which need to be known by the dancers dancing in that tradition.

John Martin, 1972 (1933).

Motivation of a technique

The hidden content of a dance technique, which is essential to hold on to in order for the form of the class, the movements and combinations themselves to retain their full significance for the dancer; said of Graham's technique and vision.

Marion North, Interview.

Codify the technique, To

A way of fixing and naming an established technique such as Bournonville by Hans Beck, or Limón by Limón Inc., in an attempt to preserve it for the next generation of dancers.

Clement Crisp, Interview.

Ossification of a technique

The process after a technique has been codified when it is in danger of keeping its form and losing its life; losing the motivation, intention, and dynamic content of a technique while retaining a repeatable pattern of exercises.

Clement Crisp, Interview.

Spiritual concomitant

The essential part of a technique which informs the athleticism.

Jane Dudley, Interview.

Dilute the school, To

The way a teacher may alter or embellish an established technique and in so doing weaken the essential qualities of it.

Clement Crisp, Interview.

Violate the material, To

What a teacher may do in relation to a tradition by adding their own material which is not rooted in the core of the tradition.

Jane Dudley, Interview.

Teaching by the book

Staying with the basic material of a tradition, not adding your own variations, transmitting the core intent.

Jane Dudley, Interview.

Repeating by rote

Teaching dance material in a tradiiton, retaining the usual form but without concern for the ideas sustaining it.

Jane Dudley, Interview.

Groove, A

The danger that either the mind or the body may be forced into an inflexible groove by prolonged technical training.

Merce Cunningham in Walter Sorell, 1951.

New language

The innovations in the vocabulary of the dancer's technique which are created to serve the innovations in form which in turn reflect the spirit of the times [Zeitgeist].

Kurt Jooss, 1935

Developing a new technique

Experiments by an artist [e.g. Graham] in "unknown specialist controls and new specialized mechanics", finding the new rituals, new use of space and dynamics, the new motivation, all in tandem with the creation of new dances.

Agnes de Mille, 1991.

Evolving a technique

A slow process which it is necessary to test over a period to ensure that all the material serves the purpose, dropping material however attractive if it does not, and discovering new ways if those need to be found to serve current choreographers.

Robert Cohan, Interview.

Graham-style class

A technique class as near as possible in form and instruction to a class taken by Martha Graham, given in preparation for dancers who are to perform a Graham work.

Robert Cohan, Interview.

Graham-based class

Technique classes founded on Martha Graham's technique but adapted to cater for a company or student in training who will dance choreographic works in other styles and so needs a safe, strong and versatile facility rather than a highly stylised one; Cohan classes at London Contemporary Dance Theatre are an example.

Robert Cohan, Interview

2.   CLASS

Class

"Class is the moment where you have to struggle to make the movements pass completely into and through the body".

Merce Cunningham in Merce Cunningham and Jacqueline Lesschaeve, 1985.

Class

The daily ritual that marks a dancer a professional and a student who may one day become a professional.

Daniel Nagrin, 1988.

Class
> The daily activity of a dancer, to warm up the body, to build stamina and strength, to learn technique.
> *Daniel Lewis,* 1984.

Class
> "...goes on all the years of a dancing life". "No dancer can rehearse until he has had at least an hour and a half of practice every day".
> *Ninette de Valois,* 1977.

Class
> The daily event which a dancer undertakes to keep his "instrument well tuned", his "technique polished", which "gets the motor running" and prepares him for his day's work.
> *Joseph Cipolla,* Interview.

Class
> "...a time to work on tools...".
> *Robert Cohan,* Interview.

Class
> "...a preparation for rehearsal and performance...".
> *Norman Morrice,* Interview.

Class
> A daily process which builds the dancer's body to do a certain kind of movement appropriate to the choreographic works of a style [e.g. ballet] or of an artist [e.g. Cunningham].
> *Siobhan Davies* in National Resource Centre for Dance, 1988.

Character class
> A class starting with barre work, moving on to centre work and enchaînements which have national character dance styles as their material.
> "A Hungarian character class, or Russian".
> *Robert Harrold,* Interview.

Company class
> Different classes offered to the men and women of a ballet company, in which in addition to the daily class content, the fluidity of port de bras is stressed for women; strength, jumps and beats being priorities for the men.
> *Monica Mason,* Interview.

Company class
> Primarily for centering and muscle toning to prepare the dancers for the 6 or so hours of rehearsal in the day ahead; using known material through which the dancers can "work internally".
> *Robert Cohan,* Interview.

Company class

"The dancer's own time, to be used for physiological and psychological preparation, a cleansing; also a time to experiment with expression and articulation".
Peter Dunleavy, Interview.

Advanced level

The company class for women principals and soloists, who work at a level which prepares them to take on the major roles in classical works, both technically and in stamina, where each works as an individual in the light of what her own instrument requires.
Monica Mason, Interview.

Repertoire-related class

A company class in which particular stylistic or difficult elements in the current repertoire might be included.
"Port de bras related to 'Swan Lake'."
Monica Mason, Interview.

Company class content

Class which may include material from repertory, or material preparing the body to cope with the style of new vocabularies or the rigours of particularly physically taxing dance; said of London Contemporary Dance Theatre's classes when "Troy Games" was in the repertory and during a Paul Taylor residency.
Robert Cohan, Interview.

Young professional

The young male 18-year-old new company member, who has to adjust to company class; from being one of perhaps 6 he is now one of 25, from being supervised and given 3 training classes a day, he now has one class designed to prepare him for his day's work.
Monica Mason, Interview.

Company class

Not a time for picking up complex materials, nor an opportunity for a performing experience, which may be a legitimate aim of student classes.
Robert Cohan, Interview.

Student class

Daily class, a place of physical and psychological safety in which dancers in training may feel able to take risks and to dare both in physical and emotional terms when they feel ready.
Erica Stanton, Interview.

Emotional content

Something to find in rehearsal and not in class, even if the class is Graham technique with a reputation for being "an emotional technique".
Robert Cohan, Interview.

Rituals

The regular verbal and motional beginning and ending episodes of a technique class, given to provide the essential warming up and warming down, and to give the teacher and the dancers the transition from daily life to class, back to daily life again.
Erica Stanton, Interview.

3. SOME AIMS AND PURPOSES OF CLASS

Aims of technique

"1) to develop bodily strength, flexibility, control, and endurance — in short, the necessary skill for performing; 2) to encourage the student toward creative use of the principles of natural movement through experiential understanding of his or her rhythmic, dynamic, and design potentials."
Ernestine Stodelle, 1978.

Aim (of ballet)

To develop the ligaments, muscles and joints.
Agrippina Vaganova, 1969 (1934).

Aim of ballet training

To give dance artists sufficient technique to use in the way that a choreographer wants, sufficient understanding of how the body works and an ability to interpret both emotion and abstract movement.
Laverne Meyer, Interview.

Educating the dancer

The part of the dancer's development which goes beyond training.
"...beyond technique into expression,
beyond doing into making,
beyond actual into virtual,
beyond the physical into the perceptual".
Rosemary Brandt, Interview.

Goal of ballet

"...to develop the musculature and maintain the physique...a supple musculature that will be responsive to choreographic demands...for both ballet and modern dancers".
Anna Paskevska, 1990.

Elements of dance

The tools which the dancer needs to acquire.
"...centering, gravity, balance, posture, gesture, rhythm, moving in space, breathing...".
Robert Cohan, 1986.

Discipline

"Your goal is freedom, but freedom may only be achieved through discipline".
Martha Graham, 1957.

Rigours of style

The disciplined movement a dancer acquires in technique training, valuable not only as a movement facility but as a way of understanding the precision of style in a dance work.
Lea Anderson, Interview.

Dance movement training

"...training the body to move with speed, flexibility and control; to move with the sustained control of slow motion, to move free of any particular style..."; a Cunningham aim.
James Klosty, 1975

Dancer's training

Educating the dancer beyond the ability to execute the steps, towards understanding how movements are structured, their simultaneous and sequential arrangement, the multi-layered content and processes of dance movement.
Rosemary Brandt, Interview.

Primary aim

To move safely, efficiently, with the least strain necessary to achieve the movement; overcoming personal habits, finding alternative ways of accomplishing the required movement.
Stephanie Jordan, Interview.

Servicing the body

What a good technique does, making the body a more expressive instrument.
Jane Dudley, Interview.

Functional use

The efficient and economical use of the body which is the aim of much technique work in dance.
Erica Stanton, Interview.

Corrective exercises

Class material given by the teacher, including company class teacher, to assist a dancer in overcoming persistent or developing technical problems; an essential safeguard against injury.
Robert Cohan, Interview.

Class (ballet for contemporary dance students)

"To learn the laws of ballet", "to build their physique", "to increase their awareness of the body in space", "to learn a particular way of moving".
Mirella Bartrip and *Teresa Kelsey,* Interview.

Traditional class

"...a balanced set of exercises to limber, strengthen, develop, relax, or make possible difficult known feats...".

Agnes de Mille, 1991.

Technical aim in a style

The overall goal of a series of technique classes, which might be to experience and master the physicality, the imagination, and the spatial parameters of the vocabulary of the style being used, and how that can be achieved by each dancer on his/her own instrument.

Erica Stanton, Interview.

Expressive motion in space

"For the ballet-artist, mastery of steps infers domination of space, as much above the floor as upon it. Limits explored are not those of extreme emotion, but of expressive motion. Determined and defined, ballet is a continuous aria of the aerial".

Lincoln Kirstein, 1976.

Sense of performance

That part of ballet training which develops musicality, focus, presentation, projection, awareness of the stage space and of the audience.

Laverne Meyer, Interview.

Rhythmic sense

A precision in timing and energy developed in class, with the ability to hold rhythmic structures across the music.

Stephanie Jordan, Interview.

True speech (of a dancer)

"A technical training is seen as freeing the socialised body and thereby increasing its capacity for 'true speech' but a performance style which depends solely on a technical vocabulary has a limited range of expressive posibilities."

Christopher Winter, 1989.

Well-prepared

"Qualities in the young dancer which should include firmness of the body, and its stability, agility and mobility."

Agrippina Vaganova, 1969 (1934).

Discover sensation, To

The aim of some technique teaching in dance in which the development of a 'predisposition' to search for the kinaesthetic experience of moving is considered important.

Erica Stanton, Interview.

Body alignment

The posture of the body which reveals feelings, which also produces feelings and which, when lifted, enables the dancer to be ready to move anywhere.
Robert Cohan, 1986.

Co-ordination

"In dance, that means unity of body produced by emotional physical balance. In technique it means so to train all elements of the body...as to make them all equally important and equally efficient."
Martha Graham, 1941.

Natural or unnatural

"The daily discipline, the continued keeping of the elasticity of the muscles, the continued control of the mind over the body's actions, the constant hoped-for flow of the spirit into physical movement, both new and renewed, is not a natural way.... But the final synthesis can be a natural result, natural in the sense that the mind, body and spirit function as one."
Merce Cunningham in Walter Sorell, 1951.

Principles of Bharatha Natyam Nritta

"Clarity", the correct and clean rendering of line; "grace", a way of resolving the abstract geometry form with the physical body; "vigorous", the strength and speed, especially of footwork; "precision", especially in the intricate timing and rhythm.
"Dance Theatre Journal", 1991.

Technique, The

The steps of ballroom dancing, their style, pathways, poise, rhythm, and hold, which a couple learn and practise rigorously.
Geoffrey Hearn, Interview.

4.   BALLET STYLES

Ballet styles

"A style is not a method of training but a particular interpretation of the classical technique..."; "Style in this sense becomes a choreographic device, which usually emphasises or exaggerates certain aspects of the technique."
"Romantic style, Kirov and Bolshoi styles, Balanchine style."
Anna Paskevska, 1990.

Classical style

Its movement is predominantly marked by "outwardness, verticality, skill, clarity, objectivity, grace.", as exemplified by a Petipa pas de deux.
Selma Jeanne Cohen, 1982.

Good classical work
> A term used, regardless of style, of a class in the Vaganova, Cecchetti, English, or American style which offers good line, musicality, excellence of class structure with a balance to its parts.
> *Monica Mason,* Interview.

Classical technique
> "...geometry imposed on the body...".
> *Norman Morrice,* Interview.

Balletic forms
> Idioms within the ballet technique such as "classical, neo-classical, contemporary ballet".
> *Anna Paskevska,* 1990.

Balletic styles
> Established ways of performing the ballet vocabulary, associated with choreographers, schools or countries; "the heroic style", "the classical style, well shaped and formed", "the romantic style", etc.; used in student classes to introduce young dancers to the ways of dancing the same movement in different styles.
> *Laverne Meyer,* Interview.

Ashtonian
> In the style of Frederick Ashton, "using the back and shoulders and arms", "an intimate quality".
> *Laverne Meyer,* Interview.

School of American Ballet style
> "Technically, the School of American Ballet students receive superb training. There are mannerisms — the arching back, the broken wrist, the exaggerated angularity... Emotionally their faces and their bodies seem to be in neutral most of the time".
> *Marcia Siegel,* 1972.

Balanchine style
> "Large, clear, accurate and unaffected, our ballet style looks — and particularly among the slender young girls remarkable for speed, toes and prowess; its phrasing is not very personal...".
> *Edwin Denby,* 1968(c).

Balanchinean
> In the style of George Balanchine "with no frills" "no romanticism".
> *Laverne Meyer,* Interview.

Bournonville school

A repertory of six classes, strictly codified sets of exercises (Monday through Saturday), developed from the daily training systems established by August Bournonville and later Hans Beck.

Vivi Flindt and *Knud Arne Jürgensen, 1992.*

Cecchetti style

A way of training in the classical ballet tradition developed in Italy by Enrico Cecchetti, "a school of bravura, virtuosity, and strength", the product of his own training with Lepui (who was a pupil of Blasis).

Clement Crisp, Interview.

Russian School

The sequence of class in the Russian School of Ballet: exercises at the barre, exercises in the centre, petit adagio, grand adagio, and allegro.

Agrippina Vaganova, 1969 (1934).

Vaganova style

A method of dance training developed by Agrippina Vaganova at Petrograd and initiated in 1918, which emphasised strength, energy, power, and a positive presentation of men and women of their time, not idealised and romanticised but nevertheless with added subtlety.

"an impregnable technique", "with a subtle voice".

Clement Crisp, Interview.

Vaganova system

A teaching method, a codified system, based on a logical progression over an eight-year programme, designed to give care to the technical side of the ballet dancer's training.

Laverne Meyer, Interview.

Guest teachers

Internationally renowned figures who teach class for a company, bringing their own style of work for 6 weeks or so, their own fresh eye to the dancers, and their own excellence; said of the company class at the Royal Ballet.

Monica Mason, Interview.

5. SOME PRINCIPLES OF BALLET

Principles

"The underlying reasons that govern all classical movements...based on both aesthetic and physical considerations".

Anna Paskevska, 1990.

Seven principles of classical ballet, The

"They are stance, turn-out, placing, laws of balance, transfer of weight, rules, co-ordination".
Joan Lawson, 1988.

Stance

"The dancer gets the best results when the spine has been straightened to its fullest. It must not be stiffened as its curves must continue to act as shock absorbers".
Joan Lawson, 1988.

Stance/posture (classical ballet)

In correct stance the weight is distributed evenly throughout the body, but for classical ballet the weight is usually carried slightly forward to facilitate the stylistic emphasis upon lightness and verticality.
Jane Carr, Interview.

Stretching up

Pulling upwards, the spine feeling released, the backs of the legs pulled up, the crown of the head lifting; the basic carriage of the body in ballet.
Teresa Kelsey, Interview.

Principles of stance and turn-out

The three planes within the mover's kinesphere, the vertical, sagittal, and horizontal planes, are the geometric model within the body on which the principles of stance and turn-out in ballet are based.
Rosemary Brandt, 1987.

Turn-out

"The turn-out must take place in the hip joints and nowhere else".
Joan Lawson, 1988.

Turn-out

The outward rotation of the legs from the hips, the heels pushing forwards together giving the sense of 'en dehors', opening out, which is essential to ballet style; rotated to 180 degrees is the ideal but each dancer works "to his own turn-out".
Mirella Bartrip and *Teresa Kelsey,* Interview.

Placing

"Each part of the body must be kept in proper relationship to the other and to the central line of balance if classical dance is to retain its purest form".
Joan Lawson, 1988.

Principle of placing, The

Although understood as a series of positions of the body, placing has spatial content related to the three planes in both motional and positional terms.
Rosemary Brandt, 1987.

Classical line

"The harmonious configurations that are pleasing to the eye..."; "...characterised by length, purity and simplicity."; "It is achieved not only by correct placement of body and limbs but more significantly through an inner tension guided by an aesthetic sense which extends the line beyond the dancer's physical limits."
Anna Paskevska, 1990.

Balance

Equilibrium in the body, the ability to arrive motionless and stable on demipointe through sensing the equalising of opposing forces in the body and a strong vertical line of energy.
Alan Dubreuil, Class.

Balance

The effort which is to be made, in the first position, to keep to the vertical axis around which the dancer's balance is built.
Agrippina Vaganova, 1969 (1934).

Aplomb

Stability; a basic concept of classical ballet for the correctly set body; the ability to stand straight on one leg.
"The stem of aplomb is the spine."
Agrippina Vaganova, 1969 (1934).

Laws of Balance

"The weight of the body must always be centred over one or both feet and the natural laws of balance be followed at all times in classical ballet."
Joan Lawson, 1988.

Laws of Balance

Usually seen as the weight centred stably over one or two feet, balance is actually achieved through a constant interplay of lability and stability.
Rosemary Brandt, 1987.

Principle of transfer of weight, The

Usually seen as the weight having to adhere to the centre line of gravity; Laban's principle of the rhythm of preparation/action/recovery invites understanding and experience of the motional and rhythmical content of transferring the weight of the body.
Rosemary Brandt, 1987.

Rules

"It is better to have a rule to break than no rules at all, if discipline is to be maintained in the class room."
Ninette De Valois in Joan Lawson, 1988.

Co-ordination
The way the articulation of one part of the body is reflected in the whole body, an essential feature of ballet style.
Teresa Kelsey, Interview.

6. SOME ASPECTS OF THE BALLET CLASS

Levels of study
"The first four years are the most critical in establishing good habits and setting the foundation for all future progress. At the intermediate level the focus shifts slightly to the acquisition of vocabulary. During the final two years of study, execution of the vocabulary is perfected."
Anna Paskevska, 1990.

Class structure
Structure of a ballet class, which, at all levels, is "barre, port de bras, center practice of barre exercises, adagio, petit allegro, grand allegro, and petite batterie".
Anna Paskevska, 1990.

Class structure
The design and progression of a ballet class; the developmental order and crucial combination of exercises that best prepare the body for what it has to be able to do.
Laverne Meyer, Interview.

Ballet terminology
A succinct means for conveying positions and places, such as "attitude", and a series of coded words such as "glissade" which gives information for what is to be done, neither of which address how they are to be done or what is to be made by them.
Rosemary Brandt, Interview.

Teaching choreologically
Working with movement principles, such as transference of weight, effort and recovery, scattering and gathering, in the dance class, combining technique or ballet with understanding movement, "which allows me to articulate explicitly how they are to be done, and what is to be made of them".
Rosemary Brandt, Interview.

Studio
A place "set apart from the environs", where young dancers can "concentrate in silence, listen and learn something very special", in an atmosphere created by "the formality of well-mannered studio behavior."
Anna Paskevska, 1990.

Silence
The traditional quietness of the ballet class, which promotes the concentration of teacher, dancer and pianist, and gives the class its atmosphere of a ritual.
Mirella Bartrip and *Teresa Kelsey,* Interview.

Barre, The

Not a physical support to grab on to, but an assistance both physical and psychological to aid you to centre your body over your legs.

Mirella Bartrip and *Teresa Kelsey,* Interview.

Barre work

A series of exercises, depending for exact content on level and aim but following the basic structure of: pliés, demi-pliés with tendus, ports de bras, battements tendus, ronds de jambe, battements fondus, battements frappés, ronds de jambe en l'air, petits battements.

Mirella Bartrip and *Teresa Kelsey,* Interview.

Port de bras

To achieve the correct shape, "The humerus is rotated inward in the shoulder socket. The rotation causes the elbow to be uplifted, then the lower arm is rotated outward in order to continue the line created by the upper arm. The hand faces front."

"To achieve fluidity and ease of execution the impulse and support for all actions of the arms comes from the torso, not the deltoids."

Anna Paskevska, 1990.

Head participation

"The head gives it the finishing touch, adds beauty to the entire design. The look, the glance, the eyes, crown it all. The turn of the head, the direction of the eyes, play decisive roles in the expression of every arabesque, attitude — in fact of all other poses".

Agrippina Vaganova, 1969 (1934).

Épaulement

"The positions of arms and shoulders which define and qualify positions of the legs...governed by the twin rules of opposition and complement, used especially in croisé and effacé positions."

Anna Paskevska, 1990.

Centre practice

Usually the first exercises in the centre, in which work done at the barre is repeated without its aid, to give a sense of the body's alignment in the space.

Mirella Bartrip and *Teresa Kelsey,* Interview.

Alignment

The relationship of hip to arm to leg and torso required by the principles of line within the body of classic ballet, whether in a pose, moving, or turning; and, the relationship of the lines in the body to the stage space and the auditorium.

Laverne Meyer, Interview.

Adage

Work in the centre which develops strength, control, and balance through sustainment in both arms and legs.

Mirella Bartrip and *Teresa Kelsey,* Interview.

Adage

The part of the class which allows the dancer to develop individual phrasing, lyrical flow and the expressive poetic qualites of ballet.

Laverne Meyer, Interview.

Adagio

Literally 'at leisure'; in ballet terminology any set of slow movements executed to develop grace, balance and co-ordination.

"...a generic term for a combination of slow and sustained movements designed to develop line and balance."

Lincoln Kirstein and *Muriel Stuart,* 1977 (1952).

Adagio

"In adagio the pupil masters the basic poses, turns of the body and the head, and in a complicated adagio develops agility and mobility of the body."

Agrippina Vaganova, 1968 (1934).

Pirouette

Spinning on one leg in ballet, which has two components, 'balance and impetus'; balance is achieved by alignment over the supporting leg and impetus by setting up a torque through pressure of feet on the floor, which is released as a spin, and by the force directed to the shoulders by the arm movement around the vertical.

Eds. from *Anna Paskevska,* 1990.

Allegro

"When the legs of the pupil are correctly placed, when they have acquired a turn-out, when the ball of the foot has been developed and strengthened, when the foot has gained elasticity and the muscles have toughened — then may we approach the study of allegro."

Agrippina Vaganova, 1969 (1934).

Petit allegro

Little jumping phrases to warm up the feet, usually in $^2/_4$ or $^6/_8$ time.

"Glissade assemblé, glissade assemblé, jeté, temps levé, pas de bourrée, changement...".

Mirella Bartrip and *Teresa Kelsey,* Interview.

Allegro

Sequences with more bounce and ballon than petit allegro, usually in $^6/_8$ or $^3/_4$ time, travelling and using diagonal alignment and directional changes.

"Demi contre temps", "ballotté", "sissones", "failli".

Mirella Bartrip and *Teresa Kelsey.*

Grand Allegro

The part of the class for large, expansive, virtuosic jumping combinations.

Laverne Meyer, Interview.

Grand allegro

Danced with the accent up and out of the floor, large movements with lability, travelling and changing direction.

Mirella Bartrip and *Teresa Kelsey,* Interview.

Final section

The last part of the class which includes, for the women, all manner of turns and turning jumps, including châiné, and piqué and fouetté turns and, for the men, all manner of multiple turns in the air and more complicated combinations of turning movements on half point; and batterie (beating steps).

Laverne Meyer, Interview.

Tours en l'air

Turns in the air, which "are the domain of the male dancer".

Agrippina Vaganova, 1969 (1934).

Male vocabulary

Dance material which includes greater emphasis on building strength to prepare for the demands of lifting a partner and, traditionally, more jumps and beats than women; trained through longer combinations and more demi-pliés, grands battements, fondus, grandes pirouettes, and tours en l'air.

Laverne Meyer, Interview.

Pointe work

Ballet 'on the toes', traditionally danced by women, "requiring strong arch and ankle, strength in the hip joints and the spine", using pointe shoes.

Anna Paskevska, 1990.

Warming down

How class ends, maybe with a port de bras, with a bow, with a reverence, according to the requirements of the participants (beginners, company members, classical dancers, contemporary dancers), and according to the emphasis of the class (to learn to take a bow, to thank the teacher, to take applause....).

Laverne Meyer, Interview.

7. SOME CONTEMPORARY TECHNIQUES

7a. CUNNINGHAM

Cunningham technique

It combines "the flexible back and changing levels of modern dance, and the upright carriage and brilliant footwork of ballet".

Sally Banes in State Univ. of New York, 1987.

Technique as dancing
"Not rhapsodic self-expression" but "the synthesis of the physical and spiritual energies."
Merce Cunningham in Walter Sorell, 1951.

Cunningham technique
Cunningham technique is "designed to develop flexibility in the mind as well as in the body."
Carolyn Brown in Roger Copeland and Marshall Cohen, 1983.

Technique and choreography
"The technique, the training method, and the choreography were intimately bound."; said by Steve Paxton of the development of Cunningham technique.
Steve Paxton, 1987.

Bounces
To loosen up the whole back, "Lengthen over, reach, don't drop in your waist."; "over the front, over the side and over the diagonal."
Albert Reed, Cunningham Studio class.

First position
In parallel, with feet below the hips, not touching.
Albert Reed, Cunningham Studio class.

Leg rotations
In parallel and out-turned.
Albert Reed, Cunningham Studio class.

Movement of the spine
Curving, rounding over, opening out, arching back, rolling through the back, lifting; reaching out, tilting, shifting; "and to the diagonal".
Albert Reed, Cunningham Studio class.

Arching
Although backward, "it's an upward forward feeling".
Albert Reed, Cunningham Studio class.

Leg movements
"Brushes, développés", "taking the leg round, in attitude, stretching and lengthening", "with flexed ankle and pointed foot", "degagé and on the floor", "in passé".
Albert Reed, Cunningham Studio class.

Leaning
Falling away from the vertical, then re-balancing.
Albert Reed, Cunningham Studio class.

Levels

The grades of proficiency in performing the Graham technique and in the visible use of principles involved; used at the Graham studio.

"Fundamental, elementary, intermediate, and advanced."

Thea Barnes, Susan Sentler, and *Brenda Baden-Semper,* Interview.

Contraction and release

A Graham term for the source of her technique and movement vocabulary which is both a physical source from which movement arises, and a spiritual/mental motivation.

"...the point of ecstasy...".

Thea Barnes, Susan Sentler, and *Brenda Baden-Semper,* Interview.

Contraction, The

"An enfoldment and a shock" (Graham), "A spasm of percussive force" (de Mille), "Proceeding from a deep emotional feeling" (Nelle Fisher), "Propelling the arms and legs" (de Mille), "It is visceral" (Graham), "Revitalized raw emotion" (de Mille).

Agnes de Mille, 1991.

Contractions

The key motivating force in Graham's movement vocabulary "in what they caused the rest of the body to do", taking place in the pelvis and diaphragm and resonating in the extremities.

Agnes de Mille, 1991.

Images

The words used to help a dancer find the motivation, dynamic and form of technical exercises, words which are images of feelings but do not necessarily demand an emotional response.

"...the passion of the inner arm...", "...contract back into the cave of the heart, and release into the night..." (Martha Graham).

Robert Cohan, Interview.

Stretching the back

In Graham technique, the pelvis goes under and then the shoulders go forward, not a hinge movement from the hip.

Robert Cohan, Interview.

Release

In Graham technique, the spine lifts and extends, the front of the torso lengthens while the muscles of the back contract. The impetus is an inhalation. The movement starts from the base of the spine. There is no drop in energy use as you come out of the contraction into release.

Alice J. Helpern, 1981.

Starting the movement
The initiation of movement, which, in Graham technique, is in the pelvis.
"It starts underneath you, right in the core, in the genitals"; "...in the groin...".
Robert Cohan, Interview.

Back, The
The part of the body which Graham technique takes as primary. One of the purposes of the technique is to strengthen the torso and provide articulation in the back.
Jane Dudley, Interview.

Ritual
The floor work in Graham technique, a performance in unison of the prescribed movements, danced as a continuous presentation.
Thea Barnes and *Susan Sentler,* Interview.

Floor work
The first part of a Graham technique class which takes place from a sitting position, in which the essential sensations of the style are experienced.
"Feel the spine, shoulders over hips, abdominals lifted, feeling the sitting bones."
Thea Barnes, Susan Sentler, and *Brenda Baden-Semper,* Interview.

"and-a"
The crucial preparation in Graham-based work.
"The most important part of the movement, the part which not only prepares but causes the main movement."
Robert Cohan, Company class.

Ground
"The ground is a spatial element, not to be resisted as in ballet, but to be used."
Martha Graham in Agnes de Mille, 1991.

Stretches
Extending, over the back, over the sides of the torso, down the length of the leg; a technical exercise especially in Graham and Graham-based work.
Robert Cohan, Company class.

Suspension
(while sitting) The lifted state before and during an arch or a contraction.
"Up, up, up, grow, don't let your waist go down."; "Stretch so the weight is pulled completely out of the pelvis."
Robert Cohan, Company class.

Leg rotations

A fundamental need for ballet and contemporary dance techniques and choreographic works using those styles, a facility playing a large part in technique classes.

"Make the muscles burn under there", said of the buttocks in Graham floor work.

Robert Cohan, Company class.

Off balance

Off the vertical; said in Graham technique in floor work where the hand is needed as a support for torso tilts.

"Reach, get as far away from your pelvis as you can".

Robert Cohan, Company class.

Spirals

The Graham movement around the spine, with all manner of variations, performed in the rhythm of "the threes and the sixes"; going around and up into the opening.

"...like a nautilus's shell...", "...like a barber's pole...".

Thea Barnes, Susan Sentler, and *Brenda Baden-Semper,* Interview.

Direction of gaze

"The gaze is around your own body in a spiral, not out there; the pelvis rotates and the top vertebrae follow".

Robert Cohan, Company class.

Hang on to, To

To hold back one part of the body, so making a counterweight against which the main movement pulls; used in Graham technique.

"Hang on to the back."; "Hang back on yourself before you come forward, you have to press."

Robert Cohan, Company class.

Centre work

The second part of a Graham class when the dancer sets up her centre in preparation for the off-balance and propulsion into the space which is to follow.

"...parallel tendus, brushes, passé, shifting into space, pliés...".

Thea Barnes, Susan Sentler, and *Brenda Baden-Semper,* Interview.

Plié

The bending of the knees, preceded and accompanied by a lifting in the waist and pulling up on the thighs; used as a means "...of reaffirming your centre..."; "...reaffirming the plumb-line...", especially after movement which has taken the body off balance.

"The lift makes the knees bend".

Robert Cohan, Company class.

Inner line of the leg

The line of the leg from groin to ankle when out-turned.
"Work on the inner line of the leg as you step forward."
Robert Cohan, Company class.

Study

A combination of from 2 to 8 different steps on a variety of Graham technique movements; "...dynamics, attacks, accents, hips shifts, off-centre work, andante or allegro".
"Attack like a viper.", "Show how you bite the apple".
Thea Barnes and *Susan Sentler,* Interview.

Going across the floor

The variety of walks, leaps and jumps in the Graham style used to travel through the space.
"...the walks on 4, circular walks, step draws, strides, low runs, skitters, prances, triplets...".
Thea Barnes, Susan Sentler, and *Brenda Baden-Semper,* Interview.

Piece of repertory

The longer studies used in a Graham class which come out of the ballets, used by teachers rather than choreographing their own material in Graham style.
"Graham-speak".
Thea Barnes, Interview.

Falls

In Graham's movement vocabulary, not yielding to gravity but "dissolving, melting, and sliding, a communion with the ground and then a recovery and regalvanizing" (de Mille), "a spring up to life" (Graham).
Agnes de Mille, 1991.

Jumps

Part of a Graham class in which the leaps and jumps from the ballets are used to go across the floor, to take you into space, flying and suspending.
"...leaps on 3, on 2, or 5 and 6...", "...bison jetés, barrel jumps, march jumps, bell jumps, tilt jumps, stag leaps, skip jumps, gallops, brush jetés". "Like a Polaroid picture, suspended in space".
Thea Barnes, Susan Sentler, and *Brenda Baden-Semper,* Interview.

7c. HUMPHREY, LIMÓN, AND LIMÓN-BASED

Humphrey terminology

"DESIGN (of movement in space), DYNAMICS, (variations in tempo and tension), ISOLATION (of single parts of the body), PHRASING (grouping of movements in rhythmically expressive sequences), REBOUND (natural release of energy in reaction to Falling, with emphasis on breath inhalation), RHYTHM (kinetic response to simple and complex sequences of stressed and unstressed beats), SUCCESSIONAL (progressive flow of related body parts), SUSPENSION (the final curve of a Rebound when recovery has been achieved and equilibrium is momentarily restored), TENSION AND RELAXATION (basic ingredients of Humphrey movements: Tension maintains the body's balance; Relaxation incurs Falling), WHOLENESS (integrated movement of the entire body...the most typical dance characteristic of the Humphrey style)."

Ernestine Stodelle, Contributed.

Humphrey technique

"Whereas other established dance techniques train the body by means of a specific code of graduated exercises from the simple to the complex, the Humphrey Technique concentrates on the movement experience throughout the developmental procedure."

Ernestine Stodelle, 1978.

Centre Work, Floor Work, Barre Work, Spatial Sequences

"The four divisions of work in a modern Humphrey-based technique class."

Ernestine Stodelle, 1978.

Rhythmic training

"Training in the 'animating force' of rhythm demands mastering complex coordination, sometimes performed in counterpoint to music".

Ernestine Stodelle, 1978.

Variation

A teaching method in Humphrey technique in which the basic exercises are enlarged in scope by the introduction of new choreographic forms, making the transition from the acquisition of skill to creative use of it.

Ernestine Stodelle, 1978.

Developing a style

Holding to principles of dance and finding an individual way to express them; said of José Limón's personal way of developing the principles he shared with Humphrey/Weidman.

Carla Maxwell, Interview.

Participate in the history, To

To be a contributing part of a tradition, or a style associated with an artist; said of participants in the Humphrey/Weidman/Limón heritage who use those principles in a way that works for each one individually; said in contrast to codifying the work of an artist and striving to avoid all personal interpretation.

Carla Maxwell, Interview.

Limón-based class

A technique class in which the traditional vocabulary developed by José Limón forms the basis, with the aim and teaching method individual to the teacher.

Erica Stanton, Interview.

Limón technique

Not a fixed class but a set of principles.

Carla Maxwell, Interview.

Limón technique

"A technique built on motion", "learning how to move through position A to position B, to position C."

Daniel Lewis, 1984.

Alignment (Limón technique)

The placement of all the body parts in relationship to each other. A standing posture in which the feet are parallel, toes pointing forward, and placed directly under the hip joints, the shoulders are lined up over the hips, the spine feels long, the head is lifted, the weight is evenly distributed over both feet. The vertical axis through the body is sensed.

Daniel Lewis, 1984.

Successions

Sequential flow through the body, especially spinal successions and successional arms.

Daniel Lewis, 1984.

Successions

A Limón term for a wealth of ways of manifesting a sequential flow in the body; "from head through to pelvis, from ribs to arms...".

Carla Maxwell, Interview.

Successional arms

A term used to describe the path of the arms in the Limón technique. "The lower arms cross, hugging the sides of the body, lift up over the head as if removing a sweater and then open out into a second position with the elbows leading."

Daniel Lewis, 1984.

Fall, rebound, and recovery exercises

Exercises which use the pull of gravity; "through using the elastic reaction in a rebound, and through passing through the bottom of the fall and continuing on in the same path", as in a swing, in the recovery.

Daniel Lewis, 1984.

Limón swing
    A fall and a recovery, achieved through acknowledging the presence of gravity and recovering into a suspension.
    Carla Maxwell, Interview.

Peak and trough
    The rhythm of suspending and dropping, resisting and using gravity, "active and passive weight" used in a Limón-based technique class.
    Erica Stanton, Interview.

High point
    The top of the suspension, especially the sternum, but will be whatever part of the body acknowledges the pull against gravity.
    Carla Maxwell, Interview.

Series
    "Plié series, lunge series, tendu series", sequences of movement which become established over time; said of Limón-based work.
    Daniel Lewis, Interview.

Co-ordination of melodies
    Progressing from the simple working together of two parts of the body in regular rhythm to the working together of three [legs, arms, torso] in mixed metre.
    "Complex orchestration."
    Erica Stanton, Interview.

Body as orchestra
    Imaging the body as analogous to the integrated instruments of the orchestra, "Timpani for the steps, strings for the arms, flute for the head, horns for the torso" or whatever instruments were imaged that day.
    Carla Maxwell, referring to José Limón's teaching, Interview.

Centre combination
    A main section of a technique class, which will locomote and go into and out of the floor.
    Erica Stanton, Interview.

Locomotor sequence
    A major part of a technique class when the dancer is fully warmed through, in which off-balance, turning, falling are main ingredients of a long phrase for which torso articulation and dynamic energy are essential.
    Erica Stanton, Interview.

Re-centre the body

To bring the body back to its correct alignment, e.g. at the end of class, often after travelling across the floor. Also to allow the muscles to release tension and the body to find its equilibrium.

Daniel Lewis, 1984.

Movement from repertory

Combinations from a Limón work such as "Chaconne", or "Missa Brevis".

Daniel Lewis, 1984.

7d. JAZZ DANCE

Jazz dance

"A fusion of African-American social dance, classical ballet, contemporary and tap dance highly stylized for use in musical theatre, cinema, cabaret and television. Amateur and professional instruction is found in studios, universities, and fitness centers around the world".

Walter Nicks, Contributed.

Jazz dance class

A technique class that prepares dancers for cabaret, Broadway, boat cruise shows, musicals, and theatre and screen entertainment generally.

Thea Barnes, Interview.

Jazz dance styles

Afro-Jazz, Afro Cuban Jazz, Modern Jazz, Funky Jazz, and Free Jazz are among the many titles advertising jazz dance instruction. The style of instruction and methodology is as varied as the instructors. Most professional training owes a debt to Katherine Dunham and Jack Cole. Famous choreographers and dancers whose successful dance companies complemented their Broadway and Hollywood production, they created pronounced individual styles".

Walter Nicks, Contributed.

Jazz dance as entertainment

"You've got to have an audience, you're communicating all the time, to your classmates, to the teacher, to the fourth wall, to the mirror, anybody; you entertain them."

Thea Barnes, Interview.

Jazz attitude

An interpretational input by the student, an essential contribution by the performer, achieved either by copying the teacher's 'attitude' or being similar.

Michael Owen, quoted by Thea Barnes, Interview.

Warm up
The first phase of a jazz class, lasting 5 minutes or more, which each teacher has as a distinct signature of his/her class; a continuous known sequence of moves performed in uninterrupted unison; may be slow and organic (Keith O'Brian), "Bang up, let's go" (Thea Barnes); a mass of isolations (Michael Owen).
Thea Barnes, Interview.

Warm-up and isolations
The movement used at the beginning of a dance class, especially in jazz dance and disco dance, to loosen the body, warm the muscles, and to gain control of the body by moving one particular part at a time, to music.
Robert Audy, 1978.

Isolations
"A section of a jazz dance class targeting specific areas of the body for improving coordination, control and flexibility. The head, chest and pelvic area are explored for increased lateral, circular and vertical movement range."
Walter Nicks, Contributed.

Centre combination
A long sequence in the space which may have a historical or topical influence; a Fred Astaire combination, or a rap adaptation, done for a proscenium stage, or a 'party' situation where students dance meeting each other, with a touch of improvisation.
Thea Barnes, Interview.

Break up in groups
The last part of a jazz dance class in which the taught combination is performed in groups, the observers watching, applauding, critiquing, encouraging during the dancing.
Thea Barnes, Interview.

8. OTHER TECHNIQUES

Normative ideal
"A principal goal of training in Hawkins technique, — to achieve the optimum standard of efficiency of movement in relation to nature and to gravity. Defined by Hawkins as the best possible standard you can achieve using your intelligence and your senses."
Mark Lintern Harris, Contributed.

Momentum paths
"Movement which flows in felt, looping pathways which, depending on the emphasis of weight, are either under-curved or over-curved; a Hawkins technique priority which is applied both to gesture patterns of the limbs and to the moving through space of the locus of the centre of gravity."
Mark Lintern Harris, Contributed.

Balanced, restful alignment

"A state of dynamic posture in stillness where the three principal weights of the body — pelvis, rib-cage, and head — are balanced in an easy, vertical alignment, directly above the centre of gravity."; a Hawkins technique principle.

Mark Lintern Harris, Contributed.

De-contraction

"A term used as an alternative to 'relax' (with its implication of passivity), to imply an active decision not to contract a muscle or group of muscles, and to help counteract any tendency unthinkingly to prioritise 'strong' movements."

Mark Lintern Harris, Contributed.

Tasselling

"A technique for the control of, and a description of, the free movement of the arms, legs and head in response to the momentum path of the movement; in the arms the movements tend to rise successively and fall simultaneously".

Mark Lintern Harris, Contributed.

Jooss-Leeder technique

The application of Laban's principles to a dance practice which employs use of weight and suspension — giving in to and defying gravity — and economy of effort, that is the use of the minimum tension and energy required by a movement to embody most effectively the intention of that movement.

Simone Michelle, Interview.

Jooss-Leeder style

Technique is not separated from dance; both arise out of inner feeling and intention.

Jane Winearls, 1958.

Studies

Short dances resulting from a series of technique classes, which have been directed toward developing one particular element of movement; for example a study on a dynamic quality or on use of double tension; an integral part of Jooss-Leeder technique.

Simone Michelle, Interview.

Holm concepts

Technique, practical theory/improvisation, composition; the three facets of Hanya Holm's work, all based around concepts of movement developed from her Laban/Wigman heritage.

Don Redlich, Informal discussion.

Diagonal forms

A range of technical exercises and invention tasks based on "the diagonal of the body and the diagonal of the room"; used by Hanya Holm.

Don Redlich, Informal discussion.

Swings
> Circular, curving movements using the body's weight; used by Hanya Holm.
> *Don Redlich,* Informal discussion.

Isolations
> Shifts of part of the body, especially the hip, pelvis, chest and rib cage; used by Hanya Holm.
> *Don Redlich,* Informal discussion.

Six swings, The
> The Laban-based directional swings, as used by Hanya Holm.
> *Don Redlich,* Informal discussion.

Horton style
> "Architectural technique" focusing on "joint mobility, developing, throwing, flinging, swinging, casting and off-balance movements"; "a logical exploration of the anatomy", "tempos, movement range, rhythmical patterns, dynamic accents" are all explored.
> *Marjorie B. Perces, Ana Marie Forsythe* and *Cheryl Bell,* 1992.

Partnering work
> The skill of working in a partnership, the "knack", especially of co-ordinating the timing and the force needed for lifts and supports and turns, a skill acquired through repetition and lengthy practice, and the 'feeling' and sensing of one another.
> *Laverne Meyer,* Interview.

Technique, The
> The steps of ballroom dancing, their style, pathways, poise, rhythm, and hold, which a couple learn and practise rigorously.
> *Geoffrey Hearn,* Interview.

Release work
> An approach to movement introduced to Britain by Mary Fulkerson, in style contrasted to the virtuosity and lifted tension of ballet-based work and other established modern dance vocabularies.
> *Stephanie Jordan,* 1992.

Release work
> "A way of working in which the misuse of tension built up in a body can literally be released; a process by which the geography of the body can be seen more clearly, can tell more, instead of having a hard muscular barrier between the dancer and the audience."
> *Siobhan Davies,* Contributed.

Bartenieff Fundamentals (TM)

A body therapy system developed by Irmgard Bartenieff from Laban's movement principles as an approach to basic body training, not as a system of set exercises, but as a way of encouraging full psychophysical functioning in body mobilisation.
Peggy Hackney, 1984.

Inner connectivity and outer expressivity

Terms in Bartenieff Fundamentals (TM) to identify the goal of the system which is to promote an integration of intent and expression in an individual's movement processes.
Peggy Hackney, 1984.

Functional integration

The name given to the purpose of the Feldenkreis method of body therapy, that is to enable you to do what you want to do and which at the start of therapy you are unable to do.
Scott Clark, Interview.

Conditioning for performance artists

Physical exercises for the body designed to develop "strength and suppleness, stamina and vitality" leading to an ability to work with "openness and elegance, and sparkle".
Helen Crocker and *Bim Mason,* Interview.

Body conditioning (aim of)

Exercises, possibly in a gymnasium, or a Pilates studio, designed to strengthen the weaker areas of the body; especially needed for the demands on male dancers for lifts in ballet and for both sexes using contemporary dance vocabularies.
Laverne Meyer, Interview.

Relaxation

A key dynamic state in Butoh, seen as contrasting to tension as a key state for contemporary Western dancers in the 1990's.
Ushio Amagatsu, Interview.

Personal vocabulary

The range of movement developed by an individual for himself through selection and emphasis of movement material suitable to his own vision and physique; said as an aim of Laban-based teaching of technique.
Marion North, Interview.

Tanagra figures

Poses used as one of the bases for the technique of Isadora Duncan, with precise stepping, arm, head and body motion, which should be "measured and uniformly executed", "connected without pausing" while "omitting all emotional interpretation"; only then when mastered, should the dancer attempt "to create beautiful things".
Irma Duncan, 1970.

Margaret Morris Technique

A system of body training, in which breathing, spinal mobility, and opposition movements form the principles.
Margaret Morris, 1972.

Figure dancer's technique

To move "hither and thither", freely and easily, with control over direction and speed, followed by mastery of timing, phrasing with the music, continuity, and the ability to dance "in concert with" fellow dancers.
Cecil J. Sharp, 1934 (1909).

9.   WORKING IN CLASS

Centre yourself, to

To get yourself together physically and mentally in the moments before a class begins, preparing yourself.
Mirella Bartrip and *Teresa Kelsey,* Interview.

Centering

Finding your own centre as a feeling and maintaining that as a means of "holding you together" as you move.
Robert Cohan, 1986.

Stillness

Being quiet inside yourself, "finding a centre", a dynamic quality, waiting, a feeling which the individual dancer has to find for himself.
Laverne Meyer, Interview

Work internally, To

What a dancer may do in class, concentrating not on the outer form of the exercise but on the particular problems of co-ordination, line, strength, balance, etc. which he has set himself.
Thomas Paton, Interview.

Internalise, To

A process of learning through isolating specific muscle action while dancing and also through making use of imagery in order to co-ordinate the energy in complex muscle action until the habit of internalising is established.
Robert Cohan, Interview.

Solving

What a dancer has to do about a technical fault once it is identified; it is his responsibility to work on it, to solve the problem.
"What are you going to do about it?"
Robert Cohan, Company class.

Positive and negative forces

Ways of using the preparation for a turn (pirouette) or jump (entrechat six) which aid the movement or hinder the movement; the efficiency or inefficiency of the preparation.

Alan Dubreuil, Class.

Refine the energies

To work in class in order to know "what to tighten, where to loosen, when to push, what to stretch, how to turn", using movement exercises which are well known, so building up the sensation of the appropriate energy use.

Robert Cohan, Company class.

Devotion

"The steadfast and willing devotion to the labor that makes the class work not a gymnastic hour and a half, or at the lowest level, a daily drudgery, but a devotion that allows the classroom discipline to be moments of dancing too."

Merce Cunningham in Walter Sorell, 1951.

Show, To

"The dancer strives for complete and tempered body-skill, for complete identification with the movement in as devastatingly impersonal a fashion as possible. Not to show off, but to show."

Merce Cunningham in Walter Sorell, 1951.

Anatomical imagery

"...focuses on the 'interior' of the body, on the workings of the joints, the physical and structural connections between body parts, the functioning of the circulatory and nervous systems and the effects their operations have on movement, and conversely the effect movement has upon them."

Sarah Rubidge, 1988.

Muscle language

A part of the verbal language in a class, useful for isolating muscle action, but only one way to sensing the movement which motional images may contribute to as usefully.

Robert Cohan, Interview.

Body concentration

The focus on sensation which a dancer needs in order to build up patterns of working in which execution is enriched by sensation.

"...don't just do it, give the directions to yourself.", "...get into the heel.", "...step on the inside of the thigh".

Robert Cohan, Company class.

Sensing the forms

"In addition to developing awareness of rhythmic-dynamic phrasing, there is emphasis on sensing the designs of the forms created in the act of 'falling and recovering'."

Ernestine Stodelle, 1978.

Experiencing

The essential way of learning movement, especially of qualities such as fall and suspension; said in contrast to attempting to imitate.

Carla Maxwell, Interview.

Inevitability

The quality of movement which has a syntax, which, for example, opens in order to close, lifts in order to plié, a quality which has to be achieved by the dancer's internal sensation of the syntax within their own body.

"As you put movements together, do they have a grammar?"; "You have to find the inevitability."

Robert Cohan, Company class.

Observing

Looking at other dancers dancing, especially in technique class, so discerning what has to be done, how different solutions are reached, and, thence, how one might achieve a solution oneself.

Stephanie Jordan, Interview.

Posture

A way of holding the body which gradually develops through using centering, balance and gravity, but which requires confirmation that what you feel your posture is is what it actually looks like.

Robert Cohan, 1986.

Adapting a technique

Within limits, adjusting a technical exercise to the possibilities of your own physique.

"How far do I cross?"; "It depends on the length of your foot".

Robert Cohan, Company class.

Reaffirmation

The commitment of each dancer to dedicate himself to strive for the ideal performer that he could become, an affirmation made at the commencement of each class.

Thea Barnes, Susan Sentler, and *Brenda Baden-Semper,* Interview.

Ideal

How a Graham dancer works, towards an unattainable ideal, with a "dedication from the soul", "a responsibility towards themselves".

Thea Barnes, Susan Sentler, and *Brenda Baden-Semper,* Discussion.

Make a statement

To use the exercises in a Graham technique class as an artistic statement of content and form, through commitment to the movement and personal investment in it.

"...to give it your 2 cents worth..."

Thea Barnes, Susan Sentler, and *Brenda Baden-Semper,* Interview.

Dramatic inference

The quality in Graham work which gives the movement a sense of dramatic content, of relationship, of oppositional tension, of vulnerability, feelings which the dancer has to find for herself within the form.

Thea Barnes, Susan Sentler, and *Brenda Baden-Semper,* Interview.

Transcend, To

The attitude in class in which the dancer works as if in a performance, transcending the physical environment of the practice studio to find the 'inner spirit' of the work.

Mirella Bartrip, Interview.

Using the technique

"Making the mechanics of movement work for you, finding the qualities in the movement, using both your intellect and your soul."

Laverne Meyer, Interview.

Interpretation

The process of giving the movement something from yourself, "...going into yourself and coming out of yourself...", "...something inside going out, not just the meat."

Laverne Meyer, Interview.

Exercise, An (in class)

More than it seems; a sequence of movement which has an image which deeply works in the body and which gives a focus to the personality of the dancer.

Jane Dudley, Interview.

Rechanneling

Releasing unnecessary stress and tension in isolated parts of the body while moving, absorbing it and redistributing it using "...the help available from the back, pectoral, and pelvic area muscles."

"Dance energy is dynamic, directed outward from the center through the limbs."

Anna Paskevska, 1990.

Instinctual dancing

"In most people, there's a split between instinct and intellect. A technique class should...put them together so that both are working in unison. Dancing is not intellectual. It is instinctual".

Merce Cunningham in Merce Cunningham and Jacqueline Lesschaeve, 1985.

Art of movement

"It is not the doing of the activity which is important but the linking of the inner being and the outer form."
Marion North, 1971.

Sense of rhythm

Something a dancer has to find in class by paying attention to complex layers of rhythm, of heart, lungs and limbs, within his own body.
Robert Cohan, 1986.

Rhythmicality

Using the musical rhythm, feeling it in the movement, neither behind the beat nor ahead of it but "in the centre of the beat".
Mirella Bartrip and *Teresa Kelsey,* Interview.

Rhythmical freedom

Within technique class, decisions made by the dancer as to timing and energy use on given technique material.
Stephanie Jordan, Interview.

Phrasing (a sense of)

The capacity of the dancer to give breath and punctuation, "a comma", to the combination, finding its dynamic qualities, possibly percussive or flowing.
Laverne Meyer, Interview.

Add to the music

"Use your musicality to both respond to the music and to take your interpretation further." "To be at one with the music's inner meaning."
Laverne Meyer, Interview.

Memory ordeal

Some sections of a technique class which tax the dancers' ability to pick up the movement and to remember it; an essential learning process in professional training.
Erica Stanton, Interview.

Motor memory

The ability to hang on to or remember rich movement fragments and combine them according to a new set of criteria.
Aileene Lockhart and *Esther E. Pease,* 1977 (1966).

Pain thresholds

The familiar horizon for dancers who have to learn, for their body, what different pains might be brought on by one role, by one incident, by one jumping variation, by one lift.
Monica Mason, Interview.

Pain

Muscle pain which is an expected experience for dancers.
"After 16 jumps, give me a slow recovery, even if your legs are burning."
Robert Cohan, Company class.

Practice time

Time set aside for individuals to work on their skills, a usual arrangement for circus skills, but less so for dance skills.
Helen Crocker and *Bim Mason,* Interview.

Tucking-under

"Tucking-under is probably the most common mistake among dancers. In an effort to achieve a straight back, in the vain hope of disguising a larger than desired posterior, in the strain of lifting a leg, the response more often than not is to tuck under."
Anna Paskevska, 1990.

Rolling in

The pronation of the knees, a danger when the feet are turned out beyond the ability of the hips to control the rotation.
"Special care and attention is directed to the knee joint each time turn-out is increased...".
Anna Paskevska, 1990.

Sickling

Pointing the foot so that it curves slightly inwards, so spoiling the line of the leg; a way of using the foot to be avoided.
Mirella Bartrip and *Teresa Kelsey,* Interview.

10. MUSIC FOR CLASS

Playing for class

The pianist's role in company class, where s/he has to respond to the instructions given to the dancers by the teacher, noting the tempo, the rhythm and the dynamic in order to support the dancers as they work; a highly skilled and specialist job.
Jonathan Higgins, Interview.

Knowing the technique

Playing with a rapport with the technique being taught, not necessarily with the teacher teaching it, so providing the right emotional support for each exercise.
Nicholas Mojsiejenko, Interview.

Music, The (of a ballet class)

What the pianist plays, can be classical in style, from shows, pop, may be from sheet music or 'out of our heads'; dependent on the taste of the teacher of the class.
Jonathan Higgins, Interview.

Music for class

Music which keeps to the rhythmic patterns that are in the ballet tradition, "$2/4$, $3/4$, $4/4$, $6/8$, a mazurka, a polonaise", not music with uneven rhythms, musique concrète or no music, leaving these forms of accompaniment to be encountered in repertory.
Laverne Meyer, Interview.

Musical means

"Heavy playing, light and rhythmical, jazzy, baroque elegance, shifting between major and minor, dense (with many notes), spare (with isolated chords), using the top and/or the bottom of the keyboard, missing out beats for jumps."
Nicholas Mojsiejenko, Interview.

Music, The (for class)

The supportive role that music plays for the dancer's daily class, which, because of the repetitive nature of the exercises, their arduous demands on the body, helps to bring expressiveness into what could otherwise be a purely physical event.
"A pianist makes or breaks a class."
Dancers, The Birmingham Royal Ballet, 1992.

Emotional playing

The variety of emotional support which an accompanist provides in a contemporary class; shifting between styles and means, according to the exercise and its place in the class overall.
Nicholas Mojsiejenko, Interview.

Live music

Music for class played by a musician, who, in jazz dance, is a percussionist and/or pianist, and who contributes to the class as an artist.
"...music with a breath in it...".
Thea Barnes, Interview.

Jazz dance music

"Most jazz dance classes are conducted with recorded music thus losing one of the most vital dynamics of jazz dance. The interaction of music and movement, the play of multiple rhythms, the counterpoint and syncopation engendered by live music is most essential."
Walter Nicks, Contributed.

Musicality

The phrasing, rhythm, and dynamics of ballet movement which is both derived from and integrated with the musical accompaniment; hence, accompaniment for class is set both in style and rhythm.
Mirella Bartrip, Interview.

Musicality (development of)

Learning to respond to music, to become aware of the sort of music it is, the character of it and what the composer is 'saying' through the music.

Laverne Meyer, Interview.

Musicality

A problematic word, used in highly contradictory ways by the dance community, in the areas of dance dynamics and phrasing, as well as the co-ordination with and interpretation of music.

Stephanie Jordan, Interview.

Anacrusis

The 'and' of class exercises, which the pianist needs to give in the musical accompaniment to support the dancer's preparation.

Mirella Bartrip and *Teresa Kelsey,* Interview.

Accompanist for class

In a Graham class, the music has "to be driven, to support the dancers, to inspire, to be rhythmically clear, to give the 'and' in preparation for the contraction, to keep the beat but vary the quality, to give an atmosphere."

Thea Barnes, Susan Sentler, and *Brenda Baden-Semper,* Interview.

Tempo of the exercise, The

A crucial dimension of each part of class, set by the teacher usually by giving it in rhythm, with regard to the maximum benefit to the dancer of the speed or the sustainment or the stamina required to do the exercise successfully.

Jonathan Higgins, Interview.

Pendular rhythms

Metres in $^3/_4$ or $^6/_8$ or other triple rhythms which accomodate the timing of swinging movements.

Erica Stanton, Interview.

Mixed metre

Rhythms in which units of 2 and 3 are mixed irregularly, in comparison with the more common regular $^2/_4$, $^3/_4$, $^4/_4$, or $^6/_8$ metres.

Erica Stanton, Interview.

Rock solid rhythmically

The essential quality of a musician when playing for class, avoiding rubato, acceleration, or pulling out the musical phrasing.

Jonathan Higgins, Interview.

Finger clicking

The beat given by the teacher to both the dancers and the musicians; Robert Cohan in London Contemporary Dance Theatre company class.

Eds.

Steady four, The

The basic beat of disco music which evens out the rhythm, so providing reliable tempo but diminishing nuance and fluctuation.

Thea Barnes, Interview.

Teacher/pianist collaboration

The relationship which the musician will build up over time with a teacher of class, learning what the teacher's taste and 'musical prejudices' are, knowing how far to 'play it straight' or embellish, interpreting verbal and non-verbal cues for a change of musical quality, with equanimity.

"steady it", "give a bit of music at the end", "more juicy".

Jonathan Higgins and *Alan Dubreuil,* Class.

Teacher/accompanist relationship

She has to convey just what she wants to the musician, "to sing the rhythm, to give the counts, to place the accents"; she may ask for particular qualitites to support the dances.

"Use the lower register.", "Use a different colour.", "We need a pretty tune now.".

Thea Barnes, Susan Sentler, and *Brenda Baden-Semper,* Interview.

Count four in, To

What a dance teacher may say to an accompanist as a request for a musical lead to an exercise.

Robert Coleridge, Interview.

Percussionist

A player of percussion instruments; in the dance domain often a musician who accompanies a contemporary dance technique class.

Eds.

Chapter 6   C O S T U M E

1.   DRESS

Appurtenances

All the paraphenalia, equipment, costume elements which are used by dancers in a particular dance or dance form; said of Morris dance.

"Coats/jackets, skirts, hat, shoes, bells, baldricks, sashes/scarves, belts, ribbons, handkerchiefs/napkins, feathers, sticks, swords/weapons; lady's, fool's, hobby horse costumes."

Michael Heaney and *John Forrest,* 1991.

Ballet wear

The wherewithal to make ballet outfits, especially for school productions.
"Shoes, clothing, sequins and trims, wigs, theatrical make-up."
Dancing Times, 1993.

Bell up, To

A Morris dance term for putting your performance clothes on; these consist in white trousers or black breeches and white shirt, possibly a black waistcoat, bell pads on the legs, a smart hat, possibly a bowler, straw hat or top hat, decorated with flowers and streamers, a baldrick that is crossed braid on the chest with a team medallion, and ribbons from the arm bands, usually black shoes; each team has its own club gear.

Roy Judge, Interview.

Dance wear

Garments worn by dance people, some of which are an obligatory uniform, some a subculture preference, some for efficiency, warmth and safety.

Eds.

Gear

What is worn by a jazz dancer as an individual statement; girls: "high-heeled character shoes, opaque tights, French-cut leotard to show the leg line, bras (not too cute), hair flying (but fixed up nice), some jewellery"; guys: "macho looking, body beautiful look, hair just right, maybe cut-up bike shorts".

"...and the right bag...".

Thea Barnes, Interview.

203

Highland dress

Recognised form of dress for male dancers in competition, the kilt and sporran, jacket, stockings with garter flash, Glengarry bonnet, black Highland dancing pumps, with jabot and ruffles and skean dhu (dagger) optional; for women the tartan skirt, white blouse, jacket, hose and dancing pumps.

Scottish Official Board of Highland Dancing, 1955.

Outfit

In Latin-American dance, the term used for costume, shoes and jewellery worn by both men and women dancers in competitions.

Ruud Vermey, Interview.

Traditional costume

Clothing worn by a community for dancing, whose cut and weight influence the movement; wide heavy skirts billow out in turning and spinning, bells on the ankle sound well when stamping, narrow skirts lead to small stepping.

Robert Harrold, Interview.

Traditional costume

The Odissi style of South Indian dance, for women, in which "a silk saree", "with silver ornaments on head and ears, wristbands, armlets, and an elaborate belt", "ankle bells", "a necklace with a locket", "an elaborate hair-do in the form of a knot", "with garlands of flowers woven into the hair", "eye and eyebrow make-up", "the vermilion spot on the forehead", "red liquid on her palms and soles".

Leela Samson, 1987.

Uniform

The obligatory ballet class clothing for girls and boys which is designed to "reduce fussing during class" to aid concentration.

Anna Paskevska, 1990.

Wearing your strides

Being dressed up to go clubbing.

Portsmouth clubbers, interviewed by Donna Taylor.

2. HEAD AND HAIR

Hair styles

The designs for the hair used in ballets as part of costume design, such as a French roll, a French pleat, ringlets; the wig master prepares the hair pieces and assists the dancers as hairdresser at each performance.

Henry Menary, Interview.

Classical hair style
The traditional female hair style for classical ballets, a centre parting with curtains of hair covering the ears pulled back into a bun at the nape of the neck, secured by a net.
Henry Menary, Interview.

Hair as a message, The
The meaning carried by the style of the hair which may typically refer to a dance genre (romantic ballet hair, wig and pigtail), be indicative of characterisation (the long-haired poet, the long-haired innocent girl), be modish (Anderson's "Flesh and Blood"), be symbolic (the plaits of the Bride in Nijinska's "Les Noces"), flout convention (Ek's "Giselle"), be individual to the dancer (Bausch), or have other functions.
Eds.

Head-dresses
All manner of designed head decoration: Isamu Noguchi's crowns and hat-pins for Martha Graham, Natalie Gontcharova's bandeaus for Nijinska'a "Les Noces", Oliver Messel's crowns and plumes for "Sleeping Beauty"; all have to take into account their danceability, i.e. what the dancer has to do in them, as well as their designed images.
Eds.

Head-dress
The decoration on the head worn for folk dance, which affects the movements that can be performed, often inhibiting the movement; the mantilla, the sombrero, the cap, the kerchief.
Robert Harrold, Interview.

Wigs
The headgear used in ballet for character roles, period works, and for uniformity in the corps de ballet, such as full wigs, half wigs which use the dancer's own hair line, tonsure wigs for a bald head effect, powdered wigs.
Henry Menary, Interview.

Wig making
Starting from a lace foundation, fitting it for the dancer's head, marking it with the dancer's hair line, pinning the foundation to a wooden wig block, knotting each hair to cover the lace, and proceeding to dress it.
Henry Menary, Interview.

Dressing a wig
The process of washing, conditioning, curling, drying, and decorating a wig or hairpiece; curling tongs, rollers, pin curls, and finger waves might all be used.
Henry Menary, Interview.

Wig galoon

A thin hollow tape sewn around the edge of a wig, especially one for female opera dancers, through which a metal spring is threaded to keep the shape of the wig.

Henry Menary, Interview.

Wearing a wig

The process, for a female dancer, of wrapping her own hair as flatly as possible round her head, securing it with tape or a stocking, putting the wig on, pinning it in place and gluing it around the lace. Another technique which can be used for both males and females is the process of pin-curling the hair prior to putting the wig on.

Henry Menary, Interview.

3.   MAKE-UP

Make-up

"A ritual, the means through which you transform yourself into the character you hope to play".

Martha Graham, 1941.

Make-up

The province of the designer, who takes hair and face design as part of her domain.

Yolanda Sonnabend, Interview.

Slap

In Latin-American dance, a term used for make-up, including both face and whole body.

Ruud Vermey, Interview.

Body painting

Literally putting paint on the dancer's body rather than on a body stocking; partial or, in the case of Keith Haring's painting of Bill T. Jones, over every surface of the nude body.

Bill T. Jones and *Arnie Zane,* 1989.

Masks

Coverings for the face which carry a range of traditional characters and arche-types and also newly created ones:

"Basle masks, character masks, Commedia masks, Asian masks."

Helen Crocker and *Bim Mason,* Interview.

Masks

Usually animal masks cum head-dresses used in English ceremonial ritual dances, the stag, the horse, the rabbit.

Hugh Rippon, 1993.

4. FOOTWEAR

Barefoot

Originally a hallmark of modern dance, beginning with Isadora Duncan who danced barefoot as a symbol of the unadorned human body. Later modern dancers decided to work barefoot as it gives a sense of being closer to the earth than when wearing shoes, and the dancer's balance, whilst barefoot, is also more sure.

Mary Kerner, 1990.

Barefoot

The usual footwear for T'ai Chi indoors, when contact with the ground is valued; for outdoors, soft flexible-soled shoes are preferred.

Katherine Allen, Interview.

Clogs

Wooden and iron-soled shoes with leather uppers, which are worn by Morris dance teams in the North West tradition.

Hugh Rippon, 1993.

Flatties

Shoes worn in contemporary and ballet work; said in contrast to pointe shoes or character shoes or barefoot.

Eds.

Jazz shoes

Soft, flat-soled shoes with tie-up laces, basically black or white, but can be any colour.

Robert Audy, 1978.

Pointe shoes

Satin ballet slippers, blocked at the toe enabling the dancer to stand on the tips of the toes, so promoting virtuoso turns and balances for the ballerina; ocassionaly worn by men for particular effect.

Michael Clifford, Interview.

Pointe shoes

Hard-toed ballet shoes, custom-made for each dancer.

"with a high vamp and square pointe", "with a flat platform and a narrow box", "leather or cardboard shank", "C width at the toe, B width at the heel", "half shank and sides cut down".

Janice Barringer and *Sarah Schlesinger,* 1990.

Preparing pointe shoes

The process of getting a shoe ready for a performance, through padding the toe, sewing the ribbons, bending the shank, flattening the box, scouring the sole, protecting and de-slipping the tip; a procedure undertaken by each dancer to her own requirements.

Janice Barringer and *Sarah Schlesinger,* 1990.

Colour intensity
An ingredient in design in which primary (intense) colours are used with a variety of techniques to create diffuse or concentrated effects.
Beatrice Hart, Interview.

Monochromatic costumes
Individual costumes with variations within a small hue range.
Beatrice Hart, Interview.

Body outline
The quality of the outline of the costumed dancer.
Beatrice Hart, Interview.

Definition
The quality of the fabric of costumes and their cut to reinforce and clarify the content and intention of the movement; said of the silk and organza fabric and bias cutting of Laurie Booth costumes.
"...the flow and pulse in the fabric...".
Laurie Booth, Interview.

Shaped fabric
Fabric which clings to the body can stretch, and is given sculptural form by the movement; said of Graham's tricot tubing costume in "Lamentation" (1930).
Agnes de Mille, 1991.

Surface design
The patternings on a costume or set design.
Beatrice Hart, Interview.

Surface decoration
One design feature in costume making; 'flesh, bone and muscle', 'physiology of the human body' treated as surface decoration by Yolanda Sonnabend for MacMillan's "Requiem".
Yolanda Sonnabend, 1985.

Hard edged
A term used to describe the sharp division between one movement and the next, and one colour and the next in the costume.
Beatrice Hart, Interview.

Still body/moving body
The two states of the body in dance, both of which are considerations in designing costume.
Beatrice Hart, Interview.

Fabric movement
The way different materials respond to the dancer's movement, a design factor which must be taken into account when selecting fabric for a costume.
Barry Kay, 1981.

Fabric qualities
Costume materials which have visual, aural, and kinetic qualities; the cellophane and silk farthingale skirts in Jooss's "Pavane" which reflect the light giving a "harshness to the courtiers" and give an aural dimension to the sharpness of their movement.
Ana R. Sanchez-Colberg, 1992.

Fabric qualities
The properties that materials for costumes have when the designer manipulates them.
"For 'La Bayadère' it had a sheen", "a scrunch", "floppy movement", "graded from solid folded texture to transparency".
Yolanda Sonnabend, Interview.

Texturing technique
The designer's skill in using devices of fabric difference, such as shiny, see-through, jewelled, to provide the desired effect.
Beatrice Hart, Interview.

Layering technique
The designer's skill of placing one fabric on another to give the desired effect.
Beatrice Hart, Interview.

Playing with the effect
The process of trying out a design idea, to see how a costume will work in motion.
Beatrice Hart, Interview.

Create a style for the dancer, To
The process whereby a style of clothing used in dressmaking and tailoring has to be radically altered to accomodate to the needs of the dancer.
Beatrice Hart, Interview.

Language of change
Using costume change and set transformation to support key developments in the plot.
"...rags to riches in 'Manon', "...the curse in 'Sleeping Beauty'...".
Nicholas Georgiardis, Interview.

Dislocation

A radical change of image used as a metaphor for a dislocation in the ballet's plot.

"...pursued out of the palace into a totally empty place...", "...courtiers are human, then baboons...".

Nicholas Georgiardis, Interview.

Rehearsal clothes

What a dancer wears for class or rehearsal, which may be used in performances, such as in some Judson Church pieces.

Beatrice Hart, Interview.

Street clothes

Normal everyday wear which can be used in some dance performances.

Beatrice Hart, Interview.

Street clothes

Costumes which look like everyday wear but are made with 'dancer's cheats', suits possibly with trousers attached to an undervest, added anchoring devices to ensure that the costume is firmly in place.

Malcolm Steed, Interview.

Ballet costuming

Using specific devices, not needed in other theatre costume work, to enable the dancer to move without restriction and to feel that the costume is secure.

"anchoring under the crutch", "built-in gussets", "a waistband with elasticated sides", "a firm waistband for partnering".

The Birmingham Royal Ballet wardrobe dept., Interview.

Conventional

Limited in imaginative innovation, an inevitable attribute of ballet costumes for the main protagonists because they have to accomodate the traditions of ballet choreography.

Nicholas Georgiardis, Interview.

Language of colour

A main means for the ballet designer, where conventions of movement lead to limitations of costume possibilites, leaving colour as a means of metaphor.

Nicholas Georgiardis, Interview.

Tutu

The traditional short skirt made on a basque, with layers of net which stands horizontally out at hip level, variously sharper or softer in line, scalloped or pointed at the circumference, made integrally with the short frilled pants; sometimes used in classical ballets, such as "Swan Lake".

Audrey Ward, Interview.

Tutu

The conventional skirt which divides the body horizontally, so providing a definite design which the choreographer works with.
Ashley Page, Interview.

Romantic tutu

The long net skirt traditonally worn in romantic ballets, such as "Giselle", which may be varied by their length and number of net layers.
Audrey Ward, Interview.

Frillies

The pants worn under romantic tutus which are made with rows of soft net frills to help the skirt to billow out.
Audrey Ward, Interview.

Doublet

A much-used basic pattern for classical ballet male costumes, constructed to avoid decoration on the shoulders and front so that nothing can catch in pas de deux partnering and lifts, often made with sleeves on an undervest.
Malcolm Steed, Interview.

Morris fool, The

Garishly dressed dancer in the Cotswold Morris who may be dressed "as a man-woman", "a circus clown", "a simple shepherd".
"Odd coloured socks, a painted face, and a cow's bladder and cow's tail attached to a stick."
Hugh Rippon, 1993.

Ambulant architecture

One of the concepts of Oskar Schlemmer's "Triadisches Ballett" (1922) in which the dancer is sheathed in cubic blocks; so using costuming to link modern man with his spatial surroundings.
Lincoln Kirstein, 1971.

Character costumes

Clothing to enhance the particular roles the dancers play in the work; in "Enigma Variations" (1968) realism of a period and mood were given by Julia Trevelyan Oman with "tact, accuracy and rightness".
"...looked as if they had been worn by individuals who chose them with care."
Lincoln Kirstein, 1971.

Conflicting costumes

Bakst's costumes for "L'Après-Midi d'un Faune" (1912) reflecting the romantic, Hellenic-inspired anti-mechanisticism and emphasis on spiritual and human content of the Art Nouveau movement through their flowing lines, contrasting with the angularity of Nijinsky's choreography.
Hans H. Hofstätter, 1984(1968).

Cross-dressing

Men wearing women's clothing and women wearing men's clothing; a device used to "defamiliarise the existing universal gender definitions". It differs from transvestism in that "the men do not stop being men" nor stop doing "manly things". However, aspects of the 'other'/female (excluded from the original representation of male) are superimposed. The conventional attitudes to gender shift via the juxtaposition created by the layering of visual signs. Related to aspects of "gaming" via the strand of costume. Said of Pina Bausch, especially when she uses onstage costume changes.

Ana R. Sanchez-Colberg, 1992.

Period style

An ingredient of many ballets around which a designer can work or between which he can choose, for both set and costumes.

"French Regency for 'Manon' but I preferred late 18th century."

Nicholas Georgiardis, Interview.

Pastiche in design

Costumes made to evoke the culture of a place and time; said of Bakst's virtuoso c.18 designs for the 1921 "Sleeping Princess" for Diaghilev's Ballets Russes, or his oriental evocation for "Scheherazade" (1910), or ancient Greece for "Daphnis and Chloe" (1913).

Richard Buckle, 1981.

Radical costuming

Marked changes in the style of costume for dancers, exemplified in the transparent draperies favoured by Isadora Duncan which were in sharp contrast to the corset, bodice, ballet tutus and shoes of her peers and which facilitated the expression of her new freedom in dance.

Michelle Potter, 1990.

Revealing

Costumes designed to show the dancer's body, through using transparent materials, employing low necklines, bare midriffs, cut out designs; said of Leon Bakst's designs which could be said to 'add to the structure of the movement' and to have possible salacious content.

Michelle Potter, 1990.

Uniforms

Unison costuming designed to completely eliminate individual differences of characterisation while allowing for some individual difference of the wearer; used by Natalie Gontcharova in "Les Noces" (1923) to contribute to the "noble starkness" of the Russian peasant in coarse brown-black and natural linen.

Lincoln Kirstein, 1971.

Tights and T-shirt

Balanchine's choice of costume for several ballets, to allow the movement and the dancers' performance of it to dominate the ballet.

Richard Buckle, 1981.

Unitard

The all-in-one leotard used as a basis for many contemporary designers; the material in which they are made, how they reflect light, as well as their cut at neck and arm, being of design interest.

Eds.

Body stocking

The all-in-one tights to which may be added (or taken away) paint, appliqué, holes, drapes, dye; Nadine Baylis's netting for Glen Tetley's "Ziggurat" (1967), Joan Miró's asymmetry in Boris Kochno's "Jeux d'Enfants" (1932), white allovers with symbolic head-dress, or scarf or minimal cloak by Jean Hugo for Roland Petit's "Les Amours de Jupiter" (1946).

Richard Buckle, 1981.

Body stocking

The all-over tights; elasticated material clinging to the contours of the body.

Richard Buckle, 1981.

Quasi-nudity

The body stocking which when introduced into costume design in the 1920's was seen as presentation of the naked body, emphasising the dancer's body, musculature and bone structure, rather than character or persona.

Richard Buckle, 1981.

Realistic costumes

Costumes which denote a place, race, status, person, courtiers, villagers, et al., so denying the audience the opportunity to discern for themselves through costumes that only suggest places etc.

Richard Buckle, 1981.

Period styles

Costumes in a historical setting (or a national setting) "from which the designer's fantasy may take over"; said of André Derein's designs for "La Boutique Fantasque" (1919).

Richard Buckle, 1981.

Spectacles

Productions like "The Sleeping Beauty" which allow the designer to provide insights into courtly splendour, such as Barry Kay's Catherine the Great/Alexander III (1967) scenes and Nicholas Georgiadis's glories of Louis XIV (1975).

Richard Buckle, 1981.

Skips

Large baskets used for the transport of costume accessories and props on tour.
Lili Sobieralska, Interview.

7. THE COSTUME AND THE DANCER

Fitting call

An appointment made by the wardrobe supervisor for the casts of a ballet in repertory to fit the costume; usually two calls are arranged.
Lili Sobieralska, Interview.

Feeling comfortable (dancer)

The dancer's need on wearing a costume, both physically and emotionally.
Beatrice Hart, Interview.

Tension

The uneasy relationship of the movement and the costume, not a matter of settling for something comfortable to wear but adding a layer, possibly conflicting, to the movement and uncomfortable for the dancer.
Lea Anderson, Interview.

Feeling exposed — vulnerable (dancer)

How a dancer can feel in costumes cut to expose the body to view.
Beatrice Hart, Interview.

Dancer's alienation

How a costume, uncomfortable either physically or emotionally, can inhibit a dancer's performance.
Beatrice Hart, Interview.

Find ways around it, To

To accomodate a costume design to the feelings of the dancer.
Beatrice Hart, Interview.

PART THREE: MOVEMENT

Collecting the entries for this part was problematic. The non-verbal nature of movement was only too evident. In the studio, efforts to communicate were often vocal, without actual words, especially for getting at the qualities of new movement-in-the-making, plus, of course, demonstration. Technical terms were the usual currency with established vocabularies, but they give us no more than well-known terminology. Images, counts with intonation, singing and clapping abounded as other means. None of this richness can be included here. It was in the coaching of repertory, in the detailed instruction in one-to-one lessons, in textbooks, in the works of kinetically educated writers, and from modern/contemporary choreographers at work that words for the ingredients of movement emerged. Sectioning these was also problematic but the well-known notion of what moves, how and where, gave the most coherent triple perspective of the efforts made to verbalise movement content. So the Chapters are THE MOVING BODY, DYNAMICS AND TIMING, SPACE-IN-THE-BODY AND THE DANCER IN SPACE. Even then, poetic movement can sound prosaic.

How movements are put together or flow together, make phrases and sequences, motifs and enchaînements, figures and routines is included in the Chapter CHOREOGRAPHIC FORM. How the dancer dances the movement is given in THE PERFORMER AND THE MOVEMENT. How it is rehearsed is in REPERTORY, REVIVAL AND TRADITION.

Documenting the movement on paper is described and discussed here in the Chapter on NOTATION; the skills involved, the established methods employed, and some idiosyncratic and supporting means are included. The sections on Labanotation and Benesh are limited since both have textbooks which discuss their grammer and orthography, thoroughly. The discussion of score writing and reading, given here, leads on to the professional practice of Benesh choreologists and Labanotators in the rehearsal studio, in reconstructions and mounting of repertoire. For those entries see the Chapter on REPERTORY, REVIVAL AND TRADITION.

Chapter 7 MOVEMENT AND THE MOVING BODY

1. MOVEMENT

Movement

"One of man's languages."
Rudolf Laban, 1966 (1939).

Dancers' language

A non-verbal but real language which includes timing, memory, placement, and risk.
David Buckland and *Siobhan Davies,* Seminar.

Movement

The primordial means of expression and communication between men, through which early man revealed his ideas.
Roderyk Lange, 1975.

Movement as dance material

"...what the dance work is made of."
Eleanore W. Gwynne, 1978.

Movement

"...a cluster of spatial and dynamic elements combined with a particular use of the body in action...".
Janet Adshead, 1988.

Moving

"Movement doesn't happen to you, you make it happen."
Rosemary Brandt, Interview.

Choreology

"...the study and description of the movements of dancing."
'Concise Oxford Dictionary', 1990.

Choreological order

The hidden rules in movement; "that which holds our movement together".
Rosemary Brandt, Interview.

Choreological terminology

Technical terms and phrases developed to address the needs of the dancer to go beyond "learning movements", and so enable the teacher and the student (equally the choreographer and the dancer) to deal with the necessary processes explicitly.

Rosemary Brandt, Interview.

Bodily actions

Movements of the whole body, "...the various articulations in the body, ...creating rhythmical and spatial patterns, but also the mood and inner attitude produced by bodily actions."

Rudolf Laban, 1950.

Five structural components of movement, The

"The five structural ingredients of movement, that is the body, the actions, the rhythm/dynamics, the space-in-the-body, relationships."

Valerie Preston-Dunlop, 1987.

'Star', The

The colloquial term for the ways a dancer can refine her movement, and can find new movement; the five points of the star are the body and its co-ordination, the actions performed, their dynamics and timing, their spatial form, the relationship within the body and with the environment; a Choreological Studies term.

Athina Vahla, Teaching.

Factors of motion

The three contributory elements of motion: spatial factors, temporal factors, force aspects.

Aileene Lockhart and *Esther E. Pease,* 1977 (1966).

Four motion factors

Weight, space, time, flow, the four factors in movement for which intention can be given by the mover — and which can be discerned by the observer or audience.

Rudolf Laban, 1971 (1950).

Motion

"Movement is the gross or general pattern of action, and motion the inner itinerary that qualifies it and distinguishes it as dance."; the ability to achieve metamorphosis resting with the dancer.

Alwin Nikolais in Murray Louis, 1980.

Kinetic values

From "...gross in character..." to "[with]...sensitivity towards the inner detail.";
"The dancer does refine certain kinetic values but too often he touches upon space, time and gravity only to the extent necessary to support his kinetic interest. Most of the rest is left to accident or subconscious experience."

Alwin Nikolais, 1964.

Action
>A movement which has intention.
>*Andrée Grau,* Interview.

Waffling around
>Moving with no clear definition: something a dancer has to learn to work through.
>*Jane Dudley,* Interview.

Integrity of the movement
>The quality of the material that a dancer has in improvisation, a quality that is based on some conceptual framework and on the sensitivity of the mover to his body.
>*Laurie Booth,* Interview.

Expressive element
>The ingredient in dance movement which emerges through details of tension, through relationship of body parts to each other and to the space, sometimes together with an image.
>*Els Grelinger,* Interview.

Narrative
>The story line of each movement in a phrase, its initiation, which gives the dancer a way of feeling, thinking, and doing.
>"...as if you are moving a curtain aside...", "...as if you are pushing away with resistance...".
>*Lea Anderson,* Interview.

Imagining
>The inner narrative of a dancer's movement given by the choreographer, or may be provided by the dancer for her/himself.
>"Throw the whole thing down."; said of an arm movement.
>*Lea Anderson,* Interview.

As if
>Words frequently used to find the intention of a gesture, to avoid simply moving the body and to achieve a movement which reads for the audience.
>"...as if something shocking has happened...".
>*Lea Anderson,* Interview.

2.   MOVEMENT VOCABULARIES

Vocabulary
>"...a set of artistic or stylistic forms or techniques, esp. a range of set movements in ballet etc."
>*'Concise Oxford Dictionary',* 1990.

Movement vocabulary

The choices of movement made by a choreographer for one work, the vocabulary of that piece.

"Small, careful, reflective movement, built up brick by brick."
Siobhan Davies, 1988.

Personal vocabularies

The movement resources which a choreographer has at his disposal and from which he will select, "possibly instinctually", for each work.

I learnt "acrobatic, ballet, tap, release work, character, had influences from Graham, the Rambert School, Sokolow, Tudor.....".
Christopher Bruce, Interview.

Idiosyncratic steps

The vocabulary developed by a choreographer and communicated to the dancers largely by demonstration, assisted by counting and words.

"...triplet but small, on the 3..."; "...chassé, chase the foot, 5, 6..."; "...lunge with her learning on your back..."; "push, hook, coupé back on the 7, coupé forward"; "parallel first, open second"; "lift your head on the 5, 2."
Twyla Tharp, Informal talk.

Lexicon

"...the vocabulary of a person, language, branch of knowledge, etc". [established, capable of being handed down as a tradition. Eds.].
'Concise Oxford Dictionary', 1990.

Idioms

Movement vocabularies and dance styles which are "products of distinct cultures and represent attitudes towards character and emotion peculiar to those cultures"; said of classical ballet, of flamenco, or jazz, or Hindu dance, et al.
Selma Jeanne Cohen, 1967.

Received corpus of steps

The footwork vocabulary of Bharatha Natyam handed down from one generation of dancers to the next.
Shobana Jeyasingh, 1993.

Physical language

Movement material in a clearly defined style, presented by one artist or one company such as Adzido, or by a group of artists as in New Dance or Physical Theatre.
Maggie Semple, 1992.

Movement language

Choices of movement material made specifically by one choreographer for one work.
Rosemary Butcher, Interview.

Existing codes

A term for vocabularies of movement which are established and recognised and which choreographers use and adapt for their own purposes.
Stephanie Jordan, 1992.

Classical language

The Bharata Natyam dance language, considered as classical because "it is traditional, not associated with an individual in its inception, specific, even rigid, a tangible base"; "It takes for granted the desirability to create an idealised body."
Shobana Jeyasingh, Interview.

Folk dance vocabulary

Runs, skips, hops, jumps, weaving steps, stamps, turns, danced according to the rhythms of the music.
"Side-behind-side-hop, side-in front-behind-step-stamp."
Robert Harrold, Interview.

Danse d'école

The traditional academic ballet vocabulary passed on and developed by the conservatoire.
"At no step in the classic pedagogy is there room for improvisation, experiment or doubt. The academy is not choreography any more than finger exercises are music. Without in themselves pretending to art or encouraging premature self-expression, both are stuff from which art derives."
Lincoln Kirstein and *Muriel Stuart,* 1977 (1952).

Science, A

The purity of the vocabulary of ballet, a rich resource from which new dance material can be found.
Ashley Page, Interview.

Material

What dances are made of; maybe viewed narrowly as specialised dance vocabularies or more widely as embracing all the actions which the body can do.
"...any movement...",
Laurie Booth, Interview.

Small material

Gestural movement which is on a particularly small scale, finger moves, eyebrow, tiny shoulder twists, and shifts of weight; movement which is just as clear in space and time as full-size movement.
Lea Anderson, Interview.

Song gestures

Movement in a performance setting which is regarded by the performers as belonging to song, a term in anthropological study.
Andrée Grau, Interview.

Alternative movement

Material which is not associated with fixed dance vocabularies but which emerges through motivations, methods and processes which deliberately conjure original movement material, possibly in association with words, props, costumes et al.

Ana Sanchez-Colberg, 1992.

Abstract movement vocabulary

"The dynamic fulfilment of a movement makes up its dramatic content. The body action — its shape, its weight, its rhythm — constitutes the movement's meaning."

Murray Louis, 1980.

Allegro

"This is the foundation of the science of dance, its intricacy and the bond for future perfection; dance as a whole is built on the allegro."

Agrippina Vaganova 1969 (1946).

Allegro

"...from the Italian, meaning lively and rather fast. Used to describe all movements of this nature."

Richard Glasstone, 1977.

Bournonville vocabulary

"A language of dance which deliberately avoids all 'excesses' of virtuosity and passion."

Erik Bruhn and *Lillian Moore, 1961.*

Categories of step in classical ballet

There are seven: 1. Poses; 2. Transitory or preparatory steps; 3. Elevation; 4. Ports de bras; 5. Batterie; 6. Pirouettes; 7. Pointe.

Joan Lawson, 1960.

Terre à terre

Literally 'ground to ground'. Applied to movements done close to and along the ground.

Richard Glasstone, 1977.

Mime alphabet

Using the human form as the starting point, movement elements used to act convincingly, in appropriate proportion to the dramatic stimulus, those actions to the point where they are not only true psychologically, but visually striking; said of Étienne Decroux's work.

Alvin Epstein, 1958.

Materials of mime

Without costuming, with a mask and with words forbidden, the mime improvises with his torso, his arms and his legs; these are his materials; said of Étienne Decroux.

Alvin Epstein, 1958.

Basic qualities of mime

"Design, rhythm and intensity are the basic qualities which motivate the work of the mime artist"; said of Étienne Decroux.
Baird Hastings, 1950.

Natural movement

"...however far the movement departs from the actual practices of life movement, however much the movement style employs formalizations and distortions in its making of 'art', it always retains a clear sense of the normal body.... The movement is able to range freely in response to inner direction because it is so closely related to natural function...".
John Martin in Walter Sorell, 1976.

Familiar motion

The basic vocabulary of Isadora Duncan "familiar to all races".
"Walking, running, skipping, jumping, kneeling, reclining, rising."
Irma Duncan, 1970.

Pedestrian movement

A source of movement for choreographers, generated from the everyday behaviour and functional motion of ordinary people going about their business.
Eds.

Mundane movement

All kinds of movement which occur in everyday living.
Paul Filmer, Interview.

Social gestures

The well-known and immediately recognisable gestures of a society which, when used in dance, communicate their meaning at once.
Doris Humphrey, 1959.

Social action

Movement which is interpersonal, which occurs in interactional exchange of a kinetic sort.
Paul Filmer, Interview.

Action without interaction

Movement which has no interpersonal content.
Paul Filmer, Interview.

Functional gestures

Gestures which have been developed for an everyday practical use placed out of context in dance.
Doris Humphrey, 1959.

Occupational rhythms

The rhythms arising from the repetition of a work action or a sequence of different work actions; these are formed into dance-like movement, as can be found in some folk dance, or could originate from urban work habits.
Rudolf Laban, 1948.

Sport

Movement material borrowed from sport...jogging, kicking, dodging, back somersault, vaults, and balances.
Deborah Jowitt, 1977.

Gym material

Movement vocabulary for a dance collected from the sparring bouts of boxers studied in a training gymnasium; used by Bhuller in "Heart of Chaos" (1993).
Darshan Singh Bhuller, Interview.

Prop-derived

Movement material which emerges from the possibilites of using an object; of a tyre in Bruce's "Waiting" (1993), rolling it, balancing on it, sitting on it, twisting it, throwing it, catching it on your foot, lying on it.
Christopher Bruce, Interview.

Repertoire of gestures

A stock of regularly used movement made from the body of signs which originate in everyday life; gestures of affection, of dominance, of childhood games, of description, of self-assertion, of bonding, of directing the traffic, of grooming, and so on.
Valerie Preston-Dunlop, Seminar.

Mimetic of the whole body

A principle of Fokine's New Ballet.
"...the new ballet admits the use of conventional gesture only where it is required by the style of the ballet, and in all other cases endeavours to replace gestures of the hands by mimetic of the whole body."
Michel Fokine, 1914.

Pantomime

"Pantomime is movements that are too representative to be part of dance....like a deaf and dumb actor."
Louis Horst, 1958.

Shadow movements

"Tiny muscular movements such as the raising of the brow, the jerking of the hand, the tapping of the foot which have none other than expressive value."
Rudolf Laban, 1971 (1950).

Habitual movement

Movement which is taken for granted, which occurs without the mover being neccessarily aware of it.

Paul Filmer, Interview.

Floor vocabulary

Movement material which arises out of a dancer's strong physical relation to the floor, with or without another dancer.

Mark Murphy, Interview.

Given an earth

Classical ballet with real jazz, the exciting mix which gives the essential vocabulary of ballet a grounding by the basic qualities of jazz movement.

Gillian Lynne, Interview.

Vernacular jazz dance movement

"The rich verbal vocabulary of vernacular jazz dance movement often reflects the movement character and body usage. Break Down, Juba, Ring Shout, Cakewalk, Coonjine, Buzzard Lope, Buck and Wing, Pigeon and Chicken Wing, Stomp, Black Bottom, Snake Hips, Fishtail, Camel Walk, Eagle Rock Charleston, and the famed Lindy Hop are just a few. Rock, Twist, Hully Gully, Pony, Monkey, Mashed Potatoes, Break Dance and Hip Hop are among the more recent examples evidencing the strength of the traditional roots and their continued influence."

Walter Nicks, Contributed.

Breaking sequences

Break dance vocabulary; the simplest version was entry (into the ring made by spectators), footwork, spin on head, shoulder or hand, freeze an individual flash of inverted stillness, and exit back into the circle.

Sally Banes in Nelson George et al, 1985.

Basic tap steps

The vocabulary is built up from elements such as the brush, the catch back, the heel drop, cells such as the shuffle, tap-step, ball change, motifs such as the time step, the break, the shim sham.

James Siegelman in Mary Clarke and David Vaughan, 1977.

Tap routines

Combinations of basic steps designed to produce distinct moods, such as the calm, soft shoe routine, the snappy carefree 3-beat treat, the energetic time step saga.

Roy Castle, 1986.

Movements (in country dance)

The actions of each individual and those which can only be done by two people which contribute the basic vocabulary with which the figures of the dance are accomplished; they include the honour, the balance, the turn, the swing, the single, the double, arming, handing, and leading.

Cecil J. Sharp, 1934 (1909).

Step figures

Country dance vocabulary.

"Promenade, balance, swing, circle singles and doubles, polka, waltz, casting right and left, advance, retire, change places, allemande."

Douglas Kennedy, 1968 (1949).

Figures

Established patterns of "concerted evolution" which provide the vocabulary of country dances in contrast to intricate step patterns.

Cecil J. Sharp, 1934 (1909).

Morris-figures

The basic vocabulary of Morris dances; although similar in type they take a different form with each team; they include the gyp, the hey, a hands-around, a back-to-back, the galley.

Peter Buckman, 1978.

Morris vocabulary

Morris dances are made up of figures, that is the way the 6 dancers make spatial paths around each other, of steps, and of hand movements which include the way handkerchiefs are moved or sticks are hit or hands clapped; these patterns are associated with particular localities, for example, within the Cotswold Morris, villages in that area.

Roy Judge, Interview.

Morris steps

The basic vocabulary of travelling steps, made up of spring doubles (or 4-step) and singles (2-step), back steps, side steps, jumps off two feet, galleys, and capers; these are combined into figures and choruses.

Anthony G. Barrand, 1991.

Highland vocabulary

Hop, assemble, disassemble, spring; change and leap from 5th position, pas de basque; the shake, the cut, the balance and the rock; the toe-and-heel and heel-and-toe touches; the shed, the shuffle and the pivot turn.

Scottish Official Board of Highland Dancing, 1955.

Steps

In Highland Dancing the step is a combination of two or more positions which form the basis on which the style is founded.

Scottish Official Board of Highland Dancing, 1955.

Foot positions

The basic material from which Highland Dancing steps are formed; the closed positions, open position in which the working foot is in contact with the supporting leg or not, ground and aerial positions in which the working leg is in contact with the ground or not, and the rear position.

Scottish Official Board of Highland Dancing, 1955.

Supporting foot, working foot

The foot which supports the weight of the body, and the foot which is gesturing.
Scottish Official Board of Highland Dancing, 1955.

Arm positions

The five basic positions which are the only ones used in Highland Dancing; hands on hips, hands over head, hands low in front and two asymmetric combinations.
Scottish Official Board of Highland Dancing, 1955.

Hold figures

Country dance vocabulary.
"Swinging, chain, right hands left hands, crossed hands, arches, ballroom hold, all join hands."
Douglas Kennedy, 1968 (1949).

Circle holds

The grasps used in folk dance with a circular formation.
"Hold on shoulders, hold the belt, the V hold, the W hold, the T hold, the front basket and back basket; opened out or tightly closed together; with little fingers only."
Robert Harrold, Interview.

Partner holds

The grasps which are used in folk and social dances.
"Back grasp, social hold, open social, courtesy turn, promenade hold, peasant hold, open shoulder and waist hold, the allemande hold, barrel hold, czardas hold."
Robert Harrold, Interview.

Irish step-dance vocabulary

From movements, such as, stepping, stamping, toe and heel drops, leaps, hops, jumps, throws, kicks, heel strikes, toe touches, tipping, cutting, batters, and rocks, etc., intricate motifs are made to fit in with the accompanying music.
Catherine Foley, 1988.

Square dance vocabulary

The figures of the 4 couples in each set of a square dance; examples are: circle left, honor, swing and twirl, do sa do, make a star, promenade, weave the ring, allemande, and grand chain.
Betty Casey, 1976.

Movement (in baroque dance)

"...a bending of the knees followed by a stretching of the knees (which could be extended by lifting the heels and standing on [demi] pointe), or a rise into the air in a spring."
Wendy Hilton, 1981.

Movement (in baroque dance)

"...a preliminary sink, a bend of both knees but with the weight on only one foot, followed by a rise and a return to the normal level."
Belinda Quirey, 1987.

Figure (in baroque dance)

A floor pattern within a baroque dance, usually completed to one musical strain.
Wendy Hilton, 1981.

Social dance as material

Vocabulary from social dance (such as the Tango, the Foxtrot, the Cancan) which is part of the movement material of a theatre work used as fragments interspersed with other material, as a source to be manipulated, and expanded or distorted, as material for one couple alongside other material by the ensemble, and so on.
Eds.

Mime-actor as prop

Becoming, not a character, but an object which is subject to powers greater than himself, earthquakes, storms, thrown into war, buffeted.
Étienne Decroux, in Alvin Epstein, 1958.

Mime actor as ideal

One of the phases in the mime's alphabet where he is transfigured, removed from the mundane, each limb seeming to have serene independence.
Étienne Decroux, in Alvin Epstein, 1958.

Figures

In ballroom dancing, the steps which constitute the basic form of each dance, taken in diagonal lines towards the centre of the ballroom or out from it.
"The feather step, reverse turn, the 3-step, the natural turn".
Geoffrey Hearn, Interview.

Fifties Rock basic

A more advanced repertoire of basic actions for the gent and lady such as the handshake, bepop, Suzie Q, cruising, stomp, rubber legs, swing.
Derek Young, 1991.

Rock basic

The six basic changes of place in Rock 'n' Roll dancing, using the basic moves of sway, step, replace, turn, and the basic partner moves of pull turns, push, catch, push, spin, and pull spin.
Derek Young, 1991.

Classical language

The vocabulary of an established dance style, such as Bharatha Natyam, the classical dance of South India.
Shobana Jeyasingh, 1993.

Bharata Natyam

The South Indian dance form, "rooted in Hindu myth and custom", in which ten body postures, steps and jumps, and the known hand positions form the central movement material.
Leela Samson, 1987.

Manipuri

A form of South Indian classical dance in which the praise of Krishna is central, and whose style is "never aggressive but tender and reticent; movements of the body are not accentuated, they are subtly suggested: tremendous effort is required to give the Manipuri style its apparent effortless quality."
Leela Samson, 1987.

Odissi

A classical Indian dance, associated with the Shiva temples, whose material is symmetric and markedly asymmetric postures "which express particular moods", together with positions of the feet and heels, kinds of gait, turns, floor patterns; it is "lyrical perhaps due to the curved, rolling and spiral nature of the style."
Leela Samson, 1987.

Aerial vocabulary

The basic movements and positions of work on a trapeze or bars, which can be used for an act, in a competition, or as part of a choreography.
"Skinning the cat, half angel, birds nest, drops, drop to half angel".
Helen Crocker and *Bim Mason,* Interview.

Manipulation

Movement material from circus which consists in the skill of manipulating two or more objects, such as juggling, devil stick, club swinging, diabolo, balancing objects.
Helen Crocker and *Bim Mason,* Interview.

Aerial work

That part of circus skills which consists in movement on static and swinging trapeze, flying, and web rope cradle.
'Fool Time', 1992/93.

Equilibrists

That part of circus skills which consists in the variety of acrobatic balancing: stilt walking, unicycling, rola bola, slack wire, tight wire, walking globe.
'Fool Time', 1992/93.

Acrobatics

The skills of tumbling, hand balances and flight, together with balances in pairs and groups, derived from circus but also used in other performance arts.

'Fool Time', 1992/93.

Physical theatre vocabulary

A movement vocabulary used by several choreographers, developed from circus and tumbling skills together with dance skills, leading to a physical vocabulary strong in acrobatic and aerial (trapeze) work.

"Dance Theatre Journal," 1992(a).

Postures

"Positions found in the Hand and Weapon Forms, often with names connected with Chinese culture and mythology, e.g. Needle at Deep Sea Bottom, Embrace Tiger, Return to Mountain, Fair Lady Works at Shuttle."

Katherine Allen, 1993.

Opening and closing

The discharging and gathering the ch'i (breath energy) connected to the differentiation of 'substantial' and 'insubstantial' weight bearing, and so to movements from down to up (opened) and from up to down (closed); said in T'ai Chi.

"When you know opened and closed then you know yin and yang".

Li I-yu in B.P.J. Lo, M. Inn, R. Amacker, and S. Foe, 1985.

Thirteen postures

The basic vocabulary of T'ai Chi made up from the eight trigrams and the five elements.

"Ward off, rollback, press, push, pull, spit, elbow, shoulder; and forward, back, left, right, and centre equilibrium."

Chang San Feng in B.P.J. Lo, M. Inn, R. Amacker, and S. Foe, 1985.

Ritual gestures

Movements that generate from religion, the ancient world, etc., such as the gesture of praying.

Doris Humphrey, 1959.

Moon walk, The

Michael Jackson's movement signature.

Oprah Winfrey in Michael Jackson, 1993.

Mixed vocabulary

Dance movement which shifts from one coded vocabulary to another, a stylistic feature of much contemporary dance; from ballet to the mundane.

"...chassé step, reach away...".

Scott Clark, Class.

Grafting

Fusing gestural material on to vocabularies of steps; said of Ashton's subtle characterisation in "Enigma Variations".
Deborah Jowitt, 1977.

Non-dancers' scope

Starting from the daily language of movement we all share, leading to body shapes, held gestures, walks; avoiding difficult co-ordination, avoiding rhythmic complexity for actors, but using it for singers; avoiding jumps and spins, but leg gestures can usually be tackled.
"Stuff that can go into their bodies."
Stuart Hopps, Interview.

3.   POSITION AND PROCESS

Positions

"Positions are places you pass through."
Rosemary Brandt, Teaching.

Position and change

"How to go from one step to another is one of the key questions of dancing. At the same time, the position, once you get where you're going, has to be clear."
Merce Cunningham and *Jacqueline Lesschaeve,* 1985.

Pattern and position

The linear pattern of the body as it moves through space; how the body goes from position to position.
"The position is the end of the movement, a way of registering a poetic image through stillness."
Doris Rudko, Interview.

Body attitude

Those qualities which are maintained in the person, in which body part relationships and tensions, spatial and shape emphases, and effort factors are held "as a kind of baseline from which a mover operates".
Janis Pforsich, Ellen Goldman, John Chanik, and *Lynn Wenning,* Contributed.

Movement processes

The body, effort, shape, and space changes which take place in the body during a movement event; said in contrast to elements which are maintained in a posture or body attitude.
Janis Pforsich, Ellen Goldman, John Chanik, and *Lynn Wenning,* Contributed.

Stillness

"...is not merely a matter of being static. It may arise from repose or...be pregnant with action."

Alan Salter, 1977.

Stillness

A major ingredient of Butcher's live installations, in which performers interact with, or are placed beside, visual installations that are still; a positive visual ingredient of a work with qualities of duration.

Rosemary Butcher, Interview.

Pause

A bodily action arrested.

Rudolf Laban, 1971 (1950).

Space hold/body hold

A concept from Labanotation used in rehearsal to clarify what is to be maintained in the next movement.

Lea Anderson, Interview.

Incomplete gesture

A movement arrested before it is finished.

Anna Markard, Rehearsal.

Arrested gesture

Using the device of interrupting a movement before it is finished, halting it halfway, which can give an impression of psychological stress; said of Douglas Dunn.

Sally Banes, 1980.

Dance gesture

"...is not a static position but a movement happening. This movement happening has inherent in it the various forms of polarity, such as stable or labile equilibrium, counter movements of body parts, symmetry and asymmetry, central and peripheral orientation, growing and shrinking, gravitational pull and levitation, recurrence and free rhythmicality, increase and decrease, relatedness and relationship."

Sylvia Bodmer, 1962.

Natural flow

The transition from one position to another which the choreographer has to find and which either goes with the momentum and weight of the movement or against it.

"If we went into it on relevé...", "I don't know where you turn from", "Yes, you would do that from there".

David Bintley, Rehearsal.

Transitions
"These are unstressed passages and their function is to lead from one statement to the other, connecting and at the same time separating the more important sections."
Lilla Bauer, 1965.

Transitions
The linking passages between one movement event and another; the way choreographers deal with transition is as much a part of their style as the making of the main material.
Valerie Preston-Dunlop, Interview.

Transition
The movement between two other movements and/or other positions; the part of the phrase which is crucial to style but often overlooked.
"Reach, then use your back to reach the other side."
Robert Cohan, Company class.

Transition
The way into a movement, the joining of one movement with another.
"That's the best way to come out of the spin. Move on into your promenade."
Geoffrey Hearn, Instructing.

Links
Transitions between movements which can lead to a continuous phrase of movement, "...one continuous linking flow."
Christopher Bruce, Rehearsal.

Linking steps
Transitional steps, possibly a pas de bourrée or glissade, often used as "preparations for something impressive" or as Balanchine choreographed them, "falls worked, so that they deserve the attention of the dancers and the audience."
Merrill Ashley, 1984.

Discrete changes
"Changes in motion which are clearly divided, (which many are not) have a starting time and place and a finishing time and place."
Valerie Preston-Dunlop, 1981.

Movement context
Movement occurring before and after a particular action of the human body, and partially conditioning it.
"A detail must be understood within the movement context. What has happened before and comes afterwards very often conditions the appearance of details."
Roderyk Lange, 1985.

Preparation

The essential beginning part of much movement, the 'and' of dance vocabularies. "...that is the preparation for the jump...".
Scott Clark, Class.

Preparation

The usual preparatory movement before the main action, but one which a choreographer sometimes decides to hide or to omit altogether.

"No preparation; go straight up."; said rehearsing Ashton's "Symphonic Variations".
Michael Somes, Rehearsal.

Active and passive movement

A distinction made between movements which initiate a change and movements which are caused to change by being pushed, carried along, dragged, touched, etc.
Rudolf Laban, 1956.

Cycle of becoming

In T'ai Chi, the way one movement quality (Yin) contains the seed of another (Yang) and becomes it in continuous exchange; contrasted to the Western concept of bipolar opposition.
Katherine Allen, Interview.

Present

The totally aware state in T'ai Chi of being in the action as it evolves, rather than moving towards a posture or moving away from the previous one.
Katherine Allen, Interview.

4.   ACTIONS

Action

One of the essential components of movement, jumping, turning, travelling, transferring weight, gesturing, twisting, contracting, extending, overbalancing, and holding still.
Valerie Preston-Dunlop, 1981.

Action-motivated movement

A dance movement, performed by a person with intention, "with a premise"; said of Limón style.
Carla Maxwell, Interview.

Simple movement

"...walking, running, sitting, lying, rolling, lunging, jumps, turns."
Sally Banes, 1980.

Activities

Basic movement material used in the preparation of physical theatre and performance art, including bending, falling, catching, lifting, sitting, kneeling, and other everyday movement categories.

Helen Crocker and *Bim Mason,* Interview.

Pure movement

Neither functional nor pantomimic, simply mechanical body actions like bending, straightening, or rotating with a neutral context.

"...movement that has no other connotations...".

Trisha Brown, 1987.

Categories of movement in ballet

In the Cecchetti method there are seven movement categories: i) plier(bend), ii) étendre(stretch), iii) relever(rise), iv) glisser(slide), v) sauter(jump), vi) élancer(dart), vii) tourner(turn).

Cyril W. Beaumont and *Stanislas Idzikowski,* 1975.

Articulation of action

Precision in what kind of action is needed to achieve the step, and in what order.

"Not turning, it's stepping and swinging. It's step, brush, kick. Do your spot turn and then change hands."

Geoffrey Hearn, Instructing.

Commitment to the action

"Hold on to the integrity of the movement — don't lose the travelling, that's the impulse for the movement; don't let the attention to detail rob the movement of its original impulse; let it all enhance the travelling."

Rosemary Brandt, Teaching.

Basic building blocks, The

The actions of which movement is comprised, investigated in the first stages of exploring in the Language of Dance Teaching Approach; also called "the raw material of movement".

Ann Hutchinson Guest, Interview.

Actions with props

An inventory of moves made with properties, such as the bricks in Wim Vandekeybus's "Roseland".

"Throw, catch, pass, carry, drop, pick up, handle, grasp, release, smooth, penetrate, surround, etc."

Eds.

4a. EQUILIBRIUM AND TRANSFERENCE OF WEIGHT

Equilibrium
The state one gains when returning to a stable base, and loses when moving into lability.
Rudolf Laban, 1956.

Stance (in Cunningham style)
"...the place from which the body can move in any direction at any speed, without hesitation, without stammering."
Edwin Denby, 1968.

Center of weight
"The center of gravity, or center of weight, is that point in the body from which or on which the body can be suspended or poised in equilibrium... The center of gravity has no fixed location in the body, its exact position depending on the build of the individual and on the position taken."
Ann Hutchinson, 1970.

Balance
What every dancer needs to find and to feel through sensing the center line through the torso and hips down to the supporting leg.
"You must be over the knee."; "Don't fall on to it."; "You'll be out of balance if you use your head like that."
Geoffrey Hearn, Instructing.

Decentralization
"The creation and use of a fluid center", "moving the center to any part of the body", "leading to the production of unpredictable and rhythmically complex movement."; said of Alwin Nikolais's work.
Murray Louis, 1980.

Mobility
Occurs in two kinds: stable and labile.
Rudolf Laban, 1966 (1939).

Labile
Those moments in movement which tend to take the body off-balance and continuously change the balance through the use of oblique directions rather than the vertical, resolving themselves into a stable state as the weight becomes vertical.
Valerie Preston-Dunlop, 1987.

Poise (in Latin American)
    The man's poise is forward, on the front of the foot, the woman's backward; close body contact, together with the line of the hold make the dancers ready to move in any direction.
    Geoffrey Hearn, Interview.

Transference of weight
    The way in which the body's weight, supported by one leg, is transferred to the other leg; or to both legs, or to the knee, or from the whole foot to the ball of the same foot.
    Rudolf Laban, 1956.

Transferring the weight
    Changing the supporting part of the body by stepping and rolling, sometimes also by sliding; stepping being regarded as any move (not only of the legs) which has a gesture, however insignificant, between each transfer, rolling being sequential transferences, and sliding being transferences with friction.
    Eds.

Transfer of weight
    In ballet, "Weight must always be transferred from one foot to the other" through the central line of balance.
    Joan Lawson, 1984.

Gestures
    Said in contrast to 'supports', that is to steps and transferences of weight. "Movements which do not support weight".
    Peggy Hackney, Sarah Manno, and *Muriel Topaz,* 1977.

Substantial and insubstantial
    Terms for the weight of the body resting on one leg (substantial), or not on that leg (insubstantial); the technique of separating a weight-bearing leg from a free leg and so enabling turns and steps to take place in balance; a T'ai Chi term.
    B.P.J. Lo, M. Inn, R. Amacker, and *S. Foe,* 1985.

Step
    A word used in many dance genres to distinguish one movement from another, it may be a leg movement or a movement of the whole body; from the French 'pas'.
    Monica Parker, Interview.

Steps (in folk dance)
    All manner of combinations of transferring weight, danced in all manner of rhythms.
    "Walks, runs, polkas, slips, steps, hops, skips are basic to folk dance."
    Robert Harrold, Interview.

Stepping
> The variety of movement forms in which the weight is transferred from one foot to the other, some forms having names and some having only longer description.
> "Sliding steps, treading, lunging, in plié, stepping over, stepping across in front and behind, prancing."
> *Laban Centre for Movement and Dance,* 1993.

Stepping
> A basic transference of weight from one foot to another which offers innumerable stylistic variations.
> "Take the weight with you as you step.", "A straight leg into it.", "Développé into it", "Delay the step."
> *The Birmingham Royal Ballet,* Rehearsal.

Full step
> After an extension, stepping to where the foot points, not just dropping it down, so passing through an off-balance state, to reassemble in the transference of weight.
> *Robert Cohan,* Company class.

Direct change of support
> A stylisation of stepping, minimising the lift of the preparatory gesture, so that going straight into the step is all that the spectator will see.
> *Anna Markard,* Rehearsal.

Undercurve and overcurve
> A transference of weight involving a particular coordination of leg and pelvis in order to make a curved rather than horizontal weight change.
> *Anna Markard,* Rehearsal.

Sliding step
> Made by passing the foot forwards so that it hardly touches the ground.
> *Pierre Rameau,* 1931 (1725).

Stamping
> Basic footwork material, danced in variety.
> "With the heel, with the whole foot, stamp into the ground and out of it, with weight and without, wearing hard shoes and soft, accented, two stamps, stamp to end the phrase."
> *Robert Harrold,* Interview.

Stylised steps
> Stepping with definite dynamic quality, body part, or patterning content; goose step, stamping, on tiptoe.
> *Jurgen Pagels,* 1984.

4b. JUMPING

Jumping

A basic action in dance, found in all styles and modes; essentially consisting in a preparation, take off, flight in the air, and a landing; interest may be in the height, the length, the footwork, etc.

"Trotting, skipping, galloping, hopping, leaping, prancing, assemblé, sissonne, sauté, temps levé, springing, saltation, elevation, bounding, a gambol, a caper, aerial work."

Eds.

Aerial work

All forms of jumps, leaps, hops, sissonnes, assemblés, sautés, in a dance vocabulary.

Eds.

Jeté

A leap from one foot to another, not necessarily in a balletic style; used also for movement in a contemporary and idiosyncratic vocabulary.

Christopher Bruce, Rehearsal.

Jumps, leaps, and hops

Basic movements of the whole body weight, called 'saltatory' movements by Laban, through flight and flinging (jeter) the weight into the air.

Rudolf Laban, 1956.

Five basic jump forms

The five combinations possible by jumping with two feet: jumping (2 to 2), hopping (1 to the same), leaping (1 to the other), assemblé (1 to 2), and sissonne (2 to 1).

Peggy Hackney, Sarah Manno, and *Muriel Topaz,* 1977.

Batterie

"Generic term used to describe all jumping movements involving the beating of the legs, either by striking one against the other as in batterie de choc, or as a result of the interweaving of the feet as in batterie à croisements."

Richard Glasstone, 1977.

Caper

The simple and complex jumping steps in Morris dancing, as the dancer rebounds and 'capers' again in a series of rhythmic leaps, the full caper and split-jump requiring an extremely strong physique.

Douglas Kennedy, 1949.

4c. TRAVELLING

Locomotion
    "The main focus is on getting from one place to another and establishing a point of arrival. There are manifold ways of doing this....crawling, prancing, creeping, shuffling, sliding, striding, rolling....running, and walking."
    Valerie Preston-Dunlop, 1963.

Running
    Basic dance material, especially in folk dance.
    "Running fast and slow, accentuated running, into the ground (Holland), out of the ground (Scottish)."
    Robert Harrold, Interview.

Travelling and in place
    Movements which locomote through the space, contrasted with those which stay on the spot; found widely in all genres.
    "Walking, running, bourrée, châiné, galloping, triple runs, crossing the floor; marking time, coupé, feet together."
    Eds.

Locomotor phrases
    "Movements which use a moving base, generally the feet, and are the means by which a dancer moves through the space."
    Aileene Lockhart and *Esther E. Pease,* 1977 (1966).

Walk
    Essentially transferences of weight and a pathway.
    "Walk, shuffle, limp, stride, march, saunter, strut, pace, on tiptoe."
    'Roget's Thesaurus', 1982.

Buoyant walk, A
    The basic and most satisfactory step for dancing, acquiring a rhythmical character and an upward and forward impulse of energy, from which alternatives and variations can be built.
    Douglas Kennedy, 1949.

Stylised walks
    "Koreans are quick to point out that their dance is characterized by walks in which the dancer steps first on the heel rather than the ball of the foot or the toe. What is unique in this movement is the way in which dancers seem almost to caress the floor with their feet, flexing their toes upward before placing the heel on the floor and then gently rolling the entire foot down.
    Judy Van Zile, 1993.

Promenade
> Walking round in a circle, part or whole; a move used in combinations.
> *Albert Reed,* Cunningham Studio class.

Swing
> The lilting quality which walks are given in folk dance.
> *Robert Harrold,* Interview.

Jazz walks
> Moving through space using a 1+ 2+ rhythm for each step.
> "The flat jazz walk, the ball drop or heel drop jazz walks, the Reggae walk, the Cuban walk, the Funky, Boogie, or Chicken walks."
> *Uta Fischer-Munstermann,* 1978.

Walking and running
> Two means of locomotion, used as examples of actions for which the Limón dancer must have a premise; "How do you receive the floor?"; "Are you coming down hard or soft?"; "How are your feet articulating and why?".
> *Carla Maxwell,* Interview.

Bent-legged bourrée
> A travelling step that became a much-used movement in José Limón's choreography.
> *Deborah Jowitt,* 1977.

Bourrée
> The travelling step in the classical vocabulary, used in variety by choreographers, with bent knees, on the spot, in a small zigzag path, with material from other vocabularies.
> *Christopher Bruce,* Interview.

4d. TURNING

Turning
> Movements of the whole body which go around its vertical axis.
> "Pirouette, pivot, fouetté, renversé, tour en l'air, swivel, whirling, twirling, spinning, change of front, slew round, revolve."
> *Laban Centre for Movement and Dance,* 1993.

Turning
> A basic folk dance step, danced alone and also in couples.
> "Pivot turn stressing one foot, swing turn, stepping between the partner's feet and turning, step-hop turns".
> *Robert Harrold,* Interview.

Turn

A change of direction in which the body rotates around a vertical central line or axis.

Jane Winearls, 1958.

Pirouette

The term for specific turns in ballet; used more broadly for a turn on one leg, possibly one knee.

Christopher Bruce, Rehearsing.

Renversé

A movement in the ballet vocabulary; the term used more generally to communicate that kind of turn, even one on the knees, to which the choreographer will give articulation.

Christopher Bruce, Rehearsing.

Change of front

Turning to face another room or stage direction.

Ann Hutchinson, 1954.

Direction of the turn

Turning to the right and the left, turning clockwise and anticlockwise, a natural and reversed turn, turning en dehors and en dedans, turning in towards and turning out from, all ways of describing the direction of the turn.

Eds.

Amount of turn

"Degree of turn can be defined in several ways: 1. Quantitatively, e.g. whole turn, half turn, quarter turn; 2. Qualitatively, e.g. a little, a lot, as many times as possible, as much as you want; 3. By the destination, e.g. turn to face downstage, turn to face your partner, turn so your back is to the center of the circle."

Ilene Fox, Contributed.

Step-turn and turn-step

Stepping before a turn, contrasted with turning and then stepping (when the turn is often experienced as a change of focus), and contrasted with an amalgamated turn where both happen at the same time, often found in the swing of ballroom dance turns.

Peggy Hackney, Sarah Manno, and *Muriel Topaz,* 1977.

Swing

Several kinds of turns with a partner where the aim is to get up a good turn of speed while holding on to each other; "In the walk swing you lean slightly away and feel a centrifugal force, in a pivot swing you move faster, rhythmically dropping onto the inside foot as you vigorously swing around each other."

Jack Hamilton, 1974.

4e. ROTATING

Rotations

Turns in and out of parts of the body, especially legs, arms, head, chest, pelvis, and torso as a whole.

"Turn out", "parallel feet", "rotate your elbows", "turn your head".

Eds.

Twists

Turns of parts of the body where the rotating action is within the part itself: twisting the chest using all the vertebrae and shoulder area; contrasted with turning the chest as a whole from the waist area only.

Els Grelinger, Interview.

Rotation and Twist

"A part of the body, such as the head, rotates in one piece. There is no twist in the part itself, the twist occuring in the joint or segment at the point of attachment. For this action the specific term 'rotation' has been chosen. Where the free end is able to rotate farther than the base, a twist within the limb itself is bound to occur. For this the specific term 'twist' is used. A few parts of the body are capable of both actions. For example there may be a twist in the torso or a rotation of the whole torso."

Ann Hutchinson, 1970.

Natural turn-out

Rotation of the legs to 90 degrees, not to the desired 180 degrees of the classical style; turning-out in the natural "hang" that the skeleton has before formal training; used in Jooss choreography.

Anna Markard, Rehearsal.

Facing

What some surfaces of the body do by their nature, the face, the palms, the front of the chest and whole front surface of the body, and which other surfaces can be asked to do through intention, or be seen to do by a notator.

"Face front", "chest facing the diagonal", "palms are up", "look over there".

Valerie Preston-Dunlop, Interview.

Somersault and Cartwheel

Rotating movements of the body as a whole around the lateral and sagittal body axes. Variations exist for the whole body and, to a limited degree for parts of the body, e.g. the pelvis, head.

Ann Hutchinson Guest, 1983.

4f. FALLING

Falling

A basic action in dance vocabularies in which gravity pulls the body downwards; may be total or partial.

"Fall, drop, tumble, dive, slump, sink down, give in to gravity, overbalance, topple over, sprawl, collapse."

Eds.

Falling

A source of movement material through the ebb and flow of dynamic arising from radical changes of balance and off-balance; all manner of falls providing the impetus for movement.

Laurie Booth, Interview.

Fall

"Falls are used primarily as preliminary to and therefore as a means of affirmation....My dancers fall so they may rise."

Martha Graham, 1941.

Falls

An ingredient in Graham vocabulary.

"back fall on 7, 4 and 3", "fall from sitting, from kneeling", "standing back falls", "4-position fall", "split fall", "pretzel fall", "travelling fall".

Susan Sentler, Interview.

Falling and its opposite

Basic motivations for movement, especially for change and continuously new impulses which gravity will promote.

"Flinging, dropping, tilting, rising; body, weight generating movement."

Trisha Brown, 1987.

Suspending

A basic action in dance vocabularies in which vertical resistance to the pull of gravity is primary; a counterpart to falling.

"Rising, lifting, suspending, pulling-up, growing, hovering, relevé."

'Roget's Thesaurus', 1982.

Lifting and lowering

Moving upwards and downwards, a combination of extending and bending actions of the body, together with awareness of a vertical rise and fall in space; also relevé and plié, stretching up and sinking down.

Eds.

Swing
> A fall and recovery, achieved through acknowledging the presence of gravity and recovering into a suspension.
> *Carla Maxwell,* Interview.

Lean on it, To
> After a leg lift to the side, to keep the leg high while pushing the weight towards it, leaning the weight on it, only then putting the leg down and stepping.
> *Robert Cohan,* Company class.

Tombé
> "Fall onto the supporting leg, you have to let gravity initiate it, you can't use the same energy as in a step. You have to give your weight to gravity so you can take it back again."
> *Rosemary Brandt,* Teaching.

4g. CONTRACTING AND EXTENDING AND AXIAL MOVEMENT

Contracting
> A basic action in dance, in which muscular and joint action work together, usually in preparation for the next action; contrasted by both releasing and extending.
> "Bending, contracting, curling in, plié, shrinking, getting smaller."
> *Eds.*

Extending
> From a closed-in position, stretching the limbs and/or torso into the space; a basic action in dance; contrasted with contracting.
> "Stretching, getting longer, tendu, pulling out, dégagé."
> *Eds.*

Lengthen the leg, To
> To extend, a movement in its own right and one made before lifting the leg.
> *Robert Cohan,* Company class.

Reach, To
> To extend into the space, used with 'into' and 'away from' and 'around', usually with some strength, but always with intention.
> *Eds.*

Curling and uncurling
> Bending in and extending out, starting with the head if it is a torso curl, or the hand if it is an arm curl.
> "Rolling down".
> *Eds.*

Contracting, extending, spreading
>The bending, stretching, and widening of limbs and trunk, independently or in co-ordinated flow.
>*Rudolf Laban,* 1956.

Flexed
>Contracted, bent, hinged; used particularly of the ankle joint as 'the flexed foot'.
>*Robert Cohan,* Company class.

Hinge
>The movement of a joint, used of the hip joint to distinguish torso tilts from torso contractions.
>*Robert Cohan,* Company class.

Leaning
>Tilting over into an oblique direction, usually the torso from the hips or the body as a whole from the feet; also called 'tilting' and 'inclining', especially in chest tilts and head inclinations.
>*Eds.*

Fan
>A movement of fingers and of toes, one digit after the other; opening fan and closing fan.
>*Robert Cohan,* Company class.

Swings
>Circular, curving movements using the body's weight; used by Hanya Holm.
>*Don Redlich,* Informal discussion.

Pendulum swing
>A movement carried out from a joint — shoulder, hip socket — in which the limb swings with weight followed by suspension, and usually, back again along the same path.
>*Simone Michelle,* Interview.

Eight swing
>An action using weight and suspension in which the limb travels inwards and outwards from the body in a figure of-eight-pattern.
>*Simone Michelle,* Interview.

Gathering and scattering
>"Shaping towards the body" and "shaping away from the body".
>*Cecily Dell,* 1970.

Scattering and gathering

Movements which go away from the centre and return, through a natural tendency in movement to flow between contending and resolving; examples are to be seen in any balletic adage.

Rosemary Brandt, Interview.

Scooping and strewing

A sequence of movements made by the arms and legs which are based upon a swinging fall of the limbs towards and away from the centre line of the body. Scooping gathers strength from the fall and holds it, while strewing is the gathering of weight in order to scatter it.

Simone Michelle, Interview.

5.   CO-ORDINATING THE BODY IN MOTION

Co-ordinating the body

The manner in which the body's parts work together as a whole, through an image or a sensation or a strategy.

Valerie Preston-Dunlop, 1981.

Co-ordination (in ballet)

A term used in ballet for the simultaneous arrangement of the different parts of the body, while sequential co-ordination is seldom explicitly addressed; what precedes and what follows is not seen as co-ordination, but: "Co-ordination is experienced in motion."

Rosemary Brandt, Interview.

How?

The body logic of what makes the next movement happen, the cause and effect in movement logic.

"There are thousands of ways of bending the knees, the question is 'HOW?'. You bend by pulling up."

Robert Cohan, Company class.

Nothing wasted

To move so that not one part of the body wastes the opportunity to be "a living part" of the dance.

"Every molecule is living."

Carla Maxwell, Interview.

Initiation

The place in the body where the movement begins, and from which the body can move into the space.

Erica Stanton, Interview.

Origin of the movement

"Work from the back, rotate the shoulders under and the palms will come up.";
"The pelvis produces the arm movement."

Robert Cohan, Company class.

Solar plexus

"The bodily habitation of the soul, the center in which inner impulse was
translated into movement."; an Isadora Duncan concept.

John Martin, 1977.

Renewal

"Movement springs from an inner impulse, then radiates and returns in a never
ending wave of renewal."

Irma Duncan, 1970.

Leading with

A part of the body preceding the rest, taking the rest with it.

Valerie Preston-Dunlop, 1981.

Central movement

Leading the movement from the centre of the body, in the central part of a limb
until the periphery "is a living part" of the centre.

Carla Maxwell, Interview.

Echo through the body

Moving so that an initial impact is reflected in the rest of the body; said of the
movement with sticks in Bruce's "Waiting" (1993) as they are slammed onto the floor.

Christopher Bruce, Rehersal.

Hierarchy of joint action

"A term used in movement which starts in the pelvis and lumbar spine and flows
out to the periphery of the body (called 'centred' movement), in which the energy or
dynamic level attenuates as it passes through each successive joint, becoming more
refined."

"Where movement at a distal point is stronger than at a proximal point, the
movement is said to be 'ex-centred', though this is not necessarily a pejorative term."

Mark Lintern Harris, Contributed.

Guidance

A surface of a limb, or the torso, guiding the movement through space, causing
twists and rotations; the sensation of guiding the movement.

Jane Winearls, 1958.

Human body as limit

"...with dancing we're locked into the fact that it's the human body doing the action. There are two legs; the arms move a certain number of ways; the knees only bend forwards. That remains your limit."
Merce Cunningham and *Jacqueline Lesschaeve, 1985.*

Body sense

Teaching dancers their movement material by both demonstration and by giving them an understanding of what one body part does in relation to another.
"Put your head under your arms."
Rui Horta, Workshop.

Body connections

Relatedness of body parts; used for co-ordination, for orientation in complex positions, and for extending vocabulary.
"Put your left ear to your right ankle" in a Graham spiral (Cohan); "Your hand is over the left elbow" (Horta); "Not cou-de-pied, put the foot past the other leg" (Bruce).
Eds.

Relatedness

"...the relation of my body parts to each other in a specific spatial orientation."
Sylvia Bodmer, 1962.

Addressing

A movement of some kind made with the aim of relating to someone or something; a connection betwen one person and another or between one body part and another, as in looking at, pointing at.
Ann Hutchinson Guest, 1983.

Near to

Almost touching, the nearness being the relationship between two parts. During movement a passing nearness may occur.
Ann Hutchinson Guest, 1983.

Touch

Physical contact with another part of the body, a person or object. Used for all manner of gestures where body parts touch or contact with the floor or an object occurs.
Ann Hutchinson Guest, 1983.

Support

Weightbearing; taking of weight by a part of the body or supporting (carrying) the weight of another, as in a duo.
Ann Hutchinson Guest, 1983.

Graining

Co-ordinating the body to echo a main movement, similar to the graining of wood, especially around a knot.

Dale Thompson, Rehearsal.

Carriage of the body

The manner of co-ordinating the body as a form, whether upright, leaning, or horizontal, by stretching into "a pin-like extension", flattening into "a wall-like surface", circling "with a ball-like shaping", twisting "with a screw-like form".

Rudolf Laban, 1950.

Organic

Developing out of the body; "I don't trust the head".

Bessie Schoenberg, Interview.

Organic relationship

The relatedness of the movement of legs to the torso and the torso to the arms so that each movement grows out of the action of another part of the body.

Erica Stanton, Interview.

Including

Inclining the torso, or chest or just the shoulder area in an arm movement, letting the body go with the arm; equally including the hip in a leg movement or the torso in a step; a notation term.

Albrecht Knust, 1979.

Channelled intention

A co-ordinating image used to help the dancer to get her body moving as one unit, unfragmented.

Anna Markard, Rehearsal.

Congruency

Moving all parts of the body with the same intention, all rising, all opening, all strongly held, and so on; a co-ordination style in expressionist dance.

Eds.

Integrated

A form of co-ordination in which the individual rhythm of the body's parts integrate without losing their own articulate; said of Limón style.

Carla Maxwell, Interview.

PGM

Posture-gesture-merger; a Warren Lamb term for the way of moving in which a gesture is supported by or merges with shadow movements of the rest of the body (the posture) so giving authenticity to the movement, because those moments are not learnt but are spontaneously generated and difficult to contrive; a concept especially useful in reading or producing authenticity of performance.

Valerie Preston-Dunlop with *Warren Lamb*, Contributed.

Within yourself, To move

Moving within the torso rather than bending in one piece from the hips.

Anna Markard, Rehearsal.

Opposition

A co-ordination principle in which the arms and legs move in opposition to each other, right leg forward and left arm forward; used in human walking, in dance to provide equilibrium and stability.

Eds.

Sensation of gravity

Moving with the feel of the actual weight in the joints, the pelvis and the head working collaboratively or against each other.

Erica Stanton, Interview.

High point

The point of the body which retains the oppositional pull with gravity and pulls vertically away from the feet.

Daniel Lewis, 1984.

Sequential movement

The activity at the starting point (usually shoulder or hip) is followed immediately by activity in each of the next joints along the line of the limb.

Jane Winearls, 1958.

Successive or successional flow

"When movement passes through the body or a part of the body in anatomical succession."

Eds.

Outward and inward succession

Sequential movements starting from the anatomical source of the body part (shoulder for arm, hip for leg, pelvis for torso), or starting at the extremity (finger tips, head).

Nona Schurman and *Sharon Leigh Clark,* 1972.

Flow of movement in the body
The manner in which movements of parts of the body precede and follow each other successively and also coincide in simultaneous flow and overlap each other sequentially or cause the flow to pause.
Rudolf Laban, 1956.

Countertension
"Movements of one side of the body are counterbalanced by resisting in the opposide side of the back. These countertensions within the body give strength to the movement and demand energy and control."
Alice J. Helpern, 1981.

Counterbalance
An ingredient of co-ordination, for example in kneeling, when the torso and head lean backwards as the knees take the weight forwards.
Anna Markard, Rehearsal.

Simultaneous and consecutive
A timing relationship of one movement to another. Simultaneous movements are those that happen at the same time while consecutive movements are those that happen one after the other.
Ilene Fox, Contributed.

Articulation
Clear co-ordination of the isolated moves in a phrase.
"Swing the arm, now the hip drops, then take the body away from the leg."
Christopher Bruce, Rehearsing.

Symmetric activity
"...has equal stress by both sides and is experienced as a state of equalness."
Valerie Preston-Dunlop, 1981.

Asymmetric activity
"One side of the body is more active than the other; it is felt as a sensation of inequality."
Valerie Preston-Dunlop, 1981.

Polykinetic
Counterpoint within one body.
Rudolf von Laban, 1928.

Split dynamics
In ballet, the fluidity of the arms used simultaneously with the strong, rhythmic, sharp, and precise leg work, a complex dynamic co-ordination.
Mirella Bartrip and *Teresa Kelsey,* Interview.

Calculated opposition

The oppositional and rhythmic relationship between arm movements and steps in baroque dance.

"The technical achievements of this style — for example...the calculated opposition of arms to step units...".

Meredith Little and *Natalie Jenne*, 1991.

6.   ISOLATIONS

Isolations

Shifts of part of the body, especially the hip, pelvis, chest and rib cage; used by Hanya Holm.

Don Redlich, Informal discussion.

Isolations

Articulation of individual parts of the body, which nevertheless are danced with awareness of the opposition in other parts; said of Limón style.

Carla Maxwell, Interview.

Nouns of movement, The

The parts of the body which move; objects which are moved; a Language of Dance Teaching Approach term.

Ann Hutchinson Guest, Interview.

Shifts

Small movements of isolated parts, especially parts of the torso and the head; used in contrast to tilts where an inclination from one joint occurs, shifts occur within the spine itself; shifts forward and back, sideways and circling shifts can be done.

Albrecht Knust, 1979.

Leave things alone, To

To allow parts of the body to remain unaffected, unaltered, while another part is actually engaged.

Yolande Snaith, Interview.

Independent co-ordination

The parts of the body moving independently of other parts, in isolations (Cunningham), in counter rhythms (Latin American), in shifts of the chest and head (Indian Classical).

Eds.

Disassociation
          The co-ordination of independent body parts, especially hips against shoulders, which is part of "true jazz dancing".
          Gillian Lynne, Interview.

Isolation of the limbs
          "One of the most exceptional features of African dance whereby every limb of the body can play in free movement, but is always held be a center which holds the individual parts together structurally and stylistically."
          Renato Berger, 1990.

Fragmentation (of the body)
          The manner in which the body's parts work independently of each other; the presentation of that independence.
          Valerie Preston-Dunlop, 1981.

Body parts as soloists
          "Not only is everybody a 'soloist' in Cunningham's choreography, every section of every body can become a soloist as well; for Cunningham often sets the head, arms, torso, and legs moving in opposition to one another."
          Roger Copeland in Roger Copeland and Marshall Cohen, 1983.

Unthought of
          Without clear intention; applied to a part of the body which the choreographer does not want the audience to notice, a deliberate unintentionality so that another part will be seen.
          Lea Anderson, Interview.

7.   BODY ARTICULATION

Body articulation
          The rhythm of the movement coming out in particular parts of the body used in the style of the dance being performed.
          "Rotate the hip.", "Get higher on your toes." (said of the Paso doble), "No, not your head".
          Geoffrey Hearn, Instructing.

Body articulation
          Isolations, and integrations, of actions of parts of the body which have their own expression; achieved through the dancer's focus and attention on individual parts.
          Carla Maxwell, Interview.

Articulation of the movement
    The manner in which a movement of the body is more finely differentiated by smaller parts playing a designated role, for example, lifting the arm with the elbow initiating the move.
    Rudolf Laban, 1956.

Exploration of joints
    The angular use of the body in Bharata Natyam style in which the geometric possibilities of the joints, even individual finger joints, is part of the vocabulary.
    Shobana Jeyasingh, Interview.

Articulation
    The key to the alphabet of the mime-actor; mime is best in articulated stillness, in stylized walks, in detached units of movement; said by Étienne Decroux in contrast to the motion, the jumps and the fluidity of dance.
    Alvin Epstein, 1958.

Focus
    "To concentrate the attention" of the movement, usually on a spatial direction or a point in space or on a fellow dancer, possibly on the audience.
    Eds.

7a. TORSO

Torso, The
    The central part of the body which makes emotion visible through both body mechanics and body chemistry — heart, lungs, stomach, viscera, spine —, the arms and face being peripheral.
    "...it is the torso which expresses...", "...the torso is the source of life...", "...the motor...".
    Martha Graham in Agnes de Mille, 1991.

Torso divisions
    The chest and the pelvis as two independent areas of the torso, the waist area used mostly for touches and holds, the shoulder area used for 'épaulement' in ballet as well as independent movements; the surfaces of the torso and its parts, used for contacts, for focus, and for 'leading with'.
    Els Grelinger, Interview.

Torso movements
    The vocabulary is found in: the torso initiating the movement (Graham), the torso held vertical (ballet), the torso pushing down into the weight (Latin American), the torso following the arm movement (Jooss), the torso suspending (Humphrey), the torso undulating (Ailey), the torso tilting, twisting within itself, and turning as a whole (Cunningham).
    Eds.

Torso movements
Movements of the whole torso and within it as isolations and successions, from standing and from lying: i.e., swinging, rotating, tilting, curling, uncurling.
Nona Schurman and *Sharon Leigh Clark,* 1972.

Spine, The
It "acts not just as a source for the arms and legs, but itself can coil and explode like a spring, can grow taut or loose, can turn on its own axis or project into space directions."
Merce Cunningham in Walter Sorell, 1951.

Movements of the back
Successional bending of the back in three directions (forward, sideward, backward); from the head inward and from the hips outward; tipping forward in one piece from the hips, bending sideways of the rib cage; stretching sideways with one arm or both over the head; body circling.
Nona Schurman and *Sharon Leigh Clark,* 1972.

Spiral
In Graham technique the spiral is created by maximum turning of the torso around its spinal axis; the Graham dancer learns to channel energy upward while turning the torso.
Alice J. Helpern, 1981.

Solar plexus
"...the motor from which all movement starts", "all the muscles run obliquely towards a center point, the solar plexus"; "start your movement from within"; an Isadora Duncan concept.
Irma Duncan, 1970.

Centres of levity and of gravity
Two centres in the body, especially evident in ballet, one in the chest and one in the pelvis; literally, a centre of lightness and a centre of strength and gravity.
Rosemary Brandt, Interview.

Centre of weight
In Graham technique, the pelvis is the location of the centre of weight, and thus mobilisation of body weight is initiated from the pelvis.
Alice J. Helpern, 1981.

Natural functioning (of the body)
"Movement starts in the body's centre of gravity and then — in correct sequence — flows into the extremeties".
Erick Hawkins in Selma Jeanne Cohen, 1977.

Contraction
A movement in which the chest and waist move towards each other in Leeder technique.
Simone Michelle, Interview.

Upper part of the body movement
The upper part of the torso, not specifically the chest only; said to describe movements of the torso used in response to what the arms are doing and so in mixtures of tilts, twists, and shifts, which are not individually analysed.
Albrecht Knust, 1979.

Participation of the trunk in arm movement
When a gesture of the arm into different directions is amplified by the inclusion of the trunk as a postural support to the arm; spiral movement may take place as well as twists and inclinations in this kind of participation.
Rudolf Laban, 1956.

Chest movement
As well as the usual turning and tilting into a direction, the chest shifts, expands and contracts, inhales and exhales, is the suspension point and can collapse.
Els Grelinger, Interview.

Rib cage
A part of the body which reflects the humanness of movement, the centre of feeling, the breath, the heart; a part which can articulate and initiate.
Carla Maxwell, Interview.

Breath, The
A source of organic movement, especially from the rib cage, which informs movement that speaks of the human condition.
Carla Maxwell, Interview.

Breast bone
Not just a bone but 'the light point' of Jooss/Leeder technique, through which the dancer feels suspension.
Anna Markard, Rehearsal.

Depth of rhythm
The feeling of rhythm of the dance (in Latin American) permeating the whole torso, reflected in the movement of pelvis and chest over the steps of the dance.
Geoffrey Hearn, Interview.

7b. LEGS

Leg movements
Pliés, relevés, on one or both feet, half or full, leg swings and kicks, bending and extending, brushes and push offs.
Nona Schurman and *Sharon Leigh Clark,* 1972.

Working leg and supporting leg
The leg which is gesturing and the leg which is supporting the body's weight; the working leg bending, stretching, rotating, and circling, in variety and combination, co-ordinated with the supporting leg, which rises and bends, in turned-out and parallel rotations.
Eds.

Leg movements
Simple moves such as "lifting the leg, turning the leg in and out, extending and bending the leg, stepping onto the leg", to movements with a rhythm and dynamic, "swing the leg, kicking, shaking the leg", to movements with a shape, "circling with the leg, extending the leg into space", to movement in a style, "rond de jambe, petit battement", "leg flicks", "capers", "figure-of-eight swings".
Eds.

Rhythm (of leg movement)
The timing in steps, gestures, jumps and their combinations made by the sequential and simultaneous flow of the weight-bearing action and the free leg; fluidity and staccato dynamic given by the sequential flow from support to gesture and by the sharp juxtaposition of support to gesture.
Peggy Hackney, Sarah Manno, and *Muriel Topaz,* 1977.

Easy knees
Walking and running with the knees relaxed and so slightly bent; said in contrast to pulled-up knees and natural walking knees.
"In folk dance, agricultural people move into the ground with bent knees, urban people with easy knees."
Robert Harrold, Interview.

Demi plié
A transitional movement in classical ballet, consolidated as a stance in South Asian dance.
Shobana Jeyasingh, Interview.

Footwork
The steps, jumps, and gestures which need to be done precisely for a dance to retain its style and technical polish.
"Really poised on the ball of the foot", "Feel it through the ankle.", "Chassée 1, chassée 2, backstep. Flick your foot twice."
Geoffrey Hearn, Instructing.

Positions of the feet

In academic classical ballet all movements begin, move through, and finish in one of the five positions of the feet or a position derived from one of them.
Richard Glasstone, Lecture.

Sixth position

Following after the five ballet positions, the sixth position is akin to a reversed fourth position progressing backwards in space.
Margaret Lloyd, 1974 (1949).

Sixth position

After the five positions of the feet, the sixth is an open diagonal fourth; a Hanya Holm term.
Don Redlich, Informal discussion.

Occupied with the floor

The main function of the legs, in getting the body around, into and along the floor, in constrast to the gestures of the arms and hands.
Yolande Snaith, Interview.

7c. ARMS

Carriage of the arms

"The manner of moving the arms gracefully in the Menuet is as important as the execution of the pas, because the arms move with the body and are its principal ornament."
Pierre Rameau, 1931 (1725).

Port de bras

Arm movementes in ballet, literally carriage of the arms.
"Arms that move gracefully with the body in dancing are like the frame to a picture. If the frame is unsuitable the picture, no matter how beautiful, loses in consequence."
Carlo Blasis, 1968 (1820).

Port de bras

Movements of the arms in the ballet style which a Feldenkreis-trained teacher would see as one way of reaching into space, reaching being a part of daily movement vocabulary, and the connection being an important part of the dancer's awareness.
Scott Clark, Interview.

Arm movements

Movements that occur in the arms, have their own rhythm, and integrate with the rest of the body as an articulated entity, with their own premise; may originate in the centre, or in any part of the arm.
Carla Maxwell, Interview.

Gesture

The shape and position of the arms and hands in relation to the rest of the body which provides definition to the activity.

Yolande Snaith, Interview.

Sequential arms

A stylistic way of moving the arms, with the shoulder-elbow-wrist-hand guidance of the gesture.

Anna Markard, Rehearsal.

Surface of the limb

One side of an arm, lower arm, hand (or leg) which is the motivating side for the shape of the movement being made; emphasising one surface to give intention to the move.

"...the inside of the arms sucked together...".

Lea Anderson, Interview.

Enter into the chest, To

Allowing an arm movement to affect the chest area, to react to it in a reflecting way.

Anna Markard, Rehearsal.

Épaulé

Literally shouldered. A position — usually arabesque — in which the shoulder girdle is rotated so that the shoulder corresponding to the downstage leg comes forward. This adds interest to the position and in motion may facilitate moments of lability.

Jane Carr, Interview.

Shoulders

Shrugging, hunched, pulled back, lop-sided, shaking.

Eds.

Shoulder isolations

Lifting, dropping, and circling, moving forward and backward, together or separately and in opposition.

Nona Schurman and *Sharon Leigh Clark,* 1972.

Hands, The

"...the subtle speaking voice of the body."

Agnes de Mille in Agnes de Mille, 1991.

Hands

An articulate part of the body, with an expressive range and an organic part to play.

Carla Maxwell, Interview.

Hand details

Beyond the basic vocabulary of hand movements, hands are able to do subtle movements which are combinations of the basics together with timing and dynamics and possibly an image; a sequential fan, a figure-eight, pointing, beckoning, 'thumbs up', 'balletic hand', make a fist, touching, caressing, picking up props, supporting dancers.

Els Grelinger, Interview.

Cupped hand

The stylistic carriage of the hand in Graham work which evolves from the contraction/release source and reads for an audience because of its context within the whole movement form; the contracted hand.

Thea Barnes, Susan Sentler, and *Brenda Baden-Semper,* Interview.

Widen the palm, To

A flattening process of the hand without necessarily widening or spreading the fingers.

Anna Markard, Rehearsal.

Finger dance

The hand and finger vocabulary of the mudra technique of India.

Karlheinz Stockhausen in Mya Tannenbaum, 1987 (1979–81).

7d. HEAD

Head movements

The head tilts and turns and shifts in fine combinations; the eyes, eyebrows, mouth, cheeks also have movement possibilities, analysed as opening, closing, widening, narrowing, or moving into a direction.

Els Grelinger, Interview.

Head signals

Familiar head movements known through behaviour, which are used in dance as choreographed material and as personal interpretation.

"Head nods, open-mouthed, shaking the head, smiling, frowning, winking, open-eyed, pursed-lipped."

Eds.

Positions of the head (Classical ballet)

Traditionally there are five positions: 1. erect, 2. lowered, 3. raised, 4. inclined, and 5. turned.

Jane Carr, Interview.

Level-eyed

Keeping the gaze horizontal, overcoming the tendency to tilt the head in sympathy with the movement.

Anna Markard, Rehearsal.

Materia technica (in connection with the face)

Horst is stressing the role of the movement of the whole body as carrying the dance message, i.e. as materia technica, not the face.

"There is theatre in dance. Dance can be its own theatre without any facial expression — Of course the face can light up but the face is not materia technica."

Louis Horst, 1958.

Gaze

Focusing, a strong carrier of intention, varying in intensity, in distance, in direction, and in support from the rest of the body; used in Nijinska's "Les Biches" by the dancers to observe each other's variations, to "train their sights on the audience, challenging, seductive, vulnerable, with sexual intent."

Lynn Garafola, 1989.

Gaze and Focus

The line of the whole face, making clear the connection with the audience, and the direction and intensity of the eyes, giving the intention of the movement.

Mirella Bartrip and *Teresa Kelsey,* Interview.

Eyelids and eyeball dance

The vocabulary of the eyes in traditional Balinese dance.

Karlheinz Stockhausen in Mya Tannenbaum, 1987 (1979–81).

Chapter 8 DYNAMICS AND TIMING OF MOVEMENT

1. DYNAMICS AND ENERGY

Dynamics of movement

Changes of movement colouring recognised and initiated by choreographers and schools according to their own view of dance; hence Cunningham's interest in time, Laban's in effort, Limón in weight, Graham in the contraction, Balanchine in musical dynamic, many dancers in emotional colouring, and so on.

Eds.

Dynamics

The texture of dance which has its equivalence in painting in "surface texture, color and intensity", in music in "timbre plus loud and soft, legato and staccato"; in movement it is "smooth and sharp" plus "variations in tempo and tension".

Doris Humphrey, 1959.

Dynamics

"One of the materials that makes the poetic image."

Doris Rudko, Interview.

Dynamics

"The expressive life of the movement", whether motivated from feelings and emotions or simply kinetic.

Doris Rudko, Interview.

Dynamic combinations

Successive or simultaneous changes of dynamic quality in the movement.

Alan Salter with *Stina Grist,* 1977.

Physical 'How' and emotional 'Why' of dynamics

The actual dynamic energies with the intentional dynamic feelings which result in the phenomenon of dance.

Alan Salter with *Stina Grist,* 1977.

'Why' of movement, The

Agnes de Mille's way of describing the dynamic intention in Martha Graham's work.

"She [Graham] got the gesture down not only to the muscles, which is 'how', but to the juices and the electricity [of the body's motor] as well, which is the 'why'."

Agnes de Mille, 1991.

Dynamics
What comes into the role when the dancer allows feeling to enter every part of the movement.
"...human feeling...".
Marion Tait, Interview.

Folk dance dynamics
The quality that the music provides and the movement follows.
"With a vibrating jig, with shaking shoulders, with heavy stamps, beats, smooth stepping, vivacious leaps, dancer's shouts."
Robert Harrold, Interview.

Dynamics
Change in energy use in motion, for which there are seven basic qualities; pendular swing, sustained movement, percussive movement, swaying, vibratory movement, collapse, ballistic movement.
Joan F. Hays, 1981.

Dynamic qualities
Qualities of dance suggested by Margaret H'Doubler: "swinging, collapsing, vibrating, suspending, percussive, pulsating."
Elizabeth R. Hayes, 1955.

Qualities
"romping", "storming", "meandering", "jerking", "quivering", "drooping", "frantic beating", "breathing stillness", "controlled fluidity", "tremendous tension", "shuddering", "whiplash", "writhing", "percussive force", words for qualities of movement used variously by Jowitt in her dance writings.
Deborah Jowitt, 1977.

Natural affinity
The tendency for dynamic qualities and spatial shapes to influence each other; viz: swing and impulse lead to spatial progression, while impact leads to body design.
Rosemary Brandt, Interview.

Attack
A dynamic point of view; the performer sets about, positively, to execute the movement with the qualities it should have.
Valerie Preston-Dunlop, 1992.

Textures
Dynamic qualities seen in the imagination as different textures with which to paint the space through movement.
Laurie Booth, Interview.

Movement colourings

Dynamic qualities, in complex variation, as subtle and varied as visual colouring in painting, for which it is necessary to know the nature of the colour, its intensity, its fluid/abrupt transition to the next colour, the durational proportions of each colour in the phrase.

Valerie Preston-Dunlop, Seminar.

Energy

The capacity of the body to move.
Daniel Lewis, 1984.

Kinetic energy

Potential energy released in motion.
Daniel Lewis, 1984.

Potential energy

The energy that is stored by the body and can be released through gravity.
"The energy of a body on the threshold of movement."
Daniel Lewis, 1984.

Dance energy

The energy use in dance, different in nature from that of other athletic activities; it is "dynamic, directed outward from the center through the limbs"; also termed 'tension'.
Anna Paskevska, 1990.

Energy quantity

The amount of energy used, only discernable generally as "with a lot" or "with a little", letting your own personal and cultural energy use serve as the base line.
Judy Van Zile, 1976.

Energy level

Raising and lowering the energy used, within one movement, and in stillness, locating the energy in the body, changing the energy level through subtle changing and marked contrast.
"...a tiny surge of energy...".
Judy Van Zile, 1976.

Use of energy

The application of vital force, in appropriate variety, by no means always "with lots of energy", but with subtle changes and sensitivity.
Rosemary Brandt, Interview.

High, medium, and low energy

The supposedly fixed texture of a dance, or of a phrase; either all high energy, bounce, and speed; or low energy, relaxed; or medium energy without variation; rather than changing energies which provides textures, hues, and timbres to material.
Joan F. Hays, 1981.

Adverbs of movement, The

The manner in which movements are performed.

"Verb modifiers; Timing and dynamic changes as well as spatial variation and physical variation to the basic alphabet of movement; a Language of Dance Teaching Approach term."

Ann Hutchinson Guest, Interview.

Apparent energy

Apparent energy is what is seen in terms of action and stillness rather than of actual work, regardless of the physiological or kinaesthetic experience of the dancer.

Yvonne Rainer, 1968.

Pared energy

The energy that is necessary to do the movement, no more.

Rosemary Butcher, Interview.

Real energy

Real energy refers to actual output in terms of physical expenditure on the part of the performer.

Yvonne Rainer, 1968.

Resonance

The energy of a movement retained in a pause.

Murray Louis, 1969.

Energy in stillness

The dropping, building, or collecting, maintaining of energy in a held position; the stillness at rest or "on the verge of going somewhere else."

Judy Van Zile, 1976.

Inner molecular activity (of dance)

Density, graining, focus, and projection into space, all vitalised by energy.

Murray Louis, 1969.

Impetus

The energy to achieve the movement, finding a preparation or an arm movement which gives the needed momentum.

"That'll put some more impetus into it."

David Bintley, Rehearsal.

Collecting the energy

Gathering in the body's power prior to more vigorous movement; said of movement with both large and subtle changes of energy.

Anna Markard, Rehearsal.

Chi

The vital energy which the practice of T'ai Chi Ch'uan cultivates in the body and which is found in the meridian channels of the body.
Katherine Allen, Interview.

Energy in the body

The localised or entire body use for energy patterns; the differences and simultanieties of energy use and level by body segments.
Judy Van Zile, 1976.

Refresh the energy or no new energy

Two contrasting ways for the dancer to begin a movement; which way it is, is crucial to the style and meaning of the movement.
Anna Markard, Rehearsal.

Energy phrasing

The possible placement of changes of energy within a movement phrase, or between phrases, achieving punctuation.
Judy Van Zile, 1976.

Surge of energy

"...as if you took a quick breath to prepare for..." the next movement; an energy build, however tiny, which is stylistically crucial; said of a Korean walking pattern.
Judy Van Zile, 1976.

Peripheral energies

The impetus for the movement coming in the peripheral parts of the body, hands, feet and head; used in improvisation.
Rui Horta, Workshop.

Impetus

The physical power to do the next move, finding where the power comes from. "Get the impetus from the shoulder."
Desmond Kelly, Rehearsal.

Momentum

"Find the momentum to help you get out of there into the next.", "...but control the momentum as you finish the turn."
Valerie Preston-Dunlop, Class.

Vocal energy

Getting the voice to provide dynamic quality: "Growl it, shout it, whisper it, gasp it", "sssssh..., ja —, tk tk tk".
Valerie Preston-Dunlop, Teaching.

Tan T'ien
> The centre of gravity, situated about 3" below the navel, the place to which the energy sinks and collects and from which it radiates out, the place to which you give your attention.
> *B.P.J. Lo, M. Inn, R. Amacker, and S. Foe, 1985.*

2. FLOW

Continuing and stopping
> "The basic polarities of the flow of movement."
> *Rudolf Laban, 1948.*

Continuous changes
> Changes which are not discretely differentiated but are ever emergent.
> *Valerie Preston-Dunlop, 1981.*

Continue, To
> A quality which a dancer should find in order to avoid stopping in a pose; "lift out of it and continue after you get there."
> *Laverne Meyer, Interview.*

Fluidity
> In ballet, to blend one position into the next.
> "...to blend the 'attitude' straight in...".
> *Desmond Kelly, Rehearsal.*

Attitude to flow
> Freeing-binding, liberating-witholding, unhampered-hampered, free-controlled, outpouring-contained, are words attempting to express the poles on the flow attitude. The mover intends in flow.
> *Peggy Hackney, Interview.*

Flow of movement
> Movement continually flows between the momentary suspension of activity and the momentary cessation of activity in a wave-like pattern, through initial accent, transitional accent, and terminal acent.
> *Jane Winearls, 1958.*

Dynamic interaction
> In T'ai Chi, the change between the gathering Yin movement and the pushing Yang movement, which are not opposites but become each other.
> *Katherine Allen, Interview.*

Flux

"The normal continuation of movement as that of a flowing stream which can be more, or less, controlled", "binding or freeing the flow".
Rudolf Laban, 1950.

Freeze it, To; Lock it, To

Two images given in rehearsal for arresting the movement; used in respect of the whole body or of a held position in part of the body while motion of the rest continues.
Anna Markard, Rehearsal.

Bound flow

Hampered continuity.
Rudolf Laban, 1950.

Free flow

Unhampered continuity.
Rudolf Laban, 1950.

Afterflow

The following flow to a main action, allowing the afterflow to occur rather than stopping the movement.
Christopher Bruce, Rehearsing.

Retention and release

The characteristic flow of baroque dance, with moments of stillness (poise) contrasting with faster-moving steps; or slow movement released into faster or freer movement.
Stephen Preston, Interview.

Motion in stillness

"The fluid, ongoing movements that appear to stop are, in reality, simply collecting energy that ultimately gently explodes, or runs over, into the next series of fluid actions. Korean dancers move through positions instead of arriving at them, creating curvilinear shapes as well as an ongoing quality of energy."
Judy Van Zile, 1993.

Swinging

"A movement quality of a pendular nature involving an easy, natural movement of the body or of its parts."
Aileene Lockhart and *Esther E. Pease,* 1977 (1966).

Swing

A basic movement quality in ballroom dancing, used specifically in each dance, "swing to close" in the waltz, "swing to go on" in the foxtrot.
Geoffrey Hearn, Interview.

Succession and continuity
The way movement unfolds from one attitude to another; the never stopping consciousness of the flow, however still or slowly moving the movement is (in Butoh).
Ushio Amagatsu, 1992.

Swing, Impulse, and Tension
Martin Gleisner (1928) described Laban's classification of three basic ways of moving with dynamic flow as "with flowing swing, an impulsive outburst, and with tension".
Vera Maletic, 1987.

Lability and Stability
The Laban terminology for overcoming of inertias which promotes movement and brings about liberation, contrasted with that which facilitates stillness, temporary rest, quietude, and equilibrium.
Vera Maletic, 1987.

3. GRAVITY, FORCE, AND TENSION

Theory of motion
"...all life fluctuates between resistance to and yielding to gravity...".
Doris Humphrey, 1959.

Gravity (as a force in movement)
The interplay of vertical movement, resisting gravity, giving in to it, and recovering again, a key motivating force in Limón's technique.
"The floor is a strong base from which the dancer rises to great heights, only to return and rise again."
Daniel Lewis, 1984.

Groundedness
A Limón term for a feeling of weight and gravity, a feeling of connection with the ground.
Daniel Lewis, 1984.

Weight falling
The understanding of how the weight of the body is connected to the floor.
"The weight is falling through the heel of the standing leg."
Gregory Nash, Interview.

Wind in the movement
The quality and density Amagatsu wants in the dancer's movement, the essential quality of the dancer's relatedness to nature.
Ushio Amagatsu, 1992.

Softness

> The giving of a little assistance to gravity using weight.
> *Jane Winearls,* 1958.

Softening

> Releasing a joint, resulting in a bend, perceived as letting go, rather than muscular engagement. (Term derived from Alexander Technique)
> *Gregory Nash,* Interview.

Fall and recovery

> The giving in to and rebound from gravity.
> *Doris Humphrey,* 1959.

Fall

> The complete release of the muscles as the body drops, giving in to gravity, and so releasing kinetic energy; a Limón concept.
> *Daniel Lewis,* 1984.

Recovery

> The catching of the potential energy released in a fall where the energy passes through the bottom of the fall and continues in the same path, as the swing of a pendulum; as used in Limón work.
> *Daniel Lewis,* 1984.

Suspension

> The moment when the body is airborne, when the body resists the pull of gravity; a key sensation in Humphrey and Limón technique.
> *Daniel Lewis,* 1984.

Feeling of suspension, A

> "The dancer often begins a movement that rises, in some fashion, and then appears to stop abruptly. The dancer remains briefly poised, as if deciding whether to lift even higher or to move on to something else. As the contained energy verges on explosion, the performer rises just a bit higher before releasing everything into a gentle downward movement. This moment of suspension — a delicate hovering — creates a strong, dynamic tension for the viewer and contributes to the visual sigh of relief."
> *Judy Van Zile,* 1993.

Breath

> The heightening of the potential energy contained within the body, the feeling of lengthening in the body, of feeling the oppositional pull between head and feet. "Breath is integral to suspension."; used in Limón work.
> *Daniel Lewis,* 1984.

Suspended

"A quality of movement that creates the impression of defying gravity; floating, effortless movement."

Aileene Lockhart and *Esther E.Pease,* 1977 (1966).

Rebound

The catching of the potential energy released in a fall where, when the falling body part reaches the limit of its stretch, the part recoils like a spring and the regathered energy is shunted in a new direction; a Limón term.

Daniel Lewis, 1984.

Ballon (Fr.)

Literally 'bounce' — refers to ease in ascent and descent in classical ballet allegro as exemplified in Bournonville style.

"The smooth falling and rising of the feet in the passage from step to step, is the ideal achievement of the classic ballet technique. The most important elements in ballon are the light ascent and the soft descent to the floor."

Lincoln Kirstein and *Muriel Stuart,* 1977 (1952).

Buoyancy

"...a light, smooth, spongy, quality..."; said of Paul Taylor's movement style.

Deborah Jowitt, 1977.

Tension/Relaxation

The Delsartian concept of Reaction, or Recoil, not as opposite states but as tendencies, of increasing and decreasing tension, which are seen as compensating qualities in the "rhythm of life".

Ted Shawn, 1963 (1954).

Spannung und Entspannung (Ger.)

Usually translated as tension and relaxation which implies two states, tense and relaxed, whereas in its original language, Spannung is an ongoing state of change, more like tensioning and releasing.

Ted Shawn, 1963 (1954).

Tension

A force which appears in a variety of forms, i.e., a muscular activeness, perceptual alertness, feeling, readiness to move, resistance to pressure and the need to accelerate.

Valerie Preston-Dunlop, 1987.

Peripheral tension

Slight tension in the hands or feet during movement which is guided by those parts.

Anna Markard, Rehearsal.

Effortless
   A way of moving which is without stress or special tension for the body, without the trained posture and body carriage of the mainstream professional dancer.
   Laurie Booth, Interview.

Release
   Letting go muscular tension. (Term derived from Alexander Technique)
   Gregory Nash, Interview.

Release
   Letting go the body's tension, so that gravity can be both felt and seen as initiation for the move and possibly as its resolution.
   Rosemary Brandt, Interview.

Collapse
   "A sinking movement involving the controlled release of tension of the entire body or any of its parts."
   Aileene Lockhart and *Esther E. Pease,* 1977 (1966).

Compress the weight, To
   The feeling in Latin American dancing where the control in the pelvis and the pushing down of the weight into the floor helps you to get the rhythm of the dance.
   Geoffrey Hearn, Interview.

Weighted movement
   "The viewer is involved in seeing the energy that presses into the floor or lifts out of it."
   Paul Taylor, in Selma Jeanne Cohen, 1977.

Weight from the torso
   Moving with the torso right behind the movement, giving it a particular emphasis, force, and depth.
   Anna Markard, Rehearsal.

Heaviness
   Assisting the strength of a movement through the use of body weight.
   Jane Winearls, 1958.

Light and heavy
   Two sensations in T'ai Chi, light through readiness to move and heavy through being rooted to the ground.
   Katherine Allen, Interview.

Contraction, The

"An enfoldment and a shock" (Graham), "A spasm of percussive force" (de Mille), "Proceeding from a deep emotional feeling" (Nelle Fisher), "Propelling the arms and legs" (de Mille), "It is visceral" (Graham), "Revitalised, raw emotion" (de Mille).
Agnes de Mille, 1991.

Contraction and release

A Graham term for the source of her technique and movement vocabulary which is both a physical source from which movement arises, and a spiritual/mental motivation.
"...the point of ecstasy...".
Thea Barnes, Susan Sentler, and *Brenda Baden-Semper,* Interview.

Emotional content

The deep emotional feeling which gave rise to Graham's contraction, the dynamic of spasm, in the pelvis.
Agnes de Mille, 1991.

Strength and Lightness

When the force of gravity is overcome and weight is resisted using a great deal of energy or using the minimum amount of energy.
Jane Winearls, 1958.

Strength

The dynamic force of movement wherein lies the life force of dance.
Mary Wigman, 1966.

Tensile strength

The use of only those muscles which make the movement happen; said in contrast to block strength when all the muscles work indiscriminately.
Robert Cohan, Company class.

Let the breath go, To

A way of getting subtle weightiness, a soft downward dynamic.
Anna Markard, Rehearsal.

Eight powers

Eight methods of interpreting and applying force, associated with the eight trigrams of the Pa Kua. The methods can be combined in an endless number of ways, limited only by the imagination and skill of the player.
Katherine Allen, Interview.

Dynamics of movement

"Shadings in the use of energy intensity or power. Subtle variations in the treatment of movement contrasts."
Aileene Lockhart and *Esther E. Pease,* 1977 (1966).

4. INTENTION AND EFFORT QUALITIES

Eukinetics
The study of expressive qualities in dance.
Vera Maletic, 1987.

Effort, Theory of
The means for describing the motivating power for movement, as it manifests in qualities of both expressive and functional movement.
Vera Maletic, 1987.

Effort
Expressive additions to the spatial texture and rhythmic patterns already essential to the performance of a movement form; movement colourings.
Roderyk Lange, 1975.

Effort elements (The four pairs of)
The primary components of movement dynamics, which are the polar elements in time (quick/slow), in space (indirect/direct), in weight (strong/light), and in flow (bound/free).
Rudolf Laban, 1950.

Intention
That which informs all movement and dictates the initiation of the movement.
Simone Michelle, 1990.

Intention
The motivation for moving; may be dramatic, literal, or purely motional; heightening the dynamic content of the phrase is achieved through volition, it has to be found by the dancer from within.
Valerie Preston-Dunlop, Interview.

Movement and image
The imagined intention of movement giving it both form and content.
"I reach for a star, straight up, to place it as a crown on her head, and I enclose her with the cloak of life"; said of the opening dynamic phrase of Graham's "Diversion of Angels".
Bertram Ross, Informal discussion.

Inner necessity
The reason for moving "like that, in that instance", which has to be found in order to give the performance a dynamic — "without dynamics it is dull, dull, dull."
Dorothy Madden, Rehearsing.

Intensity

"The depth of feeling or concentration" given to the movement.
Aileene Lockhart and *Esther E. Pease,* 1977 (1966).

Effort

"The inner impulse from which movement originates".
Rudolf Laban, 1950.

Inner attitude

The intention of the mover towards space, time, weight, and flow, giving rhythm and nuance.
Rudolf Laban, 1950.

Fighting attitude of the performer

To weight, space, time, and flow which results in firm, direct, sudden, and bound movement qualitites.
Rudolf Laban, 1950.

Yielding attitude

To weight, space, time and flow, resulting in light, flexible, sustained and free movement qualities.
Rudolf Laban, 1950.

Attitude to space

Indirect or direct, all-encompassing or pinpointed focus — words attempting to express the poles on the spatial attitude. The mover intends in space, intends that the spatial quality of the movement is evident.
Peggy Hackney, Interview.

Attitude to weight

Strong-light, fine touch-pressure, gentle-forceful, power-delicacy, are words attempting to express the poles on the weight attitude. The mover intends in weight, intends that the weight quality of the movement is evident.
Peggy Hackney, Interview.

Effort quality coaching

"The nuance of performance which an understanding of Laban's effort theory in practice helps me to achieve with my Latin couples."

"Cha, cha, CHA, but come out of it with lightness, and free flow; no, you're stopping, let it flow on. Now do it with the direct gaze, with intensity — and reflect that in your posture."
Ruud Vermey, Coaching competitors.

Basic effort actions, The eight

"In dancing, effort actions do not often appear in their undiluted or unmixed form...however, they act as recognisable landmarks in the ephemeral rhythm and flow of dance and so are identified. They are called floating, thrusting, gliding, slashing, dabbing, wringing, flicking, and pressing," in Laban terminology.

Valerie Preston-Dunlop, 1981.

Element combination

The effort and shape elements which appear together simultaneously or sequentially, in qualitative movement.

Cecily Dell, 1970.

Inner attitudes

Incomplete efforts, movement when only two motion factors "seem to give the (dynamic) shading to the movement" and in which "the following characteristics are found": space/time appears 'awake', weight/flow appears 'dreamlike', space/flow appears 'remote', weight/time appears 'near', space/weight appears 'stable', time/flow appears 'mobile'.

Rudolf Laban, 1950.

Action drive

"Basic effort actions in which the flow remains latent and only the factors of Weight, Time and Space operate". A combination of three incomplete efforts "to which it is difficult to give names" but for which "the following characteristics are found"; 'near' (not 'remote'), 'stable' (not 'mobile'), and 'awake' (not 'dreamlike').

Rudolf Laban, 1950.

Passion drive

"When flow replaces space and no particular attitude towards shape is displayed" ..."bodily actions are particularly expressive of emotion and feeling. In this case we speak of the Passion Drive". "The following characteristics are found": 'near' (not 'remote'), 'mobile' (not 'stable'), and 'dreamlike' (not 'awake').

Rudolf Laban, 1950.

Effort derivatives

Not only can effort actions combine sequentially in rhythms, but they have derivatives through emphasis being given to one element; hence a pressing effort can be emphasised in respect of force, directness or sustainment; crushing, cutting and squeezing are terms suggested for these derivatives.

Rudolf Laban, 1948(a).

Throwing

The dynamic quality of an action, as if throwing the limb or torso into the air, or onto the ground.

Christopher Bruce, Rehearsal.

Pushing

Moving against resistance which is either there anatomically or has to be created by the dancer.

"Push your knees open (in sitting)."; "Push your leg away."
Robert Cohan, Company class.

Balletic dynamic

The dynamic qualities originally given to some movements in the ballet vocabulary : "battu", "fouetté", "glissé", "frappé", "tombé", "jeté", "coupé".
Rudolf Laban, 1966 (1939).

5. TIMING AND ACCENT

Temporality of consciousness

The timing, tempo, speed of movement taken as related to the speed of other phenomena in the planet.
Ushio Amagatsu, 1992.

Natural pace

The timing of a performance work which can be forced into faster or slower, or be conceived as fast or slow, or can be allowed to settle into the pace that the activity gives it; said in relation to work which emerges from interaction with a spatial installation.
Rosemary Butcher, Interview.

Proper time

The duration and quality of timing needed to do the movement of each part of the body; hence, the timing of the steps, of the arms, of the rib cage....
Carla Maxwell, Interview.

Duration of movement, The

The relative time length of movements as shorter or longer than each other, and the organisation of their length according to counts and measures.
Rudolf Laban, 1956.

Proportion

The relative duration of movement qualities, in any proportion (uncounted), which gives effort rhythm.
Rudolf Laban, 1948(a).

Accuracy of time

The exact duration of the movement phrase, repeatable in accurate detail, as the identity of the phrase.

"Accuracy of time is necessary to maintain the designed space. Change the space and the time changes, unless the speed of the particular phrase changes in order to keep the time the same. Change the time and the space, and the movement changes."
Carolyn Brown, 1968.

Timing

In Cunningham work this refers to the precision of the duration of a phrase, remembered by the dancer's muscle memory, checked with a stop watch.
David Vaughan, Conversation.

Timing

The subtle use of time in movement.
"hesitation", "attack", "take your time", "get there on 4", "Delay your start", "now go for it", "it's 5, 1 and a 2,", "speed it up a bit", "no, exactly together."
Christopher Bruce, Rehearsing.

Attitude to time

Prolonging-condensing the movement, sustained-sudden, decelerating-accelerating, are words attempting to express the poles in the time attitude. The mover intends in time, intends that the time of the movement is evident.
Peggy Hackney, Interview.

Dual timing

Internal and external timing; the quick decision making and preparation made by the dancer in order to have the main movement on time and unhurried.
"You've got to be organised in time."
Robert Cohan, Company class.

Felt timing

"The duration and the accent of the movement, not the analysis of it into its count time".
Doris Rudko, Interview.

Decelerating-accelerating

Slowing down or speeding up within a movement and within a phrase and within a dance which alters its dynamic impact.
Eds.

Letting go

A way of increasing the speed of the movement by allowing gravity to cause acceleration.
Rosemary Brandt, Interview.

Accent

"...energy punctuated by beat...".
Doris Humphrey, 1959.

Accent

The greatest use of effort in a movement to highlight that point.
Jane Winearls, 1958.

Accents
    The stronger beats (movement beats, not necessarily musical beats) in a sequence or series of movements.
    Daniel Lewis, 1984.

Placing on the beat
    Deriving from a concept of the beat as three-dimensional, with a front, middle, and back; there are at least three places to begin or end a movement, each giving different dynamic or attack.
    Stephen Preston, Interview.

Sharpness
    The result of the ability to command quick applications of energy plus speed.
    Doris Humphrey, 1959.

Percussive
    "A movement quality of a ballistic, thrusting, aggressive nature; the quick checking of the force of the impetus."
    Aileene Lockhart and *Esther E. Pease,* 1977 (1966).

Percussive and sharp
    Two of the dynamic qualities used in the Limón technique to provide contrast in movement.
    Carla Maxwell, Interview.

Anacrusis
    "An up-beat preceding the primary accent at the beginning of a phrase; an unaccented preparatory movement."
    Aileene Lockhart and *Esther E. Pease,* 1977.

Stress and accentuation
    The strong and light stress in movement, found in stamps, claps, and taps, and in changes of muscular energy during movement.
    Rudolf Laban, 1956.

Initial accent
    The sudden gathering and release of tension, resulting in an impulsive movement.
    Jane Winearls, 1958.

Terminal accent
    The gathering of tension throughout the movement with the climax at the end, in order to attain a new state.
    Jane Winearls, 1958.

Transitional accent

The balancing of strength and weight so that neither the beginning or end of the movement is highlighted but instead the connection between the two is emphasised, as in a swing.

Jane Winearls, 1958.

Placing the emphasis

Finding the important part of a movement, wherever and whenever that might be, and giving it the subtle stress necessary.

Anna Markard, Rehearsal.

Pointers

The high points in a phrase of movement which the choreographer deliberately structures; used in tiny movement as well as full-sized.

Lea Anderson, Interview.

Impulse

A speedy initiation to the movement which then continuously decelerates, so providing a felt connection between one movement and the next.

Rosemary Brandt, Interview.

Impulse phrasing

Placing the accent at the start of the movement phrase which then dies away.

Marion North, 1971.

Impactive phrasing

A phrase which builds up to a definite movement at its end.

Marion North, 1971.

Impact

The quality of a movement which builds up to a moment of arrival often in a perceived body design.

Rosemary Brandt, Interview.

Swing

The quality of a movement which has its fastest moment in the middle, both seen and experienced as a curving spatial progression.

Rosemary Brandt, Interview.

Impulses of mime

The two poles of "shock" and "slow motion", between which are shades of quality and dynamic stylization.

Étienne Decroux in Alvin Epstein, 1958.

Continuous

The quality of unaccented movement, made at any speed, but one in which the dancer is constantly measuring the energy in order to hide the natural tendency in movement to flow between tension and release.
Rosemary Brandt, Interview.

Sustained

"A continuous controlled smooth movement quality. The amount of force is constant throughout."
Aileene Lockhart and *Esther E. Pease,* 1977 (1966).

Vibratory

"A movement quality of a staccato nature in which the energy is applied to the movement in short, sporadic bursts."
Aileene Lockhart and *Esther E. Pease,* 1977 (1966).

Vibration

A dynamic quality of movement used by Hanya Holm.
Don Redlich, Informal discussion.

Punctuate the phrase, To

To use a gesture or defined movement to produce a highlight in an activity.
Yolande Snaith, 1991.

Normal pace

Although there is no such thing as a universally agreed normality, one can say that most people's heartbeat at rest is beating normally, an unhurried walk is normal, a steady breathing rhythm is normal. If we cannot say that, then how do we recognise a hurried walk? More hurried than what? Than something we perceive as normal, presumably. These normalities are crucial datum points from which meaning is discerned.
Valerie Preston-Dunlop, 1989.

6. RHYTHM

Rhythm in bodily movement

"A continuous play of forces pulling now in harmony, now in opposition, within the space-time continuum."
F. Mary Fee, 1973.

Rhythm

"In relation to organization, rhythm may be considered as the process by which events taking place in time are marked off, related and organized."
Margaret H'Doubler, 1957 (1940).

Rhythm

The organisation of time in a way capable of being identified by the organs of perception.

Curt Sachs, in Roderyk Lange, 1975.

Rhythm

"Mostly the rhythm is dictated by the quality of the movement, but sometimes by where someone needs to be at a given time in reference to another group of dancers."

Merce Cunningham, in Merce Cunningham & Jacqueline Lesschaeve, 1985.

Rhythm

"It is the most powerful ingredient of music and dancing. It derives from the heartbeat and is basic to our natures. Breathing, walking, habit are all expressions of it. It is our constant battle with gravity, with mother earth."

Peggy van Praagh and *Peter Brinson,* 1963.

Time Rhythm

Rhythms which arise from the qualities of suddenness and sustainment and their short or prolonged duration in any sequence.

Rudolf Laban, 1948(a).

Action rhythm

The rhythm of the movement is derived from the movement itself and the dancer's sensibility to it.

"Cunningham requires of his dancers that the rhythm come from within: from the nature of the step, from the nature of the phrase and from the dancer's own musculature."

Carolyn Brown, 1968.

Action rhythm

"...rhythm comes out of the nature of the movement itself...".

Carolyn Brown, 1968.

Breath rhythm

The phrasing of the movement is determined by the breathing of the individual dancer or of the choreographer.

Doris Humphrey, 1959.

Effort rhythms

Rhythms of bodily action manifest as changes in weight, space, time and flow, in variety.

Rudolf Laban, 1950.

Emotional rhythm

Results in: ..."a dramatic rhythmic pattern"...which is used as..."The motivation for motor rhythms or gesture sequences"...in dance.

Doris Humphrey, 1959.

Psychological rhythms

Rhythms, phrasing, tempi in a dance work as a whole which are the result of a dramatic or kinetic situation, "They are not imposed, they have to come out of the dancers' inner sense of timing."
Dorothy Madden, Interview.

Rhythm as intellectual

The highly mathematical structure of Bharata Natyam rhythmic patterns, counted alike by dancer, musician and spectator and regarded as primarily intellectual rather than physicalized.
Shobana Jeyasingh, Interview.

Free rhythm

With non-recurrent elements but with a discernible phrase shaping the movement sentence.
Roderyk Lange, 1975.

Inherent rhythm

The organic naturalness of rhythm in the body through control and release, work and rest, repetition and periodicity.
"Rhythm as an experience may be said to be a measured energy."
Margaret N. H'Doubler, 1957 (1940).

Rhythm, The

The beat of a pop performer's music which dominates the dance that he does, dictating the dynamics and phrasing, while allowing him freedom to make his own style.
"You're a slave to the rhythm."
Eds, after Michael Jackson, 1993.

Metrical rhythm

Rhythms of measured time units; arising through the recurrence of units of a certain length of time in movement.
Roderyk Lange, 1975.

Metre

The organisation of counts or beats by measures.
Daniel Lewis, 1984.

Measure

A group of counts or beats, two beats, three beats, five beats.
Daniel Lewis, 1984.

Counting

"[Counting is needed] to define the beats, to clarify the transitions from one theme to the next, to be precise in giving the necessary accents, the moments of arrested movement and breathing."
Mary Wigman, 1966.

Metric rhythm

The countable rhythm of a movement phrase, one which may arise out of the movement itself resulting in a regular or mixed metric rhythm; alternatively the rhythm may be imposed on the movement by applying counts.

Erica Stanton, Interview.

Rhythmically square

Counted material; a term used to distinguish counted material from Merce Cunningham's uncounted way of using rhythm according to the actions that produce it.

David Vaughan in Richard Kostelanetz, 1992.

Multiple rhythms

Metric rhythms which keep changing, such as $^6/_2$, $^5/_4$, $^4/_4$, $^7/_4$, used as a teaching device to shift habits and open up possibilities.

Jane Dudley, Interview.

Greek rhythms

Arising from oratory in the Hellenic era, the six rhythmic forms — i.e. the iambus (of short-long durations), trochee (long-short), dactylus (long-short-short), anapaestus (short-short-long), paean (long-short-long or other combinations of five units), ionian (long-long-short-short).

Rudolf Laban, 1950.

Rhythmic patterns

The mathematical forms of the rhythm of dance, especially evident in the classical Indian style of Bharatha Natyam in which the footwork of the dance makes visible the intricate rhythmic game playing of the music.

Shobana Jeyasingh, 1993.

Motor rhythm

The rhythmic structure of movement as experienced and dictated by the body's response to a movement phrase.

Doris Humphrey, 1959.

Organic rhythm

Movements are put together so that they are joined functionally. They have muscle logic.

Paul Taylor, in Selma Jeanne Cohen, 1977.

Organic rhythm

A rhythm which emerges by the way movements are put together so that they grow out of each other. Elements such as momentum, rebound, swing, preparation into action, tension and release, occur in organically organised phrases; transitions play an important part.

Valerie Preston-Dunlop, 1992.

Mixed rhythms
Dance material, some of which is counted and some of which allows the rhythm to emerge out of the action.
Darshan Singh Bhuller, Rehearsing.

Phases of a contact
The preparation, the contact, and the release.
Rudolf Laban and *F.C. Lawrence, 1947.*

Phases of an action
The preparation, the main action and the recovery.
Rudolf Laban and *F.C. Lawrence, 1947.*

Work rhythms (as source)
Strings of action from work such as throwing, pulling, striking.
Alan Salter with *Stina Grist, 1977.*

Polyrhythm (in the dancer's body)
Two or more rhythmic patterns occurring concurrently in the dancer's body, usually between arms and weight support.
Roderyk Lange, 1974.

Rhythmic counterpoint within the body
Two or more rhythms occurring simultaneously within the body.
Doris Humphrey, 1959.

Rhythmic nuance
Rhythmic variety and subtlety.
James Klosty, 1975.

Rhythmic sources
"...the rhythm comes from within: from the nature of the step, from the nature of the phrase, and from the dancer's own musculature; not from without...".
James Klosty, 1975.

Four sources of rhythm
"1) the breathing-singing-speaking apparatus which leads to phrasing and phrase rhythm, 2) the partly unconscious rhythms of function: the heart beat, peristalsis, contraction and relaxation of muscles, waves of sensation through the nerve ends, 3) the propelling mechanism, the legs, 4) emotional rhythm: surges and ebbs of feeling, with accents...".
Doris Humphrey, 1959.

Rhythmicise

To take movement vocabulary which is unclear in its rhythm and to form its character by either finding its innate rhythm and clarifying it or by organising it according to metrical rhythmic principles.
Stephanie Jordan, 1992.

Tempo

A slow, medium or quick pace.
Rudolf Laban, 1950.

Tempo

"The speed of the beat is the tempo."
Lynne Anne Blom and *L. Tarin Chaplin,* 1982.

Tempo rubato

Elasticity and flexibility with the tempo and rhythm, taking a minute part of time from one unit and adding it to the preceding or following unit, bringing, however, the phrase back to the beat in the end.
Roderyk Lange, 1975.

Dynamics of competition ballroom dance

The flow of the weight contrasted with the rhythmicised footwork and both subtle and varied arm movements.

"Use more energy. Gently now. Now swing it. Hover. Pliable in your ankles. Cha cha cha and 2 and 3."
Geoffrey Hearn, Instructing.

Sing, To

To dance with rhythmic articulation which is both felt and performed.
Jane Dudley, Interview.

7.   PHRASING

Phrase

"...'phrase' means length of time, breath length. If you're angry it's a short breath, it's a short phrase."
Martha Graham in Elinor Rogosin, 1980.

Phrases

Movement sequences which have a start and go on until they finish; may be one breath length, last four counts, or "minutes long without stopping or slowing down".
Trisha Brown and *Yvonne Rainer* in Trisha Brown, 1987.

Phrase

"...the organisation of movement in time-design...".
Doris Humphrey, 1959.

Shape, The (of a phrase)

Not the spatial form of the phrase, but the rise and fall of energy, ebb and flow of continuity, climax and calm of the phrase.
Jane Dudley, Interview.

Breath

"...commands the function of muscles and joints...puts the breaks in the dynamic structure and dictates the phrasing of the flowing passages...".
Mary Wigman, 1966.

Movement phrase

A sequence of movements with a recognisable shape, having a beginning and an end and consisting of a variety of lengths of movement and with rises and falls in its dynamic composition.
Doris Humphrey, 1959.

Beyond the step

What there is to be learnt over and above getting the basic pattern of the movement, namely, the effort and recovery, the phrasing, the ebb and flow of energy within the phrase.
Rosemary Brandt, Interview.

Phrasing as energy change

"...the way in which energy is distributed in the executing of a movement or series of movements. What makes one kind of movement different from another is not so much variations in arrangements of parts of the body as differences in energy investment."
Yvonne Rainer, 1968.

Phrasing

"Phrasing is an organizing factor underlying the performance and perception of movement within the space-time-weight-flow continuum. The term refers predominantly to the qualitative rhythm of movement. It is differentiated from the notion of a Phrase as a shorter or longer compositional unit of movement or dance. The proposed phrasing taxonomy encompasses various groupings of movement qualities (or Efforts) in which changing or unchanging, and repetitive patterns can be identified."
Vera Maletic, Contributed.

Silent score, A

In a musicless dance work, the (silent) music that develops from the three-dimensional phrasing of the rhythm and energy of the movement, kinetic music that can be felt and hummed by the performer.
Jodi Falke, Interview.

Phrasing

"A phrase is simply two or more consecutive movements, while phrasing...refers to the manner of execution."
Yvonne Rainer, 1968.

Sequences

Movements which begin as ideas, and remain so until the dancer deals with them by finding how the constituent parts belong together, from which a sequence of dance can emerge.
Rosemary Brandt, Interview.

Sequencing and phrasing

The way movement flows and interacts between preparation, action, and recovery.
Janis Pforsich, Ellen Goldman, John Chanik, and *Lynn Wenning,* Contributed.

Sentences

Phrases of movement which have some emergent rhythmic content through the changing stresses of activity and recovery in time, flow or spatial form.
Marion North, 1971.

Movement colourings

Dynamic qualities, in complex variation, as subtle and varied as visual colouring in painting, for which it is necessary to know the nature of the colour, its intensity, its fluid/abrupt transition to the next colour, the durational proportions of each colour in the phrase.
Valerie Preston-Dunlop, Seminar.

Phrasing as change of movement shape

"...no one part of the series is made any more important than any other. For four and a half minutes a great variety of movement shapes occur, but they are of equal weight and are equally emphasized."
Yvonne Rainer, 1968.

Break, A

The ending movements of a phrase, usually one which has repeated step patterns; used in folk dance, character dance and tap dance particularly.
Robert Harrold, Interview.

Unorganic

Phrasing in which extraneous movement or a foreign insertion prevents the body from following its natural muscular path. It will look false and usually feel false for the dancer.
Paul Taylor, "Private Domain" 1987.

Random insertion

An odd movement put into a phrase which is otherwise organic gives both the performer and the audience a jolt; it adds interest into what can otherwise eventually seem predictable.

Valerie Preston-Dunlop, 1992.

Freeze, The

The main moment in a break dance sequence, in which the rapid footwork and spins common to all break dances was punctuated by a flash of stillness, the moment of individual style, intricate, witty, insulting or obscene.

Sally Banes in Nelson George et al, 1985.

Non-linear sequencing

"...progresses in units not directly related to each other." (Used by Meredith Monk).

Marcia Siegel, 1986.

Concealed punctuation

Phrasing in a dance which is hidden, giving the impression of an endless continuum of motion; said of Ian Spink's work.

Stephanie Jordan, 1992.

Chapter 9 SPACE-IN-THE-BODY AND THE DANCER IN SPACE

1. SPACE-IN-THE-BODY; CHOREUTICS

Space

A tangible element to move through, with conscious intention, a place to journey in.

Robert Cohan, 1986.

Raumkörper (Ger.)

"...the space-body...is to the dancer as substantial and real as his physical body."
Elizabeth Selden in Katharine Everett Gilbert, 1983 (1941).

Positive space

The space taken up by the body.
"...tangible, as object, as occupying a given amount of space."
Lynne Anne Blom and *L. Tarin Chaplin,* 1982.

Negative space

"...the area between objects, between the positive shapes."
Lynne Anne Blom and *L. Tarin Chaplin,* 1982.

Abstract language

"Ballet expresses itself in an abstract language of lines and volumes...."
André Levinson (1928) in Joan Acocella and Lynn Garafola, 1991.

Space-in-the-body

Shapes, designs, air patterns made by each dancer in his own kinesphere as his way of expressing finitely the infinite relationship of his body with the space.
Valerie Preston-Dunlop, 1987.

Address the space, To

To be aware of how the body is moving into the space; to present the body to the space which it is entering; to be aware of the way in which body and space interact.
Hanya Holm in Margaret Lloyd, 1986.

Space as a partner

Space as a partner in a dialogue with the moving body.
Walter Sorell, 1976.

296

Create energy, To

To enliven the space between one limb and another, to make the space around the body alive.

Gillian Lynne, Interview.

Charge the air, To

To enhance the space immediately around himself through communicating a thought-out three-dimensionality and an "eloquent interior life"; said of Laurie Booth.

Judith Mackrell, Interview.

Choreutics

The theoretical articulation of space for the practice of dance composition and research.

Vera Maletic, 1987.

Choreutics

The spatial factor in movement.

Simone Michelle, Interview.

Choreutics

"[This]...may be explained as the practical study of the various forms of (more or less) harmonised movement."

Rudolf Laban, 1966 (1939).

Choreutic discernment

The ability to distinguish between a movement and the abstract linear forms within it.

Valerie Preston-Dunlop, Interview.

Choreutic eye, To develop a

"To learn to look for line as well as flesh and blood."

Valerie Preston-Dunlop, Interview.

2. THE KINESPHERE AND ITS MAPS

Kinesphere

"...is the sphere of movement surrounding the body, which can be reached by extending the limbs without changing one's stance."

Rudolf Laban, 1948.

Individual action space

"An action space around the performer"; "This individual 'action or reaching space' Laban called a person's individual 'kinesphere': One may also call it an individual's personal space."

Irmgard Bartenieff, 1974.

Conversational space

Small-sized, intimate space contrasted with full kinesphere size; used in jazz dancing which retains the 1920's style.

Thea Barnes, Interview.

Kinesphere

"...a place with boundaries, a place to organise, a place to rotate, to diminish, to enlarge."

Valerie Preston-Dunlop, 1987.

Invisible walls

The edge or border of the dancer's own space — "the cylinder of air in which the dancer moves" —, seen through "a vortex of curves, segments of circles, arcs" of the classic ballet vocabulary.

André Levinson (1925) in Joan Acocella and Lynn Garafola, 1991.

Body image boundary

The psychological barrier which acts as a boundary around each individual to mark out the intimate space around the body regarded as 'mine', not 'yours'; the edge of the dancer's own space beyond which is the common domain.

Eds. from *Seymour Fisher* and *Sidney E. Cleveland,* 1968.

Personal space

The personal area, the imagined space which each has as his own to fill with his movement.

Valerie Preston-Dunlop, 1987.

Inhabited space

"The space which was more or less amorphous can have shape, can be not merely occupied physically but positively inhabited."

Alan Salter, 1977.

Model of space

A way of imagining the space around the body as a sphere, the inner surface of which is followed by the limbs in their circular motion.

Laurie Booth, Interview.

Spheric space

A way of visualising the dancer's space as a sphere whose centre is the centre of the dancer's body.

Rudolf Laban, 1966 (1939).

Interior body map

A conceptual framework of the dancer's own space, in which planes of latitude and longitude are imagined which serve as guidelines for movement interpretation; said of the map suggested by the Eshkol-Wachmann movement notation model.

"...mathematical weapons...."
Laurie Booth, Interview.

System of reference

The Eshkol-Wachmann map of the kinesphere in which movement is seen as planal, or conical at an angle around an axis, and rotational turning around the axis itself, with centres at moving joints.
Noa Eshkol, 1958.

Spatial orientation of the dancer

The sphere of personal space of each dancer which turns and travels with her, within the cubic space of the environment (studio, stage) which is constant.
Albrecht Knust, 1979.

Dancer's square

A Cecchetti principle for the orientation of the dancer to the audience, with the corners of the square (1–4) and the walls (5)(8).
Peggy van Praagh and *Peter Brinson,* 1963.

Dancer's square

The cubic, kinesphere-sized spatial structure which a ballet dancer works to, so that her alignment is clearly orientated wherever she is on stage.
Mirella Bartrip and *Teresa Kelsey,* Interview.

Space module

The diagram of the ballet dancer's square showing the spherical orientation of the body movement inside the cubic map for an audience-orientated technique.
Lincoln Kirstein, 1977 (1952).

Cylinder space/Square space

Images of a defined space, a particular volume, in which to work; used by Hanya Holm.
Don Redlich, Informal discussion.

Cubic space

A map of the space taken from architectural space and best fitting the dancer's environmental space rather than the dancer's personal space, for which icosahedral space is a better fit.
Rudolf Laban, 1966 (1939).

Octahedron
 A three-dimensional structure which embodies the directions high, right, forward, left, back, and deep. The octahedron is the spatial map for the basic movements of danse d'école.
 Valerie Preston-Dunlop, 1987.

Icosahedral scaffolding
 A term for the structure with which to orientate the dancers' trace forms/ pathways/patterns; the 3-dimensional form (icosahedron) which arises from turning cubic space into spheric space.
 Rudolf Laban, 1966 (1939).

Icosahedron
 A three-dimensional spherical structure used as a grid to orientate oblique and diagonal movements in relation to the three stable planes.
 Valerie Preston-Dunlop, 1984.

Territory
 A space set up by the choreographer as belonging to a dancer, a duet or a group; "...the diagonal line which is the territory of the duet..."; said of Siobhan Davies's "Rushes" (1982).
 Stephanie Jordan and *Helen Thomas, 1990.*

3.   ELEMENTS OF ORIENTATION

Geometry (in classical ballet)
 "One of the consistencies that runs through all the generations of classical ballet is a concern with geometry."
 Robert Greskovic, 1984.

Three dimensions, The
 Height, breadth, depth are the basic elements of orientation in space, each containing two opposite directions.
 Rudolf Laban, 1966 (1939).

Cardinal directions, The
 Up, down, right, left, backwards, and forwards, taken as the basic spatial orientation of the dancer's movements.
 Eds.

Basic spatial actions
 These are rising-falling, opening-crossing, advancing-retreating, and growing and shrinking.
 Rudolf Laban, 1948.

Shape-flow

A change of relationship of one, several or all of the parts of the body, in which growing or shrinking takes place, especially in the total body or the torso.

Cecily Dell, 1970.

Shape-flow

A change of relationship of one, several or all of the parts of the body, in which folding or unfolding takes place, especially in the limbs; may also be termed closing or opening.

Cecily Dell, 1970.

Verticality

The up/down dimension, which is inherent to human spatiality.

"It is not invented, you have it in you."

Rosemary Brandt, Interview.

Posture

"There is only one law of posture I have been able to discover — the perpendicular line connecting heaven and earth."

Martha Graham, 1941.

Stability

The use of movements in the cardinal directions, up, down, left, right, forward, and backward such that the centre of weight tends to remain directly over the stance, or to repeatedly return to it.

Rudolf Laban, 1971 (1950).

Three-dimensional cross

A cross formed by the six dimensional directions high, deep, right, left, forward, and backward which radiate from the centre of the body.

Rudolf Laban, 1966 (1939).

Three planes

The vertical (or frontal) plane, the horizontal plane, and the sagittal plane, also called 'the door plane', 'the table plane', and 'the wheel plane'.

Rudolf Laban, 1966 (1939).

Wheel plane

The plane which divides the space on the right from that on the left and passes through the body at the line of the spine; also known as 'the sagittal plane'.

Valerie Preston-Dunlop, 1987.

Door plane or frontal plane

The plane which divides the space in front of the body from the space behind it; also known as 'the vertical plane'.

Valerie Preston-Dunlop, 1987.

Table plane

The plane which divides the space above the waist from that below; also known as 'the horizontal plane'.
Valerie Preston-Dunlop, 1987.

Three planes, The

"Useful terms to make sure the movement is clearly located, both to the space and to the structure of my body in that space. That understanding enhances the spatial flow of the movement."
Rosemary Brandt, Interview.

On the ear, To go

A way of describing the path of an arm circle that is absolutely sideways, and done without turning the head towards the arm.
Anna Markard, Rehearsal.

Compass

The eight points of reference used in ballet's orientation to the 4 sides and 4 corners of the dancer's space.
Imperial Society of Teachers of Dancing, Cecchetti Study Day.

Directions of the body

The Cecchetti method defines eight directions of the body: croisé-devant, à la quatrième devant, écarté, effacé, à la seconde, épaulé, à la quatrième derrière, croisé derrière.
Cyril W. Beaumont and *Stanislas Idzikowski,* 1975.

Dancer's square

The dancer can be imagined as being at the centre of a square which is divided by eight lines radiating from centre to the corners and to the mid-points of the sides of the square. The dancer's positioning in relation to these directions produces the various alignments of croisé, en face, effacé, écarté, and épaulé. More accurately the dancer may be envisioned as standing at the centre of a cube which moves with the dancer.

"[The dancer]...poses or moves within an imaginary cube and it is the total movement within that cube which gives depth, height and breadth to the choreographic design."
Joan Lawson, 1960.

Basic principles of classical ballet

"...classical ballet is built on croisé and effacé. It is from croisé and effacé that the richness of its forms is drawn, and it could never blossom out so luxuriously were it confined to the tedious and monotonous direction en face (facing front)."
Agrippina Vaganova, 1969.

Effacé

Literally 'shaded', often used as a synonym for 'ouvert'.

"...a position in which the dancer stands facing one of the downstage corners with the leg furthest from the audience extended to the fourth in front, and the arm nearest the audience raised en haut, in effect 'shading' a portion of the body."

Richard Glasstone, 1977.

Ouvert

"Open. Indicates any position or pose in which the legs are not crossed in relation to the spectator."

Richard Glasstone, 1977.

Croisé

"Crossed. Used to describe any position or pose in which the dancer's legs appear crossed in relation to the audience."

Richard Glasstone, 1977.

En face

A way of presenting the dancer straight on, opening to the audience, in contrast to the customary diagonal presentation of effacé and croisé; a Bournonville style of presentation.

Clement Crisp, Interview.

Écarté

A position standing on one leg with the other leg extended to the side along a diagonal line. The rest of the body echoes this line within the vertical and horizontal planes, i.e. flat or 2-dimensional.

Richard Glasstone, 1977.

Six-diametral cross

A cross formed by the twelve oblique diametral directions which radiate from the centre of the body, towards the twelve corners of the three planes.

Rudolf Laban, 1966 (1939).

Diametral directions

Directions which contain two spatial elements: up-open, forward-left, down-forwards, right-back, up and left, etc., etc.

Valerie Preston-Dunlop, 1987.

Four-diagonal cross, The

A cross formed by the eight diagonal directions which radiate from the centre of the body, towards the eight corners of a cube.

Rudolf Laban, 1966 (1939).

Diagonal directions

Directions which contain three spatial elements: high-right-forward, deep-left-backward, etc; a term also used for the two diagonals of the stage, hence confusing.
Valerie Preston-Dunlop, 1987.

Lability

The use of movements in the diametral and diagonal directions so that the weight moves away from being above the stance, with a tendency to lose equilibrium.
Rudolf Laban, 1966 (1939).

Vertical, horizontal, and inclined linear forms

Movement forms which are either up and down, or parallel to the floor, or sloping, leaning, and oblique; they may be of any size, be placed anywhere around the body, and be danced by any part of the body.
Valerie Preston-Dunlop, 1987.

Location

A recognised place in the kinesphere which has a definite directional value, like 'high right', or 'deep forwards', or 'deep left back', or 'centre'. A location is not a rigid pin point in space. It is, rather, a small area centred on a point so that there is leeway, according to where the movement comes from and where it is going.
Valerie Preston-Dunlop, 1984.

Theory of crosses of axes

The theory that the human's concept of his orientation in space has three modes: a) the constant cross of axes, b) the standard cross of axes, c) the cross of the body's axes.
Albrecht Knust, 1979.

Body space — Stage space

A Hanya Holm term for orientating directions according to the body or to the space.
Don Redlich, Informal discussion.

Constant cross of axes

A concept of the body in space in which up/down is understood as the vertical line of gravity, and forward is designated as forward by reference to some constant feature in the environment, such as downstage in a theatre or towards the mirror in a studio space.
Valerie Preston-Dunlop, 1987.

Orientation in a studio space

Taking directions in complex combinations from the spatial landmarks in the studio.
"...reach back towards the mirrors...", "...arm slicing across towards the wall...."
Scott Clark, Teaching.

Standard cross of axes
>A concept for orientating the body in space in which up/down is understood as the vertical line of gravity and forward as the direction in front of the mover's stance, wherever he happens to be facing.
>*Albrecht Knust,* 1979.

Cross of the body's axes
>A concept of the body in space in which up/down is understood as parallel to the line of the spine (up=headward, down=seatward) and forward is the direction in front of the chest (for arm movements) or pelvis (for leg movements).
>*Albrecht Knust,* 1979.

Bodily spatial orientation
>Getting the direction of the movement in relation to your own body and/or your partner's body, rather than through the geometry of the space.
>"The line of your nose over his finger tips.", "Look through the gap between his ear and his arm.", "Go across your body.", "The arms are level".
>*Geoffrey Hearn* and others, Instructing.

4. DESIGNED MOVEMENT

Designed movement
>One which has a clear pattern from its initiation to its completion.
>"...to see the beginning and the end...."
>*Els Grelinger,* Interview.

Spatial design
>A relationship between objects in both time and space.
>*Doris Humphrey,* 1959.

Shape of the movement
>Phrases of steps seen by the choreographer as a series of shapes, which he wishes the audience to see thus also.
>*Christopher Bruce,* Rehearsal.

Alignment
>Used in two senses: for the co-ordination of the movement line in the dancer's body; and also to refer to the co-ordination of that with the lines of the stage space.
>*Mirella Bartrip* and *Teresa Kelsey,* Interview.

Aligned
>Orientated to the room/studio/stage and/or to the dancer's own body space, and/or with other people; a precise alignment especially necessary for unison work, requiring all three kinds of spatial awareness.
>*Lea Anderson,* Interview.

Spatial motifs

Movement material whose content is shape, direction, pathway, and distance.
Sally Banes, 1980(a).

Trace forms

The dancers' pathways tracing shapes in space, as living architecture.
Rudolf Laban, 1966 (1939).

Directional movement

Reaching out from yourself toward something around you in a spoke-like path or an arc-like path; or without a clear objective to reach to, moving to make a spoke-like or an arc-like path in space.
Cecily Dell, 1970.

Line of the movement

"...not only where you start and how you finish but the path you go through to get there."
Robert Cohan, Company class.

Lines

Spatial images which aid co-ordination and alignment, images of straight lines and curves which the dancer intends and the human body approximates.
"The outside of her left foot through the back to right little finger is one line, that is the sensation."
Robert Cohan, Company class.

Form and orientation of a movement line

The linaear, planar, or plastic content of a trace is its form, while the directional content of the trace could be called its orientation; since both have one- two- or three-dimensional content, there can be confusion, so we can distinguish linear (1D form), planar (2D form), plastic (3D form) from dimension (1D orientation), diametral (2D orientation), diagonal (3D orientation).
Jeffrey Longstaff, 1992.

Shaping processes

The sculptural shaping created by the moving body parts within the three planes; widening or narrowing, rising or sinking, advancing or retreating.
Cecily Dell, 1970.

Design

A technical term in Design Drawing (Labanotation) for the pattern traced in movement, that is the path drawn in space by gestures or made as a body shape in a position.
Ann Hutchinson Guest and *Rob van Haarst,* 1991.

Taking a thread through space

An image to enable the dancer to create a continuous flow of movement.
Jane Rivers, Class.

Sending the skeleton

Spatially directing the movement through and beyond the anatomy.
"...send the finger-tips."
Gregory Nash, Interview.

Central, peripheral, and transversal paths

Paths which pass through the centre, going into it or out of it radially, such as a developé leg gesture; paths which stay on the edge of the kinesphere, as most port de bras do; paths which pass through the space between the periphery and the centre, usually on a straight line.
Valerie Preston-Dunlop, 1984.

Droit, Ouvert, Rond, Tortillé

A direct path in space; a curved movement which travels from in to out, central to peripheral, as an air pattern; a circular path in space as an air or floor pattern; a twisting path in space as air or floor pattern — it can occur in a limb or can be used to describe floor patterns.
Simone Michelle, Interview.

Droit, Ouvert, Rond, Tortillé

Feuillet's terms for step forms used in his notation system 'Choréographie', and seen by Laban as fundamental forms with inherent dynamic content.
Vera Maletic, 1987.

Pin, Wall, Ball, and Screw

Fundamental forms for body carriage or body shapes, which Laban developed from Feuillet's Droit, Ouvert, Rond, and Tortillé forms.
Vera Maletic, 1987.

Curve

The basic shape of many dance movements, with four fundamental variations: circular; flattened; arched; spiral.
Valerie Preston-Dunlop, 1987.

Circle

The frequently used carriage of arms, found in most mainstream techniques, used also as a carried circle, one which is lifted over the head from one side to the other.
"Make a circle with your arms; the sun rises and sets."
Scott Clark, Teaching.

Peripheral path

One which stays on the edge of the kinesphere, as most port de bras do.
Valerie Preston-Dunlop, 1984.

Sculptural forms

The forms in space made by the dancers as they move and as they arrive.
"...lines, loops, and tangles...."
Richard Buckle, 1981.

Centripetal (gesture or pathway)

Drawn to the centre, usually associated with a circular path.
Mary Wigman, 1966.

Centrifugal (gesture or pathway)

Fleeing from the centre, usually associated with a circular path.
Mary Wigman, 1966.

En dedans

Ballet term, meaning literally 'inwards', usually indicating movements which circle or turn towards the central axis of the body.
Jane Carr, Interview.

En dehors

Ballet term, meaning literally 'outwards', usually indicating movements which circle or turn away from the central axis of the body.
Jane Carr, Interview.

Choreutic unit

The simplest spatial form in the body, a line or a curve, which has a size, a position in/around the body, and is somehow presented to the audience as motion or position.
Valerie Preston-Dunlop, Interview.

Manner of materialisation

The distinction between the physical properties of the movement and the perceived qualities of it, in terms of the way spatial lines (choreutic units) are physically done and perceptually received.
Rosemary Brandt, 1987.

Spatial Progression

Spatial progressions must move, but not all moves are spatial progressions; only those which convey a moving spatial message. A run may be spatial progression if it conveys a line in space, but not if it conveys 'escaping' or 'as fast as possible'.
Valerie Preston-Dunlop, Interview.

Spatial Tension

"A plié in second position can give off spatial tension if it is so danced that the line between the knees is what is seen. It can give off spatial progression if a fluid lowering and lifting is what is the thing. If the end position is given emphasis, then that body design is what is conveyed."

Valerie Preston-Dunlop, Interview.

Spatial tension

The relationship between people, seen spatially, or between parts of the body so that the space between them is energised.

Lea Anderson, Interview.

Spatial Projection

Sending the energy into space beyond the body's limits.

Valerie Preston-Dunlop, 1981.

Spatial projection

The shape of the movement or the shape of the body, projecting out into the space.

"They were a series of vertical lines, projecting up through the head."

Lea Anderson, Interview.

Projecting lines inwards

The arms and hands curve so that they direct lines of energy, through the fingers, towards the dancer; said of Baroque dance.

Stephen Preston, Interview.

Body Design

A line or a curve which is made evident to the audience through the actual design of the body; the form is in the body itself rather than in its movement.

Valerie Preston-Dunlop, 1981.

Arabesque

For Blasis an infinite number of sculpture-like poses — arabesques are now usually understood to be a codified set of poses on one leg with the working leg extended most often to the back and the arms gesturing to complement the 'line'.

"...inspired by the bas-reliefs of antiquity and fragments of Greek painting, as well as by the delightful frescoes from Raphael's drawings...."

Carlo Blasis, 1968 (1820).

Attitude

A pose standing on one leg with working leg bent and one arm (or sometimes both) extended up. While the support is held over the central line of gravity, the arms and legs reach into the three dimensions against a vertical axis.

"In my opinion it is an adaptation of the much admired pose of the celebrated Mercury of Bologna."

Carlo Blasis, 1968(1820).

Architecture (of bodies in space)
The carving out of spatial forms and the creating of bodily design within the space, using pathways, gestures performed en masse, and group forms.
Walter Sorell, 1976.

Chord
A combination of two or more movements constituting together a particular entity.
Rudolf Laban, 1956.

Simultaneous clustering
Said of choreutic units, that is lines in space, and the manner of materialisation with which they occur at the same time and belong together, e.g. as in an arabesque or an attitude.
Rosemary Brandt, 1987.

Size
Working with both large and small movement in phrase making, seeing them as complementary elements and dynamic contrasts.
"From a big design to a small detail."
Rui Horta, Workshop.

Size of movement
Large and small are used to describe the size of steps and pathways, wide and narrow are used for the distance between two feet or any two parts, extended and contracted are used for leg and arm gestures; long and short are also used for the size of steps.
Peggy Hackney, Sarah Manno, and *Muriel Topaz,* 1977.

Spatial range
The relative extent of space or scope of movement; the distance between two extremes of a movement.
Aileene Lockhart and *Esther E. Pease,* 1977 (1960).

Single-space design
The design in space which a dance has at one moment in time, the snapshot view, including the design of one body through to the designs of several groups.
Doris Humphrey, 1959.

Shape of the phrase
The time-shape of the movement which is more than bits of designed movement put together like a mosaic, being tied to the breath.
"Movement...is influenced by the powerful emotional shape of the breath phrase."
Doris Humphrey, 1959.

Design in time

The shapes of movement which emerge over time, ranging from one changing transition in one body to a shape of a phrase, to the shapes in time of groups and a full-length dance.

"One space design will follow another and there will be a shape in their successions in time."

Doris Humphrey, 1959.

Sequential clustering

Said of choreutic units, that is lines in space, and the manner of materialisation in which they occur one after the other in phrases which belong together, seen as a way of providing the experience of co-ordination rather than an understanding of the working together of parts.

Rosemary Brandt, 1987.

5. SPACE AS A HARMONIC SYSTEM

Space harmony

A system of harmonic relations in the kinesphere, analogous to the organisation of pitch harmony in music, encompassing both dissonant and consonant designs; a system recognised in classical ballet and further developed in choreutics.

Rudolf Laban, 1966 (1939).

Harmony

The symmetry of designs.

Lucas Hoving, 1969.

Harmonic opposite

A direction of energy into the opposite direction to the first, creating a balanced form; seen in positions and in movements and between people.

Valerie Preston-Dunlop, 1984.

Harmonic opposite

"It is not symmetry, it is 3-dimensional balance, it's about the balanced functioning of the body in 3-dimensional space."

Rosemary Brandt, Interview.

Harmonic laws

Laban's term for the relationships which he saw as existing between the spatial structure and the dynamic content of movement.

Vera Maletic, 1987.

Parallel and perpendicular
Elements of spatial design used as floor patterns in which distance between the dancers and length of pathway are the variables.
Sally Banes, 1980.

Dynamic tensions
The spatial relationships which occur between movements going into different directions.
Roderyk Lange, 1975.

Dynamics of space
The inherent power of spatial forms, e.g. circles and squares.
Hanya Holm in Walter Sorell, 1976.

Symmetry
The simplest form of body harmony.
Marion North, 1971.

Lateral symmetry
Right-left equality.
Valerie Preston-Dunlop, 1981.

Vertical symmetry
Up-down equality (between arms and legs) or rising balanced by lowering.
Valerie Preston-Dunlop, 1981.

Sagittal symmetry
Forward-back symmetry, in a position or through a repetition.
Valerie Preston-Dunlop, 1981.

Transposing
Changing the orientation of a form and finding another version of it. This is done vertically, every direction upwards goes downwards and vice versa; horizontally, every direction to the right now goes to the left and vice versa; sagittally, every direction forwards now goes backwards and vice versa.
Valerie Preston-Dunlop, 1984.

Asymmetrical use of the body
When one side of the body is unequal to the other, usually a state which promotes motion, while symmetry in the body tends to make the movement come to a stop.
Valerie Preston-Dunlop, 1987.

Asymmetrical
"An unbalanced proportion in the design."
Aileene Lockhart and *Esther E. Pease,* 1977(1966).

Dissonance in dance

Consciousness of tension within the body evident in design.

"It is not consonance gone cockeyed; it tends to move, to distort, to make its own space designs."

Louis Horst, 1957.

Chordic shapes

"We don't make shapes singly in space, not one at a time, but because of the structure of our bodies we operate chordically, polydirectionally, as simultaneous pathways, designs, projections. As we move, the movements are perceived as discordant or harmonious."

Rosemary Brandt, Interview.

Spatial interval

The tension between one direction and another; the 180° tension is 'opposite', the 90° tension is 'at right angles' and intervals are the rest, each kind carrying their own content.

Valerie Preston-Dunlop, Seminar.

Oppositional and successional

"...lines are either opposed, in a right angle, or are flowing, as in a curve...."
Doris Humphrey, 1959.

Elegant balance

The harmonic relationship between upper body and lower body movement.
Madeleine Inglehearn, Interview.

Scale or Ring

Choreutic units arranged serially so that they return to the starting point, forming a triangle, or a pentagon, or a figure eight, or a circle, and danced as expansions of port de bras sequences; a Laban term.

Valerie Preston-Dunlop, 1984.

Axis and equator forms

"Design elements in which circular and curved forms (equator) surround a line which goes through it (axis); most frequently seen as a horizontal circle around a vertical line but all manner of other axis/equator relations are embedded in dance."

Valerie Preston-Dunlop, Seminar.

Yin Yang of direction

The concept that when one moves upwards, the move contains the notion of downwards at the same time, and so on for all directions.

"Up or down, front or back, left or right are all the same."

B.P.J. Lo, M. Inn, R. Amacker, and *S. Foe,* 1985.

Spatial counterpoint
> Using the harmonic properties of spatial movement choreographically.
> *Valerie Preston-Dunlop,* Seminar.

6.   SPACING

Spacing
> The organisation of the dancers in the space and their awareness of where they should be.
> *Anna Markard,* Rehearsal.

Facings and placings
> Precise spatial orientation and positioning required for clear form, but crucially so in all group work, especially in unison.
> *Lea Anderson,* Interview.

Alignment (sequence dancing)
> This is understood as three things: 1. The relationship of the feet to the body; 2. the relationship of the body to the ballroom; 3. the pattern of a series of steps or a movement in relationship to the ballroom.
> *Victor Silvester,* 1942.

Mark, A
> A place in the rehearsal room, on walls, a door et al, to which dancers orientate but which will not be there on stage.
> *Lea Anderson,* Interview.

Flat diagonal; steep diagonal
> Imagined floor pattern lines across the stage used in rehearsal for orientation.
> *Anna Markard,* Rehearsal.

Quarter line, eighth line, centre line
> Marked lines in the upstage/downstage direction used in rehearsal for spacing a work.
> *Anna Markard,* Rehearsal.

Make a dance mark on the stage
> To place dancers on the stage as one would plot co-ordinates on a graph.
> *Siobhan Davies,* Seminar.

Stage directions
> Upstage, Downstage, Stage left (that is performer's left and audience's right), Stage right.
> "Exit stage left.", "You're too far up.", "Pass downstage of him.".
> *Elizabeth Keen,* Rehearsal.

Cubical space

Oskar Schlemmer's concept of the theatre space in which man, the dancer, stands at the centre of a space which is criss-crossed by visually perceived/imagined lines which he described as related by "Laws of cubical space".
Tut Schlemmer, 1958 (1924).

Calligraphy of a dance

The intentional patterns made by the traveling paths in a dance, which may "...have some special symbolic intention that makes the pathways traveled by the dancer as important as the movements of the dancer's body itself."
Joan F. Hays, 1981.

Curved paths

Travelling on a circular pathway for which you need to know the direction of circling (clockwise or anticlockwise), the amount of circle, the size of the circle, the situation of the circle in relation to where you start (is it beside you, behind you, etc.?).
Peggy Hackney, Sarah Manno, and *Muriel Topaz,* 1977.

Presence (baroque)

Historically, the place occupied by the audience of the highest rank; in current practice the term is used to indicate the front of the dancing area and the performing focus of the dance.
Wendy Hilton, 1981.

Space/shape relationship

Shapes in space — volumes, linear boundaries etc. that the dancer makes in response to the requirements of that specific space.
Alwin Nikolais, 1963.

Fixed and fluid space

"The space could be constantly fluid, instead of being a fixed space in which movements relate. We've grown up with ideas about a fixed space in the theatre to which spectator and dancer refer. But if you abandon that idea you discover another way of looking. You can see a person not just from the front but from any side with equal interest."
Merce Cunningham in Merce Cunningham and Jacqueline Lesschaeve, 1985.

Multidirection

"In applying chance to space I saw the possibility of multidirection. Rather than thinking in one direction i.e. to the audience in a proscenium frame, direction could be four-sided and up and down."
Merce Cunningham in Francis Starr, 1968.

Defocused space
"...the most revolutionary features of the (spatial) organization are its open-endedness, pushing out the proscenium frame.... And the all-over, open-field situation which so often obtains when the dancers are moving independently about the space.... The space is de-focused and the values are equalized."
Jill Johnson in Carolyn Brown, 1968.

Decentralisation
"...any place in space is of interest; this opens the choreography to a multi-directional, multi-facing point of view, including the illusion that the dance continues offstage as well...at variance with the central perspective of classical ballet...."
Carolyn Brown, 1968.

Multiple centres of attention
A term applied to Merce Cunningham's use of the stage space, in contast to certain points on the stage being more important than others and one centre of attention at a time being offered to an audience.
Stephanie Jordan, 1992.

Multiplicity of centers
For Cunningham there is not one center to a space, but a "multiplicity of centers, connected and equal in value."
Calvin Tomkins, 1974.

Levels
The stratification of the space into three levels, which a choreographer may use quite specifically as a design ingredient.
"Work in the upper level."
Rui Horta, Workshop.

Choreographic formulae
How the danced use of space is conventionalised, viz: the stage diagonal for demonstration of skill, the circle as symbol of impenetrability, the line as confrontational presentation.
Norbet Servos and *G. Weigelt,* 1984.

Violating the proscenium
"The dancers repeatedly approach the proscenium,...unexpectedly confronting the viewers with unusual requests; the dancers sit on the edge of the stage and eye the audience, intoning fragments of monologue."
Norbert Servos and *G. Weigelt,* 1984.

Deconstructing theatrical space
"Dance practice which abandons the proscenium arch to integrate the performer with the audience and everyday movement with technical movement."
Paul Filmer, Interview.

Dead centre

"...there are at least eleven lines converging on it, plus the psychological security of the symmetrical design...it is the most powerful single spot on the stage...."
Doris Humphrey, 1959.

Direction and position (in the space)

Where the dancer moves in the performance space, considered from the audience's point of view, and the power of theatrical spaces to influence that view.
Doris Humphrey, 1959.

Spatial dominance

Parts of the dancer's canvas becoming more dominant than other parts through two, or more, dancers being close together in it, charging it, while other dancers are more scattered or isolated.
Laurie Booth, Interview.

Hierarchic use of stage space

"[the]...distribution of dancers in the performing space...in terms of a hierarchy of significance, beginning with the center stage as the area of greatest prominence and moving outward in diminishing intensity."
Don McDonagh, 1969.

Volumetric choreography

Choreography in which the depth of the performing space is more important than conventional concepts of hierarchy.

"He [Taylor] choreographs like a sculptor, filling the stage not hierarchically but volumetrically."
Nancy Vreeland Dalva, 1989.

7.   THE DANCER IN THE PERFORMANCE SPACE

Dancer-space relationship

The dancer's awareness of himself as more than just a presence in space, of himself as existing in a dynamic relationship with the space.
Alwin Nikolais, 1963.

Aesthetics of space

The feeling properties of the space; "It is a living, sentient thing."
Doris Rudko, Interview.

Spatial dynamic

The interaction of performers in a work when the space between them and around them becomes dynamically charged.
Rosemary Butcher, Interview.

Dynamics of the space

The quality of distance and nearness which actions spell out, providing the dance with content beyond the movement itself.
Bessie Schoenberg, Interview.

Imagined space

"The infinity of imagined space, extending beyond the limited, tangible space of reality, erasing the boundaries of corporeality and turning a gesture into an image of seeming endlessness."
Mary Wigman, 1966.

Inside out and outside in

The dancer's relationship to space.
"What is physically there as space, and also space created by the imagination of dancers and how they throw their bodies into the space."
Siobhan Davies, Contributed.

Terrain

The imagined landscape in which dance improvisation can take place, an environment which can alter in the performer's imagination, so providing an internal venue for radical shifts in his movement material.
"...interior landscape...."
Laurie Booth, Interview.

Canvas

What the space is, for the dancer, on which, or in which, he moves leaving traces of his activity.
"Nothing can eradicate an action."
Laurie Booth, Interview.

Stage as canvas

[Taylor] "...uses the whole stage as a canvas. Stop most of his dances anywhere, and the stage is as composed as a canvas by the seventeenth-century French painter Poussin."
Nancy Vreeland Dalva, 1989.

Shared space

The space beyond each kinesphere — the dance area, the delineated space — shared by performers and by performers/audience.
Valerie Preston-Dunlop, 1987.

Centre and periphery

Areas of stage space used for floor pattern designs in which groups cluster, disperse, and regroup; said of Lucinda Childs's work.
Sally Banes, 1980.

Dancing space

> A space which has light, sound, colour, and movement, explored through time.
> *Fiona Burnside,* 1990.

Using the space

> The possibilities the dancer has of engaging with the performance space.
> "...to enter, exit, fill, cross, invade, evacuate, jam up...."
> *Valerie Preston-Dunlop,* Class.

Molecules, The

> An image given of the content of the space with which the dancer can work to find the intention required and the resulting movement style.
> "Slip between the molecules", for fluidity; "Now move more molecules", for solidity.
> *Lea Anderson,* Interview.

Occupy a space, To

> To feel a sense of ownership of a space.
> "...to be in it, enter and exit from it, to use it, to have one's whole life in it for a while, to live and be in it."
> *Valerie Preston-Dunlop,* 1987.

Moving through space

> A quality in ballroom dancing associated with 'swing' which gives the participants a motional pleasure not available in the mundane use of space, together with a feeling of freedom and power.
> *Helen Thomas,* Interview.

Create energy, To

> The way dancers are able to enliven the space, to give energy to a part of the stage that they are not in themselves.
> *Gillian Lynne,* Interview.

Animate the space, To

> To use devices which bring a quality of interest into the space through which the dancers move; said of Richard Alston, Balanchine, and Siobhan Davies.
> *Judith Mackrell,* Interview.

Charged

> What the space becomes through the energy and action of dancers in it, especially the space between dancers.
> *Laurie Booth,* Interview.

Inherent force of space

What a choreographer has to deal with when he places movement and dancers in a space, so that the space works with the idea.
Dorothy Madden, Interview.

Protagonist (space as)

The principal character in the dance being, at times, the space in which the dance takes place, its power and ability to contribute meanings of dominance and vulnerability to dancers by where they are in the space.
Laurie Booth, Interview.

Expressive motion in space

"For the ballet-artist, mastery of steps infers domination of space, as much above the floor as upon it. Limits explored are not those of extreme emotion, but of expressive motion. Determined and defined, ballet is a continuous aria of the aerial."
Lincoln Kirstein, 1976.

Dynamics in the space, The

Where in the stage space the main action is taking place, and its nature; how the action shifts from place to place in the whole stage picture.
"...busy downstage right, or circular motion to exit left...."
Stuart Hopps, Interview.

Kinetic architecture

Movement which has spatial content, and is seen to relate to the actual architecture of the performance space.
Laurie Booth, Interview.

Fourth wall, The

The nickname for the proscenium arch.
"Working with the 4th wall or without it."
Helen Crocker and *Bim Mason,* Interview.

Chapter 10   N O T A T I O N

1.   SOME NOTATION SYSTEMS

Choreography
　　"Choreography...is the art of setting down dances by the aid of different signs, just as music is written down with the help of figures or characters called notes...."
　　Jean Georges Noverre, 1986 (revised original 1803).

Choreography
　　It now designates the planning and composing of a ballet or a dance, but it has been employed to designate the drawing of figures and symbols of movements which dance composers or choreographers jotted down as an aid to memory.
　　Rudolf Laban, 1956.

Orchésographie
　　A book in which the dances of the 16th century are written in words with musical measures and tunes, together with a verbal description of the manners and context.
　　Thoinot Arbeau, 1925 (original 1588).

Fully fledged system
　　A term used to distinguish early verbal or visual indication systems from those which translate movement into a rule-governed symbol system; the first quoted is Feuillet's "Chorégraphie, L'Art de Décrire la Danse", Paris, 1700, probably devised by Beauchamps.
　　Ann Hutchinson Guest in Mary Clarke and David Vaughan, 1977.

Beauchamps-Feuillet system (1700)
　　The most highly developed track-drawing system, which had widespread use throughout Europe in the 18th century, depicts the path across the floor. On this path are drawn indications for step direction, turns, beats, and other intricate footwork and simple arm movements.
　　Ann Hutchinson Guest, 1989.

Stepanov notation for movement
　　A system devised by Vladimir Stepanov (1866–1896) based on a study of anatomy and anthropology; he used modified musical notes on three staffs to indicate flexion, rotation, abduction, etc.; used to notate ballets in Russia in the early 20th century.
　　Alexander Gorsky, 1978.

Nijinsky's system of Dance Notation

In this system, based on the Stepanov system, timing is indicated by the appropriate music note which is placed on an adapted music staff representing the main body sections. Direction is shown by placement of the notes on the lines and spaces of the staff. Limb flexion and rotation are marked on the stem of the note. Stage orientation and direction of travel are shown by numbers.

Ann Hutchinson Guest and *Claudia Jeschke,* 1990.

Conté system (1931)

A system based on music notes which uses numbers for directions and semi-abstract signs for other movements. Ballet based, it was used for Conté's own compositions. There has been a recent move in France to develop it further.

Ann Hutchinson Guest, 1989.

Eshkol-Wachmann System

A movement notation system which arranges parts of the body on a vertical line and time on a horizontal line on the manuscript page; movement of the body is analysed as shifts of the longitudinal axes of the limbs in relation to a spherical system of reference and classified as 'Rotatory', 'Plane', and 'Curved'. Positions and magnitude of movement (intervals) are expressed by numbers (numerical values).

Noa Eshkol and *Abraham Wachmann,* 1958.

Notation systems

Linguistic constructions designed to record dance and movement in a grammatically governed system of symbols, whether Labanotation, Eshkol-Wachmann or Benesh.

Janet Adshead-Lansdale, Interview.

Requisite properties of good notation system

Unambiguity and syntactic and semantic disjointedness and finite differentiation.

Nelson Goodman, 1969.

2.   BENESH NOTATION SYSTEM

Benesh notation

"...is based on a five-line horizontal staff that becomes a matrix for the human figure as seen from the back. The bottom line represents the floor, and the others from bottom to top represent the knee, waist, shoulder and top of the head."

Anya Peterson Royce, 1974.

Five line stave

The stave, similar to a music stave, used by Benesh notators, which provides a framework of reference; each line coinciding with visually distinctive features of the human body.

Monica Parker, Interview.

View the movement from behind the dancer, To

To read or write notation as seen from the performer's viewpoint.
Monica Parker, Interview.

Movement lines: limbs and parts of limbs

In Benesh notation, lines drawn on the stave from one position to another providing a visual aid and summarising a series of intermediary positions.
Monica Parker, Interview.

In front of, level with and behind the body

In Benesh notation, the identification of the relationship of the limbs to the body.
Monica Parker, Interview.

Tilt, turn and bend

The three basic forms of movement of the head and body used in the analysis of dance and movement and for which signs are given.
Monica Parker, Interview.

Stepping, sliding, jumping

The three forms of travelling for which signs are given and from which steps are built up.
Monica Parker, Interview.

Plotting extremities

The way in which the feet and hands are represented on the stave in terms of their position and of the line of movement taken to arrive there.
Monica Parker, Interview.

Rhythmic structure and phrasing

The rhythmic structure of movement is shown by in-stave and, where necessary, above-stave information. Where musical accompaniment exists, its relationship to movement is shown, generally by including music bar lines in the dance score. Movement phrases are identified where appropriate.
Monica Parker, Interview.

Zoning and surfacing

These indicate the specifics of a body part through attention to details of the area of that part (e.g. in a touch) or the surface of the part.
Monica Parker, Interview.

Static and linking information

Used to describe the positions arrived at and passed through and the connecting movements between them in sequences of dance or motion.
Monica Parker, Interview.

Dynamic markings

The same dynamic markings are used as in music notation (p, f, and their variants). They are placed above the stave to give indications of the dynamic colouring of the movement.

Monica Parker, Interview.

Direction and location

The terms used to describe where the dancer faces and the whereabouts of the dancer in the performing space, respectively.

Monica Parker, Interview.

Dancers' counts

The manner in which dancers count the music in phrases which may differ from the counts of the written musical phrase.

Monica Parker, Interview.

3.   LABANOTATION

Laban's system of movement notation

The dance and movement notation system invented by Rudolf Laban, published in 1928, and subsequently developed by Albrecht Knust, Maria Szentpál, Ann Hutchinson et al. Known as "Kinetography Laban" and/or "Labanotation".

Rob van Haarst, Contributed.

Labanotation/Kinetography Laban

This is a movement script. It records the progression of movement, showing its dynamic content by portraying the functioning of the human body in space and time. First published in 1928, it has been constantly developing over the years involving contributions from many people and is used world-wide in many different dance and movement contexts.

Roderyk Lange, 1985.

Kinetogram

Graph including a movement staff and abstract symbols which represent a dance or movement sequence; term used by practitioners of Laban's system of movement notation.

Rob van Haarst, Contributed.

Four principles (of Laban's notation)

The shape of the signs answers "what action?", signs beside each other or following above each other answer "when?", their length answers "how long?", and their placement in a stave answers "what body parts?".

"1) What happened? 2) When did it happen? 3) How long did it last? 4) Who (or what body part) did it?"

Albrecht Knust, 1979.

Staff, The

An arrangement of vertical columns into which the symbols for actions are placed: central columns are for the body as a whole, the second columns to right and left are for leg gestures, the third columns are for trunk, chest and upper part of the body movements, the fourth are for arm movements.

Albrecht Knust, 1979.

Motion characters

"Motor symbols", "signs for movement" forming part of a movement notation, each representing the fundamental movement of a definite part or parts of the body, and in combination capable of rendering both the external effect seen by the observer and the flow of the movement progression felt by the mover.

Rudolf Laban, 1956.

Movement Type

Movement indications mainly comprise the following types:

Tilting (inclining, 'taking a direction'), which involves the length of a limb or body section slanting into a particular direction.

Rotating, which occurs around one of the axes of the body-as-a-whole or of a body part, includes turning, somersaulting, and cartwheeling. Twisting is a rotation in which the extremity of the limb or body part rotates to a greater degree than the part near the base.

Shifting, which is usually seen as a minor displacement in space of a part in its entirety, in contrast to a tilt in which the extremity of the body part moves farther than the parts nearer the base.

Flexion of the joints of the body, which may produce contraction, folding, or adduction; in extension the reverse occurs as elongating, unfolding, or abduction.

Ann Hutchinson, 1970.

Direction signs

"The chief kinetographic signs" of the Laban system which describe the directions of the movement "as they relate to the front of the performer"; direction signs for supports indicate the "direction of progression" [e.g. step forwards], and for gestures they indicate the "direction of the inclination" [e.g. incline the arm sideways-down moving from the shoulder].

Albrecht Knust, 1979.

Levels

The three levels, "high, medium, and low", are shown by shading the direction signs; "High supports are performed on the toes and ball of the foot with heels raised and knees straight (on half point), low supports are on the whole foot with slightly bent knees (demi plié); high level for arm gestures is above shoulder level and low level is below it; and so on for all parts of the limbs.

Albrecht Knust, 1979.

Place

Place is the central point from which directions are defined. For supports it is the point where the vertical line meets the supporting surface; and for gestures it is the moving joint at which the vertical, sagittal and lateral dimensions intersect.
Ann Hutchinson, 1970.

Directional movement

Directional movement is concerned with displacement of the body-as-a-whole, or of its parts, into a particular direction, as in taking a step or as in shifting the head into a direction. Directional movement for the limbs is seen as the arrival of the extremity of the limb (or limb segment) at a destinational point, the body part visibly establishing that directional line.
Ann Hutchinson, 1970.

Motion toward, motion away

Movement description may be of 'motion toward' or 'motion away from' a point in space, a part of the room, a part of the body, there being no defined amount of motion or arrival point.
Ann Hutchinson, 1970.

Free end and fixed end

The two ends of a limb (or the torso and its parts), terms used to distinguish the end of the limb that stays fixed in space and the other end which moves in space. Used as reference points by which the direction of a gesture is judged.

"Since the whole arm moves from the shoulder joint and its free end is the hand, the relationship between the hand and the shoulder tells us its direction and level in space."
Ilene Fox, Contributed.

Design Drawing (Formerly called Shape Writing)

A feature of Labanotation contributed by Ann Hutchinson Guest, which describes the shape or design of a movement in terms of tracing the path of the extremity in the air.
Ann Hutchinson Guest and *Rob van Haarst,* 1991.

Design (Shape)

Indication of a design (shape) formed by the body or by one or more of its parts.
Ann Hutchinson Guest and *Rob van Haarst,* 1991.

Timing

Timing is concerned with when a movement occurs, the simultaneous or sequential occurrence of actions, and their duration, that is the amount of time taken from the start of each movement to the finish. Also considered is the duration of inaction, the amount of time taken between one movement and the next.
Ann Hutchinson, 1970.

Relative and measured timing

Actions may be of relatively longer or shorter durations than each other. The durations may be measured as in music through establishing regular beats, with bar lines used to mark the beats into groups (measures).

Ann Hutchinson, 1970.

Time dot

An indication of that moment when a particular action occurs, begins, or ends. On the movement score this indication is used to show exactness of that moment, or that the moment may be flexible because of the size of stage or other factors; a way of writing contributed by Maria Szentpál.

Ann Hutchinson, 1970.

Center of Gravity

"...that point in the body from which or on which the body can be suspended or poised in equilibrium.... The center of gravity has no fixed location in the body, its exact position depending on the build of the individual and on the position taken."

Ann Hutchinson, 1970.

Supports

The progression of the body as a whole, the shift of the weight of the body from one foot (or part) to another; jumping and retaining the weight on a body part are considered under 'supports'.

Albrecht Knust, 1979.

Paths

A path in dance is the track across the floor made as a result of the body-as-a whole moving through space. The shape of the path may be straight, circular, or meandering. Its destination may be a particular location on stage, or proximity to another performer.

Ann Hutchinson, 1970.

Additional path indications

Statement of the leader may be necessary in group paths. Orientation may be in relation to a path or to a focal point, rather than to the more usual performance front; for example, in ballroom dancing the Line of Dance (L.O.D.) around the room is the path to be followed and the dancers' orientation is understood in relation to this line.

Ann Hutchinson, 1970.

Supporting on various parts of the body

Combining the methods of writing supports with the methods of writing parts of the body to indicate kneeling, sitting, lying, rolling, cartwheels and somersaults, handstands, walking on all fours, etc.

Albrecht Knust, 1979.

Body signs

The symbols for the various parts of the body which are categorised as: 1) joints (e.g. knee); 2) limbs (e.g. lower leg); 3) surfaces (e.g. the back of the hand); 4) details of surfaces (e.g. just below the knee); 5) area (e.g. the chest); 6) small parts (e.g. thumb, mouth).

Eds. from Albrecht Knust, 1979.

Hand movements

The many motional possibilities of the hand are analysed as flexing, stretching, curling in, uncurling, rotating as a whole, twisting, narrowing, widening, moving into a direction as a whole, separate finger movements, bringing the fingers together.

Els Grelinger, Interview.

Four principles of turning

1) the direction of turn (right or left, clockwise or anticlockwise) is shown by the shape of the turn sign; 2) the degree of turn is shown by black pin signs; 3) the duration of turn is shown by the length of the sign; 4) the position of the turn sign on the staff indicates on which foot the body turns.

Albrecht Knust, 1979.

Rotation

Two basic signs indicate rotation to the left or right and mean a turn of the whole body when written in the support column, or a twist of the body part when written in a gesture column; a pin sign placed in the rotation sign indicates the degree of the turn or twist.

Sally Archbutt, Interview.

Relation signs

Signs, and their rules, which indicate the spatial and weight relation of body parts to each other and to the surroundings; touching, carrying the weight of, addressing, being near, surrounding, meeting; and their duration.

Albrecht Knust, 1979.

Touching and sliding

A touch is the contact between two parts of the body, between a body part and the floor, an object, or another person. It may be brief or retained. In dance, the most common form of touching and sliding is contact of the foot on the floor. Notating these requires detailed knowledge of the timing of the contact, the parts of the foot involved, and whether the movement is weight-bearing or not.

Ann Hutchinson, 1970.

Indication for Dynamics

Special signs can be used to show the strength or lightness with which the movement is performed.

Sally Archbutt, Interview.

Floor plans

Diagrams which indicate on paper a bird's-eye view of the performing area. On these are written the entrances and exits of the performers, their locations, where they are facing (their relationship to the established front of the performing area) and the paths used as they move. When paths cross, indication is given of who passes downstage. Traditionally the performance area has been the proscenium arch stage.

Ann Hutchinson, 1970.

Scoring

Drafting onto paper the movement patterns of the performers. Separate staves are used for each performer moving individually; unison movement being written on one stave. Scoring includes indication of relationship of the choreography with the accompanying music (or specific indication of the passage of time) as well as with floor plans which indicate entrances, exits and spatial changes in placement of the performers in the performing area.

Ann Hutchinson, 1970.

Scoring

Writing a score, organising the staffs to show entries and exits, to show who is dancing what movement material, drawing accompanying floor plans and indications of the musical accompaniment (if any), adding whatever verbal comments, images, advice might be helpful to the reader.

Albrecht Knust, 1979.

Score, The

The dance equivalent to a music score. A choreographic record written in dance notation which usually includes historical background, production notes, casting requirements, and all other information needed for research into the choreographic structure and the original production of the work or for the purpose of mounting as faithful a reproduction of the work as possible.

Ann Hutchinson, 1970.

4. WRITING

Orthography

The rules and grammar of a notation system.
Andy Adamson, Interview.

Autography

The hand writing of a notation system.
Andy Adamson, Interview.

Means in a system, The

The abilities of a system of notation to describe movement according to its degree of development.

"Insufficiently developed range (of Nijinsky's system)."
Ann Hutchinson Guest, Interview.

Structured description

The use of Laban's system of movement notation to give a "...description of movement in clearly defined, measurable terms." "Such a complete method of description is needed for writing specifically structured exercises, whether these have been formulated for remedial, practical, or artistic reasons. It is essential for the preservation of folk and ethnic dances and choreographic works"; distinct from Motif Description and Effort-Shape Description.

Ann Hutchinson, 1970.

Notating

The optimal process for writing a work which requires that the notator is in on the choreographic process while the piece is being set, to hear what is said as well as see and hear what is done, to keep notes of images, dynamics, etc.

Jean Johnson-Jones, Interview.

Notator's contribution

"Notators have been considered to be either objective observers or faithful translators for the choreographer. Too many factors enter the equation, however, for the notator to be wholly one or the other. Instead, the notator may record perceptible movement and translate the choreographer's intention with the tools that are available, but inevitably adds something of him- or herself to the product."

Sheila Marion, 1990.

Safeguard the material, To

This is regarded as the job of the notator, to record the dance material and not to allow its detail to be blurred or lost during rehearsal by the dancers' inaccurate performance of it.

Monica Parker, Interview.

Grammar of the piece

The set of rules embedded in the choreography which should dictate to the notator which analytic method to use to record the piece.

Jean Johnson-Jones, Interview.

Idealist and materialist dance scores

A concept used by Jack Anderson for reconstruction from the score, but one which notators may use when writing the score so that a strictly structured description (materialist) or one which contains suggestions for choices, images, moods, intentions (idealist) may be used appropriately.

Sheila Marion, 1990.

Authentic dance

"A dance written down in notation which can be reproduced as closely as possible in style, steps, figures, and music."

Madeleine Inglehearn, Interview.

Build a record, To

To make a notated score of a ballet which faithfully puts the work down on paper, gradually, layer by layer.

Monica Parker, Interview.

Decision-making process of the notator

Thinking through "the best way of conveying what you want to say in the most economical way".

Monica Parker, Interview.

Conflicting grammars

The tension that arises between the need for any notation system to retain a tight control of its rules in the service of readability, and the need to notate innovative dance work for which innovative writing rules may seem preferable.

Jean Johnson-Jones, Interview.

Notating from the dancer's point of view

A research process in which the orthographic choices within a notation system are used and, if necessary, added to in order to obtain a record of the dance as near to the way the dancer understands it as the notation system can allow.

Andrée Grau, Interview.

Aide memoire

The initial marks on paper made by a notator during rehearsal to record the critical information for use later in writing the actual score. Can also refer to condensing patterns, counts, etc. onto a single page as an aid in the reconstruction process.

Monica Parker, Interview.

Physical awareness

Essential awareness in the body by a notator of what the choreographer has made so that s/he can demonstrate it and also so that s/he can write it.

Monica Parker, Interview.

Knowing the music

A responsibility that the notator has prior to rehearsal, especially in the case of a highly musical choreographer, such as Antony Tudor, who will not count, but sing.

Muriel Topaz, 1986.

Critical information

Essential data collected by a Benesh notator during a rehearsal of a new work so that what has been made can be faithfully kept and brought to the next rehearsal, especially those things which dancers may not remember, e.g. details of grips and timing.
Monica Parker, Interview.

Nuance

The details of movement style which the notator must grasp when writing a work in which essence or meaning is encapsulated in the 'proper' execution of the steps.
Muriel Topaz, 1986.

Structured choreography

In a rehearsal, those parts of an emerging ballet which appear to be ready and should be recorded; they are set for that day but may be dropped, kept or changed the next day.
Monica Parker, Interview.

Moment in a phrase

An element in a phrase of dance of a work being notated that the choreographer might want to retain; a moment which the notator must notice, physically absorb and retain for future reference.
Monica Parker, Interview.

Completed score

A dance score able to be read and used by any trained notation person; an aim of the Dance Notation Bureau of New York.
Ilene Fox, Interview.

Score contents

The comprehensive contents of a Dance Notation Bureau accredited score, including all information contributing to an artistically satisfying record of the work of use to reconstructors.
Dance Notation Bureau, 1993.

Primary function of a score

The authoritative identification of a work from performance to performance.
Nelson Goodman, 1969.

LabanWriter

A computer-based graphics editor developed to produce a dance score of publication quality from a handwritten document. Its use at the Dance Department, University of Ohio is described.
Dance Notation Bureau, 1987.

Making a camera-ready score
Making neat, reproducible copy of a dance score. May be done using the computer program LabanWriter.
Ilene Fox, Interview.

Calaban
Computer-Aided-Labanotation: a computer-based tool to facilitate the process of producing publication quality Labanotation scores which includes editing facilities to move, copy, mirror, and erase individual and groups of symbols.
Andy Adamson, 1992.

Libraries
Groups of regularly used movement patterns, notated and stored in the Calaban system, which can be recalled, manipulated, and edited.
Andy Adamson, 1992.

MacBenesh
A Macintosh computer application developed to assist notators in the production of Benesh scores.
Rhonda Ryman, 1990.

Dance library
A collection of notated dance scores as both a circulating resource for dance companies and schools to hire, and a resource for dance scholars.
Dance Notation Bureau, 1992.

5.   READING

Choreologist
The name given to a dance notator and reconstructor using the Benesh system.
Monica Parker, Interview.

Fluency and credibility
The capacities essential for a notator in the process of teaching the work to dancers from the score, knowing the work so that s/he can convey it stylistically and musically.
Monica Parker, Interview.

Reading a score
To personalise the reading of a score so that from the beginning the reader imagines the unfolding of the movement as something he is doing himself.
"I am swaying.", "On count four I lift my shoulder to the ceiling, sharply.", "I inhale on the right step, exhale on the left.".
Els Grelinger, Interview.

Reading partner work

Interpreting the score instructions in the light of a new cast, whose heights and physiques inevitably alter the original spatial relationships, as written.

Jean Jarrell, Interview.

Accessibility (of information in a score)

The ease with which the choreographic pattern emerges from the written document and is recognisable to the reader.

Monica Parker.

Fundamentals

The essential ingredients of a choreographic phrase which can be read first, layers of stylistic features being added as the reader becomes more efficient.

Jean Johnson-Jones, Interview.

Decoding phase (of reading scores)

The technical phase where the reader associates the written symbols with the movement, the position, the movement sequence and dance; one phase in reading and performing a score.

Einya Cohen, 1990.

Comprehension phase (of reading scores)

The reader learns to 'grasp the meaning' of the movement phrases, to make sense of the material; this is another phase of reading and performing a score.

Einya Cohen, 1990.

Dig, To

A way of reading a dance score to find from it not only the moves to be done, the co-ordination and the shape of it and the counts, but the motivation behind the movement, its intended expression; shown in a good score in the detail of the flow and in the orthographic choices made by the notator.

Els Grelinger, Interview.

Interpreting the notation

Reading dances in Beauchamps-Feuillet notation in the light of verbal, manuscript evidence, in order to reconstruct as closely as possible to the original.

Madeleine Inglehearn, Interview.

Showing, A

An informal presentation of a reconstructed dance, an intermediary process prior to its reaching performance level.

Ann Hutchinson Guest, Interview.

6. SPECIALISED NOTATIONS

Motif writing
> The notation system derived from Labanotation which writes the movement intention, not the movement itself, thus inviting several interpretations in dance material.
> *Valerie Preston-Dunlop,* 1987.

Effort notation
> The shorthand invented by Rudolf Laban for writing the subtleties of effort combinations in a person's movement phrases.
> *Marion North,* Interview.

Chumm charts
> The system of documenting the clusters of spatial elements in dance movement, writing the spatial progression, spatial projection, body design, and spatial tension units of the limbs and body. (Choreutic unit and manner of their materialisation)
> "Does that design end with your finger tips or go way out into space?"
> *Valerie Preston-Dunlop,* 1981.

Camera script
> The shot-by-shot plan of a video dance or a dance on video, created by pre-visualising everything from the camera's point of view.
> *Gillian Lynne,* Interview.

Camera script, The
> The document which contains the shots in order, and beside that the action, that is the indication of the dance content written in an in-house language understood by all participants and not in technical dance language.
> "Step, step, Devil in behind, wiggle, turns and walks L."
> *Bob Lockyer,* Camera script.

7. VERNACULAR SCRIPTS

Dance manuals
> Instructions written by dancing masters in the Renaissance and Baroque period and today by leading teachers of the various subdivisions of dance activity, written in vernacular languages with terminologies specific to each activity.
> *Roderyk Lange,* 1988.

Story board the music, To
> The preparations a choreographer makes for work in musical theatre and film, writing crucial moves in the musical score, and literally drawing a sequence of pictures which show the progression of the number.
> *Stuart Hopps,* Interview.

Video or notation?

The preservation of a dance work by filming it or by notating it; the issue of which to use, or both, centres on understanding "just what is to be preserved", a question that generates a layered discussion of purpose and product.
Jack Anderson, 1993.

Video record

Filmed fragments of movement material for dances, an inadequate record on their own but useful together with detailed notes of the motivation of the movement, without which they are useless.
Lea Anderson, Interview.

Production notes

The personal notes of a choreography and the notes of the production as a whole sharable by the team of collaborators, the latter usually written in an expanded musical score for continuity.
"...my black books, the double page musical score...."
Stuart Hopps, Interview

Score

Usually applied to a notated score but also to meticulous records of a dance through other means, such as Lucinda Childs's score of "Melody Excerpt" (1977) which is a systematic graphic representation of floor plans, or her score of "Street Dance" which is minute/second outline of what the audience should look at in the street.
Sally Banes, 1980(a).

Diary books

Notes of observation recorded primarily in drawings associated with dates, notes which get translated into movement material and images of a dance work.
"...blowing out the candles on Teresa Barker's birthday cake...."
Lea Anderson, Interview.

Performer charts

A record of who is dancing what, whose material has been eliminated/included, in order to avoid a star system creeping in by default when an egalitarian message is intended.
Lea Anderson, Interview.

Aide memoire

A term used for the purpose of Lionel Bacon's "Handbook of Morris Dances", the established notated dictionary of steps and figures, the teams relying largely on the oral tradition and the common memory of the team.
Roy Judge, Interview.

PART FOUR: CHOREOGRAPHY

The Chapter CHOREOGRAPHIC FORM develops further the entries on genres listed in THE DANCE DOMAIN by giving terms for individual dances, the term being indicative of their content, or possibly of the attitude to the dance work of the person who coined the term. Titles for structural and narrative parts of works follow, showing how people from different dance traditions speak about the way in which a dance work is constructed.

The section on "Formal devices" could have been placed in the chapter on CHOREOGRAPHIC PROCESSES, or here on choreographic products, which in the event is where it is. In it are an alphabetically listed collection of the diverse choreographic structural methods used to turn movement material into a work.

Chapter 12 contains entries that specifically deal with issues of group and ensemble work, duos and couples, and a few on the solo dance. It is here that the languages of traditional dance forms are contributed by interviewees and writers from the community dance domain. Discussion on the sensitivity needed to dance together is interspersed with the form, and significance for the spectator, of group and duet dances.

The Chapter CHOREOGRAPHIC PROCESSES has entries which show the diversity of methods and purposes of dance makers. Some insight into how people begin their works, how they plan them, how they use their dancers, emerges from the melange of entries from contributing choreographers. The dancer's point of view of these processes is found in the Chapter on THE PERFORMER AND THE MOVEMENT, especially in the section on "Working with a Choreographer".

Chapter 11 CHOREOGRAPHIC FORM

1. KINDS AND FORMS OF DANCE WORKS

Abstract dances

Cunningham "tends to eliminate overt human motivations in his dance so that everything emotional (or as much of everything as he can reasonably manage) has to be seen into it by the observer."
Clive Barnes, 1968.

Accumulation pieces

Works which use mathematical formulae as the way of structuring dance material in the gradual addition of elements to, say, 30 pieces of material accumulated in 18 minutes; said of Trisha Brown's "Primary Accumulation" (1972).
Lise Brunel, 1987.

Big band features

A piece structured on the format of big band concerts, which feature separate songs (dances), with no costume change, no exits and entrances.
Lea Anderson, Interview.

Cabaret-like

A show with clearly distinguished and unconnected acts, each with its own kind of music, humour, and form; a structure which can be adapted to choreography.
Lea Anderson, Interview.

Chamber ballets

Dance works requiring small scale resources; used of Tudor's "Fandango" and "Continuo".
Muriel Topaz, 1986.

Choreo-symphony

"...by making the music visible, by reproducing it in dance form, he [Balanchine] creates a choreographic symphony that will produce, through the dance pattern alone, the same emotional effect as non-programmatic music."
Natalia Roslavleva, 1964.

Chorische Spiele (Ger.)

Large group works for non-professional dancers, first used by Laban in the 1920's.
Lucas Hoving, 1969.

Collage

"An asymmetrical network of surprises, without climax or consummation."
Susan Sontag in Stephanie Jordan, 1990.

Compulsory dances

In ice dance, the figures which must be skated.
"The pattern of each dance, the path the couples should take around the ice, indeed the precise steps and timing of switches from edge to edge of the skate, are laid down in the rules."
Mark Burton, Contributed.

Contemporary forms of ballet, Three

"...the narrative form, the mood form, the abstract form..."
Peggy van Praagh and *Peter Brinson,* 1963.

Conventional dance

"His [Taylor's] work is ordinarily composed toward the front with conventional dance sense."
Don McDonagh, 1969.

Conventional duration

The length of time of a dance work which, in mainstream ballet, is a full evening three-acter, or a 20/30 min. each in a triple bill, or shorter in a showpiece pas de deux.
Rosemary Butcher, Interview.

Conventional piece

A work which fits easily into the repertoire of a company, is not controversial or subversive to the genre.
Ashley Page, Interview.

Court dances

A term used in television, film, and theatre for dances to be performed by actors in period pieces, dances which cannot and do not attempt authenticity but which convey the flavour of the period and situation and enable the action of the play to continue through them.
Geraldine Stephenson, Interview.

Dance arrangements

A term used by Antony Tudor of his "Little Improvisations" and other chamber works which are brilliant but unadorned arrangements of classroom steps.
Muriel Topaz, 1986.

Dance-opera

A subtitle given by Pina Bausch to several of her works that are based on operatic texts.
Pina Bausch, 1976.

Dance oratorio

The fusion of movement, music and the spoken word; a dance form used by Laban as experiments towards the "formal heightening of the opportunity for human expressiveness in artistic performance" (trans.).

Mary Wigman, 1921.

Dance study, The

A series of movement sequences or phrases composed to form a complete artistic unit with the emphasis on a particular element of movement principle.

Geraldine Hurl, 1986.

Dance theatre

A work with narrative, text, found movement, props that invade the space, a heavy ingredient of design; said of Spink's work for Second Stride Company.

Stephanie Jordan in National Research Centre for Dance, 1988.

Democratic dance form

The form of dance works which reflects the democratic structure of society, so challenging the 'étoile' (star) system of classical ballet.

Peter Brinson, Interview.

Duet

The easiest bit of a dance to do, which almost makes itself.

"An encounter between two human beings, endlessly fascinating."

Ashley Page, Interview.

Ensemble dance

A choreographic work for a group in which the form of the work reflects the democratic procedures of society rather than the hierarchic procedures which ballerina and corps de ballet reflect.

Doris Humphrey, 1959.

Equipment pieces

Dance works centring on use of a specially designed set which enables dancers to find new movement and present audiences with new perceptions of dance; said of Trisha Brown's work of 1968.

Trisha Brown, 1987.

Events

"Presented without intermission, these Events consist of complete dances, excerpts from dances from the repertory, and often new sequences arranged for the immediate performance and place, with the possibility of several separate activities happening at the same time — to allow for not so much an evening of dances as the experience of dance."

Merce Cunningham, late 1960's.

One-act and three-a
"The mood b
works; they are the one
form in which develop
Peggy van Pr

Pantomime ballet
"The pantomi
is the main aspect of
making a serious dram
up. The audience watcl
Edwin Denby,

Performance event
A dance wor
according to a series o
matic.
Laurie Booth,

Performance piece,
A dance worl
audience.
Laurie Booth,

Physical drama of s
In non-dramat
the essential elements
David Buckla

Pluralistic dance
Dances which
"...to me, the
I'm hoping to make ot
Paul Taylor, "

Pot boiler
A dance pop
included in many tour
of its popularity it inl
experimental works.
Norman Mor

Female dance work
Pieces for the Cholmondeleys which reflect the all-female company, so including in the work their mutual support and desire to 'take the movement further'.
Lea Anderson, Interview.

Formalist, autonomous dance work
"Content...dissolved so completely into form that the work of art or literature cannot be reduced in whole or in part to anything not itself."
Clement Greenberg in Stephanie Jordan, 1990.

Four-walled activity
A dance work which is destined for a theatre space, the choreographer working with a 'one viewpoint' eye during rehearsal, namely 'out front'.
Mark Murphy, Interview.

Framework theme, A
"There is no notion of the progress of time as a constant, nor of narrative propulsion, only the few abrupt shifts forward into a new period and place suggested by the dawn of a new episode."; said of Richard Alston.
Stephanie Jordan, 1992.

Free dance routine
A meticulously prepared sequence of ice skating which combines "grace, sport, art, and two lives merging into one."; said of Jayne Torville and Christopher Dean.
Andrew Longmore, Contributed.

Gig, A
An improvisation session, with audience.
Laurie Booth, Interview.

Happening
"Can be anywhere, any time, of any duration", "it may be spontaneous, it may be formal, it may be anarchistic"; it is an event in which "the spectator can be jolted eventually into new sight so that he wakes to the life around him."
"Behind the happening is the shout, 'Wake up!'."
Peter Brook, 1990 (1968).

Improvisational form
Setting a structure by deciding to work on X, Y, or Z material in a certain way, within clear boundaries.
Trisha Brown, 1987.

Issue-based work
Choreographies and performance art pieces which deal with current socio/sexual/political agendas; said of the work of Lloyd Newsom, Mark Murphy, Emilyn Claid, Nigel Charnock, amongst many.
Chris de Marigny, 1993.

Literary ballet

A ballet in wh

"The danger, i

purely literary and unh

without the use of wor

Frederick Ash.

Major piece

A work which

ments on the social or

achieves a timelessness

Ashley Page, l

Male dance work

Pieces for the

their humour and their

Lea Anderson,

Miniatures

Concise dance

human body and the h

Jane Dudley, l

Montage principle

A way of deve

scenes which are impo

"Kontakthof".

Norbert Servo.

Montage

A literary, mus

'Webster', 199

Mood ballet

"...presents a

characters are less indi

Peggy van Pra

Movement choir pla

Large works f

for an audience, design

meaningful art works.

Rudolf Laban,

Crowd scene

Ensemble work for large numbers for which the choreographer may subdivide the crowd, appoint leaders to each group, teach them the material and appoint them to be responsible for their group; a Laban method.

Geraldine Stephenson, Interview.

Dance interludes

Decorative dances between acts in operas; with the 'inner necessity' advocated by Wassily Kandinsky and his colleagues from 1911, these became redundant as inappropriate in the changing culture of the 1920's.

Ana R. Sanchez-Colberg, 1992.

Divertissement

A section of a ballet which does not further the plot but which acts as an opportunity for pure dancing.

Glossary in Mary Clarke and David Vaughan, 1977.

Dream sequence, A

A section of a dance work or musical which takes the audience out of the narrative context into the imagination or fantasy of the protagonists.

Eds.

Enchaînements and Variations

These are distinguished by the former constituting exercises for the classroom and the latter choreography suitable for the stage.

Kirsten Ralov, 1979.

Episodes

Clearly distinguished scenes in a dance which have some overarching common theme but are each highly individual in structure; said of Bausch's "1980", "Bluebeard", "Café Müller".

Eds.

Fights

The name given to combative sections of narrative ballets, such as the one in "Romeo and Juliet", for which specialist fight arrangers are employed who use mnemonic terms as rehearsal aids.

"Twyla. Door frame. Tennis match. Frantic five. Zig-zag. High and low curves."

Alan Dubreuil, Interview.

Movement moment, The

An episode in an opera or musical or theatre work, which the director will designate as belonging to the choreographer or movement director, leaving him to initiate the ideas and make it work.

Stuart Hopps, Interview.

Movement scene

Part of a play, in which a scene with movement and/or dance predominates, and for which a movement specialist is engaged.

Geraldine Stephenson, Interview.

Dance sequence

A term used in the film industry for a section in a film which features dancing, for which dancers and choreographers would be employed.

Dorothy Madden, Interview.

Production

Any part of a ballet which is not set as a dance; crowd scenes, mime scenes, entrances and exits.

Diana Childs, Interview.

Production numbers

A way of presenting song, dance, and music in which a story line is given which provides an overall movement environment in which the song and dance are supported.

"high jinks and nonsense", "horseplay and fisticuffs", "waltzing, drinking, and flirting".

Geraldine Stephenson, Interview.

Scène d'action

"...where the dance should speak with fire and energy; where symmetrical and formal figures cannot be employed without transgressing truth and shocking probability, without enfeebling the action and chilling the interest."

Jean Georges Noverre, 1966 (1803).

Setting the crowd scenes

Deciding on the moves of crowd scenes in a ballet, such as Bintley's "The Snow Queen", which are interspersed with dances which have a basis of steps, for example "The Stamping Dance".

Lisa Conway, Interview.

Show piece dance

The main solos and pas de deux of a classic ballet production, which offer the soloists the opportunity to display both their virtuosity and their interpretive capacities; said of the National Ballet of St. Petersburg.

John Percival, Contributed.

Transitions

Organic, gradual or abrupt linking of one episode in a work with another.

Susan Sentler, Interview.

Pas de deux
"...the pas de deux generally holds pride of place in a ballet, or act, because it contains not only the best dancing by the best dancers but is the emotional centre of the piece."
Peggy van Praagh and *Peter Brinson,* 1963.

3. THE NARRATIVE ELEMENT

Pas d'action
Movements which tell the story of the work, which carry the narrative of the ballet.
Peggy van Praagh and *Peter Brinson*, 1963.

Ballet d'action
"...it should be divided into scenes and acts, and each scene should possess, like the act, a beginning, central portion and conclusion; that is to say, its introduction, plot and climax."
Jean Georges Noverre, 1966 (1803).

Recitatif scenes
In ballets in the traditional repertoire, scenes in which the story is furthered through mime, interspersed into dancing scenes; said of Petipa's works.
Peggy van Praagh and *Peter Brinson,* 1963.

Thematic dance
"Thematic dances are concerned with content that refers to some definite situation or story."
Margaret H'Doubler, 1957 (1940).

Drama in dance
"Normally, drama is produced by contrast, something against something else followed by a resolution out of it one way or another."
Merce Cunningham and *Jacqueline Lesschaeve*, 1985.

Excerpt
"Conventional dramatic structure with a beginning, a turning point and an ending is completely abandoned by Bausch in favour of a form which appropriates reality by means of excerpt-type individual situations."
Hedvig Müller and *Norbert Servos,* 1984.

Conventional mime
The story-telling means used in classical works, such as "The Sleeping Beauty".
Peggy van Praagh and *Peter Brinson,* 1963.

Business

What character dancers are concerned with more than physically challenging dance work, the acting part of ballet; said of Carabosse in "Sleeping Beauty", or the Ugly Sisters in "Cinderella".
Ashley Page, Interview.

Representative dances

"Representative dances may...be classified into two orders: thematic dances and dances of characterization."
Margaret H'Doubler, 1957 (1940).

Interior and exterior existence

The complexity of a dance work, with 'in' jokes and references understood only by those informed in dance, together with its overt existence, its accessible narrative and form.
Ashley Page, Interview.

Narrative form

A way of working preferred by Gillian Lynne; even where the work is ostensibly abstract, she will provide for herself an emotional context from which her creative fluidity can begin.
Gillian Lynne, Interview.

Narrative

"Graham's narratives, constructed in 'acts' like a classical tragedy, or in 'tableaux', are (in some respects) much closer to the purely theatrical than to narrative proper."
Laurance Louppe, 1989.

Narrative

"...the way in which narrative is used in French choreography is not in essence theatrical. It deals with given narratives in which the stage, for want of anything better, becomes the framework."
Laurance Louppe, 1989.

Narrative dance

A piece based on a situation or a premise, with a thread of continuity and purpose running through it, leading to a denouement.
Doris Humphrey, 1959.

Narrative thread

Some sense of narrative offered to the audience in a work, but not in logical time, the 'thread' being interrupted and reappearing in episodic structures.
Mark Murphy, Interview.

Signs as choreographic tools

"The choreography is composed totally of rhythms and signs which form a perfect combination."; said of Lea Anderson's "Flag".
Bernadette Benis, 1989.

Illustrative gesture

Movements to accompany songs which pick up the meaning in the lyrics, a device which may be appropriate to reinforce the narrative for the audience, but may be 'over the top'.
Margot Sunderland with *Kay Pickering,* 1989.

Moment of drama (in a ballet)

In a narrative ballet, a punctuation of the dancing with movement/stillness/an exit/an entrance, etc. which highlights the dramatic thread of the characters.
David Bintley, Rehearsal.

Theatricality

The aspects of a dance work which distinguish it from a pure movement piece, integrating "dance movement with straight acting in an interactive set with a sound score."
Mark Murphy, Interview.

Paramount role of dance in ballet

"Consciously, all through my career, I have been working to make the ballet independent of literary and pictorial motives.... If the ballet is to survive, it must survive through its dancing qualities...it is the dance that must be paramount."
Frederick Ashton in Zoe Dominic and John Selwyn Gilbert, 1971.

Images

The suggested characterisation which appears, disappears, and reappears through the articulation of posture and gesture.
"...sternness, mirth, urgency, inebriation, pedantry."
Sally Banes, 1980(a).

Scenic progression of images

Said of Bausch's treatment in "Arien".
"Patterns of behaviour, gesture, "actions" from different points in time, and various social clichés, telescope into one another; the distinction between what is real and what is not is suspended."
Norbert Servos and *G. Weigelt,* 1984.

Semi-allegorical form

Dances which are halfway between narrative and non-narrative.
Don McDonagh, 1969.

4. FORM

Form
> The structure of the dance brought about through the relationships between the components of the dance.
> *Janet Adshead*, 1990.

Structure
> The way a dance is put together which, if successful, speaks to both the dancers who perform it and the audience who watch it.
> *Bonnie Bird,* Interview.

Structure
> "A synthesis of form and content, in which action motifs must be extended into phrases and sequences, spatial and dynamic shapes must be developed with changing patterns, contrasting formations, and qualitative changes into organic rhythms of purposeful intent."
> *Hettie Loman,* 1991.

Morphological elements and cells
> The smallest units of form in dance material; elements are single kinetic units of material, cells are more than one that irrevocably appear together.
> *Roderyk Lange,* 1981.

Thematic material
> Movement made for a dance which has fertile possibilities for development and manipulation; a Louis Horst term.
> *Jane Dudley,* Interview.

Motif
> "...distinctive bit of movement that can be formally manipulated."
> *Alan Salter,* 1977.

Motif
> "Motifs are organising devices that give the artist's imagination a start, and so 'motivate' the work. They drive it forward and guide its progress."
> *Susanne K. Langer,* 1953.

Motif
> "It arises through the linking of dance gestures. At least two dance gestures are needed to form a motif. They may be similar, contrasting or even identical in character. The way in which the dance gestures are joined in sequence reveals the content."
> *Sylvia Bodmer,* 1962.

Concentrated beads
Stylistically tight strings of movement, made as core material for a work.
Lea Anderson, Interview.

Choreographic material
Movement motifs which recur during a work and which build up the character of the role; said of Jooss's "The Green Table".
Anna Markard, Rehearsal.

Passage
A small section of a work.
Bessie Schoenberg, Interview.

Phrase
A phrase covers several movements which, by themselves, may not be meaningful, movements which, in context with one another, may become meaningful, through relationships, change, and contrast.
Valerie Preston-Dunlop, 1987.

Phrase shape
"A good dance then should be put together with phrases and the phrase has to have a recognisable shape, with a beginning and an end, rises and falls in its overall line and differences in length for variety."
Doris Humphrey, 1959.

Phrase
"A phrase is the smallest and simplest unit of form. It is a short but complete unit in that it has a beginning, middle and end. Every phrase...contains this basic structure."
Lynne Anne Blom and *L. Tarin Chaplin,* 1982.

Strings
Phrases of movement created in a style as a starting point for a choreography, from which selections will be made for the work itself.
Lea Anderson, Interview.

Routine
In Latin American dance, a term used for the extended sequences composed for competition purposes.
Ruud Vermey, Interview.

Formula
A structural unit, elicited because of its persistent character within a compositional mode of a dance. It constitutes a cultural trait.
Roderyk Lange, Interview.

Two measure requirement, The

One of the restrictions put by Louis Horst in his Pre-classic Forms course, that the thematic material created should use and be complete in two bars of the given music.

Jane Dudley, Interview.

Form as the shape of content

"Inspiration has to be present to make the form come alive.... Form without content becomes form for the sake of form."

Hanya Holm in Walter Sorell, 1976.

Structure

"The movements must build up to a climax. There must be a beginning, a rise to the turning point and a resolution."

Margaret H'Doubler, 1957 (1940).

Rounded off

The edges of each section of a dance which separate it from the next, sections which do not organically grow out of each other.

Lea Anderson, Interview.

Free association

For Bausch, "Beginning and end no longer represent the temporal frame for the development of characters. Instead, separate scenes are joined in a loosely associative sequence. The aim no longer is a logical, accurate development of a plot and character, but an unfolding of lines of free-association with images and actions."

Hedvig Müller and *Norbert Servos,* 1984.

Theme

"The idea should be developed through an introduction, development and finale. The introduction should state the theme, present the characters and place them in a situation which they have to resolve. The middle section should develop the theme and situation, exploring and deepening the conflicts between the characters which the situation has created. The finale should provide the climax which resolves the situation and makes clear the author's intention."

Peggy van Praagh and *Peter Brinson,* 1963.

Logical development

If the constructional elements of motifs, developments, variations, contrasts, climaxes or highlights, and above all transitions are successfully employed, then the dance appears to have logical development which in turn produces unity.

Jacqueline M. Smith, 1980.

Essential ingredients

"All the forms and transitions serve the idea: the action is not interrupted by superfluous ornament."

Hettie Loman, 1992.

Unity

"...the oneness that results from the organisation of many parts."
Janet Adshead, 1986.

Balanced

The composition of a baroque dance as a whole shows a balance of interest between step patterns and figures; contrast between curves and straight lines, fast steps and slow steps.

"...the essentials of the baroque dance style are containment, harmony and balance...."
Philippa Waite, Interview.

Design coherence

The essential principle of form and the basis of style developed through the manipulation of the factors of "symmetry, balance, emphasis, proportion, unity and harmony", to produce a whole.
Aileene Lockhart and *Esther E. Pease*, 1977 (1966).

Seamless

A quality of the transition between sections of a work. "They happen without your noticing it."
Dorothy Madden, Interview.

Chance methods

"Cunningham uses chance much as he might a magnet, to draw possibilities to him from beyond his reach, and to arrange his materials, like iron filings, into relationships he might not otherwise have seen."
James Klosty, 1975.

Structural tension, A

A tension in a work which arises through the conflict of two elements such as a tempestuous content presented in a tightly confined form.
Stephanie Jordan, 1992.

5.   FORMAL DEVICES

Formal devices

Established ways of handling movement material in dance making, such as repetition, canon, theme and variations.
Stuart Hopps, Interview.

Choreographic choices

The means a choreographer chooses to create the kind of work envisaged, such as "spacing, grouping, energy ricocheting, movement texture", rather than the formal devices of repetition, retrograde, accumulation; said of Gillian Lynne's work.
Gillian Lynne, Interview.

ABA dance

A trio of movement phrases where the beginning motif is repeated and becomes also the last, giving the dance a cyclical structure.

"Thoroughly formal...suited to the non-dramatic dance...."
Doris Humphrey, 1959.

ABA form

A choreographic form borrowed from music in which the theme A, manipulated, is followed by a contrasting theme B, with a return to a somewhat differently treated A.

"The most deeply instinctual aesthetic form; a beginning, a middle and an end; this is the universal pattern of life itself, we are born, we live, we return to the unknown."
Louis Horst and *Carroll Russell,* 1961.

Abstraction

"...1. to distill to essence, and 2. nonverbal, sentient..."; said of Alwin Nikolais's choreography.
Murray Louis, 1980.

Abstraction versus realism

"With realism the brain can tell the senses what they have felt; with abstraction the senses can stimulate the brain into non-literal imagery."
Murray Louis, 1980.

Accumulation

Joining short phrases or individual movements to make a continuous phrase, acquiring a kind of logic through the working process.
Gregory Nash, Interview.

Augmentation

"The act of enlarging or increasing the amount, degree, size or time value of a movement."
Aileene Lockhart and *Esther E. Pease*, 1977 (1966).

Balleticise, To

To use two of the essential qualities of classic ballet, skill and clarity, to tame and refine authentic folk dance steps until they no longer violate the style of the ballet in which they appear; to have applied other essential qualities such as lightness and delicacy would be "inconsistent with the peasant aura" and would "infringe on the character of the steps."
Selma Jeanne Cohen, 1982.

Binary form

The AB compositional form.

"The first section A is contrasted by a new section B, but both have a common thread which binds one to the other...."
Jacqueline M. Smith, 1980.

Breaking a phrase

Cutting a phrase in two, three or more fragments, choosing where the breaks shall come; a device used when several phrases are to be made by combining fragments chosen from more than one original source.

Rui Horta, Workshop.

Broken form

A composition of movements alienated from their original affinities, being made up of non-sequiturs.

Doris Humphrey, 1959.

Canned chance

A Duchamps term in which one purposely divorces oneself from one's own perspective through allowing chance to be contained in the work.

Doris Rudko, Interview.

Canon in time

The same motif is performed by the subdivisions or individual participants of a group one after the other.

Albrecht Knust, 1979.

Central focus

Giving the audience clear indications of where they should look by giving key choreographic passages in the central area, a device used in conventional ballets; said in contrast to devices which decentralise the space and defocus the audience's attention.

Valerie Preston-Dunlop, Seminar.

Changing your space

While playing with made material, allowing directional change, distance, orientation and proximity to generate material.

Yolande Snaith, Interview.

Change the space, To

A choreographic device in which the movement material is danced with some spatial alteration, such as a change of front, or a change of place in the space.

Dorothy Madden, Interview.

Choreographic complexity

The increase in the number of possible steps and figures used in the routines of ballroom dancing and Latin American dance, through changes in the rise and fall, amount of turn, and speed of movement.

Geoffrey Hearn, Interview.

Choreographic formulae

How the danced use of space is conventionalised by Bausch, viz: the stage diagonal for demonstration of skill, the circle as a symbol of impenetrability, the line as confrontational presentation.

Norbert Servos and *G. Weigelt,* 1984.

Climax

"...can reach its peak at any stage of the composition, but in the simplest forms it very often comes at the end as a conclusive statement."

Lilla Bauer, 1965.

Composition by fragment

A method of composition associated with Robbins.

"...a collage approach to both popular dance movement and the classical vocabulary, as well as the body language linked with daily life."

Millicent Hodson in Janet Adshead, 1987.

Cumulation

Successive additions to a movement or rhythm.

Aileene Lockhart and *Esther E. Pease,* 1977 (1966).

Cyclic

The formal structure of a work; used in Ohad Naharin's "Mabul" (1993) as a metaphor for ritual, rebirth, a recurring journey.

Susan Sentler, Interview.

Decentralisation

A move away from the dominance of the human figure and the necessity for time-space logic. The absence of literal continuity in order to achieve a balance between theatrical elements.

"...I was not concerned about the figurative presence of the dance but the dancer simply as completely released from that into the next phase: a freer instrument of motion rather than a dancing emoting figure."

Alwin Nikolais in an interview with author, Sali Ann Kriegsman, 1981.

Deconstruction and reconstruction

Taking apart phrases of movement into units of material which can be altered, augmented, allowed to mutate, and then be constructed anew in a different form.

Laurie Booth, Interview.

Deformation

"...a reversal or turning inside out of the expected leads to synthesis of old and new."

Lincoln Kirstein, 1959.

Development
> "The expansion and elaboration of thematic material."
> *Aileene Lockhart* and *Esther E. Pease*, 1977 (1966).

Developing
> Extending thematic material in rhythm, in space, and through devices specific to each choreographer.
> *Jane Dudley*, Interview.

Distortion
> "The act of exaggerating or twisting the original form or shape."
> *Aileene Lockhart* and *Esther E. Pease*, 1977 (1966).

Duchampian games
> Choreographic experiments inspired by the Dadaesque ideas and chance elements of Marcel Duchamps in the 1920's.
> *Doris Rudko,* Interview.

Duration (as an organising structure)
> Cunningham is concerned with "...time as structure...how length of time can alter movement and change space...."
> *Carolyn Brown,* 1968.

Dynamic excitement
> The level of dynamic energy in a work which is heightened and lowered by changes in the ingredients.
> "Lifts look especially energetic combined with turns."
> *Stephanie Jordan* and *Helen Thomas,* 1990.

Elements of construction
> 1. Motif; 2. Repetition; 3. Variation and contrasts; 4. Climax and highlights; 5. Proportion and balance; 6. Transition; 7. Logical development; 8. Unity.
> *Jacqueline M. Smith,* 1980.

Enhancing a gesture
> Building from a gesture into a movement with both visual and aural design, by defining the shape, elaborating the configuration by what precedes or accompanies it, giving it a pattern in time, building it into a phrase, sharpening the contrasts of dynamics within it.
> *Selma Jeanne Cohen,* 1967.

Exposing structural devices
> Presenting a work in such a way that the devices and processes used in its making are not hidden but overtly presented; for example, by calling out instructions, or inviting the audience to read out a task; said of Rosemary Butcher.
> *Stephanie Jordan,* 1992.

Extend the material, To

To start with movement material, however simple, and work with it, reiterate it, develop it, present it as duo material, as disintegrating and re-forming, with various music, in several styles of behaviour.

Susan Sentler, Interview.

Field perspective

"I think the way people pay attention now is gradually changing. Young people don't think in terms of linear thinking. They don't have to go from one thing to another. They can follow a field. They can see it all, it doesn't have to be linear. That's part of what we've been involved with choreographically, allowing something like a field situation."

Merce Cunningham in Merce Cunningham and Jacqueline Lesschaeve, 1985.

Force-field

The ingredients in a dance used by the choreographer, variously, to set up forces between dancers, or between dancers and space, or within one body.

Stephanie Jordan and *Helen Thomas,* 1990.

Fugue structures

Choreographic devices which follow the fugue structures of the musical world; used in group work.

Stephanie Jordan, 1992.

Gaming

Using a strategy to destabilise and open up the sign-signifier relationship of distinct parts of the dance material by altering for example the movement's timing, the space, the body part, etc., enough to make a deliberate shift in connotation.

Ana R. Sanchez-Colberg in Stephanie Jordan and Dave Allen, 1993.

Gaming with time

A theatrical device which breaks the traditional dramatic line and linear chronological time, in which for example: the denouement of the work is known to the audience before it is developed in the work; in Death's inevitable victory in Kurt Jooss's "The Green Table", also applicable for example to Bausch's fragmented "narrative" in "Lament of the Empress".

Ana R. Sanchez-Colberg, 1992.

Ground bass

"A form in which the basic theme is repeated again and again serving as a background for other thematic materials."

Aileene Lockhart and *Esther E. Pease,* 1977 (1966).

Increase and decrease

One of the polarities of the dance gesture, that concerned with growth, which ensures that the gesture moves and is not a position or pose.

Sylvia Bodmer, 1962.

Insertion

Interrupting an existing movement phrase with material from another source.
Gregory Nash, Interview.

Kinetic blocks

Movement structures which are architectural, with clear starts and finishes and solidly meshed together activity, contrasted with movement that shifts, is unequal in density and comes and goes; said of Nijinsky's "Le Sacre du Printemps" (1913).
Millicent Hodson, 1986.

Layering

A choreographic process whereby activities, each one a mix of movement/person/sound, are juxtaposed or interwoven; as the work proceeds it may seem to unravel, revealing each layer.
Yolande Snaith, Interview.

Layering

A term in dance video/film making in which images are edited on top of each other to build up a complexity of meanings.
Chris de Marigny, 1992.

Layering

A process of building on original material, by enriching the sources, the performance, through the sound, the inferences, secondary movement material, costume metaphors.
Susan Sentler, Interview.

Loop structure

A choreographic structure in which a phrase returns like a loop to its starting place, so that the main progression of the work can continue.
Stephanie Jordan, 1992.

Lyrical intensification

A device in a non-dramatic dance in which the single feeling being explored (spiritual courage, romantic love, affirmative resolution) is developed over time through ranges of intensification rather than through the sequential definition of successive feelings that are required in a dramatic work.
Selma Jeanne Cohen, 1967.

Manipulation

"Manipulation is using thematic material through inversion, reversion and repetition."
Louis Horst, 1958.

Manipulating

Rearranging material already made, according to known processes such as repetition and rhythmic change, different direction, or focus.

Jane Dudley, Interview.

Minimalist studies

Dance explorations which focus on one dance problem, through repetition with minimal changes, leading to a short work on that theme which may be a preparatory study for a work or sufficient in itself; said of Simone Forti's work.

Eds. from Simone Forti, 1974.

Modules of time

Uninflected movement material of a given length, which is capable of repetition with minimal transitional devices such as change of front, which can be danced anywhere in the space, any number of times; said in contrast to phrases of movement material which are constructed to have a-beginning-a-middle-and-an-end, with criteria such as climax or accent.

Sally Banes, 1980(a).

Multi-layering of rhythms

Superimposing choreographically the pattern of one dancer on that of another in Bharatha Natyam style which is based on mathematical rhythmic patterns of music and footwork.

Shobana Jeyasingh, 1993.

Naturalistic yet ritualistic

A critic's description of the mix of mundane choreographic material with choreographic devices associated with ritual, contained in the choreographic style of Pina Bausch; said of "Orpheus and Eurydice".

Nadine Meisner, Contributed.

Patchwork quilting

A device in dance making in which different phrases of movement material already established are structured together with, substantially, an eye for the overall image envisaged.

Stuart Hopps, Interview.

Polychory

Choreographic counterpoint, the dance equivalent to musical polyphony.

Joan Benesh in article by Fernau Hall (1964) in Roger Copeland and Marshall Cohen, 1983.

Polyphony
"One pair of dancers or the soloists alone start the theme (in movement), then other choreographic 'voices' join in, catching up with them or blending together in a new theme..."
Natalia Roslavleva, 1964.

Quote, To
To include fragments of movement from earlier works in a new work, to refer back through elements of the design to earlier works; part of the interior life of a work.
Ashley Page, Interview.

Radical juxtaposition
"...choreographic structure in post modern dance using collage which replaced chance methods."
Sally Banes in Janet Adshead, 1986.

Real Time
The timing that is needed to do the movement, no more and no less, and the duration needed to perform the work, not cut off or drawn out by conventional ideas of the length of a dance work.
Rosemary Butcher, Interview.

Reconstructed
A choreographic device in which phrases and fields of movement are stated, broken down, and constructed afresh; said of Lucinda Childs's work.
Sally Banes, 1980.

Recurring theme
A motif which appears in many variations.
Doris Humphrey, 1959.

Reiteration
"Anderson's choreography uses reiteration first, to shed light on the construction of the phrase and clarify its elements and then, to aid, emphasise and bolster its total strength and force."
Sophie Constanti, 1987.

Repetition
"...essential to the function of a motif."
Alan Salter, 1977.

Repetition
"...implies that the material is manipulated to 1) Restate; 2) Reinforce; 3) Re-echo; 4) Re-capitulate; 5) Revise; 6) Recall; 7) Reiterate."
Jacqueline M. Smith, 1980.

Repetition

"...can serve to enforce the discreteness of a movement, objectify it, make it more object-like...literally making the material easier to see."
Yvonne Rainer in Roger Copeland, 1986.

Repetition, with changes

The variety of ways in which repetition can be handled, especially by not repeating when the music does, by repeating a fragment of a phrase only in order to keep the momentum of the work going.
"...not a pure repeat...."
Ashley Page, Interview.

Repetition with minimal changes

Repeating motifs but changing their length, their inversion, their rhythm so slightly that the audience is hardly able to discern what has changed; said of Nijinska in "Les Noces".
Valerie Preston-Dunlop, 1981.

Repetitive structure

A choreographic device in which the various kinds of repetition comprise the basis of the work's form; repetition, reversal, symmetric repetition, transposition vertically, sagittally and laterally, and their combinations.
Sally Banes, 1980(a).

Rhythm, A

Adding a count to movement material which has been created from improvisation in a free rhythmic form, to come up with a metered phrase, probably of uneven lengths.
"We have 8, 8, 5, don't we?"
Rui Horta, Workshop.

Rhythmic intensity

The putting together of elements and cells in small moments, in passages, and in the whole work to give different layers of rhythmic interest and density.
Judith Mackrell, Interview.

Rhythmic patterns

Recognisable and repeatable movement rhythms which constitute the base from which the rhythmic structure of a dance is made.
Jane Dudley, Interview.

Rhythmic structure

"The life blood in the movement", the way time accent, metre, ebb, flow, and climax are used through rhythmic patterns.
Jane Dudley, Interview.

Rhythmical counterpoint
   Using two rhythmic elements (movement and sound, dancer and dancer, group and soloist, etc.) to interact contrapuntally.
   Valerie Preston-Dunlop, Interview.

Rondo
   "A dance form of three or more themes with an alternating return to the main theme."
   Aileen Lockhart and *Esther E. Pease*, 1977 (1966).

Saturation
   High intensity of information throughout the four strands of the medium, at any given point of the dance, in order to give the audience an overload of sensory information "so that the silences can be more readily heard."; a Bauschian term.
   Ana R. Sanchez-Colberg, 1992.

Schematic fragmentation
   A choreographic device of breaking up group forms, not from organic dissolution but from a predetermined rationally devised scheme; said of Nijinsky and Stravinsky in "Le Sacre du Printemps".
   Millicent Hodson, 1986.

Slow motion device
   A compositional device used, in a variety of ways, to distort both natural time and metric time, to give theatrical import to material or to invite the audience to attend to it anew.
   Eds.

Spatial counterpoint
   Several dancers presenting different material at the same time, perhaps differentiated in travelling direction and level; said of Siobhan Davies's work.
   Stephanie Jordan, 1992.

Spectacle
   An element of visual excitement in choreographing a musical which may be needed to raise the energy level of the show, possibly of a finale.
   Margot Sunderland with *Ken Pickering*, 1989.

Staggered
   A piece of material learned in unison, which is then presented with one dancer after another, unevenly timed and spaced.
   Christopher Bruce, Rehearsing.

Stylisation

The abstraction and removal of movement from its normal context.
Doris Humphrey, 1959.

Stylisation

The use of choreographic devices to clarify and enhance the sign value of the movement, but also to allow the choreographer to comment with his own signature through his choice of devices.
Selma Jeanne Cohen, 1967.

Subversive

Dropping unconventional material into a conventional work, so inviting the spectator to look freshly at the conventions; falls, floor work inserted into ballet vocabulary.
Ashley Page, Interview.

Symmetric repetition

A laterally symmetric repeat in which movements to one side are then performed to the other.
Ann Hutchinson, 1954.

Symmetrical

"A balanced, even design; an even correspondence of design, space, rhythm, or position of the body."
Aileene Lockhart and *Esther E. Pease,* 1977 (1966).

Take it away, To

Discarding movement which the choreographer does not like; something which may be done for the original production but also in a revival.
David Bintley, Rehearsal.

Tasks

Methods of generating or manipulating movement phrases within defined structuring parameters.
Gregory Nash, Interview.

Ternary form

"A division into three parts; a compositional form of three phrases or sections such as the ABA."
Aileene Lockhart and *Esther E. Pease*, 1977 (1966).

Textural density

The shifts and changes in the balance of the elements of the work (large and small movement, unison and counterpoint, crowd and duet/solo combinations, compact and linear movement) which give the work its substance.
Stephanie Jordan, 1989.

Theatricalisation of folk dance
Bringing folk dances into the theatre by modifying their form through choreographic devices to the expectation of Western dance theatre audiences.
Paul Filmer, Interview.

Theme and variation
A choreographic form borrowed from music.
"...a statement of a theme of some length, say 8 measures, upon which any number of variations can be built in completely different styles so long as the thematic material is always indicated."
Louis Horst and *Carroll Russell,* 1961.

Tight editing
A term in video making which describes the juxtaposing of short takes from different angles or times, a method which distorts the continuity in time and space of dance.
Chris de Marigny, 1992.

Time as dramatic method
"The perception of time as a subjective phenomenon is the most striking aspect of her dramatic method."; "Graham's theatrical dances are cinematic not only in their rapid succession of episodes but in their use of flashbacks, flashforwards, and merging events."
Joseph Mazo, 1977.

Transformation
Visibly changing the way of moving during a dance so that one distinct image is seen to turn into another; said of Michael Clarke's transformation from a non-gender-specific, black-veil-draped figure into a figure whose movement quality gave representation of masculinity.
Helen Thomas, Interview.

Translation of behaviour patterns
"The choreographer's [Lea Anderson's] repertoire of repetitions, inversions, and spatial reorientations are used to reveal the behaviour patterns, observed by the artist, to the audience."
Fiona Burnside, 1990(b).

Travel, To
The process of "raw material being moulded and shaped into a production" when that material has been originated in another continent and another culture; said of classical dance forms from Africa for Western European audiences.
Maggie Semple, 1992.

Understatement

"The act of minimising the representation of a movement idea, the low-keyed treatment of a movement statement."
Aileene Lockhart and *Esther E. Pease*, 1977 (1966).

Unison

A device to amplify small gestural vocabulary.
Lea Anderson, Interview.

Unpredictable

Movement material which does not follow sequential rules that can be read easily by an audience; several simultaneous strategies are adopted to structure the work and so avoid predictability.
Trisha Brown, 1987.

Variation

"An embellishment of the theme for the sake of variety."
Aileene Lockhart and *Esther E. Pease,* 1977 (1966).

6. CHOICES DURING THE PERFORMANCE

Base line phrases

Movement material created by the choreographer and transmitted to the performers, to be used as core material to be deconstructed, mutated, and reconstructed during the performance.
Laurie Booth, Interview.

Decision-making in performance

A choreographic device in which the performers have the task to decide on ways of dancing, ordering material, exits and entrances for example, which gives the work a particular excitement and freshness.
Stephanie Jordan, 1992.

Depersonalisation of a dance

"...everyone...is free to choose spontaneously in performance what parts of it...to perform...it is a dance which can be done by any number of dancers and the whole is never jeopardised by the departure of any one dancer..."; said of one of Cunningham's works.
James Klosty, 1975.

Events

"...in each place it's different; though the material is the same, the order is different, they have to rethink the way they will operate...."
Merce Cunningham in Merce Cunningham and Jacqueline Lesschaeve, 1985.

Exit and entrance

When improvising, using leaving and entering the canvas of the space as material of the dance.

Laurie Booth, Interview.

Free canon

A choreographic device used in the creation of a group work, in which learned movement material is danced by the performers in their own timing.

Dorothy Madden, Interview.

Give rules, To

A choreographic device which allows dancers to present given and learnt material in rule-determined orders, so that the work changes with the changes of rules supplied for each performance; a Rosemary Butcher device.

Stephanie Jordan, 1992.

Ghosting

A device used in group improvisation in which one dancer picks up the spirit of the material of another, dancing it in a diminished but nevertheless articulate way.

Laurie Booth, Interview.

Indeterminacy

When dancers are allowed to make certain choices of their own during the performance.

"I was...interested in the idea of indeterminacy, of giving dancers a certain freedom, not about the movements themselves but about tempo, direction, and whether to do certain movements or not."

Merce Cunningham in Merce Cunningham and Jacqueline Lesschaeve, 1985.

Improvised dance form

The joint production between Kathak dancer and musician, bringing together their distinct learned skills in a unique moment of performance, for which rehearsal can be no preparation.

Alpana Sengupta, Interview.

List format

"...a basic set of instructions governing one or more aspects of a work."

Sally Banes in Janet Adshead, 1986.

Macro form

The overall form of an improvised performance piece which is determined before the event as a kinetic field but whose micro forms are left open to the decisions of the moment.

Laurie Booth, Interview.

Prefabricated dance

A term used by Richard Alston for a dance in which movement material already made was ordered in performance by the dancer who chose the continuity of sections.
Stephanie Jordan, 1990.

Shadowing

A device in group improvisation in which one dancer picks up the material of another dancer, performing it in their own part of the space but in the same time span.
Laurie Booth, Interview.

Spontaneous determination

A choreographic method associated with Yvonne Rainer, which combines both chance and indeterminacy.
Sally Banes in Janet Adshead, 1987.

Stay with it, To

To used choreographic freedom without wandering off the theme: said of a choreographer and of perfomers in structured improvisation.
Dorothy Madden, Interview.

Chapter 12   SOME ENSEMBLE, GROUP, DUO AND SOLO DANCE CONCERNS

1.   ADAPTING, RESPONDING, PARTNERING

Adaptation to partners
Dancing with others — playing with differences and similarities of shape and dynamic quality and learning to lead, to respond, and to follow.
Rudolf Laban, 1948.

Affiliation
The quality of the interaction of two people in terms of the high or low content of support or aggression their behaviour exhibits; expressed in subtle to stark exchange of dominance and submission.
Michael Argyle, 1967.

Commitment to another dancer
"...the state of mind and body which develops through experiencing and participation in partner dances — rather than merely co-operating as spectators of each other's dance."
Alan Salter, 1977.

Contribute, To
A desirable characteristic of an ensemble dancer or an actor in a crowd scene, essentially an ability not to be 'a star' but to know their place as one of a large group.
Geraldine Stephenson, Interview.

Cue off one another
The essential trust and sensitivity which people dancing together have to develop.
Twyla Tharp, Informal talk.

Developmental vocabulary
The basic movement experiences for children in relationship play.
"Cradling, rolling over, sliding over, tunneling under, balancing on, clinging on, jumping over, being swung, pushing against, escaping from."
Veronica Sherborne, 1990.

Duo relationships

Partnerships in which the man and woman may be technically related, as in Balanchine's "Agon", or emotionally related, as in Graham's "Night Journey".

Of Graham: "The love duet structured as a flashback and fractured by tensions of remembrance represents…woman as lover and beloved, simultaneously wife and mother, serving the marriage bed and the cradle".

Selma Jeanne Cohen, 1982.

Energetic connection (or relationship)

A performance skill in which dancers show a relationship or connectedness with each other, which cannot be reduced to obvious things like spatial design or gaze.

Gregory Nash, Interview.

Feeling the reciprocity

The ebbing and flowing of energy between a couple, "…as it flows out of my hand you should receive it and give it back, it is one energy not two, not yours and mine but one functioning energy that we share."

Rosemary Brandt, Teaching.

Gel together, To

How two dancers in ballroom or Latin American dance are said to gradually work until they dance as a couple.

British Broadcasting Corporation, 1992.

Invisible threads

The relationship between baroque partners, enabling a conscious drawing of symmetrical figures in floor patterns.

Madeleine Inglehearn, 1993.

Kinaesthetic empathy

Awareness empathetically of the kinaesthetic experience of another person (dancer): bridging the gap of awareness between one person's movement and another's perception of it as bodily experience.

Valerie Preston-Dunlop, 1980.

Leading

The man dominates the partnership, the lady moving at his suggestion through the slight pressure of arm and weight; said of ballroom dancing.

Geoffrey Hearn, Interview.

Listening ability

Dancers' awareness of what other dancers are doing.

Angela Kane, 1990.

Partnering

The essential sensitivity to weight, alignment, timing, and style which a ballroom couple need to find in each other.

"Let me lead you there. Encourage her over. Keep the big distance between your heads and now swing."

Geoffrey Hearn, Instructing.

Partnership

The intuitive rapport which two dancers need to develop in order to be able to respond to the choreographic requirements of a classical pas de deux efficiently and expressively.

Laverne Meyer, Interview.

Rapport

The essential relationship which ice dancing partners must have to achieve the "magic" of "perfection" which championship demands.

Andrew Longmore, Contributed.

React, To

An image used to aid a dancer move visibly in response to another dancer or to an event on stage.

Anna Markard, Rehearsal.

Respond, To

How a choreographer might want dancers to take the choreographed duo material, to inform the movement by their individual response to each other, giving it a quality over and above the steps and so go beyond the established vocabulary from which the material comes.

"...affection, trust...."

Siobhan Davies in National Resource Centre for Dance, 1988.

Signals

What partners give to each other as cues in a pas de deux; a signal in preparation before a pirouette or a lift, signals for timing, may be focus or weight or subliminal communication.

Marion Tait, Interview.

Withs

Two people who, by their reciprocal behaviour, are seen to be attached to each other as a pair.

Eds. from Albert Scheflen (1972).

Yielding

A response to a partner/opponent in T'ai Chi in an attack and defence exchange in which the yield follows the other's movement, not in weakness, but by mirroring his direction rather than countering it.

Katherine Allen, Interview.

Democratic duet form

The partner work introduced by Steve Paxton in Contact Improvisation.

"...accommodate the movement of their partner and together...discover a course of action for mutual movement."

Steve Paxton in Stephanie Jordan, 1992.

Contact improvisation

"...displays real interaction between performers in place of the carefully choreographed or contrived interactions between dancers which characterize the more conventional forms of modern dance."

Sarah Rubidge, 1986.

Capoeira play (Jôgo de capoeira)

Movements of 'powerful attack', 'skilful defence', and 'cunning positioning' in relation to your opponent, encircling, trapping and feigning, working within the circular space created by the encounter, cartwheeling, jumping, slicing in attack, used with a high level of creativity to gain control of the encounter.

Bira Almeida, 1986.

2. GROUP/ENSEMBLE WORK

Group

Three or more dancers related so as to act as a unit of some sort.

Jane Rimmer, 1991.

Group work

The manner in which the corps is choreographed, primarily through working out the pattern of the dance, which may be formal, have no formal pattern, or even be apparently random.

Monica Parker, Interview.

Group body

A group functioning as one body.

"An individual body can stretch, bend, twist, turn, jump, fall, etc. A group body can form circles and lines, break up and come together, move with or without a leader, etc."

Barbara Mettler, 1980.

Synchronised group

A group of dancers whose movements are uniform, the group moves en masse.
Jane Rimmer, 1991.

United group

A group made up of individuals representing one or more factions, unified in style and intent.
Deborah Jowitt, 1988.

Mass/voluntary associations

"The break-up of mass into its essential units of force and their reassembling into more intelligent voluntary associations for joint effort."
John Martin in Deborah Jowitt, 1988.

Communal participation

The group acting as a social unit, not necessarily through unison movement, but with unison intent, as in Bausch's "Rite of Spring".
Ana R. Sanchez-Colberg, 1992.

Community texture

The overall treatment in a work in which group choreography is a major feature, solo and couple sections being short-lived and drawn back into the general group structure.
Stephanie Jordan, 1992.

Enlarge through unison, To

A device in which disparate or canon movement of a group is brought together in a unison movement, increasing legibility through its replication on several bodies.
Stephanie Jordan, 1992.

Ensemble design in Ailey's choreography

Stark contrasts of unison or individualism, "...either everyone is doing the same thing or no one is doing anything that relates to anyone else."
Kenneth LaFave, 1989.

Occasional unison

Unison used from time to time, possibly for one movement only, as a choreographic device to heighten a moment in a group work.
Christopher Bruce, Rehearsal.

Chorus

"A company of singers and dancers in Athenian drama participating in or commenting on the action; also, a similar company in later plays."
'Webster', 1993.

Chorus

A group structure used in Martha Graham's choreography, viz. "Diversion of Angels", and more widely in the choric works of Ausdruckstanz choreographers, and latterly by Pina Bausch in her treatment of the group.

Eds.

Expressiveness

A principle in Fokine's New Ballet.

"The new ballet...in developing the principle of expressiveness, advances from the expressiveness of the face to the expressiveness of the whole body, and from the expressiveness of the individual body to the expressiveness of a group of bodies and the expressiveness of the combined dancing of a crowd."

Michel Fokine, 1914.

Interplay of numbers

Shifting between ensemble, solo, duet, solo figure against ensemble, then crowd against two, so that aspects of social dynamics are presented in a work; said of Kurt Jooss's work.

Ana R. Sanchez-Colberg, 1992.

Disintegrated group

In a piece for an ensemble, each dancer acting as a single entity, in multiple unsynchronised activity; said of Bausch's "Arien".

Johannes Birringer, 1986.

Rhythmic layering

In Cunningham work, "...there is the possibility that they can be doing different movements in different rhythms, then that is where the real complexity comes in, adding this kind of material one on top of and with another...."

James Klosty, 1975.

Groups forming

Patterns arising in group compositions as the relationships between dancers form, grouping, elongating, dissolving, and re-forming; separating, collecting, crowding together.

Valerie Preston-Dunlop, 1987.

Social order

The formation that groups of people spontaneously adopt, so giving off signals of their intention and relationship to each other and to those not in the group; used intentionally in ensemble works especially those with a narrative base.

Eds. from Albert Scheflen, 1972.

Loosely-knit groups

[Anderson's "Clump" shows use of] "...the loosely-knit groups which can be observed on almost any social occasion."

Fiona Burnside, 1990(b).

Mingling

The overall look of one kind of group planning which gives an effect of chance itineraries.

Dorothy Madden, Interview.

Group formations

Spatial arrangements of dancers which reflect the relationship the participants have to each other and to the surrounding space.

Roderyk Lange, 1975.

Group frieze

A two-dimensional, stationary arrangement of figures.

Jane Rimmer, 1991.

Frieze effect

"It is typical of the neo-classical choreographers for great importance to be placed on floor patterns.... [Ashton] appears to be particularly anxious to avoid the two-dimensional frieze effect sometimes to be found in expressionist choreography."

Clive Barnes, 1961.

Key formations

Places in the dance where the group shape is central to the form and its meaning.

Lea Anderson, Interview.

Mapped pathways

Predetermined schematically arranged floor patterns for several dancers who, through changes of front, are alternately in unison, diverge, interweave, and intersect; said of Lucinda Childs's work.

"...circles, semicircles, straight lines, zigzags, spirals; triangular, square."

Sally Banes, 1980(a).

Spatial relationships of groups

Formations such as lines, blocks, circles, spaced out, in loose groups, in pairs, scattered, concentrated, divided, confrontational.

Valerie Preston-Dunlop, 1981(a).

Rank or File

An arrangement of dancers in a line, either side by side or one behind the other.

Albrecht Knust, 1979.

Circling and Wheeling for a group

Terms to distinguish everyone travelling as an individual around a centre of his own from concentric travelling around a common centre.

Albrecht Knust, 1979.

Snaking
>Moving as a file in a winding pathway.
>*Albrecht Knust,* 1979.

Canon in space
>A group arrangement in which the subdivisions or individual participants perform related but different movements at the same time, resulting in a graduation within the shape of the group.
>*Albrecht Knust,* 1979.

Group patterns
>The movements of groups on stage that have a visual form which the audience can recognise, rather than seeing a moving mass or chaotic change.
>*Stuart Hopps,* Interview.

Asymmetry in classical ballet
>The manner in which the corps is grouped which, in the classic genre, is less usual than symmetric form.
>*Monica Parker,* Interview.

Group form
>An arrangement in space of dancers in which the shape, facing, number of and distance between dancers is visible and reads for the audience.
>*Valerie Preston-Dunlop,* 1980.

Group form tasks
>Exploring the import of the number of dancers dancing, for example: "Discovering the difference between two duets that happen to be a quartet, and a quartet that happens to be two duets."
>*Doris Rudko,* Interview.

Group forms
>The basic 'traffic' movements which a choreographer in film, and theatre, and opera will have as staple beginning material; for group work the circular form, the linear form, the travelling form, the back-on-itself form,
>*Stuart Hopps,* Interview.

Traffic control
>A major job for the choreographer in theatre, opera or film where large numbers of non-dancers are required to move as groups, such as a country square coming to life.
>*Stuart Hopps,* Interview.

Spatial architecture

A term used of Bronislava Nijinska's choreography, especially "Les Noces", in which she masses her ensemble into "human pyramids, phalanxes, mounds", as a metaphor for the absence of individuality in Russian peasant culture.
Lynn Garafola, 1989.

Open up the stage space, To

"The dance's many entrances and exits are an attempt to give an illusion of a larger cast than five and to open up the stage space so that the dance will seem to be happening in a larger one than is bounded by the proscenium."
Paul Taylor, "Private Domain", 1987.

Holes

The spaces between dancers which individuals can use as routes by which to travel through each other.
Rui Horta, Workshop.

Physical vocabulary

Movement which arises from people being physically in contact with each other, movements for which there is no adequate verbal vocabulary.
Mark Murphy, Interview.

Working with weight

Touching, lifting, pulling, pulling apart, supporting, leaning, catching, heightening the physicality of the material.
Valerie Preston-Dunlop, Interview.

Group flow

The flow of the design of the movement, its energy, passing from person to person, making connections between the dancers of a sequential sort.
Valerie Preston-Dunlop, Interview.

Relationships of time

Synchronising the timing and rhythms of the groups or leaving chance timings, but making time devices a feature of the ensemble work.
Valerie Preston-Dunlop, Interview.

Group timing

The co-ordination of a series of moves by individuals which have to be timed precisely for the scene to work.
"Roll in to Karen, put it on Andrew, lift it off Kenny, now come in...too late."
Christopher Bruce, Rehearsing.

Common tempo

Intuitively shared tempo felt by a group of dancers working together.
Jane Rivers at Imperial Society of Teachers of Dancing, Study Day on Dalcroze.

3. GROUP IMPROVISATION

Group improvisation
   Moving in response to other dancers on a shared theme, without a preconceived outcome.
   Valerie Preston-Dunlop, 1981(a).

Group feeling of a company
   The sensitivity of each member of the company to his/her part within the group, especially needed in improvisatory works and in works built on an egalitarian system of casting.
   Dorothy Madden, Interview.

Dancing together
   Paying attention to the activity of other dancers working in the same space at the same time.
   "...overlap, intervene, coexist, initiate, follow, collide, respond, avoid."; said of Douglas Dunn.
   Sally Banes, 1980(a).

Out and in, To be
   In group improvisation in which exits and entrances are part of the process, the attitude of the dancer when he has gone out of the spatial canvas is that he is still in the field of activity.
   Laurie Booth, Interview.

Macroform
   The overall plan of a group improvisation so that the movement is left open but the clustering and dispersal of performers is given, together with cues for the introduction of new bodies of material.
   Laurie Booth, Interview.

Organised improvisation
   A Margaret Morris Movement term for a system of "ways" in which group improvisation might be structured, such as "Lines and Clumps Alternating", "Domination and Subjection", "Enter and Exit."
   Margaret Morris, 1972.

4. TRADITIONAL GROUP DANCE FORMS

Dance types
   Categories and sub-categories of dances within a genre according to the format of the dance material itself; such as the "round dance, processional dance, combative dance" types of the Morris.
   Michael Heaney and *John Forrest,* 1991.

Formations in country dance
The three basic group arrangements in country dances: the round, the square, and the longways, each danced by two or more couples.
Cecil J. Sharp, 1934 (1909).

Country dance forms
The round, the farandole, and the hey, being the original forms from which modern country dance forms eventually evolved.
Hugh Rippon, 1993.

Figures and choruses
Groups of steps with floor patterns which make up a Morris dance, collections of which tend to be specific to a team or a location, or specific to a tune; figures and choruses are 'called' by the No. 1 dancer either as a reminder of what is to come or because a pre-set pattern is not customary to that team.
Anthony G. Barrand, 1991.

Figures
Traditional moves in the Morris for six dancers: who move as three pairs in approach, separate and go-around figures; in two rows of three in which the 'hey', a figure-of-8 pattern, is common; or all together in circular or linear figures.
Anthony G. Barrand, 1991.

Concerted evolutions
A term used in country dancing to refer to the pathways made by the participants in performing the figures of a formation dance.
Cecil J. Sharp, 1934 (1909).

Hey, The
The rhythmical interlacing in serpentine fashion of two groups of dancers moving in single file and in opposite direction; a figure occurring in country dances in straight and circular formations.
Cecil J. Sharp, 1934 (1909).

Line dances
A form in which the dancers relate to each other side-by-side, thus establishing a common front for something to be faced, met, or fought against.
Roderyk Lange, 1975.

Circle dance
An ideal group form in which all the dancers are on equal terms in relation to the centre of the circle and to each other; a form which shares an internal focus and excludes those outside the circle.
Roderyk Lange, 1975.

Round dance

A circular dance form, which may be without a central focus, or with a lady in centre or a maypole; associated with early Morris or country dance.
Michael Heaney and *John Forrest,* 1991.

Chain dance

An open circular form with the emphasis on progression rather than a shared focus (as in a circle dance), there is one leader and spiral and serpentine forms emerge.
Roderyk Lange, 1975.

Chain and round dances

"...dances performed by more than three people in a linked formation, e.g. open or closed circle, line, or winding chain...no couple dance figures should be present; it is essential that all participants perform basically the same step pattern."
Lisbet Torp, 1986.

Corner dances and column dances

Two types of dances for a Morris side of 6 dancers, with typical figures and floor patterns which reflect their titles.
Roy Judge, Interview.

Processional dances

A form intended to transfer the group from place to place, with forward steps predominating over sideways, which predominate in circle dance forms.
Roderyk Lange, 1975.

Processions

How Morris dances used to be performed, giving rise to 'procession on' and 'procession off' dances in Cotswold Morris team's repertoire.
Hugh Rippon, 1993.

Processional Morris dance

At least 8 men, processing in 2 lines twirling brightly coloured slings or ribbon sticks; stopping, performing set figures, and moving on.
Hugh Rippon, 1993.

Garland dance

A specialised dance form danced by eight men in the North East of England, an example of the urban revival dances which reappeared after Cecil Sharp's seminal work of collecting English folk song and dance.
Theresa Buckland, Interview.

Handkerchief dances

One of the main groups of dances in the Morris, in which two handkerchiefs are held by each dancer, wrapped round the middle fingers, and lifted and dropped down with strong movements of the hand and arm during the figures.
Anthony G. Barrand, 1991.

Combative dances

A dance type in the Morris, in which a fighting element is present in the movement, not simply fighting equipment, as in a sword dance, being part of the costume or a prop.

Michael Heaney and *John Forrest, 1991.*

Stick dance

One of the main kinds of Morris dance, in which short or long sticks are held by the dancers who hit each other during the dance.

Roy Judge, Interview.

Sword dances

Six dancers with swords, linked together, weaving in and out of each other, clashing and locking the swords together, ending with a decapitation of 'the Captain', a seventh dancer who later comes back to life again; a Yorkshire dance; traditionally danced on Boxing Day.

Hugh Rippon, 1993.

Reels

Scottish dances in which setting steps on the spot alternate with travelling steps, danced by 3, 4, 6, or 8 persons, usually including a change of time and tempo, starting with the slow Strathspey and changing to the quicker reel.

Yves Guillard, 1989.

5.   DUET FORMS

Duet frameworks

Exploring the import and movement potential inherent in duet form, "Exploring what is in two bodies but not three"; "What is in a trio, not a duet"; "You can't braid with two."

Doris Rudko, Interview.

Basic duet form

The fundamental material of the contact improvisation 'pas de deux'.
"...touch, give weight, lift, carry, wrestle, fall, re-balance."

Steve Paxton in Sally Banes, 1980(a).

Double-work

The study of the skills and sensitivity required in the supported adage and lifts of pas-de-deux.

Nicolai Serrebrenikov and *Joan Lawson, 1978.*

Double act

A performance for two people in which the basic routine is fixed, the personas are developed, but the timing and audience relationship are fresh with each performance.

Helen Crocker and *Bim Mason,* Interview.

Couple, A

The smallest group unit, in which the dancers move around and alongside their common axis, often concerned with their own interaction and unconcerned with other dancers.

Roderyk Lange, 1975.

Partnership

The material which comes from "learning to dance with other people", from "trust", from understanding "counterpoint", from "the brutal process of the studio, going over and over again to make it work."

Twyla Tharp, Informal talk.

Big partnership, A

A pas de deux pair who stay with each other for some time, benefiting from the opportunity to develop their roles; a partnership in which the pair "look good together physically, work well physically", "get on well", and "have a chemistry."

Joseph Cipolla, Interview.

Partner, To

A male dancer's job; in a company to know a pas de deux role and be able to dance it with several female soloists; learning how each partner dances the role.

"Which way do you turn in the 'Blue Bird'?", "I do it by myself, not pulled by you.", "That felt comfortable, you didn't knock me off balance."

Marion Tait, Rehearsal.

Pas de deux

Traditionally, a duo in ballet with an opening adagio section when the man supports the woman in slow movements, a solo by each, ending with a faster dance together.

Glossary in *Mary Clarke* and *David Vaughan,* 1977.

Cavalier and Porteur

The terms used to describe the male partner in pas de deux, indicating first the kind of gallantry that is associated with partnering in ballet, and secondly an old-fashioned term indicating the diminished role of the male dancer early in the century as the carrier of the ballerina.

Glossary in *Mary Clarke* and *David Vaughan,* 1977.

Grand pas de deux

This balletic duo follows a set pattern: "entrée, adage, solo, solo, coda."

Peggy van Praagh and *Peter Brinson,* 1963.

Pas de deux look

"A visually stark contrast between the sexes, dramatic tension between the male and female, with sensitivity but not so sympathetic that the male image is difficult to achieve."

Joseph Cipolla, Interview.

Descriptive language of pas de deux

A kind of slang language unique to each pas de deux based usually on the visual images of the movement or the relationship, used for ease of rehearsal communication.
"the carrot turn", "the flip."
The Birmingham Royal Ballet, Rehearsal.

Danse à deux (baroque)

A ballroom dance to be performed by one couple at a time; usually of symmetrical figuration.
Wendy Hilton, 1981.

Adherence

"Maintaining relaxed, sensitive contact with your opponent in order to detect his intentions", in T'ai Chi Ch'uan.
Katherine Allen, 1992.

Bizarre relationships

Partner work which challenges stereotypical large-small, male-female relationships by presenting all manner of interactions between all manner of persons, in dance.
Lea Anderson, Interview.

Bodily contact

All kinds of touches and supports, on another person, caressing, hitting, patting, embracing, slapping, tickling, and so on, a principal signal-giving means in social interaction.
Michael Argyle, 1967.

Body against body

The confrontational and co-operative dance work of same sex duos; said of Bill T. Jones and Arnie Zane.
"Daring, skill, playfulness; attack, support, share; weight and balance; aggression and dependency."
Bill T. Jones and *Arnie Zane,* 1989.

Body to body

Working with another person without losing contact; visceral not cerebral.
Bessie Schoenberg, Interview.

Bonding behaviour

Interacting movement between partners which expresses the wish to or the fact of belonging; touching, grooming, looking, eyebrow flashing, smiling are examples (used in dance, especially pas de deux and partner work).
Eds. from Albert Scheflen (1972).

Circle holds

The grasps used in folk dance with a circular formation

"Hold on shoulders, hold the belt, the V hold, the W hold, the T hold, the front basket and back basket; opened out or tightly closed together; with little fingers only."

Robert Harrold, Interview.

Competitive language

Duo material based on movements of competition in sport, wrestling, boxing, fighting, and social interaction.

Eds.

Conversation on stage

Two people "talking" in movement, like one sound against another in an orchestra.

Siobhan Davies in National Resource Centre for Dance, 1988.

Conversational timing

The timing in a duo (or trio, etc.) in which duration, tempo and interruption reflect verbal conversation timing.

Valerie Preston-Dunlop, 1981(a).

Dyadic interaction

The behaviour of two people in a social encounter who use signals of territoriality, of bonding, and reciprocals of aggression and support.

Eds. from Albert Scheflen 1972.

Giving and taking weight

A basic theme for the interactive improvisation of two or more dancers.

Laurie Booth, Interview.

Kinesics

Units of movement behaviour which, in a context, are meaningful and can be read by an interacting partner.

Ray L. Birdwhistell, 1971 (1970).

Lifts

All manner of lifts, usually man lifting woman, but not always, which have to appear effortless and whose phrasing and breath control have to be found for a successful outcome.

Bonnie Bird, Interview.

Lifts

All manner of ways of supporting and carrying.

"...a bell lift..."; "Make a torque..."; "...back to back, now 'straight up'"; "Take hold of her pelvis...."

Twyla Tharp, Informal talk.

Pas seul

A solo dance in ballet, especially a solo within a large work.
Peggy van Praagh and *Peter Brinson*, 1963.

Not quite a solo

A work for one character supported intermittently by secondary characters; Maurice Béjart's "Sissi — Anarchist Empress" for Sylvie Guillem (1993), billed as a "ballet for one woman".
John Percival, Contributed.

Solo figure

One dancer contrasted with the ensemble; Lisa Minelli in "Cabaret", The Infanta in Jooss's "Pavane", The Bride in Nijinska's "Les Noces"; used for formal and dramatic impact.
Eds.

Solo format

Said of Bharatha Natyam which is traditionally a dance for one who commands the space without moving far in it.
Shobana Jeyasingh, 1993.

Einzeltanz (Ger.)

Solo dance, a title given to the solo dance recital, a popular form of theatre in Europe in the early 1900's; Niddy Impekoven, Gertrud Bodenwieser, Alexander von Swaine, Yvonne Georgi, Harald Kreutzberg, as well as Mary Wigman's early appearances, are examples.
Hermann Aubel and *Marianne Aubel,* 1930.

Jig

A solo Morris dance, which may be learnt from traditional notation sources, or be adapted from such sources, or be newly invented; "The Pipe Dance", "The Fool's Jig", "Go Enlist for a Soldier", "Fiddler's Jig" are all titles for established jigs.
Anthony G. Barrand, 1991.

Characters

In Bharatha Natyam, the several roles that traditionally the soloist takes on in one dance.
Shobana Jeyasingh, 1993.

Chapter 13   CHOREOGRAPHIC PROCESSES

1.   CHOREOGRAPHY

Choreography
"The art of making dances."
Doris Humphrey, 1959.

Choreography
"The art of planning and arranging dance movements into a meaningful whole;
the process of building a composition; a finished dance work."
Aileene Lockhart and *Esther E. Pease*, 1977 (1966).

Making a work
"Like sculpting, where all the elements of the materials come into play and shape
towards your idea."
Dorothy Madden, Interview.

Choreography
"...is about saying something and yet hiding it, giving it depth."
Stuart Hopps, Interview.

Choreograph, To
"To choreograph a dance is to design it in the process of making it, for we can
hardly conceive of an art-making process which is not a designing activity as well."
George Beiswanger quoted in Judith Genova, 1979.

Choreography
"...charges steps, movements and patterns with thoughts and emotions so that
spectators are stirred as by a painting or poem."
Peggy van Praagh and *Peter Brinson*, 1963.

Choreography
A complex process with cultural, intellectual and aesthetic content.
Richard Ralph, Interview.

Choreography
"...a kind of physicalized writing."
Robert Dunn in Janet Adshead, 1986.

Dance making

A process "totally wrought out of your body" with "intelligence, culture, and imagination."

Jane Dudley, Interview.

Choreography

In the movie world, the term used not only for making dances but for directing battle scenes, fights, and any movement of persons which has a structure.

Stuart Hopps, Interview.

Choreograph for the camera, To

To structure a dance work with the technique of film and video making forming part of the creative process, from the beginning.

Chris de Marigny, 1992.

Choreograph an eyebrow, To

To treat the smallest movement and the smallest expressive parts of the body as dance material for video because of the "power of the close up" to communicate.

Bob Lockyer, Interview.

Constant, The

In dance on video and video dance, the basic ongoing theme which guides the shooting and post-production editing, that is the movement, not the story nor the music which may be the case in other video works.

Bob Lockyer, Interview.

Composing

"Composing means creating form, which in turn means pattern making, and the realization of this fact means the inevitable inclusion of an attitude of craftsmanship."

Lilla Bauer, 1966.

Creativity versus choreography

"Creativity is a source. Choreography is a skill."

Murray Louis, 1980.

Creating a dance

"The choreographer selects, manipulates, combines and structures specific components" so that they "exhibit the character, qualities and meaning pertinent to the choreographer's own purposes."

Pauline Hodgens, 1988(a).

Create and act, To

In circus-derived work, to learn technical skills, to create a routine on them, and with performance skills transform the routine into an act of performance.

Helen Crocker and *Bim Mason*, Interview.

Composition

"A learnt skill, a taught craft", "which is the means and the method to structure creativity."

Murray Louis, 1980.

Craftsmanship

"The shaping and forming of the created movement, the structuring of the movement into an entity, the objective and subjective ordering process."

Murray Louis, 1980.

Craft of choreography

"What can be taught; it is up to the gods if you can use it."

Dorothy Madden, Interview.

Choreography

Consists of creativity and craft; "the first you can only awaken, the second you can teach."

Doris Rudko, Interview.

Invention

Given the choreographic 'gift', invention takes two forms: the discovery of new movement and the arrangement of old movement in original ways.

Peggy van Praagh, and *Peter Brinson*, 1963.

Churning it out

Making dance after dance after dance, on demand, in a style which has proved interesting to sponsors; used to describe what can befall a young innovative choreographer working in a modish style, who is given no time to recharge his/her creativity.

Jane Nicholas, Interview.

Journey, The

"What you and the dancers go through while a work is in progress."

David Buckland and *Siobhan Davies*, Seminar.

Start choreographing

A process of discovery; how to run a rehearsal, how you ask the dancer to do it, how to find movement which is not out of class, with turning points in growth towards "a public making of a very private piece of information."

Siobhan Davies in National Resource Centre for Dance, 1988.

Choreographic task

A problem set for student choreographers which becomes an exploration of possibilities; "A study for two bodies in constant contact with one another."

Bessie Schoenberg, Interview.

Setting spatial tasks

A way of sensitizing the young choreographer to the complexity of space through giving choreographic tasks on: "How it feels to recede and to advance"; "The import of a diagonal"; "Speaking through movement to the 'world out there', to infinity"; "Speaking to each individual out there"; and so on.

Doris Rudko, Interview.

Choreographic tools

Devices which the choreographer has at his finger tips which he uses both in prepared and in immediate dance making situations.

Stuart Hopps, Interview.

Tight framework

A limitation in which to work, in order to explore the possibilities within it, not running away from it but keeping to the task, tightly.

Doris Rudko, Interview.

Organic form, Finding

To allow the dance to find its own organic form, as the motivation and treatment of the idea demands it.

Doris Rudko, Interview.

Go beyond the intent, To

How a choreographic work develops during its making, ending with a different image from that with which it first began.

Beatrice Hart, Interview.

Re-do a number from scratch

When, in the rehearsal of a new work, the steps are not working, the choreographer abandons the rehearsal, beginning with a new approach in the next rehearsal.

Monica Parker, Interview.

Re-work, To

To edit out, to elaborate, to develop, to find the central idea; part of the compositional process.

Doris Rudko, Interview.

Abandon, To

A process in the development of a choreographer when one successful way of working has to give way to a new impetus.

Siobhan Davies in National Resource Centre for Dance, 1988.

Gestation period

A time when a new work is in process, not an active rehearsal period but nevertheless a time of progress.

"Somewhere on a subliminal level you're still working with it."

Dorothy Madden, Interview.

Experimental phase
> A period of time in a choreographer's output when he or she is primarily testing new avenues of working method rather than making works intended to be sustained repertory pieces; said of Matthew Hawkins's early work.
> *Ashley Page*, Interview.

Time to explore
> What a choreographer can do when working with her own company and not when creating with a large repertory company where time is at a premium.
> *Siobhan Davies* in National Resource Centre for Dance, 1988.

Making it work
> The continuing process of making a ballet, in which the material found from working out the mechanics is repeated and adjusted until the meaning begins to emerge from the steps and the choreographer is satisfied.
> *Monica Parker*, Interview.

Producing the work
> The choreographer's job which involves not only making the movement, casting and rehearsing the dancers, but also putting it on the stage, and turning it from steps into a ballet.
> *Monica Parker*, Interview.

Choreographic product
> The made dance.
> *Janet Adshead* and *June Layson*, 1983.

Product, The
> The final work, when all the collaborators have worked it through to get the images intended, defined and refined.
> *Mark Murphy*, Interview.

2.   THE IDEA/SOURCE/CONCEPT/MOTIVATION

Idea of the dance
> What a director of a play hopes to achieve by a movement scene in a play, an idea which is conveyed to the movement director (or choreographer) and may be sketchy or precise.
> "They dance", "Swirling skirts fill the TV screen", "Provocative dance in a dragon costume by two people".
> *Geraldine Stephenson*, Interview.

Concept, The
> The overall idea behind an opera production which all the staff involved, including the choreographer and movement rehearsal director, are aware of and may contribute to; said of the Wagner Festival production of "Parsifal", Bayreuth.
> *Teresa Kelsey*, Interview.

Cerebral start

A way to begin working, from an idea in the head, which the body must follow, so that the dance exploration becomes totally sensory, "of all the senses".
Bessie Schoenberg, Interview.

Collaborative concepts

The choreographer/designer work together, which may begin at the same time for both with the original concept, but may be delayed until the choreography is complete; the dance itself, if a movement piece, may not have a clear concept, but the designer has to provide one.
Liz da Costa in Roy Strong et al., 1981.

Chain-reaction

"The aim is to do the most magical work you can — to permit the chain-reaction of movement ideas, which spring from the original concept.... If dance is too logical, it becomes expected and predictable; then it can lose its life."
Paul Taylor in Selma Jeanne Cohen, 1977.

Formal ideas

Ideas of form for a work which may emerge from the literal ideas which initiate it; the cyclic idea of seasons and reproduction giving rise to the formal constraints of cyclic movement phrases, continuity of flow, uninterruptible motion.
Darshan Singh Bhuller, Rehearsal.

Set of ideas and references

What a choreographer will generate out of the collaborative discussions with the director and musical director; these may be sparked off by the setting, by the narrative, by the music, or a mixture, and will guide his movement choice.
Stuart Hopps, Interview.

Set of ideas, A

The researched starting point for a Butcher work from which the visual installation will be decided and put in place; in response to that a set of instructions to the performers emerges.
Rosemary Butcher, Interview.

Set of ideas

Several interlinking ideas which give the work its style.
"Chagall look, definite characters, Czech and Russian feel, cartoon qualities, the darker side of weddings"; said of "Les Noces" for Gulbenkian Ballet (1980's).
Christopher Bruce, Interview.

Sources and resources

Possible ideas for dances, either in the movement itself or ideational, which have to be researched by digging into yourself, into the idea, into the movement, into the music, until resources for the work itself emerge.
Dorothy Madden, Interview.

Starting points

Thinking about the idea over a period of a month, communicating informally and intensively with the collaborators, until confusing, unrelated images, even filmic scenes, begin to emerge as ways to commence rehearsals.

Mark Murphy, Interview.

Starting point

Della Davidson's way of beginning:

"...getting the dancers drawing with crayon on paper to see how they worked, so that casting could come first, then movement", for "Judith" (1991).

Bonnie Bird, Interview.

Dance idea: music idea

A conflict in which the music for a dance idea is sought and found which, when studied, provides quite another dance idea; a conflict which can resolve itself surprisingly and satisfactorily.

Ashley Page, Interview.

Image

Whether narrative or abstract, a good ballet has to have something to project and develop, which shows some progress in time, some image.

"...the spirit behind all choreography...."

Ninette de Valois, 1977.

See images, To

The creative imagination at work.

"I started with the image of flight of a flock of birds, the men flying in.", "...sad warriors...."

Christopher Bruce in Clement Crisp and Mary Clarke, 1974.

Inspiration

"A ballet for me has to have a personal fount of inspiration even if that's never going to be communicated to the audience."

Frederick Ashton in David Vaughan, 1977.

Inspiration

"Inspiration is for the very young. Necessity, rather than inspiration, is the source of choreography."

George Balanchine in George Balanchine, 1984.

Imagination

"The core of making dances", together with knowledge of composition and a resource of vocabulary.

Christopher Bruce, Interview.

Impulsion to move, The

The catalyst which starts "the motor of the soul" (Duncan); this may be music, pictures, sculptures, direct elemental personal experience, or self-induced emotional states.
John Martin, 1977.

Emotion as stimulus

"Emotion is the stimulus which gives the movement its colouring, its reason for being."
Hanya Holm in Walter Sorell, 1976.

Dramatic imperative

"One place that dances come from."
Twyla Tharp, Informal talk.

Conception

"To compose is not an inspirational experience. Composition is based on only two things, a conception of a theme and the manipulation of that theme."
Louis Horst and *Carroll Russell*, 1961.

Source material

Sources on which to base period dance style in modern stagings, including original music scores, and notation of dances similar in character to the new choreography.
Stephen Preston, Interview.

Subject matter

"...the older I get the less interested I am in ballets of the pests, persecutions and cynicism of contemporary life.... A re-statement of one's own personal idiom of the classical ballet is all I wish to achieve."
Frederick Ashton in David Vaughan, 1977.

Theme

"No theme is inappropriate to ballet if it can be expressed visually through movement."
Peggy van Praagh and *Peter Brinson*, 1963.

Theme and form

"The theme of each piece calls for its own particular forms. As in life, the inner and the outer are linked and continuously affect one another."
Hettie Loman, 1992.

Drawing ideas out of the object

A meditative process with an object whereby the performer identifies ideas, situations, actions, smells, etc. associated with the object and subsequently responds spontaneously to those associations, without the object.
Yolande Snaith, Interview.

Minor themes of a work

"Ashton's attention to minor themes is not a waste on his part. His gift for detail and intimacy is something very affecting — rare in so grandiloquent a form as classical ballet."

Alistair Macaulay, 1988.

Scenario

What the theme for a ballet has to become, a carefully written scheme of events for the ballet.

Peggy van Praagh and *Peter Brinson*, 1963.

Libretto

The choreographic plan, based on the scenario provided by the ballet's author; a detailed preparation for the work used by the composer, designers, as well as the choreographer.

Peggy van Praagh and *Peter Brinson*, 1963.

Note book, A

The sketch book vital for the preliminary image making of a visual artist, which for Rosemary Butcher is not written or drawn in a book but is the working period with one dancer when she plays by giving instructions and watching the outcome until the image emerges to form the basis of the piece.

Rosemary Butcher, Interview.

Erect the scaffolding, To

To know what has to be done, what story to be told, what characters to be created, what formal dances to be composed; said of the creation of a ballet.

Frederick Ashton in Mike Davis, 1958.

Taking a risk

The way in which a choreographer in the classic genre goes beyond the traditional confines of that genre through choice of movement, use of vocabularies from other genres, subject matter and costume.

Monica Parker, Interview.

Fresh path

A radical shift in choreographic convention; said by Nijinska of her lifting of the corps de ballet from its customary supporting role to a 'place of authority' in "Les Noces".

Bronislava Nijinska in Clement Crisp and Mary Clarke, 1974.

Parameters of the fields

What the collaborating artists have to define before rehearsals of an improvisatory work can begin, deciding on the limitations and freedoms allowed for movement, for sound, for the designer of the set and costumes.

Laurie Booth, Interview.

Motivation
       "...a complete array of reasons, involuntary or voluntary, physical, psychical, emotional or instinctive...leading to movement."
       Doris Humphrey, 1959.

Curiosity of the body
       A visceral interest in finding out the movement possibilities of the body. "Let movement beget movement."
       Bessie Schoenberg, Interview.

Sensorial route
       One route to successful choreography, by learning to trust an intuitive intelligence, by finding pregnant movement, and, only then, beginning to find structuring form.
       Doris Rudko, Interview.

Body, A
       What a choreographer works with, his source; it may be his own, an assistant's, or directly with his dancers' bodies.
       Jane Dudley, Interview.

Contemporary
       The quality of an idea which might move a choreographer to make a dance.
       "...it speaks of NOW..."; "...city traffic patterns and people sleeping in cardboard boxes on the street...."
       Twyla Tharp, Informal talk.

Flavour of the idea
       The beginning of the choreographic process, before movement material has been found, when the parameters of the idea, its 'taste' are being explored by choreographer and dancers together.
       Erica Stanton, Interview.

Piece-dependent
       Ways of working which are specific to each piece being made, developing out of the distinct nature of the excitement that precedes a period of creative dance making.
       Jodi Falk, Interview.

Psychological themes
       The kind of idea for a ballet used by Kenneth MacMillan instead of the more traditional narrative or musical themes.
       Monica Parker, Interview.

Archetypal emotions
       The feelings in the narrative of Bharatha Natyam work, "grand, highly charged emotions", which suit the mythology and legend of the tradition.
       Shobana Jeyasingh, 1993.

"What if?"

The basic start of much movement exploration, trial and error on ideas and movement themes.

Erica Stanton, Interview.

Human being

The central force in Tanztheater, the corporeality which affects the gesture formation of the work; contrasted with the 'human form' and the shapes in which it can be placed, a distinctly different choreographic focus and intention.

Ana R. Sanchez-Colberg, 1992.

Feeling tone, A

An attitude such as lethargy, irritability, excitement, from which movement material is discovered; a state a dance maker has to create and then objectify through movement.

Jane Dudley, Interview.

Dance gesture

"...the first building stone in the art form of dance."

Sylvia Bodmer, 1962.

Emotion as stimulus

"Emotion is the stimulus which gives the movement its colouring, its reason for being."

Hanya Holm in Walter Sorell, 1976.

Emotional source

The beginning of a dance, coming out of a feeling state, possibly autobiographical, from which imagery emerges with an emotional flavour.

Erica Stanton, Interview.

Dance menu

The choice of bits and bytes of movement from which a choreographer may choose to compose on screen through the computer program "Compose" (now developed as "Life Forms" (ed.)).

Dierdre Kelly, 1990.

Listening to the music

A way of starting a work, during which "a shape forms", a subconscious process quoted by Kenneth MacMillan.

"When I go into rehearsal I always think I have no idea what I am going to do. In fact I find I do know...in the sense of shape though not of precise steps."

Kenneth MacMillan in Clement Crisp and Mary Clarke, 1974.

Come out of the music, To

To work sufficiently with the sound so that movement related to it is discovered.
Jane Dudley, Interview.

Block out the music, To

To listen to music and write down its structure in terms of "what it is doing", "what it sounds like", using metaphors: "a siren", or personal technical terms: "a double fugue."
Ashley Page, Interview.

Working with the soul

A term coined by Isadora Duncan to convey the way in which she found her dance material.

"Listen to the music with your soul. Now, while listening, do you not feel an inner self awakening deep within you — that it is by its strength that your head is lifted, that your arms are raised?"
Isadora Duncan in Walter Sorell, 1981.

Arc of the music

"I don't always know how my ballets are going to end...I do have a conception...of the total arc of the music."
Jerome Robbins in British Broadcasting Corporation, 1959.

Imagined location

To find a 'place' in which the dance exploration begins, a context, "a setting where it is all happening."
Erica Stanton, Interview.

Set as stimulus

Having the set already in place when rehearsals begin, so that the movement can emerge from the physical relationship of performer and environment.
Mark Murphy, Interview.

Collaboration

A close working partnership of two artists; of choreographer and designer Kenneth MacMillan and Barry Kay. The ideas may spring from either and be integrated into the production "so that you can't tell from where it originated."
Barry Kay, 1981.

Designing for dance

Not just making costumes for moving bodies or providing a location in which they move, but testing the assumptions: exits and entrances — why not on a bicycle? musician — why not on stage? Why not sitting on a brick wall?
Liz da Costa, 1981.

Know what it is about, To

To have a firmly rooted image, series of images from which to start work; said in contrast to starting with movement material and allowing the images to develop out of it.

Jane Dudley, Interview.

Content determining form

The guiding principles of a work which develops from the choreographer's idea, themes, and attitudes; these informing the choices he makes in the use of the dance medium, so dictating the form that the work eventually takes.

Kurt Jooss, 1933.

Purpose of the dance

"The creative process demands first an understanding of the purpose of the dance. Is it to express love, hate, anger, what?"

Peggy van Praagh and *Peter Brinson*, 1963.

Choreographing for a dancer

When a choreographer knows a company well, making a dance, or a role, around a particular dancer's strengths.

"He has done it specially for her", said of David Bintley for Samira Saidi.

Anita Landa, Rehearsal.

Pragmatic choreography

Making a dance for practical reasons such as the need for a company to have a role for a new dancer; completing or altering the dance with practical concerns paramount.

Valerie Preston-Dunlop, Interview.

Associative process

An indirect process whereby individuals respond to a catalyst (object, picture, sound, topic, etc.) to generate dance play associating with the catalyst but not directly reflecting it or using it.

Yolande Snaith, Interview.

Structuring a state

A way of forming a multi-media piece which opens with text as the main ingredient and ends with movement as the main ingredient, having an intricate exchange en route.

"...going from one state to another...."

Ian Spink in National Resource Centre for Dance, 1988.

Keep your integrity, To

Not to alter a planned dance work to suit the space available, but rather to allow the dance to dictate the space it needs; similarly not to alter its duration to one expected of a dance by convention, rather to allow it to take as long or as short a time as it will.

Rosemary Butcher, Interview.

Dance scribbling

"The idea is to see action rather than shape or line. It works best for fast movement.... It looks anything but two-dimensional."; said of making "Junction" (1961).
Paul Taylor in Selma Jeanne Cohen, 1977.

Work meditatively, To

To meditate 'on your feet', to work in the studio on an image until material associated with that image comes up.
Yolande Snaith, Interview.

Replace the image

To allow the image with which you started improvising to fade and be replaced by the sensation of the action itself; this may in turn fade and be replaced by the image.
Laurie Booth, Interview.

Become blocked, To

During improvisation, allowing yourself to lose your spontaneity by becoming static, repetitive, intellectual, losing contact with your catalyst.
Yolande Snaith, Interview.

Barrier of boredom

An important moment in improvisation when the performer becomes 'fed up' with the activity, and works on through this obstacle to find 'good things'.
Yolande Snaith, Interview.

Chance procedures

"...it is not subject to a prearranged idea as to how it should go.... It can take a momentum of its own.... That leaves open the possibility of surprise (chance) and that is essential...."
Merce Cunningham, 1968.

Chance procedures

A process whereby chance (toss of a coin, etc.) is used to determine the kind of movements used, their order, tempi, entry and exit, etc.; used to make decisions which are then permanent.
Millicent Hodson in Janet Adshead, 1986.

Accidents

Spontaneous happenings in a workshop, which produce material for a piece.
Yolande Snaith, Interview.

Shared Map

A model of space which two or more dancers both use during improvisation; in so doing they are able to read each other's movements and interact without effort.
Laurie Booth, Interview.

Landscapes
Contexts for dance, especially for improvisations in which objects, sets, poles, light and sound in variety are both the catalyst and the context for movement.
Miranda Tufnell and *Chris Crickmay*, 1990.

Working alongside another performer
An improvisatory process in which performers use their lateral vision to become aware of the others' material, allowing outsiders (audience) to see relationships occurring spontaneously which are not necessarily experienced by the performers.
Yolande Snaith, Interview.

Contamination
How the movement of one dancer is affected by that of another in improvisation.
Rui Horta, Workshop.

Merging and evading
Two fundamental images used in group improvisation in which dancers interact without "destroying the integrity" of the other person's material.
Laurie Booth, Interview.

Spark off, To
An improvisatory process whereby performers work alongside each other and allow the others' dynamics, timing and material to initiate the expansion of their own material.
Yolande Snaith, Interview.

Infectious
The qualities of the movement of one performer being picked up by another, the likelihood that this process will take place in improvisation.
"...movement is viral...."
Laurie Booth, Interview.

Putting it down
The moment when the creative process, of all the elements of the work, comes together as product.
David Buckland and *Siobhan Davies*, Seminar.

Put something down, To
After lengthy structured improvisation in preparation for a work, the process of selecting from the material generated by this manner to form the work itself.
Yolande Snaith, Interview.

6. CHOREOGRAPHIC DEVICES

(*see* Chapter 11 Choreographic Form: Formal Devices.)

7. SOME WAYS OF WORKING

Working with the body

Choreographing with instructions for the body itself and its parts, and the actions it should do.

"Take the head with it, throw the head."; "Join your arms, go on to your toes, take this hand to that one, lock the foot behind the knee, move your head into your hand."

Richard Alston, Rehearsing Darshan Singh Bhuller.

Working with images

Choreographing so that images emerge from the movement.

"Hover there."; "You can't see, there, or there."; "Reach up to hold onto something."; "...strangeness..."; "...rocking..."; "Something startles you."

Richard Alston, Rehearsing "Perilous Night" (1993).

Working on movement logic

Having a broad idea of what the movement flow is, going on to work on how the dancer's body can achieve it.

"...so it has to be the left leg in front..."; "It'll be right/left."; "Get your balance and then go."; "Use the floor there."

Richard Alston, Rehearsing Darshan Singh Bhuller.

Working on structure

Choreographing a piece with one of the concerns being its overall form.

"This is the slow section."; "It comes to a stop there."; "Go on the next phrase."; "Can I have that movement in here again?"; "...a collage ending."; "Now it picks up the energy."; "Do that 3 times with a $1/4$ turn."

Richard Alston, Rehearsing "Perilous Night" (1993).

Working with music

Choreographing with the music/movement/dancer interdependence in mind.

"The low note is your cue there."; "Go from your last musical cue"; "...strange movement for that strange reverberation..."; "Nick [conductor] will start when you start."; "There's a repeat in the music, we can't cut it."; "Listen for the hard piano sound."

Richard Alston, Rehearsing Darshan Singh Bhuller.

Audience's focus

What a spectator will be able to see, and will be encouraged to look at.

"He is downstage, centre stage, lit, moving slowly, we are looking at really small things."

Richard Alston, Rehearsing "Perilous Night" (1993).

Body language

"Anderson relies heavily on body language as her means of expression, so it is not surprising that cultural codes and conventions are an area of exploration for her."

Angela Kane, 1987.

Break out, To
In choreographing a work, to limit yourself to given parameters in order to forge the style of the work, and then to let it overflow beyond them.
Lea Anderson, Interview.

Social interaction as movement material
"Look at sport or just people, how they interact, and see it as movement, which is what you are doing; your craft is movement."
Lea Anderson, 1990.

Uncomfortableness
Creating a style of moving which feels odd to the dancers; chosen as a challenge to the convention of ease and fluidity.
Lea Anderson, Interview.

Folk dance vocabularies
Some vocabularies used by Frederick Ashton in "La Fille Mal Gardée".
"...the Cumberland Reel, the Sword Dance routines, and an authentic Highland Fling."
Ninette de Valois, 1977.

Creative process
"He shows the dancer what to do." "The mechanics are simple, the creative process invisible."; said of Balanchine's working process.
Nancy Goldner, 1973.

Themes
"love and fear", "longing and loneliness", "frustration and terror", "man's exploitation of women"; said of Pina Bausch.
Norbert Servos and *G. Weigelt*, 1984.

Organic process
A way of working which allows the piece to grow gradually, costumes come from the movement not through a designer, the structure emerges gradually from the chaos of trial and error rehearsal.
Pina Bausch, Conversation with audience.

Footwork composition
One of the tasks of a choreographer working in the Bharatha Natyam style, to work, like a musical composer, to create the intricate rhythmic patterns of the footwork.
Shobana Jeyasingh, 1993.

Altered vocabulary
Using the classical vocabulary, but altering the spacing or the timing or the arms, so that the classicism is not obvious and the role comes through.
David Bintley, Rehearsal.

Risk taking

To explore movement possibilities which might be regarded as on the threshold of danger physically, especially in off-balance movement, but also conceptually by undertaking roles which require a shift in the normal way of working for that individual, especially in improvisation.

Laurie Booth, Interview.

Setting priorities

Finding a style of movement and a source for movement making in which limits are imposed, and the priorities of traditional style are set aside and replaced by others.

"Let gravity do the work; verticality not important; not only on the feet."
Laurie Booth, Interview.

Catch movement, To

To remember movements of improvisation which seemed worthwhile and retain them as formed material for a work; a way of working which develops from structured improvisation.

Trisha Brown in Trisha Brown and Yvonne Rainer, 1987.

Set a rhythm, To

"To give yourself a metre, a beat, a tempo, for a section of a dance, on which you and the dancers can work; one needs a pace, a momentum, an energy level to work with."

Christopher Bruce, Interview.

Set of 8's

The customary counts used as a base on which steps are set, which enable complex counterpoint in group work to function, and everyone to know where they are for rehearsal purposes.

Christopher Bruce, Rehearsing.

Creating ambiguity

An evocative style built up during the making of a work, for which the aim is not total directness, "allowing images which produced movement to be forgotten while the movement remains", juxtaposing them with movement material arising from other images, "deliberately not clarifying a character, a relationship"; masking a direct statement through choreographic devices and production techniques.

Christopher Bruce, Interview.

Try out an idea, To

To experiment in the studio with the dancers, possibly for extra material for a scene nearly complete, to keep or to throw out.

"Something that suggests firing a gun, really swing it, go forward, hip-hip, fall back, give a break in the hip."; "One, pull-and-a-three."
Christopher Bruce, Rehearsing.

Rhythm and phrasing

An important element in choreography, through which the dancers can relate to the sound score, the dancers having their own phrasing over the music, and counterpoint between each other and between the movement and the music.

Christopher Bruce, Interview.

Develop a vocabulary

To find a movement style which suits your purpose, one which has clear structure, limitations, and motivations.

"...a new dance grammar...."

Trisha Brown in Trisha Brown and Yvonne Rainer, 1987.

Preparatory work

Studio work undertaken by the choreographer before he starts rehearsals with his dancers; with Claude Brumachon the material is worked out on his and a partner's body, precisely, during these preliminary and between-rehearsal work periods; it is then taught to the dancers.

Bonnie Bird, Interview.

Push the boundaries, To

To work choreographically at testing the validity of the conventions of movement material for dance, of theatrical time and space, of the expected roles of the audience, the performers, and the collaborators.

Rosemary Butcher, Interview.

Work independently, To

To attempt to make pieces ('live installations') "when I want to, in the way I want to", more with the timetable of a painter or a sculptor than of a company-based, theatre-related choreographer, inevitably thereby schedule-dominated.

Rosemary Butcher, Interview.

Finding the language

Researching the work-specific dance material in practice; for "Body as Site" the language started with a concern for urban landscape, for which a visual grid system was drawn out on the dance floor, with improvisation on pedestrian and functional movement, tearing the space, subdividing it, and structuring with continuity and radial shifts.

"Crawling, shoving, knocking, pushing, tearing."

Rosemary Butcher, Interview.

Composition by field

"...making a piece in which something is exactly what it is in its time and place and not in its having actual or symbolic reference to other things. A method of spontaneous operation with an emphasis on space, clearing the ground for creative perception."

Merce Cunningham in Millicent Hodson, 1987.

Step

"I 'step' with my feet, legs, hands, body, head — that is what prompts me, and out of that other movements grow, and different elements (theatre) may be involved...."
Merce Cunningham in Selma Jeanne Cohen, 1968.

Composing by computer

Using the "Life Forms" computer program of three-dimensional animated figures, on which "you can make movement", adding the Time Grid and the Space Grid facilities, and tracking the figures as a video camera might; said of Cunningham.
Janice Berman, 1991.

Preliminary composition

Using the "Life Forms" computer facility, creating phrases from the menu of movements, putting them into the computer memory for future use in the studio with dancers; a Cunningham exploration.
Robert Greskovic, 1991.

Having movement in mind

Contrasted with having movement already made in the body, a way of working which requires that the choreographer is able to pull the actual movement out of the dancers, before refining it and reworking it; said of Della Davidson's way of working on "Judith" (1991).
Bonnie Bird, Interview.

Spread and focus

Two contrasting uses of space, of idea, of time, used by Siobhan Davies in her work; said of "Wyoming" (1988).
Siobhan Davies in National Resource Centre for Dance, 1988.

Superkinespheric moments

Moments in a dance when falling is imminent, when the "fundamental limits of balance of the human body are transgressed", achieved by using Laban's choreutic model of the dancer in space and reassigning its centres infinitely throughout the body instead of using one centre, the body's own centre; said of one of William Forsythe's processes.
Patricia Bandoin and *Heidi Gilpin*, 1989.

Studies

Dance explorations which focus on one dance problem through repetition with minimal changes, leading to a short work on that theme which may be a preparatory study for a work, or sufficient in itself; said of Simone Forti's work.
Simone Forti, 1974.

Symbolic device

A means of transforming a literal image into a choreographic image; said of Martha Graham.

"...an open mouth, cupped shaking hands to symbolise sound, both a call and a scream."

Agnes de Mille, 1991.

Rhythmic base

The essential beginning in choreographing ballroom dancing, where the eight-bar phrases in the specific rhythm and tempo of the dance form give the underlying structure, so that, whatever music is played, the routine can flow with it.

"The motivation is the music, the feeling is the rhythm."

Geoffrey Hearn, Interview.

Build up steps, To

To work with performers giving them a gradually increasing repertoire of material for which names may be given, 'the cherry basket', 'the trencher', before settling on who will do what, in which order, where and when.

Stuart Hopps, Interview.

Immediacy in film making

In film making, the extremely brief rehearsal time which means that the choreographer has no time to reflect on what he has made, no time to make a mistake, and has to "think on his feet" in terms of what will be effective to the cameras wherever they are placed.

Stuart Hopps, Interview.

Pick up, To

What a choreographer does from the improvised material provided by dancers, choosing those coincidental flashes which provide him with what he is looking for in his piece.

"Choose what triggers for me."

Rui Horta, Workshop.

Energies, The

The changing dynamic qualities of movement, which the choreographer passes on to his dancers through demonstration and through his voice.

"...te ha, lazy and hup, hup."

Rui Horta, Workshop.

Theatrical

A style of movement material contrasted with 'abstract' which can be read by an audience easily; used in this instance occasionally to provide connotation in material which is otherwise formal.

Rui Horta, Workshop.

Deconstruct a tradition, To

To take apart a dance in Bharatha Natyam style into a set of elements, which in the tradition are strictly ordered, to change from a solo performer to a quartet, to change the facings and directions.

Shobana Jeyasingh, 1993.

Breaking the form

Choreographing with a received dance vocabulary, altering, modifying it to the individual artist's taste, challenging those spectators who are emotionally involved with the original form and its received emotional content.

Shobana Jeyasingh, Interview.

Work from the character, To

To choreograph from the roles which are to be played, leading to steps and original movement being found to accommodate the characters.

Gillian Lynne, Interview.

Original choreography

Making movement for a musical show which is not based on any known vocabulary but comes right out of the imagination of the choreographer in the light of the production as a whole.

"For 'Cats', I had to make it all up to go with the T.S. Eliot poems."

Gillian Lynne, Interview.

Energy ricochet

The way the dynamics of a dance shifts across the space from one performer to another, one ingredient in the choreographer's palette.

Gillian Lynne, Interview.

Adjustment

The way in which Kenneth MacMillan varies traditional steps, or his own invented steps from previous ballets.

Monica Parker, Interview.

Mould, To

One method in making a work in which the choreographer literally bends the dancer's body into the shapes he wants to see; said of Kenneth MacMillan.

Ashley Page, Interview.

Physical

A quality in some choreographers' work, passionate, athletic, with the movement coming from within the dancer; said of Ivan Marko's "Tannhäuser Bacchanale" choreography.

Teresa Kelsey, Interview.

Open vocabulary

Working so that the kind of dance material is not predetermined or spoken about in a way which might close options, avoiding a hard-edged delineation of possibilities.
Mark Murphy, Interview.

Emergent dynamic

Working reflectively and deeply to find the timing and dynamics which the scenario demands.
"Chase the truths down to what the idea is."
Mark Murphy, Interview.

Basics, The

In choreography, movement as the basic medium, together with and supported by the aural and visual elements; working choreologically with the central component of dance, that is movement; said of Ohad Naharin's "Mabul" (1993).
Susan Sentler, Interview.

Generating material

Creating a body of raw dance material before the processes of structuring and refining.
Gregory Nash, Interview.

Transference of image

The placing of a literal image into the language of steps; said of the image of combing the Bride's tresses in "Les Noces."
"Their dance on pointe and the Bride's dance will express the rhythm of plaiting."
Bronislava Nijinska in Clement Crisp and Mary Clarke, 1974.

Rhythmic formalism

Said of Nijinsky's choreographic method where "he replaced traditional pas with an essential 'posture' from which he constructed the design of movement on the body", extending it to groups and ground patterns of groups; this formal method is then rhythmicised in relation to the music as in "Le Sacre du Printemps."
Millicent Hodson, 1986.

Significant posture

A body position set up by a choreographer which becomes the root of the whole work; said of Nijinsky's method in "Le Sacre du Printemps" and "L'Après-midi d'un Faune", in which the positions chosen restrict the body, giving it coherent style, and essentially function expressively for the work's themes.
Millicent Hodson, 1986.

Non-literal device

Means by which a choreographer and composer can mix the abstract with the denotive.
Alwin Nikolais, 1963.

Dehumanisation

"A choreographic method by which the body or any part need not remain in its physically real identity; it can become a free agent by withholding its motion and intermingling it with other dance figures and objects."

Alwin Nikolais, 1963.

Extending

Taking movements for ballet, such as a port de bras, and altering the accompanying movement, the torso, the head, to present the familiar material anew.

Ashley Page, Interview.

Visualise, To

To see in the imagination how the dance will look while listening to a known piece of music, not visualising the music in movement, but rather visualising an independent dance structure which nevertheless comes from the music.

Ashley Page, Interview.

Pure invention

Working towards new dance material without starting from a known and shared vocabulary, such as ballet, or character steps, or Graham technique, starting with the idea and the body.

Ashley Page, Interview.

Strategy of denial

Yvonne Rainer's method of work which signalled Post-modernism.

"No to spectacle, No to virtuosity.... No to glamour.... No to involvement of performer.... No to moving and being moved."

Yvonne Rainer, 1966.

Get steamed up, To

Having warmed up, to work at a pace and with energy in order for the movement possibilities of the body to be explored honestly.

Bessie Schoenberg, Interview.

Work honestly, To

"...to penetrate the real ore, the gold, to find the seam in a heap of movement; material that is not only fun or fresh but to the point and experienced."

Bessie Schoenberg, Interview.

Dig, To

The process a choreographer has to undertake, "to dig deeper into the self", and wider into the arts "to painting to see how your eye is taken over the canvas and brought back to a focus."

Bessie Schoenberg, Interview.

Way of working

A Snaith term for the choreographic process: a lengthy period of structured play used to generate dance material for a piece.

Yolande Snaith, Interview.

Endings

"My works never have real endings, they just stop and fade out because I don't believe there is any final solution to the problems of today."

Anna Sokolow in Selma Jeanne Cohen, 1977.

Dancer/choreographer collaboration

Movement material that dancers offer to choreographers who then accept or discard it, using their own discretion and taste; said of Glen Tetley's and Kenneth MacMillan's working process.

Ashley Page, Interview.

Contrapuntal rhythmic play

A choreographic device used by Antony Tudor in which the rhythm of movement and the music are equally clear metrically, never the same, but clearly interwoven in fine detailed phrasing.

Muriel Topaz, 1986.

Honing

Sharpening the detail of a work; an essential early process in Antony Tudor's rehearsals, where he "does not sketch or block...but instead works and reworks like a jeweler...each perfect detail."

Muriel Topaz, 1986.

8.   THE CHOREOGRAPHER'S EYE

Choreographer's eye

"The thing that a choreographer really needs is an eye. He has to do his training through his eye. It's not a thing you can teach.... I think I learned to be a choreographer through watching other choreographers work."

Frederick Ashton in Zoe Dominic and John Selwyn Gilbert, 1971.

Critical eye

The choreographer's discernment of the emerging work as he seeks to define the statement.

Mark Murphy, Interview.

Evaluating

While running a work-in-the-making, the choreographer distancing himself as far as possible from the action, possibly watching it in the mirror, to get a sense of the whole, in order to judge its value.

"It's a good sketch — a possibility."
Richard Alston, Rehearsal.

It

What the choreographer is looking for, the right movement for that place in the ballet.

"That's it!"
David Bintley, Rehearsal.

Stand back

To move back from the dancers to review the work being made.
"...to see if I like what I've made...."
Christopher Bruce, Interview.

Testing material

Using the combination of a jazz class to judge whether the dance material given would make successful choreographic material; class used as a testing ground by the teacher/choreographer.
Thea Barnes, Interview.

Timing

A sense of what to do, and when; a desirable ability for both choreographer and performer.
Dorothy Madden, Interview.

Interplay

"You feel-think and you think-feel; it has to be an interplay of subjectivity and objectivity, always."
Doris Rudko, Interview.

Elimination

The choreographic practice of refining choreographic ideas and/or material.
"The score [for 'Apollo'] was a revelation. It seemed to tell me that I too could eliminate. I began to see how I could clarify by limiting, by reducing to the one possibility that is inevitable."
George Balanchine in George Balanchine, 1984.

Overcomplicate, To

A tendency in making dances, when searching for the right movement, to 'tinker' with the arms, the timing, the focus until it is impossible for the dancers to make sense of it.
"Am I overcomplicating this?"
David Bintley, Interview.

Refining

Elimination of the parts of the generated material which don't fit in with the choreographer' s vision for the piece.
Gregory Nash, Interview.

Orchestrate the detail, To

To work on the movement material of a group of dancers, refining the kinetic message rather than working on meanings which casting, especially mixed gender casting, will provide.
Shobana Jeyasingh, Interview.

Simplification

"It's not what you put into a ballet, it's what you take out."
Frederick Ashton in Clive Barnes, 1961.

Simplification

"When one begins to do things one is apt to overcharge everything, and if things are too intense, one blurs the vision of the audience. By simplifying, you make it easier for an audience to take in your intentions."
Frederick Ashton in Zoe Dominic and John Selwyn Gilbert, 1971.

Simplification

A choreographic process by which choreographic material is pared down to essentials.

"He is constantly trying to fine down his choreography and to achieve the flow that gives the dance its vital sense of spontaneity."
Clive Barnes, 1961.

Narrowing down

"In every section I narrowed down the possibilities of movement, really tightly restricted them in some way — it's a very particular way of moving." (referring to "Flesh and Blood").
Lea Anderson, 1990.

Economical

"Not making superfluous movement for movement's sake."
Christopher Bruce in Clement Crisp and Mary Clarke, 1974.

Visual competition

When staging a number with several individual characters, allowing each one enough space and time to be presented as separate characters, so that the audience is not confused visually with competing images.
Margot Sunderland with *Ken Pickering*, 1989.

Put something in there, To
> To see a gap in a solo or pas de deux or ensemble, and to make movement to fill it; occurring in the original creation or in revival.
> *David Bintley*, Rehearsal.

Too close to the idea, To be
> What a choreographer may be, too subjective, and so having difficulty in distancing himself from what he has made.
> *Dorothy Madden*, Interview.

Judge, To
> "Saying you like it or not before you have let it be born"; what an inexperienced choreographer might say too soon of her own emerging movement.
> *Doris Rudko*, Interview.

Unaware egotism
> The subjective perspective that a student might have on another person's choreographic work.
> *Bessie Schoenberg*, Interview.

Working from the outside or inside
> The director's view of the work as outside, the performer's view of the work as inside; the dance theatre artist (such as Snaith) shifting from one role to another while working on a piece.
> *Yolande Snaith*, Interview.

Bridge the distance, To
> To make work which takes account of the space between stage and audience of a large house, so that a work made for a smaller house may not 'carry'; said of "Bridging the Distance."
> *Siobhan Davies* in National Resource Centre for Dance, 1988.

Pluralistic
> A quality of taste developed by a choreographer through working in two genres which both have a clear aesthetic; said of Shobana Jeyasingh' s classical Indian/Western theatre dance experience and, thence, of the development of her critical judgement.
> *Shobana Jeyasingh*, 1993.

Jar on the eye, To
> To see a moment of imbalance in the spatial dynamic patterns of a scene, which seems 'out of tune' with the rest.
> *Stuart Hopps*, Interview.

Avoiding cliché

Seeing the emergence of a well-known, much-used image, which would be out of place in the work, and replacing or diffusing it.

"You are rocking — no, that's a cliché; make it much smaller, can you lift your knees off the ground?"

Richard Alston, Rehearsing "Perilous Night".

Get outside your own physicality, To

To work choreographically on the dancers' bodies rather than your own to overcome your inherent stylistic and physical limitations and so to use your eye as well as your kinetic judgement.

Erica Stanton, Interview.

See the orchestration, To

To look at the stage for the duration of a scene, maybe 10 minutes, and to hold in your eye the simultaneous shifting strands of activity to sense the rightness of the various 'voices', i.e. movement strands, or their imbalance.

Stuart Hopps, Interview.

Delicate balance

In dance/movement work in theatre, film or opera, the balance which has to be struck between movement material which is simple enough to be learned quickly and performed by non-dancers but is not banal but effective and 'fresh'.

Stuart Hopps, Interview.

Criteria

The qualities which a critic or a teacher might look for in a promising young choreographer's work.

"...a freshness in choice of material, an arresting vocabulary, a uniqueness in the shaping of the work as a whole, its structure, the treatment of their idea; the way they work with their dancers..."; "...something which triggers my attention to watch the work...."

Bonnie Bird, Interview.

Stereotyped work

In a workshop, the kind of response from dancers to an improvisation situation which the choreographer wants to avoid, against which he gives clues to the kind of work which he will not accept.

"No steps; not a naive image of fish."

Rui Horta, Workshop.

Dotting the i's and crossing the t's

To make a dance 'plain and obvious' for a first viewing, so that the audience appreciates the work's meaning at their first (and possibly only) view of it.

Norman Morrice in Clement Crisp and Mary Clarke, 1974.

Deadly middle

"...too much of the moderate pace, too much symmetry, too-even rhythm and accents, too much horizontal design and so forth...".
Doris Humphrey, 1959.

Neat dance

"Some people feel they have to fix a dance, they have to make it neat. No, it's better to have disordered life but to have life."
Anna Sokolow in Selma Jeanne Cohen, 1977.

Rebirth

A process in the making of a Butoh work using the changing dynamic state of the body as a floating foetus through the developmental stages of babyhood and childhood of lying, sitting, crawling, standing, walking, running, balancing, etc.
Ushio Amagatsu, Interview.

PART FIVE: THE DANCE SOUND AND THE DANCE SPACE

While compiling entries on the sound in dance, interviews were held with both musicians and dancers. The Chapter THE DANCE SOUND is primarily about generating a sound track, and what might be used to make one, together with elements that composers use in structuring scores. Some entries on how composers set about their work are given. The dates of the entries give insight into the shifts, over time, in the interaction between choreographer and composer from the latter's point of view, and in the relationship of their products.

The Chapter THE SOUND AND THE MOVEMENT looks at how these two parts of the choreographed work function together. A few entries point to the differences and the similarities of the two media, but the bulk of the chapter contains entries on how dance people use and respond to the aural element. Very different perspectives and needs emerge. Entries on the two extremes, music visualisation and co-existence of sound and movement, are both given sections. The co-operation of the two creative artists, and of the dancer with the music, complete the chapter, in diversity.

For THE DANCE SPACE, places that people use to dance in and on are named. The kind of work presented in them is intimated, too. The designer's point of view on how to transform a space into a place, and the lighting designer's language, have entries. Both artistic imagination and structural means were talked about in the interviews and collected on stage. Video is given a section here, where video time and space are introduced, as well as some techniques of camera and editing for dance, collected from experienced video experts as well as relative beginners, from the dancer and the video artist's point of view.

Chapter 14 THE DANCE SOUND

1. MUSIC

Music

"Music is an involvement with sound."
Alwin Nikolais, 1963.

Music and dance in the new ballet

"In contradistinction to the older ballet it does not demand "ballet music" of the composer as an accompanist to dancing; it accepts music of every kind; provided only that it is good and expressive."
Michel Fokine, 1914.

Absolute music

Contrasted with ballet music, to encompass musical works written with no intention of accompanying dance, autonomous works of music.
Dale Harris in Mary Clarke and David Vaughan, 1977.

Applied music

Music which serves a function, often to help the dancer in class, and is not designed for listening; also found in music for television and film which underscores the action content.
Robert Coleridge, Interview.

Ballet music

Music especially written to accompany the theatrical presentation of dancing, usually regarded with low esteem by musicians until Diaghilev's collaboration with Ravel, Prokofiev, etc., Balanchine's with Stravinsky, Graham's with Horst, and Cunningham's with Cage.
Dale Harris in Mary Clarke and David Vaughan, 1977.

Capoeira Sound, The

The berimbau rhythms, singing of traditional folkloric and improvised song, clapping, and the playing of percussive instruments which initiate and direct the movements of the two participants into the different styles of combat and harmony of the "jôgo".
"...transporting the capoeiristas to another level of consciousness."
Bira Almeida, 1986.

Club sound

"...acid, hard core, jungle, industrial, techno, trance, club, 'progressive', and... garage."; "...rap, swing and ragga..."; music which the DJ spins and mixes for the clubbers.

"Touch", 1993.

Dance music

Popular music, much of which is used for dancing as well as listening, divided into Rock, Folk, and Jazz.

"Time Out", 1993.

Developmental music

Music for a dance work in which the opening thematic material is developed through compositional devices, i.e. music which is not static or unchanging in mood/dynamics/texture, etc.

Robert Coleridge, Interview.

Disco

A style of popular music which must have a steady danceable beat, usually in $^4/_4$ time, mostly produced electronically with a synthesizer.

Lani van Ryzin, 1979.

Dramatic dance (music for)

"Dramatic music has to make its point 'now'. It is given no time for musical form to develop, so it becomes gestural."

Norman Lloyd, 1963.

Electro-acoustic music

Music composed by combining, or electrically manipulating, naturally created sound material with electrically generated sound.

Philip Chambon, Interview.

Evocative music

Music which assists the audience to read the work without being imitative or obvious; said with reference to a way of using a folk-derived sound source.

Chris Benstead, Interview.

Gebrauchsmusik (Ger.)

Literally translated as "utility music" (in 'Grove'), a term first introduced by Hindemith for a special kind of music written for amateurs; used also by Copland, Milhaud, Weill and Orff. "Workaday music" is an alternative term suggested by Eric Blom.

Eds. from 'Grove', 1980.

Gebrauchmusik (Ger.)

Music composed solely for performance with dance. Quoted as a tendency at Bennington Summer Schools ca. 1935–37.

"...music for an occasion, written to serve the dance and not intended for an independent life...."

Sali Ann Kriegsman, 1981.

Hip-hop (music)

One of the most popular styles of music in the (Portsmouth) club scene. "It has a $^4/_4$ metre and a very strong beat which is emphasised in dance with the focus on the footwork."

Donna Taylor, Interview and observation.

Hoedown

The traditional fiddle band music for square dancing.

Betty Casey, 1976.

Irregular patterns of melos

The overall sound of a work, which in Stravinsky's "Rite" and "Noces" is folk-like without actual folksong material being used, whose patterns are continually shifting, changing and being renewed.

Eric Walter White, 1979.

Jazz styles

"...cool jazz, be bop jazz, mainstream jazz, swing, popular 50's music, rap...."

Thea Barnes, Interview.

Musique concrete

"What was made by slowing, speeding, filtering, rearranging, overlaying, direct-ing, etc. I had the values of a whole instrument combine at my one-man-manipulatable disposal."

Alwin Nikolais, 1963.

Narrative piece

Music which supports the narrative of a dance work, using leitmotif methods to highlight characters and clear mood changes, possible allusions and images.

Chris Benstead, Interview.

Poppy and arty

Two contrasting qualities of music, the one related to popular music, 'the pop scene', the other art music; qualities which a composer may move between.

Philip Chambon, Interview.

Sampling

In the pop music scene, recording fragments of other people's tracks in order to manipulate them into sound for dancing; used in clubs.

Annabel Scott and *Tim Godwin*, Interview.

Soundscape

    Music which is densely textured, appealing to the ear, but which has rhythms that you would never dance to.

    Ashley Page, Interview.

Tape suite

    A collage of already recorded music which is assembled, for a given duration, to complement a dance work; said of Peter Gordon's compositions.

    Peter Gordon in Bill T. Jones and Arnie Zane, 1989.

Tunes

    What musicians in the Morris play, usually the traditional melodies collected by Cecil Sharp but, for revival Morris teams, it also may incude new tunes invented by the musician.

    Roy Judge, Interview.

2. SOUND

Sound source

    Anything which produces sound; a term used to refer, primarily, to unconventional sources of sound, not that of musical instruments.

    Robert Coleridge, Interview.

Amplified feet

    The noise made by dancers on the floor, especially in tap dancing or step dancing, which is electrically enlarged to form the sound score of (that part of) the work.

    Philip Chambon, Interview.

Becoming a sound track

    Performers using voice, body sounds, and object sounds to create a layer of sound for a work.

    Yolande Snaith, Interview.

Dance text

    Poetry, dialogue, monologue or any verbal text which is spoken during the performance; said of Jones's and Zane's "Blauvelt Mountain" (1980) when the text was spoken intermittently 'sotto voce'.

    Bill T. Jones and *Arnie Zane,* 1989.

Narration

    A possible sound track for a dance, spoken live or taped, with the narrator a visible or invisible part of the event.

    Dorothy Madden, Interview.

Prompt caller
>   Instructions given to the dancers in social dancing while it is going on, just in time to remind the dancers what the next figure is.
>   "Set to partners and circle left.", from 'The Quaker's Wife'.
>   *Jack Hamilton*, 1967.

Patter calling
>   Directions to the dancers given by 'the caller' in a rhyming language made up of instructions and comments; used in Western square dancing, and country dancing generally.
>   "Lady goes right and gent goes left,
>   And away you go around the town."
>   *Bob Cann*, 1989.

Word as sound score, The
>   The spoken word used as an extension of the musical score, as Graham did with Emily Dickinson's words in "Letter to the World", and Humphrey did with Federico Garcia Lorca's lines in "Lament for Ignacio Sanchez Mejias."
>   *Walter Sorell*, 1971.

Inventory of sounds
>   The culture-based inventory of sounds regarded as possible or likely by a composer, viz. a Western inventory, a South Asian inventory, which can be widened through cross-cultural collaborations: "listen to the city sounds of Birmingham with Indian ears."
>   *Shobana Jeyasingh*, Interview.

Tone
>   The part of a sound track of verbal and vocal materials which is not words, but the tone of voice with which it is produced; said of Meredith Monk's work.
>   "...listening to songs and speeches in non-sense language, we realize that verbal content is only part of meaning."
>   *Sally Banes*, 1980(a).

Verbal and kinetic script
>   Strategies for movement and sound for Post-Modern dance events which include "verbal arguments, laughter, and mistakes".
>   *Sally Banes*, 1980(a).

Distorted language
>   "The dancers scream, moan, groan, pant, giggle, laugh, screech, utter primal sounds (in Bausch's 'Bluebeard')."
>   *Norbert Servos* and *G. Weigelt*, 1984.

Found sounds

Raw aural material obtained from mundane objects.
Philip Chambon, Interview.

Sound set

A set which is constructed of materials that make the sound-track of the piece through their acoustic properties; said of Marian Bruce's set made of corrugated iron, wood, and a steel barrel, used by the dancers and a musician to create a sound score in Christopher Bruce's "Waiting" (1993).
Marian Bruce, Rehearsal.

Shoe music

The rhythmic sound patterns made in dances, such as Irish jigs, English clog dance, or by tap dancers.
James Siegelman in Mary Clarke and David Vaughan, 1977.

Tap mat

A piece of hardboard or blackboard or, preferably, linked strips of board which can be unrolled/rolled up after use, used for practice in order to maximise the sound of the taps.
Roy Castle, 1986.

3.   ELEMENTS AND STRUCTURE OF MUSIC AND SOUND

Language of the musician

The way the musicians in musical theatre or the composers of music for dance works talk about their music, the technical vocabulary of the score, the structure and dynamic, a language which choreographers need to know for collaborative work.
Stuart Hopps, Interview.

Studio

The workplace of the electro-acoustic composer.
"Three samplers, two synthesisers, an 'Apple' computer with a sequencer program, 16-track mixing desk, reverb. unit, digital delays, speakers, a classical guitar, electric guitars, percussion instruments, kitchen utensils, and singers."
Philip Chambon, Interview.

Basic elements of sound

The four basic elements of contemporary sound are time and pitch, timbre and amplitude.
John Cage, 1963.

Defined musical language

A musical composition in which the harmonic modes, rhythmic structures, instrumentation, associations are clearly defined; one in which consistence of vocabulary and style is heard.

Robert Coleridge, Interview.

Tonality

The sound quality of a work, of a section of a work.

"In $^1/_4$, a series of notes, played as chords all together, changing slowly, imperceptibly, with no harmonic modulation"; "Made from voice, chiming, orchestration".

Philip Chambon, Interview.

Rhythmical quality

The precise rhythmical content of the music brought out by the choice of instrumentation; said of Kurt Jooss's choice of two pianos to "reinforce" the rhythmical quality of the scores for his works.

Kurt Jooss in Ana R. Sanchez-Colberg, 1992.

Binary and ternary beats

A beat may be called binary if it is divisible into two equal parts, and ternary if it is divisible into three equal parts.

'Grove', 1980.

Rhythmic devices

The way time units are used in musical composition to create rhythms and to develop them through augmentation, retrograde, repetition with addition, deletion, and so on.

Robert Coleridge, Interview.

Rhythm as number

The attitude to rhythmic structures in Bharata Natyam music, which, having no harmonic content, develops complex number-based calculations and mathematical games of percussive and rhythmic patterns.

Shobana Jeyasingh, Interview.

Association of rhythms

The rhythmic patterns of music carry with them associations of time and place, such as ragtime, the waltz, the tango, a march, such that the audience of a dance work will locate the movement in a particular time and place.

Robert Coleridge, Interview.

Metronomic

Rhythm organised metrically in a regular pace; used particularly in some types of electro-acoustic music making.

Philip Chambon, Interview.

Counts and no counts

Rhythmic organisation according to metred counts provided by the choreographer or, according to the emotional base of both dance and sound, uncounted.
Philip Chambon, Interview.

Time structures

"What brought about the falling apart of time structures? The introduction, perhaps, of space into our concept of time."
John Cage, 1963.

Driving bass line

The part of a musical composition which has high energy momentum conveyed through the notes in the lower register, giving a sense of driving forwards, e.g. bass riffs in jazz and rock, boogie-woogie piano, etc.
Robert Coleridge, Interview.

Isolated chords

A musical gesture whose essence is a group of chords surrounded by silence; one example of what is meant by a musical gesture.
Robert Coleridge, Interview.

Harmonic tension

The quality of chord clusters in which the sound begs for a resolution of some sort from the polytonal dissonance.
Eric Walter White, 1979.

Harmonic fields

Fixed groups of notes/chords which are dwelt upon long enough to become perceptible as a unit — a feature of much contemporary music where chords are used as sonorities and not in relation to one another as in functional tonal harmony.
Robert Coleridge, Interview.

Modal

Working with one of the modes, that is with a selected series of intervals in an octave; not modulating from one diatonic key to another.
"It hovers around B minor."
Philip Chambon, Interview.

Wall of sound

One quality of sound which a composer can bring to a work; said of Benstead's composition for Robert North's/Bridget Riley's "Colour Moves".
"...colour, splashes of colour, sustained, modal..."; "...the vibraphone, piling up the notes, hovering, creating a suspension."
Chris Benstead, Interview.

Static

A quality referring to the harmonic structure of a musical work in which key change is not a feature; said in contrast to 'moving', in which key modulation is used for harmonic progression.

Philip Chambon, Interview.

Atonality

The absence of tonality; "...the relationship of one sound with another has been eradicated as an integral part of musical composition...", which deprives sound of the groundedness of tonal music, and creates an "...inconstant, unreal space...."

Hanns Hasting (1931) in Valerie Preston-Dunlop and Susanne Lahusen, 1990.

Timbre

Timbre is the bodily experienced part of music.

"When we listen we discover timbre. We discover that our ears are on either side of our head, that duration is not an image, that rhythm is not durational but kinaesthetic and gravitational."

Norman dello Joio, 1963.

Associations of instrumentation

The fact that instruments conjure up associations which most listeners will share, such as the romanticism of strings, the jazz association of the saxophone, harps and angelic music.

"Instruments contain their own history."

Robert Coleridge, Interview.

Hearing music

Listening to music not for its notes and counts but to perceive its interior qualities, possibly "attenuated", "delicate", "intense."

Jane Dudley, Interview.

Density

The vertical or horizontal thickness of the sound, through degree of contrapuntal detail, providing a dense or sparse score.

Robert Coleridge, Interview.

Musical space

The way in which spatial terms are used to describe music, chords as narrow and wide, pitch as high and low, quality as contained or spacious, the material as stretched or compact.

Robert Coleridge, Interview.

Musical contour

The overall magnitude and texture of a musical work which a choreographer will work with or "transmute into dancing".

"...lyricism, grandeur and bravura of Tchaikovsky's Second Piano Concerto."

Noël Goodwin, 1988.

Sound and time

"We thought that sounds took place in time. We see they're vibratory movements of particles in air. Each one, setting out from its point in space, gets to all its arrivals from a single departure. Thoughts about time simply drop off."

John Cage, 1963.

Silence

Absence of deliberately made sound; a part of a musical composition whose presence can be emotionally highly charged.

Robert Coleridge, Interview.

Musical structure

The ideas on which the melodic, rhythmic, and harmonic aspects of a musical composition are chosen and co-ordinated, one example being "singular elements expanding, increasing in number and interacting in more complex ways over time."

Bill T. Jones and *Arnie Zane,* 1989.

Themes or cells

Fragments of note clusters with rhythmic and harmonic form, usually only of four notes (in "Rite of Spring") or three (in "Les Noces") which form the basic material of the (Stravinsky) work.

Eric Walter White, 1979.

Development

Rearranging the time values and the notes of the cell minimally to avoid literal repetition.

Eric Walter White, 1979.

Foreground and background

Layers in a sound composition so that some features are clearly heard above others in the overall texture.

Robert Coleridge, Interview.

Collage

A musical score put together from a variety of sources from differing styles and periods, usually from pre-existing music and sound recordings; said of Bausch's "1980".

Raimund Hoghe, Interview.

Fragmentation

Playing a pre-existing score intermittently during a dance work; used by Bausch in "Café Müller", Rui Horta in "Mozart".

Eds.

Aural line
      The continuity of sound of the choreographic work, made up of whatever mix the collaborators have decided upon, of pre-recorded music, body sound, song, vocalisation, live instrumental music, traffic noise, et al.
      Ana R. Sanchez-Colberg, 1992.

Cinematic sound track
      The kind of aural composition/compilation, for a dance, which is constructed using the techniques of film sound score.
      Mark Murphy, Interview.

Sound, The
      The music, lyrics, dialogue et al which come first before the dance material is made for the movement scenes in plays and films; especially deciding where in the music the narrative will break up a formal dance.
      Geraldine Stephenson, Interview.

Soundscape
      Collected sounds, creating an environment.
      Fiona Burnside, 1990(a).

Spatial sound
      A held sound, such as a chord on a harmonium, which fills the entire surrounding space.
      Mary Wigman, 1966.

Music as decor
      The way the associations of the sound used in a dance can turn a space into a place, thus serving a similar function as decor.
      Robert Coleridge, Interview.

Surrounding
      How music can be played to enhance a dance work, literally coming from all directions.
      Lise Brunel, 1987.

Score
      Usually the manuscript of a musical composition, but in electro-acoustic music it is the work itself for which no written version is possible.
      Philip Chambon, Interview.

Manuscript notes
      Traditional musical notation used as an organising means to work out the aural material for a composition, which may end up as a multi-layered electro-acoustic work, for which no notation is adequate.
      Philip Chambon, Interview.

4. COMPOSING

Commissioned score
A piece of music or sound asked for and paid for to be part of a particular choreographic work.
David Buckland and *Siobhan Davies, 1991.*

Commissioned music
Music composed for a ballet or a dance; in electro-acoustic genre more quickly available for the choreograher than music written in note form, the latter being exceptionally difficult for the choreographer to work with collaboratively.
Christopher Bruce, Interview.

Scenario of a theatre work
The basic plan of a composition decided upon, usually in collaboration, in the form of titles and order of different episodes which encapsulate the action envisaged.
Eric Walter White, 1979.

Working titles
Names given to parts of a dance work which both the choreographer and the composer use.
"the eights", "cane dance", "slow interrogation", used in Christopher Bruce's "Swan Song."
Philip Chambon, Interview.

Preparation
The work undertaken before commencing a musical score for a dance work; may involve "watching and absorbing dance rehearsals; allowing that to pass into the brain, to get a shape of an aural palette."
Philip Chambon, Interview.

Aural palette
A self-imposed limitation from the multitude of possible sounds which a composer seeks to identify through his preparatory work, and which will guide the style of the composition.
"harsh metallic sounds, voice and flute-type sounds" for the opening of "Swan Song."
Philip Chambon, Interview.

Minutage
A prepared list given to a commissioned composer showing the exact length of time each number should last.
David Vaughan, 1977.

Composer's instructions

Preparatory notes given by the choreographer to the composer stipulating the quality of sound, the speed, the atmosphere, the instrumentation, and sometimes even the counts required.

Ashley Page, Interview.

Adding cues

Layering in additional occasional sounds, after the completion of a composition which is found to be difficult for the performers to work with.

Philip Chambon, Interview.

Additional music

Sound needed by a choreographer when his work cannot be completed with music as written.

"Give me another minute and a half", said by Christopher Bruce to Errollyn Wallen (composer) for "Waiting" (1993).

Christopher Bruce, Rehearsal.

Aural images

The expressive sound images which a composer may start with, and structure into a multi-layered complex sound image for the listener.

"Sea rolling, whales, pushing forward and back, underwater breathing and sucking."

Philip Chambon, Interview.

Collaborative languages

The choreographic, musical and verbal language used by the choreographer and the composer in the planning dialogues for a work, languages which each has to understand for smooth collaboration; said of Chris Benstead's and Janet Smith's work.

Chris Benstead, Interview.

Collaborating

A choreographer working with a composer, possibly from scratch, but also in order to add to or alter an already written composition; said of Ashley Page and Colin Matthews in "Pursuit."

Ashley Page, Interview.

Come off the page, To

To hear music for the first time, an especially tense moment for the composer of an orchestral work, where the orchestral call may be the first time he hears what he has created, having to decide there and then what, and if, anything needs reworking.

Chris Benstead, Interview.

Compose for the performer, To

To provide the level of musical obviousness or subtlety which is required by the expertise of the performers; said of the music for the scenes for children participating in Janet Smith' s "Trio for Dance Construction" and the professional dancers' scenes.
Chris Benstead, Interview.

Composing chronologically

Writing the music for a dance work by starting at the beginning of it and continuing through the dance until the end, a process not necessarily, even not often, followed.
Philip Chambon, Interview.

Composing for dance

"The music was written after the dance was composed, writing a section as each new part of the dance was complete."
Vivian Fine, 1963.

Composing intuitively

Allowing sounds to arise from an emotional response to the dance for which it is made; said in contrast to working mathematically, which some serial and minimalist composers do.
"...yearning, strong and defiant...."
Philip Chambon, Interview.

Compositional solution

A decision on what devices and sound qualities to use for a section of a work after a period in which the tonality of the music for the dance could not be imagined.
Philip Chambon, Interview.

Conjured up

Said of sounds which are allowed to emerge in response to the images of a dance work.
"a sparkling, shimmering sound in response to the beam of light in a dark cell", "the physical properties of light", "a ray of hope."
Philip Chambon, Interview.

Cut the music, To

Shortening a musical composition to accommodate the needs of the movement in a choreography.
Robert Coleridge, Interview.

Doodles

What a composer might start with in a collaborative work, share them with the choreographer, and out of that discussion discover the composition's direction, jettisoning the doodles en route; said of Orlando Goff's collaboration with Ashley Page.
Ashley Page, Interview.

Dressed in orchestral colours
The change of sound quality which a composer hears when his work is transferred to orchestral scoring, having started life on the limited canvas of a piano.
Robert Coleridge, Interview.

Drone
A sound used as a continuous bass around which other sonorities will be composed.
Philip Chambon, Interview.

Hi-tech means
The electro-acoustic, computer-aided studio equipment which enables intuitive and felt aural inspiration to be manipulated into a composition.
Philip Chambon, Interview.

Homework
Working in the electro-acoustic studio to find rough ideas which might not be used in the final work but which serve to tune the ear to the emergent aural style.
Philip Chambon, Interview.

Information
A term in electro-acoustic music for the computer-recorded notes generated by playing the keyboard, of which length, dynamic and 'where in the bar' can be changed individually.
Philip Chambon, Interview.

Look at movement, To
What a composer for dance has to learn to do, for which playing for class is one way.
Chris Benstead, Interview.

Manipulate sounds, To
To make "real sound and human sounds" into "surreal sounds" through the use of electro-acoustic means.
Philip Chambon, Interview.

Mixing
A computer-aided compositional device in electro-acoustic music in which individual tracks of sound are superimposed on one another, in a multitude of possible ways.
Philip Chambon, Interview.

Mock up on a piano, To
The first provisional compositional stage of a musical work which will eventually be orchestrated.
Robert Coleridge, Interview.

Music as a mirror of dance

"The music of a ballet should be its most faithful mirror, a spontaneous creation of the deeper subconscious powers of the choreographer, read intuitively by the composer."

Norman dello Joio, 1963.

Musical characters

What a composer for a narrative ballet has to create aurally for the principal characters in the work.

Peggy van Praagh and *Peter Brinson*, 1963.

New ballet

"...I emphasised the total freedom of the composer of the music to express whatever he feels and however he feels about it.... I never specified nor ever wished to consider the number and kind of measures he needed to accomplish this end. It was on the basis of such principles that the new ballet and the music for it was created. Becoming free, the music grew richer and enriched the dance itself."

Michel Fokine, 1961.

Parameters of sound

The possible limitations and freedoms set by collaborating artists or by the composer alone before the creation of a sound score or the live improvisation of a sound accompaniment.

"...for example: mundane sound, stretched technologically.'

Laurie Booth, Interview.

Put down a track, To

Composing in a recording studio; especially needed for works on small budgets where the composer may have to lay down each track himself, playing different instruments, finding sound sources, vocalising etc. himself, and mix one on top of another.

Chris Benstead, Interview.

Quantizing

A device in electro-acoustic music making in which the duration and regularity of the notes recorded in their raw state are partially or completely regularised, eliminating the natural irregularities of playing.

Philip Chambon, Interview.

Released sound

"Sounds freed of their actual physical derivation by speeding, filtering, etc."

Alwin Nikolais, 1963.

Rewriting music

Composing a score based on music which a choreographer likes and has partially choreographed with, but which is unsuitable for completion of the work.

"Working from rough recording of the rehearsal pianist so far, analysing the speed changes and structure, respecting the requirements of the choreography, finding a satisfactory tonality."

Philip Chambon, Interview.

Sampling

Digital recording of the raw state sounds for later manipulation into a musical work.

Philip Chambon, Interview.

Sampling

A way of composing music more like a film score, where themes come and go rather than develop.

Rosemary Butcher, Interview.

Sensation

A feeling, a mood, which the composer with the choreographer seek to find for a collaborative choreographic work; (giving the example of one which commenced with the designs).

"Bridget Riley's designs for five backdrops pinned up and spread around."; "...looked at and looked at..."; "first, an order, a series of moods, a sense of stillness."

Chris Benstead, Interview.

Sense of spaciousness

An ambience which is helpful to a composer, leading to a frame of mind in which musical ideas might be generated; a feel for the rate at which ideas/material will unfold in time; an awareness of the physical space in which a piece of music will be performed and how its architecture and acoustics will influence it.

Robert Coleridge, Interview.

Sound luminosity and transparency

"We're no longer satisfied with flooding the air with sound from a public address system. We insist...that sounds will arise at any point in space bringing about the surprises we encounter when we walk in the woods or down the city streets."

John Cage, 1963.

Subliminal manipulation

Layering, changing, speeding up, slowing down, distorting in such a way that the listener is not aware of the crafting process.

Philip Chambon, Interview.

Tandem, In
Working closely with a composer where the music and dance need to coincide; said by Shobana Jeyasingh of her work with Kevin Volans on "Correspondences".
Shobana Jeyasingh, 1993.

Try out musical gestures, To
To try fragments of sound which have some similarity of essence to see how they will function in an emerging dance work, prior to writing the composition as a whole.
Robert Coleridge, Interview.

Vertical and horizontal dimension of music
An allusion to the way music is written, in that all sounds which occur at the same time are written one above the other, and those that occur one after the other appear in succession from left to right on the stave.
Robert Coleridge, Interview.

Write for a space, To
To have in mind a particular dance space/theatre/studio/venue in which the choreographic performance will be premiered, and for which the musical score will be written.
Robert Coleridge, Interview.

Chapter 15   THE SOUND AND THE MOVEMENT

1.   THE FUNCTION OF SOUND IN DANCE

Generate energy, To
>The overall function of music in some dances.
>*Robert Coleridge,* Interview.

Limited audience perception
>"If one really looks can one listen and if one really listens can one look?"
>*Gertrude Stein* in Louis Horst, 1963.

Three way focus
>A dance and a concerto, such as Ashton/César Franck "Symphonic Variations", or MacMillan/Prokofiev "Triad", which give the audience not only the two (ear and eye) attention modes but a third, the solo instrument, which the choreographer has to take into account.
>*Noël Goodwin,* 1988.

Opaque music
>Sound which is so dense with notes that there is no room for the dance to find a place in it, or for the listener to pick out many individual details.
>*Robert Coleridge,* Interview.

Transparent music
>"Music should be transparent, open and spacious so that the audience can see the dance through it."
>*Louis Horst,* 1963.

Aural wallpaper
>What much music is to dance, simply something repetitive which fills the sound space or may "provide a means of propulsion".
>*Noël Goodwin,* 1989.

Parallel the movement, To
>The way a sound score works with the movement of a dance by the composer and choreographer sharing an attitude to their materials, or a structural plan of the piece, but not aiming for a note-to-note correlation.
>*Robert Coleridge,* Interview.

Weight of the music

A crucial ingredient to a satisfactory music/movement correlation in a dance where special attention to the type of density of chords and loudness of dynamics is concerned.

Robert Coleridge, Interview.

Structural relationship

A variety of ways in which music and dance function together in a choreographic work, such as reflect, reinforce, or coexist, but also relationships of phrase lengths, macro- and micro-structural features, etc.

Robert Coleridge, Interview.

Physio-psychological entrée

"[Dance and music both have their] own physio-psychological entrée into the mind of the receiver."

Alwin Nikolais, 1963.

Tonal embellishment/independent element of content

In contrast to the frequently supplementary function as a tonal embellishment in classical ballet, in "Bluebeard" the music has the status of an independent, indispensible element of content of equal rank with the other scenic elements.

Norbert Servos and *G. Weigelt,* 1984.

General/specific continuum, The

A continuum of the way the sound might complement the movement in dance, from broad similarities to details of reinforcement.

Robert Coleridge, Interview.

Accompaniment

Music which is closely associated with a dance, which is always, or nearly always, played when that dance is danced; can be applied to most genres of dance.

Michael Heaney and *John Forrest,* 1991.

Frame for dance, A

"Music is a frame for dance to set off a dance already created."

Louis Horst, 1958.

Music as source

Creating a ballet to existing music, and so limiting the free development of the movement and the imagination of the collaborating creators, including the designer, especially by having a time structure which cannot be changed.

Nicholas Georgiardis, Interview.

Arbitrary combinations

Clusters of movements and movements with sounds, arrived at through chance methods which linked material of different ilks, quirky moves with dance-technical steps, screams with mumbles; said of Yvonne Rainers's 1961 work.

Sally Banes, 1980(a).

Experiments in accompaniment

Sound accompaniment to a dance work; in Simone Forti's "Bottom" (1967) this consisted in frenetic drumming, then a single sung and constant chord, then a vacuum cleaner, a simple repeated whistled melody, all accompanying 4 slides projected for 5 minutes each.

Jonas Mekas, 1967.

Movement accompaniment

Instead of a musical accompaniment for dance, the process is reversed; music is played and a simple movement activity (sitting on and winding and unwinding a rope loop) accompanies it; said of Simone Forti's work of 1961.

Eds. from Simone Forti, 1974.

Leitmotif

A musical phrase which is a signature tune for an individual character in a ballet. Found in Ashton's "La Fille Mal Gardée" where Lise, Colas, and the Widow all have musical and set/props signatures.

Eds.

Musical pulse

The regularity of a pulsed sound, which is there for both the choreographer and the audience, there for the movement to "duck in and out of."

Ashley Page, Interview.

Musical structure

The ideas on which the melodic, rhythmic, and harmonic aspects of a musical composition are created, are selected and co-ordinated as a choreographic device, one example being "singular elements expanding, increasing in number and interacting in more complex ways".

Peter Gordon in Bill T. Jones and Arnie Zane, 1989.

Rhythmic connection

The rhythm of the music and the rhythm of the dance synthesized, not by reiterating each other but by reinforcing the essentials of each, by mood, by structure, by leitmotif; said of Kurt Jooss's and F. A. Cohen's work.

Anna Markard in Ana R. Sanchez-Colberg, 1992.

Dance to music

The engagement of the dancer with the musical score, not Mickey Mousing but expressing the feeling of the rhythm in the body.

Judith Mackrell, Interview.

Go against, To

    A way of contrasting dance and music, as opposed to balancing working 'sympathetically' .

    Lea Anderson, Interview.

Layers

    Combination of music and dance, each with its own contribution to evoking the period and attitude of a work; further layers (in the Jagger/Bruce "Rooster") are added by the dance "enlarging and extending the references in the lyrics".

    John Percival, 1993.

Utilitarian material

    "Tapes of rushing water, an orchestra warming up, the tick of a metronome, the whining of a movie projector", accompanied by movements of a similar source, "handling a prop, lying down, abstract jumps".

    Douglas Dunn in Sally Banes, 1980(a).

Dialogue

    The speech during dances which occur in film and television and dances in plays, in which dancers and actors have to cope with the rhythm of the movement, which is very different from the rhythms of speech.

    Geraldine Stephenson, Interview.

Drama inherent in music

    "It is part of Ashton's strength that he does not overload drama onto the music's structure, but rather reflects the actual drama inherent in the music, giving it physical form and shape."

    Clive Barnes, 1961.

Music illumination

    Choreography which aims to clarify the music, using its structure and content as its base (as in Balanchine's use of Stravinsky).

    "I had to try to paint or design time with bodies in order to create a resemblance between the dance and what was going on in sound."

    George Balanchine in Edwin Denby, 1968.

Silences

    Moments, in a dance work, without aural accompaniment, which serve a distinct purpose in the overall performance; possibly a respite, a transition, a heightened climax.

    Eds.

Duet of music and dance

    "When a choreography stems from the music — but then goes off into areas of the choreographer's alone."

    Norman dello Joio, 1963.

Interrelatedness of dance and music

"In the free interweaving of movement and sound there lies a deeper rhythm. Free of superficial points of rhythmic contact, music and dance create patterns of interrelatedness that enhance the total work."
Vivian Fine, 1963.

Make events collide

To make a series of small events, small structural units, and to put them together with the music so that they seem to pursue it and collide with it.
Ashley Page, Interview.

Contrapuntal

"The dance moves in counterpoint to the music rather than following it literally."
Robert Starer, 1963.

Cross rhythm/counter-rhythm

An intentional choreographic device in baroque dance, placing the accents of the steps against those in a measure of music.
Wendy Hilton, 1981.

Crossing the music

A term in Rock 'n' Roll for allowing yourself extra time in lifts and drops instead of sticking with the basic rule of dancing in time; that is beginning your steps on the final beat of the bar.
Derek Young, 1991.

Structural tension between music and dance

"By alternating contradiction with agreement, I hope to establish structural tensions and unexpected contrasts."
Paul Taylor, "Private Domain", 1987.

Music as point of departure and point of return

"Ashton himself does not tie himself to the quivering quaver...he uses the music's rhythm as a sheet anchor for his choreographic variations, a point of departure and a point of return. He has a very sensitive feel for the shape of music."
Clive Barnes, 1961.

Synthesis of dance and music

"...the dancer not following the music slavishly but providing a synthesis between dance and accompaniment, through opposition and counterpoint."
Louis Horst, 1963.

Point of tension in music/dance relationship

"The dance should be the centre of interest, the point of tension."
Louis Horst, 1963.

Music and dance fit

"It is not necessary for the music to fit the dance like a glove; in fact it should not fit too tightly."
Louis Horst, 1963.

Emotional essence of music

That which the choreographer should try to capture rather than confining his attention to its technical structure.
Norman dello Joio, 1963.

Literal device

Means by which a choreographer and composer mix the abstract with the denotive.
Alwin Nikolais, 1963.

Musical choreographer

One who brings out the emotional content of the music, not the counts.
Norman dello Joio, 1963.

Paraphrasing of the music

"The way a choreographer can expand or concentrate the meaning of the music, reinterpret it in a different perspective, add an extra dimension that the music cannot have."
Gunther Schuller, 1963.

Dance rhythm

A recognisable musical and dance structure, which gives a name to a dance with a specific character, said of Baroque and contemporary ballroom dances.
"Students tend to think there's a dance called the bourrée, sarabande, etc. What I have to get over is that it's the rhythm that makes it a bourrée or sarabande, not the steps."
Madeleine Inglehearn, Interview.

Calling

The special terminology of square dancing, called out as the dancing is taking place, each call taking the dancers away from and back to their home base on the square.
Betty Casey, 1976.

Call, A

Rhythmicised instructions on the figures and steps of a square dance so the gent and lady of each pair know what to do.
"Each Gent bow and swing your maid,
Put her on your right and promenade."
Betty Casey, 1976.

Boogie woogie
>   The music for the jitterbug which has a particular tempo with the typical rhythm and accents and continuity in the pianist's left hand.
>   *Derek Young*, 1991.

Swing beat
>   A favoured music style to dance to. It is a mellow form of Hip-hop, with a $^4/_4$ metre but with a steadier tempo. Focus of the dance to Swing beat is in the movement of the arms and hands, with the torso reflecting that movement.
>   *Donna Taylor,* Observation.

Hip-hop (dance)
>   The style of dance performed to Hip-hop music. The focus of attention is on the footwork, the feet moving with the beat of the music.
>   *Donna Taylor,* Observation and interview.

Tempo
>   The speed at which the music is played; the best speeds for dancing are slow rock at 36–40 bars per minute, and fast rock at 48 bars per minute.
>   *Derek Young,* 1991.

B.P.M.
>   Bars per minute, the pace of the dance music which is gradually raised by a skilful disc jockey during the evening as the adrenalin begins to run in the dancers.
>   *Annabel Scott* and *Tim Godwin,* Interview.

Slows and Quicks
>   A step taking two beats of music or a step taking one beat; the terms have no reference to the speed of the music but only to the number of beats of the music used.
>   *Derek Young,* 1991.

4.   MUSIC VISUALISATION

Music visualisation (in 1915)
>   "The dancer heard some music that made him feel like moving and he interpreted what he heard."
>   *Louis Horst,* 1963.

Music visualisation
>   "Music visualisation in its purest form is the scientific translation into bodily action of the rhythmic, melodic, and harmonic structure of a musical composition, without intention to 'interpret' or reveal any hidden meaning apprehended by the dancer."
>   *Ruth St. Denis* (ca 1915) in Suzanne Shelton, 1981.

Parallel of the music

"Dance which translates the music into physical movement."
Gunther Schuller, 1963.

Dance score

The annotated movements of head, arms, feet, and whole body which connect with each musical layer, instrumental and rhythmic.
"The movements connect directly with the musical adventure."
Karlheinz Stockhausen (ca 1980) in Mya Tannenbaum, 1987.

Interpretive dancing

"Interpretive dancing is just interpreting the music."
Louis Horst, 1958.

Redundancy of mood

"When both the music and the dance are simultaneously full of emotional connotation."
Louis Horst, 1963.

Unison of dance and music

"There are times when dance and music unison is desirable for strength and dramatic effect."
Louis Horst, 1963.

Synchoric orchestra

A Ruth St. Denis term for a dance work in which each individual dancer represents one instrumental line of an orchestral music work, the resulting movements being fused together into a choreographic entity.
Walter Sorell, 1981.

Take one's lead from the music, To

"...taking one's lead directly from the music...this is the method which I now prefer. Through it one gets the purity of the dance expressing nothing but itself, and thereby expressing a thousand degrees and facets of emotion and the mystery of poetry of movement; leaving the audience to respond at will and to bring their own poetic reactions to the work before them."
Frederick Ashton in Walter Sorell, 1951.

Music and movement

"Music is to dancing what words are to music; this parallel simply means that dance music corresponds, or should do, to the written poem and thus fixes and determines the dance's movements and actions."
Jean Georges Noverre, 1966 (1803).

Musicality

The phrasing, rhythm, and dynamics of ballet movement which is both derived from and integrated with the musical accomaniment; hence, accompaniment for class is set in style and rhythm.

Mirella Bartrip and *Teresa Kelsey,* Interview.

Movement which is right for the music

"...movement which is uncannily right for the music. I mean by this not merely phrasing but the right weight and emphasis of steps within the phrase...the lightweight and feathery texture of the batterie and intricate footwork at which he excels emphasised by the light and crisp rhythms of Hérold or Auber...".

Richard Alston, 1984.

Rendering the music

"...dancing with action is the instrument, or organ, by which the thoughts expressed in the music are rendered appropriately and intelligibly."

Jean Georges Noverre, 1966 (1803).

Mickey Mousing

The movement following the music note for note, phrase for phrase, dynamic for dynamic.

David Bintley, Interview.

Mickey Mousing

A Nikolais term for slavishly following the music in the dance.

Alwin Nikolais, 1963.

"Boom-with-boom"

What concentrating on the minutiae of the music-dance relationship can lead to, beat for beat.

Merce Cunningham in Walter Sorell, 1951.

Articulation

Marking the upbeats and downbeats of a measure of music with the 'movements' (sinking and rising) of baroque step-units.

Meredith Little, 1991.

Abstract ballet

"Dancing becomes a thing in itself; its movements stem only from the music as if all the symbols on the musical stave had come to life on stage. Instead of becoming a means of portraying characters or evoking a mood, it becomes the end product."

Peggy van Praagh and *Peter Brinson,* 1963.

Berimbau rhythms
   The named rhythms played on the Berimbau which direct the Capoeira participants to "work co-operatively to compose harmonious form" or to confront each other in "strategies, physical skills and intuitions in the spirit of the fight", in "slow motion counterattacks of cunning and knowledge".
   "The one-string bow-shaped instrument that establishes the speed and style of the 'jôgo de capoeira' encounter."
   Bira Almeida, 1986.

5. COEXISTENCE

Coexistence of music and dance
   "The common denominator between music and dance is time...the two arts could exist together using the same amount of time, each in its own way, one for the eye and the kinesthetic sense, the other for the ear."
   Merce Cunningham in Merce Cunningham and Jacqueline Lesschaeve, 1985.

Coexistence of sound and movement
   "They exist together as they move forward in time."
   Louis Horst, 1963.

Sever the connection, To
   Liberating the choreographer from the constraints of working with a set musical score while simultaneously denying the dancer the opportunity to show the feeling of the musical rhythm in the body.
   Judith Mackrell, Interview.

Autonomous (dance, of music)
   "Ideally, dance uses no music at all but the sound of the feet and breathing is heard by the audience."
   Louis Horst, 1963.

Coexistence
   "The relationship between the dance and music is one of co-existence, that is being related simply because they exist at the same time."
   Merce Cunningham in Francis Starr, 1968.

Independence of movement
   "Dancing has a continuity of its own that need not be dependent upon either the rise and fall of sound or the pitch and cry of words."
   Merce Cunningham in Francis Starr, 1968.

Dance as an autonomous art

"Dance is an art independent of music."
Mary Wigman in Louis Horst, 1963.

Autonomous dance

"The only true autonomous dance is one which is unaccompanied."
Gunther Schuller, 1963.

Dance without music

"Dance without music is an ideal, a tough ideal."
Louis Horst, 1958.

Aural decor

Music as a coexistent element, a frame.
"[Music for Merce Cunningham is] aural decor."
Noël Goodwin in Clive Barnes, Noël Goodwin and Peter Williams, 1965.

Phrasing

"...the rhythms and phrasing come from the movement, not from musical accompaniment...."
James Klosty, 1975.

Dance as a lesser art

"Dance has no life of its own disassociated from music; it derives its stimulus from music."
Norman dello Joio, 1963.

Independent art form of dance

"Dance is an independent art form and its motivation should be the feeling of the choreographer, not of the music."
Louis Horst, 1963.

Adding a layer of dance

A choreographic process in which the movement is made after the music, to become one layer of the aural/visual/kinetic whole which will be the finished work.
Robert Coleridge, 1992.

6.   DANCER/MUSIC AND CHOREOGRAPHER/COMPOSER RELATIONSHIP

Musicality

A problematic word, used in highly contradictory ways by the dance community, used with reference to dance dynamics and phrasing as well as to their co-ordination with the interpretation of music.
Stephanie Jordan, Interview.

Bol
      Communication in percussion and speech, in which dancer and musician convey to each other the rhythms they intend to use.
      Alpana Sengupta, Interview.

Challenging music
      The dancers have first to learn to listen to the musical counts, then ally that with the movement; said of "Agon" and "Les Noces" (Stravinsky).
      "...repeat the 7,7,6...."
      Monica Mason, Interview.

Counts, The
      The means used to get the steps in the right rhythm, with the music; what the dancer has to work with and through until counting disappears and musicality takes over.
      Marion Tait, Interview.

Dance with the music, To
      Said in contrast to dancing on the music, which is synchronising counts of movement with beats of music, but rather giving a sense of movement phrasing and musical phrasing and feeling how they interweave.
      Thomas Paton, Interview.

On the melody
      Dancing with the melodic line as the musical feature that the dancer follows; used in folk dance.
      Robert Harrold, Interview.

Dancing behind the music
      The way dancers take the cues from the music, instead of anticipating the tune, the tempo, the rhythm, waiting until they hear it before getting going.
      Jonathan Higgins, Interview.

Dancing over the music
      The skill of the dancer in coping with choreographic material where the time values of the dancing and the time values of the music bear no relationship, and yet arriving at a point in the score where accurate correlation is demanded.
      Bonnie Bird, Interview.

Engage with music, To
      The way an Indian dancer establishes a fundamental and essential relation with the musician with whom s/he shares rhythmic patterns and tempo.
      Shobana Jeyasingh, 1993.

Following

Response to the rhythm and phrasing of the dancer by the musician, especially in folk dance styles with an element of improvisation and temperament, such as flamenco.
Robert Harrold, Interview.

Break, A

A sequence of movements which signals to the musician that a change of rhythm is about to begin; used in Spanish dancing with communication between the dancer, who may be clapping, and the guitarist.
Robert Harrold, Interview.

Folk dance dynamics

The quality that the music provides and the movement follows.
"With a vibrating jig, with shaking shoulders, with heavy stamps, smooth stepping, vivacious leaps."
Robert Harrold, Interview.

Iron out, To

To lose, through the course of time, the subtlety of the relation of music and dance, with the dancer reverting to a more conventional way of doing the step.
Michael Somes in David Vaughan, 1977.

Keep the rhythm, To

The capacity of the Graham dancer to hold the rhythm of the movement within herself, independently of the musical accompaniment, through familiarity with the exercises and their traditional tempo and beat.
Thea Barnes, Susan Sentler, and *Brenda Baden-Semper,* Interview.

Laya and Layakari

Tempo of the rhythmic cycle (tal): basic ones being vilambit (slow), madhya (moderate), and drut (fast); improvisation when the performer is able to show a range of different tempi (laya).
Alpana Sengupta, Interview.

'Lift'

The musicians' responsibility, not only to play the tunes at a tempo right for country dancing, but with the lift which carries the dancers along above the metrical beat.
Douglas Kennedy, 1949.

Listening

Hearing music rather than counting beats, an essential process for the dancer and especially so with modern music where beats vary, are uneven in pace and metre and counting is counter-productive.
Jonathan Higgins, Interview.

Live interaction

Interaction between music and dance through musicians and dancers both present on stage; said of Jonathan Lunn's "Modern Living" (1992).

Nadine Meisner, Contributed.

Musicality

An intuitive and physical response to music, a physical and spiritual awareness of it; "not with the ear and the foot, but with the whole being."

Laverne Meyer, Interview.

Performance tempo

Not the slower tempo at which dance material may be learnt but the speed at which the performance of dancer and musician will be given.

Anna Markard, Rehearsal.

Playing for rehearsal

Working with a piano reduction from the orchestral score of the work, picking out the threads of the music which the dancers will hear in the full orchestral version, paying especial attention to tempo.

Jonathan Higgins, Interview.

Props music

A sound score made by dancers using props; said of Bruce's "Waiting" (1993) with London Contemporary Dance Theatre, where sticks are used to beat the corrugated iron set and the floor, in rhythmic layers.

Christopher Bruce, Rehearsal.

Pulse

"Pulse to a dancer is not only being in time with the music, nor only syncopated beat. It is the source of energy and character because it represents the natural human reaction to the rhythmic qualities in music. Audiences react to it as strongly as dancers. Hence pulse is an expression of the primitive link between the community, music and dance."

Peggy van Praagh and *Peter Brinson,* 1963.

On the pulse

Dancing with the beat of the music, its pace and weight reflected in the dance steps; used in social and folk dance.

Robert Harrold, Interview.

Reworking

What both the choreographer and the composer need to be prepared to do when both are creating the work, allowing for flexibility in the relationship, and mutual influence in what is and is not right.

Chris Benstead, Interview.

Rhythm

"As important as good technique, the rhythm of the music must flow from the dancer so that he/she does not move on the beat but in it."
Walter Sorell, 1976.

Rhythmic slave

A dancer who allows himself to be totally dependent on the music's rhythms.
Louis Horst, 1963.

Tal

The rhythmic cycle of a specific number of beats (16, 12, etc.) within which the dancer and musician improvise rhythmically, observing strict rules.
Alpana Sengupta, Interview.

Visible player

A musician who is on stage and part of the action of a dance work; said of percussionist Simon Limberick in Bruce's "Waiting" (1993).
Christopher Bruce, Rehearsal.

Working with music

The range of possible ways of relating sound and movement, basically: an intimate relationship, and in-and-out relationship, an "I do my thing, you do yours" relationship, all of which a dancer has to learn to cope with.
Bonnie Bird, Interview.

Chapter 16   THE DANCE SPACE

1. SPACE FOR DANCE

Space
>   The place of performance, its elements of light, decoration, ground, and air.
>   *Fernando Crespo*, 1988.

Performance space
>   The place in which a dance work is presented; for Nicky Smedley's "Rock" (1993) it was a curtained-off section of the leisure centre's sports hall, the back of which was a climbing wall, used as the main prop of the piece.
>   *Ian Bramley,* 1993.

Accidental space
>   Contrasted to a ritual space; "one which you make, you change it and you alter it by the dance".
>   *Shobana Jeyasingh*, Interview.

Interactional space
>   The space in which and with which people interact in the mundane situation of everyday; that same space seen in dance interactions, between dancers and between dancer and audience.
>   *Paul Filmer* and *Valerie Preston-Dunlop*, Discussion.

Studio, The
>   The place where class and rehearsal happen, which should be regarded as a theatre, so that every move is an act of performance.
>   *Bonnie Bird,* Interview.

Ballet studio
>   The space for class and for rehearsals in which a sprung floor, mirrors, barres, and a piano are the essential features, with sufficient height for lifts and sufficient size for company calls.
>   *Eds.*

Orchestra
>   From the Greek, meaning a dancing-place.
>   *Jane Harrison,* 1918.

Prompt side and O.P. side

The sides of the stage, that is the left side from the dancer's point of view is the prompt side, the side where the stage manager has the control desk; a term used in opera and theatre, and so in large ballet companies.

John Hart, Interview.

Stage left and stage right

Stage directions taken from the performer's point of view, used by most dance companies.

Anthony Bowne, Interview.

Down stage and up stage

The area towards the audience is 'down' and the area towards the back of the stage is 'up'; taken from when stages were always raked, that is sloping, down towards the audience.

Eds.

Getting in and getting out

Putting the scenery on stage and removing it after the show; the shifts from store to stage and store again.

Brian Baxter, Interview.

Set and strike, To

To put the scenery in place for the show and to get it off the working area; processes which the crew undertake, usually masked by the tabs, or when the house is closed, but may also happen as a scene change in full view.

John Hart, Interview.

Pit

The space for the orchestra in the major theatres and opera houses, designed for the conductor and orchestral players, arranged so that the conductor can see both the players and the dancers on stage.

Eds.

Fly floor

A gallery roughly level with the borders, used by the crew members when controlling the counterweight system for the flown scenery.

The Birmingham Royal Ballet crew, Rehearsal.

Hang, To

To attach on to the cross bars in the flies, that is in the large space above the stage, scenery which is to be lowered into place and raised out, known as flying scenery.

John Hart, Interview.

Bars

Cross-stage bars onto which the flying scenery — cloths and borders — and lights are attached, numbered from downstage to upstage; bars which are raised and lowered by the crew on the fly floor.

"Have Act II No. 4 Border on 31.", "Put the gauze on No. 2.", "Give me 37 for Act III."; "...the 'special' on No. 1 bar.".

John Hart, Rehearsal.

Drop in, To

To lower any piece of flown scenery or equipment to near ground level in order to adjust or change the set or the rig.

John Hall, Rehearsal.

Cloths

Large painted canvases extending to the full visible height and width of the stage; hence usually "a sky cloth", "a back cloth", "a front cloth."

John Hart, Interview.

Borders and banners

Decorated and functional flown scenery; borders extend across the whole width of the stage, while banners do not.

John Hart, Rehearsal.

Tormentors

The extreme downstage wing, semi-permanent, at each side, usually plain in colour, which serves to mask lighting equipment, especially needed in a theatre where the front rows of the audience and boxes would otherwise see into the wings.

John Hart, Interview.

Teaser

A horizontal border immediately behind the front tabs, intended to mask the overhead lamps of the stage.

John Hart, Interview.

French flats

Solid pieces of scenery which fly, while most flying scenery is (soft) canvas.

John Hart, Interview.

Legs

Curtains hung at the side of the stage to mask exits and entrances; may be decorated or plain.

John Hart, Interview.

Blacks

Surrounding black curtains.

John Ashford, Interview.

Built set
>   A set which is constructed and not a series of painted flats, borders, and banners.
>   *Barry Kay*, 1981.

Materials
>   What sets are made of: painted canvas, iron, wood, plastic, net.
>   *Eds.*

Mechanical devices
>   Possible inclusions in a set design, such as lifts, rotating floors, moving plat-
forms, flying objects.
>   *Eds*.

Cyclorama
>   A featureless, usually white, floodlit curved or flat vertical rear surface to the
set, primarily intended to give the illusion of great distance.
>   *John Hart,* Interview.

Floor
>   A vinyl mat which covers the stage for dance performances, made in several
colours, which is put down before the stage is set, and struck afterwards, and may be
changed during the evening.
>   *John Hart,* Interview.

Sprung floor
>   Structural floor specially prepared for dance.
>   *Eds.*

Sight lines
>   The lines of vision of the audience, taken from the outermost seats, usually of
the front stalls, lines which determine the area of the stage which is a) visible to the entire
audience, b) invisible to the entire audience.
>   *John Hall*, Interview.

Spiking
>   Putting tape on the floor of the stage to mark exactly where the set, the legs, the
dancers, or anything on stage must be located, especially so that the lighting will function
as planned, to the quarter inch.
>   *Dorothy Madden,* Interview.

Hold it on wheels, To
>   To keep the set of a ballet in the truck until it is needed again; a term used in a
company with repertory and who tour.
>   *Brian Baxter,* Interview.

Technical rehearsal

Practice for the setting and striking of sets, synchronising with lighting changes; especially needed when scene changes are in full view.

John Hart, Interview.

4. TRANSFORMING THE SPACE

Transform a space

To use lighting, curtains, theatrical devices to turn the available space into the desired illusory place.

Dorothy Madden, Interview.

Fictionalise the space, To

To transform it from its actual self to an imagined domain.

John Ashford, Interview.

Place, A

Floor cloths and front cloths, the design of the dancers' floor and of the front of stage curtain which turns the space into a place.

David Buckland and *Siobhan Davies,* Seminar.

World, A

What the designer needs to create for a dance, a context for it to take place in.

Ashley Page, Interview.

Special place, A

What the lighting designer and the choreographer want to create for the dance; "is it friendly, cold, clean, open, threatening?"

Anthony Bowne, Interview.

Create an environment, To

What a lighting designer for dance does, turning "the grey box" he starts with into a "special place", particularly the province of the lighting designer for dances which are apparently abstract.

Anthony Bowne, Interview.

Design, The

The designer's product, the making of a place out of a space.

David Buckland and *Siobhan Davies,* Seminar.

Primary definition

The first decision an artist has to make on a commission for a ballet design is whether he will tell the story of the location of the work through a descriptive design or make it an abstract place, a psychological place.

Nicholas Georgiardis, Interview.

Theatre design

"It experiments, manipulates, plays with quotation, reference, style and pastiche."
Yolanda Sonnabend, 1985.

Scenography

"The international term for all aspects of design where the visual environment is an integral constituent of the production rather than a decorative addition."
Francis Reid, 1992.

Visual design

All the design elements, the venue, the stage, the lighting, the set, which constitute both a context for the work and an ingredient of the work.
Ashley Page, Interview.

Researching a space

Looking at examples of the kind of space you want to create, what the materials are it is made from, the variety of textures, and decoration; the people in it.
"For MacMillan's 'Playground' it was steel mesh, concrete, graffiti, children in old clothes, tacky shirts, dirty sweet bags, a drain pipe, big overhead lights."
Yolanda Sonnabend, Interview.

Box, The

The square model of the theatre in which the designer first puts her ideas into practice, starting with the boldest flights of imagination.
Yolanda Sonnabend, Interview.

Knowing the theatre

Being aware of the problems, dimensions, limitations and opportunities of each theatre and so designing for "that theatre", not any theatre.
"There is no wing space at Covent Garden."
Yolanda Sonnabend, Interview.

Rough sketches

The second stage of designing for a major dance work, after the initial imaging and mulling, a stage when the ideas are emerging and can be either torn up or shared with the choreographer.
Barry Kay, 1981.

Drawings

A stage in ballet design in which many sketches are made of ideas for costumes and set, and discussed with the choreographer, prior to model making and detailed designs for the wardrobe production department.
Nicholas Georgiardis, Interview.

Model making

The first stage of designing for the theatre, making an accurate scale version of what the set will be, and from which the decision will be made to accept or reject the designer's offering.

Yolanda Sonnabend, Interview.

Model

The model of the set, made by an assistant, built on 1:25 scale, preceded by ground plans and elevations in scale; "a means of tying you down, helping you to decide, and, when accepted, completely tying you down."

Nicholas Georgiardis, Interview.

Model showing

Presenting the box in which the model of the proposed set has been made, to the group of people concerned with the work in question, choreographer and all heads of departments; an occasion on which decisions are made as to whether or not the set will be approved for a production.

Yolanda Sonnabend, Interview.

Model showing

A meeting in which a model of the proposed set for a new ballet is shown by the designer to the heads of departments of the company with a view to deciding whether the company should proceed with constructing it, or not; usually 1–2 years before a scheduled opening of the work.

Diana Childs, Interview.

Plan-making

Turning a three-dimensional model into plans for the workshop to use in construction; a job which might be done by an assistant to the designer or by the model room of a large opera house such as Covent Garden.

Yolanda Sonnabend, Interview.

Take over, To

The job of the workshop department of a theatre, such as Covent Garden, who take charge of the actual construction of the set through the plans made of the agreed model.

Yolanda Sonnabend, Interview.

Competing for time

In an opera house in which new works in both the opera and ballet departments are being made, finding yourself in competition with the opera design, which tends to have priority.

Yolanda Sonnabend, Interview.

Monitoring

Checking the way in which the construction of the set is progressing, undertaken by the designer with assistants, by visiting the several venues in which specialised work is being undertaken.

"all over London", "metal workshop", "paint shop", "making the tent", "the stairs."

Yolanda Sonnabend, Interview.

Scheduling

The timing of the set construction which usually takes place well before the ballet is made, while the costumes may remain flexible until after visiting many rehearsals and fittings begin.

"I have to set where they are living first."

Yolanda Sonnabend, Interview.

Working periods

For sets, the period is months, even years, to give time for budgeting as well as scheduling construction, while costume making occurs in the last few weeks before the production, when casting is known.

Barry Kay, 1981.

Art movement designs

Costumes and/or set designs by artists who are working in an established style of art and who bring that style to theatre design; cubist sculptor Henri Laurens for "Train Bleu" (1924), surrealist Joan Miró for "Romeo and Juliet" (1926), constructivist Yuri Yakulov for "Les Pas d'Acier" (1927) are examples, all for Diaghilev.

Richard Buckle, 1981.

Ballet design priorities

The dancer's needs which constitute restraints and necessitate pragmatic decisions in the design of the set.

"She needs an interval — to change from her sweaty costume after the big solo, so we can't have the 2nd and 3rd acts continuous."

Anthony Dowell quoted by *Yolanda Sonnabend*, Interview.

Bare box

The stage, unadorned and opened up to reveal the box-like form of its structure.

Ashley Page, Interview.

Burden of description

For ballet, which uses no words to describe the place in which the action happens, the job of giving the audience a sense of location falls on the designer, so limiting his freedom.

"...dull place, lovely setting, luxurious palace...."

Nicholas Georgiardis, Interview.

Breathing of the space

The way the space has life through moving, 'living' elements such as trickling sand and water, and slowly swinging objects, which assist and reflect the dancer's conscious relatedness to the earth.

Ushio Amagatsu, Interview.

Cavernous

The quality of a large, black, empty stage, into which a design element can be placed to "create a world".

Ashley Page, Interview.

Cinematic projections

Filmed images, moving or stills, projected, usually on to a backcloth or cyclorama, as a means of designing the space; first presented by Tchelitchev for "Ode" (1928) for Diaghilev.

Richard Buckle, 1981.

Constructions

Ways of breaking up the space through placing modernist free-standing sets on stage; said of Naum Gabo and Anton Pevsner's transparent mica set for "La Chat" (Balanchine) in 1927 and Henri Laurens's geometric sets for "Le Train Bleu" (Nijinska) in 1924.

Lynn Garafola, 1989.

Contradictory elements

More than one image in a design, which arise out of different stimuli but nevertheless have to fuse in some kind of tension.

Yolanda Sonnabend, Interview.

Dance space, The

The problem for the ballet/dance designer who has to keep the space quite free for the dancers to move in while creating a convincing location.

Barry Kay, 1981.

Decorless

The trend in new dance works to abandon set and decor and replace them with a location suggested by minimal means, simply a place for dancers to be in; George Balanchine is the prime example.

Richard Buckle, 1981.

Design elements

Physical properties of a design such as levels on which performers can climb, a set made in separate pieces which can change in form during the work, together with the image properties of the design, made to look like or serve as a bed or a room or an internal theatre box; said of Bruce McLean's design for "Soldat".

Ashley Page, Interview.

Designing from a scenario

A method used in narrative works, such as "Isadora" (1971), where the designer has to accommodate many scene changes dictated in the script of the scenario.

Barry Kay, 1981.

Design/choreography

Works in which the design is not a context or location for the dancing but is part of the choreography; examples are Nadine Baylis/Norman Morrice's "Hazard" (1967), Isamu Noguchi/Martha Graham's "Cave of the Heart" (1946), Alwin Nikolais's "Scenario" (1971), Rouben Ter-Arutunian/Glen Tetley's "Pierrot Lunaire" (1962).

Mary Clarke and *Clement Crisp,* 1978.

Diminished

How an imaginative and daring design may become lessened over time through financial and touring constraints.

"Seven great glass columns in fibreglass lit to perfection.... one plastic column."

Yolanda Sonnabend, Interview.

Dislocation

A radical change of image used as a metaphor for a dislocation in the ballet's plot.

"...pursued out of the palace into a totally empty place...", "...courtiers are human, then baboons...."

Nicholas Georgiardis, Interview.

Disturb the space

A function of the design for a work, achieved by breaking up the bare space with elements, probably asymmetrically placed, "a column, a ladder", and by lighting.

Ashley Page, Interview.

Domestic scenario

A set which is devised as a territory for dance using ordinary furniture and images of domestic architecture, internal walls, doors, a kitchen, a living room.

Mark Murphy, Interview.

Double meanings

Sets which offer the audience two images; used of Barry Kay's designs for "Anastasia" (1970), a ship/a birch forest, and a ballroom/a revolutionary barricade.

Richard Buckle, 1981.

Durability

A prime requirement in ballet sets and costumes which will be played many times, stored and toured, a consideration informing decisions on materials and construction.

Nicholas Georgiardis, Interview.

Effects

Theatrical set transformation to create illusions, quite usual in musicals but rare in ballets; used in "Ondine" (1958) by Lila de Nobili for the shipwreck in Act 2.

Mary Clarke and *Clement Crisp*, 1978.

Emotional landscape

The atmosphere achieved by Isamu Noguchi for Martha Graham through his abstract sets which nevertheless provoked emotional metaphors when his pieces became the dancers' landscape.

Walter Sorell, 1971.

Filmic

"As used by Alwin Nikolais refers to his use of projections as a means of changing the environmental setting within a dance."

Nancy Zupp, 1976.

Form of the design

The designer's response to both the choreography in rehearsal and the music, giving rise to the elements which, together, give the design a form.

"Tchaikovsky's 'Swan Lake', beautiful, strange, unbearable", "a kind of hysteria, despair and nervousness".

Yolanda Sonnabend, Interview.

Hard architecture

The set, bare stage, or decor; what is actually in the space, for the lighting designer to light.

Ross Cameron, Interview.

Human body on stage

The artistic interaction of the body and space which has two "primordial conditions: lighting that will enhance the body's plasticity, and a plastic configuration of the setting such that it will enhance the body's postures and movements."

Adolphe Appia (ca 1910) in Denis Bablet and Marie-Louise Bablet, 1982.

Images and materials

The two essential ingredients of design; for "Danse Concertante" at Hong Kong it was "abstract and elegant, classic, for which I gave a scroll in pink and gold rope, and an Art Deco staircase."

Yolanda Sonnabend, Interview.

Inexplicable decor

A space to dance in, which has non-narrative content, containing elements which change during the performance, which emerge but are not directly symbolic.

Ushio Amagatsu, Interview.

Physical field of action, A

"The only scenery is a layer of earth covering the floor of the stage, transforming it into a timeless archaic arena in which will be fought a battle of life and death ('Rite of Spring'); a sea of flowers ('Carnations') in which the dancers romp; a huge pool of water ('Arias'); a foggy landscape ('On the Mountain a Cry Was Heard')."; said of Pina Bausch.

Norbert Servos and *G. Weigelt,* 1984.

Playground

A set in different spatial planes, with which performers interact, moving in and on it, and also moving it.

Mark Murphy, Interview.

Psychological

The properties of a space over and above its physical properties, its poetics, its inherent and created atmospheres, tensions and energies; said contrasting the studio space with the stage space.

Doris Humphrey, 1959.

Putting a mark down

Making an image which impinges on the audience; the image may be photographic or movement or decor, or the tension between, to make a place for the dancer to inhabit.

David Buckland and *Siobhan Davies*, Seminar.

Redesigning

Creating a second design for the same classic ("Swan Lake" or "Sleeping Beauty"), for either a revival or a new production, by seeing the work another way, using the challenge with greater experience.

"...a stronger and simpler statement...."

Nicholas Georgiardis, Interview.

Reinterpret, To

The job of the designer of a classic work, to be engrossed in the work and find new images within it.

Yolanda Sonnabend, Interview.

Restricted space

The limited part of the stage available to the ballet designer, the sides and no more than $\frac{1}{5}$ of the floor space at the back, the rest being required by the performers.

Nicholas Georgiardis, Interview.

Reviving a design

Remaking designs for a ballet created decades before; a problematic request which the span of time exacerbates partly through changing taste, "it looks dated", and through changes in the designer's vision, "I have no conviction for it now."

Nicholas Georgiardis, Interview.

Rhythmic spaces

A term of Adolphe Appia (c. 1910).

"...platforms at various levels of different shapes, thus creating a 'living space' for the moving singer/actor/dancer."

Walter Sorell, 1981.

Rhythmic spaces

Rhythmic geometry translated into sets for movement: a term coined by Adolphe Appia for his sets for Jaques-Dalcroze.

"...primary forms, timeless walls, staircases, slopes...", "...meant for the enhancement of the human body...."

Adolphe Appia (ca 1910) in Denis Bablet and Marie-Louise Bablet, 1982.

Risks

Experiments of both imagination and materials that have not been tried before and which constitute an unknown quantity and therefore a financial as well as artistic speculation.

Yolanda Sonnabend, Interview.

Scene painting

Putting paint on whatever surfaces are in use to get the desired image, painting and scratching corrugated iron sheets, wooden structures, a barrel, for Bruce's "Waiting" (1993).

"...black with a touch of red...."

Marian Bruce, Rehearsal.

Scenic dance, A

The movement of the set in a visible transformation from one scene to another.

Yolanda Sonnabend, Interview.

See, To

The designer's essential means, tempered by the kind of theatre she works in; hence Sonnabend, as a designer working primarily in the proscenium theatre, sees in terms of "planes and perspectives", with "images built up from related fragments".

Yolanda Sonnabend, 1985.

Set materials

"...cloths, painted canvas, wood, hardboard and painted canvas to look like old wood, varnish, metal, gauzes, and so on...."

Nicholas Georgiardis, Interview.

Set revivals

Reviving a ballet decades later, including the set and costumes; a problematic situation in which changing fashions and taste have to be considered.

Nicholas Georgiardis, Interview.

Spontaneous image

The occasional instantaneous image which comes into a designer's head in response to the discussions with the choreographer.

"...for MacMillan's 'Song of the Earth" it was a clear image of a black cloud with gradation into grey...."

Nicholas Georgiardis, Interview.

Spatial metaphor

Using the spatial content of set designs to communicate; said of the Curse in 'Sleeping Beauty' for which the vertical houses shift sharply to slant obliquely, and of the unreal proportions of the houses to give the fairy-tale essence.

Nicholas Georgiardis, Interview.

Strip it bare, To

To reveal the back wall of the theatre, to leave it as an untransformed space.

John Ashford, Interview.

Tent the stage, To

A design which involves an enveloping cloth over the ceiling of the stage, used by Yolanda Sonnabend with a huge pleated curtain suggesting ink-spattered Japanese rice paper for part of MacMillan's "Rituals" (1975).

Mary Clarke and *Clement Crisp,* 1978.

Textures

The actual roughness and smoothness of walls and columns; the perceived textures achieved through paint and illusion.

Nicholas Georgiardis, Interview.

Transitions

In costume and set, the changes from one texture to another, either sharp or gradual.

"...from solid to wispy...."

Yolanda Sonnabend, Interview.

Unpredictable decor

Design elements which move during the performance in unpredetermined patterns; said of Andy Warhol's silver, helium-filled pillows which moved around the stage on their own terms in the Cunningham/Cage/Rauschenberg piece "Rainforest" (1977).

James Klosty, 1975.

Versions

Different constructions of the same set design to cope with different venues, for which large variations are ineviable.

"...an out-of-doors version of 'Swan Lake' at Palermo...."

Yolanda Sonnabend, Interview.

Virtual architecture
What lighting provides to the hard architecture by transforming it into illusory space.
Ross Cameron, Interview.

Visualise a totality, To
The need for a designer of a full-length ballet to image the whole work, how one scene will follow another and avoid the temptation to see it in sections, a process of gestation taking weeks, "preferably months of mulling over".
Barry Kay, 1981.

Working direct
"...not using a model but working yourself with the materials of the set, creating and decision-making as you go...."
Marian Bruce, Rehearsal.

Working with a set
Usually making the dance first, using the central space, having the set for the onstage rehearsals, or, interacting with the set from the beginning, where it has to be conceived of as portable, strong and stable enough for dancers to handle.
Christopher Bruce and *Marian Bruce,* Rehearsal.

5. LIGHTING

Luminaires
The international term for stage lights, divided into floodlights to light large areas, focus spots to give large or small beams, fresnel spots to give soft-edged beams, beam lights for straight intense white light, projectors for use with slides and film.
Ross Cameron, Interview.

Lighting rig
The placing of lanterns, of all kinds, in the positions needed for the performances being prepared; such as a spot bar, a batten, the boom towers, a following spot, and 'specials' for each dance.
John Hall, Rehearsal.

Rig
The mounting and aiming of lamps to light the show.
John Hart, Interview.

House equipment
The resident lighting rig of a theatre which a large touring company will not use, bringing their own, while a small company will.
Anthony Bowne, Interview.

Boxed

Pre-set lighting bars which are boxed up for touring, unpacked, hung, and connected to the touring company's own dimmers and lighting board; a method used by a large dance company.

Anthony Bowne, Interview.

Boom towers

The tall light stands on wheels which are placed in the wings with up to four lanterns on each, such as cantatas, silhouettes, shins.

John Hall, Rehearsal.

Light sources

The quality of the light is determined to a large extent by the type of lamp, it may be an intense hard white light from a discharge source, such as an H.M.I., or a warmer, more yellow light from an incandescent source, such as a quartz/halogen lamp.

Anthony Bowne, Interview.

Colour temperature

The warm or cool qualities of a white light source given through the kind of lamp used (tungsten, quartz, iodine, or fluorescent) over which colour choices are made.

Peter Mumford, 1985.

Light quality

Soft and hard light; a fresnel gives unfocused soft-edged light, a profile gives a sharp-edged clear-cut quality; useful for creating mood.

Anthony Bowne, Interview.

Gels

Pieces of coloured transparent thin sheet, in a range of hues and depth, that can be put into individual stage lights to make the beam coloured.

John Dunlop, Interview.

Overall lighting score

What the lighting designer writes to produce his vision of the changing ambience of the dance, taking into account the groups, patterns, exits, and entrances of the dancers, the changing dynamics and moods, the musical contour, and the choreographer's vision of the imagined location; said of Ross Cameron's design for Dale Thompson's "Monolith".

Ross Cameron, Interview.

Luminous narrative

"A lighting designer usually tries to make a luminous narrative occur. Lights come up — areas feed in — spots fade in and out — pools isolate a single figure — silhouettes emphasize a sculptural pattern — and other devices give eloquence to the stage space."

Murray Louis, 1980.

Flow of light
　　A coherence in the composition of the lighting design, a definite direction of light, not an arbitrary collection of lighting angles.
　　Anthony Bowne, Interview.

Initial design drafting sheet
　　A rough plan of the lighting for a show before it is translated into a moment-by-moment cue sheet.
　　Ross Cameron, Interview.

Lighting plot
　　A written chart of the successive settings of the lighting controls throughout a performance, stated in terms of the cue number, the light number or group of lights, their intensity on a 10-point scale, and the speed of change from one setting to another; transferred to computer for the run.
　　"195 at 6. 2 second fade. A snap cue. A cross fade. 45, 48, 50 and 153 at 7. Bring in the colour change. Group 502. Lose a point on 194.".
　　John Hall and *Hermann Markard,* Rehearsal.

Focusing
　　"...the process of adjusting the direction and beam of spotlights to give a clearly defined image on stage."
　　Francis Reid, 1992.

Focusing
　　A process directed by the chief electrician in conjunction with the lighting designer on the precise aiming, tilting, masking, width adjustment of all the lights especially those for special effect.
　　"Keep inside the black [legs].", "Chop off the top.", "Give its smallest form.", "It's clipping the border.", "Swing left a touch.", "Sharp on the edge.", "Go a bit bigger.", "Put the shutter right in.".
　　John Hall, Rehearsal.

Hot spot
　　The centre of the area of the beam from a lantern on the stage, used for precise aiming.
　　John Hall, Rehearsal.

Cross fading
　　Changing a light state by decreasing the intensity of some channels and increasing others to give a second state; used also with two projected slides so that one fades into the other.
　　Francis Reid, 1992.

Blackout

Lowering of the stage lighting to zero; this must include the working lights on back stage, so that the visible stage is in total darkness; can be immediate or gradual.

"Kill the flies. Kill the round stage."

John Hall, Rehearsal.

Gauze

A cloth of open weave which may be painted and when lit from the front is opaque; when it is not lit, the scene behind is visible.

John Hart, Interview.

Dissolve

Fading the light on a gauze (by which it was made to seem opaque) so that the scene behind it is made visible.

Francis Reid, 1992.

Light line

A line within which the dancers must stay in order to be lit, especially concerned with side lighting.

Anna Markard, Rehearsal.

Light the dance, To

The job of the lighting designer.

"...to show the dance happening...".

Arch Lauterer, 1959.

Light versus lighting

"Light is what the dancer looks for onstage; lighting is what the audience sees. The dancer responds physically to light while the audience responds artistically to lighting."

Murray Louis, 1980.

Invisible

"Light is invisible until there is something to light."

Ross Cameron.

Make tangible, To

The lighting designer's job, to make the space have a volume and a texture, tangible for the audience.

Anthony Bowne, Interview.

Light and movement

Two media which "exist on the same terms".

"They live in time, they move in space, they vary in texture, and they arouse emotional response."

Arch Lauterer, 1959.

Lighting states

"The points in a dance performance which are given frame by the lighting design which creates atmosphere, energy, place."
David Buckland and *Siobhan Davies*, Seminar.

Physical space

The performance area which through the use of lights, gauzes, cellophane, and negatives is transformed into a place for dancers to work in.
David Buckland and *Siobhan Davies*, Seminar.

Floor colour

The black, grey or white dance floor which absorbs or reflects colour differently; "dancers stand out from a black floor, contrast too much, it's difficult to create an environment with black, you can't paint it."
Anthony Bowne, Interview.

Paint the floor, To

The lighting designer's approach to the floor as a surface to paint, lighting it independently of the dancer, and so preferring a grey floor to a black one.
Anthony Bowne, Interview.

Wash

Giving the dance floor an overall colour wash through back light, so enabling the designer to light the dancers separately and with a different colour and intensity.
Anthony Bowne, Interview.

Architectural definition

Lighting which is used on a bare stage to give an impression of a 'place' in which the action occurs.
Ana R. Sanchez-Colberg, 1992.

Gobos

Projecting shapes and forms on a grey floor, or on the backdrop, to give a focus for the dancers, possibly an image for the audience; "a colonnade on the floor" for Erica Stanton's piece.
Anthony Bowne, Interview.

Texture

Qualities in the space which the lighting designer creates, through seeing space as volume, contrasting light with shade, using gobos, split colours, linear diffusion; said of Anthony Bowne's work.
Anthony Bowne in Michael Sommers, 1990.

Scenic lighting
>Lighting which creates landscapes, rooms, prison cells, and intellectual/emotional concepts: isolation, hope, time passing.
>*Peter Mumford,* 1985.

Isolate a space, To
>To define a part of the dancing area by colour and focus.
>*Ross Cameron,* Interview.

Light
>The medium of lighting used by designers, who create with the intensity of the luminaires, the colour of the gels, the direction of the beam, the form of the pools of light, the diffused or hard-edged quality of the beam, the motion of the lantern, and the ability of the technology to group these into consecutive and concurrent light states.
>*Ross Cameron,* Interview.

Supportive element
>What the lighting designer sees lighting as, supporting the choreographer's work and subordinate to it.
>*Ross Cameron,* Interview.

Eye of the audience
>The lighting designer's view of the work at its last rehearsal stages, in anticipation of its being presented to an audience.
>*Ross Cameron,* Interview.

Illuminating a dance
>Simply adding lighting to movement, which is not how a lighting designer sees his contribution; rather, it is bringing shape, composition, and dynamics to the work.
>*Ross Cameron,* Interview.

Illuminating a dance
>To use colour, direction, intensity, motion and form of light to reveal meaning in the dance, not merely to give it light.
>*Anthony Bowne,* 1989.

Integral designs
>The collaborative preparatory work of choreographer and lighting designer which gives rise to a lit environment with which the dance can interact, using cue structures as creatively as a musical score, so making the lighting integral to the work.
>*Peter Mumford,* 1985.

Atmosphere
>What the choreographer wants the lighting designer to create after consultation on colour and intensity.
>
>"The atmosphere must be in the air for me."
>*Gillian Lynne,* Interview.

Underscore, To
>What light can do for a dance, reinforcing qualities in it.
>
>"You can't wait until the dress rehearsal to use light."
>*Arch Lauterer,* 1959.

Macro- and micro-cosmic
>Two qualities of lighting, the overall atmosphere and style for the work, together with the detailed changes of the individual dancer in space and time.
>*Ross Cameron,* Interview.

Model the body, To
>What light does to the dancer, by top lighting it, front lighting it, or whatever combination is decided upon.
>
>"Low-level side lights sculpt the body."
>*Ross Cameron*, Interview.

Silhouette the figure, To
>A lighting design technique for which the outline of the costume will be a clear image.
>*Beatrice Hart,* Interview.

Fabric colour under lights
>The way dyes and fabric type react differently to light, so that apparently similar colours in daylight become differentiated under stage light.
>*Beatrice Hart,* Interview.

Cue-to-cue lighting
>Lighting design which responds to movement or musical cues.
>*Ross Cameron,* Interview.

Counterpoint lighting
>When the lighting design has a life of its own.
>*Ross Cameron,* Interview.

Klieg
>"Blinding light concentration from side lighting", which "can push or pull the strongest technician from his balance."
>*Murray Louis,* 1980.

Shin busters
Side lighting at knee level, which is able to avoid lighting the floor and so focus just off the floor on the dancers; it also increases the apparent height of the performers.
Anthony Bowne, Interview.

Field lighting
"We never like lighting to focus, to dramatize something...the lighting isn't meant to support the dancers and their movement. They light a field rather than any specific parts of it."
Merce Cunningham in Merce Cunningham and Jacqueline Lesschaeve, 1985.

Cross lighting
Lighting a drop in collaboration with the set designer from the side, to bring out its texture.
Ross Cameron, Interview.

Cross lighting
Lighting from the side, high up, at least 12 foot, which aims to reveal the plasticity of the forms on stage.
Anthony Bowne, Interview.

Lighting as weather
Shifting climatic conditions used as an image for a lighting design, either pre-set before the performance or used as an improvisatory field during a gig.
Laurie Booth, Interview.

Special effect
Special lighting effects which may be used as an integral part of a production such as "The Nutcracker", or 'Starlight Express", or a pop concert, to give particular illusory states such as fire, smoke, ripples, flickering, twinkling stars, bangs and flashes, psychedelic projections, laser beams, et al.
Francis Reid, 1992.

Lighting style
A combination of design imagination and technology which is recognisable as one designer's work.
"...strong back light, with high cross lighting..." (Tipton); "...carving up the space with corridors and rectangles..." (Read); "...white, with bursts of unusual colour in strong patterning..." (Mumford).
Ross Cameron, Interview.

House style, A
A recognised style of lighting design usually associated with a company; said of John B . Read's lighting, or Peter Mumford's.
"...a Jenny Tipton piece...".
Ross Cameron, Interview.

6. VIDEO SPACE AND TIME

Alternative canvas

The screen as another sort of space for dance works.
The Video Place, 1993.

Broader canvas

Video space for dance which provides all the layers which video camera and editing techniques provide.
The Video Place, 1993.

Screen space/theatre space

"...a basic and essential premise: that the dancing area of the camera is a triangle in depth, from the lens to the background, narrow at the front, wide to the rear. To that you add camera moves, but with that you begin. In the theatre you start with a rectangular stage area, a shape encouraging movement from side to side; whereas for camera, dance is better from rear to front (or vice versa), with the image growing in strength as it approaches the lens."
Colin Nears in Stephanie Jordan and Dave Allen, 1993.

Frame, To

To place the dancer somewhere in the camera viewfinder; the way the director almost choreographs the spatial patterns of the dance in the same way as the choreographer places the dancer on the stage.
Bob Lockyer, Interview.

Three-dimensionality

The spatial problem for the choreographer of dance on the two-dimensional screen of the video.
Bob Lockyer, 1983.

Camera space

The fundamental dimension in video space is foreground-background, while the cross-stage lateral dimension is the fundamental space of theatre work.
Bob Lockyer, Interview.

Foreground and background

The main spatial dimension of video dance used by Merce Cuningham by directing the viewer's eye to individual events within the group formation of his dancers.
Merce Cunningham and *Charles Atlas,* 1981 and 1987.

Cone, A

The field of view of the camera, and so also of the viewer, of video dance.
Bob Lockyer, 1983.

Shooting for the record or Videotaping for the record

A process which usually involves one camera and one operator whose responsibility is to record every aspect of a dance so that it can be re-created in the future.
Daniel Nagrin, 1988.

Video dance — space

An example of Cunningham's decentralisation and demagnetisation of the space, made possible by camera movement.

"[Video]...opens up the conventional stage space."
Merce Cunningham in Merce Cunningham and Jacqueline Lesschaeve, 1985.

Performance space

A term used in dance video and film making for the spaces created by the way the film studios are structured and lit, and by the angle and movement of the camera shots of them.
Chris de Marigny, 1992.

Studio floor

The performance space and the surrounding space where the camera crews are for the shooting of a video dance.
Bob Lockyer, Interview.

Space as field

Space unconfined by theatrical limitations of a front, sides and back.
"Using the space as a field makes it easier to shift the direction of the camera."
Merce Cunningham in Merce Cunningham and Jacqueline Lesschaeve, 1985.

Anywhere, To be

The power of the camera to interrupt the continuity of space, by cutting from one location to another, from one view of a dancer to another, so transposing the dance from place to place.
Bob Lockyer, Interview.

$2/3$ $1/3$ problem, The

The difficulty of adjusting the amount of visible space in the shot in ratio to the size of the movers in wide angle shots; part of "camera knowledge" essential in the collaboration of video and dance.
Bob Lockyer, Interview.

Image size

"Size of image leads to another point: the full figure, the total dancer, hands, arms, legs, feet, body, head, is small on the television screen.", "Furthermore, if you begin to shoot more than a couple — three, four or more dancers — their size reduces and so does their impact."
Colin Nears in Stephanie Jordan and Dave Allen, 1993.

Invisible walls of camera space

The edges of camera space; inside the perimeter you are in the shot, you can exit or enter, penetrating the invisible walls, from many directions, from behind the camera, from on top of it, as well as from left and right.

Bob Lockyer, Interview.

Shatter the illusion, To

To destroy the image created by one camera by cutting to another's view of the same event, a view in which the power of the space is inevitably different.

Bob Lockyer, Interview.

P. O. V., The

The point of view, the view that each camera has at each moment of the dance, a view of people in space quite different from that of the stage space frontal p. o. v.; a view in movie making which the performers and choreographer have to bear in mind constantly.

Stuart Hopps, Interview.

7. CAMERA AND EDITING

Time jumps

The ability of video editing to disrupt the continuity of time, leaping forwards or backwards in the time sequence of the dance, so juxtaposing images and movements which cannot be juxtaposed in real time.

Bob Lockyer, Interview.

Components of time in video dance

Elements drawn from both video technology and choreography.

"...tempo, movement and stillness of both media, length of shot and of dance phrases, transitions between shots and dance phrases, sequencing...".

Jayne Dowdeswell, 1993.

Rhythmic tool

The shot used sometimes as a means to enhance the dynamics of movement in video dance, and to add a whole 'dimension' of time manipulation not available in live performance.

Hilary Harris, 1967.

Cutting on the beat

A device in video dance in which the musical rhythm is emphasised by the editing video technique, coinciding and intensifying sound with motion.

Hilary Harris, 1967.

Montage

A compositional tool in film and video, achieved through editing in which the filmed material is rebuilt in its own rhythmic sequence; examples are Terry Braun and Peter Mumford's staccato sequencing in "Dancelines", Vandekeybus's frenetic energy in "Roseland".

Jayne Dowdeswell, 1993.

Iso, switch and mixed feed

Three editing devices, basic ways of relating camera shots of dance; to isolate the feeds from the cameras, to change cameras by cutting, to mix one feed with another.

Bob Lockyer, Interview.

Reflect and counterpoint

The camera movement going with or against the dancer's movement, in space or time.

Michelle Fox, 1991.

Pixillation and retrograde

Photographing the dancer at 1 shot per second, giving an interrupted rhythm to the dance; and backwards giving a view never possible in reality.

Michelle Fox, 1991.

Camera left and right

Left and right sides of the camera seen from the cameraman's point of view; opposite to stage left and stage right which are from the performer's point of view.

Bob Lockyer, Interview.

In the box

In the booth where the output of the cameras is seen and mixed in a multi-camera shooting; the director's domain.

Bob Lockyer, Interview.

Camera case, The

A rationale for the choices to be made by a TV director and the cameraman on the transfer of a dance work to video.

David Buckland and *Siobhan Davies*, Seminar.

Cutting criteria

The reasons for video editing.

"Analysis, musicality, recognition of choreographic phrasing, perception of dramatic development, awareness of human relationships on stage are needed."

Colin Nears in Stephanie Jordan and Dave Allen, 1993.

Camera work
A video/film making term which encompasses the techniques available to the camera through lens, focus, and angle, prior to editing.
Chris de Marigny, 1992.

Panning problem
The way camera panning distorts/loses the spatial pathways of a dance work, overcome by having a complex set in the background against which the dancers can be seen to move in foreground.
Jayne Dowdeswell, 1993.

Shots
The repertoire of possibilities for the camera's distance, width, and height.
"Close up tight", "mid-shot", "wide shot", "with headroom".
Bob Lockyer, Interview.

Poetic video
Videotape of dance that uses the full resources open to the camera eye, the imagination of a videographer and the sensitivity of an editor to re-create the physical impact and meaning of a live performance.
Daniel Nagrin, 1988.

Anchoring
A device in video dances for relating one shot to another so that a dance or dancer appears to have continuity.
"...if you look at a television screen, and you see someone on it, and suddenly he appears elsewhere, you get lost. You have to try to anchor what appears on the screen. We tried to get a sense of space by coloring two walls differently."
Merce Cunningham in Merce Cunningham and Jacqueline Lesschaeve, 1985.

Chroma-keying
A technique for superimposing one image on another from multi-camera shooting and with colour equipment, providing special effects which can combine and separate movement events; in Merce Cunningham and Charles Atlas's experimental piece "Blue Studio/Five Segments" (1975).
Nancy F. Becker, 1982 (1975).

Video graphic time-space-dynamics
The amalgam of video technology's manipulation of the time and space structures of dance with human movement's timing and dynamics.
Jayne Dowdeswell, 1993.

PART SIX: THE DANCE EVENT

This Part opens with the rehearsal process and the issues of overcoming the ever-present tendency of dance works to alter and to disappear. There are entries on coping with problems of REPERTORY, REVIVAL AND TRADITIONS. The live situation of on-going rehearsals is given by the language of company staff, collected largely as they worked in the studio and on stage to a precise schedule. The combined entries from all involved gives some insight into the processes of putting works on in a theatre. The language of refining and coaching, and of the performance itself are given. Dancers, repetiteurs, choreologists, choreographers, and backstage crew all contribute.

The Chapter on the NEXUS AND THE EMERGENCE OF STYLE shows how people see the elements of the dance coming together in all manner of diverse mixtures. The language of style was collected largely from dance research sources. Some examples, of how people recognise style in an artist's work, show how the nexus of elements is given distinctive individuality by different collaborators and choreographers.

Whether the dance communicates or not, how choreographers concern themselves with their audiences, or do not, is given in COMMUNICATION. To that end the role of the audience is given pride of place here. How spectators contribute to the event has been collected together.

Chapter 17 REPERTORY, REVIVAL, AND TRADITION

1. THE SCORE

Dance score, The
The title given by a Benesh notator to a notated document of a ballet (not necessarily completed).
Monica Parker, Interview.

Established version of the work
The work as performed on opening night; the full detail of which will be written as the score, opening night being regarded as a deadline.
Monica Parker, Interview.

Choreographer's image
A direct quotation of a choreographer's verbal instruction to highlight the movement, written above the stave by the notator.
Monica Parker, Interview.

Structure of the music
The musical structure in terms of phrases and time signatures which provides essential information for the dance notator in writing the dance score.
Monica Parker, Interview.

Stylistic development of the work
Details of movements which become integral to the work during the choreographic process and are recorded in the master score.
Monica Parker, Interview.

Score, The (Labanotation)
"A well-written score contains the movement form and the movement intent, together with details of the character and the relationship of the roles."
Odette Blum, 1990.

Score, The (Labanotation)
"It provides the bodily, spatial, rhythmic relationship and overall dynamic elements of the work as closely to the choreographer's image of the work as it is possible to do at this time."
Odette Blum, 1990.

Book, The

    The dance score of a work written during the making of the ballet, the means of carrying the work on to the next revival.

    "It is the literal truth"; "Is that correct?", asked of the notator in rehearsal of a revival.

    David Bintley, Interview.

Book, The

    The name given to the score of a completed ballet during the process of recon-struction: it is the true record, the "Bible".

    Monica Parker, Interview.

Inviolate

    The accuracy of the movement, and the notation of it, in works in which the steps themselves embody the character being portrayed; the reconstructor has to regard the score as leaving him/her no rights of alteration.

    "no leeway".

    Muriel Topaz, 1986.

Test of the score, A

    When dancers learn their parts from the score independently of the notator or reconstructor; the score information and readability is seen through the detail and sense of the danced material.

    Ann Hutchinson Guest, Interview.

Interpretation of a role

    Seen by the notator as the performance differences brought by the individual artists over and above the work itself; these will differ with each casting and are not generally included in the score.

    Monica Parker, Interview.

Licensing

    The arranging of permission to perform a creative work under copyright, usually undertaken by publishers or performing rights societies. In the case of notated dances, such permission will be negotiated by the Dance Notation Bureau on behalf of those choreographers who request it.

    Muriel Topaz, 1986.

2. REPERTORY, REVIVAL WITH AND WITHOUT A SCORE

Maintain the repertory, To

    To keep works in the repertory, to revive works made a few years ago; a process efficiently done in the ballet world through choreologists and the independence of the choreography from one set of principals.

    Judith Mackrell, Interview.

Abandon the repertory
> To fail to maintain works in the repertory, which many modern dance groups do because the works are dependent on the original casting, were made to be of their time, and have not or cannot be notated.
> *Judith Mackrell*, Interview.

Reconstruction
> The term used for remounting a ballet from the written score.
> *Monica Parker*, Interview.

Reconstruction process
> The ordered sequence of work which a reconstructor undertakes in order to achieve a 'good performance' of a dance reconstructed from the score; preparation from the score, familiarity with the music, casting the work, teaching the material, coaching the style, overseeing costuming, set and lighting, and bringing it up to performance level.
> *Els Grelinger*, Interview.

Reconstructing a dance work
> The process of setting a ballet from a notated score.
> *Sheila Marion*, 1990.

Knowing a work physically and visually
> For construction purposes, to know what it feels like to do and how it should look overall in order to teach and rehearse it adequately.
> *Monica Parker*, Interview.

Score reading
> Interpreting the choreographer's intention through attention to the analysis of the work inherent in a well-written score; said in contrast to a geometric analysis of the dancers' movement which a surface reading of the score could bring.
> *Ray Cook*, 1981.

Off the page
> The notated movement got into the body and memory of the dance director, and no longer only in the score; a stage in mounting a work from the score.
> *Ray Cook*, 1981.

Getting it into movement
> The essential process of translating the notated dance from the page into the body; the reconstructor's job before teaching the movement, to be completed by the dancers after learning it.
> *Ann Hutchinson Guest*, Interview.

Teaching it from the book
A weak reconstruction process where the reconstructor fails to get the written material into movement before teaching it, hence teaching one piece of information at a time without first finding the sense of the whole.
Ann Hutchinson Guest, Interview.

Notation-based version
The transmission of dance repertory from one cast to another through the use of a notated score, in contrast to the transmission through relying on the memory of performers.
Ann Hutchinson Guest, Interview.

Rehearsing a reconstruction
The choreographer's process, after the work is set on the new cast by the choreologist and/or member of staff, whereby s/he decides upon the best solutions for the present soloists and the space in which it will be performed.
Monica Parker, Interview.

Setting the work
In a reconstruction, the process undertaken by the choreologist of teaching the work to a new cast, using the score as a correct record.
Monica Parker, Interview.

Revival, A
The process of taking the dance, 'the lump', off the video recording of an earlier performance and starting the journey anew.
David Buckland and *Siobhan Davies*, Seminar.

Revival, A
Reworking of a ballet by the choreographer, getting the life back into it and adjusting to the new performers.
David Bintley, Interview.

Revival criteria
To keep the work artistically alive, by playing with a balance between retaining unchanged what is essential to the work, its images, and by substituting one movement with another more suited to the new cast, a jump for a jump, a turn for a turn.
"...to play with the material, to rediscover the material, to keep the clear imagery, another jump will do."
Stuart Hopps, Interview.

Identity
The spirit of a work, understanding of which is essential for a successful revival so that the dancers can 'get under the skin of' the characters of their roles created decades previously.
Judith Mackrell, Interview.

Identity

"Identity in dance is that through which we recognise multiple performances of a dance work as performances of the *same* work, even if they differ in detail. Identity is not necessarily located in the material features of a dance work (steps, etc.). Some (e.g. Baugh) have suggested that it lies in the 'organising principle' of the work. Criteria of identity are not uniform, either across genres or even across an individual artist's body of works. Some dance works can accommodate quite major changes in individual instantiations (productions or performances) without endangering the identity of the work itself."

Sarah Rubidge, Contributed.

Convincing

The quality of a revival which is remounted by understanding the spirit of the original, the motivation and dynamic of the movement, so that the dancers can 'get under the skin of' the original performers; said as necessary for Nijinska's "Les Biches" revival.

Judith Mackrell, Interview.

Reviving a work

Re-staging of a ballet by the choreographer himself, giving the work its original life. Sometimes a 'revival' is staged by people closely associated with the choreographer.

Clement Crisp, Interview.

Choreography

Both setting the piece and producing it, an essential dual process to be undertaken by the choreographer himself, even in revivals.

Christopher Bruce, Interview.

Directing revivals

Remounting of works, such as "Cats" or "Phantom of the Opera" in other cities with new casts, where the structure remains constant, the movements are set by assistants, and for which the director (Gillian Lynne) works for 2 weeks to "mould the dancers, to make them be more wonderful than they have ever been."

Gillian Lynne, Interview.

Directorial skills

The skills required by the person directing a restaging or reconstruction of a work; includes the ability to work with the dancers to create a performance with the proper dramatic quality, style, line, musciality and artistry. Also includes the ability to oversee aspects of the technical production. If staged from a dance score, notation skills are also needed.

Ilene Fox, Interview.

Definitive

Said of a re-staging of a ballet when the lineage from the first performance is continuous through the first-hand knowledge of the work by the rehearsal director.

Michael Somes, Rehearsal.

Interpretation by a dancer or dance director

A considered portrayal of the dance based on the extensive knowledge of the choreographer's repertoire and of the stylistic conventions of the period in which it was made.

Janet Adshead and *June Layson*, 1983.

Authenticity of lineage

The means by which a dance work is retained and re-staged, after the choreographer is no longer able to re-stage it himself, through a combination of dancers remembering the feel of it, through video recordings of the look of it, dance and music scores of its structure, and personal knowledge of the style and identity of the work.

Anna Markard, Interview.

Corrupting the identity

A way of re-staging a work, or performing it, which ignores the tradition in which it is placed.

Clement Crisp, Interview

Lyricise

Over time, to smooth out and lose the multiple dynamics of a style, a tendency which a company has to combat, so that the dynamic intention, and its relation to the point of view of the dance, is not lost.

Carla Maxwell, Interview.

Working to the bone

Teaching material which is in tradition with stringent concern for the authenticity of your approach, both for the movement and for the idea of the originator; said of teaching Louis Horst's "Pre-classic Forms".

Jane Dudley, Interview.

True version

A problematic term focusing on the tension between regarding the dance as consisting in steps which carry ideas, or ideas carried by steps, and thence, on what might be a true revival, emphasis on original steps or on original ideas.

Jack Anderson, 1983 (1975–76).

Idealist (a) and Materialist (b) reconstructions

(a) Reconstruction in which the idea and effect of the original is primary although some steps may be different provided they further the idea; (b) Reconstruction in which an assemblage of specific steps and movements is primary, from which ideas or effect may result but may have a different effect through changed context.

Jack Anderson in Sheila Marion, 1990.

'Real' style

A version of baroque style which, although it may not conform with the sources in all respects, is theatrically convincing because it is kinaesthetically understood.

Stephen Preston, Interview.

Authenticity issues

The problems surrounding a revival of a dance work, with or without a score, including those of changing cultural taste.

"Now it seems over-romantic, even vulgar", said of the Stokowski version of Bach for a Humphrey work.

Stephanie Jordan, Interview.

Eroding

Losing the original choreography of a work by reviving it with emphasis on the ideas behind it rather than the steps that made it.

Jack Anderson, 1983 (1975-76).

Museum piece

A revival of a work in which authenticity of form is the main criterion, for which the dancers can only act their roles by copying the movement forms.

Judith Mackrell, Interview.

Motivation

"The reason for the gesture."

Murray Louis, 1980.

Fabric for revivals

The sensitivity to the use of fabric needed for revivals.

"They've gotten the wrong...weight and texture.", "When you're using fabric to accompany you, you've got to get the right partner."

Murray Louis, 1980.

Transferring a design

Remounting a ballet in another city, in another decade, with another company and artistic direction, and another audience, with original designs; a problematic request which the designer may decline to comply with.

"The 'Nutcracker' of 1966 which Rudolf Nureyev wanted for Paris."

Nicholas Georgiardis, Interview.

Change a work, To

The adaptations which have to be made in the re-staging of a work on a different size of stage to that of the original; the stated number of dancers, length of pathways, and grouping may not work in the new size; change of cast brings the questions: is gender crucial or not, is age important, how to re-stage an improvised phrase, how to cope with a virtuoso solo by a different kind of virtuosic technician.

Ray Cook, 1981.

Re-create, To

The process of revival: "...to revive a work properly one cannot bring the work out of the past to create, but instead one has to go into the past to re-create it."

"Nostalgia, sentiment and the safety of distance can be disastrous for revivals."

Murray Louis, 1980.

Re-creating a dance work

The process of re-mounting a dance work for today's audience, whether from the notated score or from dancers' memories or the choreographer's notes etc., etc., and in so doing providing a question as to the authorship of the re-created work, because of the inevitability of a chain of interpretation en route.

Sheila Marion, 1990.

Choreographic ownership

The concept that dance works are the property of their choreographer, who may make changes, re-do, "fuss with it", but that no one else may "touch it"; a problem in company repertoire.

Jack Anderson, 1983 (1975–76).

Restoring (a ballet)

Re-working a ballet by someone other than the choreographer with every attempt made to go back to the first night of the original production.

Clement Crisp, Interview.

Re-creating (a role or ballet)

Re-staging and re-working a role where there is a breakdown in continuity between the original work and the present production; said in contrast to reviving and to restoring.

Clement Crisp, Interview.

Reconstruction

To mount a work thought to be lost by gathering bits of evidence from a variety of sources and individuals, collaborating with artist/researchers in music/design/dance to attempt to find a way of presenting the work for today's audience; said of the Hodson/Archer reconstruction of Nijinsky's "Rite of Spring".

John Percival, 1993.

Deform the past, To

To change the formal features of a dance work in re-staging processes, however slight these may seem, sufficiently to lose the essential qualities of the original; said also of a teacher's/ballet master's treatment of a technique.

Clement Crisp, Interview.

Common memory, The

The term used of the oral tradition of a Morris club who together keep the traditional dances in repertoire.

Roy Judge, Interview.

Total recall

The memory of a performer for a work that he or she has danced; a memory which may not be adequate to re-stage the work, for the view of one performer of one performance may not be equivalent to the choreographer's view of several performances, even several re-stagings.

Ray Cook, 1981.

Discrepancies
Differences between one re-mounting of a work and the original performance, or from some evidence of the original such as a film.
"How many small differences can you have before the dance is structurally and qualitatively different?"
Ray Cook, 1981.

Memory-based version, A
The transmission of dance repertory from one generation of dancers to the next, relying on the memory of performers, rather than on a dance score.
Ann Hutchinson Guest, Interview.

Staging a work from film or video
"One does not know whether one is observing the choreography as intended, the director's interpretation, or the dancer's performance."
Odette Blum, 1990.

Film/video record
A recording of one performance of a dance work, by one cast, directed by one person who may not be the choreographer and, hence, an unreliable source for future reconstruction of the work; said of a recording of Doris Humphrey's "Day on Earth".
Jean Jarrell, Interview.

New production of a classic
Usually associated with the name of the artist/producer/choreographer in charge, a reconstruction of a classic ballet in which new structures are introduced beyond what would simply be termed a reconstruction or re-mounting of an existing work.
Monica Parker, Interview.

Transfer the work to the screen, To
The process of taking a stage work and with more or less adaptation "reshaping it to suit the camera".
Bob Lockyer, Interview.

Adaptation
Shifting a dance from stage to video and vice versa, a complex process which is not always possible because of the differences between the techniques of camera work and of theatre space.
"'A Simple Man' works. Not all do."
Gillian Lynne, Interview.

Reverence for the work
The feeling that a choreographer or the performers may have for a staged dance work which may be a problem when the dance is to be adapted for a television version and they hold to the original without appreciating the inevitable impact of the TV medium on it.
Bob Lockyer, Interview.

Rough edit, A
> The first edit in which the director and the choreographer view the new version to consider the role that the filming has played on the shifting identity of the work.
> *Bob Lockyer*, Interview.

3. STARTING REHEARSALS

Scheduling
> Timetabling the rehearsals and calls for a company in relation to performances and class, visiting choreographers, number of studios, injuries, availablity of staff and principals.
> "...allowing the pas de deux 40 mins. and the fight 30 mins. for the first run, put together in the second rum in 30 min."; "the Forsythe must be soon after class".
> *Monica Mason*, Interview.

Call sheet
> A schedule for the company giving times, places, people, ballets, class, costume fittings.
> *The Birmingham Royal Ballet.*

Casting
> Working with a company or student group to see the physique, the skills and strength of each dancer in preliminary workshops, and their physique, in order to relate each dancer to the roles which have to be filled.
> *Els Grelinger*, Interview.

Rehearsing
> The process, in re-staging a ballet, which begins with "steps, counts, spacing, and the beginning of style" and goes on to the "coaching of style, production, and development of stamina".
> *Judith Maelor Thomas*, Rehearsal.

Getting the steps
> The first stage in a rehearsal of a ballet in which the movement is learnt, using demonstration, counting, naming steps in rhythm, and using words for spacing.
> "chassée step step", "and-a-li-ft", "1, 2 you're turning 3 and a 4", "step assemblé, saut de basque". "just tombé on it and piqué", "downstage with the right leg", "on the open leg".
> *Judith Maelor Thomas*, Rehearsal.

Getting the steps
> The preliminary process of setting a dance.
> "Don't ask why, just do it."
> *Twyla Tharp*, Informal talk.

Rehearsal technique

For small material, learning the movement on a larger scale at first, gradually diminishing the size while retaining the clarity and intention; a technique to overcome the memory problems associated with very small movement.

Lea Anderson, Interview.

With the music

After learning the steps, to dance the material with the rehearsal pianist playing, using agreed cues.

Judith Maelor Thomas, Rehearsal.

Spacing

An essential early rehearsal concern for some ballets; the way dancers orientate themselves in relation to each other and to the stage.

Judith Maelor Thomas, Rehearsal.

Spacing

"use your tram lines", "get back to your slot", "straight across the back", "a shallow diagonal", "go in to your partner", "don't kill the centre couple".

Judith Maelor Thomas, Rehearsal.

Kill another dancer, Don't

To avoid dancing in front of another performer so that the audience cannot see them; said particularly to ensure that lead roles are visible at the appropriate times.

Judith Maelor Thomas, Rehearsal.

Put it together, To

To take what has been learnt separately and to dance it in the right spacing and grouping.

Judith Maelor Thomas, Rehearsal.

Transmitting dance material

Processes which teachers, choreographers and reconstructors devise and use in order to build up the style of a work in the dancers' performance.

"Give the overall design, then the exact shapes, the rhythms and counts, and then go for the quality and expression: finally put it in the space."

Els Grelinger, Interview.

Respect for the material

The attitude of dancers towards a piece being reconstructed, especially one several decades old and from a culture different from their own, which the reconstructor has to engender.

"I find hostility to doing something simple."

Els Grelinger, Interview.

Communicate the style, To
      The job of the reconstructor who has to set not only the steps, movements, pathways, and grouping of the work, but also provide the motivation out of which the original dance emerged.
      Els Grelinger, Interview.

Humphrey warm up
      Exercises which a reconstructor of a Doris Humphrey work may start with in order to prepare the dancer for the technical demands of the dance as well as its style and quality of movement.
      Els Grelinger, Interview.

Gestural work
      Movement material which has behavioural content, for which the dancer's intention, inner attitude and focus are an essential ingredient and must be elicited by the reconstructor.
      "You've got to be fierce, be mean and nasty"; said of Charles Weidman's "Lynch Town".
      Els Grelinger, Interview.

Narrative image
      The supporting dramatic idea which enables a dancer to give substance to the shapes and rhythms of the movement he has to perform in a work, especially in a reconstruction.
      Els Grelinger, Interview.

Rehearsal atmosphere
      The way a choreographer works with his dancers in the creation or restaging of a ballet: whether he explains the roles or not, wants overt 'acting' or requires the dancers to 'become the characters' in the manner of Stanislavsky, whether improvisation is used, etc.; what a reconstructor may need to re-create in order to find the work.
      Muriel Topaz, 1986.

Keep going, To
      To dance what has been learned in a rehearsal, from beginning to end, ignoring memory lapses and mistakes of spacing and timing.
      Michael Somes, Rehearsal.

See a sketch, To
      Said by a producer, to watch a dancer's first attempt at a section before the expression and finesse is studied.
      Anna Markard, Rehearsal.

Marking
      What dancers do as one process of learning material, walking it through without high energy or personal commitment, concentrating on various aspects of what has to be danced.
      Eds.

Run through, A

Dancing through a work in rehearsal, usually for a particular purpose, such as for memory, for cues, for lighting, for a stand-in, for a new space, for costumes, or for full out.

"We'll do an easy run for memory."
Elizabeth Keen, Rehearsal.

Keep it on hold, To

To retain material learnt in rehearsal with the expectation that something will be altered in a later rehearsal, such as timing.
Judith Maelor Thomas, Rehearsal.

Bring it back with you, To

What dancers need to do at the next rehearsal, to be able to perform the material with all its complexity of content and finesse of style.
Anna Markard, Rehearsal.

Get the steps back, To

A run through at the beginning of the rehearsal to give the dancers an opportunity to bring back what they learned in the previous rehearsal.
Judith Maelor Thomas, Rehearsal.

From the top

From the beginning; said in rehearsal for a run.
Christopher Bruce, Rehearsing.

Counts, The

The means used to get the steps in the right rhythm, with the music; what the dancer has to work with and through until counting disappears and musicality takes over.
Marion Tait, Interview.

Your tune

Said in rehearsal; what the dancers have to recognise as a musical cue and as the sound with which they will eventually dance.
Anna Markard, Rehearsal.

Orchestration

"Here, it's on the horn."; "It's in the percussion."
Monica Mason, Interview.

Visual cue, A

Knowing when to move on with the next material, not by counting or from a sound, but by some apparent visual information.
Anna Markard, Rehearsal.

Talk the rhythms, To
>To aid dancers learning new material, to count it through with the phrasing and accents in the voice.
>*Anna Markard*, Rehearsal.

Cues
>"Take it from the 3 4's."; 'Take it from the top."; said in rehearsing London Contemporary Dance Theatre.
>*Christopher Bruce*, Rehearsal.

Cues for the rehearsal pianist
>"Straight in at chunka, chunka, chunka", "From the second window".
>*Desmond Kelly*, Rehearsal.

Musical lead to come on stage
>The music which accompanies an entry, the dancers picking up the phrase in the wings to enter in mid-movement.
>*Anna Markard*, Rehearsal.

Straight on it
>No introductory music or counts in; said in rehearsal when repeating material to be learned.
>*Anna Markard*, Rehearsal.

Markings
>Names given to short sections of the choreography, written in both the piano rehearsal score and the dance score, to facilitate rehearsals.
>*The Birmingham Royal Ballet.*

Music library
>The piano scores of the ballets in the company's repertory, marked up with dance cues in order to have known places "where you can rehearse from", without confusion.
>*Jonathan Higgins*, Interview.

Piano reduction
>A version of an orchestral piece rendered into a score for a rehearsal pianist; usually difficult to play and not easily providing the dancers with the cues and qualities that they will hear in performance, but adequate for rhythm and tempo.
>*Jonathan Higgins*, Interview.

Tempos
>The pace which the conductor will provide at the performance of a ballet, which may not be the same as that of the rehearsal pianist, providing the dancers with a problem.
>"The trouble we had...", "That speed...it never is."
>*David Bintley*, Interview.

Performance tempo
Not the slower tempo at which dance material may be learnt but the speed at which the actual performance will be given.
Anna Markard, Rehearsal.

Fiddle, To
To make a transition work, often by taking an extra step, turning the other way, or changing feet.
Judith Maelor Thomas, Rehearsal.

Risk, To
To move without keeping total control, to give the movement a daring quality, by placing the body so as to allow a loss of equilibrium, or some lability.
Anna Markard, Rehearsal.

Qualify for the audience, To
A way of performing movement material with some showmanship, rather than identifying with the role honestly.
Anna Markard, Rehearsal.

All the concern (of the dancer)
The dancer's focus of attention, what he has to commit himself to, in image and motion; said as a way of overcoming fragmented or ornamented moving habits.
Anna Markard, Rehearsal.

Images
Words said in order to provide the performer with a way into subtle co-ordination and dynamics, in this case of two arm and body gestures.
"A sigh" and "concerned".
Anna Markard, Rehearsal.

Open-eyed gaze
A particular focus without blinking which brings an intensity to the performance.
Anna Markard, Rehearsal.

Gracious, To be
Said to a male partner on the manner in which he should relate to his female partner during a pas de deux (of Ashton's "Symphonic Variations").
Judith Maelor Thomas, Rehearsal.

Absolutely there, To be
A way of performing, to get to the position so that it registers immediately.
Michael Somes, Rehearsal.

Attitude
The dancer's intention reflected in the way s/he supports the gesture with the torso.
Anna Markard, Rehearsal.

Compromise, To

To simplify or modify a movement pattern in reconstructing dances, from a score, for dancers whose technique is not identical to that of the original cast, so that the essential message of the work is retained rather than slavishly working for exact replication of form.

Els Grelinger, Interview.

Descriptive language of pas de deux

A kind of slang language unique to each pas de deux, based usually on the visual images of the movement or the relationship, used for ease of rehearsal communication.

"the carrot turn", "the flip".

The Birmingham Royal Ballet, Rehearsal.

Tracking

A term used with flying apparatus by the crew who control the cross-stage track from which the aerialist is supported.

"...track back now, keep it smooth; as I spin bring the track stage right...".

Darshan Singh Bhuller, Rehearsal.

Flying techniques

The collaborative control of the ropes of the flying rig attached to a flying harness, by which cross-stage motion and rise and fall motion are co-ordinated with the movements of the dancer who is 'flying'.

"I'm giving you my weight."; "Lift me slowly as I reach Peter."

Darshan Singh Bhuller, Rehearsal.

In-house language

The language developed during the rehearsing of a work, between choreographer and dancers which is particular to that work only; also the slang used by dancers about their theatres, such as Colly (Coliseum) or The Garden (Covent Garden).

Lynn Robertson Bruce, Interview.

Rehearsal language

A jargon invented while the ballet is being made, which is retained and used to indicate a reference point during rehearsal.

Marion Tait, Interview.

Learning traditional dances

Ways of transmitting indigenous dances, by either 'traditional' modes or 'modern' modes: the demonstrator is a friend/relation or a teacher, the transmission takes place when you like or at a fixed time and place, the dance is one that is familiar from one's culture or a new dance, chosen by the teacher; it is to be danced with friends and relatives, or to be danced with classmates.

Alexis Raftis, 1990.

Rehearsal sets

      The full performance sets which some theatres, such as the Bayreuth Festival Theatre, have for rehearsals, so that all preparatory work is done with the levels and staging that will be in place for the performance.

      Teresa Kelsey, Interview.

Place the singers, To

      In opera, to give the singers their grouping on the set, taking into account their voice range, their height, and their movement ability; the job of the rehearsal director for movement.

      Teresa Kelsey, Interview.

4.   COACHING AND THE LAST STAGES OF REHEARSING

Coaching

      What the ballet staff or choreographer or rehearsal director undertake, to refine the ballet after the dancers have "got the steps under their belts".

      Marion Tait, Interview.

Coaching

      Refining the ballet, getting the line as well as the role, through images, acting, or corrections of position, or demonstration.

      "you're misinterpreting the position", "really Bolshoi, feel Russian, just feel it", "right shoulder back", "no, like this".

      Desmond Kelly, Coaching.

Coaching methods

      Individualised ways of working with dancers, taking into account that some like to be told, others not, some can be corrected while dancing, others not till they have finised the variations, some like to run the scene through, others take it bit by bit.

      Monica Mason, Interview.

Producing the dancers

      Working with them to "get the steps right" and to get the qualities, the dramatic content, through the movement itself.

      "Sit, look straight out, take longer, just turn to see her; make more of it so that I see that the foot has gone through for a reason."

      Christopher Bruce, Rehearsing Kenneth Tharp.

Refine a role, To

      Working with a coach, to go beyond the steps to the character.

      "shyer, more tentative", "too percussive", "soften it down", "play with it more".

      Desmond Kelly, Coaching.

Getting the image

Rehearsing the dancers to refine the articulation, qualities, and intentions.

"Let the sand trickle through your fingers, do it one finger at a time, then let your gaze level out."; "I miss the volume of the leg movement."; "Too contrived, should be playful, so let the flow continue."

Christopher Bruce, Rehearsing.

Third eye, The

The eye of the coach, additional to that of the choreographer and the dancer's own image of himself in the mirror, a judgement for which the dancer must feel trust in order to commit himself.

Joseph Cipolla, Interview.

Texture work

Rehearsals which deal with the dynamics, timing, and phrasing of a piece or a number, essential work on the very essence of a role.

Gillian Lynne, Interview.

My girls

The pas de deux partners of a male soloist; after learning a particular coaching point with one female soloist, he may "pass it on to my girls".

Desmond Kelly, Coaching.

Finding your way into the dance drama

What dancers have to do in works which have dramatic content and character roles, finding the integration of personal interpretation with the constraints of style which constitutes successful identification with a work.

Anna Markard, Rehearsal.

Getting it right

Rehearsing a movement using various means to help the dancer achieve what the choreographer wanted: demonstration, description of what to do, of what another part of the body should do, its dynamic, its image.

"drop it", "a bit more 'back'", "it's quite heavy" said of an arm movement; "opening that way, pointing to the future" said of a focus and arm movement; "I'm accelerating on the second soutenu".

Samira Saidi and *David Bintley*, Rehearsing.

Over-analyse, To

A process in rehearsal when the performer and coach concentrate too long on how the movement should be done, so that the capacity to dance it goes, temporarily.

Anna Markard, Rehearsal.

Feed back system

A rehearsal technique in which performers are critiqued for their skills, their routines, and their act, an essential learning process.

Helen Crocker and *Bim Mason*, Interview.

Coaching the style

Getting the essential quality and expression of a choreographer's work; "Cut through the space", "feel heavy", "be simple", "be direct"; images used for reconstructions of Doris Humphrey's work.

Els Grelinger, Interview.

Style precision

Refining movement material so that, through its detail, its style and content emerge; said of the 18th century movement in Claude Brumachon's "Naufragés" for Transitions Dance Company.

Bonnie Bird, Interview.

Run, A

Dancing a ballet without interruption on stage, with lighting, with or without costume, with piano accompaniment rather than orchestra; the last stage before the dress rehearsal or 'general'.

The Birmingham Royal Ballet.

Placing

When transferring a work from studio rehearsals to the stage, determining exact positions for the dancers in relation to the set and the lights.

"Move forward to the first hard leg." "Feel where the light is." "Which wing should Death be in?" "In between the two flats." "Go toward that lamp."

Desmond Kelly and *Alan Dubreuil*, Rehearsal.

Varied runs

To run a work through in the final stage of rehearsal with different ideas in mind, "Send yourself across a very large area"; "concentrate on that detail", "an idea personal to each dancer" in order to discover different layers in the material.

Siobhan Davies in National Resource Centre for Dance, 1988.

Dress rehearsal

One of several rehearsals on stage after the lighting plot is complete, at which attention may be given to co-ordinating the dancers with the lighting cues, entrances and exits in blackout, following spots, placing dancers in relation to 'specials' for which marks are put on the floor, where the ballet demands it such as Jooss's "The Green Table".

The Birmingham Royal Ballet.

Cueing arrangements

Deciding who takes their time from whom in synchronised events, needing collaboration between the dancers, the musicians/conductor, the stage manager who cues the lighting changes and the stage crew; the cueing decisions are put in 'the book'.

The Birmingham Royal Ballet.

Looks fine from the front

What may be said with regard to a problem on stage, to reassure that it is not a problem from the audience viewpoint.

Lynn Robertson Bruce, Interview.

Cover, To

To work at the back of the studio, behind the first cast, and possibly the second, and learn the part in the ballet being rehearsed, to be ready 'to jump in' if required.

Lisa Conway, Interview.

Full call, A (of a ballet)

A rehearsal with the choreographer, the notator, the ballet master, the rehearsal pianist, the stage manager, the conductor, the full cast of the ballet and the covers; each contributing their skills to the rehearsal process.

The Birmingham Royal Ballet.

Put the ballet on stage, To

The final stages of rehearsing a new work or a reconstruction to make it work in the specific performing area.

Monica Parker, Interview.

Production

"Putting the dance work into a particular space, a space with particular facilities; working with whatever there is to make the work come alive."

Dorothy Madden, Interview.

It doesn't work in the space

What sometimes happens when the dance rehearsed for an opera is put on stage for the first time, and dancers encounter the set, the chorus, and the soloists.

Lynn Robertson Bruce, Interview.

General Rehearsal, The

The final rehearsal with costumes, orchestra, lighting, and set of the performance; sometimes open to an invited audience.

Diana Childs, Interview.

Notes

Drawings, words, images given to each performer prior to a performance to remind them what the essential motivation for the piece is.

Lea Anderson, Interview.

Opening night

The first night of any production.

Lynn Robertson Bruce, Interview.

5.   THE PERFORMANCE

Incoming show
> A dance production, a visiting dance company, a solo evening, or whatever, that the production manager of a theatre has to oversee, satisfying both the performers, their management and the audience so that they will all come back again.
> *Ross Cameron*, Interview.

Technological support
> What the production manager supplies to incoming artists, giving maximum access to sound technology, set, costume, programme, production, and box office.
> *Ross Cameron*, Interview.

Programme
> The document offered at a performance, giving the details of the artists and management involved in the dance work(s) to be seen, and in some cases an explanatory note or quotation.
> *Dorothy Madden*, Interview.

Warm up
> Provided by the head of movement, to suit the dancers, before rehearsals and performances, in opera works.
> *Lynn Robertson Bruce*, Interview.

Come in for the warm up, To
> What a dancer does before a performance or rehearsal.
> *Lynn Robertson Bruce*, Interview.

Preparation for performance
> The activities before a dance performance which are regarded by some communities as inseparable from the performance itself and are seen as part of it.
> *Andrée Grau*, Interview.

Practice time
> In Latin American dance, a term used for the rehearsal in public of routines in preparation for competitions.
> *Ruud Vermey*, Interview.

Rounds and exemptions
> The eliminating stage of a ballroom dance competition; some couples, because of their status as past winners, are allowed to pass through a round, to be exempted from competing in it.
> *British Broadcasting Corporation*, 1992(a).

Set the show, To

  The term used by the costume, wig, and shoe departments of a ballet company for placing what is to be worn in the dressing rooms of the artists before a performance.
  Michael Clifford, Interview.

Break shoes in

  The process of beating new pointe shoes against a hard surface, concrete stairs backstage for example, a regular pre-performance activity in a ballet company; also canvas shoes and character shoes are broken in and stretched before the performance.
  Michael Clifford, Interview.

Placing call, A

  A call on stage to space the dancers prior to a first performance in a new venue, and also an emergency call 'at the half hour' to give a spacing rehearsal to the cover dancers who will be performing that evening.
  Lisa Conway, Interview.

Cover call, cover principals, cover showing

  A rehearsal in which the people covering soloists and dancers and chorus perform.
  Lynn Robertson Bruce, Interview.

Setting up

  What a musician does before the performance to make sure that his/her instruments, music and lights are in place.
  Robert Coleridge, Interview.

Sound check, A

  What a musician does before the performance, to test volume and equipment/ instruments/microphone/speakers, etc. in each performance space.
  Robert Coleridge, Interview.

Wearing black

  The traditional colour of clothing for musicians, ranging from dress suit/long skirt to black shirt and jeans.
  Robert Coleridge, Interview.

House is now open, The

  Said by the front of house manager over the back-stage tannoy to inform the performers and crew that the public would be entering the auditorium.
  The Birmingham Royal Ballet, Performance.

Prompt desk

A work station used by the stage manager, situated in the down stage left wing, from where communication with everyone concerned in the performance is made in relation to 'the book' compiled by the stage manager in rehearsals.

Diana Childs, Rehearsal.

On the book

The stage management person who has the information on all aspects of the performance and is sitting on stage left.

Lynn Robertson Bruce, Interview.

Call the show, To

To given the cues for all concerned in a show, from front of house to lighting crew, stage crew, dancers, musicians, and backstage assistants. Usually done by the stage manager in a large theatre, and the lighting technician in a small theatre.

Ross Cameron, Interview.

Lighting cues

A series of numbered lighting events controlled by the stage manager and written on the musical score, which constitutes 'the book', put into effect in the performance and used in the final stages of rehearsing.

"Go back 2 cues", "Pick it up at cue 58".

Diana Childs, Rehearsal.

Stand by

"The signal given shortly before a cue, to warn an operator that the cue is imminent."

Francis Reid, 1992.

Prop table

A table in the wings on which all stage properties are placed, and from which dancers take their props before entrance, and to which they return them, afterwards. There is always one prop table stage R and one stage L.

Lynn Robertson Bruce, Interview.

Resin box

The box of resin dust in every ballet studio and in the wings, into which dancers dip their shoes in order to gain more friction with the floor.

Eds.

Five minute call

The warning broadcast to performers before a performance.

Lynn Robertson Bruce, Interview.

Transformation, The

The process just before a performance when the dancer becomes the role.
"to accept the becoming".
Joseph Cipolla, Interview.

Go up, To

To go from the dressing room to the stage.
Lynn Robertson Bruce, Interview.

Beginners

What is called when the performance is about to begin. The 'Beginners' are those who are onstage at the start of the performance.
Lynn Robertson Bruce, Interview.

Ritual centring

The preparation for performance which some dance directors require; standing in a circle in silence holding hands, on stage, during the overture, then breaking to warm up individually on your place; said of Ivan Marko at Bayreuth.
Teresa Kelsey, Interview.

Stand by

The instruction to performers to be in readiness to begin, to be ready for their cue.
"Stand by on sound", "Standing by on lights".
Elizabeth Keen, Rehearsal.

Take the floor, To

In Latin American dance, a term used to start a practice session or a competition, inviting the couples to walk onto the dance floor and commence when the music begins.
Ruud Vermey, Interview.

Calling the show

"Start with a preset, warmers on the tabs.";
"Lose the house lights.";
"Dancers in place, please.";
"Lose the warmers.";
"Lose the tabs."
"Cue 1 go.".
Ross Cameron, Interview.

Find your mark, To

To enter the stage in a black out and find a luminous tape spot marked in rehearsal as 'your spot'.
Ross Cameron, Interview.

Blue spotters
>Lights which performers can see to help them orientate when semi-blinded by the stage lighting.
>"...blue spotters on the quarter line...".
>*Ross Cameron*, Interview.

Do your business
>What you do on stage, the dancing, movement, singing, speaking, or whatever has been rehearsed.
>*Lynn Robertson Bruce*, Interview.

Relay, A
>A live television transmission of a dance performance as it is given in the theatre, with audience.
>"A 'football match' covering".
>*Bob Lockyer*, Interview.

Premiere
>The presentation of a dance production for the first time (according to country or the world); the event may be regarded as constituting the authentic performance of the work.
>*Anatole Chujoy* and *P.W. Manchester*, 1967.

Premiere
>The first night of a production: "...an occasion where the audience may dress up and be as much performers as the singers and dancers."; said of the Wagner Festival Bayreuth.
>*Teresa Kelsey*, Interview.

Immediate rehearsal process, The
>The brief and concentrated rehearsal time usually immediately prior to shooting which takes place in movie making and video making; contrasted with the lengthy rehearsals in theatre work.
>*Stuart Hopps*, Interview.

Miss a call, To
>To miss an entrance on stage; the unforgivable sin in theatre.
>*Lynn Robertson Bruce*, Interview.

Hard show, A
>One in which there is a lot of work for the dancers in musical theatre.
>*Lynn Robertson Bruce*, Interview.

Take a call, To

To take a bow at the end of the performance, which dancers in opera may or may not be required to do.

Lynn Robertson Bruce, Interview.

Take applause, To

To know how to anticipate and to accept the clapping of the audience, a crucial part of the preparation of performance artists.

Helen Crocker and *Bim Mason*, Interview.

General notes

After a rehearsal and a performance, a verbal report to chorus and dancers on their work, giving improvements and changes.

Lynn Robertson Bruce, Interview.

After life (of an event)

The buzz around a dance event, the discussion and argument following it to which a dance journalist contributes through her review.

Judith Mackrell, Interview.

Hornet's nest

The buzz surrounding a confrontation of traditionalist critics with a production that breaks new ground; said of Anthony Dowell's restaging the production by Mikhail Baryshnikov of the "Don Quixote" with stark designs by Mark Thompson.

Allen Robertson, 1993.

Bomb, To

To fail; to experiment with design ideas, new music and choreographic ideas, which, when put together, worked only in part; said of the Pilobolus production of "Nutcracker" which juxtaposed Tchaikovsky and Ellington, and a design which was Art Deco, going into cartoon fantasy.

Yolanda Sonnabend, Interview.

Get out, The

The period (usually overnight) after a show has ended its run when it has to be cleared out of the theatre; either packed away for storage, or loaded into vans ready to move to the next venue.

Jane Nicholas, Interview.

Chapter 18 THE NEXUS AND THE EMERGENCE OF STYLE

1. THE NEXUS

Nexus

"a connected group or series".
'Webster', 1993.

Nexus

"a bond; a connection."
'Concise Oxford Dictionary', 1990.

Mix

"Art form, cultural activity, recreation or whatever, dance has to consist of performers, moving, with some sort of sound and in a space; the magic is in the mix."
Valerie Preston-Dunlop, Seminar.

Ingredients of dance

"Dance, like magic and ritual, contains ingredients — aural, temporal, and visual things, not to mention the dancer — that must be combined just so and in precise proportions or it doesn't work, there is no magic."
Paul Taylor, "Private Domain" 1987.

Materials of the dance, The

The things that are used "to create something over and above what is physically there."

"...the dancers' bodies, ...the cloth that drapes them, ...the floor, ...the ambient light; musical tone, ...the forces of gravity, ...other physical provisions."
Susanne K. Langer, 1957.

Alleged incidentals

"It is quite true that we ordinarily talk as if there were some central notion of the dance work — the movement — with respect to which such factors as stage effects, music, and specific performers are incidental. Closer inspection shows that this view is not so plausible as it seems. The main focus of choreography *is* movement, but in a given work, the quality of the movement may be drastically changed by variation of one of the alleged 'incidentals'."
Adina Armelagos and *Mary Sirridge*, 1978.

Identity of a work

"...to suggest that a simple appeal to 'the movement' is likely to prove inadequate for purposes of establishing a work's identity. The crucial role played by such elements as we list (movement style, individual performance style, music, costuming, lighting) cannot simply be treated as an extreme example of the importance of display conditions. A painting in darkness is still the painting it was; a dance performance with a change in one of the alleged 'incidentals' may not be a performance of the work at all."

Adina Armelagos and *Mary Sirridge*, 1978.

Interrelations

The web of relationships between the components which make up the form of the dance.

Janet Adshead, 1988.

Strands of the dance medium, Four

The performers, the movement, the sound, the space, and their visual, aural and kinetic sub-strands.

Laban Centre for Movement and Dance, 1992.

Text of a work

It is much more than the score; it is the steps, the relationship to the music, the decor, the inner life of the ballet, and the style of the performers.

Clement Crisp, Interview.

Art of ballet

"The art of ballet...is the perfect theatrical blending of four component arts: drama, music, design, and dance."

Peggy van Praagh and *Peter Brinson*, 1963.

Bharata Natyam form

A South Indian dance form which includes "melody, rhythm, poetry, drama, and mime", as well as dance movements themselves.

Leela Samson, 1987.

Elements of theater

For Cunningham these are: movement/stillness, sound/silence, lights/absence of lights, costumes/absence of costumes, set/bare stage.

Merce Cunningham and *Jacqueline Lesschaeve*, 1985.

Multiple complexity of theater

"The energies and dynamics of motion, light, color, sound, sculpture, architecture, design, and voice, all become part of his creative palette."; said of Alwin Nikolais.

Murray Louis, 1980.

Basic elements of the dance

"I see the basic elements of the dance in its aesthetic manifestations, that is, in the beauty of the movement, in the unfolding of the rhythmic patterns, and not in their possible meaning or interpretation."

George Balanchine in Walter Sorell, 1951.

Trappings of dance

"...communicating different kinds of emotion with steps depends more on how the steps relate not just to the music but to all the dance's trappings — its title, gestures, images, decor."

Paul Taylor, "Private Domain" 1987.

Inner life of a ballet

The complex web of qualities which make the ballet what it is; much more than the steps; that which answers the question 'What is it about?'.

Clement Crisp, Interview.

Provoking a metaphor

The complex mixture of form and content, performer and movement, image, costume, sound, audience, setting, et al, which together give some meaning to the dance.

"I maintain that critics too often report a metaphor before they are fully aware of what provoked it."

Marcia Siegel, 1972.

Making a work work

Using the nexus of performer, movement, space, lighting and decor, and sound, to provide an audience with an experience.

David Buckland and *Siobhan Davies*, Seminar.

Stagecraft in Performance Art

The art and skill of using the performance space include entrances and exits, eye contact with the audience and other performers, intimacy and complicity between performers, in order to become "a performer".

Helen Crocker and *Bim Mason*, Interview.

Locked away

The quality of a performance created in a particular designed place with particular dancers, which can never be re-found.

David Buckland and *Siobhan Davies*, Seminar.

Placement

The way a figure is put in relation to the set, to generate a relationship, a tension, or a fusion.

David Buckland and *Siobhan Davies*, Seminar.

Feed into the work, To
How the supportive production elements of lighting and costume contribute to the overall content of the choreographic work.
Ross Cameron, Interview.

Anchor
The concept or tradition that gives the designer something around which to work for each ballet.
"Western fairy-taile tradition"; "'The Prince of the Pagodas' is a mix of 'Cinderella', 'King Lear', and 'Beauty and the Beast'"; "The music of 'Sleeping Beauty' is heavily stamped with 19th century style".
Nicholas Georgiardis, Interview.

Resources
The requirements for music, set, costume, stage size and equipment, and performers, which a reconstructor has to ensure are available before commencing the mounting of a work.
Els Grelinger, Interview.

Ballets in rep.
Works which have been performed by the company already and for which the resources of musical score, dance score, costumes, and set exist.
Jonathan Higgins, Interview.

Unity
"There has to be a relationship between the parts."
Louis Horst, 1958.

Disintegrated
Of a Cunningham work, "It is a disintegrated spectacle in which the elements are independent of each other"; said in contrast to "the integrated spectacle of Diaghilev's time".
David Vaughan, 1974.

Autonomy
"...the official Cage-Cunningham dogma requires the autonomy and freedom of each theatrical element — movement, light, sound, and decor...".
James Klosty, 1975.

Alliance of dancing with other arts
A principle of Fokine's New Ballet.
"The new ballet, refusing to be the slave either of music or of scenic decoration, and recognising the alliance of the arts only on the condition of complete equality, allows a perfect freedom both to the scenic artist and to the musician."
Michel Fokine, 1914.

Added media

Cunningham's co-existence concept.

"Why not add in all possible media, from music (and musicians as visible performers), to paintings and sculptures, to film and television?"

Sally Banes in State Univ. of New York, 1987.

Disco dancing

A social dance style of the 1960's, for couples and single dancers, in which individuality is based on the simple vocabulary of steps, turns, and breaks done together and individually, to disco music, in a disotheque with disco lighting.

Jack Villari and *Kathleen Sims Villari*, 1979.

Scottish dancing

A recreational social dance form using all manner of reels, largely organised in clubs and danced in the kilt for a foursome, a sixsome, or an eightsome, traditionally to the bagpipes or the fiddle.

Peter Buckman, 1978.

Parallel elements

The interrelatedness of the elements of a Butoh work which, although rehearsed separately, are created to provide a unified whole, each element containing similar essential qualities; the trickling sand, the dripping water, the slowly turning egg, the movement taking time.

Ushio Amagatsu, Interview.

Total stage realisation

Said of Alwin Nikolais's work.

"Props grow into sets, sets may be used as props, and both are born as the total stage realisation of a unified visual image which defies departmentalisation in movement, decors, projection, light and sound."

Walter Sorell, 1971.

Kathakali

A style of classical South Indian dance for men, "a total drama" with an "explicit language of gesture", "elaborate and imaginative facial expression"; accompanied by verses sung by two musicians which tell the poetic situation, mood and impersonation; the performers wear "magnificent costume, head-dresses and elaborate facial make-up, and masks and long ornamental hair"; the performance begins after dark and lasts until dawn.

Leela Samson, 1987.

Theatrical totality

"His [Robbins's] greatest achievement was in remaining faithful to the ballet and pantomime concept in the course of the drama, in characterizing the actor-singer-dancers through gesture and movement taken from everyday life, but heightened through stylization. He thus achieved a unique theatrical totality."

Walter Sorell in Eugenia Volz Schoettler, 1979.

Popular style

An ingredient in some folk song and dance ensembles' work, presented as a popular art form with comic turns, choruses, flashing sabres, and a blaze of colour in costume and light.

"...knotty squats and falls, flying splits and whirls..."; said of the Red Army of Russia Ensemble.

Nadine Meisner, Contributed.

Dance drama

The synthesis of the formal coherence of ballet with the emotional content of Ausdruckstanz (Ger.=expressionist dance) which Kurt Jooss aimed for in his choreographic style.

Kurt Jooss, 1933.

Theatrical synthesis

The balance of the elements of theatre so that no one part dominates or confuses the others.

Doris Humphrey, 1959.

Centrifugal work

A ballet whose momentum gathers in scattered departments, the dancers, the set makers, the wig master, the lighting designer, the wardrobe, the press, etc., increasingly as the premiere approaches.

"You have to keep its centrifugal tendency under control."

Nicholas Georgiardis, Interview.

Synthesis

The plot, character, costume, locale, music, dance, and lyrics of a work integrated together to give a style; said of Michael Jackson's and Michael Peters's pop video "Thriller" (1984) which captured the style of a Hollywood musical.

"Screen", 1986.

Interdependence

The nature of the relationship between the kinetic, aural, and visual elements of the dance, in almost infinite variety.

"Most dance works don't operate on a coexistence of all their elements, nor a dependence of one element on another, but by the subtle interdependence of all the ingredients in layers."

Valerie Preston-Dunlop, Seminar.

Apollonian/Dionysian dichotomy

The complementary polarities "in art and human experience' where matters of form and reason contrast with those of content and passion, seen in dance in stability/lability, ordered/chaotic structure, spatial form and dynamic flux.

Ana R. Sanchez-Colberg, 1992.

Formal function of a feature
The purpose of a feature of the dance (a step, a focus, size, duration, an off-balance turn, a partnering lift, etc.) within the structure of the dance, so that it defines the elemental use which constitutes the style of the work.
Ana R. Sanchez-Colberg, 1992.

Expressive function of a feature
The purpose of a feature of the dance (its length, energy level, movement vocabulary, lighting, etc.), to define the content of the work.
Ana R. Sanchez-Colberg, 1992.

Authentic style
A way of moving which re-creates as closely as possible in today's conditions, based on detailed historical knowledge of steps, costume, department, and the dance area.
"One has to start off being as authentic as possible before choreographing in the correct style."
Madeleine Inglehearn, Interview.

Period style
Choreography which attempts to follow the period sources as closely as possible in costume design, staging, and dance technique.
Stephen Preston, Interview.

Noble style
The embodiment of aristocratic behaviour and values within a 17th/18th century ballroom and professional theatrical technique; the style aimed at by current practitioners.
Wendy Hilton, 1981.

Dance pastiche
Dance created deliberately in the style of another choreographer or time period.
Eds.

Hold a piece in trust, To
The responsibility which a company has towards a choreographed work in their repertoire, so that the identity is maintained and the work is held together in totality, including such elements as the lighting design.
Marion North, Interview.

3.   EXAMPLES OF HOW INDIVIDUAL STYLE IS DESCRIBED

Fashions in abstract ballet
Changing styles in non-narrative ballets.
"...dreamy-lovers-and-Romatic-music...", "...neat-geometrics-to-Baroque-concerti...".
Jack Anderson, 1975–76.

Afrocentric and Eurocentric American dance modalities

A distinction made of two modalities of dance, irrespective of the background or skin colour of the dancers, which distinguish those forms of dance which share the dynamic qualities of African-generated dance from those which share the dynamic qualities of European-generated dance.

Brenda Dixon Gottschild, 1990.

Leanness

Said of Rambert Dance Company style under Richard Alston's influence.

"Easing the body onwards into space, lengthening across and down the back and up the back and head."

Stephanie Jordan, 1992.

Cholmondeleyism

The shrewd observation producing witty gestural phrases, perfect comic timing and skilful manipulation of the relative heights and shapes of the dancers (in Lea Anderson's company The Cholmondeleys).

Fiona Burnside, 1990(b).

Dichotomy of movement styles

"...a dichotomy between balletic footwork and the manic floundering of the rest of the body."; said of Anderson's "Fish Wreck".

Sophie Constanti, 1987.

Ashton's English style

A style of ballet developed by Ninette de Valois and Frederick Ashton.

"simple, pared down, restraint", "emphasis on line and musicality", "no broken wrists".

Michael Somes, Rehearsal.

At the cutting edge, Working

Choreographers who are on the threshold of contemporary styles, experimenting with new approaches to the art of dance; the avant garde.

Eds.

Neo-classical

The style of a Balanchine work in the classical repertory, concerned with energy and dynamics, musicality and rhythmicality, but with arms not conforming to the classical norm.

Monica Mason, Interview.

Law and logic (of style)

Two ingredients of classical ballet "...pertaining to a body moving in space with the aim of creating beauty by organised dynamism", any departure from the law and logic being apparent to the spectator.

André Levinson (1992) in Joan Acocella and Lynn Garafola, 1991.

Style changes
     The way the hold in ballroom dancing has lifted and broadened, the movement has become bigger, and the lady has been given more opportunity to be expressive with her body and head, dancers move across the floor more broadly, a gradual change over the last twenty years.
     Geoffrey Hearn, Interview.

Fundamental action
     The ingredients of the style of ballroom dancing in Sport Dance, which starts with the steps, the line in the space, the swing quality, the rhythm, the poise of the weight in the body, the partnership, the holds, the line of the back, the use of the music, and fine details of performance.
     Geoffrey Hearn, Interview.

Bausch's undance-like theater of movement
     "A theater of situations in which time stands still; the game can begin at any time and go on indefinitely.... She selects a cross section of daily behavioural realities and examines them microscopically in stages which are then duplicated, accelerated, or performed in slow motion."
     Norbert Servos and *G. Weigelt*, 1984.

Naturalistic yet realistic
     A critic's description of the mix of a mundane choreographic material with the choreographic devices associated with ritual, which constitutes the choreographic style of Pina Bausch.
     "...truth and simplicity..." of 'Orpheus and Eurydice'.
     Nadine Meisner, Contributed.

Gender-specific movement
     "Bausch's men and women have different repertories of movements strongly re-miniscent of Ausdruckstanz, the men, for example, being characterised by almost aggres-sively powerful leaps."; said of "Rite of Spring".
     Norbert Servos and *G. Weigelt*, 1984.

Nourishing style
     A way of moving which promotes the health of the body and prepares it for a lifetime of dancing, rather than a short spell of exceptional virtuosity and taxing skill.
     Laurie Booth, Interview.

Bournonville partnering style
     A way of the male and female dancers working together to present companion-ship and equality of the sexes, so emphasising the respectability of female dancers.
     Clement Crisp, Interview.

Bournonville style

A characteristic way of choreographing ballets in which lightness, bounce, and a generous way of travelling across the stage is typical. Also implicit is a sense of drama and mimetic gesture largely used. c.f. "Napoli", "La Sylphide".
Clement Crisp, Interview.

Bournonville style

A dance training method and a style of choreography developed by August Bournonville between 1830 and 1877, which presented an enobling view of life, a moral stance between men and women, an equality of the sexes in the dramatic structure of his ballets, and preserved and developed the French technical style of Auguste Vestris that Bournonville learned in Paris in 1823–29.
Clement Crisp, Interview.

Freeze

The main moment in a break dance sequence, in which the rapid footwork and spins common to all break dances is punctuated by a flash of stillness, the moment of individual style, intricate, witty, insulting or obscene.
Sally Banes, 1985.

Layered

In "Naufragés" (Claude Brumachon) the 18th century style of movement, the images of disintegration of that culture, the metaphors of shipwreck in the movement, the violence of the dynamic of movement and music, the Fragonard paintings as source, the "shipwreck" of sexual exchange between men and women, the emphasis and harsh rhythm of the repetitious structuring.
Bonnie Bird, Interview.

Blatant

A word used by Butcher of her own 1990's style: pared down to the limit, without compromise, simply showing what is to be shown, doing what is to be done; an example:
"...a crowd jostling, on and on and on, as is."
Rosemary Butcher, Interview.

Performance installation

A Rosemary Butcher term for the style of her work which took place in a non-conventional dance place, lasted for a non-conventional duration, collaborating with a non-theatre designer, but danced by experienced conventionally trained dancers; said of "Body as Site" (1993).
Rosemary Butcher, Interview.

Contemporary styles

Styles of dance technique and of choreographing which include mainstream American and European work and the more recent innovations of individual artists; styles which, although clearly different from each other, are seen as a group distinct from the classical ballet technique and way of choreographing.

Marion North, Interview.

Style of a Cunningham work

Through dance techniques, any body part can be used, in combination with any other(s), to make any movement, at any speed, in any stage space.

Sally Banes in State Univ. of New York, 1987.

Awkwardness

"...to ballet's virtuosity and grace, to Graham's implosive intensity, he added the possibility of awkwardness...his choreography is the first to honor equally the arabesque and the limp..."; said of Merce Cunningham.

James Klosty, 1975.

Independence of elements (in choreographic style)

"What we have done in our work is to bring together three separate elements in time and space, the music, the dance, and the decor, allowing each one to remain independent. The three arts don't come from a single idea which the music supports and the dance demonstrates, but rather they are three separate elements, each central to itself."

Merce Cunningham in Merce Cunningham and Jacqueline Lesschaeve, 1985.

Intricate tangles (of the aural/visual/kinetic style)

A complex mix of "sound, movement, color, line of energy, and shape and design"; said of the way that Cunningham's dances "lack of overt expressionism focuses attention on 'intricate tangles' which this mix creates."

Sondra Fraleigh, 1991.

Movement impulse

The movement impulse comes from the arm and pelvis, leading to a flexible use of the upper body and an emphasis upon a central and successive use of the spine; Siobhan Davies's style.

Angela Kane, 1990.

Fleetness

Used of Siobhan Davies's style.

"Rapid detailed work of the feet and lower legs, neat small jumps as well as major elevation and a fast torso."

Stephanie Jordan, 1992.

Folk dance styles

Qualities in national folk dances which reflect the terrain in which they are danced and the clothing worn, as well as the musical instruments and rhythms essential to their performance.

"The jumped styles of Polish and Czech Mountaineers, and the Scottish Highland dancers. Strong accents of Hungarians, wearing boots. The vastness of Russian countryside."

Robert Harrold, Interview.

Gesamtkunstwerk (Ger.)

A total work of art, a work in which many media are used as a total work of theatre; said of Wagner's concept of opera, of Kandinsky's "Der Gelbe Klang" (1914), of Laban's "Sang an die Sonne" (1917), of Schoenberg's "Die Glückliche Hand" (1914).

Eds. from Walter Sorell, 1971.

Early Graham

"Early Graham style had the purity of an earth-sky rite, with its rooted look, pounding feet, stiffly vertical posture, arms that branched occasionally into angular gestures. Austere, hopeful, unambiguous dancing that reflected her ruthless asceticism and her desire to purge dance of all trivialities of movement."

Deborah Jowitt, 1977.

Undecorated

The quality of Hanya Holm's work, clean and clear.

Don Redlich, Informal discussion.

Kathak

A style of classical South Indian dance, not associated with ritual, with two forms, the Lucknow gharana which is "graceful" and with "sophisticated rhythm" and the Jaipur gharana "known for its speed and rhythmic challenge", "complicated and repetitive style of pure dance" in which both improvisation and "set items" are used, especially dance interspersed with spoken verse.

Leela Samson, 1987.

Laban Kammertanz style (ca. 1924)

"...the style consists in congruent body co-ordination, intense commitment to the movement, deeply felt performances, a high level of group sensitivity and adaptability, contrasted with grotesque and comic use of mundane gesture, contracontextual and broken-affinity modes."

Valerie Preston-Dunlop, 1988.

Personal dance language

"...from a classical step, to a pedestrian shrug, to...", said of Mark Morris's "New Love Song Waltzes" (1993).

Judith Mackrell, Interview.

Lyrical physicality

Movement qualities which are "athletic, aggressive, fiery, and passionate", but which are also "rooted in a lyrical base"; said of Mark Murphy's style.
Mark Murphy, Interview.

Manoeuvres

Dance material which manipulates one dancer against another, ducking, weaving, hurtling like a missile, where risk, danger and reflex dominate the encounter; said of Mark Murphy's work.
Judith Mackrell, Interview.

Repetition with minimal changes

Repeating costumes but with one slight difference (head-dress in "Les Noces"), repeating the set for two scenes with slight differences (1 window or 2 in "Les Noces"), repeating musical motifs as well as dance motifs with slight changes of rhythm; said of Nijinska, Gontcharova, and Stravinsky structural style.
Valerie Preston-Dunlop, 1981.

Contact improvisation

"A dance form with: democratic duet format, incorporating elements of martial arts, social dancing, sports, and child's play."; said of Steve Paxton's contact work.
Sally Banes, 1980.

Physical theatre vocabulary

A movement vocabulary, used by several choreographers, developed from circus and tumbling skills together with dance skills, leading to a physical vocabulary strong in acrobatic and aerial (trapeze) work.
"Dance Theatre Journal", 1992(a).

Flat continuity

A process of composing in which varied movement material is used, even virtuosic in content, but with no variation in dynamic and phrasing; said of Ian Spink's work.
Stephanie Jordan, 1992.

Bare

A quality of the movement/sound material of a work, uncluttered by overtones of expression or characteristation; said of Snaith's own work.
Yolande Snaith, Interview.

Snaithism

[Snaith] "...uses objects to create environments, situations, worlds"; a comment on her spatial signature.
Sarah Rubidge, 1988.

Corporeality

Emphasis on the bodily rather than the mental or the spiritual; a term used of the style of German New Dance in the 1920's and of Tanztheater since the 1970's, especially of things bodily being the source of movement, the crux of the expression.

Ana R. Sanchez-Colberg, 1992.

Dualities

"Dualities occur in Tharp's works with regularity. She effortlessly contrasts styles of movement, such as show dancing and ballet, or music of a classical composer with that of a popular writer."

Don McDonagh, 1976.

Eurocrash

"The pell-mell, athletic, confrontational-brinkmanship style deployed so effectively by Vandekeybus and others."

Mary Brennan, 1992.

Cutting style

The style of a video dance director who develops a personal way of relating shots, the zoom, the crash, the order, the duration, and so on, such that this structuring of shots has formal content over and above what is being filmed.

Bob Lockyer, Interview.

Chapter 19 COMMUNICATION

1. AUDIENCE/SPECTATOR/JUDGE AND HOW THEY RESPOND

Audience
> People who assemble to view, participate in, share or hear a performance in any setting.
> *Eds.*

Look at, To
> Not glance, or scan, or view, or observe, or criticise, or respond, but attend to.
> "If you are going to look at dance, you have to REALLY look at it."
> *Louis Horst*, 1958.

Spectator as an individual
> "Each spectator as an individual can receive what we do in his own way and need not see the same thing, or hear the same thing, as the person next to him."
> *Merce Cunningham* in Merce Cunningham and Jacqueline Lesschaeve, 1985.

Peer group audience
> Spectators who belong to the same culture or sub-culture as the performers; said of contemporary dance audience.
> *John Ashford*, Interview.

Gallery audience
> People who look at exhibitions of paintings and also at live works of art presented in a gallery, and so treat the live art as they would a painting, by looking at it for as long or as short a time as it interests them, then moving on.
> *Rosemary Butcher*, Interview.

Outsider
> The audience, onlooker, anyone seeing the work, including the director.
> *Yolande Snaith*, Interview.

Acceptable
> What an audience will tolerate, the threshold which an avant garde choreographer pushes so that what an audience thought of as unacceptable becomes acceptable.
> *Trisha Brown*, 1987.

548

Audience expectation

The preconceptions that the public bring with them to a performance.

"They come with a set of expectations regarding the nature of the dance event they are going to experience. These expectations contain within them an implicit set of criteria upon which they base their interpretations and evaluation of the event. Both expectations and criteria are grounded in the social, cultural, artistic and historical milieux of which the individual has experience, as well as in experiences of a more personal nature. The more distanced a work is from these expectations the more active a role the spectator must take in order to engage in the world/s the work is projecting."

Sarah Rubidge, Contributed.

Baggage

The personal response which a spectator might bring to a work, and so make an issue out of items which are not an issue for the company, usually of a stereotypical sort.

Lea Anderson, Interview.

Ballet design, Impact of the

The abiding impression given to an audience in a ballet performance.

"When the curtain rises on a ballet, the first thing that strikes the public's eye is the design".

Clement Crisp, 1985.

Body, The

The first visual material that the audience responds to, but unless it is "stunning, worrying, or unpleasant" they move on quickly to the next stage of appreciation which is the dancing.

Judith Mackrell, Interview.

Boredom reiterated

How some people see abstract works which have no narrative element to which the audience can turn.

"...have to wait 40 bars before the audience has a gem."

Gillian Lynne, Interview.

Catch on, To

The response of the audience to a Trisha Brown game-playing dance, when she is toying with the audience's ability to follow what she is doing; if they do, she shifts her ground plan, or stands still.

Trisha Brown, 1987.

Celebrate, To

To participate in a work as a performer or as a spectator with the purpose of acknowledging its quality; rather than seeking its message, or its entertainment value, or the quality of its referent.

Eds.

Chemical change

The effect that an audience has on performers, especially in group improvisation, when the dancer's bodily sensation is enlivened by the presence of spectators.

Laurie Booth, Interview.

Co-creating audience

Not only perceiving the dance in front of us by aural, visual, and kinetic means, but simultaneously imaginatively responding to it deeply and so completing what the choreographer has begun.

Francine M. Watson Coleman, 1986.

Composition by field

"[A piece in which]...your eye can jump from one point to another, you don't have to be led any longer from one point to another...".

Merce Cunningham in Merce Cunningham and Jacqueline Lesschaeve, 1985.

Contemporary popular culture

A term used for the taste of the general population of today; the audience taste which a choreographer may wish to bear in mind when presenting dance works.

Eds. from David Jary and Julia Jary, 1991.

Constructing identity

"When I look at a dance I perceive something of the work's identity, its individuality. Not only do I perceive it — I consciously construct it. That is, I imbue the work with the meaning I find there as a viewer (or critic). This requires both my perceptual grasp and conscious integration of the work."

Sondra Fraleigh, 1991.

Dialogue with self, To have a

In Butoh, the intention of the director as to how the audience should respond to the work, not to receive a message or comprehend but to respond with a feeling which initiates a self-discussion.

Ushio Amagatsu, Interview.

Drawn, To be

The eye of the spectator to be attracted by the performer to focus on the face, arms and chest, the centre of human feeling.

Carla Maxwell, Interview.

Educate the audience, To

One function of a choreographer, to present the audience with unfamiliar circumstances for the familiar, to prod them into re-evaluating conventions, to wake them into active appreciators of dance.

Ashley Page, Interview.

Emotional experience
     How some choreographers want their work to be perceived/received by the audience. The work is not an "objet-trouvé" with an existence outside of the artist-performance-audience context; said of the Ausdruckstänzer and Tanztheater artists.
     Ana R. Sanchez-Colberg, 1992.

Engage your audience, To
     To intrigue your spectators through a level of sophistication and direction.
     Judith Mackrell, Interview.

Enjoy, To
     To take pleasure in the movements of a dancer, in the harmony of a pose, in the contrast of curve and line, in the swift-sharp-soft fluidity of a phrase, and so on, for their own sake without feeling the need to define their meaning.
     Selma Jeanne Cohen, 1967.

Entertainment value
     The quality in a work from the audience's point of view, that a choreographer bears in mind; said of a work which holds their attention immediately.
     "Is it getting boring?", "Is it uncomfortably going on a bit?".
     Gillian Lynne, Interview.

Expectation, of the audience
     The preconceptions that the public bring with them to a performance.
     "[They come] with a set of expectations regarding the nature of the dance event they are going to experience. These expectations contain within them an implicit set of criteria upon which they base their interpretations and evaluation of the event. Both expectations and criteria are grounded in the social, cultural, artistic and historical milieux of which the individual has experience, as well as in experiences of a more personal nature. The more distanced a work is from those expectations the more active a role the spectator must take in order to engage in the world/s the work is projecting."
     Sarah Rubidge, Contributed.

Express, To
     "To express or to give form to something to be received by an other, whether in words or in movement, is to manifest one's body toward the other. The knower (the other) and the known (the dancer) become dynamically interrelated in a communicative process through the object (the dance), which mediates what can be known (the substance of the dance)."
     Sondra Fraleigh, 1987.

Focus on, To
     To attend to; to converge on; a way of looking by the audience which the designer is concerned to influence by making the set and costumes readable.
     "They should focus on what I want them to focus on."
     Nicholas Georgiardis, Interview.

Frontality

Facing the audience, a traditional way of presenting the dancer in Bharata Natyam, where it is regarded as rude to "turn your back on your audience — they feel slighted".
Shobana Jeyasingh, Interview.

Go with it, To

As a spectator, to be engaged with the dance, to be brought into it and along with it by the artist.
Bessie Schoenberg, Interview.

Idealist

What Jack Anderson calls a dancegoer who regards dance as the incarnation in movement of ideas or effects, who does not object to steps being changed in revivals so long as the central concepts and the same overall effect are given.
Jack Anderson, 1975-76.

Images

"The dancer deals not just with movement, but with the motivational source, idea, or metaphor behind the movement, that which the movement will bring to mind. Even if the dance is stylistically abstract, it will draw our attention to its unique unfolding of movement patterns in space-time. Movement patterns are also images, and they impress the imagination, as the word 'image' implies."
Sondra Fraleigh, 1991.

Imaginary world

"Every dance invites the audience to enter an imaginary world. A dramatic dance is an invitation to enter a world of people, actions, thoughts and feelings, to ponder upon the events which unfold and their social significance."
Hettie Loman, 1988.

Imaginative participation

A way of appreciating dance works which is intimate and personal, involving the spectator's will to engage with the two intellectually, through kinaesthetic empathy, through emotional involvement and through allowing his imagination to respond to the work.
Francine M. Watson Coleman, 1986.

Impact of the music

Audience's response to the music of a choreographic work, their memory of a work by its music.
"...the one with funky bass line...", "...the one with the jazzy rhythm...", "...the one with the singer...".
Nicholas Mojsiejenko, Interview.

Instinctive or retrospective

The quality of a response to a dance performance, immediate through viewing of it, or the quality that emerges from a study of it through which the layers of structure become available.

Judith Mackrell, Interview.

Interest

The quality of attention brought to a performance by the audience and maintained by the quality of the work itself, so that what is in it is not obviously given but must be sought by the audience themselves.

Selma Jeanne Cohen, 1967.

Joy of dance

An experience for both dancer and spectator.

"The result of what I do, of dancing well and expressing what I want to get across."

Peter Dunleavy, Interview.

Kinaesthetic or emotional perception

The inexpressible dialogue occurring between dancers, and between dancers and audience; the experienced sensation over and above what can be reiterated in words.

Walter Sorell, 1976.

Kinetic empathy

"...the inherent contagion of bodily movement which makes the onlooker feel sympathetically in his own musculature the exertions he sees in somebody else's musculature."

John Martin in Roger Copeland and Marshall Cohen, 1983 (1946).

Kinetic responsiveness

"...the brand of empathy that most directly unites the dancer and his or her audience."

Roger Copeland in Roger Copeland and Marshall Cohen, 1983.

Labelling

What an audience does while looking at a work, putting it in a category, "ballet, South Asian, jazz, African", and so seeing it as a much more culture-specific work than it in fact is.

Shobana Jeyasingh, Interview.

Look anew

To create a work which so presents familiar and unfamiliar material that the audience are possibly made uncomfortable, and in any case are forced to look 'with new eyes' at dance material.

Ashley Page, Interview.

Materialist

What Jack Anderson calls the dancegoer who regards dance as an assemblage of specific steps from which ideas or effects may be derived, who expects exact replication of those steps in a revival, and anticipates and tolerates the inevitable different effect.

Jack Anderson, 1975-1976.

Metakinesis

Muscular and kinaesthetic sympathy linking the dancer's intention with the viewer's perception of it.

John Martin, 1972 (1933).

Motor responsiveness

The appreciation of a dance work through responding bodily to it, in opposition to, or along with, intellectual knowledge of the work.

John Martin, 1972 (1933).

Move the spirit, To

The objective of art work; said of choreographies which attend to the aesthetic experience of the audience, in contrast to the lack of communication of many postmodernist dance pieces.

Peter Brinson, 1991.

Movement thinking

Receiving and issuing sophisticated meanings communicated through movement which convey self-expression of a kind which cannot be verbalised, in a more rapid and compact manner than speech.

Roderyk Lange, 1975.

Movement which tells

Not narrative movement but material that demands an emotional response from the audience.

Siobhan Davies, 1988.

Not communicating

"When the choreographer presents movement in and for its own sake, he is not communicating. Such movement has its own significant purpose of filling the audience with wonder and delight."

Erick Hawkins, 1966.

Participate, To

To take part in a dance; said of a performer, and of spectators when they see themselves as part of the work itself.

Eds.

Participating audience

Taking part in the dance event as a spectator by clapping, singing, shouting encouragement, possibly joining in; a social dance occurrence.

Robert Harrold, Interview.

Pleasurable

The response of the audience to the sensuality of a dancer moving, through the shared physicality of humanness.

Francine M. Watson Coleman, 1986.

Polyattentiveness

A John Cage term.

"...the simultaneous apprehension of two or more unrelated phenomena."

Roger Copeland in Roger Copeland and Marshall Cohen, 1983.

Pop dance

Dance which "never confronts the audience with anything heavy" and "which aims to offer that kind of gratification."

Marcia Siegel, 1979.

Prediction and speculation

Attitudes of audience members towards the way in which recognised movement material may appear, or may be resolved; ways in which they guess or imagine what might be going to happen.

Lucinda Childs in Sally Banes, 1980.

Psychological time of a work

The density of experience in the allotted time span of a work, duration filled with experience.

Robert Coleridge, Interview.

Reassemble meaning, To

What an audience may seek when confronted by material which is disjointed, which comes from different sources, and has a Dadaist and Surrealist structuring.

Ian Spink in National Resource Centre for Dance, 1988.

Recognition

"[Anderson's 'Clump']...relies upon the audience's recognition of those aspects of society upon which it comments."

Fiona Burnside, 1990.

Repetitive structuring

Work in which material is repeated, not in variety, but straight so that it appears to be a series of beginnings and endings; said of work presented in a gallery which, while being continuous for hours on end, is cut up so that spectators are guided in when to come and go.

Rosemary Butcher, Interview.

Rhythmic discipline

The experience of rhythm in the body by the audience as well as by the performer, which transforms the spectator from a "passive" observer to one who feels himself "to be the work of art"; said referring to Jaques-Dalcroze's Eurhythmics.

Adolphe Appia in Denis Bablet and Marie-Louise Bablet, 1982.

Seeing and knowing

"The eye tries to recognize what it already knows. It is like security.... It takes anybody a long time to really see something new."

Merce Cunningham in Merce Cunningham and Jacqueline Lesschaeve, 1985.

Superimposing

Projecting on to the dance that we see indefinable qualities which are its meaning, not any qualities but those which, by analogy, we feel intuitively to be there; hence in the "Dying Swan" we participate in the death and do not see a woman representing in ballet a bird dying.

Francine M. Watson Coleman, 1986.

Take notice, To

An audience's response to a work which has some ability to arouse, through shock, through discomfort, through hilarity, through curiosity.

Mark Murphy, Interview.

Time goes into slow motion, When

The experience of the audience when the density of the event being watched and heard is so great that one minute of it contains as much psychological experience as much, much longer of clock time. There is one other way of achieving this — long drones in which nothing happens also achieve similar effects.

Robert Coleridge, Interview.

Two-way current, The

The quality of an actor affecting an audience, their concentration affecting the actor's performance.

Peter Brook, 1990 (1968).

Understanding a dance

Noticing the features (formal and otherwise) of the dance — in the light of the traditions and conventions of the artform — so as to be able either to make sense of the dance or to recognise a critic's 'reading' of that dance as encapsulating (or beginning to encapsulate) one's own view. Understanding dances should be recognised as typically only partial, since understanding is not 'all-or-nothing' — thus one may begin to understand a dance, or understand only part of it.

Graham McFee, 1992.

Unforgiving work

One which is hard on the audience, demanding concentration from beginning to end.

Ashley Page, Interview.

Union

One kind of relationship of an audience to the performer, a process of being 'in the same field' as the performer, generating a sense of wonder in the spectator.

Jodi Falk, Interview.

Visually literate

A quality in an informed audience who can read the metaphors embedded in the design; equally, visually illiterate for those who cannot.

Nicholas Georgiardis, Interview.

Voyeuristic

An attitude in a spectator towards the dance and dancers of a performance which is one of a prying observer, an attitude caused by the contextuality of a production in an unsuitable venue.

Maggie Semple, 1992.

Watching to wonder at

Show pieces, often in the ballet genre, which exploit the athleticism of dancers, providing audiences with the opportunity to "wonder at and share kinaesthetically the achievement of human bodies" but fail to stir the mind.

Peter Brinson, 1991.

Adjudication

What judges do at a dance competition, holding up number cards if an open marking system is used.

Derek Young, 1991.

Technical merit

In Latin American dance, a term used by juries to denote excellence in tacitly agreed performance criteria associated with details of steps, body carriage, rhythm, etc.

Ruud Vermey, Interview.

Artistic merit

In Latin American dance, a term used by juries to denote aspects of the couples' routines which are not covered by Technical merit, but what these qualities are is not agreed or stated.

Ruud Vermey, Interview.

Merit

The essential qualities in competitive dance, when the 'fundamental action' of each dance is something precious to maintan and the 'characterisation through personality' is the way each couple makes it their own.

Geoffrey Hearn, Interview.

Evaluating a dance

Using criteria of value, either stated or implicit, judging the dance against those criteria, defending the judgement in terms sharable with others who might see the work.

Pauline Hodgens in Janet Adshead, 1988.

2. SPECTATORS' VIEW/PERFORMERS' VIEW

Two simultaneous experiences

What the artist making the work experiences and what the audience sees, two distinct and disparate perceptions but both of which the choreographer plays with.

Trisha Brown, 1987.

Emotional place, An

An illusory ambience which a dance creates, a place which the choreographer might not fully anticipate but which emerges through the process of work up to and beyond the premiere.

Siobhan Davies, 1988.

Formal separation

Even when touching or weight bearing, there is a difference between the onlooker's perception of it as personal closeness and the experience of it as a formal choreographic device.

Alan Salter, 1977.

Self-expression

"Because a choreographer is deeply motivated, he feels what he is saying and thinks he is communicating to the audience, but if he is not aware of how what he wants to say is expressed in its physical form, they won't get it."

Doris Rudko, Interview.

Sensation of proximity

What a performer experiences as clear awareness of another's presence across the space between them, contrasted with what is perceived by an onlooker as separateness and distance.

Alan Salter, 1977.

Expression and impression

The power of movement to be a means of expression of the individual as artist and as person together with its power to impress both the person moving and the spectator through its kinetic experience and kinetic images.

Marion North, Interview.

Private image, A

The dancer's own image, not intended to be communicated as a legible sign, but nevertheless infusing her movement with interest.

Stephanie Jordan, 1992.

Interpretations

The concept that a dance work will say different things to different people at different times and that to look for one meaning, the 'truth' of the work, is misguided.

Chris Challis, 1991.

Emitters and Receivers

The terms for the artists creating a work and the spectators of it when the work intends to communicate a message; a term from semiotics.

Eds.

Virtuosity

A display of skill for its own sake that stirs a kinesthetic response of wonder and delight in the viewer.

Selma Jeanne Cohen, 1982.

3.   LEGIBILITY

Issue of 'legibility'

"Searching for ways of maintaining the viewer's understanding of structure whilst challenging their perception."

Stephanie Jordan, 1992.

Dance literacy

The ability to read a dance, to discern its syntax, its organising structures, its means of communication.

Shobana Jeyasingh, Interview.

Meanings given off

What a dance work provides for an audience, whether the choreographer intended them or not.

Dorothy Madden, Interview.

Credibility
>   The quality and references within a work which enable the audience to believe in it.
>   *Mark Murphy*, Interview.

Speak, To
>   "Dance is communication and the great desire is to speak clearly and beautifully and with inevitability."
>   *Martha Graham*, 1957.

Reading movement
>   Understanding the content of the movement of a dance through the music with which it is presented.
>   "You read movement according to your ears."; "The music gives the sentiment."
>   *Twyla Tharp*, Informal talk.

Neutrality
>   The materials of the dance, the actual steps, the dynamics, the dancers etc. carry meaning which is distinct from meaning provided by the spectator himself and by the context of the performance.
>   *Pauline Hodgens* in Janet Adshead, 1988.

Understanding a dance
>   Interrelating the knowledge of the dance which is derived from its socio-cultural background, its context, its genre, and its style, all of which contribute to its meaning.
>   *Pauline Hodgens* in Janet Adshead, 1988.

Dance message, The
>   The content of the work, as intentionally given by the artists and received by the audience; either in the form of 'the medium as message' or as carrying a message by the medium.
>   *Valerie Preston-Dunlop*, Interview.

Picture, A
>   An image for an audience which the dancer achieves through precise timing and spatial form, together with narrative content.
>   *Lea Anderson*, Interview.

Graphic
>   Narrative work in a ballet which is explicit in its references; said of MacMillan's "Manon" and "Mayerling".
>   *Ashley Page*, Interview.

Readability
Consistently overt ways of using features of form to tell a narrative; in Christopher Bruce's "Swan Song": the prisoner's chair as a safe haven, threat of force given by the warders tap dancing in unison, the shaft of light as a message of release, the red nose as a symbol of ridicule.
Valerie Preston-Dunlop, Interview.

Work for an audience, To
The choreography and the dancers' interpretation together have to convey for the spectator what the idea is; the slight gestural movement, the tension of the back of a neck or of a touch can overdo or underplay the incident so that it does not read for the audience.
Maude Lloyd, 1984.

Character and mood
The two sorts of things that a moving dancer can convey: what kind of person he is, and, what state of feeling he has at that moment, in various stages of particularity or abstraction.
Selma Jeanne Cohen, 1967.

Emotional nudity
Feeling expressed in the raw, bare and undressed, a feature of expressionist dance; to be presentable, feeling needs abstraction and restrain.
Margaret N. H'Doubler, 1957 (1940).

Communicability of dance
The inherent ability of dance to communicate through the mix of performer and movement.
"By failing to find a completely objective approach, and by failing to disguise the dancer's individual body language, my awareness of the communicability of dance has increased."
Paul Taylor, "Private Domain", 1987.

Reading a work's body politics
Deconstructing the body politics of a dance work through the movement choices in the choreography; said of the reciprocal relationship of men and women in Siobhan Davies's work seen through the equal giving and taking of bodily weight by both partners.
Helen Thomas, Interview.

Communication in dance
A sensual way of people reaching each other, not literal, but one of feeling, of "touching personal moods"; said of the work of some community choreographers.
Peter Brinson, 1991.

Direct physicality

The language of a dance, its vocabulary, which is overtly sensual and to which an audience has a direct response; said of Meg Stuart's work.

Mary Brennan, 1992.

Movement sense

A movement makes sense only if it progresses organically in a natural succession.

Rudolf Laban, 1966 (1939).

Dance logic

The relations in a dance which appear to appear; why something apparently alien is seen to belong and provide a logic which is not cerebral but visceral.

Bessie Schoenberg, Interview.

Action moods

Expressions of mood created by the combination of how the body is used, spatially or rhythmically such as lyric, solemn, grotesque, serious.

Rudolf Laban, 1971 (1950).

Inevitability

An "elusive quality" best described as the quality of a work which "flows with a mad logic of its own" and gives "absolute certainty and rigor of its conception" and is thus readable while resisting literal translation; said of Bill Jones and Arnie Zane.

Alan M. Kriegsman, 1984.

Posture pattern interpretation

The way in which postures are 'read', the reading is culture-bound and is interpretable by individuals who share the same cultural code or conventions.

Warren Lamb and *Elizabeth Watson*, 1979.

Relate to an audience on a human level, To

"We don't dance mechanically, we're not fictitious. We relate on a very human level.... I do think the people who come to see us get the feeling it could be them we're talking about, or dancing about."

Alvin Ailey in Elinor Rogosin, 1980.

Speaking through the movement

Communicating by the movement itself by the endowment that the performer gives; the dramatic subtext inevitable by a human being, a person, dancing the dance; said of Limón works.

Carla Maxwell, Interview.

Human element

The ingredient in a ballet which can touch the audience, the feelings generated between people which can become an overriding factor of dance, shifting the emphasis from appreciation of the movement per se.

Ashley Page, Interview.

Graham vocabulary

A lexicon of movement developed to communicate human feeling in the most economical way by reflecting the body in states of emotion.

Bonnie Bird, Interview.

Assault the audience's eye, To

Violent dance reflecting the violence of popular culture, in contrast to work which requires careful looking.

"...coming at you with hammer and tongs...".

Jane Dudley, Interview.

Dancers as people

"Robbins's 'Fancy Free' was completely realistic in its portrayal of how people lived in America."

Edwin Denby, 1968.

Formal language

A dance vocabulary in which "every movement has an understood meaning, like some oriental dances" (not what Jooss used himself).

Kurt Jooss, 1933.

Cultural idiosyncracies

"The confusion in communication arises when audiences feel that hand gestures (of Bharata Natyam) always convey literal 'one to one' meanings. The reality is that they can also be used in an abstract way to add expressive detail to the body."

Shobana Jeyasingh, Interview.

Speak, To

The ability of movement to have a "clear meaning", not in terms of a fixed formal language, used to convey stories and moods exactly, but in terms of a movement reaching an audience as containing legible content of some kind.

Kurt Jooss, 1933.

Natural affinities

An affinity between the movement and the context in which it is done, so that it falls within the accepted norms of behaviour; the movement is easily read and suggests no ambiguity.

Norbert Servos, 1980.

Macro-context and Micro-contexts

The context of a whole dance, or the contexts within a dance, even of one movement, which provide some means of reading the dance.

Valerie Preston-Dunlop, 1987.

Reading non-literal ballet

"It [the audience] does not identify the gestures with reference to real life, it does not search in each pose for a distinct descriptive allusion. It watches the movements in sequence as a dance...when the dance is over one understands it as a whole...".

Edwin Denby, 1968.

Abstract form

A dance which does not lead the audience to interpret it in terms of a connection to human feeling and the human condition.

Doris Rudko, Interview.

Image of intention

The meaningful statement which dancers can make with formal movement, intending nothing more than to do that which is in the shape and rhythm of the material.

Robert Cohan, Company class.

Anatomical statements

What a dancer can communicate by paying attention to the syntax of a movement language, such as that of Graham's technical vocabulary.

Robert Cohan, Company class.

Title

It should identify the work.

Monica Parker, Interview.

Title

"A title is a lifeline thrown to the audience."

Louis Horst, 1958.

Titling

Indicating to the audience one aspect of content which might be in conflict with other aspects; said of Lea Anderson's "Pastorale", made after the hurricane in which pastoral scenes were devastated; hence the restricted costume, and harsh music, spatial squashedness.

Lea Anderson, Interview.

Title

A description of the work's content with possibly more than one layer for the audience to hold on to.

"'Fall Like Rain' — falling mansoon train, falling in love, falling into and onto, falling over...".

Darshan Singh Bhuller, Interview.

Titles as puns
> Titles which suggest more than one layer of content; said of Emilyn Claid's "For Play", Nicky Smedley's "Rock".
> *Ian Bramley*, 1993.

Program notes
> Short explanation of a ballet, put there to aid the audience; a practice which some choreographers regard as unnecessary.
> "I believe the stage action should be totally explanatory...movement should not be less total than is a score of a piece of music."
> *Anthony Tudor* in Muriel Topaz, 1986.

Programme note
> Additional words written in the programme beyond the title and credits, that "give the audience information that makes them feel comfortable", but "will influence the way they look at the work".
> *Richard Alston*, Conversation with Darshan Singh Bhuller.

At the cutting edge
> Said of work which is made for the immediate present, made to be seen now in the mood of the moment; which begs the question: "will it be relevant in 15 years' time?".
> *Judith Mackrell*, Interview.

Comtemporariness
> A quality in a choreographic work which speaks of today.
> *Bonnie Bird*, Interview.

4. OPENING THE MEANING

Keep open the meaning, To
> A way of choreographing in which the spectator's "distilling process" can operate; said in contrast to making work in which the spectator has little room to use his imaginative interpretation.
> *Ana R. Sanchez-Colberg*, 1992.

Manifestative
> A term used for that part of a work which expresses a subjective way of experiencing rather than one which represents the world through clearly grasped references; the manifestative meanings in dance are realised through the imagination.
> *Margaret N. H'Doubler*, 1957 (1940).

Audience's attention

"She [Tharp] is less and less interested in the formal separation of audience and performer and has begun to create her works more and more in such a manner that an audience, which may not see all of a work, will pay more attention to what it can see."
Don McDonagh, 1969.

Impressionistic

The overall style of a dance work, not one which is expressive of clearly denotive images, nor one that is a formal work, but one which offers images for which an audience can find their own meanings within a given range.
Laurie Booth, Interview.

Journey, A

What a successful choreographer can take the audience on, a varied yet organic experience distinct from a logical narrative.
Susan Sentler, Interview.

Ambiguity

The presentation of dance material as having more than one meaning through using devices which disintegrate what would otherwise be a unified expression, or inserting and omitting material which will make the spectator question his reading of the work.
Eds.

Ambiguity

The intentional quality of a work which, within limits, allows the audience to see more than one meaning in a work, see something else on second viewing, see something different from another viewer, see early images which the choreographer himself has forgotten are in it.
Christopher Bruce, Interview.

Shadowy piece

A description by Richard Alston of his work-in-the-making, "The Perilous Night" to Cage's score of the same name; intended to be clear in its overall mood, "a troubled piece", but open to interpretation by its mix of formal material, of changing speeds and dynamic, with occasional behavioural signs.
Richard Alston, Rehearsing with Darshan Singh Bhuller.

Evocative work

A dance which avoids direct statement but gives an overall texture through which a situation, a feeling, can be aroused.
"Are they children, grownups, dancers, militant South Africans, or angry young men? Whichever, it is a violent, unsolvable situation."
Christopher Bruce, Interview.

Audience choices

Leaving the audience free to interpret the dance fragments in their own way, not because the material is 'abstract' but because of its intentionally fragmented and jumbled structuring.

Ian Spink in National Resource Centre for Dance, 1988.

Dual-visual level of expressionist dance

The real central figure, the unreal actions, abstract in character, causing a confused message, demanding two levels of communication from the audience.

Alwin Nikolais, 1963.

Contra-contextual

When the movement and the context or the performer appear to be inappropriate or alien, giving contrary messages to each other.

Laban Centre for Movement and Dance, 1991.

Multiplicity

Layers of meaning in a work in which many "meaningful associations" are offered for the audience to interpret as they will; said of Pina Bausch.

Raimund Hoghe, 1980.

Unpredictable

Movement material which does not follow rules that can be read by an audience, so that several simultaneous strategies are accepted to structure the work and avoid predictability.

Trisha Brown, 1987.

Presentational form

Cunningham term.

"We have to meet the artist halfway. We have to bring something before we can bring something away. More and more the artist is a man bringing something to our attention just to make of it what we will or perhaps just what we can."

Clive Barnes, 1968.

What dance is 'about'

"Cunningham himself does not think his dances are 'about' anything, but he is willing to accept the fact that others may find specific ways to interpret them."; "The meaning is there if that's what you want." (Cunningham).

Calvin Tomkins, 1974.

Deny all outside reference, To

To make dance works on the assumption that they can be 'abstract', that is that they refer to nothing but themselves, despite the fact that audiences will read some meaning into them, come what may.

Rosemary Butcher, 1988.

Emotional wash through movement or music

"In dance there are many roles that are not specifically dramatic. But there is a sort of emotional kind of wash, like a hue or color, that comes through choreographically in the movements or through the music."
Elinor Rogosin, 1980.

Non-literal sound

"A whole level of sound which causes emotional response but which cannot be identified in words."
Alwin Nikolais, 1963.

5. WAYS OF COMMUNICATING

Expression in dance

A species of the expressiveness of the arts in general, involving the recognising of a dancework as art (and as intended as art) in ways which permit the spectator to make sense of that work — typically requiring that the spectator make sense of the features of the work (formal and otherwise) against a background of the traditions and conventions of the artform.
Graham McFee, 1992.

Movement emphasis

The chosen emphasis in the means of communication of a choreographic work:-
"In Transitions, we can't carry sets, or elaborate projections, or pay for extravagant costuming."; "We emphasise the dancers' experience of communicating through movement — mixed media pieces may come their way later."
Bonnie Bird, Interview.

Gestural language

"...the gestural communication within a culture...differences in the profound symbolic meaning of cultural systems of gesture bring about different dance styles."
Suzanne Walther, 1979.

Semiotic content of space

The shared meanings which space contains and adds to dancers' movement, for an audience, according to where the performers are in relation to each other and in relation to the audience, especially in proscenium space.
Laurie Booth, Interview.

Signification

One manner in which meaning is transmitted to an audience, through signs embedded in the dance medium which can be read; said of the strained body posture used by Nijinsky in "Le Sacre du Printemps" to embody 'ordeal' which ceremonies and sacrifices and ritual games contain.
Millicent Hodson, 1986.

Dance sign and symbol

The denotative features of a work (signs) and the connotative features (symbols), that is those features which provide an unmistakable meaning and those which suggest an area of meaning.

Helen Thomas, Interview.

Spiritual sign

What dance can be in liturgical dance, a "sign of the spirituality of matter and a means of offering spiritual/physical wellbeing."

J.G. Davies, 1984.

Symbolic vocabulary

Movement material carrying meaning, material which stands for something significant; said of Graham's "Heretic" (1929) when she uses mechanical movement reminiscent of the machine to stand not for machinery but for the mechanical tradition of mindless bureaucracy and formula — "straight lines, angular gestures, geometric formation".

Agnes de Mille, 1991.

Virtuosity as symbol

The human desire to soar, to reach for the moon, to climb the mountain, expressed in virtuosity, and danced with that intention.

Akim Lvovitch Volynsky, 1972 (1925).

Metaphors of orientation

Devices in a dance work in which 'upside down' or 'up the wall' or 'beside yourself' are conveyed through both movement and manipulation of the set.

Mark Murphy, Interview.

Metaphors of the skill

The use of traditional circus skills such as juggling, aerial work, balancing, not for their trick value but as metaphors for the hazards of daily life.

"...juggling with alternatives, walking on a tightrope...".

Helen Crocker and *Bim Mason*, Interview.

Aerialist skills

Using a circus artist's skills in theatre or opera as a metaphor; said of the movement material on trapeze in Janacek's "The Cunning Little Vixen" choreographed by Stuart Hopps.

Stuart Hopps, Interview.

Movement lie

"I eventually appreciated the artistry of a movement lie — the guilty tail wagging, the overly steady gaze, the phoney humility of drooping shoulders and caved-in chest, the decorative-looking little shuffles of pretended pain, the heavy, monumental dances of mock happiness."

Paul Taylor, "Private Domain", 1987.

Dance illusion

What is set up by the dance.
Murray Louis, 1969.

Illusion making

Knowing what has to happen onstage in order to "lead people into believing" that something else is happening.
Peter Dunleavy, Rehearsal.

Spatial illusions

Using movement, focus, grouping, entrances and exits, lighting, to give an impression of space as infinite, then space as enclosed, space as "a place".
Susan Sentler, Interview.

Break the dance illusion

To bring reality into the dance by using words.
Murray Louis, 1969.

Secondary affinities

Movement material which draws on gesture, body language and interpersonal behaviour but distorts one aspect of it so providing it with a strangeness; an ingredient in the defamiliarisation process used by Bausch.
Ana R. Sanchez-Colberg, 1992.

Defamiliarisation

A device in which movement material, or gender roles, which have a social norm, are altered in one aspect to make the audience look at familiar things anew; for example, in a foxtrot hold, touching the partner's forehead instead of hand, embracing but with straight arms, dressed in male attire but with one high-heeled woman's shoe.
Norbert Servos, 1980.

Subvert, To

To choreographic device in which a domestic set, such as a living room, and the movement in it, is put on its side or upside down, so that the audience, having a bird's eye view, are invited to see the world in another way.
Mark Murphy, Interview.

Stake the territory, To

To focus the audience in the opening section of a dance on the subject matter to be explored in the work as a whole.
Judith Mackrell, Interview.

Hold an audience, To

The entertainment strength of a dance or a musical, in the sense of engaging the interest and feelings of the spectators throughout the performance, through what there is to be done and by how that is done by the cast.
Gillian Lynne, Interview.

Demands of the stage

What a theatrical situation demands and must be accepted, namely pacing, rhythmic vitality, humour, and content, in order to hold the audience's attention, not private meditation.

Jane Dudley, Interview.

Density of dance information

The amount and complexity of information in dance material which an audience can absorb; the way a choreographer can increase the density with audiences who know his work or who are well informed in dance.

Stephanie Jordan, 1992.

Ambush the onlooker's imagination, To

What experimental choreography can do when it succeeds in reaching an audience unexpectedly caught by innovation.

Mary Brennan, 1992.

Shock, To

To provide an audience with a work which tests the unspoken etiquette of ballet or of a particular company's use of ballet.

Monica Parker, Interview.

Clichés

Movements in dances and well-known dance solos "which are done to death"; "like the story of Krishna stealing butter", and the "Sugar Plum Fairy" in ballet, which become clichéd and difficult to present with freshness.

Shobana Jeyasingh, Interview.

Demasculinise choreographically

A way of presenting a man in dance through giving him movement material which is traditionally female, a device used by Michael Clarke and further supported by cross-dressing.

Helen Thomas, Interview.

Plotless ballet

"Even plotless ballet, which is nothing but men and women dancing, is anything but non-representational or 'non-human'...", "...here the dramatic element can be isolated as it were from narrative and specifics...".

Clive Barnes, 1961.

Space conscious

"...aware of the dramatic implications of the vision of the individual pitted against the universe...space [as] a protagonist in the dance...".

Hanya Holm in Walter Sorell, 1976.

Path traveled

"The road we travel, our path in space, indicates where we are going, where we come from, and who we are. In and of itself, the path that the dancer travels is a contributing factor to the dance."

Lynne Anne Blom and *L. Tarin Chaplin*, 1982.

Unintended undercurrents

"Somehow in the process of working out the dance I've found that certain unintended emotional undercurrents have cropped up. Moving slowly to fast music sometimes seems to give the dancer a look of inner excitement, and its opposite—".

Paul Taylor, "Private Domain", 1987.

Play of environment

The chance coexistence of elements in the spatial environment which play on the moving figure, so adding an ingredient which influences the content of the dance for the audience: OR environmental influence by design, such as Meredith Monk's use of three environments in the same dance.

Doris Rudko, Interview.

Particularised moods

"...Taylor's dances have moods — moods usually established, enhanced, and particularized by their sets, costumes and lighting."

Nancy Vreeland Dalva, 1989.

Expressive unit

The bit of dance which is capable of being read by an audience, which, if pantomime, is small (one look, one gesture), but is more likely to be as long as a phrase or even an extended passage.

Selma Jeanne Cohen, 1967.

Organic form

"...is significant form. It is a fusion of outward form with inner imagery."

Margaret H'Doubler, 1974.

Form

"True form comes from reducing reality to its essential shape; form is emotional, exciting."

Anna Sokolow in Selma Jeanne Cohen, 1977.

Consistency of movement quality

The way the dynamic and spatial qualities are set up and retained throughout a dance/variation/solo, so that, however 'abstract' it sets out to be, meaning emerges because the dance qualities suggest qualities of human behaviour; without consistency no meaning is suggested.

Selma Jeanne Cohen, 1967.

Emotional gesture

The patterned and recognisable movements of emotional states.
Doris Humphrey, 1959.

Independent and interactional

Two modes of interpersonal behaviour in which the body movement of one person gives off information to another on a preference to function together or a preference to function alone; the information is supplied by moving according to the natural affinities of space and dynamics in movement (interactional) or against the affinity (independent); a concept especially useful in coaching dance expression for performance.
Valerie Preston-Dunlop with *Warren Lamb*, Contributed.

Spiritual in dance, The

"The arts...are never a religion in themselves, never objects of worship, but are the symbol and language for communicating spiritual truths."
Ruth St. Denis in Walter Sorell, 1951.

Climax

In cross-art forms, where the traditional climax of skill and, for clowns, of the expectation of failure, is replaced by 'emotional climax' or the climax of theatrical tension.
Helen Crocker and *Bim Mason*, Interview.

Distillation of ballet steps

"They [ballet steps] have become so distilled that people now have a distance from that kind of movement vocabulary."
Twyla Tharp in British Broadcasting Corporation, 1983.

Performance

That part of working in circus and physical theatre which turns technical expertise into an act of communicative theatre.
Helen Crocker and *Bim Mason*, Interview.

Dance discourse

The dances within an event which are purposefully arranged in an order and regarded as having some communicative function.
"The hierarchical, structural, and semantic unit composed of all dances performed at a certain event."
Anca Giurchescu, 1987.

Hum surrounding a work

A term used by Jowitt to describe the reactions and responses to a work.
"Critical writing, along with the responses (public and private) to what is written, lobby conversations, interviews, dancers' tales and so on cling to a dance performance, making it resonate in the memory, prolonging its life."
Deborah Jowitt, 1985.

Self-expression
        "Self-expression is an expression of life and comes from within...the visible expression of our invisible selves...".
        Diana Jordan, 1938.

6.   COMMUNICATING THROUGH VIDEO/FILM/TV

Television
        A medium which treats the narrative elements of a dance immediately through direct imagery and which finds non-narrative works difficult.
        "A story-telling medium."
        Bob Lockyer, Interview.

Active and passive observer
        The camera, shifting from passive in long shot, full view of the dance, to active in close up by 'choosing' what to observe.
        Jayne Dowdeswell, 1993.

Identify with, To
        What video audiences do with the people in the works they watch, much influenced by the way the camera work gives importance to one performer or another.
        Bob Lockyer, Interview.

Viewer manipulation
        Camera work in dance and music videos which direct the viewer to look at the movement from one performer's point of view; said of the duet "Running up that Hill" (1985), music video of Kate Bush.
        Jayne Dowdeswell, 1993.

Zooming in
        Using a zoom lens to 'home in' on one point or performer, which the viewer is then able to see intimately and invited to identify with; illustrated by Yolande Snaith's and Terry Braun's "Step in Time Girls" (1988).
        Jayne Dowdeswell, 1993.

Language of dance
        The structure and images in dance which the video director and cameraman need to understand in order to let the choreography "speak for itself".
        Bob Lockyer, Interview.

Camera views
        Worm's eye view, bird's eye view, tilted view, low and high view, as well as camera focus, so dictating the viewers' perception of the dance and creating illusions; used in Vandekeybus's "Roseland" (1989), Belinda Neave's "The Dance House Project" (1992), Lea Anderson's "Flesh and Blood" (1990).
        Jayne Dowdeswell, 1993.

Mutual performer
　　The camera used as a performer by approaching and retreating, tilting, tracking, and panning, giving the viewer a sense of mingling with the dancers in their space; used by Cunningham in "Channels/Inserts".
　　Jayne Dowdeswell, 1993.

Compress the space, To
　　What one view of a dance may do, giving the appearance of a tight group of people compressed together; "to cut up wide" would open the space, spoil the image and show little figures in a large space.
　　Bob Lockyer, Interview.

Screen time/stage time
　　The contrast between the way the video cuts dictate the spectator's viewing of the work, while in the theatre the spectator's eye can roam and select at will, at his own pace.
　　Bob Lockyer, Interview.

Video dance — dynamics
　　The dynamics of the dance work dictated by the camera work.
　　"On stage, as opposed to video, the dynamics do not depend on the camera; it's in the look of the dance."
　　Merce Cunningham in Merce Cunningham and Jacqueline Lesschaeve, 1985.

Interrupted flow
　　The disjointedness of the dancer's continuity which occurs during the filming of a dance for TV, video, or film and which alters the meaning of the work.
　　Siobhan Davies, Seminar.

PART SEVEN: DANCE RESEARCH

Some approaches to research in dance and dancing are given here, divided according to the traditional disciplines from which researchers come, and according to the newer disciplines emerging from within dance practice. Conflicting viewpoints can be found and a sense of a developing body of knowledge, mixing theory and practice, emerges. Some more esoteric areas of research complete this overview. Inevitably there is an emphasis on British-based work, for pragmatic reasons.

Chapter 20 DANCE RESEARCH

1. DANCE SCHOLARSHIP

Dance scholarship
"A partnership between verbal and non-verbal knowledge, requiring a balance between theory and practice and a broad interdisciplinary approach."
Peter Brinson, 1991.

Dance scholarship
A refreshingly young, even naïve, domain, compared with that of English literature, for which the established modes of discourse have yet to be rewritten for dance to find its own scholarly language and concepts.
Judith Mackrell, Interview.

Preliteracy of dance
The period of dance history before literacy was possible through adequate dance notation systems; by these, dance 'texts' could be studied and with a strong critical tradition be analysed; said with knowledge that notation is "not yet a widespread tool of dance scholarship".
Peter Brinson, 1991.

Schrifttanz
A word created by Laban in 1928 to express dance literacy or literate dance discourse, not confined to issues of notated dance but to issues in serious dance debate in which dance notation was automatically a part.
Valerie Preston-Dunlop and *Susanne Lahusen*, 1990.

Interlocking disciplines
A network of approaches to the study and research of dance, given titles such as 'sociology of dance', 'a feminist perspective', 'politics of dance', 'anthropology of dance', 'aesthetics of dance', each providing means of study which relates to other means.
Janet Adshead-Lansdale, Interview.

Mentalities
Ways of coping and perceiving which are expressed as images by Laban to denote:
i) people who imbue movement subjectively with emotional content; ii) people who analyse movement with so-called objective precision; iii) people who spontaneously experience the movement event bodily.
"The emotional dreamers, the scheming mechanics, the biological innocents are three human mentalities all necessary to the study of movement."
Rudolf Laban, 1966 (1939).

Movement thinking

Gathering of impressions of happenings for which nomenclature is lacking.
Rudolf Laban, 1971 (1950).

Verify a method in practice, To

A dance researcher has to relate always to the empirical basis, to direct dance experience, and to adjust procedures accordingly.
Roderyk Lange, Interview.

Objectivity

"A principle which has to be followed in scholarly dance research, with appropriate methods applied. However, an absolute degree of objectivity is not attainable, nor even desired, as the analyst has to view the progression of a dance through his own movement experience."
Roderyk Lange, Interview.

Choreographic research

Research undertaken by a choreographer in the making of a new work. "It must be a criss-cross between tangible research of sources and creative insight, and used for continuous enrichment and clarity."
Dorothy Madden, Interview.

Choreography as research

The notion that the process of creating a dance work of substance can constitute research.
Marion North, Interview.

Choreography as research

An area of dance studies in need of investigation to determine the way in which the dance work as both process and product can be made available for public discourse.
June Layson, Interview.

Practical research

Critical, intellectual reflection by a dance artist on what s/he has done and could do, without interfering with the creative choreographic process itself.
Richard Ralph, Interview.

Constellation of human behaviors

A term used in anthropological investigation of dance to indicate the necessity for holistic study methods, because dance is "...not only product but behavior and concept, too...", "...a constellation of human behaviors."
Alan Merriam, 1974.

2. CHOREOLOGY

Choreology
> A scholarly domain which uses specific tools and workable methods within the range of its subject, dance.
> *Roderyk Lange*, Interview.

Choreology
> "Choreology in its broadest sense is the scientific study of dance and thus has very wide applications."
> *Benesh Institute*, 1993.

Choreology
> "Deals with the logic and balancing order of dance" (1927), "the theory of the laws of dance events manifested in the synthesis of spatial and temporal experience" (1929).
> *Rudolf Laban* (translated by Vera Maletic) in Vera Maletic, 1987.

Choreology
> A kind of grammar and syntax of the language of movement dealing not only with the outer form of movement but also with its mental and emotional content.
> *Rudolf Laban*, 1966 (1939).

Choreology
> "...a term commonly associated with Benesh Movement Notation...".
> *Benesh Institute*, 1993.

Choreology
> According to the documentation on the Choreological Laboratory in Moscow in 1923–1928, choreology is the theoretical and practical study of the 'art of movement', by using experiments in rhythm and plasticity and searching for a means of recording movement, using cinema, photography, graphics, paintings and sculpture.
> *Nicoletta Misler* in Nancy van Norman Baer, 1991.

Ethnochoreology
> The study of dance parallel with that of music in ethnomusicology; a term originating in the field of anthropology and ethnology.
> *International Council for Traditional Music*, 1993.

Choreological studies
> An intrinsic theoretical and practical study of dance form and content, focusing on a structural study of the medium of dance, that is the performer, the movement, the sound, and the space, using four interdependent modes of investigation: experiential, exploratory, analytic, and documentary. Seen as complementary to such extrinsic studies as politics of dance, sociology of dance, aesthetics of dance, which bring the methodology of their own discipline to bear on dance.
> *Valerie Preston-Dunlop*, 1987.

Technology of dance
        The precursory contribution of Rudolf Laban to choreological study methods through his notation system, and his choreutics and eukinetics, by which tangible data on the movement texture of the dance can be collected.
        Roderyk Lange, Interview.

Notation systems
        Linguistic constructions designed to record dance and movement in a grammatically governed system of symbols, whether Labanotation, Eshkol-Wachmann or Benesh.
        Janet Adshead-Lansdale, Interview.

Notation-based
        Dance research in which the material collected is written in notation, usually Labanotation or Benesh; a kind of research tool regarded as essential by choreologists.
        Andrée Grau, Interview.

Theory of choreography
        "The Theory of Choreography is concerned with the acquisition of knowledge of the movements of the body, and the principles and rules which govern the elaboration in every form and style."
        Leonide Massine, 1976.

Intrinsic method
        A term used in choreological and sociological study of dance to refer to the ways in which the features of form of a dance work or event are found, the way those are structured together, and function as a means of interpreting the conditions of the culture in which the dance is made.
        Paul Filmer and *Valerie Preston-Dunlop*, Discussion.

Dissection and articulation
        Two operations (identified by Barthes) essential to the choreological analysis of a dance work, dissection being the operation of identifying parts of the whole: articulation is the operation of associating the parts through finding the rules which relate them and so identify their place in the work.
        Ana R. Sanchez-Colberg, 1992.

Choreological order
        The hidden rules and structures in movement which, when consciously mastered, make movement penetrable, meaningful and understandable.
        Rudolf Laban, 1966 (1939).

Research scores

Scores of dances using detailed descriptive notation written by research choreologists with the purpose of providing data; said in contrast to repertoire scores which use prescriptive notation, i.e. notation within a "language".
Andrée Grau, Interview.

Breaking the code

The moment in deciphering an unknown notation system (e.g. Nijinsky's) when well-known movements, such as ballet barre work, are recognised, enabling the system's code to be understood.
Ann Hutchinson Guest, Interview.

Choreotechnical characteristics

Defining properties of a given dance style.
"A particular style of dance is based on specific choreotechnical characteristics. Therefore, when analysing and notating it, the particular 'code' on which this style or dance is based has to be broken."
Roderyk Lange, 1985.

Verify a translation, To

To find visual confirmation, such as photographs, of what has been discovered to be in a piece of notated dance material written in an unfamiliar system (e.g. Nijinsky's).
Ann Hutchinson Guest, Interview.

Dance score analysis

A combination of Labanotation and Effort/Shape concepts used with a Labanotation score toward the discernment of "stylistic and expressive aspects of a dance work."
Elizabeth Kagan, 1978.

Notation research

A forum for re-evaluating notation systems, stretching them to cope with different movement forms, for eliminating convenience signs; said of the International Council for Kinetography Laban.
Jean Johnson-Jones, Interview.

3.   ANALYTIC METHOD

Analytic method

An established way of setting about a dance analysis, carefully chosen to illuminate the problem to hand, selected from several possible alternatives, probably using more than one method.
Valerie Preston-Dunlop, 1991.

Analysis of movement

The various modes of taking movement apart to find out what it consists in; a process by which artists come to find their own grammar; said of Kenneth King.

"...kinetic, theatrical, and poetic points of view...".

Sally Banes, 1980(a).

Stating the aims

"One does not analyse for the sake of it but because one wants to discover something; so you set about it by clarifying what it is that is puzzling or what it is that is as yet unknown to you. Then and only then can you choose a method."

Valerie Preston-Dunlop, Seminar, 1991.

Neutral

A quality in analysis which is never present; the method is not neutral, the observer is not neutral; both are the result of personal and cultural histories.

Janet Adshead-Lansdale, Interview.

Movement descriptions

Movement descriptions are only an adequate record if they include views of the movement from the dancer's point of view (inner) and from several other viewpoints.

"Movement is, so to speak, living architecture. An architect can only show the plastic image of the 3-dimensional whole by both inner and outer views, ground plan and at least two elevations."

Rudolf Laban, 1966 (1939).

Tripartite relationship

The choreographer/dancer/viewer relationship as author/text/reader, knowledge of which can inform an analysis.

Stephanie Jordan and *Helen Thomas*, 1990.

Describing the components of the dance

A stage in analysis in which discerning differences in the elements of the dance, describing them, and naming them are the essential skills.

Janet Adshead, 1988.

Language of description, The

An inherently problematic area in analysis of dance, in that the choice of descriptive language is itself an interpretation, a selection of terms from many alternatives, each culturally dependent.

Janet Adshead-Lansdale, Interview.

Dance-specific

A term applied to analytic methods which may have been regarded as universal but which are found to be culturally based, and therefore have to be treated as choreographer-specific or even piece-specific to be of any use.

Janet Adshead-Lansdale, Interview.

Interpretative dimension
  A continuous and persistent perspective in analysis, present in description through to evaluation.
  Janet Adshead-Lansdale, Interview.

Terminology
  The verbal currency for discourse which dance history academics and scholars must address in order to develop a means of furthering their subject through overcoming the misunderstandings that occur in the dialects of the various branches of dance activity.
  June Layson, Interview.

Choreological terminology
  Technical terms and phrases developed to address the needs of the dancer to go beyond "learning movements", and so enable the teacher and the student (equally the choreographer and the dancer) to deal with the necessary processes explicitly.
  Rosemary Brandt, Interview.

Value judgements
  Choices that analysts make which colour the three layers of analysis: description, interpretation and evaluation; judgements which reflect a position held, possibly feminist, socialist, moral.
  Janet Adshead-Lansdale, Interview.

Data collection
  Having decided on what categories of data are needed to address the question put to the dance, data collecting is the process by which this information is gained, usually through watching/listening/sensing many times and using some symbol system to aid the recording of what is found as it is found.
  Valerie Preston-Dunlop, Interview.

Collecting and processing of data
  Procedures in the study of dance, for which methods of recording and documenting are essential.
  Roderyk Lange, 1980.

Data, The
  The information about a dance collected by the dance researcher to which the notated dance score contributes; data is in a form which can be studied by other researchers in order to verify interpretation or come to other conclusions.
  Andrée Grau, Interview.

Dance text
  A problematic term, inherently unstable; possibly specific to each work, or each artist; a term used sometimes for the notated score but only possible to use in that way for some dances and impossible for others.
  Janet Adshead-Lansdale, Interview.

Information

Data and views about a dance, provided to the researcher by informants in verbal, kinetic, or oral forms, which may prove confirmatory or contradictory.

Andrée Grau, Interview.

Open interpretation

The concept that there cannot be one interpretation which is the definitive interpretation, but that there are many, possibly conflicting, which will continuously emerge.

Janet Adshead-Lansdale, Interview.

Informant

The title given to the person who provides information for the dance researcher; this may be the dance maker, the dancer, but also non-dancers including audience members.

Andrée Grau, Interview.

Discrete units (of motion)

A term for independent units of motion which carry symbolic meaning and appear in conglomerates within a dance style.

Roderyk Lange, Interview.

Interpretation

The process in dance analysis which follows description of the formal features by 'making sense' of them by knowledge of the context in which the dance exists, this being both tacit within a shared culture and stated in research.

Janet Adshead, 1990.

Understanding the dance

Seeing and hearing the work in the light of the traditions and conventions of dance, so that both the intended expressiveness of it (ling-comm) and the unintentional expressiveness given off by it (perf-comm) are given meaningful interpretations by each spectator.

Graham McFee, 1989.

Meaning

A problematic concept, in that there is no such thing as the meaning of a work but rather several possible meanings, depending on what the observer decides to look for and how s/he gets at it.

Janet Adshead-Lansdale, Interview.

4. MORPHOLOGY OF DANCE, STRUCTURAL METHODS, AND DANCE STUDIED AS A LANGUAGE

Morphology (of dance)
The study of the size, shape, and structure and relationship of the parts (of a dance).
'Encyclopædia Britannica', 1986.

Morphological analysis
A method borrowed from musicology which choreologists use to discern the structure and form of dance material.
Roderyk Lange, 1980.

Analysis of form
The tracing of the relationships existing between the components of the movement, the dancers, the visual setting and the aural elements.
Janet Adshead, 1988.

Analysis of form
Form analysed through relations between the moment and the linear development of a piece. The analysis of form through "the impact of a set of relations at a movement in time" viewed within the context of the dance and its continuing development.
Janet Adshead, 1988.

Form analysis of dance
"The study of form", "the form of a dance, in the sense of the inner organization of its segments and units, is the most easily comprehensible phenomenon through which dance becomes an artistic product".
Folk Dance Study Group of the International Folk Music Council, 1974

Form analysed through relations at a point in time
The freezing of a dance in order to analyse the relationships across the components at a particular moment and then analyse the visual impact of sets of complexes or components as they occur.
Janet Adshead, 1988.

Macroanalysis of style
A method focusing on the use of the four strands of the dance medium, and the process/production of a work, with substrands, features, subfeatures, aspects, and subaspects through a glossary of stylistic features.
Ana R. Sanchez-Colberg, 1992.

Formal relationships
"...the connections or associations made as the elements come together in the art object."
Eleanore W. Gwynne, 1978.

Cluster

"...the simultaneous occurrence of a number of elements."
Janet Adshead, 1988.

Clustering

The simultaneous or consecutive linking of elements in the dance which belong together in a work; a term used in music for chord and melodic clusters, and in dance for clusters of elements of motion, rhythm and position.
Valerie Preston-Dunlop, 1991.

Nexus

The web of interrelationships which exist in a dance work through the essential choices made on how strands and sub-strands of the dance medium link; coexisting dance and sound, dancers contributing movement material, sound made by the dancers are examples.
Valerie Preston-Dunlop, 1991.

Form

Form comes out of that to which it is related — subject matter—; that which causes the behaviour causes the form.
Hanya Holm in Walter Sorell, 1976.

Form

"Form is a pattern, a plan, in its outer aspect; an order, structure; with feeling within it. Form is deliberately made and abides by the rules decided upon."
Louis Horst, 1958.

Structural analysis

The study of the manner in which dance material is put together in elements, cells, motifs, phrases, sections, dances, suites, cycles and events.
Anca Giurchescu, 1987.

Structural analytic methods

A developing group of analytical approaches used in the study of dance material, which look for such elements as 'regularites', e.g. within the performances of a dance by different dancers, 'formal structural units', 'units with symbolic, encoded meaning', 'dance types', 'dance dialects', etc.
Roderyk Lange, 1980.

Structuralism

"Not a single theoretical framework but best described as a method of inquiry."
Stephanie Jordan and *Helen Thomas*, 1990.

Processive symbolic form (in a dance work)

Metaphors in a dance work which become legible as the work proceeds through elements which although meaningless in isolation appear again and again and so build up meaning through their contexts.
Anita Donaldson, 1992.

Conformant symbolic form (in a dance work)

Metaphors in a dance work which are legible because they conform to the conventions already established in a dance genre.

Anita Donaldson, 1992.

Hierarchic symbol form (in a dance work)

Meaning in dance which is found by the way in which apparently meaningless elements of the dance cluster to give a metaphor, several of which cluster to give a further metaphor, and so on until the meaning is presented by the whole.

Anita Donaldson, 1992.

Movement

"One of man's languages."

Rudolf Laban, 1966 (1939).

Language of Dance

Investigation into the content and structure of movement patterns in terms of the use of the movement alphabet, i.e. the root actions and elements (nouns, verbs, adverbs), their arrangement, weighting (emphasis), the resulting rhythmic structure (timing, duration, stress), and the initiation or motivation from which the movement emanated.

Ann Hutchinson Guest, Contributed.

Syntax of the movement, The

"The way the formal elements of the composition are developed and juxtaposed," being "part of the meaningful content of the work, even though we may not be able to translate this into words"; said referring to Humphrey's "The Shakers" (1930).

Suzanne Youngerman, 1978.

Break the code, To

What the analyst has to do to reveal the deep structure of dance material.

Roderyk Lange, Interview.

Kinetic units

Discrete parts of dance material identified in the structural analysis of dance.

Roderyk Lange, 1980.

Surface structure

The final form of the medium, synthesized in actual phrased movements articulate in style, mood, dynamic, rhythm, design, providing the manner in which the deep structure is transmitted.

Valerie Preston-Dunlop, 1987.

Surface structure

The part of a dance which is externally revealed, can be analysed morphologically, and recorded in a dance notation system.

Roderyk Lange, Interview.

Deep structure

The particular coherence of the elements of the dance material which give the essential intended meaning of the dance, dance section, or dance statement, in a work functioning linguistically.
Valerie Preston-Dunlop, 1987.

Deep structure (of dance)

A hidden dimension of a dance, not externally revealed, that which structural analysis can reveal, namely the encoded compositional norms.
Roderyk Lange, Interview.

Dance dialect, A

Versions of dance which, although discernibly different, have the same fundamental determinants, the same deep structure.
Roderyk Lange, Interview.

Kinemic and morphokinemic

The names given to the first two analytic levels of Tongan Dance in the structural method devised by Adrienne Kaeppler (1967); these levels "...are comparable to the phonemic and morphemic levels of linguistic analysis."
Anya Peterson Royce, 1974.

Motif

"A dance phrase which combines certain morphokines in characteristic ways and is verbalised by the people as dance movement."; said of Adrienne Kaeppler's structural method for the analysis of Tongan Dance.
Anya Peterson Royce, 1974.

Full graphic movement notation

The property of a given movement notation system to be seen to function analogously to phonetic script, i.e. to represent human movement as a series of minimal significant elements or 'phonemes', there being a finite number of phonemes, represented by the graphic symbols of the script.
Roderyk Lange, 1985.

Dance as language/movement as language

The problematic issues thrown up by the concept that 'movement' is synonymous with 'dance', and hence that discussion surrounding movement as a language might equate with those on dance as a language.
Valerie Preston-Dunlop, Seminar.

Arts as a language, The

The false thesis that an art form (dance) is a language, although works "may be made to perform linguistic or symbolic functions" and "particular works may possess the property of serving some linguistic or symbolic function".
Anita Donaldson, 1993, quoting Joseph Margolis (1974).

5.   DANCE ANTHROPOLOGY/ETHNOLOGY

Dance anthropology

The study of the meaning of dance in human existence, within the socio-cultural context.

Roderyk Lange, Interview.

Dance ethnology

"The study of dance forms in relation to other aspects of culture."
Samuel Marti and *Gertrude Prokosch Kurath*, 1964.

Folkloristics

An American term for the study of folklore which centres on the performance of an event and works out from that point, rather than starting with the broader social cultural context of an event and gradually narrowing down.

Theresa Buckland, Interview.

Archeo-choreology

"The reconstruction of obsolete or obsolescent dances."
Samuel Marti and *Gertrude Prokosch Kurath*, 1964.

Choreometrics

"[A method of]...describing dance patterns so that they could be consistently compared cross-culturally, grouped into their regional or functional families and thus studied in their cultural and historical contexts."

Irmgard Bartenieff in Janet Adshead, 1988.

Choreometric profile (of a dance)

The coding of dances for their movement patterns, such as: "i) most active body parts, ii) number of body parts, iii) body attitude, iv) shape of main activity, v) energy of transition, vi) energy in main activity, vii) degree of variation, viii) spread of flow through the body."

Anya Peterson Royce, 1974.

Dance typology

A system of groupings of dances which reveal relationships existing between them. Dances of the same type have specified attributes, mutually exclusive and collectively exhaustive.

Roderyk Lange, 1975.

Ethnic dance

A view held by anthropologists that all dance forms, including mainsteam ballet and contemporary dance, are ethnocentric.

"All dances are ethnic dances, they are all made by people."
Andrée Grau, Interview.

Ethnocentric
> Viewing the world (of dance) through the norms of one's own culture.
> *Roderyk Lange*, Interview.

Phenomenon, The
> Activity within a community which might or might not be a dance; that which is to be studied in anthropology.
> *Andrée Grau*, Interview.

Contextural approach to dance
> Viewing the dance object within the social and cultural context; what it means to people according to the cultural norms of their own society.
> *Roderyk Lange*, Interview.

Functional analysis
> An approach, common in the human sciences, used in anthropological dance research to establish the role of dance within a social group system.
> *Roderyk Lange*, 1980.

Construct a model, To
> What an anthropologist does, in order to understand the dance being studied, through the interpretation of what is seen and talked about, rather than imposing an already constructed model.
> *Andrée Grau*, Interview.

Field work
> What a dance researcher undertakes on location.
> *Roderyk Lange*, Interview.

Data check list
> A framework for a particular fieldwork project in dance, which supplies cues which will be turned by the researcher at the particular location into questions concerning the dance material itself and the informant, when conducting the interview.
> *Roderyk Lange*, 1984.

Biased background
> The anthropologist's educational/cultural background which will colour the way s/he sees the activities of the community being studied, especially relevant to the view of the community's dances.
> *Andrée Grau*, Interview.

Bi-musicality
> A term, analogous to 'bilingual', to describe people who can understand two distinct musical cultures and vocabularies; the use of the term was extended by John Blacking to include dance.
> *Andrée Grau*, Interivew.

Dance transmission

The way dances are passed down from one person or group or generation to another; a concept which might be significant in anthropological study.

Andrée Grau, Interview.

Dance status

The value given to a dance by authoritative figures or groups, or to dancers, compared with other activities and persons; a concept which might be significant in anthropological study.

Andrée Grau, Interview.

Dance ownership

The concept that a dance belongs to someone, to its creator or its dancer; a concept which might be significant in anthropological study.

Andrée Grau, Interview.

Participant-observer

A researcher who studies, amongst other things, the dances of a community by participating, where appropriate, as well as observing, in order to find out what is regarded as essential vocabulary or valued performance.

Andrée Grau, Interview.

Find the boundaries of a movement system, To

To participate in a dance, to provoke a response from those who know it, by making mistakes or adding movements; one way of finding out what is acceptable as within the operative rules of the system; one of several methods used in anthropological study.

Andrée Grau, Interview.

Setting

The term for the nature of a dance event, who sponsored it, the occasion that the dance was part of, significant key figures and ingredients of the environment; used of traditional dance.

Michael Heaney and *John Forrest*, 1991.

Ideological manipulation

The political use "of dance forms for nationalist agendas" currently problematical in folk dance and music.

Colin Quigley, 1993.

Researcher's responsibility

Ethical problems of the impact on indigenous dance of research activity and of the essentially personal nature of the description and discussion of dances which a researcher cannot avoid.

Theresa Buckland and *Anca Giurchescu* in Colin Quigley, 1993.

6. NON-VERBAL COMMUNICATION THEORIES AND DANCE

Proxemics

The study of the use of space and time in social interaction, e.g. distance, orientation between people, conversational timing, hesitancy, interruption, tempo, duration, which convey social relationships.

Edward T. Hall, 1966.

Proxemics in dance

The study of spatial and temporal relationship between dancers with a view to understanding the possible interpretations audiences might give to a work, and to possible proxemic devices a choreographer might use in duo and group works.

Milca Leon, 1993.

Kinesics

The study of the movement that is used as a means of non-verbal communication in interpersonal behaviour, together with the context in which it takes place.

Valerie Preston-Dunlop from *Ray Birdwhistell*, 1970.

Interpersonal behaviour studies

Research from a psychological viewpoint of the motivation to interact and the social techniques used to interact.

Michael Argyle, 1967.

Social order

The subject of how order in society is maintained through tacitly agreed non-verbal codes, by which members of a society understand each other's movement signals and respond appropriately.

Eds. from *Albert Scheflen*, 1972.

Movement profiles

Descriptions of the personality of individuals through the data of the rhythms and phrases of their shadow movements, a method developed by Marion North from Rudolf Laban's preliminary research; used in interpretation of a role, casting, teaching, and dance therapy.

Marion North, 1972.

Action Profiling

A system of analysis of body movement derived from Laban's principles of movement and developed by Warren Lamb and Pamela Ramsden in which patterns of integrated body movements are observed, recorded and analysed to reflect aspects of an individual's 'cognitive style', that is their decision-making processes.

Deborah du Nann Winter, 1987.

Davis Non-Verbal Communication Analysis System (DaNCS)

A method for coding non-verbal aspects of the interaction of individuals, using relationship, position, action, and dynamic quality, as complementary aspects of movement behaviour.

Martha Davis, 1982.

Trinitarian basis

The Delsarte view of the human being as intellectual, emotional and physical, expressed through the natural laws of time, motion and space, for which he proposed nine laws of gesture and posture.

Walter Sorell, 1981.

7. SOCIOLOGY OF DANCE AND DANCE POLITICS

Sociology of dance

A discipline which analyses the relations between dance and society.

Paul Filmer, Interview.

Sociology of dance

An extrinsic study of dance by tradition.

"...for the most part, sociology studies art in terms of a reflection of something outside itself, such as the social conditions or authorial intentions without attending to the specificity of the form itself."

Helen Thomas, 1986.

Extrinsic and intrinsic methods

Two methods used in the sociology of dance which look at the way society produces and interprets dances beside the way the condition of the culture is embedded in dance work.

Paul Filmer, Interview.

Extrinsic and intrinsic perspectives

The sociological context for a dance work and the qualities of the dance, its movement, music, decor, etc., which constitute it, studied to uncover its symbolic character and elucidate its potential for meaning.

Helen Thomas, 1991.

Culture-bound

Said of ballet, but true of all forms of dance. Values and conventions reflect the dance culture, and the wider cultural context.

Janet Adshead-Lansdale, Interview.

Reflexive representation
A term used in sociology of dance to refer to how the structure of dance as we see it might structure our ideas about the society in which the dance takes place.
Paul Filmer, Interview.

Dance politics
The study of power in dance activity.
Peter Brinson, Interview.

Dance politics
The study of the way society structures and funds our opportunities both to dance and to produce dances.
Paul Filmer, Interview.

Politics of dance
The study of the influence of power structuring on the form of dance works.
"Manipulation of power — by royalty, theater management, or private patronage, vitally affects the spectacle produced."
Lincoln Kirstein, 1971.

Dance politics
The study of political survival mechanisms in a culture which traditionally marginalises dance.
Marion North, Interview.

Advocacy of dance
The ability of dance people and dance productions to speak for the value of their art for society generally, and in society generally.
Peter Brinson, Interview.

Produce a rhetoric, To
To create a jargon, a discourse, around a concept or area of dance, such as video dance.
John Ashford, Interview.

Dance power
The empowerment of the individual and communities through the participation in creative dance activities, thus finding their own potential for creativity.
Peter Brinson, Interview.

Dance power
The study of the power that dancers and choreographers have to influence the public through their performance.
Peter Brinson, Interivew.

Freedom of dance artists

The ability of dance people to say what they want to say in their art medium, without constraint from powerful critical circles.

Peter Brinson, Interview.

Dominant body politic

The attitude to issues of the body by the establishment, attitudes which it often appears that classical ballet tends to reflect but which Balanchine's particular use of his women dancers deconstructs.

Helen Thomas, Interview.

Body politics

Methods which look at how the body is represented and evaluated in the different contexts of each usage, of which dance provides many examples.

Helen Thomas, Interview.

Politics of the body

The study of the place of the body in dance where it becomes both the mode of expression and the instrument of production.

Paul Filmer, Interview.

Feminist theory and dance

The variety of approaches emanating from feminist literature and experience which informs scholarly analysis and reviews of performances of dance works and dance people and historical periods.

Alexandra Carter, Contributed.

Feminist dance scholarship

The issues in politics generally of concern to the feminist movement, taken up by dance scholars since dance, with its inevitable content of a gendered body, is an exemplar for feminist concerns.

Helen Thomas, Interview.

Feminist analysis

An analysis of a dance work using the insights of feminist theory as a way of seeing that challenges orthodox methodologies.

Helen Thomas, Interview.

8.   DANCE HISTORY

Dance history

An area of dance research which uses procedures from history generally, while foregrounding dance. Currently it needs to develop further specific methodologies for studying dance of the past.

June Layson, Interview.

Dance history

"The interpretation of material, usually in a literary form, with a view to explaining the historical development of dance, or of a particular aspect of the dance."
Ivor Guest, Contributed.

Historical subject matter

"Dance ideas, dance people, and dance events."
June Layson, Interview.

Dance history research methods

A learned craft, based on knowledge of the whereabouts of sources, the organisation of material, making a judgement on the reliability of sources.
Ivor Guest, Contributed.

Dance historian

"...a wanderer searching to find and to point to a life that once was, and to the ways in which it manifested itself...casting the dance as the leading character."
Walter Sorell, 1981.

Literary art

What dance history is, since it offers the reader, inevitably, an individual perception, that is the fruits of personal research filtered by judgement and by values, and influenced by the writer's imagination, communicated through clear and vivid writing.
Ivor Guest, Contributed.

Historical dimension

"The time, the dance style, and its context": the three aspects of dance which provide the structural framework for an infinitely complex study of it.
June Layson, Interview.

Context

The relevant areas of a dance topic essential for the study of dance historically, including the musical, artistic, social and political background.
Ivor Guest, Contributed.

Traditional dance history

An approach to events in which objectivity is the prime aim, a subject in which students often encounter what seem to be predetermined facts which are not presented as open to further interpretation.
June Layson, Interview.

New dance history

An approach in which the changing referential frameworks of study are as significant as the events themselves, giving rise to historical views which are contested, and essentially open to interpretation and re-interpretation.
June Layson, Interview.

Engagement

The relationship of the dance historian to the dance being studied, combining the rigours of objectivity with an unsuppressed subjective view based on a passionate engagement with the subject.

June Layson, Interview.

Historians

"...products of their own society..." "...viewing the artistic and cultural achievements of the past under the influence of their own sociocultural and aesthetic currents."

Walter Sorell, 1981.

Developmental categories

Ways of tracing the growth of ballet by commenting on works over a period of decades under the following headings: Priority (of choice of work), Precedent (from which it emerged), Politics (as it affects the work), Plot or Pretext (of the movement), Production (of the movement).

Lincoln Kirstein, 1971.

Exposition of sources

The uncovering of primary information, biographies, careers, chronologies, making use of modern retrieval and communication systems.

Richard Ralph, Interview.

Preliminary scholarly research

The basic treatment that dance history requires, which other disciplines reached decades, even centuries, ago, the finding and ordering of essential factual information.

Richard Ralph, Interview.

Pre-interpretative research

The first stage of scholarly work in which the critical faculty is primarily focused on the ordering of sources but too early a stage for specialist interpretation, such as feminist or deconstructionist.

Richard Ralph, Interview.

Date

When a dance was performed; may be an exact date or a movable feast (such as Whitsun) or a season; part of the essential historical data surrounding a performance.

Michael Heaney and *John Forrest*, 1991.

Silence of dance, The

The lack of references to dance in historical accounts of past eras, which in no way suggests that dance was not happening, rather that it was not relevant to record; contemporary dance historians need to "read into the silence".

June Layson, Interview.

Iconography of dance

The pictorial representations of dance, such as paintings, drawings, sculptures, of value as supplementary sources to evidence of the progression of movement recorded by a notation system.

Roderyk Lange, 1980.

Choreochronicle

The chronological organisation of the choreographic output or oeuvre of a dance artist.

June Layson, Interview.

9.   DANCE RECONSTRUCTION

Retrieving a work

The painstaking process of re-finding a dance work thought to be lost, by re-searching visual, aural, and written evidence, interviewing performers, amassing ephemera, studying works by the same choreographer to give a framework for reconstruction.

Ray Cook, 1990.

Historical perspective

The educational purpose of reconstructing dances on student groups in order for them to have direct experience of the physicality and style of movement vocabulary of the dance heritage, an understanding which complements what can be gained from books.

"...to put meat on the bones...".

Els Grelinger, Interview.

Sources

The resources which a choreographer in plays and films will research prior to creating movement scenes, in order to sense the style and ambience for the dances.

"Museums, photographs, books, paintings, biographies, and music of the period."

Geraldine Stephenson, Interview.

Re-creating

A process undergone in re-presenting Laban's Kammertanz repertoire (1922–28) through researching process and context where the product was lost.

"Clearly, one cannot reconstruct on the evidence available, nor would accuracy and authenticity of steps be sensible criteria."

"...structured improvisation was part of the way of working; the dancers should be prepared to work with as little clothing as possible, and every attempt should be made to build up a sense of community through sharing everything from food and drink, to space, to responsibility...".

Valerie Preston-Dunlop, 1988.

Reconstruction

"...I have worked to reconstruct the original choreography of "Le Sacre", I have been fascinated by the contemporary look of Nijinsky's dance. From the notes and memoirs of his collaborators and peers, from visual records and press clippings, from interviews with performers and spectators who have survived from the première, and talks with relatives and protégés of some who have not, I have collected clues to the choreography and plotted them, measure for measure, in my reconstruction book. Fragments of the lost masterpiece have gradually reassembled, and they shock me sometimes with their familiarity."
Millicent Hodson, 1985.

New productions

As attitudes change toward interpreting choreographic works with greater freedom, it may become possible for productions to depart from the original image and, using the choreography as recorded in a notated score, realize it from different individual points of view and contemporary interpretations.
Ann Hutchinson, 1970.

10. DANCE PHILOSOPHY AND AESTHETICS

Philosophy of dance

In popular parlance, an individual's beliefs and value-commitments about dance (c.f. X's 'philosophy of life'); more strictly, a theoretical activity dealing by means of reasoned argument with second-order questions, i.e. those concerned primarily with issues of meanings and justification:

the concept of dance and related concepts (e.g. form, rhythm);

the logical relationship(s) between such concepts (e.g. between artistic meaning and linguistic meaning, expressiveness in dance and in ordinary life);

the nature of various assertions commonly made about dance in general, dance works and performances;

the assumptions and beliefs underlying such assertions; and

the nature and types of evidence and reasoning for their justification.
Betty Redfern, Contributed.

Dance aesthetics

A term with varied meanings which deals inter alia with the "philosophy of art and dance", with concepts of "beauty" in dance, with "creative processes" in dance, with problems of "truths" in performance, with "criteria of excellence", with "aesthetic attitude".

"[Philosophical] expertise alone is not enough, for the problems that require mental ingenuity also require a sense of physicality, a grasp of kinesthesia without which any theory of dance must remain hopelessly isolated from reality."
Selma Jeanne Cohen, 1983.

Aesthetics

A branch of philosophy dealing, traditionally, with beauty, but increasingly since the nineteenth century more broadly with the arts and art criticism, especially problems of meaning, interpretation and evidence. Often mistakenly identified with philosophy of art, so that (1) other sources of aesthetic interest and (2) Post-modern forms of art are neglected or implicitly devalued "...the philosophy of art must leave aesthetics in order to cope with art which is not fundamentally aesthetic."
H.B. Redfern, 1986, quoting *Timothy Binkley*, 1976.

Aesthetic judgement

A mainly technical or semi-technical term originating in the eighteenth century (=Kant's 'judgement of taste') and heavily laden with historical overtones: traditionally, the claim that something is beautiful, but later extended to a range of aesthetic qualities. Typically, not an assessment or grading in terms of merit, but appraisal as discernment.
Betty Redfern, 1983.

Aestheticism

The view deriving from the nineteenth-century movement "Art for Art's Sake" (more accurately, 'art for aesthetic's sake' (*Terence J. Diffey*, 1967)) that art should be concerned primarily with beauty and that any other interest (e.g. moral, social) is superfluous, even possibly detrimental to its value as art; in its extreme form, the doctrine that art must not serve any extra-aesthetic ends. Sometimes extended to life in general, i.e. one devoted to the pursuit of beauty and the arts.
R.V. Johnson, 1969.

Subjective aspect

(a) the individual encounters the object at first hand, and (b) his/her response has an affective, personally significant dimension.
Betty Redfern, from *Roger Scruton*, 1974.

Objective aspect

(a) attention is centered, not on a private sensation or passive reaction, but on something in the public world, which (b) when regarded aesthetically is susceptible to rational discussion and appraisal. (Hence, aesthetic awareness is modifiable and educable).
Betty Redfern, from *Roger Scruton*, 1974.

Aesthetic attitude

A mode of awareness involving an active, feeling response to something directly apprehended such that (positively) it is enjoyed and valued as an imaginative construct for its own sake or (negatively) found repulsive or distasteful. There are thus both objective and subjective aspects.
Betty Redfern, referring to *Roger Scruton*, 1974.

Aesthetic qualities in dance

Two strands present in a dance performance, the qualities of the dance itself and the qualities of the spectators' experience of the dance: the so-called aesthetic qualities of the work and the aesthetic experience of the audience.

Pauline Hodgens in Janet Adshead, 1988.

Aesthetic qualities

In a narrow sense, qualities such as beauty, ugliness, elegance, hideousness. More widely (1) qualities requiring for their discernment "the exercise of taste, perceptiveness or sensibility, of aesthetic discrimination or appreciation" (*Frank N. Sibley*, 1959);

(2) all those qualities ascribed to something regarded from an aesthetic point of view (see "Aesthetic attitude").

Betty Redfern, Contributed.

Subjectivist accounts of the aesthetic

Accounts centring on the view that there are no specifically aesthetic qualities, but "an infinite elasticity of possibly aesthetically forceful features" (*Ruby Meager*, 1970); aesthetic claims are thus appropriate or inappropriate, reasonable or unreasonable, rather than true or false.

Betty Redfern, 1983.

Objectivist accounts of the aesthetic

Accounts centring on the view that aesthetic qualities are of a distinctive kind, able to be recognised by a special sort of perception; aesthetic claims are thus true or false.

Betty Redfern, 1983.

Second-order features

Qualities or characteristics of an object such as beauty, tenderness, unity, for which there are no standard tests of verification, but which are nevertheless discernible in certain circumstances; they are dependent on ('emergent' from) first-order features (q.v.), which thus provide a basis for possible agreement.

Betty Redfern, 1983.

First-order features

Qualities or characteristics of, e.g. movement or sound, which are straightforwardly discernible and for which there are standard tests of verification (e.g. angularity, loudness).

Betty Redfern, 1983.

Persuasive definition

"A verbal formula that endows a word, usually one with emotional overtones (e.g. 'art', 'dance', 'creativity'), with a particular meaning which the author tries to get others to accept as the 'real' or 'true' or 'essential' meaning."

H.B. Redfern, 1986, quoting *Charles L. Stevenson*, 1938.

Essentially contested concepts

"Concepts in general use, typically involving some kind of valued achievement (e.g. art, history, democracy) but not amenable to strict definition; they are complex, appraisive concepts which not only happen to engender constant dispute, but of their nature are not resolvable by argument — rather are sustained by it."

H.B. Redfern, 1986, quoting *William B. Gallie*, 1956(a) and 1956(b).

11. DANCE CRITICISM

Dance criticism

Writing about a dance event which probes original insights, in relation to other works or through detailed illustration; writing which carries a point of view which is acknowledged through its 'up frontedness'.

Judith Mackrell, Interview.

Dance criticism

A task in which the critic is asked to evaluate a work "according to his personal standards which originate in the present" while using his knowledge of both history and art theory.

Roger Copeland and *Marshall Cohen*, 1983.

Dance criticism

"I often feel as if I am pursuing a dance with words...in an attempt to define precisely what struck me as important or interesting about that work.", "to help to evoke experience again", "to provide fodder for argument".

Deborah Jowitt, 1977.

Criticism

A written or verbal account of a dance which is deeply coloured by the personal value system and history of the reviewer.

Janet Adshead-Lansdale, Interview.

Dance criticism

Taking André Levinson as exemplary, 'real' criticism should, as he did, "review dance consistently as choreography rather than merely performance, argue from principle rather than merely from taste, and draw those principles from within dance itself."

Joan Acocella and *Lynn Garafola*, 1991.

Accounts, The (of a work)

The movement account, which attempts to display the meaning and significance of the dance, and verbal account which aims to pinpoint and describe the meaning and the significance.

Pauline Hodgens in Janet Adshead, 1988.

Objectivity
What a dance critic hopes to contribute, alongside a personal aesthetic, through articles which add material, argument, and illustrations to the discussion of an event, acknowledging other perspectives as well as her own.
"...a semblance of objectivity...".
Judith Mackrell, Interview.

Critical games
The ploys of some scholars who apply their theoretical disciplines using dance simply as critical fodder; said of a feminist analysis of "Swan Lake".
Judith Mackrell, Interview.

Dance appreciation
An examination of the appropriateness of elements to the whole and of the value and significance of individual dances.
Janet Adshead and *June Layson*, 1983.

Choreographic values
Changing and possibly conflicting criteria of goodness, criteria which reflect the changing value systems of the culture generally and the specific values of the sub-culture associated with the dance work.
Michael Huxley in Janet Adshead, 1988.

12.   SEMIOLOGY OF DANCE

Semiology of dance
The science of the sign systems which emanate from a dance work or from dance practice, generally studied in relation to the culture to which the signs belong.
Eds.

Decoding a dance
Looking for the shared, culturally-agreed signs within a work, a process which can illuminate the work but also restrict the appreciation of it, if that method (a semiotic method) is the only one used.
Helen Thomas, Interview.

Signs
Information emanating from an act of communication, including a work of art, which may be referential, emotive, injunctive, metalinguistic, phatic, or poetic. [applied to the analysis and making of dance works, developing Jacobson's model of the double function of language. Eds.]
Pierre Guiraud, 1975.

Referential and poetic functions

The denotative function of some elements of a dance work (which clearly refer to some meaning outside the work itself) and the connotative function of elements which provide a poetic symbol more open to interpretation; a semiotic method.

Helen Thomas, Interview.

Privilege

To give weight to one mode or ingredient of analysis over another, such as privileging the referential function of communication over the poetic and therefore looking for and seeing denotive elements.

Stephanie Jordan and *Helen Thomas*, 1990.

Frames

First identified by Bateson (1973) as the boundaries which define the perception of any given activity. The signs which provide the "rules" for any interaction and is central to the concept of "gaming".

Ana R. Sanchez-Colberg in Stephanie Jordan and Dave Allen, 1993.

Action signs

Movements which comprise a dance system, being moves which carry semiological content, that is they act as signs carrying agreed meaning.

Drid Williams in Andrée Grau, Interview.

Tripartition

The three semiotic systems operating in a musical work, those known to the composer in the genesis of the work, those embedded in the organisation of the work, those arising through the perception of the work by listeners. [A concept applied to dance analysis and making. Eds.]

Jean Jacques Nattiez, 1990.

Deconstruction (of dance)

The detailed description of conventions governing the use of signs in a particular work (i.e. a structuralist approach), and an examination of the ways the work itself, through various devices, apparently outplays the very codes on which it relies.

Jonathan Culler, 1983.

Deconstruction of dance

An analytical method based on such a degree of relativism that evaluation of a work is reduced to a ludicrous level of impossibility.

"...anything goes...".

Helen Thomas, Interview.

13. PHENOMENOLOGY AND PROPRIOCEPTION

Phenomenology of dance

A study of dance which centres on dance as a phenomenal presence and which gives an exacting descriptive account of our experience of dance, both as spectator and as dancer.

Maxine Sheets-Johnstone, 1979 (1966).

Horizon of time

The ways in which time is lived — compressed, elongated, endless, a long time, a short time, barely enough time, etc. Lived time does not refer to clock time, but to how time feels. A concept applied to "existence and the arts".

Sondra Fraleigh, 1991.

Phenomenological experience and time

"Central to phenomenology is the understanding that we never perceive a phenomenon in static unchanging perspectives, but rather as existing through time. Time and motion are ever present conditions influencing attention and perspective. Nevertheless, consciousness can unify experience."

Sondra Fraleigh, 1991.

Phenomenological construct of time

The phenomenological construct of time describes a totality whose substructures — past, present, future — form distinct but interrelated units. Their interrelationship is internally rather than externally defined: they do not exist as an isolated series of "nows", but as units whose meaning derives from their being intrinsic to the whole.

Maxine Sheets-Johnstone, 1979 (1966).

Original temporality and objective time (or internal and external time consciousness)

Two modes of experiencing time: through an internal consciousness of the temporal flow of the dance, its felt temporal dynamics; through an external or objective consciousness of the measured and measurable durations and tempos within the dance, which for dancers may be a matter of seconds, counts, bars, etc. In the first mode, movement creates its own time; in the second, movement takes place *in* time as in a container.

Maxine Sheets-Johnstone, 1979 (1966).

Phenomenology

This "...strives to capture pre-reflective experience, the immediacy of being-in-the-world. I think of this initial impulse of phenomenology (the basis of phenomenological reduction) as poetic and subliminal, containing moments of insight into an experience when the details of 'being there' are vivid in feeling, but have not had time to focus in thought."

Sondra Fraleigh, 1991.

Subjective experience

"The direct experience of a phenomenon, a state of awareness that has a particular irreducible content" [applicable to the experience of one's own movement and the experience of seeing/hearing a performance, Eds.].

'Encyclopædia Britannica', 1986.

Bodily schema

Any living experience of the body incorporates a pre-reflective awareness of its spatiality through the bodily schema. We know ourselves to be spatially present not through a factual part-by-part inventory of ourselves, but through a pre-reflective awareness of ourselves as a spatially present totality, whose posture, orientation, and comportment are aspects of that totality.

Maxine Sheets-Johnstone, 1979 (1966).

Original spatiality and objective space

Two modes of experiencing space that are akin to the two modes of experiencing time: through an awareness of oneself as a dynamically moving spatial presence; through an awareness of oneself as an objective, purely physical thing, a body whose shape, linear contours, proximity to other objects, and the like, are measured and measurable, and whose movements are similarly measured or measurable in terms of the distance they cover, their size, the specific linear patterns they describe, and so on. In the first mode, movement creates its own space; in the second mode, movement takes place *in* space as in a container.

Maxine Sheets-Johnstone, 1979 (1966).

Orientation of the body in space (temporary)

Temporary orientation achieved when the person (dancer) attends to the events and objects in the space at that moment, leading to awareness of diagonals, planes and lability, other movers' situation, placement of sounds, etc.

Valerie Preston-Dunlop from *James J. Gibson*, 1966.

Orientation of the body in space (permanent)

Permanent orientation to the earth through gravity providing the mover's sense of the vertical, and to the earth's surface (the floor) providing the mover's sense of the horizontal plane (also called the stable spatial framework).

Valerie Preston-Dunlop from *James J. Gibson*, 1966.

Perception of the body's movement in space

Achieved through a combination of systems: joints registering relative position and movement of bones (articular), muscles and tendons registering effort (muscular), inner ear registering head movement (vestibular), skin registering touch and pressure (cutaneous), eyes registering motion (visual).

Valerie Preston-Dunlop from *James J. Gibson*, 1966.

Kinaesthetic spatial cognition

The perception of, memorising of, retrieval from the memory of spatial information in the mover's own body, applied to spatial forms in dance material.
Jeffrey Longstaff, Interview.

Somatosensory research

A field of research which incorporates the perception of movement from a propriocentric perspective with a connection to the physiology of movement, exemplified by the work of Edrie Ferdun.
Ana R. Sanchez-Colberg, Interview.

Kinesiology

The study of the mechanics of body movement.
'Concise Oxford Dictionary', 1990.

14. LABAN'S MOVEMENT ANALYSIS

Laban Movement Analysis (LMA)

"LMA can mean any and all concepts for describing body movement found in the formal systems by Rudolf Laban and his students. In practice LMA people concentrate primarily on the qualitative aspects of movement."
Martha Davis, 1987.

Labananalysis

The name given in the U.S.A. to the two analytic systems started by Laban, his notation system (Labanotation) and Effort/Shape.
Lynn Renee Cohen, 1978.

Labananalysis

"A systematic vocabulary and methodology for the description of movement."
"Interpretation of the movement requires recourse to other frameworks such as aesthetics or psychology or psychoanalysis."
Suzanne Youngerman, 1978.

Labananalysis

"...a system for the observation, description, and notation of all forms of movement..." which "...derives from the work of Rudolf Laban, his associates, and his students. It combines the concepts of Labanotation, Effort/Shape, Space Harmony (also known as Choreutics), and the Fundamentals of Body Movement."
Suzanne Youngerman, 1978.

Movement thinking

"To think in Laban's way requires two critical figure-ground shifts. The first is from focus on static positions (or end points) to concentration on the movement." The second is to see the 'how' of the movement as figure and the 'what' as ground, "that is to see the process rather than the goal" of the movement.

Martha Davis, 1974.

Movement analysis

The process of looking at movement (movement observation) in order to yield meaning; a problematic process in which attempts at objectivity are undermined by the essentially subjective process of interpretation.

Ann Daly, 1988.

Shaping processes

The sculptural shaping created by the moving body parts within the three planes; widening or narrowing, rising or sinking, advancing or retreating.

Cecily Dell, 1977.

Shape (of Effort/Shape)

An analysis which identifies Shape Flow (growing and shrinking), Directional Movement (arch and spoke), and Shaping Movement (carving); part of Labananalysis.

Lynn Renee Cohen, 1978.

Effort/Shape

"...a systematic method of observing, recording, and analyzing the qualitative aspects of body movement."

Lynn Renee Cohen, 1978.

Effort

A system of dynamic qualities which, far from being universal, is an aesthetic language developed from a particular cultural context.

Janet Adshead-Lansdale, Interview.

Core principle (of Effort/Shape analysis)

"...the interrelation of spatial adaptation and organisation of the rhythmic elements of space-force-time."

Irmgard Bartenieff, 1974.

Categories of Effort/Shape analysis

Body attitude/effort/shape/spatial orientation/initiation of movement/sequence configuration/phrasing, this being Bartenieff's category interpretation of Laban's analysis.

Janet Adshead, 1988.

Psychophysical determinants of movement, The
      That for which Rudolf Laban searched and which are embodied in his theory of effort.
      Vera Maletic, 1987.

Holistic theory of dance
      The view held by Laban of the unity of the spirit/mind and body in dance and/or of the unity of motion and emotion and/or of movement engaging the mind and the body.
      Vera Maletic, 1987.

Four psychic functions, The
      A Jungian term for the powers of thinking, sensing, intuiting, and feeling which Laban associated with the space, weight, time, and flow elements in movement.
      Vera Maletic, 1987.

15.   NATURAL LAWS OF MOVEMENT

Natural laws of movement
      "The physical laws of tension and relaxation, action and rest, reaction and impetus which govern body movement and our well-being, simultaneously guide the conservation and release of mental energy in emotional and imaginative activity (for there is no division between body and mind)."
      Diana Jordan, 1938.

Natural sequences of stress
      Those sequences which arise out of the inevitable compensations in bodily action, rising after going down, releasing after tension, and so on.
      Roderyk Lange, 1975.

Laws of tension and relaxation
      There are four rules: i) Tension as outward expansion results in lightness, ii) Tension as inward contraction results in strength, iii) Relaxation as inward deflation results in heaviness, iv) Relaxation as outward release results in softness.
      Jane Winearls, 1958.

Geophysical rhythms
      The period cycles in the physical world, the seasons, day into night, rain into dry, which dance rhythms reflect.
      Roderyk Lange, 1975.

Rhythm
      "Organically, rhythm is a fundamental tendency in all our responses and is a principle of action in our physical organism...it is a constant principle of muscular action, which is control and release, work and rest."
      Margaret H'Doubler, 1974 (1940).

Theory of natural movement, The (Humphrey)
Fall and recovery seen as the all-inclusive rhythmic base of breathing, standing, walking, running, and leaping, the natural actions of the body.
Ernestine Stodelle, 1978.

Helping or hindering
The ways in which the body as a whole responds to the movement of one of its parts; the body cannot be neutral, it either helps or it hinders the successful completion of a move.
Scott Clark, Interview.

Natural affinities
The observation that the motion factors of weight, time and space are naturally affined with the direction and actions of rising-sinking, advancing-retreating, and opening-closing.
Rudolf Laban, 1948.

Space/effort affinities
"The dimension up-down...affines with the struggle with gravity — strong/light; the direction to right or left affines with spreading or narrowing the body; the direction forward (advancing) and back (retreating) affines with the effort attitude of time — sustaining, lingering or suddenness in the use of time."
Irmgard Bartenieff, 1974.

Theory of space relations
The relationship between the tensions to which all body parts can be subjected and the maximum amount of air-space that the body can occupy is found to be a fixed quantity defined by proportional relations.
A.V. Coton, 1946.

Interdependence of space and time in movement
"...accuracy of time is necessary to maintain the designed space. Change the space and the time changes...change the time and the space, and the movement changes...".
Merce Cunningham in James Klosty, 1975.

Lability and Stability
The Laban terminology for overcoming of inertia which promotes movement and brings about a temporary sense of freedom and loss of equilibrium, contrasted with that which facilitates stillness, temporary rest, quietude, and equilibrium.
Vera Maletic, 1987.

Nine Laws of Motion
François Delsarte's "law" governing movement of the body as a whole, based on the concept of the nine-fold accord, the nine states of being brought about by the relation between the mind, the body and the soul.
"1. Altitude, 2. Force, 3. Motion, 4. Sequence, 5. Direction, 6. Form, 7. Velocity, 8. Reaction, 9. Extension."
Ted Shawn, 1963 (1954).

16.   CHOREUTICS

Choreutics

The study of the harmonic content of spatial forms and the manner in which they materialise in movement.

Valerie Preston-Dunlop, 1984.

Choreutic form

A Laban term for one kind of harmonic arrangement of directional energy and spatial interval which has been identified and given a name.

Valerie Preston-Dunlop, 1984.

Choreutic practice

"The experiencing of trace forms from several viewpoints, integrating the bodily perspective, the dynamic feeling and the controlling faculties."

Rudolf Laban, 1966.

Spatial laws

The explanation of the way in which spatial forms exist in plants, crystals, and animals and in the way human movement is organised.

Vera Maletic, 1987.

Five regular solids (Platonic solids)

The tetrahedron, cube, octahedron, icosahedron, and dodecahedron, which Plato classified and which Laban took as models for the design and practice of choreutics.

Vera Maletic, 1987.

Ch.U./M.m. Choreutic Unit and Manner of Materialisation

A method for finding out how the shapes and patterns, both actual and virtual, in a dance work (Choreutic Units) are made available to the audience through the dancer's performance of them (Manner of Materialisation). Known as "Chumm". Used practically in studio work for refining performance and with a symbol system for style analyses.

Valerie Preston-Dunlop, 1981.

Spatial progression, spatial projection, spatial tension, and body design

These are the terms for the "Manner of Materialisation" theory in the Ch.U./M.m. method, that is, ways of describing how lines of energy in space are conveyed to an audience through the movement.

Valerie Preston-Dunlop, Interview.

Geometry (in classical ballet)

"One of the consistencies that runs through all the generations of classical ballet is a concern with geometry."

Robert Greskovic, 1984.

Cross of axes

A theoretical construct consisting of three axes intersecting at one point and perpendicular to each other, used for the determination of locations in three-dimensional space as a basic analytical principle in Laban's system of movement notation.

Rob van Haarst, Contributed.

17. DYNAMIC LAWS OF HARMONY

Dynamic laws of harmony, The

The laws of harmony in organic and inorganic forms, including movement, music, architecture, crystals, visual arts, hieroglyphic signs, indigenous dance.

Vera Maletic, 1987.

Harmonic principles

Principles of ratio, balance/imbalance, unity/discord, symmetries, and so on which can be found in movement through its spatial and temporal content.

Valerie Preston-Dunlop, 1984.

Harmony

"Harmony consists of a visual entity of two or more parts of the body in motion simultaneously resulting in a posture. The curves or angles formed through the flexion, extension and elevation of the limbs of the body employed singly or in opposition of one to another are the basis of harmony."

Leonide Massine, 1976.

Harmony

No aspect of the dance medium achieves precedence over the others: the dance and music become one, there is an equal relationship between partners, spatial harmony in the figures, harmony between upper body and step patterns.

"...the essentials of the baroque dance style are containment, harmony, and balance...".

Philippa Waite, Interview.

Eukinetics

The study of the laws of dynamic harmony apparent in movement, and the relationship between the spatial and dynamic qualities of an action.

Rudolf Laban, 1966.

Yin Yang

"The theory of complementary opposites which interact in a never-ending cycle of becoming. All T'ai Chi movements contain elements of Yin and Yang. Also, any movement which becomes strongly Yang, changes to Yin when Yang reaches its zenith and vice versa."

Katherine Allen, 1993.

Yin and Yang

Concepts of correspondences, soft and hard, negative and positive, passive and active, female and male, not as polar opposites but as complementary parts of the same whole; the essential concept in the practice of T'ai Chi Ch'uan.

B.P.J. Lo, et al., 1985.

Consonant

"Harmoniously in balance; agreeably pleasant and benign. The opposite of dissonant."

Aileene Lockhart and *Esther E. Pease*, 1977 (1966).

Dissonance

"Movement or harmony that produces an effect of strangeness and tension: clashing and disquieting effects. The opposite of consonance."

Aileene Lockhart and *Esther E. Pease*, 1981.

Opposition

An organising principle of classical ballet derived from the classical ideal of contrapposto (literally "opposite" in Italian) whereby balance and harmony of the body parts are achieved.

Joan Lawson, 1979.

Placement (classical ballet)

The correct positioning and co-ordination of the body parts with reference to the principles of stance, épaulement and turn-out.

Jane Carr, Interview.

Principles of classical ballet

There are seven: 1. Stance/posture; 2. Turn-out; 3. Placement; 4. Laws of balance; 5. Rules of the head, body and arms; 6. Co-ordination; 7. Transfer of weight. These principles underlie every movement in the classical vocabulary.

Joan Lawson, 1979.

18. CHOREOSOPHY

Choreosophy

"...a term first used by the disciples and followers of Pythagoras." [choreosophia].

"...the wisdom to be found through the study of all the phenomena of circles existing in nature and in life." (1939).

A concept and term applied by Laban to the study of the connections between the phenomena of circles and human movement.

Eds.

Choreosophy
>   A Laban term.
>   "The idea that dance has a spiritual and philosophic aspect which puts the human being in contact with nature, life, and 'the core of all being'."
>   *Miriam Huberman Muñiz*, 1990.

Choreosophy
>   A study initiated by Rudolf Laban which consists in:
>   "a reverence to nature and life as the origin of dance", "faith in the spiritual, healing and creative powers of dance", "capacity of dance to...integrate and bring wholeness", "a mission...to the spiritual development of the individual and to the creation of a new social order".
>   *Miriam Huberman Muñiz*, 1990.

Choreosophy
>   "The wisdom that may be found in dance is the basic philosophy and faith of the dancer."
>   *Miriam Huberman Muñiz*, 1990.

Choreosophy
>   The beliefs and assumptions of the dancer in the spiritual content of the dance (1920), the knowledge of the spiritual relationships of the dance content (1927), the theory and aesthetics of the new dance and dance education (1929).
>   *Rudolf Laban* (translated by Vera Maletic) in Vera Maletic, 1987.

Chirosopher
>   The Hellenic name for a dancer, for whom 'significant gesture' was a subject of study.
>   *André Levinson* (1922) in Joan Acocella and Lynn Garafola, 1991.

Sacred geometry
>   The number symbolism derived from Pythagorean cosmology, by which metaphysical significance is given to theories of mathematical proportion; use of these theories can be found recurring spasmodically in dance practice; an example is Beaujoyeulx's "Balet-Comique".
>   *Françoise Carter*, 1992.

Rituals and ceremonies
>   Ways of empowering an individual to reach the "altered states of consciousness" (ASC) and "shamanic states of consciousness" (SSC), ways which have a lesser or greater ingredient of dance, often accompanied by rhythmic sound; a process in shamanism.
>   *Jean Houston* in Shirley Wheaton, 1987.

Shaman dancing

"...when the spirits take over the shaman's body...".
Judy Van Zile, 1993.

Whirling dervishes

The Mevlevi, members of the religious order started by Jalal ad-Din ar-Rumi, whose dance "art of centralisation" takes the form of a solemn procession — "...each dancer crosses his arms over his breast and clasps his shoulder", filing past the Shaykh; "...and each dancer, as he enters the orbit of the Shaykh's presence, begins to unfold his arms and turn his body round, slowly at first but soon more quickly with his arms now stretched out on either side to their full extent, the right palm upwards as receptacle of Heaven and the left palm downwards to transmit Heaven to earth...".
Martin Lings, 1975.

Cosmic harmony

The harmonic relationship of the various orbits in space of the planets, seen as the archetype of round dances on earth.
E.M.W. Tillyard, 1944.

Rhythmic forces

"Rhythm is primarily within each one of us, used to conserve energy, to bring movement into harmonious relationship with the vital organs of the body and to bring ourselves into closer contact with the greater rhythmic forces of the world."
Diana Jordan, 1938.

Taoism

"An ancient Chinese religion/philosophy which seeks to establish harmony between man and nature. A Taoist sage of the 13th C, Chang San-feng, is the semi-legendary founder of T'ai Chi Ch'uan, which accords with the Taoist teachings and can be seen as an expression of Taoist philosophy through movement."
Katherine Allen, 1993.

T'ai Chi Ch'uan

The Chinese martial art form which embodies the Yin-Yang philosophy of comlementary forces, or principles, which "make up all aspects and phenomena of life".
'Encyclopædia Britannica', 1986.

Five elements

"Earth, fire, water, metal, and wood." In T'ai Chi theory, from Wu Chi (nothingness) came T'ai Chi, the mother of Yin and Yang. The interaction of Yin and Yang produced the Five Elements which represent the various processes in the world. The Five Elements interact continuously in certain ways, and in T'ai Chi Ch'uan represent the Five Directions: Metal represents Forward; Wood represents Back; Water represents Left; Fire represents Right; Earth represents Centre.
Katherine Allen, 1992.

BIBLIOGRAPHY

Acocella, Joan and **Garafola**, Lynn (Eds.). *André Levinson on Dance / Writings from Paris in the Twenties.* Hanover NH: Wesleyan Univ. Press, 1991.

Adamson, Andy. Leaflet "Documenting Dances / an application of computer-aided-design for the implementation and analysis of / Labanotation scores". Birmingham: Univ. of Birmingham, Dept. of Drama and Theatre Arts, 1992.

Adshead, Janet and **Layson**, June (Eds.). *Dance History / A Methodology for Study.* London: Dance Books, 1983.

Adshead, Janet (Ed.). *Choreography: Principles & Practice.* Guildford: National Resource Centre for Dance, 1987. (Contains papers from the 'Fourth Study of Dance Conference' 1986)

Adshead, Janet. *Dance Analysis / Theory and Practice.* London: Dance Books, 1988.

————— "Dance Analysis or Movement Analysis? Some distinctions", 5th Hong Kong International Dance Conference Papers, 1990.

Adzido Pan African Dance Ensemble. Flyer, 1993.

Allen, Katherine. "T'ai Chi Ch'uan". Unpublished note for students, Cranbrook, ca 1992.

Almeida, Bira. *Capoeira: A Brazilian Art Form.* Berkeley CA: North Atlantic Books, 1986.

Alston, Richard. "Appropriate Steps", *Dance Theatre Journal,* Vol. 2, No. 3, 1984.

Anderson, Jack. "Idealists, Materialists, and the Thirty-Two Fouettés", in **Copeland**, Roger and **Cohen**, Marshall (Eds.). *What is Dance? / Readings in Theory and Criticism.* New York: Oxford Univ. Press, 1983. (article orginally pubd. in *Ballet Review,* 6:4, 1975–76)

————— "*London Contemporary Dance Theatre: The First 21 Years,* by Mary Clarke and Clement Crisp" (Review), in *Dance Chronicle: Studies in Dance and the Related Arts,* Vol. 13, No. 2, 1990.

————— "Putting Dances in a Safe Place", *The New York Times,* Aug 1, 1993.

Anderson, Lea. *Flesh and Blood,* video. London: Arts Council of Great Britain, 1990.

Animated, "Dance within a mixed media project", Summer 1992.

Arbeau, Thoinot (Tr. Beaumont, C.W.). *Orchesography / a Treatise in the Form of a Dialogue / Whereby all manner of persons may easily acquire and practise the honourable exercise of dancing.* London: Cyril W. Beaumont, 1925. (original in French, 1588)

Argyle, Michael. *The Psychology of Interpersonal Behaviour.* London: Penguin, 1967.

Armelagos, Adina and **Sirridge**, Mary, "The Identity Crisis in Dance", *J.A.A.C.,* Vol. 37, No. 2, 1978.

Arts Council of Great Britain, Dance Department. Press Release, July 1993.

Ashley, Merrill. *Dancing for Balanchine.* New York: E.P. Dutton, 1984.

Ashton, Frederick. "Notes on Choreography", in **Sorell**, Walter (Ed.). *The Dance Has Many Faces.* Cleveland: World Publishing, 1951.

Aubel, Hermann and **Aubel**, Marianne. *Der künstlerische Tanz unserer Zeit.* Königstein im Taunus & Leipzig: Karl Robert Wiesche Verlag, 21–28 thou. 1930.

Andy, Robert. *Jazz Dancing / How to teach yourself.* New York: Vintage Books, a division of Random House, 1978.

Bablet, Denis and **Bablet**, Marie-Louise. *Adolphe Appia 1862–1928, actor – space – light.* Publication in association with an exhibition promoted by Pro Helvetia, Zürich, 1982.

Bachmann, Marie-Laure (Tr. Parlett, David). *Dalcroze Today: An Education through and with Music.* Oxford: Clarendon Press, 1991.

Baer, Nancy van Norman (Ed.). *Theatre in Revolution / Russian Avant-Garde Stage Design / 1913–1935.* New York: Thames and Hudson / The Fine Arts Museums of San Francisco, 1991.

Balanchine, George (Ed. Schoff, Thomas). *By George Balanchine.* New York: San Marco, 1984.

Bandoin, Patricia and **Gilpin**, Heidi. "Proliferation and Perfect Disorder. William Forsythe and the Architecture of Disappearance", English text in Book 2 of the proceedings of William Forsythe / Reggio Emilia Festival Danza. Reggio Emilia: I Teatri di Reggio Emilia, 1989.

Banes, Sally. *Terpsichore in Sneakers / Post-Modern Dance.* Boston: Houghton Mifflin, 1980(a).

———— Judson Dance Theater: Democracy's Body 1962–1964. Ph.D. thesis, New York Univ., 1980(b).

———— "Cunningham's Legacy", in Leaflet *Merce Cunningham and the New Dance / the modernist impulse in dance.* (A Publication of the State University of New York) Albany NY: State Univ. of New York, 1987.

Barnes, Clive. "Frederick Ashton", *Dance Perspectives,* No. 9 (Winter 1961).

————, **Goodwin**, Noël and **Williams**, Peter. "Taylor from three sides", *Dance and Dancers,* Jan 1965.

Barnes, Clive. "Essays, Stories, and Remarks about Merce Cunningham", *Dance Perspectives,* No. 34 (Summer 1968).

———— "Twyla Tharp and the Modern Classicism", *Dance and Dancers,* Sep 1987.

Barrand, Anthony G. *Six Fools and a Dancer / The Timeless Way of the Morris.* Plainfield VT: Northern Harmony Publishing Co, 1991.

Barringer, Janice and **Schlesinger**, Sarah. *The Pointe Book / Shoes, Training & Technique.* Princeton NJ: Dance Horizons / Princeton Book Co., 1990.

Bartenieff, Irmgard. "Effort/Shape in Teaching Ethnic Dance", *CORD Research Annual* VI (1974). (Proceedings of the third conference on research in dance 1972 "New Dimensions in Dance Research: Anthropology and Dance — The American Indian")

Barton, Anna. *Spirit of Dance / The Next Steps.* Forres, Scotland: Findhorn Press, 1992.

Bateson, Gregory. *Steps To an Ecology of Mind.* London: Paladin Books, 1973.

Bauer, Lilla. "Dance Composition", *Laban Art of Movement Guild Magazine,* No. 35, 1965.

Bausch, Pina. Programme "Seven Deadly Sins", 1976.

Beaumont, Cyril W. and **Idzikowski**, Stanislas. *A Manual of the Theory and Practice of Classical Theatrical Dancing / (Classical Ballet) / (Cecchetti Method)*. London: C.W. Beaumont, Revised edn., 1932. (original edn. 1922)

Becker, Nancy F. "Dance and the Media: A conversation with Charles Atlas", *Dance Theatre Journal*, 1982, No. 3.

Bell, Michael. *Community Dances Manual 5*. London: The English Folk Dance and Song Society, 1977. (Original pub. 1957)

Benesh, Rudolf and **Benesh**, Joan. *An introduction to Benesh Movement-Notation / Dance*. New York: Dance Horizons, 1969. (first pub. 1956)

Benesh Institute, The. "Benesh Movement Notation", *in Touch*, Royal Opera House Education, Covent Garden, 1993.

Berger, Renato. "Katherine Dunham - An Ingenious Dancer and Choreographer Devoted to Traditional, Modern and Avant-Garde Dance", *Ballett International*, June/July, 6/7, 1990.

Berman, Janice. "Cunningham Enters The Computer Age", *New York Newsday*, Mar 17, 1991.

Bernstein, Penny Lewis. *Theoretic Approaches to Dance Movement Therapy, Vol. II*. Dubuque IA: Kendall Hunt Publishing Co., 1984.

Best, Penelope A. "Dance Movement Therapy: State of the Art:", *Movement and Dance Quarterly*, Vol. 12, No. 2, Summer 1993.

Binkley, Timothy. "Deciding about art", in **Aagaard-Mogensen**, L. (Ed.). *Culture and Art*. Atlantic Highlands NJ: Humanities Press, 1976.

Birdwhistell, Ray L. *Kinesics and Context / Essays on Body-Motion-Communication*. London: Allen Lane, 1971. (first pub. 1970)

Birringer, Johannes. "Pina Bausch: Dancing Across Borders", *Drama Review*, Vol. 30, No. 2 (Summer 1986).

Blasis, Carlo. (Tr. Evans, Mary Stewart) *An Elementary Treatise upon the Theory and Practice of the Art of Dancing*. New York: Dover Publications Inc., 1968. (original 1820)

Blom, Lynne Anne and **Chaplin**, L. Tarin. *The Intimate Act of Choreography*. Pittsburg: Univ. of Pittsburgh Press, 1982.

Blum, Odette. "Developing Characterizations from the Dance Score", 5th Hong Kong International Dance Conference Papers (Notation Papers) 1990.

Bodmer, Sylvia. "Dance Composition", *Laban Art of Movement Guild Magazine*, No. 28, May 1962.

Bowne, Anthony. "Lighting Design and Contemporary Dance", *Sprung Floor*, June 1989.

Bramley, Ian. "Zero gravity and gratuitous violence", *Dance Theatre Journal*, Vol. 10, No. 3, Spring/Summer 1993.

Brandt, Rosemary. An approach to the teaching of dance: / an application of Rudolf Laban's principles of human movement to the generating principles of classical ballet. Unpublished M.A. dissertation, Laban Centre for Movement and Dance, 1987.

Brennan, Mary. "Glasgow / New Moves Across Europe", *Dance Theatre Journal*, Vol. 9, No. 4, Summer 1992.

Brinson, Peter. *Dance as Education / Towards a National Dance Culture.* London: Falmer Press, 1991.

British Broadcasting Corporation. "The Choreography of Jerome Robbins", BBC 2, 1959.

———— "The Catherine Wheel", Arena, BBC 2, 1983.

———— "Soundings", BBC Radio 3, 11 Feb 1991.

———— "Come Dancing", BBC TV, 1992(a).

———— "Dancemakers", BBC TV, 22 Aug 1992(b).

Brook, Peter. *The Empty Space.* Harmondsworth: Penguin, reprint 1990. (originally published 1968)

———— *The Shifting Point: Forty years of theatrical exploration 1946–1987.* London: Methuen, 1988.

Brown, Carolyn. "Essays, Stories, and Remarks about Merce Cunningham", *Dance Perspectives,* No. 34 (Summer 1968).

Brown, Trisha. "Improvisations and structures", in *Trisha Brown.* Paris: Éditions Bougé (Series "L'atelier des chorégraphes"), 1987.

———— and **Rainer**, Yvonne. "Conversation about 'Glacial Decoy'", in *Trisha Brown.* Paris: Éditions Bougé (Series "L'atelier des chorégraphes"), 1987.

Bruhn, Erik and **Moore**, Lillian. *Bournonville and Ballet Technique / Studies and Comments on August Bournonville's Études chorégraphiques.* New York: Dance Horizons Republication, undated. (original publication, 1961)

Brunel, Lise. "From forest to loft: journey to the core of a tree", in *Trisha Brown.* Paris: Éditions Bougé (Series "I'atelier des chorégraphes"), 1987.

Buckland, Theresa. "Traditional dance: English ceremonial and social forms", in **Adshead**, Janet and **Layson**, June. *Dance History / A Methodology for Study.* London: Dance Books, 1983.

Buckle, Richard. "Modern Ballet Design: 1909–1980", in **Strong**, Roy, et al. *Designing for the Dancer.* London: Elron Press, 1981.

Buckman, Peter. *Let's Dance / Social, Ballroom and Folk Dancing.* London: Paddington Press, 1978.

Burnside, Fiona. "Inside the Magic Box" (Review of Siobhan Davies), *Dance Theatre Journal,* Vol. 7, No. 4, 1990(a).

———— "British Spring Load", *Dance Theatre Journal,* Vol. 8, No. 1, 1990(b).

Butcher, Rosemary. *Arnolfini Dance Diary.* Arnolfini Gallery, Bristol, 1987.

———— Programme Note (1988), quoted in **Jordan**, Stephanie, *Striding Out.* London: Dance Books, 1992.

Cage, John. "Symposium on 'composer/choreographer'", *Dance Perspectives,* No. 16 (1963).

Cann, Bob. *A Dartmoor Country Dance Party.* Stowmarket: Veteran Tapes, 1989.

Carter, Françoise. "Number Symbolism and Renaissance Choreography", *Dance Research,* Vol. X, No. 1, Spring 1992.

Casey, Betty. *The Complete Book of Square Dancing (and Round Dancing).* Garden City, NY: Doubleday, 1976.

Castle, Roy. *Roy Castle on Tap.* Newton Abbott: David & Charles, 1986.

Challis, Chris. "Dance — the philosophically neglected art", *The Joan Russell Memorial Journal* (**Harris**, Mark Lintern, Ed.). London: Dance and the Child International (UK) Ltd., 1991.

Chase, Marion. Untitled papers in *Journal of the American Association for Health, Physical Education, and Recreation,* Mar 1952.

Chiang, Ying-Pi. An Examination of the possible contribution of choreological studies to the education of dancers in vocational dance conservatories. Unpublished M.A. dissertation, Laban Centre for Movement and Dance, 1991.

Chujoy, Anatole and **Manchester**, P.W. *The Dance Encyclopedia.* New York: Simon & Schuster, revised edn. 1967. (original edn. 1949)

Clarke, Mary and **Vaughan**, David (Eds.). *The Encyclopedia of Dance & Ballet.* London: Peerage Books / Rainbird Reference Books, 1977.

Clarke, Mary and **Crisp**, Clement. *Design for Ballet.* London: Studio Vista, 1978.

———— and ———— *Ballerina / The Art of Women in Classical Ballet.* London: BBC Books, 1987.

Clarke, Mary. "Birmingham Royal Ballet and Royal Ballet in London", *Dancing Times,* Apr 1993.

Coe, Robert. *Dance in America.* New York: Dutton, 1985.

Cohan, Robert. *The Dance Workshop.* London: Unwin Paperbacks, 1986.

Cohen, Einya. "On teaching Eshkol-Wachman Movement Notation to Academic Students", 5th Hong Kong International Dance Conference Papers (Notation Papers) 1990.

Cohen, Lynn Renee. "An Introduction to Labananalysis: Effort/Shape", *Dance Research Annual,* IX, 1978 (CORD).

Cohen, Selma Jeanne (Ed.). *The Modern Dance / Seven Statements of Belief.* Middletown CT: Wesleyan Univ. Press, 1966.

Cohen, Selma Jeanne. "A prolegomenon to an aesthetics of dance", in **Beardsley**, M.C. and **Schueller**, H.M. (Eds.). *Aesthetic Enquiry, Essays on Art Criticism and the Philosophy of Art.* Dickenson Pub. Co. Inc., 1967.

———— *Next Week, Swan Lake / Reflections on Dance and Dancers.* Middletown, CT: Wesleyan Univ. Press, 1982.

———— "Present Problems of Dance Aesthetics", *Dance Research,* Vol. 1, No. 1, Spring 1983.

'Concise Oxford Dictonary'. *The Concise Oxford Dictionary of Current English.* Oxford: Clarendon Press, 8th edn. 1990.

Constanti, Sophie. "Easing the Load / The Spring Loaded Season at The Place", *Dance Theatre Journal,* Vol. 5, No. 2, 1987.

Cook, Ray. *The Dance Director.* New York: published privately, second edn. 1981.

———— "'Dawn in New York' — Researching a Lost Masterpiece", 5th Hong Kong International Dance Conference Papers (Notation Papers) 1990.

Copeland, Roger. "Merce Cunningham and the Politics of Perception", in **Copeland**, Roger and **Cohen**, Marshall (Eds.). *What is Dance? / Readings in Theory and Criticism.* New York: Oxford Univ. Press, 1983. (quoting Martin, John, 1939)

———— "The Objective Temperament / Post-Modern Dance and the Rediscovery of Ballet", *Dance Theatre Journal,* Vol. 4, No. 3, 1986.

——— "The Black Swan and the Dervishes / Cross-Cultural Approaches", *Dance Theatre Journal,* Vol. 9, No. 4, Summer 1992

——— and **Cohen**, Marshall (Eds.). *What is Dance? / Readings in Theory and Criticism.* [contains various articles by named authors] New York: Oxford Univ. Press, 1983.

CORD. (Committee on Research in Dance) *Institute of Court Dances of the Renaissance and Baroque Periods.* New York: **CORD**, 1972. (relates to meetings in 1970 and 1971) (now regarded as *Dance Research Annual* IV, CORD)

Coton, A.V. *The New Ballet / Kurt Jooss and his work.* London: Dennis Dobson, 1946.

Crespo, Fernando. A justification for the inclusion of the strands of the dance medium in dance analysis. Unpublished M.A. dissertation, The Laban Centre for Movement and Dance, 1988.

Crisp, Clement and **Clarke**, Mary. *Making a Ballet.* New York: Macmillan Publishing Co. Inc., 1975.

Crisp, Clement. "Yolanda Sonnabend's Designs for Ballet", in *Yolanda Sonnabend / Stage designs and Paintings.* London: Serpentine Gallery, 1985.

Culler, Jonathan. *On Deconstruction: Theory and Criticism after Structuralism.* London: Routledge & Kegan Paul, 1983.

Cunningham, Merce. "Space, Time and Dance" (1952), in **Kostelanetz**, Richard (Ed.). *Merce Cunningham / Dancing in Space and Time.* Chicago: a cappella books, 1992.

——— Programme note, late 1960's.

——— "Two Questions and Five Dances", *Dance Perspectives,* No. 34 (Summer 1968).

——— "Commentary for a Video Event", *C.B.S. Camera,* III, 1974.

Cunningham, Merce and **Atlas**, Charles. *Fractions I.* Video, 1977

Cunningham, Merce. "Humans Doing Something", *Christian Science Monitor,* May, 1979.

Cunningham, Merce and **Atlas**, Charles. *Channels/Inserts.* Video, 1981.

Cunningham, Merce and **Lesschaeve**, Jacqueline. *The Dancer and the Dance.* London: Marion Boyars Publishers Ltd., 1985.

Cunningham, Merce. Program, New York, 1993.

Da Costa, Liz. "On Designing for Ballet Today", in **Strong**, Roy, et al. *Designing for the Dancer.* London: Elron Press, 1981.

Dalva, Nancy Vreeland. "The Right Mix", *Dance Magazine,* Apr 1989.

Daly, Ann. "Movement Analysis: Piecing Together the Puzzle", *Drama Review,* Winter 1988.

Dance and Dancers. "Curtain Up" (Editorial), Feb 1988.

Dance Notation Bureau. Program for "Labanwriter". New York: Dance Notation Bureau, 1987.

——— *Notated Theatrical Dances.* New York: Dance Notation Bureau, 3rd edn. 1991 (1985).

Dance Theatre Journal. "Getting off the Orient Express, Classicism East to West", (Editorial matter), Vol. 8, No. 2, Summer 1991.

——— Vol. 9, No. 4, Summer 1992.(a)

———— (Editorial matter) Vol. 10, No. 1, Autumn 1992.(b)

Dance UK (Ed. **Brinson**, Peter). Pamphlet "A dancers' charter for Health and Welfare". London: Dance UK, 1992.

Dancing Times. Listings and advertisements, Passim.

Daniels, Fred and **Morris**, Margaret. *Margaret Morris Dancing.* London: Kegan Paul, Trench, Trubner, ca 1926.

Davies, J.G. *Liturgical Dance, an historical, theological and practical handbook.* London: SCM Press, 1984.

Davis, Siobhan. Interviewed by Stephanie Jordan in "Partners in Dance 1988 Digital Award Winners", Guildford: National Resource Centre for Dance, 1988.

Davis, Martha. "Movement as Patterns of Process", *Main Currents in Modern Thought,* Vol. 31, No. 1, Sep–Oct 1974.

———— "An Introduction to the Davis Non-Verbal Communication Analysis System (DaNCAS)", 17th Annual Conference of American Dance Therapy Association, New York, 1982.

———— "Between Glassy Eyes and Sweaty Palms", *Movement Studies,* Vol. 2, 1987.

Davis, Mike. *The Royal Ballet.* London: Oldbourne, 1958.

De Marigny, Chris. Laban Centre Education Notes. London: Laban Centre for Movement and Dance, 1991.

———— "Pernicious Technology / The IMZ Dance Screen Festival, Frankfurt", *Dance Theatre Journal,* Vol. 10, No. 1 (Autumn 1992).

———— "Life and Art at the Cutting Edge", *Dance Theatre Journal,* Vol. 10, No. 3, Spring/Summer 1993.

De Mille, Agnes. *Martha / The Life and Work of Martha Graham.* New York: Random House, 1991.

De Valois, Ninette. *Step by Step / The formation of an establishment.* London: W.H. Allen, 1977.

Dell, Cecily. *A primer for movement description / using Effort/Shape and supplementary concepts.* New York: Dance Notation Bureau, 1970.

Dello Joio, Norman. "Symposium on 'composer/choreographer'", *Dance Perspectives,* No. 16 (1963).

Denby, Edwin. "Essays, Stories, and Remarks about Merce Cunningham", *Dance Perspectives,* No. 34 (Summer 1968)(a).

———— "How to Judge a Dance", in *Looking at the Dance.* New York: Horizon Press, 1968(b). (originals various dates 1936 et seq)

———— "Ballet — The American Position", in *Looking at the Dance.* New York: Horizon Press, 1968(c). (originals various dates 1936 et seq)

———— "Bright Plumage", in *Looking at the Dance.* New York: Horizon Press, 1968(d).

"**Diaghilev/Cunningham**". Catalogue of exhibition. Hempstead NY: Hofstra Univ., 1974.

Dice. Issue 19, July 1992. Community Dance and Mime Foundation.

Dickie, Sheila and **Sayers**, Lesley Anne. "The origins of the ISTD: part 4", *Dance Now,* Vol. 1, No. 4 (Winter 1992/93).

Diffey, Terence J. "Evaluation and aesthetic appraisals", in *The Republic of Art and Other Essays.* London: Peter Lang, 1991. (originally pub. 1967)

Dixon Gottschild, Brenda. "'Up from Under' — The Afrocentric tradition in American Concert Dance", 5th Hong Kong International Dance Conference Papers 1990.

Dominic, Zoe and **Gilbert**, John Selwyn. *Frederick Ashton: A Choreographer and his Ballets.* London: Harrap, 1971.

Donaldson, Anita. The Choreutic Parameter: A Key Determinant of Choreographic Structural Style. Unpublished Ph.D. Thesis, Laban Centre for Movement and Dance, 1993.

Dowdeswell, Jayne. Videodance: and the influence of video on creating dance for this purpose. Unpublished B.A. dissertation, Laban Centre for Movement and Dance, 1993.

Duncan, Irma. *The Technique of Isadora Duncan.* New York: Dance Horizons, 1970 (1937).

Dupuis, Simone. "Interview / Jérome Robbins", *Les saisons de la Danse,* No. 189, 15 Jan 1987.

Eddy, Martha (Ed.). *The LMA Compendium.* New York NY: Laban/Bartenieff Institute of Movement Studies, Inc., 1990.

Ellenberger, H. *The Discovery of the Unconscious: The history and evolution of dynamic Psychiatry.* New York: Basic Books, 2nd edn. 1970.

Ellis, Havelock. *The Dance of Life.* Boston: Houghton Mifflin, 1923.

'Encyclopædia Britannica'. *The New Encyclopædia Britannica.* Chicago: Encyclopædia Britannica Inc., 15th edn., printing of 1986.

English National Ballet. "Dance Resource Material for Primary Schools", *DICE,* Issue 19, July 1992.

Epstein, Alvin. "The Mime Theatre of Étienne Decroux", *Chrysalis — the pocket revue of the arts,* 1955, Vol. XI, Nos. 1–2.

Eshkol, Noa. *Movement Notation.* Holon, Israel: The Movement Notation Society, 1958.
——— and **Wachmann**, Abraham. *Movement Notation.* London: Weidenfeld and Nicolson, 1958.

Espinosa, Édouard. *The Elementary Technique of Operatic Dancing.* London: *The Dancer,* Revised edn. 1935.

Fee, F. Mary. "Discovering Rhythm through the Senses: A Theory of Rhythmic Perception", *Dance Research Monograph One 1971–1972.* New York: CORD, 1973. (now regarded as *Dance Research Annual* V, CORD)

Feldenkreis, Moshe. *Awareness through Placement.* San Francisco: Harper & Row,1984 (1972).

Fine, Vivian. "Symposium on 'composer/choreographer'", *Dance Perspectives,* No. 16 (1963).

Fischer-Munstermann, Uta (Ed. Williamson, Liz). *Jazz Dance & Jazz Gymnastics / including disco dancing.* New York: Sterling Publishing, 1978. (German original 1975)

Fisher, Seymour and **Cleveland**, Sidney E. *Body Image and Personality.* New York: Dover, 2nd edn. 1968.

Flindt, Vivi and **Jürgensen**, Knud Arne. *Bournonville Ballet Technique / 50 enchaînements selected and reconstructed.* London: Dance Books, 1992.

Fokine, Michel. Letter to *The Times,* Jul 6, 1914. reprinted in **Copeland**, Roger and **Cohen**, Marshall. *What is Dance? / Readings in Theory and Criticism.* New York: Oxford Univ. Press, 1983.

Fokine, Michel (Ed. Chujoy, Anatole) (Tr. Fokine, Vitale). *Fokine: Memoirs of a Ballet Master.* London: Constable, 1st English edn. 1961.

Foley, Catherine. Irish Traditional Step Dancing in North Kerry: A Contextural and Structural Analysis. Unpublished Ph.D. thesis, Laban Centre for Movement and Dance, 1988.

'Fool Time'. Prospectus 1992/3. 'Fool Time' The Centre for Circus Skills and Performing Arts, Bristol.

Forti, Simone. *Handbook in Motion.* Halifax: Press of the Nova Scotia College of Art and Design / New York: New York Univ. Press, 1974.

Fox, Michelle. Cine and Video Dance. Unpublished M.A. dissertation, Laban Centre for Movement and Dance, 1991.

Fraleigh, Sondra. *Dance and the Lived Body / A Descriptive Aesthetics.* Pittsburgh PA: Univ. of Pittsburg Press, 1987.

———— "A Vulnerable Glance: Seeing Dance through Phenomenology", *Dance Research Journal,* 23/1 (Spring 1991).

Fraser, Richard et al. *Dancers on a Plane.* London: Anthony d'Offay Gallery, 1989.

Gallie, William B. "Essentially contested concepts", *Proceedings of the Aristotelian Society,* LVI, 1956(a).

———— "Art as an essentially contested concept", *Philosophical Quarterly,* 6, 1956(b).

Garafola, Lynn. *Diaghilev's Ballets Russes.* New York: Oxford Univ. Press, 1989.

Gellerman, J. "The Mayim pattern as an indicator of cultural attitudes in three American Hasidic communities / A Comparative Approach based on Labananalysis", *Dance Research Annual* IX, CORD, 1978.

Genova, Judith. "The Significance of Style", *Journal of Aesthetics and Art Criticism,* Vol. 37, No. 3 (Spring 1979).

George, Nelson, **Banes**, Sally, **Flinker**, Susan, and **Romanowski**, Patty. *Fresh: hip hop don't stop.* New York: Random House / Sarah Lazin, 1985.

Gibson, James J. *The Senses Considered as perceptual systems.* Boston: Houghton Mifflin, 1966.

Gilbert, Katherine Everett. "Mind and Medium in the Modern Dance", in **Copeland**, Roger and **Cohen**, Marshall (Eds.). *What is Dance? / Readings in Theory and Criticism.* New York: Oxford Univ. Press, 1983. (article originally pubd. 1941)

Ginner, Ruby. *The Revived Greek Dance: its art and technique.* London: Methuen, 3rd enlarged edn. 1944.

Giurchescu, Anca. "The Dance Discourse. Dance Suites and Dance Cycles of Romania and elsewhere in Europe", *Dance Studies,* Vol. 11, 1987.

Glasstone, Richard. *Better Ballet.* London: Kaye & Ward, 1977.

———— "Ashton, Cecchetti and the English School", *Dance Theatre Journal,* Vol. 2, No. 3, 1984.

Goldberg, RoseLee. *Performance / Live Art 1909 to the Present.* London: Thames and Hudson, 1979.

Goldner, Nancy (Ed.). *The Stravinsky Festival of the New York City Ballet.* New York: Eakins Press, 1973.

Goodman, Nelson. *Languages of Art.* London: Oxford Univ. Press, 1969.

———— *Languages of Art.* Indianapolis: Hackett Publishing Co. Inc., 2nd edn. 1976.

Goodwin, Noël. "Three Way Partnership", *Dance and Dancers,* Apr 1988.

———— "A Matter of Form", *Dance and Dancers,* Feb 1989.

Gorsky, Alexander. (Tr. Wiley, Roland) *Two essays on Stepanov Dance Notation.* New York: CORD, 1978.

Graham, Martha. "A Modern Dancer's Primer for Action", in **Rogers**, Frederick Rand (Ed.). *Dance: A basic educational technique / A functional approach to the use of rhythmics & dance as prime methods of development & control, and transformation of moral & social behavior.* New York: Macmillan, 1941.

———— *A Dancer's World.* Film with Martha Graham and Company, Nathan Kroll, 1957.

———— "A Dancer's World", *Dance Observer,* Jan 1958. (Script of the film *A Dancer's World* (1957))

———— and **Sorell**, Walter. "Martha Graham Speaks", *Dance Observer,* 84, 1963.

Graham, Martha. *Blood Memory.* New York: Doubleday, 1991.

Greskovic, Robert. "Thoughts on Classicism and Ashton", *Dance Theatre Journal,* Vol. 2, No. 3, 1984.

———— "Dancing With a Mouse", *Los Angeles Times,* May 5, 1991.

'Grove'. *The New Grove Dictionary of Music and Musicians.* London: Macmillan, 1980.

Guillard, Yves. "Early Scottish Reel Setting Steps and the Influence of the French Quadrille", *Dance Studies,* Vol. 13, 1989.

Guiraud, Pierre (Tr. Gross, George). *Semiology.* London: Routledge & Kegan Paul, 1975. (original pub. 1971)

Gula, Denise A. *Dance Choreography for Competitive Gymnastics.* Champaign IL: Leisure Press, 1990.

Hackney, Peggy. "Bartenieff Fundamentals (TM)", (unpublished document). Seattle WA, 1984.

————, **Manno**, Sarah and **Topaz**, Muriel. *Study Guide for Elementary Labanotation.* New York: Dance Notation Bureau Press, 2nd edn. 1977. (original edn. 1970)

Hall, Edward T. *Hidden Dimension.* New York: Doubleday, 1966.

Hamilton, Jack (Ed.). *Community Dances Manual 6.* London: The English Folk Dance and Song Society, 1964.

———— *Community Dances Manual 7.* London: The English Folk Dance and Song Society, 1967.

———— *English Folk Dancing.* Wakefield: EP Publishing Ltd., 1974.

Hamilton, Stanley. "Statue to Stillness" — an outdoor dance meditation. Publicity material, 1992.

Harris, Hilary. "Cine-dance", *Dance Perspectives,* No. 30, 1967.

Harrison, Jane. *Ancient Art and Ritual.* London: Williams and Norgate, 1918.

Hastings, Baird. "Étienne Decroux and his mime", *Dance and Dancers,* June 1950.

Hawkins, Erick. "Pure Poetry", in **Cohen**, Selma Jeanne (Ed.). *The Modern Dance / Seven Statements of Belief.* Middletown CT: Wesleyan Univ. Press, 1966.

Hayes, Elizabeth R. *Dance Composition and Production / for High Schools and Colleges.* New York: The Ronald Press Company, 1955.

Hays, Joan F. *Modern Dance / A biomechanical approach to teaching.* St. Louis MO: C.V. Mosby Co., 1981.

Hazzard-Gordon, K. *Jookin' the rise of social dance formation in african-american culture.* Philadelphia PA: Temple Univ. Press, 1990.

Heaney, Michael and **Forrest**, John. *Annals of Early Morris.* Sheffield: The Centre for English Cultural Tradition and Language, Univ. of Sheffield; with The Morris Ring, 1991.

Helpern, Alice J. The Evolution of Martha Graham's Dance Technique. Ph.D. thesis, New York Univ., 1981.

Hilton, Wendy. *Dance of Court and Theater: The French Noble Style 1690–1725.* London: Dance Books, 1981.

Hodgens, Pauline. "Interpreting the dance", in **Adshead**, Janet (Ed.). *Dance Analysis / Theory and Practice.* London: Dance Books, 1988(a).

————— "Evaluating the dance", in **Adshead**, Janet (Ed.). *Dance Analysis / Theory and Practice.* London: Dance Books, 1988(b).

Hodson, Millicent. "Composition by Field / Merce Cunningham and the American fifties", in **Adshead**, Janet (Ed.), *Choreography: Principles & Practice.* Guildford: National Resource Centre for Dance, 1987.

————— "Ritual Design in the New Dance / Nijinsky's 'Le Sacre du Printemps'", *Dance Research*, Vol. III, No. 2, Summer (cover marked 'Autumn') 1985.

————— "Ritual Design in the New Dance / Nijinsky's Choreographic Method", *Dance Research,* Vol. IV, No. 1, Spring 1986.

Hofstätter, Hans H. *Art Nouveau / Prints, Illustrations and Posters.* London: Omega Books, 1984. (German edn. 1968)

Hoghe, Raimund. "The Theatre of Pina Bausch", *Drama review,* Vol. 24, No. 1 (Mar 1980).

Horst, Louis. Lecture Notes from Horst's "Modern Forms" course, 1957. Private collection of Dorothy Madden.

————— Tape from Univ. of Maryland, Nov. 1958. Private collection of Dorothy Madden.

————— *Pre-Classic Dance Forms.* New York: Kamin, 1960. (original edn. 1937)

————— and **Russell**, Carroll. *Modern Dance Forms / in Relation to the Other Modern Arts.* San Francisco: Impulse Publications, 1961.

Horst, Louis. "Symposium on 'composer/choreographer'", *Dance Perspectives,* No. 16 (1963).

Houston, Jean. "The Mind and Soul of the Shaman", in **Nicholson**, Shirley (Compiler). *Shamanism / An Expanded View of Reality.* Wheaton IL: The Theosophical Publishing House, 1987.

Hoving, Lucas. "Random Notes from a Contemporary Romantic", *Dance Perspectives,* No. 38 (Summer 1969).

Huberman Muñiz, Miriam. Rudolf Laban and the concept of Choreosophy. Unpublished M.A. dissertation, Laban Centre for Movement and Dance, 1990.

Humphrey, Doris (Ed. Pollack, Barbara) *The Art of Making Dances.* New York: Rinehart & Co., 1959.

Hurl, Geraldine. The dance study as a means to dance experience in a community context. Unpublished M.A. dissertation, Laban Centre for Movement and Dance, 1986.

Hutchinson, Ann. *Labanotation.* New York: New Directions, 1954.

———— *Labanotation.* New York: Theatre Arts Books, revised and expanded edn. 1970.

Hutchinson Guest, Ann. Contributions to **Clarke**, Mary and **Vaughan**, David (Eds.). *The Encyclopedia of Dance and Ballet.* London: Peerage Books / Rainbird Reference Books, 1977.

———— *Your Move / A New Approach to The Study of Movement and Dance.* London: Gordon and Breach, 1983.

———— *Choreo-graphics.* London: Gordon and Breach, 1989.

Hutchinson Guest, Ann and **Jeschke**, Claudia. "An Introduction to Vaslav Nijinsky's System of Dance Notation", 5th Hong Kong International Dance Conference Papers (Notation Papers) 1990.

Hutchinson Guest, Ann and **van Haarst**, Rob. *Shape, Design, Trace Patterns* (Advanced Labanotation (Ed. **Hutchinson Guest**, Ann), Vol. 1, Part 2). Chur: Harwood Academic, 1991.

Huxley, Michael. "A history of a dance: an analysis of 'Dark Elegies' from written ciriticism", in **Adshead**, Janet (Ed.). *Dance Analysis: Theory and Practice.* London: Dance Books, 1988.

H'Doubler, Margaret N. *Dance / A Creative Art Experience.* Madison: Univ. of Wisconsin, 1957. (original edn. 1940)

Imperial Society of Teachers of Dancing. Publicity material. 1993(a).

———— Leaflet "Tap Branch/Modern Theatre Dance", 1993(b).

———— Leaflet "Modern Theatre Dance Branch", 1993(c).

———— Leaflet "Sequence Dance Branch", 1993(d).

———— Leaflet "Classical Greek Dance Association Branch", 1993(e).

———— Leaflet "Classical Ballet/Cecchetti Society Branch", 1993(f).

International Folk Music Council (Folk Dance Study Group of). "Foundations for the analysis of the Structure and Form of Folk Dance", *I.F.M.C. Yearbook,* Vol. 1974.

Jackson, Michael. "The Michael Jackson Interview". British Broadcasting Corporation, BBC 2, 15 Feb 1993.

Jary, David and **Jary**, Julia. *Collins Dictionary of Sociology.* London: Harper Collins, 1991.

Jeyasingh, Shobana. Conversation with Ann Nugent on "Correspondences". Issued by Shobana Jeyasingh as publicity material, 1993.

Johnson, R.V. *Aestheticism.* London: Methuen, 1969.

Jones, Bill T. and **Zane**, Arnie (Zimmer, Elizabeth and Quasha, Susan, Eds.). *Body against Body.* Barrytown NY: Station Hill Press, 1989.

Jooss, Kurt. "The Dance of the Future" (Interview by Derrada Moroda), *Dancing Times,* Aug 1933.

———— "Die Sprache des Tanztheaters" (1935), reprinted in *Ballett Jahrbuch des Tanzarchiv,* Vol. 34, No. 6 (1986).

———— *Stage Dancing in Germany.* Darmstadt: Neue Darmstädter Verlag, 1956.

Jordan, Diana. *The Dance as Education.* London: Oxford Univ. Press, 1938.

Jordan, Stephanie. "Siobhan Davies: Two for LCDT" (Reviews), *Dance Theatre Journal,* Vol. 5, No. 1, (1987).

———— "Siobhan Davies Company 1988", *Dance Theatre Journal,* Vol. 6, No. 4, (1989).

———— "British Modern Dance: Early Radicalism", 5th Hong Kong International Dance Conference Papers 1990.

———— and **Thomas**, Helen. "Gender and Structuralism: Combined perspectives", 'Man and Woman in Dance — Conference of European Association of Dance Historians', Leuven, Nov 1990.

Jordan, Stephanie. *Striding Out / Aspects of Contemporary and New Dance in Britain.* London: Dance Books, 1992.

Jowitt, Deborah. *Dance Beat / Selected Views and Reviews 1967–1976.* New York: Marcel Dekker, 1977. (Contains items with various original dates)

———— *The Dance in Mind.* Boston: Godine, 1985.

———— *Time and the Dancing Image.* New York: W.M. Morrow, 1988.

Kaeppler, Adrienne L. "Method and Theory in Analyzing Dance Structure with an Analysis of Tongan Dance", *Ethnomusicology,* Vol. XVI, No. 2 (May 1972).

Kagan, Elizabeth. "Towards the Analysis of a Score", *Dance Research Annual* IX, CORD, 1978.

Kane, Angela. "Six Companies", *Dancing Times,* May 1987.

———— "Siobhan Davies / Family Connections", *Dancing Times,* Mar 1990 (in Dance Study Supplement between pp. 592 and 593).

Kauffmann, S. "West Side Glory" (Review of Movie), *Dancing Magazine,* Vol. XXXV, No. 10, Oct 1961.

Kay, Barry. "On Designing for Ballet Today", in **Strong**, Roy, et al. *Designing for the Dancer.* London: Elron Press, 1981.

Kealinohomoku, Joann. A Comparative Study of Dance as a Constellation of Motor Behaviors Among African and United States Negroes, Unpublished M.A. thesis, Northwestern Univ., 1965.

———— "An Anthropologist Looks at Ballet as a Form of Ethnic Dance" (1969–70), in **Copeland**, Roger and **Cohen**, Marshall. *What is Dance? Readings in Theory and Criticism.* New York: Oxford Univ. Press, 1983.

Kelly, Deirdre. "Dancing bits and bytes add up to grand jetes and arabesques", *The Globe and Mail* (Toronto), Apr 14, 1990.

Kennedy, Douglas. *England's Dances / Folk-dancing to-day and yesterday.* London: G. Bell & Sons, Ltd., 1949.

Kennedy, Douglas (Ed.). *Community Dances Manual 1.* London: The English Folk Dance and Song Society, 1968. (originally pub. 1949)

Kennedy, Peter (Ed.). *Community Dances Manual 3.* London: The English Folk Dance and Song Society, 1964.

Kent County Council. Adult Education Programme 1992/93: West Kent.

Kerner, Mary. *Barefoot to Balanchine / How to Watch Dance.* New York: Anchor, 1991.

Kirstein, Lincoln. "Classic and Romantic Ballet" (1939) from *Ballet Alphabet* in *Three Pamphlets Collected* (1967), reprinted in **Copeland**, Roger and **Cohen**, Marshall. *What is Dance? Readings in Theory and Criticism.* New York: Oxford Univ. Press, 1983.

————— and **Stuart**, Muriel. *The Classic Ballet / Basic Technique and Terminology.* London: A&C Black, 1977. (original pub. 1952)

Kirstein, Lincoln. "What ballet is about: An American Glossary", *Dance Perspectives,* No. 1 (Winter 1959).

————— *Movement & Metaphor / four centuries of ballet.* London: Pitman, 1971.

————— *The New York City Ballet.* New York: Alfred A. Knopf, 1973.

————— "Classic Ballet: Aria of the Aerial", *Playbill*, May 1976, reprinted in **Copeland**, Roger and **Cohen**, Marshall. *What is Dance? Readings in Theory and Criticism.* New York: Oxford Univ. Press, 1983.

Klosty, James (Ed.). *Merce Cunningham.* New York: E.P. Dutton and Co., 1975.

Knust, Albrecht. *Dictionary of Kinetography Laban (Labanotation).* Plymouth: Macdonald & Evans, 1979.

Kochno, Boris. *Diaghilev and the Ballets Russes.* New York: 1970. (original in French 1954)

Kostelanetz, Richard (Ed.). *Merce Cunningham / Dancing in Space and Time.* Chicago: a capella books, 1992.

Kriegsman, Alan M. Review of Bill T. Jones and Arnie Zane, *Washington Post,* 1984.

Kriegsman, Sali Ann. *Modern Dance in America, The Bennington Years.* Boston: G.K. Hall, 1981.

Laban, Rudolf von. "Grundprinzipien der Bewegungsschrift", *Schrifttanz,* 1928, No. 1, July.

Laban, Rudolf (Tr. and Annot. Ullmann, Lisa). *A Life for Dance / Reminiscences.* London: Macdonald & Evans, 1975. (orginally published in German as **Laban**, Rudolf von. *Ein Leben für den Tanz.* Dresden: Carl Reissner Verlag, 1935.)

Laban, Rudolf (Annot. & Ed. Ullmann, Lisa). *Choreutics.* London: Macdonald & Evans, 1966. (mainly written in 1939)

Laban, Rudolf and **Lawrence**, F.C. *Effort.* London: Macdonald & Evans, 1947.

Laban, Rudolf. *Modern Educational Dance.* London: Macdonald & Evans, 1948(a).

————— "President's Address", *Laban Art of Movement Guild News Sheet,* No. 1 (1948)(b).

————— *The Mastery of Movement on the Stage.* London: Macdonald & Evans, 1950.

————— *Principles of dance and movement notation.* London: Macdonald & Evans, 1956.

————— (Rev. Ullmann, Lisa). *The Mastery of Movement.* (3rd Edn.) London: Macdonald & Evans, 1971.

Laban Centre for Movement and Dance. Choreological Studies syllabus, 1992.

————— Prospectus 1992/93.

————— Choreological Studies syllabus, 1993.

LaFave, Kenneth. "Reviews — Kansas City" (Reviews of Alvin Ailey), *Dance Magazine,* Mar 1989.

Lahusen, Susanne. "Oskar Schlemmer: Mechanical Ballets?" *Dance Research,* Vol. IV, No. 2, Autumn 1986.

Lamb, Warren. *Posture and Gesture / An Introduction to the Study of Physical Behaviour.* London: Duckworth, 1965.

————— and **Watson**, Elizabeth. *Body Code: The Meaning in Movement.* London: Routledge & Kegan Paul, 1979.

Lange, Roderyk. *The Nature of Dance / An Anthropological Perspective.* London: Macdonald & Evans, 1975.

———— "The Development of Anthropological Dance Research", *Dance Studies,* Vol. 4, 1980.

———— "Semiotics and Dance", *Dance Studies,* Vol. 5, 1981.

———— "Guidelines for Field Work on Traditional Dance Methods and Checklist", *Dance Studies,* Vol. 8, 1984.

———— "Laban's System of Movement Notation", *Dance Studies,* Vol. 9, 1985.

———— "Dance Notation and the Development of Choreology", *Acta musicologica: Musica Antiqua VIII.* Vol. 1. (Poland, 1988).

Langer, Susanne K. *Feeling and Form / A Theory of Art Developed from Philosophy in a New Key.* London: Routledge & Kegan Paul, 1953.

———— *Problems of Art.* New York: Charles Scribner's Sons, 1957.

Lauterer, Arch. Several contributions to *Impulse: The Annual of Contemporary Dance,* 1959. (the whole issue is titled "Arch Lauterer — Poet in the theatre")

Lawson, Joan. *Classical Ballet / Its Style and Technique.* London: A&C Black, 1960.

———— *The Principles of Classical Ballet.* London: A&C Black, 1979.

———— *Ballet Class / Principles and Practice.* London: A&C Black, 1984.

Leibowitz, Judith and **Connington**, Bill. *The Alexander Technique.* London: Souvenir Press, 1991.

Leon, Milca. Proxemics in dance: a theoretical and practical investigation of the role of non-verbal communication in narrative theatre dance, with special reference to the spatial manifestation of power. Unpublished M.A. dissertation, Laban Centre for Movement and Dance, 1993.

Levin, David Michael. "Post modernism in Dance: Dance Discourse and Democracy", in **Silverman**, Hugh J. *Post modernism, Philosophy, and the Arts.* London: Routledge, 1990.

Lewis, Daniel. *The Illustrated Dance Technique of José Limón.* New York: Harper & Row, 1984.

Lings, Martin. *What is Sufism?* London: Unwin Paperbacks, 1975.

Little, Meredith and **Jenne**, Natalie. *Dance and the Music of J.S. Bach.* Bloomington and Indianapolis: Indiana Univ. Press, 1991.

Litvinoff, Valentina. "In Search of First Principles", *Dance Research Monograph One 1971–1972.* New York: CORD, 1973. [now regarded as *Dance Research Annual* V, CORD]

Lloyd, Margaret. *The Borzoi Book of Modern Dance.* New York: Dance Horizons, reprint 1974. (original 1949)

Lloyd, Maude. "Some Recollections of the English Ballet", *Dance Research,* Vol. III, No. 1, Autumn 1984.

Lloyd, Norman, "Symposium on 'composer/choreographer'", *Dance Perspectives,* No. 16 (1963).

Lo, B.P.J.; **Inn**, M.; **Amacker**, R.; and **Foe**, S. (trans.). *The Essence of T'ai Chi Ch'uan: The Literary Tradition.* Berkeley CA: North Atlantic Books, 1985.

Lockhart, Aileene S. and **Pease**, Esther E. *Modern Dance / Building and Teaching Lessons.* Dubuque: Wm. C. Brown, 5th edn. 1977. (1st edn. 1966)

Lockyer, Bob. "Dance and Video: Random Thoughts", *Dance Theatre Journal,* 1983, Vol. 1, No. 4.

Loman, Hettie. Programme "Ophelia", 1988.

———— Programme "Once I Had Laughter", 1991.

———— Programme "The Moon and the Fisherman", 1992.

Longstaff, Jeffrey. Kinesphere and Dynamosphere, Trace Forms and Shadow Forms and the Affinities. Unpublished Ph.D. paper, Laban Centre for Movement and Dance, 1993.

Louis, Murray. "Forward is Not Always Going Ahead", *Dance Perspectives,* No. 38 (Summer 1969).

———— *Inside Dance.* New York: St. Martin's Press, 1980.

Louppe, Laurence. "French Dance: The New Narrative / Its Literary and Cinematic Roots", *Dance Theatre Journal,* Vol. 7, No. 1, 1989.

Macaulay, Alistair. *Some Views and Reviews of Ashton's choreography.* Guildford: National Resource Centre for Dance, 1988.

Mackintosh, Peri. "This is Theatre...Jan Faber and Company" (Review), *Dance Theatre Journal,* Vol. 1, No. 4 (1983).

Mackrell, Judith. "Post-modern Dance in Britain", *Dance Research,* Vol. IX, No. 1, Spring 1991.

Magri, Gennaro (Tr. Skeaping, Mary). *Theoretical and Practical Treatise on Dancing.* London: Dance Books, 1988. (original 1779)

Maletic, Vera. *Body – Space – Expression / The Development of Rudolf Laban's Movement and Dance Concepts.* Berlin: De Gruyter, 1987.

Margolis, Joseph. "Art as a Language", *The Monist,* 58:2 (1974).

Marion, Sheila. "Authorship and Intention in Re-created or Notated Dances", 5th Hong Kong International Dance Conference Papers (Notation Papers) 1990.

Marti, Samuel and **Kurath**, Gertrude Prokosch. *Dances of Anahuac: The choreography and music of pre-Cortesian dances.* Chicago: Aldine, 1964.

Martin, John. *The Modern Dance.* New York: Dance Horizons, 1972. (first pub. 1933)

———— *Introduction to the Dance.* New York: Dance Horizons, 1965. (first pub. 1939)

———— *The Dance / the story of the dance told in pictures and text.* New York: Tudor, 1946.

———— "Isadora and Basic Dance", in **Magriel**, Paul (Ed.). *Nijinsky, Pavlova, Duncan / Three Lives in Dance.* New York: Da Capo Press, 1977. (originally pub. 1947)

Martin, Marianne W. "The ballet parade: A dialogue between Cubism and Futurism", *Art Quarterly,* 1, No. 2 (Spring 1978).

Massine, Leonide. *Massine on Choreography: Theory and Exercises in Composition.* London: Faber & Faber, 1976.

Mazo, Joseph. *Prime Movers / The makers of Modern Dance in America.* London: A&C Black, 1977.

McDonagh, Don. "New York / Moderns over the river", *Dance and Dancers,* Mar 1969.

———— *The Rise and Fall and Rise of Modern Dance.* New York: E.P. Dutton, 1970.

———— *The Complete Guide to Modern Dance.* New York: Doubleday, 1976.

McFee, Graham. *Understanding Dance.* London: Routledge, 1992.

Meager, Ruby. "Aesthetic concepts", *British Journal of Aesthetics,* 10, 1970.

Meisner, Nadine. "Dance Umbrella / DV8" (Review), *Dance and Dancers,* Mar 1989.

Mekas, Jonas. "Movie Journal", *Village Voice* (New York), Dec 7, 1967.

Merriam, Alan P. "Anthropology and the Dance", *CORD Research Annual* VI (1974), (Proceedings of the third conference on research in dance 1972 "New Dimensions in Dance Research: Anthropology and Dance — The American Indian")

Mettler, Barbara. *The Nature of Dance as a Creative Art Activity.* Tuscon: Mettler Studios, 1980.

Misler, Nicoletta. "Designing Gestures in the Laboratory of Dance", in **Baer**, Nancy van Norman. *Theater in Revolution; Russian Avant Garde Stage Design, 1913–1935.* New York: Tharmes and Hudson and The Fine Arts Museums of San Francisco, 1991.

Moore, Jack. "Journal for Dollard", *Dance Perspectives,* No. 38 (Summer 1969).

Morris, Margaret. *Creation in Dance and Life.* London: Peter Owen, 1972.

Movement and Dance Quarterly. Vol. 12, No. 2, Summer 1993. (pub. Laban Guild)

Müller, Hedvig and **Servos**, Norbert. "Expression in Dance / Expressionism? 'Ausdruckstanz' and The New Dance Theatre in Germany", *Dance Theatre Journal,* Vol. 2, No. 1 1984.

Mumford, Peter. "Lighting Dance", *Dance Research,* Vol. III, No. 2, Autumn 1985.

Nagrin, Daniel. *How to dance forever / Surviving Against the Odds.* New York: William Morrow, 1988(a).

———— "Nine Points in making your own Dance Video", *Dance Theatre Journal,* Vol. 6, No. 1, Summer 1988(b).

Nattiez, Jean Jacques. *Music and Discourse.* Princeton NJ: Princeton Univ. Press, 1990.

Nears, Colin. "Bridging a Distance / Television and Dance", in **Jordan**, Stephanie and **Allen**, Dave (Eds.). *Parallel Lines / Media Representations of Dance.* London: John Libbey & Co. (for The Arts Council of Great Britain), 1993.

'New Dance'. *New Dance, a celebratory weekend publicity leaflet.* New Dance Dances and Mime, 1986.

Niclas, Lorrina. *IIIes Rencontres Chorégraphiques internationales de Bagnolet, 1992.* Seine Saint Denis: Centre international de Bagnolet pour les oeuvres chorégraphiques, 1992.

Nikolais, Alwin. "Symposium on 'composer/choreographer'", *Dance Perspectives,* No. 16 (1963).

———— "Basic Dance and Sensory Perception", *Dance Observer,* Jan 1964.

———— Contribution to *Dance Perspectives,* No. 48 (Winter 1971). (whole issue entitled "Nik, a documentary")

North, Marion. *Composing Movement Sequences.* London: privately, 1961.

———— *Introduction to Movement Study and Teaching.* London: Macdonald & Evans, 1971.

———— *Personality Assessment through Movement.* London: Macdonald & Evans, 1972.

Novack, Cynthia J. *Sharing the Dance / Contact Improvisation and American Culture.* Madison: Univ. of Wisconsin Press, 1990.

Noverre, Jean Georges (Tr. and Ed. Beaumont, Cyril W.). *Letters on Dancing and Ballets.* New York: Dance Horizons, 1966. (revised French original 1803)

Odom, Selma Landen. Book Review "What is Dalcrozian?", *Dance Research,* Vol. X, No. 2, Autumn 1992.

Oesterley, W.E.O. *The Sacred Dance: A study in comparative folklore.* New York: Dance Horizons, reprint 1968. (original 1923)

Ortega y Gasset, José. "On Point of View in the Arts", quoted in **Copeland**, Roger and **Cohen**, Marshall (Eds.). *What is Dance? / Readings in Theory and Criticism.* New York: Oxford Univ. Press, 1983.

Overby, Lynette Young. "The Relationship of Dance Training to the Body Image / A Review of the Literature", 5th Hong Kong International Dance Conference Papers 1990.

Page, Ralph. *The Ralph Page Book of Contras.* London: The English Folk Dance and Song Society, 1969.

Pagels, Jurgen. *Character Dance.* Bloomington IN: Indiana Univ. Press, 1984.

Palmer, Elsie. "Mind and Body = A new Humanism", Papers of The Conference of Educational Associations. Addlestone: Laban Art of Movement Guild, Jan 1958.

Paskevska, Anna. *Ballet / From the First Plié to Mastery / An Eight-Year Course.* London: Dance Books, 1990.

Paxton, Steve. Programme Note (1988), quoted in **Jordan**, Stephanie. *Striding Out.* London: Dance Books, 1992.

Payne, Helen (Ed.). *Dance Movement Therapy: theory and practice.* London and New York: Tavistock/Routledge, 1992.

Perces, Marjorie B., **Forsythe**, Ana Marie, and **Bell**, Cheryl. *The Dance Technique of / Lester Horton.* Princeton NJ: Dance Horizons / Princeton Book Co., 1992.

Percival, John. Reviews in *Dance and Dancers,* March 1993.

Peterson Royce, Anya. "Choreology Today: a Review of the Field", *CORD Research Annual* VI (1974). (Proceedings of the third conference on research in dance 1972 "New Dimensions in Dance Research: Anthropology and Dance — The American Indian")

Phillips, Andrea. "European dreamtime" (Wim Vandekeybus in Glasgow), *Dance Theatre Journal,* Vol. 9, No. 4, Summer 1992.

Phillips Barker, E. "Folk Dancing", in *Encyclopædia Britannica,* 1929 edn.

Pineapple Dance Studios. Publicity material, 1990.

Polanyi, Michael. *Personal Knowledge: Towards a post-critical philosophy.* London: Routledge & Kegan Paul, 1983. (original edn. 1958)

Potter, Michelle. "Designed for Dance: The Costumes of Léon Bakst and Art of Isadora Duncan", *Dance Chronicle: Studies in Dance and the Related Arts,* Vol. 13, No. 2, 1990.

Preston, Valerie. *A Handbook for Modern Educational Dance.* London: Macdonald & Evans, 1963.

Preston-Dunlop, Valerie. An investigation into the spontaneous occurrence of fragments of choreutic forms in choreographed dance works. Unpublished M.A. dissertation, Goldsmiths' College, London, 1978.

———— *A Handbook for Dance in Education.* Plymouth: Macdonald & Evans, 1980.

———— The Nature of the Embodiment of Choreutic Units in Contemporary Choreography. Unpublished Ph.D. thesis, Council for National Academic Awards, 1981.

————— "Choreutic Concepts and Practice", *Dance Research,* Vol. I, No. 1 (Spring 1983).

————— *Point of Departure: The dancer's space.* London: Valerie Preston-Dunlop, 1984.

————— *Dance Is A Language, Isn't It?.* London: Laban Centre for Movement and Dance, 1987.

————— "Laban's Kammertanzbuhne Revisited", *Laban Art of Movement Guild Magazine,* No. 77, May 1988.

————— "Choreological Image", Oublie et Memoire Conference Papers, Arles, 1990(a).

————— "Suspension Fall and Recovery of Laban's Dance Notation in the Weimar Republic and Third Reich", 5th Hong Kong International Dance Conference Papers (Notation Papers) 1990(b).

————— and **Lahusen**, Susanne (Eds.). *Schrifttanz.* London: Dance Books, 1990.

Preston-Dunlop, Valerie. Choreological Studies Seminar. Laban Centre for Movement and Dance, 1991.

————— Choreological Studies Document. Laban Centre for Movement and Dance, 1992.

Prickett, Stacey Lee. The Dance as a Weapon In The Class Struggle: / The revolutionary dance movement in America 1932–1937. Unpublished M.A. dissertation, Laban Centre for Movement and Dance, 1987.

Quigley, Colin. "International Council for Traditional Music / Study Group on Ethnochoreology, 17th Symposium", *Dance Research Journal,* 25/1, Spring 1993.

Quirey, Belinda. *May I Have the Pleasure: The Story of Popular Dancing.* London: Dance Books, new edn. 1987.

Raftis, Alkis. "A Call for a New Breed of Folk Dance Teachers", *Dance Studies,* Vol. 14, 1990.

Rainer, Yvonne. "A Quasi Survey of Some 'Minimalist' Tendencies in the Quantitatively Minimal Dance Activity Midst the Plethora, or an Analysis of Trio A", in **Battcock**, Gregory (Ed.). *Minimal Art / A Critical Anthology.* New York: E.P. Dutton, 1968.

————— in **Brown**, Trisha and **Rainer**, Yvonne. "A Conversation about 'Glacial Decoy'", in *Trisha Brown.* Paris: Éditions Bougé (Series "L'atelier des chorégraphes"), 1987.

Ralov, Kirsten. *The Bournonville School / Part 1 The Daily Classes.* London: Dance Books, 1979.

Ralph, Richard. "Spotlight on Christopher Bannerman; Professor of Dance", *Dancing Times,* Apr 1993.

Rameau, Pierre (Tr. Beaumont, Cyril W.) *The Dancing Master.* London: Cyril W. Beaumont, 1931. (original 1725)

Rao, U.S. Krishna. *A Dictionary of Bharata Natya.* London: Sangam Books, 2nd edn. 1990.

Redfern, Betty. *Dance, Art and Aesthetics.* London: Allen & Unwin, 1986.

Redfern, H. B. *Questions in Aesthetic Education.* London: Allen & Unwin, 1992.

Reid, Francis. *The ABC of Stage Lighting.* London: A&C Black, 1992.

Rimmer, Jane. "The Methodology for the Analysis of Group Forms (with special Reference to 'Rushes' — Siobhan Davies, 1982)", *Working Papers in Dance Studies* (Laban Centre for Movement and Dance), Vol. 2 (1989).

Rippon, Hugh. *Discovering English Folk Dance.* Princes Risborough: Shire Publications, third edn. 1993. (first edn. 1975)

Robertson, Allen and **Hutera**, Donald. *The Dance Handbook.* Harlow: Longman, 1988.

Robertson, Allen. *Time Out,* Apr 1993.

Rogers, Frederick Rand (Ed.). *Dance: A basic educational technique / A functional approach to the use of rhythmics & dance as prime methods of body development & control, and transformation of moral & social behavior.* New York: Macmillan, 1941.

'Roget's Thesaurus'. *Roget's Thesaurus / of English words and phrases.* Harlow: Longman, New Edn. 1982.

Rogosin, Elinor. *The Dance Makers / Coversations with American Choreographers.* New York: Walker, 1980.

Royal Academy of Dancing. International Summer School Prospectus, 1993(a).

———— Advertisement. *Dance and Dancers,* Mar 1993(b).

Rubidge, Sarah. "Steve Paxton", *Dance Theatre Journal,* Vol. 4, No. 4 (1986).

———— "Danger! Women at Work at the QEH", *Dance Theatre Journal,* Vol. 6, No. 3 (1988).

Russell, Joan. *Modern Dance in Education.* London: Macdonald & Evans, 1958.

Ryman, Rhonda. "Creating Benesh Notation on a Macintosh Personal Computer", 5th Hong Kong International Dance Conference Papers, 1990.

Sachs, Curt (Tr. Schönberg, Bessie). *World History of the Dance.* New York: Norton, 1937 (reprinted 1963). (original in German, 1933)

Salter, Alan with **Grist**, Stina. *The Curving Air / Dance and its Making.* London: Human Factors Associates, 1977.

Samson, Leela. *Rhythm in Joy / Classical Indian Dance Traditions.* New Delhi: Lustre Press, 1987.

Sanchez-Colberg, Ana R. German Tanztheater: Traditions and Contradictions / A Choreological Documentation of Tanztheater from its Roots in Ausdruckstanz to the Present. Unpublished Ph.D. Thesis, Laban Centre for Movement and Dance, 1992.

———— "You can see it like this or like that / Pina Bausch's 'Die Klage der Kaiserin'", in **Jordan**, Stephanie and **Allen**, Dave (Eds.). *Parallel Lines / Media Representations of Dance.* London: John Libbey & Co (for The Arts Council of Great Britain), 1993.

Sayers, Lesley-Anne. "'Dance' Theater at Dance Umbrella / from DV8 to Second Stride", *Dance Theatre Journal,* Vol. 6, No. 4 (1988).

Scheflen, Albert. *Body Language and Social Order / Communication as behavioral control.* Englewood Cliffs NJ: Prentice-Hall, 1972.

Schlemmer, Tut (Ed.). *Oskar Schlemmer: Briefe und Tagebücher.* München, 1958.

Schmais, Claire. "Dance Therapy in perspective", in **Mason**, K. (Ed.). *Dance Therapy: Focus on Dance VII.* Washington DC: American Association for Health, Physical Education, and Recreation, 1974.

Schoettler, Eugenia Volz. From A Chorus Line to "A Chorus Line": The emergence of dance in the American Musical Theatre. Unpublished Ph.D. thesis, Kent State Univ., 1979.

Schoop, Trudi. *Won't you join the dance? A dancer's essay into the Treatment of Psychosis.* California: Mayfield, 1974.

Schuller, Gunther. "Symposium on 'composer/choreographer'", *Dance Perspectives,* No. 16 (1963).

Schurman, Nona and **Clark**, Sharon Leigh. *Modern Dance Fundamentals.* New York: Macmillan, 1972.

Scottish Official Board of Highland Dancing. *Highland Dancing.* Edinburgh: Thomas Nelson and Sons Ltd., 1955.

Screen. Vol. 27, No. 1, 1986.

Semple, Maggie. "African Dance and Adzido / Fresh answers to ancient questions", *Dance Theatre Journal,* Vol. 10, No. 1 (Autumn 1992).

Serrebrenikov, Nicolai and **Lawson**, Joan. *The art of Pas de deux.* London: Dance Books, 1978.

Servos, Norbert. "The emancipation of dance: Pina Bausch and the Wuppertal Dance Theater", *Modern Drama,* Vol. 13, No. 1 (Mar 1980).

———— and **Weigelt**, G. *Pina Bausch Wuppertal Dance Theater / or The Art of Training a Goldfish / Excursions into Dance.* Köln: Ballett-Bühnen-Verlag, English edition 1984.

Shahn, Ben. *The Shape of Content.* Cambridge MA: Harvard Univ. Press, 1957.

Sharp, Cecil J. *The Country Dance Book,* Parts 1 & 2. London: Novello, 2nd edn. 1934.

Shawn, Ted. *Dance We Must.* London: Dobson, 1946.

———— *Every Little Movement / A Book About François Delsarte.* Pittsfield MA: privately, 2nd edn. 1963. (1st edn. 1954)

Sheets-Johnstone, Maxine. *The Phenomenology of Dance.* London: Dance Books, 2nd edn. 1979. (1st edn. 1966)

Shelton, Suzanne. *Divine Dancer: A biography of Ruth St. Denis.* New York: Doubleday, 1981.

Sherborne, Veronica. *Developmental Movement for Children.* Cambridge Univ. Press, 1990.

Sibley, Frank N. "Aestheic concepts", in **Margolis**, Joseph (Ed.). *Philosophy Looks at the Arts.* New York: Scribners, 1962. (originally pub. 1959)

Siddall, Jeanette. "Fair play?", *Dance Theatre Journal,* Vol. 9, No. 4, Summer 1992.

Siegel, Marcia B. "Agents of Change", *Dance Perspectives,* No. 38 (Summer 1969).

———— "Nik, a documentary", *Dance Perspectives,* No. 48 (Winter 1971).

———— *At the Vanishing Point / A Critic Looks at Dance.* New York: Saturday Review Press, 1972.

———— *The Shapes of Change: Images of American Dance.* Boston: Houghton Mifflin, 1979.

———— "Evolutionary Dreams", *Dance Theatre Journal,* Vol. 4, No. 3, 1986.

Silvester, Victor. *Modern Ballroom Dancing.* London: Herbert Jenkins, 1942.

Smith, Jacqueline M. *Dance Composition: A practical guide for teachers.* London: Lepus, 1980.

Sokolow, Anna. "The Rebel and the Bourgeois", in **Cohen**, Selma Jeanne. *The Modern Dance / Seven Statements of Belief.* Middletown CT: Wesleyan Univ. Press, 1966.

Sommers, Michael. "Shadow on a shoestring", *Lighting Dimensions,* Jan/Feb 1990.

Walther, Suzanne. "A cross cultural approach to dance criticism", *Dance Research Annual,* X, 1979 (CORD).

Watson, Keith. "Potty about Props", *Hampstead and Highgate Express,* Mar 10th, 1989.

Watson Coleman, Francine M. "The Imaginative Appreciation of Dance", in Dance: The Study of Dance and the Place of Dance in Society, *The Proceedings of the VIII Commonwealth and International Conference on Sport, Physical Education, Dance, Recreation and Health, 1986, Glasgow.* London: E. & F.N. Spon, 1986.

'Webster'. *Merriam-Webster's Collegiate Dictionary.* Springfield MA: Merriam-Webster, 10th edn. 1993.

White, Eric Walter. *Stravinsky / The Composer and his Works.* London: Faber and Faber, 2nd Edn. 1979.

Wigman, Mary. "Aus 'Rudolf von Labans Lehre vom Tanz'", *Die neue Schaubühne,* 2./3. Heft, 3. Jahrgang 1921 (Feb).

Wigman, Mary (Tr. Sorell, Walter). *The Language of Dance.* London: Macdonald & Evans Ltd, 1966. (original in German, 1963)

Willis, Paul. *Profane Culture.* London: Routledge & Kegan Paul, 1978.

Winearls, Jane. *Modern Dance: The Jooss-Leeder Method.* London: A&C Black, 1958.

Winter, Christopher. "Love and Language / or only connect the prose and the passion", *Dance Theatre Journal,* Vol. 7, No. 2, 1989.

Woodworth, Mark, et al. *On the dance of Erick Hawkins* (5 essays). New York: Foundation for Modern Dance, (undated).

Woolf, Janet. *Feminine Sentences: Essays on Woman and Culture.* Cambridge: Polity Press, 1990.

Young, Derek. *Rock 'n' Roll Dancing: a step by step guide.* Volume One. Stockport: Capri Publications, 2nd impression 1991.

Youngerman, Suzanne. "The Translation of a Culture into Choreography", *Dance Research Annual,* IX, 1978 (CORD).

Zupp, Nancy. An analysis and comparison of the choreographic processes of Alwin Nikolais, Murray Louis, and Phyllis Lamhut. D.Ed. Thesis, Univ. of Carolina, 1978.

ORAL CONTRIBUTORS

Brief biographical notes of the people who have contributed orally through interview, or whose words have been collected directly from rehearsals, coaching, classes, workshops and seminars which Valerie Preston-Dunlop has attended.

Adams, Carolyn. Dancer, Paul Taylor Dance Company. *Lecture/demonstration at Laban Centre for Movement and Dance, London, 1983.*

Adamson, Andy. Designer of Calaban, Head of Dance Univ. of Birmingham. *Interview, Birminghan, Sep 1992.*

Adshead-Lansdale, Janet. Head of Department and Professor of Dance, Univ. of Surrey, Guildford. *Interview, Guildford, June 1993.*

Allen, Katherine. T'ai Chi Ch'uan teacher, Kent. *Interview, Cranbrook, Jan 1993.*

Alston, Richard. Artistic Director of the National Centre for Contemporary Dance, The Place, London; Choreographer, associated with Rambert Dance Company and London Contemporary Dance Theatre. *Conversation with Darshan Singh Bhuller, Sep 1993; Rehearsing Darshan Singh Bhuller, London Contemporary Dance Theatre, Sep 1993; Rehearsing "Perilous Night", 1993.*

Amagatsu, Ushio. Director and choreographer of Sankai Juku company. *Interview, Bagnolet, Paris, 1992.*

Anderson, Lea. Indepedent choreographer; Artistic Director "The Cholmondeleys" and "The Featherstonehaughs", London. *Interview, London, June 1993.*

Archbutt, Sally. Authority on dance works of Hettie Loman, for whose companies she worked as principal dancer; Labanotator and reconstructor from 1951 to 1993; former Head of Dance at Nonington College. *Interview, Sep 1993.*

Ashford, John. Director, The Place Theatre, London. *Interview, The Place Theatre, London, June 1993.*

Baden-Semper, Brenda. Graham-trained instructor/choreographer/performer, working primarily in New York and Trinidad. *Interview, Laban Centre for Movement and Dance, London, Mar 1993.*

Barnes, Thea. Formerly dancer with Alwyn Ailey, Dance Theater of Harlem, Martha Graham Co.; teacher of Graham and jazz techniques. *Interview, Laban Centre for Movement and Dance, London, Mar and July 1993.*

Bartrip, Mirella. Head of undergraduate studies, Laban Centre for Movement and Dance, London; trained as a dancer in classical ballet at Arts Educational School, London. *Interview, London, May 1993.*

Bassett, Peter. Senior Librarian, Laban Centre for Movement and Dance, London. *Interview, London, Dec 1992.*

Bausch, Pina. Choreographer, Artistic Director Wuppertal Tanztheater, Wuppertal. *In conversation with the audience, Brooklyn Academy of Music, 20 Oct 1985, collected by Ana Sanchez-Colberg.*

Baxter, Brian. Stage Director, The Birmingham Royal Ballet. *Interview, Birmingham, Sep 1992.*

Beckett, Stuart. Formerly dancer with Sadler's Wells Royal Ballet; ballet teacher in vocational dance colleges working internationally. *Teaching ballet, London, 1992.*

Benstead, Chris. Composer, accompanist, and dancer; has composed extensively for both large- and small-scale companies. *Interview, London, Oct 1993.*

Bhuller, Darshan Singh. Choreographer, dancer, assistant rehearsal director London Contemporary Dance Theatre. *Rehearsing "Fall Like Rain", Sep 1993; Interview, London Contemporary Dance Theatre, Sep 1993.*

Bintley, David. Indepedent choreographer, working internationally. *Interview, Birmingham, Sep 1992; Rehearsal of "The Snow Queen", The Birmingham Royal Ballet, Sep 1992.*

Bird, Bonnie. D.Arts, Principal Lecturer and Consultant Laban Centre for Movement and Dance, London; Founder and Artistic Director Transitions Dance Company; member Martha Graham Dance Company; performed, choreographed, taught throughout U.S.A. *Rehearsal and interview, London, Apr 1993 and Oct 1993.*

Birmingham Royal Ballet, The. *Performance at Birmingham Hippodrome, 17 Sep 1992; Weekly list of calls, Oct 1992.*

Birmingham Royal Ballet, The: **Crew.** *Rehearsal, Birmingham Hippodrome, Oct 1992.*

Birmingham Royal Ballet, The: **Dancers.** *Birmingham, Sep 1992.*

Birmingham Royal Ballet, The: **Wardrobe Department.** *Birmingham, Sep 1992.*

Booth, Laurie. Independent choreographer and performer. *Class and Interview, London, Jan 1993.*

Bowne, Anthony. Lighting designer; Manager Transitions Dance Company, Laban Centre for Movement and Dance, London. *Interview, London, Oct 1993.*

Brandt, Rosemary. Classical dance teacher and practical choreologist. *Interview, London, 1990, Mar 1994; teaching, Mar 1994.*

Brinson, Peter. International dance consultant, writer and lecturer. *Interview. Limerick/London, Mar 1993.*

Bruce, Christopher. International choreographer, Artistic Director Rambert Dance Company, London. *Rehearsing and Interview, London Contemporary Dance Theatre, Sep 1993; Rehearsing Kenneth Tharp, Sep 1993; Creating "The Message", Sep 1993.*

Bruce, Marian. Artist, set designer. *Rehearsing, London Contemporary Dance Theatre, Sep 1993.*

Buckland, Theresa. Dance ethnologist, Senior Lecturer in Dance, Univ. of Surrey, Guildford. *Interview, London, Nov 1992; Contributed, Feb 1994.*

Burton, Mark. Writer for The Independent. *Contributed, Jan 1994.*

Butcher, Rosemary. Dance Co-ordinator; Artist in Residence Holborn Centre for the Performing Arts, London. *Interview, London, June 1993.*

Cameron, Ross. Design consultant; Technical Director, Bonnie Bird Theatre, Laban Centre for Movement and Dance, London; M.Sc. in Architectural Lighting. *Interview, London, June 1993.*

Carr, Jane. Dance Co-ordinator for Morley Adult Education College, London. *Interview, London, 1991.*

Carruthers, Julia. Administrative assistant, The Arts Council of Great Britain. *Contributed, Oct 1993.*

Carter, Alexandra. Principal Lecturer, Institute of Dance, Middlesex University; special interest in the application of feminist methodologies to the study of dance. *Contributed, Feb 1994.*

Chambon, Philip. Composer in the electro-acoustic genre. *Interview, London, July 1993.*

Childs, Diana. Stage Manager, The Birmingham Royal Ballet. *Interview, Sep 1992; Rehearsal, Birmingham Hippodrome, Oct 1992.*

Cipolla, Joseph. Principal dancer, The Birmingham Royal Ballet. *Interview, Sep 1992; Rehearsal and Interview, Birmingham Hippodrome, Sep 1992.*

Clark, Scott. Independent dancer, dance teacher, Feldenkreis practitioner. *Interview, July 1992; Teaching, Lewisham College, London, Mar 1993.*

Clarke, Mary. Editorial Director The Dancing Times, London. *Contributed, Feb 1994.*

Clifford, Michael. Shoemaster, The Birmingham Royal Ballet. *Interview, Birmingham, Sep 1992.*

Cohan, Robert. Formerly soloist Martha Graham Company, and Artistic Director, London Contemporary Dance Theatre; choreographer. *Company class and Interview, London, Sep 1993.*

Coleridge, Robert. Composer; Musical Director, Laban Centre for Movement and Dance, London. *Interview, London, May 1992.*

Conway, Lisa. The Birmingham Royal Ballet artist. *Interview, Birmingham, Sep 1992.*

Coyne, Kate. Dancer, London Contemporary Dance theatre. *Rehearsing Darshan Singh Bhuller's "Fall Like Rain" for London Contemporary Dance Theatre, Sep 1993.*

Crisp, Clement. Ballet critic Financial Times, London; dance historian. *Interview, London, Sep 1992.*

Crocker, Helen. Former dancer, aerialist, and gymnast; course director "Circumedia", the Academy of Circus Art and Physical Theatre, Bristol.

Davidson, Della. Independent choreographer. *Rehearsal, Transitions Dance Company, London, 1990.*

Davies, Siobhan. Choreographer for Second Stride; Choreographer/Director Siobhan Davies Dance Company. *Seminar, Dance Research Society, London, 1991.*

De Marigny, Chris. Editor Dance Theatre Journal, London. *Interview, London, June 1993.*

Dubreuil, Alan. Ballet Master, The Birmingham Royal Ballet. *Men's class, Sep 1992; Interview, Birmingham, Oct 1992.*

Dudley, Jane. Choreographer, international teacher of choreography, and formerly soloist in the Martha Graham Company. *Interview, London, Sep 1992.*

Dunleavy, Peter. Dancer, London Contemporary Dance Theatre. *Interview, Sep 1993.*

Dunlop, John. Formerly amateur stage electrician, Cambridge Univ. *Interview, Ightham, Sep 1993.*

English National Ballet, Education Office. *Contributed, 1993.*

Falk, Jodi. Danced with Kei Takei's Moving Earth; independent choreographer and dancer; currently teaching at Laban Centre for Movement and Dance, London. *Interview, London, June 1993.*

Filmer, Paul. Sociologist, Goldsmiths' College, Univ. of London; writing widely on sociological theory. *Interview and Discussion with Valerie Preston-Dunlop, London, Nov 1992.*

Fox, Ilene. Executive Director, Dance Notation Bureau, New York; certified professional notator. *Interview, Dance Notation Bureau, New York, Sep 1993.*

Geogiardis, Nicholas. Artist, theatre designer. *Interview, London, July 1993.*

Glasstone, Richard. Ballet teacher, The Royal Ballet School. *Lecture, London, 1989.*

Gough, Marion. International specialist in dance education and teaching studies, based at Laban Centre for Movement and Dance, London. *Correspondence, Aug 1993.*

Grau, Andrée. Anthropologist, Research Fellow in Dance at Roehampton Institute, London; Benesh choreologist. *Interview, London, July 1992.*

Grelinger, Els. Dance notator and reconstructor. *Interview, London, Feb 1993.*

Guest, Ivor. Dance historian; Chairman of The Royal Academy of Dancing, London, 1969–1993. *Contributed, 1993.*

Hackney, Peggy. Laban/Bartenieff Movement Analyst. *Telephone interview, Seattle, Dec 1993.*

Hall, John. Chief Electrician, The Birmingham Royal Ballet. *Interview, Birmingham, Sep 1992.*

Hamilton, Jack. Community dance caller, writer. *Interview, Ightham, May 1993.*

Harris, Mark Lintern. Dancer/choreographer working in Europe, with an acknowledged aesthetic and technical debt to Erick Hawkins. *Contributed, Mar 1994.*

Harrold, Robert. President National Dance Branch of The Imperial Society of Teachers of Dance; international teacher of folk and national dance forms. *Interview, Dulwich, July 1993.*

Hart, Beatrice. Designer and design teacher. *Interview, London, Apr 1992.*

Hart, John. Master Carpenter, The Birmingham Royal Ballet. *Interview, Sep 1992; Rehearsal, Birmingham Hippodrome, Oct 1992.*

Hearn, Geoffrey. International teacher of Ballroom and Latin American dancing, The Spencer Dance Centre, London. *Instructing at The Spencer Dance Centre, Nov 1992.*

Higgins, Jonathan. Company pianist, The Birmingham Royal Ballet. *Interview, Birmingham, Sep 1992.*

Hoghe, Raimund. Writer and dramaturge, working with Pina Bausch. *Interview, Bagnolet, Paris, 1992.*

Holm, Hanya. Choreographer and dance teacher. *Technique class, and interviewed by Dorothy Madden, New York, 1951.*

Hopps, Stuart. Independent choreographer in opera, musical theatre, film. *Interview, London, Dec 1992.*

Horta, Rui. Choreographer working in Europe. *Workshop, Laban Centre for Movement and Dance, London, Jan 1993.*

Hutchinson Guest, Ann. Author, teacher, researcher into systems of dance notation and movement analysis; world authority on Labanotation; recipient of two honorary doctorates for her contributions to dance literacy. *Interview, London, May 1992.*

Imperial Society of Teachers of Dancing. *Remarks at Cecchetti Study Day, London, 1992.*

Inglehearn, Madeleine. Professor of Early Dance, Guildhall School of Music and Drama, London. *Interview, London, Jan 1993.*

Jarrell, Jean. Tutor at the Laban Centre for Movement and Dance, London in charge of Labanotation, advising students on notating and reconstructing contemporary Western theatre dance. *Interview, London, June 1993.*

Jeyasingh, Shobana. Bharata Natyam and contemporary London-based choreographer. *Interview with Sarah Rubidge, London, Oct 1993.*

Johnson-Jones, Jean. Director Labanotation Institute, Univ. of Surrey, Guildford. *Interview, Guildford, June 1993.*

Jordan, Stephanie. Professor of Dance Studies, Roehampton Institute, London; dance critic and author. *Interview, Roehampton, July 1993 and Mar 1994.*

Judge, Roy. Morris dancer, folklorist, social historian. *Interview, London, May 1993.*

Keen, Elizabeth. Choreographer; teacher Juilliard School of Performing Arts, New York. *Rehearsals, Laban Centre for Movement and Dance, London, June 1992; Interview, New York, Sep 1993.*

Kelly, Desmond. Assistant Director, The Birmingham Royal Ballet. *Rehearsals, Birmingham, Sep 1992.*

Kelsey, Teresa. Choreographic Assistant at the Bayreuthe Festspiele; formerly professional dancer; currently teaching classical ballet at the Laban Centre for Movement and Dance, London, *Interview, London, May 1993.*

Laban Centre for Movement and Dance, London. *Rehearsal, 1992.*

Lahusen, Susanne. Pilates teacher; dance historian. *Class, Laban Centre for Movement and Dance, London, Apr 1993.*

Landa, Anita. Ballet Mistress, The Birmingham Royal Ballet. *Rehearsal of "The Snow Queen", Sep 1992.*

Lange, Roderyk. Dancer; dance anthropologist; Professor of Ethnology, London and Poland. *Interview, London, July 1992.*

Layson, June. First univ. professor of Dance in the United Kingdom; Emeritus Professor at the Univ. of Surrey. *Interview, Guildford, May 1993.*

Lockyer, Bob. Producer, Music and Arts, for the British Broadcasting Corporation. *Camera script for "Soldat" with Rambert Company and the British Broadcasting Corporation; Interview, the British Broadcasting Corporation, Kensington House, London, Dec 1992.*

London Contemporary Dance Theatre. *Rehearsals, London, Sep 1993.*

Longstaff, Jeffrey. Doctorate student at the Laban Centre for Movement and Dance, London; Certified Laban Movement Analyst. *Interview, London, June 1993.*

Lynne, Gillian. Choreographer; Television director for ballet and musical theatre. *Interview, London, Feb 1993.*

Mackrell, Judith. Dance critic The Independent; dance historian. *Interview, London, Apr 1993.*

Madden, Dorothy. Founder of Dance Department, Univ. of Maryland and of Maryland Dance Theater; Professor Emerita Univ. of Maryland; international teacher of choreography. *Interviews, London, Sep 1992, Nov 1992 and Feb 1993, and Ightham, Aug 1993 and Apr 1994; Rehearsing, Zwolle, Oct 1992.*

Maelor Thomas, Judith. Resident choreologist, Dutch National Ballet. *Rehearsal of Ashton's "Symphonic Variations", The Birmingham Royal Ballet, Sep 1992.*

Maletic. Vera. Teacher, writer and researcher; Dance Department, Ohio State Univ. *Contributed, Feb 1994.*

Mannion, Mickie. Lighting designer; Technical Manager at the Laban Centre for Movement and Dance, London; M.Sc. in Architectural Lighting. *Interview, Feb 1994.*

Maree, Lynn. Dance Officer, Southern Arts (the Arts Development Agency for the South of England). *Contributed, July 1993.*

Markard, Anna. Production director of Kurt Jooss repertory, working internationally with major ballet companies. *Conversation with Ana Sanchez-Colberg, Wiesbaden, 1990; Rehearsals and Interview, The Birmingham Royal Ballet, Sep 1992; Rehearsal of Jooss's "The Green Table", Birmingham Hippodrome, Sep 1992.*

Markard, Hermann. Artist; lighting designer; collaborator with Anna Markard (see details above). *Rehearsal, The Birmingham Royal Ballet, Oct 1992; Instructions to electricians' control box, rehearsal, The Birmingham Royal Ballet, Birmingham Hippodrome, Oct 1992.*

Mason, Bim. Solo performer in physical comedy; independent theatre director; heading performance studies "Circumedia", the Academy of Circus Art and Physical Theatre, Bristol. *Interview, Bristol, Dec 1992.*

Mason, Monica. Assistant Director, The Royal Ballet, London. *Interview, London, May 1993.*

Maxwell, Carla. Artistic Director, Limón Dance Foundation, New York. *Interview, New York, Sep 1993.*

Meisner, Nadine. Dance critic The Times; Deputy Editor Dance and Dancers.; *Contributed, Feb 1994.*

Menary, Henry. Wigmaster, The Birmingham Royal Ballet. *Interviews, Birmingham, Sep and Oct 1992.*

Meyer, Laverne. Director, The Legat School of Classical Ballet; international teacher of ballet. *Interview, Wadhurst, Feb 1994.*

Michelle, Simone. Choreography consultant, Laban Centre for Movement and Dance, London; formerly Director Sigurd Leeder School of Dance. *Interview, London, 1990.*

Mojsiejenko, Nicholas. Musical Director, London Contemporary Dance Theatre. *Company class, London Contemporary Dance Theatre, and Interview, Sep 1993.*

Morrice, Norman. Head of choreographic studio, Royal Ballet School; Director of The Royal Ballet Choreographic Group. *Interview, London, Apr 1993.*

Muldoon, Royston. Independent choreographer of amateur dancers. *Class and Interview, Guildford, Mar 1993.*

Murphy, Mark. Artistic Director, V-TOL Dance Company, London. *Interview, London, May 1993.*

Nash, Gregory. Choreographer and teacher. *Interview with Larraine Nicholas, June 1993.*

Nicholas, Jane. First Dance Director of the Arts Council of Great Britain. *Interview, London, Apr 1993.*

Nicks, Walter. New York based master teacher and choreographer of Jazz dance, working internationally. *Contributed, Essen, Mar 1994.*

North, Marion. Director Laban Centre for Movement and Dance, London. *Interview, London, Dec 1992.*

Page, Ashley. Principal character artist, The Royal Ballet, London; choreographer. *Interviews, London, Apr and May 1993.*

Parker, Monica. Benesh choreologist; repetiteur for the MacMillan repertoire. *Interview, Benesh Institute, London, Feb 1991.*

Percival, John. Editor Dance and Dancers; Dance Critic The Times. *Contributed, Feb 1994.*

Pforsich, Janis, **Goldman**, Ellen, **Chanik**, John, and **Wenning**, Lynn. Current faculty members of the Laban/Bartenieff Institute of Movement Studies, New York. *Contributed, Apr 1994.*

Preston, Stephen. Baroque dancer. *Interview by Larraine Nicholas, Apr 1993.*

Preston-Dunlop, Valerie. International teacher and writer on Choreological Studies, based at the Laban Centre for Movement and Dance, London. *Classes and Choreological Studies seminars, Dec 1990, Jan 1991, Apr 1992, May 1992, Oct 1992, and 1993; Interviews with Dorothy Madden, Ightham, Aug–Oct 1993, Feb 1994.*

Purnell, Derek. Administrator, The Birmingham Royal Ballet. *Interview, Birmingham, Sep 1992.*

Ralph, Richard. Principal London Contemporary Dance School. *Interview, London, June 1993.*

Redfern, Betty. Educationist, with special interest in dance and aesthetics. *Contributed, June 1993.*

Redlich, Don. Choreographer, dancer and international teacher; Artistic Director, Don Redlich Dance Company. *Informal discussion with Dorothy Madden, New York, Sep 1993.*

Reed, Albert. Dancer and teacher, Merce Cunningham Studio, New York. *Cunningham Studio Class, New York, Sep 1993.*

Robertson Bruce, Lynn. Dancer in opera and musical theatre. *Interview, London, May 1992.*

Rogers, Chris. Teacher of Early Dance. *Conversation with Larraine Nicholas, June 1993.*

Ross, Bertram. Formerly principal dancer and soloist, Martha Graham Company, New York. *Informal discussion, New York, Sep 1993.*

Rubidge, Sarah. Dance educator, associated with Rambert Dance Company and Siobhan Davies Dance Company; teacher of advanced choreography, Laban Centre for Movement and Dance, London. *Contributed, Feb 1994.*

Rudko, Doris. International New York based teacher of composition and choreography. *Interview, New York, Sep 1993.*

Saidi, Samira. First soloist, The Birmingham Royal Ballet. *Rehearsal of "The Snow Queen", Sep 1992.*

Saunders, Ron. Barn dancer. *Interview, Trottiscliffe, Apr 1993.*

Schoenberg, Bessie. International New York based teacher of choreography. *Interview, New York, Sep 1993.*

Scott, Annabel, and **Godwin**, Tim. Clubbers. *Interview, New Cross, June 1993.*

Sengupta, Alpana, Performer and teacher of Kathak dance. *Interview with Larraine Nicholas, Mar 1993.*

Sentler, Susan. Formerly dancer Martha Graham Ensemble, and Graham faculty; master instructor on technique and choreography working in Europe, especially Italy. *Interview, Oct 1993.*

Smith-Autard, Jacqueline. Dance educator and write on Dance in Education, Bedford College of Higher Education. *Interview, Bedford, Sep 1993.*

Snaith, Yolande. Independent theatre dance practitioner. *Workshop and Interview, London, Feb 1991.*

Sobieralska, Lili. Head of Running Wardrobe, The Birmingham Royal Ballet. *Interviews, Birmingham, Sep 1992.*

Somes, Michael. Formerly principal dancer, The Royal Ballet, London. *Rehearsal while restaging Ashton's "Symphonic Variations", The Birmingham Royal Ballet, Sep 1992.*

Sonnabend, Yolanda. Artist, stage designer for ballet and theatre. *Interview, London, July 1993.*

Stanton, Erica. Teacher and independent choreographer. *Technique class, Laban Centre for Movement and Dance, London, 1991; Interview, London, Dec 1992.*

Steed, Malcolm. Costume Cutter, The Birmingham Royal Ballet. *Interview, Birmingham, Sep 1992.*

Stephenson, Geraldine. Choreographer and Movement Director in television and musical theatre. *Interview, London, Feb 1993.*

Svenheim, Hans Atle. Physiotherapist. *Seminar, Laban Centre for Movement and Dance, London, 1992.*

Tait, Marion. Principal dancer, The Birmingham Royal Ballet. *Rehearsal of MacMillan's "Romeo and Juliet" with Joseph Cipolla, and Interview, Birmingham, Sep 1992.*

Taylor, Donna. Dance teacher, specialising in sub-culture and youth groups. *Interviews with Portsmouth Clubbers, Oct 1992, Mar 1993, Sep 1993; Observation, "5th Avenue Club", Portsmouth, Oct 1992.*

Tharp, Twyla. Choreographer; sometime dancer/choreographer Twyla Tharp Dance and artistic associate American Ballet Theater. *"Twyla Tharp and Dancers", an informal talk and performance, City Center, New York, Sep 1993.*

Thomas, Helen. Sociologist, Goldsmiths' College, Univ. of London. *Interview, London, Aug 1993.*

Thomes, Kaery. Dancer, Laban Centre for Movement and Dance, London. *Demonstration, Laban Centre, 1992.*

Thompson, Dale. Choreographer, dancer, teacher. *Interview, London, 1992; Rehearsal, Laban Centre for Movement and Dance, London, 1992.*

Tomkins, Alysoun. Head of Community Dance, Laban Centre for Movement and Dance, London. *Interview, London, 1993.*

Vahla, Athina. Choreographer and dancer; currently teaching repertory and choreological studies at the Laban Centre for Movement and Dance, London. *Teaching, London, Jun 1993.*

van Haarst, Rob. Labanotator and linguist. *Contributed, Jan 1991.*

Vaughan, David. Archivist, Cunningham Dance Foundation Inc., New York; author. *Conversation with Valerie Preston-Dunlop, New York, Sep 1993.*

Vermey, Ruud. International Holland-based judge and coach for Latin American dance. *Coaching competitors, Alphen a/d Rijn, Oct 1990; Interview, Alphen a/d Rijn, Dec 1990.*

Waite, Philippa. Baroque dancer. *Interview with Larraine Nicholas, Jan 1992.*

Ward, Audrey. Costume Cutter, The Birmingham Royal Ballet. *Interviews, Birmingham, Sep and Oct 1992.*

Watson Coleman, Francine M. Formerly dancer associated with Orff Institute and Salzburg Festival Opera; currently lecturer, teacher, and dance consultant combining practice with a specialism in aesthetics. *Interview, Laban Centre for Movement and Dance, London, May 1993.*

Williams, Drid. Dance scholar. *Quoted by Andrée Grau in Interview, July 1992.*

Permission to use material from the following publications is gratefully acknowledged:

Joan Acocella and Lynn Garafola (Eds.). *André Levinson on Dance / Writings from Paris in the Twenties*, copyright 1991 by Joan Acocella and Lynn Garafola, Wesleyan University Press by permission of the University Press of New England.

Bira Almeida. *Capoeira: A Brazilian Dance Art Form*, North Atlantic Books, 1986, reprinted with permission of North Atlantic Books, PO Box 12327 Berkeley CA 94701.

Denis Bablet and Marie-Louise Bablet. *Adolphe Appia 1862–1928, actor – space – light*, publication in association with an exhibition promoted by Pro Helvetia, Zürich, 1982, by permission of the authors.

George Balanchine. *By George Balanchine*, San Marco, 1984; © The George Balanchine Trust, by permission of Thomas Schoff and the George Balanchine Trust.

Sally Banes. *Terpsichore in Sneakers / Post-Modern Dance*, Houghton Mifflin, 1980; Judson Dance Theater: Democracy's Body 1962–1964, Ph.D. thesis, New York Univ., 1980; and "Cunningham's Legacy", in leaflet *Merce Cunningham and the New Dance / the modernist impulse in dance* (A Publication of the State University of New York), 1987; all by permission of the author.

Clive Barnes. "Frederick Ashton", in *Dance Perspectives*, No. 9 (1961); and "Essays, Stories, and Remarks about Merce Cunningham", in *Dance Perspectives*, No. 34 (1968); both by permission of Dance Perspectives Foundation.

Anthony G. Barrand. *Six Fools and a Dancer / The Timeless Way of the Morris*, Northern Harmony Publishing Co, 1991, by permission of the author.

The Benesh Institute. "Benesh Movement Notation", in *in Touch*, Royal Opera House Education, Convent Garden, 1993, by permission of The Benesh Institute.

Lynne Anne Blom and L. Tarin Chaplin. *The Intimate Act of Choreography*, by permission of the University of Pittsburg Press. © 1982 by University of Pittsburgh Press.

Carolyn Brown. "Essays, Stories, and Remarks about Merce Cunningham", in *Dance Perspectives*, No. 34 (1968), by permission of Dance Perspectives Foundation.

Trisha Brown. "Improvisations and structures", in *Trisha Brown*, Éditions Bougé, 1987, by permission of the author.

Trisha Brown and Yvonne Rainer. "Conversation about 'Glacial Decoy'", in *Trisha Brown*, Éditions Bougé, 1987, by permission of the authors.

Lise Brunel. "From forest to loft: journey to the core of a tree", in *Trisha Brown*, Éditions Bougé, 1987, by permission of the author.

John Cage. "Symposium on 'composer/choreographer'", in *Dance Perspectives*, No. 16 (1963), by permission of Dance Perspectives Foundation.

Roy Castle. *Roy Castle on Tap*, David & Charles, 1986, by permission of the publishers.

Mary Clarke and David Vaughan (Eds.). Glossary in *The Encyclopedia of Dance & Ballet*, Peerage Books / Rainbird Reference Books, 1977, by permission of the authors.

Mary Clarke and Clement Crisp. *Design for Ballet*, Studio Vista, 1978; and *Ballerina / The Art of Women in Classical Ballet*, BBC Books, 1987; both by permission of the authors.

Selma Jeanne Cohen. "A prolegomenon to an aesthetics of dance", in M.C. Beardsley and H.M. Schueller, *Aesthetic Enquiry, Essays on Art Criticism and the Philosophy of Art*, Dickenson Pub. Co. Inc., 1967, originally published in *The Journal of Aesthetics and Art Criticism*, by permission of the Editor of the journal.

651

Selma Jeanne Cohen. *Next Week, Swan Lake / Reflections on Dance and Dancers*, Wesleyan Univ. Press, 1982, by permission of the author.

Roger Copeland. "Merce Cunningham and the Politics of Perception", in Roger Copeland and Marshall Cohen (Eds.). *What is Dance? / Readings in Theory and Criticism*, Oxford Univ. Press, 1983, by permission of the author.

Roger Copeland. "The Black Swan and the Dervishes / Cross-Cultural Approaches", in *Dance Theatre Journal*, Vol. 9, No. 4 (1992), by permission of the author.

Clement Crisp and Mary Clarke. *Making a Ballet*, Macmillan Publishing Co Inc, 1975, by permission of the authors.

Clement Crisp. "Yolanda Sonnabend's Designs for Ballet", in *Yolanda Sonnabend / Stage designs and Paintings*, Serpentine Gallery, 1985, by permission of the author.

Merce Cunningham. "Two Questions and Five dances", in *Dance Perspectives*, No. 34 (1968), by permission of Dance Perspectives Foundation.

Merce Cunningham and Jacqueline Lesschaeve. *The Dancer and the Dance*, Marion Boyars Publishers Ltd., 1985, by permission of Cunningham Dance Foundation Inc.

Nancy Vreeland Dalva. "The Right Mix", *Dance Magazine*, Apr 1989, © 1969 *Dance Magazine*, by permission of the Editor of the magazine.

J.G. Davies. *Liturgical Dance, an historical, theological and practical handbook*, SCM Press, 1984, by permission of the publishers.

Agnes de Mille. *Martha / The Life and work of Martha Graham*, Random House, 1991, by permission of Harold Ober Associates.

Ninette de Valois. *Step by Step / The formation of an establishment*, W.H. Allen, 1977, by permission of David Higham Associates.

Edwin Denby. *Looking at the Dance*, Horizon Press, 1968 (original essays various dates 1936 et seq), by permission of Rudolph Burckhardt.

Havelock Ellis. *The Dance of Life*, Houghton Mifflin, 1923, by permission of Constable Publishers.

Alvin Epstein. "The Mime Theatre of Étienne Decroux", *Chrysalis — the pocket revue of the arts*, 1955, Vol. XI, Nos. 1–2, by permission of Baird Hastings and Alvin Epstein.

Vivian Fine. "Symposium on 'composer/choreographer'", in *Dance Perspectives*, No. 16 (1963), by permission of Dance Perspectives Foundation.

Catherine Foley. Irish Traditional Step Dancing in North Kerry: A Contextual and Structural Analysis, unpublished Ph.D. thesis, Laban Centre, 1988, by permission of the author.

James J. Gibson. *The Senses Considered as perceptual systems*, Copyright © 1966 by Houghton Mifflin Company. Used with permission.

Martha Graham. "A Dancer's World", film with Martha Graham and Company, Nathan Kroll, 1957, copyright the Martha Graham Trust, all rights reserved.

Martha Graham. *Blood Memory*, Doubleday, 1991, by permission of Bantam, Doubleday, Dell Publishing Group, Inc.

Peggy Hackney, Sarah Manno and Muriel Topaz. *Study Guide for Elementary Labanotation*, Dance Notation Bureau Press, 1977, by permission of Dance Notation Bureau.

Hilary Harris. "Cine-dance", in *Dance Perspectives*, No. 30 (1967), by permission of Dance Perspectives Foundation.

Baird Hastings. "Étienne Decroux and his mime", *Dance and Dancers*, June 1950, by permission of Baird Hastings and Alvin Epstein.

Michael Heaney and John Forrest. *Annals of Early Morris*, Univ. of Sheffield with The Morris Ring, 1991, by permission of the authors and The Centre for Cultural Tradition and Language, The University of Sheffield.

Alice J. Helpern. The Evolution of Martha Graham's Dance Technique, Ph.D. thesis, New York Univ., 1981, by permission of the author.

Wendy Hilton. *Dance of Court and Theater: The French Noble Style 1690–1725*, Dance Books, 1981, by permission of the publishers.

Lucas Hoving. "Random Notes from a Contemporary Romantic", in *Dance Perspectives*, No. 38 (1969), by permission of Dance Perspectives Foundation.

Doris Humphrey. *The Art of Making Dances* (Ed. Barbara Pollack), Rinehart & Co., 1959, by permission of Princeton Book Company, Publishers.

Margaret N. H'Doubler. *Dancer / A Creative Art Experience*, The University of Wisconsin Press, 1957, by permission of the publishers.

Imperial Society of Teachers of Dancing. Leaflets "Tap Branch/Modern Theatre Branch", "Modern Theatre Dance Branch", "Sequence Dance Branch", "Classical Dance Association Branch", "Classical Ballet/Cecchetti Society Branch" — all by permission of the Society.

Bill T. Jones and Arnie Zane. *Body against Body* (Elizabeth Zimmer and Susan Quasha, Eds.), Station Hill Press, 1989, by permission of Bill T. Jones.

Kurt Jooss. *Stage Dancing in Germany*, Neue Darmstädter Verlag, 1956, by permission of Anna Markard.

Stephanie Jordan. *Striding Out / Aspects of Contemporary and New Dance in Britain*, Dance Books, 1992, by permission of the publishers.

Douglas Kennedy. *England's dances / Folk-dancing to-day and yesterday*, G. Bell & Sons Ltd., 1949, by permission of Peter Kennedy.

Douglas Kennedy (Ed.). *Community Dances Manual 1*, The English Folk Dance and Song Society, 1968, by permission of the publishers.

Lincoln Kirstein. "Classic and Romantic Ballet", 1939; *The New York City Ballet*, Alfred A. Knopf, 1973; "Classic Ballet: Aria of the Aerial", *Playbill*, May 1976; all by permission of the author.

Lincoln Kirstein. "What ballet is about: an American Glossary", In *Dance Perspectives*, No. 1 (1959), by permission of Dance Perspectives Foundation.

Lincoln Kirstein. *Movement & Metaphor / four centuries of ballet*, Pitman, 1971, by permission of Pitman Publishing.

Lincoln Kirstein and Muriel Stuart. *The Classic Ballet / Basic Technique and Terminology*, A&C Black, 1977, by permission of Lincoln Kirstein.

Albrecht Knust. *Dictionary of Kinetography Laban (Labanotation)*, Macdonald & Evans, 1979, by permission of the author's estate.

Rudolf Laban. *Modern Educational Dance*, 1948; *The Mastery of Movement on the Stage*, 1950; *Principles of dance and movement notation*, 1956; *Choreutics* (Annot. & Ed. Lisa Ullmann), 1966; *The Mastery of Movement*, 3rd Edn. (Rev. Lisa Ullmann) 1971; *A Life for Dance / Reminiscences* (Tr. & Annot. Lisa Ullmann), 1975 — all Macdonald & Evans, and all by permission of Etelka von Laban and Roland von Laban.

Rudolf Laban and F.C. Lawrence. *Effort*, Macdonald & Evans, 1947, by permission of Etelka von Laban and Roland von Laban.

Roderyk Lange. *The Nature of Dance / An anthropological Perspective*, Macdonald & Evans, 1975, by permission of the author.

INDEX OF NAMES